DEMOCRATIC REPRESENTATION

Reapportionment in Law and Politics

ROBERT G. DIXON, Jr.

NEW YORK

OXFORD UNIVERSITY PRESS

LONDON   TORONTO

1968

Copyright © 1968 by Oxford University Press, Inc.
Library of Congress Catalogue Card Number: 68-18563
Printed in the United States of America

To three generations of voters who prayed
that this work might be completed
before there was a fourth—
My Father and Mother
Claire
Janet, Barbara, Laurie

Foreword

Fruitful theorizing about social or political affairs often awaits an explosion, whether it be an economic crash or racial violence, to stir the social scientists to basic thinking. This phenomenon has occurred in the philosophy of political representation, hard upon the Supreme Court's decision on reapportionment. In the recent literature on representation and apportionment the present volume is outstanding for its rare combination of sharp theoretical analysis and solid empirical study, its fusion of the expertise of the lawyer and the skills of the political scientist.

It is a cardinal merit of Professor Dixon's work that he steadily poses the central issue in the reapportionment cases, a question that was rather more begged than confronted in the decisions: whether the right involved is an individual voter's personal claim to a fractional participation in his legislative district equal to that of a voter in another legislative district, or is a claim of the aggregate voters of a district to fair representation in the legislative assembly. While by no means unsympathetic to the role of the Court in treating the issue of malapportionment as justiciable, Professor Dixon points out that the adoption of the first way of looking at the problem has resulted in some oversimplification of the problem of representation, some rigidities of standards in judging the validity of apportionment plans, and some puzzling problems of how to avoid the simplistic "one man-one vote" formula in elections for collegial bodies that are not representative in the legislative sense.

Along the way we are given an intimate view of the strategies of counsel, the important role performed by the Solicitor General as amicus curiae, and the practical working of the reformed practice in the various states.

The fluidity of the exposition conceals the intensive research that informs every passage.

While the major outlines of the reapportionment doctrine may be settled, there remain a host of questions still unresolved: its application to local government, the legal status of gerrymandering, the limits on multimember districts, the use of weighted or fractional voting in the legislature. On all of these the analysis offered will be of great interest to legislators and judges no less than to students of government. To adopt a phrase of Chief Justice Hughes, the author has shown himself to be an uncommon master of both the microscope and the telescope.

PAUL A. FREUND

Harvard Law School
March 1968

Preface

Since 1962 the United States has been in the midst of a "crisis of representation" touched off by the Supreme Court decision in *Baker* v. *Carr*.
Apportionment and districting practices, which are the formal side of
political representation, have become a constitutional question subject not
only to judicial review but to significant judicial direction and compulsion.

Despite literally hundreds of court hearings, legislative sessions and
adoptions of reapportionment plans, *in early 1968* as this book goes to
press *almost as many state legislatures are unconstitutional under the 1960
census as were unconstitutional before Baker v. Carr*. (The degree of unconstitutionality—in terms of district population disparity—is, of course,
substantially reduced.) It seems inevitable that virtually all state legislative
and congressional districts will be invalid under the figures of the imminent
1970 census. The reason is that no firm standard of constitutional rectitude
has yet been announced by the Supreme Court. The implications of the
Court's 1967 decisions (Chapter XVII) are that tolerance limits on population inequality in legislative districts are far narrower than most courts
have been applying. To this status of unconstitutionality may soon be added
thousands of local government legislative districts (Chapter XX).

Because representation involves both consent and direction, and ideally
a consensus-creating deliberative process too, it goes to the heart of any
governmental system. In scope, therefore, this work has sought to range
beyond the court decisions and legislative battles which provide the fire-
works of the "one man-one vote" revolution to incorporate significant
elements of representation theory.

The great merit of *Baker* v. *Carr* was in opening the way for judicial action to galvanize the political branches into more effective discharge of their

political function of working out viable representation systems. But a tendency to focus almost exclusively on equalizing legislative district population as the guide to achieving a fair and effective political representation system puts "one man-one vote" on too narrow a base. As G.D.H. Cole, the English Fabian Socialist, perceptively observed: "What is represented is never merely the individual, but always certain purposes common to groups of individuals."

From a slightly different perspective, democratic citizenship itself connotes a feeling of belonging, a sense of meaningful and effective participation in governing processes. The drive of populous suburbs to gain representation, of ruralites to hold at least an effective voice, of center city Black Power leaders for legislative spokesmen of their own, and of political parties to remain viable and competitive—all these and more make up the web of representation for which "one man-one vote" has become both the moral incantation and the rallying cry.

While this work has not involved methodological innovations, it has required use of techniques for developing, maintaining, and subjecting to critical evaluation a fifty-state file covering congressional districting and local apportionment in addition to the main theme of state legislative apportionment. Formal materials such as legislative and study commission reports, court briefs and opinions, published comments of participants, have been only a beginning. Two chapters (IX and X) are the product of a modified "case study" approach. Each of the "big six" reapportionment cases of 1964 was subjected to detailed description and critique based not only on the briefs and opinions in the lower courts and in the Supreme Court, but also on correspondence and interviews with counsel and others, and on personal observation of Bench-counsel repartee in Supreme Court oral argument. The author has been present for all of the major oral arguments in the Supreme Court in apportionment cases since *Baker* v. *Carr*.

Three additional chapters (XII, XIII, XIV)—based in part on visits to many states—present a series of vignettes on state discharge of the reapportionment duty imposed by the Supreme Court's 1964 rulings. Because of the ongoing nature of the reapportionment revolution with constitutional standards still in a developmental state—particularly regarding districting options and gerrymandering—a detailed sequential treatment of judicial-legislative roles in a novel area of constitutional decision-making has been possible.

Empirical analysis of reapportionment impact, and the representation process in general, is a virtual terra nova, despite the growing number of studies which at least in microcosm seek to analyze particular elements of political behavior. Some of these studies, with suggestions for the future now that some new apportionment patterns are stablizing, are incorporated in Chapter XX.

To the Rockefeller Foundation I owe a primary debt of gratitude for sustaining me on a year's leave of absence in 1964–65, and providing travel funds, immediately after the Supreme Court's *Reapportionment Decisions* required revision of most American legislative and congressional districts. Significant assistance came from other sources including summer support in 1965 from the American Philosophical Society and in 1966 from the Relm Foundation. Research and secretarial assistance in initial phases of the project was provided by the Rockport Fund of the National Law Center of George Washington University. In the latter phases my mainstay has been the *Washington Evening Star*–George Washington University Research Fund. I must enter a word of special gratitude to Dean Arthur E. Burns of the Graduate School and Robert Kramer of the National Law Center of George Washington University not only for general encouragement but also because their status as successful intermediaries to various grant funds made them precious beyond price.

So many have helped in so many ways in this project extending over several years that a full list of personal indebtedness would be a chapter in itself. Through travels in approximately fifteen states, and delivery of papers at annual meetings of the Conference of Chief Justices, National Association of Attorneys General, National Municipal League, and various other groups, the author has had the benefit of both information and critique from innumerable judges, attorneys general and their staffs, attorneys, private litigants, members of interested organizations such as the leagues of women voters, chambers of commerce, unions. Reapportionment consulting for the Preparatory Committees for the New York and Pennsylvania Constitutional Conventions, the Legislative Committee of the Maryland Constitutional Convention, the New York Office for Local Government, and for various law firms has provided many insights.

Within the academic community a full list of indebtedness would include most members of two professions—law professors and political science professors or bureau directors—who have been directly or indirectly involved in apportionment litigation or research. One of the heart-warming aspects of the lengthy period of effort from which this book now emerges is the courtesy and responsiveness, often as the cost of some effort, with which my repetitive requests for information on new reapportionment developments were greeted. My law and political science colleagues at George Washington, being within easy reach, have served as convenient guinea pigs for various hypotheses, some now incorporated, some discarded.

In the course of this work I naturally draw in various ways upon my

series of reapportionment articles over the past few years in several journals. I wish to thank their editors for permission to quote, paraphrase, or
condense material from their pages: "Legislative Apportionment and the
Federal Constitution," 27 *Law and Contemporary Problems* 329 (1962
Symposium); "Representation Goals: Majoritarianism of Consensus?" 52
National Civic Review 543 (1963); "Apportionment Standards and Judicial
Power," 38 *Notre Dame Lawyer* 367 (1963 Symposium); "Reapportionment: What the Court Didn't Do," *The Reporter* magazine (1964);
"Reapportionment in the Supreme Court and Congress: Constitutional
Struggle for Fair Representation," 63 *Michigan Law Review* 209 (1964
Symposium); "New Constitutional Forms for Metropolis: Reapportioned
County Boards; Local Councils of Governments," 30 *Law and Contemporary Problems* 57 (1965 Symposium); "Reapportionment Perspectives:
What Is Fair Representation?" 51 *American Bar Association Journal* 319
(1965); "The Reapportionment Amendments and Direct Democracy," 38
State Government 117 (1965 Symposium); and in addition my chapter
on "Colorado Apportionment," in Rocco J. Tresolini and Richard T. Frost,
editors, *Cases in American National Government and Politics* (Englewood Cliffs, N.Y.: Prentice-Hall, Inc., 1966).

Within the "workshop" where again the list of research and secretarial
assistants becomes too long to enumerate, I do wish to recognize specially
my three primary research assistants of the past years: W. Theodore Pierson, Jr., J. McDonald Williams, and Gordon W. Hatheway, all of whom
were law students at George Washington during their period of service.
To Mr. Hatheway in particular, who has seen all chapters take final form,
is due the accolade of ever-helpful literary midwife. The work of two
earlier assistants on certain charts, Sam S. Crutchfield, Jr., and Miss Dulcey
A. Brown, has been brought forward with minor changes and verification.

In the final phases of manuscript preparation I have been assisted by
Mrs. Ella Louise Belk and Mrs. Katherine B. Lazerow, selflessly and at odd
hours, as only they and my long-forbearing family know. They supplemented the work of the many pretty girls in the Law School secretariat
whose interest and helpfulness also were unfailing. Needless to say, any
errors and misinterpretations are my own: one man-one vote; one man-
one book.

ROBERT G. DIXON, JR.

Washington, D.C.
March 1968

Contents

a One and One-Half Party State. New Jersey: Bipartisan Model for
a Two-Party State. Backdrop for the Constitutional Convention.
Bipartisan Commission and Tie Breaker. The Superiority of New
Jersey's System. INFORMAL BIPARTISAN APPORTIONMENT. Con-
necticut: Party Agreement. Washington: Governor–Legislature
Tug of War. Minnesota: Governor–Legislature Tug of War. NEW
YORK'S "BIPARTISAN" APPORTIONMENT BY AD HOC JUDICIAL COM-
MISSION. "Talking" to the Court Through Enactment of Alterna-
tive Plans. The Four Plans. Evaluating the Tactic. Ping Pong
Litigation. Courts in Conflict. Final Deadlock and Resolution.
The Special Judicial Commission. Reapportionment in the 1967
New York Constitutional Convention.

Note on Abbreviations

In footnotes a short style has been used for some citations. The following forms are illustrative: *American Bar Association Journal* (*A.B.A.J.*); *American Political Science Review* (*Am. Pol. Sci. Rev.*); *Congressional Quarterly Weekly Report* (*Cong. Quart. Weekly Report*); *Congressional Record* (*Cong. Rec.*); *Law and Contemporary Problems* (*Law & Contemp. Prob.*); *Michigan Law Review* (*Mich. L. Rev.*); *National Civic Review* (*Nat. Civ. Rev.*).

DEMOCRATIC REPRESENTATION

I

Introduction

OVERVIEW

Really profound revolutions are those which change *ideas* men live by, not just *power* men live under. The American legislative reapportionment revolution of the 1960s and the "second round" due after the 1970 census is this kind of revolution. It is the product of radically new conceptions of equality and also of technological change which has produced dynamically shifting urban masses.

In the space of five years reapportionment virtually remade the political map of America. There are three key dates. In 1962 the United States Supreme Court entered that part of the political thicket of representative democracy known as "apportionment and districting" in the now famous Tennessee case of *Baker v. Carr*.[1] In a decision comparable in significance to *Marbury v. Madison* [2]—the 1803 decision which effectively created the American system of judicial review—the Court overruled earlier precedents and authorized judicial review of apportionments and districts which determine the composition and political control of state legislatures. The reapportionment revolution was born. In June of 1964 in a packet of cases [3] headed by *Reynolds v. Sims* from Alabama the "one man-one vote" rule that all legislative bodies must be based substantially on population was announced. By coincidence, in the fall of the same year, the Goldwater debacle in the presidential election had the side effect of

1. 369 U.S. 186 (1962).
2. 1 Cranch 137 (1803).
3. Reynolds v. Sims, Vann v. Baggett, McConnell v. Baggett, 377 U.S. 533 (1964); WMCA v. Lomenzo, 377 U.S. 633 (1964); Maryland Comm. for Fair Representation v. Tawes, 377 U.S. 656 (1964); Davis v. Mann, 377 U.S. 678 (1964); Roman v. Sincock, 377 U.S. 695 (1964); Lucus v. Colorado Gen. Assembly, 377 U.S. 713 (1964).

ousting 500 Republican state legislators from office[4] at the very time when legislative reapportionment, and potential future control of the legislature for years to come, was by judicial order in top position on most state legislative calendars. By the election of 1966, the equal population rule had affected virtually every state legislative seat and congressional seat in the nation; had abolished the weighted voting system (county-unit system)[5] Georgia had used for its governorship; and had reconstituted a fair number of city council and county board seats as well.[6]

This American reapportionment revolution may be as significant for development of the theory and practice of representative democracy as the equally bloodless Glorious Revolution of 1688 in England. That revolution confirmed a new concept of consensual government centering on legislative power; implicitly it is the starting point for reapportionment and districting problems in modern times.

In the long view, perhaps the first crisis for representative democracy was simple failure to create it, as replacement for direct democracy, in time to save the ancient Greeks. The parochial Greek city-states met their downfall because of failure to conceive of federated, representative democracy as a defense against unified Rome. Since this downfall, Democratic Man, in those relatively few areas and times where democratic forms have flowered, really has been *represented* man. He has been represented well or ill through a variety of institutions, formal and informal, which express his consent to government, his occasional direction of it, and his ultimate control of it. Among formal institutions of representation, the legislature traditionally is accorded pre-eminence. Apportionment and districting practices, which determine the legislature's political complexion and operation, are products of the level of representation theory of a society and of tactical capacity to implement that theory. Surprisingly, neither the content of representation theory, nor ways to implement

---

4. Figures compiled in *The Congressional Quarterly* (Vol. XXII, No. 47, Part I, 2709, November 20, 1964), indicate that Republicans lost 541 seats in state legislatures (445 in the lower houses and 96 in the upper houses) in the national election of November 3, 1964.
   Republicans controlled both houses of the legislature in 18 states before the election. After the election, they controlled both houses in only six states and one house in 9. There were ties in the upper house of two states, with Democrats controlling the lower house in one of the states and the Republicans controlling the lower house in the other. These figures do not include Minnesota and Nebraska, which have technically nonpartisan legislatures. *Ibid.*
5. Gray v. Sanders, 372 U.S. 368 (1963).
6. Josephine Y. King, "The *Reynolds* Standard and Local Reapportionment," 15 *Buff. L. Rev.* 120 (1965); address by Milton Alpert, Annual Meeting of the New York State Bar Association, Municipal Law Section (February 4, 1966). See generally, Joseph S. Ferrell, *Cases and Materials on Local Apportionment* (Chapel Hill: Institute of Government, University of North Carolina, tentative ed., 1965).

it, have been featured in political philosophy above the level of emotive generalities.

The current American reapportionment upheaval has obvious underpinnings in those aspects of twentieth-century technology related to population growth and shift, and to communication. Static legislative districts, whether or not equal in population when devised, are speedily unbalanced by population mobility and the population explosion. Rural America recorded its last majority in the federal census in 1910. But as late as 1920 the Bureau of the Census [7] reported that America was 48.8 percent rural even under a definition that allocated towns as small as 2500 to the "urban" category. Cities of 100,000 or more accounted for only 26 percent of the total population.[8] By 1960 the rural proportion had shrunk to 37 percent under the old definition and to 30.1 percent under the new definition.[9] Of the 69.9 percent classified as urban under the revised definition, 41 percent was located in 132 cities of 100,000 or more, and 23 percent was clustered in 21 areas of 500,000 population or more.[10] Shifting to a metropolitan area concept, the Bureau reported that 64 percent of the total population in 1960 was grouped in 216 Standard Metropolitan Statistical Areas (central city of 50,000 or more plus surrounding territory).[11] Improved communication also invites a fresh look at apportionment and districting practices grounded solely on considerations of accessibility and representation of "natural" communities.

By far the more significant aspect of the reapportionment revolution is the ideological aspect. When reapportionment purposes and goals have been articulated in other than arithmetic terms, the focus has been on improving representation—in the sense of power—in the legislature of identifiable parties, sections, or groups. As one might expect, the plaintiffs in reapportionment cases tend to be Democrats in areas of Republican legislative dominance, Republicans in areas of Democratic legislative dominance, and urban-suburban-oriented in virtually all areas. Plaintiffs have sought representation in the legislature more nearly in proportion to their statewide popular strength than that afforded by existing apportionment and districting systems. They have sought to achieve this goal almost exclusively through equalization of population of legislative districts —a device which often, but not always, produces the desired results.

"One man-one vote" thus has become the political equality symbol of

7. U.S. Bureau of the Census, *Statistical Abstract of the United States* 4 (Washington, D.C.: U.S. Government Printing Office, 1965).
8. *Ibid.*
9. U.S. Bureau of the Census, *Statistical Abstract of the United States* 14–15, 17 (Washington, D.C.: U.S. Government Printing Office, 1964).
10. *Id.* at 17.
11. *Ibid.*

the 1960s. The rigidity with which the equality idea is being applied in reshaping legislative districts, coupled with possible applications to such governmental areas as the electoral college, judgeship elections, voting practices inside legislatures, and local government, is a major event in America's long romance with the principle of egalitarianism.

The idea of equality, of course, is not new. In the Western tradition three concepts have provided the basis for the bulk of philosophic discourse: liberty, equality, justice. The words are so familiar as to seem self-defining. Yet each is infinitely subtle, not only in its internal meanings and contradictions but in its interactions with the other two. Development of the equality concept is especially fascinating.

The Founding Fathers, without blinking an eye, subscribed wholeheartedly to the "all men are created equal" concept of the Declaration of Independence. They did so in the face of an expanding institution of Negro slavery, class and wealth limitations on the franchise, and the presence of "rotten boroughs" as one basis for legislative representation in the states as well as in England. By the 1960s, however, the equality concept had become a foundation for numerous affirmative state obligations, such as the obligation to assist indigent accused by providing free counsel and free trial transcripts,[12] and obligations to equalize racial opportunity in such fields as education and voting.[13] It also became the foundation for judicial rules of legislative apportionment under which even slight district population deviations have been viewed as suspect by some courts. The term "equality" is the same; the meaning obviously is radically altered.

To dismiss the basic terms of political philosophy as being vague, however, would be to miss their central characteristic. Basic terms of political philosophy, "equality" included, are not so much vague as developmental. They describe an ideal immanent rather than imminent, because the ideal itself changes as men's aspirations and perceptions evolve.

---

12. Griffin v. Illinois, 351 U.S. 12 (1956).

13. *Education*: Federal guidelines for speedier implementation of the constitutional rule, 45 CFR 181 (1966); U.S. Commission on Civil Rights Staff, *Civil Rights U.S.A.: Public Schools, Cities in the North and West* (1962); Alexander M. Bickel, "The Decade of School Desegregation," 64 *Colum. L. Rev.* 196, 212–18 (1964); Craggett v. Board of Educ., 338 F. 2d 941 (6th Cir. 1964); Bell v. School City of Gary, Indiana, 324 F. 2d 209 (7th Cir. 1963); Dowell v. Board of Educ., 244 F. Supp. 971 (W.D. Okla. 1965); Fuller v. Volk, 230 F. Supp. 25 (D.N.J. 1964); Taylor v. Board of Educ., 195 F. Supp. 231 (S.D.N.Y.), aff'd., 294 F. 2d 36 (2d Cir.), cert. denied, 368 U.S. 940 (1961). *De facto segregation is not unconstitutional*: Downs v. Board of Educ., 336 F. 2d 988 (10th Cir.), cert. denied, 380 U.S. 914 (1965). *Voting*: South Carolina v. Katzenbach, 383 U.S. 301 (1966); Louisiana v. United States, 380 U.S. 145 (1965); United States v. Mississippi, 380 U.S. 128 (1965).

DOCTRINAL HIGHLIGHTS — ENDURING ISSUES

The history of reapportionment since 1962 has been kaleidoscopic: new cases, new doctrines, new possibilities, and new insights follow each round of experience. A modified "federal plan," approaching county equality in one house of a state legislature, was a viable option under Justice Tom C. Clark's 1962 concurrence in *Baker*.[14] It was buried in 1964 when *Reynolds*[15] produced the rule of equal population districts for both houses of a state legislature. Likewise a somewhat flexible constitutional standard based on due process considerations of fairness, or on equal protection considerations of reasonable classification, seemed to remain a viable option up to the 1964 *Reynolds* decision.[16] In that case an equal protection principle—in the relatively rigid form it has assumed for racial matters —emerged as the touchstone of decision for reapportionment too. Despite the Court's disclaimers on the score of rigidity, the 1964 rule was frequently interpreted as being a no-exceptions, no-classifications rule of mathematical equality in lower court decisions.

And yet in 1965 and 1966 in noncontrolling side statements in cases from Georgia[17] and Hawaii,[18] the Court seemed to recognize under fair representation considerations, the possible unconstitutionality of mathematically equal plans. The possibility thus re-emerged of instituting a meaningful dialogue on the relation of apportionment to fair representation—in short, of approaching this most fascinating and political of issues forthrightly as a crisis in democratic politics rather than as a mere legalism of numbers.

Throughout the sweep of cases from *Baker* in 1962 to the present—and looking forward to the "second round" three years hence, after the 1970 census—problems of proof and of allocation of "burden of proof" have been critical. In cases up to and including the 1964 reapportionment victory in *Reynolds*, plaintiffs could establish their cause simply by showing mathematical inequality in existing districts. Census data were all that was needed. Victory then was theirs unless the state could show that all deviations from mathematical equality were the reasonable result of a rational plan. The burden proved to be insurmountable.

We now have a new breed of plaintiffs who seek to challenge alleged

14. 369 U.S. 186, 251 (1962).
15. 377 U.S. 533 (1964).
16. In a speech after the *Baker* decision, the Solicitor General of the United States speculated that the Court might permit meaningful political subdivision recognition in one house if the other were population-based. 30 *Tenn. L. Rev.* 28 (1962).
17. Fortson v. Dorsey, 379 U.S. 433 (1965).
18. Burns v. Richardson, 384 U.S. 73 (1966).

nonmathematical inequities in some of the new apportionment plans, but the burden of proof has shifted and now runs against the plaintiff's side. Under the dicta of the 1965 and 1966 cases, mathematically equal apportionments are presumed to be constitutional unless challengers can show that mathematically equal districts nevertheless are discriminatory in operation and prevent fair representation. This burden may not prove to be insurmountable; yet it is certainly a heavy one. Unless the Court recants the side statements in the Georgia and Hawaii cases, such challenges seeking certain representation goals of fairness and political equity along with mathematical equality can be expected to continue.

Major apportionment issues for the late 1960s, and particularly for the "second round" reapportionment cases after the 1970 census, will include: (1) gerrymandering, whether political, racial, or regional; (2) relation of various districting practices—single-member, multimember, floterial, mixed—to fair representation; (3) permissibility of apportionment bases other than population or more recent than the decennial census; (4) devices for avoiding or breaking reapportionment deadlocks; (5) the ultimate issue of more clearly identifying representation goals and relating particular apportionment-districting practices to these goals.

NATURE OF REAPPORTIONMENT STRUGGLE

The ultimate rationale to be given for *Baker* v. *Carr* and its numerous progeny is that when political avenues for redressing political problems become dead-end streets, some judicial intervention in the politics of the people may be essential in order to *have* any effective politics. In Tennessee, at the time its legislative composition was challenged in *Baker*, there was a history of several years of unsuccessful state court litigation and unsuccessful efforts for corrective legislation. Voters in state senate districts varied from 131,971 to 25,190 and in lower house districts from 42,298 to 2340. Counties with 37 percent of the population could elect 20 of the 33 members of the senate; counties with 40 percent of the population could elect 63 of the 99 members of the lower house.[19] Similar statistics, some even more extreme, were available in a vast majority of the states. In California, a rule that no county could have more than one senator and that no more than three counties could be combined into a single senatorial district produced a Los Angeles senatorial district of over six million and a Mono, Iyo, Alpine senatorial district of 14,294.[20] In Florida, population disparities in senate districts ranged from 935,047 down to 9543 and in

19. Record, pp. 25–31, Baker v. Carr, 369 U.S. 186 (1962).
20. Silver v. Jordan, 241 F. Supp. 576, 579 (S.D. Calif. 1964).

house districts from 311,628 down to 2868, so that under a theoretical control index the senate and house could be controlled respectively by 12.3 percent and 14.7 percent of the population.[21] (The theoretical control index, also called electoral percentage, is computed by cumulating the population represented by that half of the legislative house in question which comes from the smaller districts.) In Vermont, the town representation system produced a district population range in the lower house from 33,155 down to 238, and an electoral percentage for that house of 11.6 percent.[22]

It does not take much insight to observe that politically frozen apportionment systems yield only to extraordinary methods of change. Beneficiaries of an existing apportionment-districting system cannot be expected to vote themselves out of office, except under severe external pressure. What has not always been adequately perceived is that *Baker* and the wave of litigation it inspired involve *representation* as well as right to vote; and that using the judiciary as the lever for change leads to a radically different kind of exercise of the power of constitutional interpretation and enforcement than known heretofore, thus bringing courts to a new level of judicial review.

a. *Reapportionment and Fair Representation*

Regarding the *representation* aspect of the reapportionment struggle, the matter was phrased most aptly by Justice Felix Frankfurter in his opinion in the *Baker* case:

> What is actually asked of this Court in this case is to choose among competing bases of representation—ultimately, really, among competing theories of political philosophy—in order to establish an appropriate frame of government for the State of Tennessee and thereby for all of the States of the Union.[23]

Although he dissented on the issue of whether the courts should enter this political thicket, he did correctly perceive that the whole problem of democratic institutional arrangements was involved.

In broad perspective, an apportionment case raises basic questions concerning conditions of political allegiance and modes of expression of public will and opinion. Reapportionment invites fresh analysis of bicameralism; the single-member district system; the possible role of such devices to "hear from the minority" as cumulative voting, limited voting, and modified forms of proportional representation; the role of the gover-

21. Sobel v. Adams, 208 F. Supp. 316, 320 (S.D. Fla. 1962).
22. Buckley v. Hoff, 234 F. Supp. 191, 194 (D.Vt. 1964).
23. 369 U.S. 186, 300 (1962).

nor as legislative leader; the institutional, geographic, and population bases of political parties and conditions for maintaining a two-party system; the weight to be accorded traditional patterns of thought and practice keyed to counties and other political subdivisions as representation units; and the problem of political artificiality in arithmetically equal but frequently modified districts. Unicameralism has not yet come to the fore.

Reapportionment also pushes to the fore unresolved conflicts of principle underlying our expedient arrangements of election districts and legislative assemblies, and the institutions and political practices derived therefrom. As Robert A. Dahl has noted in his provocative work on Madisonian democratic theory, a "preoccupation with the rights and wrongs of majority rule has run like a red thread through American political thought since 1789." [24] It can be phrased as an issue between majoritarian democracy and consensus democracy. In other words, shall 51 percent rule, subject only to the occasional check of judicial review? Or shall there be attempts to work a compromise between the power of majorities and the power of minorities, denying to the former the full sweep of sovereignty and denying to the latter a plenary vote?

In the past a concern for consensus, that is, an attempt to work a compromise "between the political equality of all adult citizens on the one side, and the desire to limit their sovereignty on the other," [25] has dominated American thought and practice. A distinguishing feature of our system, perhaps impelled by heritage of sectional division and heterogeneity, is that our governmental structure, institutional habits, and political parties with their internal factional divisions, have combined to produce a system in which major programs and major new directions cannot be undertaken unless supported by a fairly broad popular consensus. This normally has been far broader than 51 percent, and often bipartisan as well.

The components of this traditional consensus democracy are several. They include federalism, separation of powers, the bicameral structure of legislatures, with each house representing a somewhat different electorate and requiring a double scrutiny of all measures, the committee and seniority systems used within legislatures, the state-based rather than nation-based political party system, requirements for extraordinary majorities to enact certain kinds of measures, the executive veto power and the power to override it with an extraordinary majority, and numerous other formal arrangements and informal practices. Some forms of malapportionment likewise are classifiable here, e.g., the common guarantee in pre-*Baker* state constitutions of at least one representative per county in one house

24. Robert A. Dahl, A *Preface to Democratic Theory* 4 (Chicago: University of Chicago Press, Phoenix ed., 1963).
25. *Ibid.*

of the legislature, and a restriction on the number of representatives which may be apportioned to a single county no matter how large its population.

These arrangements and practices normally have not operated to give a popular minority an affirmative power to govern, even in such severely malapportioned states as California, where Los Angeles with 6,380,711 population and Mono, Iyo, Alpine counties with 14,294 population each had one senator. The legislative role of the governor always imposes a majoritarian influence, and seldom have both houses been apportioned on a substantially nonpopulation basis. (Important exceptions to this statement noted subsequently, mostly Southern, would include Florida, Georgia, and perhaps Tennessee at the time of the *Baker* case.)

These varied arrangements have given popular minorities some defensive power in regard to major policy issues against a numerical majority, or against the balance of power minority in control of a numerical majority. It is a political fact of life that although the large passive core of both political parties may be moderate, an activist labor-liberal minority on occasion may rule through control of the Democratic party, and a corresponding conservative minority on occasion may rule through control of the Republican party.

A few years ago Ernest S. Griffith, then director of the Legislative Reference Service of the Library of Congress, compared British politics and political structure to the American scene. He was impressed, unfavorably, by the rigid majoritarianism of the British operation in contrast to our much more complicated but also more tolerant consensus system. More recently Sidney Hook's *The Paradoxes of Freedom* prompted a reviewer to express a similar thought:

> It is evident that Washington politics today are, to a very great extent, group politics. Homogeneous majorities rarely face homogeneous minorities. There are instead temporary majorities formed by an alliance of groups which then disperse to form new alliances, what Professor Holcombe long ago called majorities of the moment. In this context, democracy is largely measured in terms of the ability of all groups to participate in the process of alliance building. Surely, even the purist theories of majoritarian democracy presuppose fair representation for minorities so that they may participate in majority making.[26]

In similar vein Morris Ernst suggested after the Supreme Court's reapportionment rulings of 1964 that the "right to be heard" is a proper concern along with the "right to vote," and lies a step beyond the "one

26. Martin Shapiro, Book Review, 51 *Colum. L. Rev.* 255, 259–60 (1963).

man-one vote" concept.[27] For this reason Mr. Ernst has suggested to newly formed nations a formula that minority parties might get in toto one-third of the votes (legislative seats), a figure insufficient to express power, but sufficient to give people that "tender and essential feeling of having a spokesman of their choosing in the halls of the mighty."

Reapportionment has an obvious impact on this large issue of majoritarianism versus consensus. Taken as a simple, absolutistic formula, "one man-one vote" and its resultant mandate of equal population districts as a universal rule clearly is a majoritarian and anticonsensus doctrine. It is designed to place both legislative houses on a straight majoritarian-population basis, as the governorship already is. The actual sweep of the new doctrine's majoritarian tendency will turn, however, on several additional factors.

One factor is the question whether the "one man-one vote" principle eventually is to be applied against any official device which impedes or thwarts effectuation of dominant political will. Any such thwarting obviously would undercut the representative function. Viewed thusly, a number of antimajoritarian rules and practices in legislatures are suspect under "one man-one vote," functionally viewed. These would include, at the very least, the following: (a) the filibuster; (b) seniority custom in "electing" committee chairmen; (c) seniority custom in committee assignments; (d) powers of committee chairmen to delay or block action; (e) all extraordinary majority requirements in legislative voting; (f) inequitable staffing for committees and legislators individually.

Another factor is the question whether the "one man-one vote" principle as applied to actual apportionment and districting practices will be turned into a command, not just of arithmetically equal districts, but of fair and effective representation as an end result. If the latter, then the command may bring to the fore such antimajoritarian features as subdistricting to break up large, winner-take-all, multimember districts, policing of majority party gerrymandering, and use of special devices to ensure minority representation.

b. Uniqueness of a Reapportionment Case

As already noted, a reapportionment case is a critically different kind of case and brings judicial review to a new level. Reapportionment cases call on courts to sit in judgment on possession and distribution of political power. In the context of more than a century and a half of judicial review this is something distinctly new in the function of constitutional interpretation and enforcement. Preceding cases were of two major types. The larger and more conventional cluster consists of cases in which the Court

27. Letter to Editor from Morris Ernst, 51 A.B.A.J. 508 (1965).

has limited the *ends* which may be sought by the holders of political power. Examples are numerous. In the ill-fated *Dred Scot* [28] decision, the Court invalidated the end of dividing the West into free states and slave states under the Missouri Compromise. It invalidated numerous state laws regulating business and employment in the heyday of "substantive due process" when, over Justice Holmes's protests, it seemed to read Herbert Spencer's *Social Statics* into the Fourteenth Amendment.[29] It invalidated numerous New Deal measures in the 1930s by a restrictive reading of several constitutional concepts.[30]

The smaller cluster of constitutional cases, posing more difficult problems of enforcement, encompasses cases invalidating racial segregation practices. These cases set a standard of constitutional validity so at variance with existing practice, particularly in regard to schools, as to require major adjustments in government finances, programs, and administration in order to achieve compliance. The Court itself recognized the compliance problem in the *Desegregation Decisions* by inserting the "all deliberate speed" proviso in 1955.[31] These racial desegregation cases differ markedly from the earlier and primary cluster of constitutional cases in their impact on government because they impose a *duty to act*, rather than a *duty to desist*. But they have this much in common with previous exercises of the power of judicial review: *they leave intact the distribution and possession of political power.* (Negro voting cases may become an exception to this statement, but only a partial exception because the effect is slight as yet, and the problem is regional.[32])

By contrast, reapportionment cases represent *judicial transfer of political power.* They question the legitimacy of arrangements by which legislative office is defined and filled. This constitutes a major innovation, not only for judicial review but for democratic theory and practice.

To speak thus in terms of distribution of political power is to talk not of legislative acts, nor of judicial acts in the previously accepted meaning of the term, but of *constitutive acts.* Reapportionment, whether by legislative action, constitutional amendment, or judicial action, restructures

28. Dred Scott v. Sanford, 60 U.S. (19 How.) 393 (1857).
29. New State Ice Co. v. Liebman, 285 U.S. 262 (1932); Adkins v. Children's Hosp., 261 U.S. 525 (1923); Adair v. United States, 208 U.S. 161 (1908); Lochner v. New York, 198 U.S. 45 (1905). *Contra*, Muller v. Oregon, 208 U.S. 412 (1908).
30. See, e.g., Carter v. Carter Coal Co., 298 U.S. 238 (1936); United States v. Butler, 297 U.S. 1 (1936); Schecter Poultry Corp. v. United States, 295 U.S. 495 (1935).
31. Brown v. Board of Educ., 349 U.S. 294 (1955), which amplifies the substantive requirements of desegregation of schools announced in 1954 (Brown v. Board of Educ., 347 U.S. 483 [1954]).
32. See, e.g., South Carolina v. Katzenbach, 383 U.S. 301 (1966); Louisiana v. United States, 380 U.S. 145 (1965); United States v. Mississippi, 380 U.S. 128 (1965).

government at the core. Significantly, of all the vital compromises at the Constitutional Convention of 1787, only the one concerning the basis of representation is entitled to be called the Great Compromise.

Apportionment and districting decisions are primary determinants of the quality of representative democracy. From popular suffrage derives the majoritarian principle of democracy. The majoritarian principle could be served simply by having all legislators elected at-large. All having the same constituency, there would be little reason to have more than a few. But from apportionment and districting derive the more personalized and balanced representation features which temper majoritarianism with requirements of deliberation and consensus.[33]

Despite this critically political—indeed, constitution-shaping—nature of reapportionment litigation, it is one of the marvels of the decade that this revolutionary process of judicial action has proceeded with such speed, magnitude, and general acceptance. Whatever the merits or demerits of the multitude of particular rulings and legislative enactments, their existence testifies to the continued acceptance of a broad power of judicial review and to the stability of our system. This acceptance now extends to reshaping and transfer of political power—indeed to judicial restructuring of sister organs of government—as well as to mere particularized restraints on unchallenged possessors of public office. The process of reapportionment litigation has continued unchecked and unmodified by constitutional amendment, although discussions of amendments introduced by Senators Dirksen, Javits, and Church consumed much time in three successive sessions of Congress between 1964 and 1966. Criticisms of judicial activism are occasionally intense, as illustrated by the remonstrance to the Supreme Court by the Chief Justices of the states in 1958 against a line of decisions checking state power,[34] and more recent suggestions to strip the Court of appellate power over reapportionment.[35] But the general posture of the public toward the Supreme Court is characterized more by reverance than by rejection, even in troublous times in regard to novel and sweeping rulings.

This very veneration, and the unlikelihood of modification of Court rulings by constitutional amendment, are in themselves weighty reasons for the Court to exercise great care in its rulings on larger political and social

33. For discussion of this point see Ch. 3.
34. Conference of Chief Justices, "Report of the Committee on Federal-State Relationships as Affected by Judicial Decisions," and Resolution of Adoption, 32 *State Government* 60, 74 (1959).
35. The congressional reaction to the *Reynolds* decision, including the Dirksen-Mansfield resolution calling for a moratorium on further reapportionment litigation and the Tuck bill seeking to shrink Supreme Court appellate jurisdiction, are discussed in Ch. 15.

questions of the day. In the Court's nonreviewability there is not only an awesome power, but also an awesome responsibility: a responsibility not to any electorate but to the high duty of preserving and enhancing a constitutional system where majority rule and minority rights exist in constant tension.

THEMES

The themes of this book are several and transcend the commonly voiced thought that "one man-one vote" reapportionment is not only a long overdue but also a self-sufficing remedy for all of the ills of representation in a burgeoning, urban-based mass democracy. To stress the relation of the reapportionment revolution to continued development of an American ideal of equal personal status vis-à-vis government is essential for an appreciation of the vigor of the movement, and for an understanding of the terms within which the political and legal dialogue have been cast. It explains certain forms state legislative reapportionment and congressional redistricting have taken, particularly the near-exclusive stress in some lower courts on equalizing population of legislative districts down to the level of miniscule variations.

To stop at this point, however, is to remain at the level of abstract mathematics and of fictional voter power. To stop with arithmetic equality is to fail to relate current apportionment and districting efforts to the nature and needs of representative government and of party democracy, and to basic elements of democratic political theory.

When Herman Finer in his first major work forthrightly entitled a key chapter "Representative Government is Party Government," [36] he was saying something meaningful to the reapportionment issue. It also may be said that a two-party system is an unstable equilibrium, always tending to one-party dominance unless carefully nurtured.[37] This thought also is directly relevant to the forms and patterns of reapportionment. In practice, in the first years of the unfolding reapportionment revolution, little attention has been given to considerations of party balance, to apportionment devices providing a base for fair and effective party competition, to devices designed to ameliorate majoritarianism with some requirements of consensus, or to avoidance of a fresh round of gerrymandering and a resultant new political freeze.

Future historians may wonder whether the relative lack of concern for

36. Herman Finer, *Theory and Practice of Modern Government* 237 (New York: H. Holt, rev. ed., 1949).
37. See generally, V.O. Key, *Politics, Parties, and Pressure Groups* (New York: Thomas Y. Crowell Co., 5th ed., 1964).

considerations of party government and for conditions of effective party competition was related in any significant way to the nature of the initial leading cases and the composition of the Supreme Court Bench itself. All three of the ex-politicians on the bench—ex-Senator Hugo L. Black, ex-Governor Earl Warren, and ex-Attorney General Tom C. Clark—were products of the one-party South or the no-party California. Also, of the nine leading cases in the period between 1962 and 1964, only two,[38] the New York case and the Colorado case, came from states with a tradition of a vigorous two-party system. The other four leading cases in the June 1964 package [39] which yielded the "equal population for districts in both houses" rule were from Alabama, Virginia, Maryland, and Delaware. The case which first opened the political thicket in 1962 was from Tennessee.[40] It was followed by a 1963 case invalidating Georgia's county-unit system for selecting such statewide officers as governor and U.S. Senator.[41] An early 1964 case, again from Georgia, concerned population inequalities in congressional districting.[42]

In democratic political theory the people, i.e., population or voters, are pre-eminent. The "consent of the governed" is certainly a people-based concept. Admittedly, the term "people" in political theory traditionally has denoted only that portion of the total populace who were politically active or enfranchised—barons in King John's day, middle and higher classes in the Glorious Revolution of 1688, and middle and higher classes in America prior to Jacksonianism. But as the political base has broadened and the franchise has been extended in the nineteenth and twentieth centuries, to men generally, the "people" whose consent to government is relevant, who therefore have representation needs, and who therefore need be considered in formulae for apportionments and districting, came to comprise virtually the entire populace. (Possible distinctions between gross population as an apportionment base and narrower measures such as registered voters are considered in Chapter XIX.)

The *first theme* of this work, therefore, is that population commands a prominent place, indeed a pre-eminent place, in any representation formula. If one were to prescribe an apportionment formula for a virgin ter-

---

38. WMCA v. Lomenzo, 377 U.S. 633 (1964); Lucas v. Colorado Gen. Assembly, 377 U.S. 713 (1964).
39. Reynolds v. Sims, 377 U.S. 533 (1964); Davis v. Mann, 377 U.S. 678 (1964); Maryland Comm. for Fair Representation v. Tawes, 377 U.S. 656 (1964); Roman v. Sincock, 377 U.S. 695 (1964).
40. Baker v. Carr, 369 U.S. 186 (1962).
41. Gray v. Sanders, 372 U.S. 368 (1963).
42. Wesberry v. Sanders, 376 U.S. 1 (1964).

ritory with no developed population centers, no developed and traditional political subdivisions, no identification of different clusters of economic or vocational interests (e.g., commercial fishing, farming, manufacturing) —which was the situation underlying the Northwest Ordinance of 1787 —one probably would prescribe, as did the drafters of that Ordinance, that population should be the sole consideration in apportionment. Absent a fairly rich institutional development, including the rise of a party system, the only relevant apportionment factor is population.

A *second theme*, offered despite the realization that some commentators feel no further themes are necessary, is that in reapportionment more is involved than the self-centered constitutional right of a voter to cast a vote which, at least in mathematical, nonfunctional terms, is weighted equally with votes of others throughout the districts which comprise the total legislative constituency. That "more," to quote Chief Justice Warren in his basic reapportionment opinion of 1964, is "fair and effective representation."

The point can be simply illustrated, although its total dimensions are large and means of achieving fair and effective representation are most subtle and difficult. A statewide election at-large of all members of a legislature would place each voter on the same plane vis-à-vis the legislature. All votes would be "weighted" equally. The majority will would prevail, insofar as there were an identifiable will on various issues within legislative purview. In terms of "fair and effective representation," however, and in terms of incentives to maintain a two-party system, the at-large voting device leaves much to be desired. At-large systems are winner-take-all systems and offer the prospect that a bare 51 percent statewide popular vote will be magnified into 100 percent representation. This would constitute a new form of "malapportionment," a new form of overrepresentation and of underrepresentation of identifiable portions of the electorate. Likewise, the effect on the party system could be devastating. As illustrated in the history of some American constituencies, particularly some city constituencies, effective party competition ceases when the minority party has little prospect of obtaining seats roughly approximating its popular vote strength.

A *third theme* is that components of fair representation are several, and that at least some of them are as amenable to judicial purview as the equal population standard. If the ultimate goal be identified as "fair and effective representation," then some judicial sensitivity to the motives underlying a given apportionment plan, and particularly to the manner of operation in practice of the plan, is essential to achieving that goal.

This is so for two reasons. First, an almost infinite number of apportionment and districting plans are available if one adopts population as a sole factor in apportionment formulae, ignores pre-existing districts, political subdivisions, and natural boundaries, and draws fresh lines on a virginal map. Second, all district lines drawn on an apportionment map are political lines in the sense that they group or separate partisans of one persuasion from fellow partisans in the same area. This grouping and separation occurs whether or not the reapportioner is aware of what he is doing. Whether by chance or by design, the possibility arises that an existing apportionment plan, however equal on a purely mathematical basis, will nevertheless overrepresent or underrepresent identifiable groups of voters. In effect, a reliance on a fairly rigid population standard for apportionment—which requires maximum sacrifice of other considerations such as political subdivision groupings—coupled with lack of meaningful judicial review of the resultant apportionment and districting scheme, can operate to maximize gerrymandering freedom.

The *fourth theme* is that gerrymandering hazards associated with allowing or compelling reapportioners to reapportion solely on a population basis may be minimized if there is a preservation, insofar as feasible, of such common state apportionment rules as maximum preservation of county lines (or other political subdivision lines) in districting. Although such rules are not necessarily antigerrymandering rules, their general thrust is in the direction both of preserving communities of interest which tend to be associated with political subdivisions, and of channelizing the work of the reapportioning body.

The *fifth theme* is that although simple census numbers should not be the exclusive consideration in approaching the task of working out actual apportionment and districting plans, exigencies of the political process normally will prevent reapportioners from making substantial progress unless they do have a mathematical outer boundary within which to work out compromises and adjustments equitable to the two major political parties and other relevant groups. Paradoxically, a precise, mathematical, constitutional limitation on apportionment discretion, which thus restricts the range of possible combinations, may be a sine qua non first, for enabling reapportioners to identify the available mix of population and relevant nonpopulation considerations (including the extent to which county lines can be preserved); second, for avoiding the gerrymandering freedom associated with a simple 100 percent mathematical equality policy; and third, for laying the basis for intelligent compromise leading to an agreed plan. When given clear mathematical guidelines, few legislatures have failed to accomplish reapportionment. For example, in September of 1965 after months of futile legislative effort, the California Supreme Court gave a new deadline and two main guidelines: no district could deviate by more than 15 percent from the average district; the electoral percentage in each house had to be 48 percent or higher.[43] In a month reapportionment was accomplished, and there was no appeal.

The *sixth theme* is that the task of apportionment, awkward and difficult as it may be, should remain in the hands of the legislature or the courts (aided perhaps by bipartisan devices), and should not be transferred to so-called "nonpartisan" boards of commissions or "nonpartisan" computer systems of apportioning and districting. This theme flows naturally from the foregoing themes. All legislative district lines being political in nature—favoring one group of partisans more and another group less —the only route to fair and effective representation is by utilizing a process which will at least make known relevant political factors, and will enable working out a balanced compromise between gains of one party and losses of another.

Beyond the exigencies of reapportionment itself, only by having such information can the forces of public opinion operate and voters make informed judgments on reapportioners' discharge of their trust. Such informed and explicit consideration of democratic political realities is guaranteed by use of true bipartisan commissions, frequently may result from consideration by legislative process, and may result from a judicial process utilizing devices either of pre-trial conference or of special master and fact finder. Politically uninformed districting solely on the basis of symmetry, compactness, and population equality, with the aid of computers, can only lead to a chance goodness or badness, or to a bad plan which is the product of hidden special motives cloaked in the guise of population considerations alone.

The *seventh theme* is not so much theme as rebuttal of one argument which can be leveled against the call made here for explicit recognition of political factors in reapportionment. Against the kind of political awareness suggested here it can be said that it is one thing to enter the political thicket, quite another to "wallow" in it. But this is more cute than perceptive. The courts are in the political thicket whenever they adjudicate and make any order relevant to apportionment. All apportionment being fully political, any order made by a court has a significant political impact. Therefore the only relevant question is whether the concededly "political" judicial order is good or bad, fair or unfair, equitable or inequitable. Such ascertainment is not advanced by putting on blinders and excluding certain kinds of relevant evidence, or even certain kinds of relevant, albeit

43. Silver v. Brown, 63 Cal. 2d 270, 46 Cal. Rptr. 308, 405 P.2d 132, 138–39 (1965).

politically embarrassing, questions, on the ground that to consider such evidence or to consider such questions would be to "wallow" in the political thicket.

More perceptively, this additional observation may be made. In some instances, and the Maryland case (in the course of which the "wallow" comment was made) is one example,[44] a limited, strictly mathematical entry into the political thicket may be all that is needed to give plaintiffs the political gains they seek. Taking off the blinders, i.e., wallowing a bit, may lead to trimming some of the political excesses in the plaintiffs' gains. In Maryland a judicially ordered apportionment added many legislative seats to large suburban counties around Baltimore and Washington. Stopping at this point, and letting the state's traditional county-at-large (winner-take-all) voting system fill these seats, might greatly magnify not only the voice of these areas in the legislature but, expressly, the voice of one wing of the Democratic party in state politics. To proceed beyond this point—to wallow—might lead to judicial orders requiring subdistricting and perhaps modest policing of excesses in subdistricting. The enlarged voice of the suburban areas in the legislature might then continue, but the minority Republican party might hold some of the seats more nearly in proportion to its strength and the basis would be laid for more effective two-party state politics. In the event, in Maryland, the legislature itself broke new ground by requiring partial subdistricting.[45] But in Iowa there was no subdistricting for enlarged urban-county delegations until the State Supreme Court "wallowed" a bit, went beyond simple mathematics and the precedents of the United States Supreme Court, and ordered some subdistricting.[46]

As Harry Truman once said, if you cannot stand the heat don't go into the kitchen. The fatal flaw in the reasoning of those who favor judicial reapportionment but deplore "wallowing," or those who pursue will-o-the-wisp nonpartisan reapportionment, is that they fail to perceive that it is not possible to depoliticize apportionment simply by depoliticizing the *instrument* that does the apportionment work, and/or by truncating the data considered by such instrument. The basic commitment was made in *Baker* in 1962 when reapportionment was held to be a justiciable issue. For all his stress on judicial restraint in his *Baker* dissent, it is doubtful that Justice Frankfurter, had he lived to participate in the post-*Baker* litigation, would have been content to operate semi-blindly on an issue such as reapportionment, which not only affects a certain species of voter

44. Alfred L. Scanlon, Attorney for Plaintiffs, Maryland Committee for Fair Representation v. Tawes, in the course of oral argument before the Supreme Court.
45. Annot. Code of Maryland, Art. 40, § 42(E)(A-1) (1957).
46. Kruidenier v. McCulloch, 142 N.W.2d 355 (Sup. Ct. of Iowa 1966).

equality but also has a block-buster effect on the composition of the legislature, on the conditions of political party competition, on the arrangement and rearrangement of communities of interest—in short, the core of the policy-making process.

The *eighth theme*, and perhaps a less controversial one, is that judicial procedures are inadequate to the task of illuminating relevant issues and possibilities in an apportionment case, adducing and comprehending relevant evidence, and constructing and policing appropriate remedies. Yet courts paradoxically are the best backstop, and necessarily the ultimate backstop, when the political processes fail to accomplish apportionment and districting. The way out of the dilemma is to recognize explicitly, as many judges fortunately have done, that a reapportionment case is sui generis. It calls not only for easing conventional rules about standing to bring suit, but also for a rather free intervenor and amicus policy so that issues and data not relevant to the original parties' interests, or not well handled by them, can be presented to the court by others.

To a degree, all public law cases concerning larger issues of public policy in such fields as antitrust and transportation transcend the interests and talents of plaintiff and defendant. The subtleties of representative government make this factor especially crucial in apportionment cases, and demand a corresponding judicial flexibility of procedure. The conventional adversary method is at its best in private law disputes; it is at its worst, if not eased, in public law disputes touching basic policies of society.

The *ninth theme*, Janus-faced, looks both to the past and the future. It is that except for the South, with its long history of political pathology, and except for some very interesting local government developments, there has been surprisingly little empirical proof, or even argumentative proof, of the supposed "bad" effects on government and public policy flowing from malapportionment, or the supposed "good" effects produced by reapportionment. Of course, if substantial voter equality vis-à-vis the state legislature be taken as a personal civil right, then such proof or lack thereof becomes irrelevant. We do not measure the free speech right of a soap-boxer by the content of his expression, at least not until it reaches an extreme point.

But even viewing the self-centered voter equality aspect of the earlier *Reapportionment Decisions* as being pre-eminent, a conceptual problem remains. The surprising weakness of the few malapportionment-"bad government" correlations which have been attempted—coupled with the traditional doctrine that even such vital personal civil rights as free speech are not absolute—would suggest at the very least the irrelevance if not the futility of being intensely concerned about such relatively minor percentage variances in district populations as three, five, eight, or perhaps even ten percent in some situations. Yet, with straight faces and high zeal, more than a few reapportioners and judges have scrutinized and compared plans on just this basis—and on a census already several years old.

If incongruity is the essence of humor, reapportionment has its aspects of jollity as well as its philosophic complexities and its deep political import.

The *tenth theme* is that the task of making good on "one man-one vote," translated as fair and effective representation, is not exclusively and perhaps not even primarily a judicial task. Courts have created and guided the reapportionment revolution because the normal political forces were locked in by frozen malapportionment systems. Now the freeze is over; the "stranglehold," as a court in Alabama once put it, is released. Needed—indeed, long overdue—is a fresh dialogue on the basics of representative democracy among both political theorists and constitutional lawyers. Man is a political animal, as well as a census statistic for inclusion in an equal population formula.

In summary, it is becoming critically important to begin to move from the rather narrow concern over *malapportionment of people* which has characterized the first years of the reapportionment revolution to concern for *malrepresentation of interests*. Political scientists have known for years that a district system of legislative election is a very inexact method for taking the popular pulse and representing popular will. All district systems of electing legislators—including equal population district systems—may yield unequal and distorted representation. District lines frequently carve up and submerge identifiable interests, sometimes unavoidably. The balance of power position of better organized interests frequently leads to exaggeration of their influence. Those interests which constitute a locked-in minority in a series of districts will, realistically speaking, get little effective representation on policy matters, and no representation at all in terms of power to participate in organization of the legislature.

In short, now that the first round of reapportionment has been accomplished, there is need to talk "one man-one vote" a little less and to talk a little more of "political equity," and of functional components of effective representation. A mathematically equal vote which is politically worthless because of gerrymandering or winner-take-all districting is as deceiving as "emperor's clothes." To solve the problem of malrepresentation of interests, and to make good on Chief Justice Warren's call for "fair and effective representation," additional standards must be devised, both constitutional and statutory, laying down ground rules of political equity. This task has barely begun.

II

Representation in the Grand Tradition: Issues and Values – English

> "I am to look, indeed, to your opinions; but to such opinions as you and I *must* have five years hence. I was not to look to the flash of the day."
>
> Edmund Burke

The relevance of the writings of the great political theorists to the precise issues of reapportionment in America in the 'sixties and 'seventies, and to the fundamental components of a system of fair and effective representation, is not readily apparent. Their focus is on "grand design," on the larger issues of representative democracy and its contrast with nondemocratic systems. There is much on leadership in general, on separation of powers, on conflict between the aristocracy of the intellect and the political equality of men as an ideal. There is little on implementation, on actual experience of mature domocratic states, on the crucial role of political parties, and on the striking contrasts in party style inside democratic systems.

But particular apportionment and districting practices, and the varied conditions of political contest and majority rule which derive therefrom, are the structural heart of the "grand design" of representative democracy. Therefore the "grand design" writings cannot be ignored. A concern for the goals of representative democracy is essential to an assessment of the extent to which the several kinds of "one man-one vote" readjustment may serve or impede the cause of representative democracy.

THE ROLE OF REPRESENTATION IN TRADITIONAL POLITICAL THEORY

Neither the Greeks nor the Romans developed representation forms of major relevance to twentieth-century legislative systems either in America

23

or elsewhere.[1] The Greeks faded in part because they failed to move from the direct democracy of the city-state to representative democracy forms which would have permitted a continuation of consensual government on a substantially enlarged territorial basis. The reason may have been partly psychological, i.e., a Grecian inability to move from a sense of community as an intimate association to a sense of community as an attenuated association resting on trust.

With representation, of course, comes impersonalization. One (the legislator) stands in place of another (the voter). With representation also comes inexactness. The single legislator cannot subsume in his being all of the conflicting aspirations of the plural electorate which stands behind him. On any issue the voters of a given constituency respond with only a melange of tongues; their elected representative can respond with only one voice—or abstain.[2] From this necessary impersonalization and inexactness, which are necessary corollaries of a representation system, may flow an explanation for the lack of appeal of representative democracy in certain times, and the Greek rejection of it. It takes a rather high level of political sophistication, and also a negative assessment of alternative systems, to transcend the traditional personal nature of rulership (found both in kingship and direct democracy) and to create political allegiance to representative democracy with its necessary delegations of trust to a wide range of intermediaries.

When we move to more recent times and the birth of modern styles of representative democracy in the English upheavals of the seventeenth century, we find the discussion colored in part by long-dead issues of outright tyranny and repression, the nature of political obligation and justification for obedience, the scope of the rule of law and ruler subserviance to it, the scope of the electorate and continuance of class representation, tolerance of political dissent, and so on, down a long list of free-government norms now accepted unquestioningly.

From the divine right of kings to the full sweep of "one man-one vote" may seem like a millennial transition. Yet in one generation in seventeenth-century England we find the pretensions of the Stuart, James I, answered by democratic "extremists" in the army of Cromwell, who de-

1. George H. Sabine, A History of Political Theory Ch. 7 (New York: Holt, Rinehart & Winston, rev. ed., 1950); Frank Tenney, "Representative Government in Ancient Politics," 14 Classical Journal 533 (1919); Robert M. MacIver, The Web of Government 164–66, 178–81 (New York: Macmillan, 1947).
2. See Robert G. McCloskey et al., "Issue Conflict and Consensus Among Party Leaders and Followers," 54 Am. Pol. Sci. Rev. 406 (1960); Charles E. Gilbert, "Operative Doctrines of Representation," 57 Am. Pol. Sci. Rev. 604 (1963); McCloskey, "Consensus and Ideology in American Politics," 58 Am. Pol. Sci. Rev. 361 (1964); James B. Christoph, "Consensus and Cleavage in British Political Ideology," 59 Am. Pol. Sci. Rev. 629 (1965).

feated and beheaded James's son, Charles I. As late as 1616 James could charge his judges in Star Chamber as follows:

> That which concerns the mystery of the king's power is not lawful to be disputed; for that is to wade into the weakness of princes, and to take away the mystical reverence that belongs unto them that sit in the throne of God.[3]

Three decades later, in the course of the civil war upheavals of the 1640s, a regimental spokesman, probably a member of the Leveller movement, could tell the Army Council—and be heard if not accepted:

> Really I think that the poorest he that is in England has a right to live as the greatest he; and therefore truly, Sir, I think it's clear, that every man that is to live under a government ought first by his own consent to put himself under that government; and I do think that the poorest man in England is not at all bound in a strict sense to that government that he hath not had a voice to put himself under.[4]

The Levellers were made famous by the flamboyance and persistence of their renowned leader, "Freeborn John" Lilburne, who twice used the jury system to appeal to popular sentiment and win acquittals in political trials. But they were not destined to remake English society overnight, nor to control the Commonwealth which preceded the Stuart Restoration in 1660. The Leveller movement did serve to popularize advanced views of individualism, universal suffrage, the supremacy of the people, and the subjection even of legislative power to the controlling mandates of a written constitution.[5] The Levellers, in one draft of their proposed Agreement of the People, even specified a detailed mathematical legislative apportionment based on population. Leveller ideas perhaps had some impact on John Locke later in the century, but found far more congenial ground in the conditions of colonial America and in the inclinations of such men as William Penn and Roger Williams.

HOBBES

Also a product of the English civil wars of the 1640s was the work of the dour Thomas Hobbes, who makes an odd decade-mate with John Lilburne, but perhaps no more odd are the contending democratic, fascistic, oligarchic, and communistic theories of our own era. At first blush one would not think that the work of Hobbes, who was obsessed with the

3. *The Political Works of James I* 333 (New York: Russell & Russell, 1918), cited by Sabine, *supra* note 1, at 396.
4. *Id.* at 483.
5. Theodore C. Pease, *The Leveller Movement* (New York: Peter Smith, 1916).

idea that society's greatest need was to create an all-powerful sovereign who could control miserable mankind and make civil war henceforth unthinkable, would have any relevance to a discussion of representation. However, as pointed out in the work of Professor Hanna Pitkin, an idea of representation—albeit of a rather special kind—is a key element in Hobbes's developed political system.[6]

Indeed there is a marked parallelism in one respect between the system of Hobbes and the later system of the ambiguous Rousseau. Both sought to lay a basis for viewing the individual as participating in society's rules without necessarily controlling them, or even being consciously in accord with the rules. Hobbes achieved the goal by a theory of irrevocable delegation, with the subject retaining his own occasionally deviant political will. Rousseau achieved it by a fiction of duality of wills. Each individual, in addition to his personal, erratic will, also has a "real (true) will." This "real will" is part of society's purified "general will," which by definition is not necessarily the majority will but rather the will which expresses the best interest of society at a given time.[7] For Rousseau, representation is the slippery process, never ever clearly articulated, of bringing to the fore the "general will." And Rousseau's dualistic concept of the individual's will leads directly to his famous and also treacherous principle that when the individual is repressed by the authorized agents of the "general will," he in reality loses nothing; he is simply being "forced to be free," that is, being forced to honor his own best interest or "real will." [8] In Machiavellian hands such a construction of a theory of political obligation can lead to an inquisition or to fascism as readily as to representative democracy.[9] By contrast with Rousseau's moral slipperiness, Hobbes emerges as an

6. Hanna Pitkin, "Hobbes's Concept of Representation," 58 *Am. Pol. Sci. Rev.* 328 (1964).
7. "It follows from what has been said above that the general will is always right and ever tends to the public advantage. But it does not follow that the deliberations of the People are always equally beyond question. It is ever the way of men to wish their own good, but they do not at all times see where that good lies . . .
"There is often considerable difference between the will of all and the general will. The latter is concerned only with the common interest, the former with the interests that are partial, being itself but the sum of individual wills." J. J. Rousseau, *The Social Contract* 168, 193 (London:J. M. Dent & Sons, Everyman's Library edition, 1947).
And again, "Left to themselves, the People always desire the good, but, left to themselves, they do not always know where the good lies. The general will is always right, but the judgment guiding it is not always well informed. It must be made to see things as they are, sometimes as they ought to be." *Id.* at 204.
8. "To the benefits conferred by the status of citizenship might be added that of Moral Freedom, which alone makes man his own master. For to be subject to appetite is to be a slave, while to obey the laws laid down by society is to be free." *Id.* at 186.
9. The problem is well discussed in G.D.H. Cole's introduction to Rousseau, *The Social Contract* (London: J. M. Dent & Sons, Everyman's Library edition, 1935).

honest authoritarian. In Hobbes, representation is simply sovereign exercise of conferred authority.

In a critical sense Hobbes's concept of representation does relate directly to one facet of twentieth-century representation—and apportionment-districting problems—once the essence of his concept is grasped. His purpose was not only to create overwhelming authority in the ruler, but also to relate the subject to that authority in such a way that the sovereign will could also be viewed as binding on the subject. His ploy was to devise a special agency concept. He identifies as "actor" one who does an act and as "author" one on whose "authority" the act is done. The author, in a sense, owns the act which is done by his authority; it is his act, and he is bound by it. Hence, the famous language of Hobbes's so-called social contract:

> I *authorize* and give up my right of governing myself, to this man, or to this assembly of men, on this condition, that thou give up thy right to him, and *authorize* all his actions in like manner . . . . (Emphasis added.) [10]

Thus is created the authority of the ruler *and also*, at least for Hobbes, the principle that the ruler has plenary, nonreviewable power of action—nonreviewable because by definition the ruler's acts are "owned" by the subjects. The sole question becomes authorization, not manner of exercise of authority. The question of whether or not a man is authorized to act as legislator is a legitimate Hobbesian question; the question of how he performs as legislator is out of bounds. As Professor Pitkin has noted, Hobbes's concept of representation is incomplete both as a general philosophic concept and as a political concept. Nevertheless his concept of representation as centering on the question of authorization of the representative's action has passed into common usage and has been followed by numerous political writers and scholars. For example, for Karl Loewenstein the essence of representation is,

> . . .that the representatives—whatever the manner of their investiture—are authorized in advance to act conjointly in behalf of their constituents and bind them by their collective decisions.[11]

This stress on authorization as the key concept in representation is the aspect which relates directly to present-day reapportionment discussions and litigation. The essence of recent reapportionment rulings by American courts is that under a system of malapportioned legislative districts,

10. Sabine, *supra* note 1, at 468.
11. Pitkin, *supra* note 6, at 340.

the initial commission to act as legislator is tainted.[12] There is no need to get to, or even ask, the question of whether the legislator per se has performed well or ill. Legislators elected from malapportioned districts, that is, districts of unequal population, lack "authorization" to act as legislators and the manner of their conduct in office is immaterial. This approach accords with the almost exclusively mathematical stress in most of the reapportionment opinions and the almost complete absence of a concern either by the litigants or by the courts for data bearing on the question of legislative performance. Under an "authorization approach," such data are irrelevant.

This conclusion of tainted authority flowing from the unequal population of legislative districts depends upon two premises. The major premise is the political equality of man. The minor premise is that the principle of political equality of man requires not merely a system of majority rule, but also a system under which no legislative district—and therefore no man or set of men—has a mathematical relation to the legislature substantially different from the relation of other men.

Obviously, a primary stress on the premise of political equality of men can provide a basis for questioning the "representative authority" of legislators in a malapportioned legislative body, even though they may be performing well in regard to such corollary tests as providing fair and effective representation of the various interests and parties in the state as a whole. At the same time, these considerations of fairness and of operating effectiveness in a representation system remain, even if the initial commission to act as legislator is untainted by any mathematical malapportionment of particular districts. These considerations also may be relevant to the question of how substantial is the "substantial equality" of district population required by the premise of political equality of man.

Hobbes was an ad hoc philosopher who set out to create a formal theory of political authority.[13] His formal theory had little relation to the affairs of men either in times of strife or in times of peace. Behind his "verbal game," as Professor Pitkin put it, "there lies a real problem of the creation of political consensus, the peaceful settlement of disputes, the

12. Karl Loewenstein, *Political Power and the Government Process* 38 (Chicago: University of Chicago Press, 1957). Additional examples of such usages found by Professor Pitkin include the writings of Avery Leiserson, Edward Sait, Ernest Barker, Hans Wolff, George Cornwall Lewis, John Plamenatz, Joseph Tussman, Eric Voegelin. For references to the writings of these men see Pitkin, *supra* note 6, at 337, fn. 31. See also Judith N. Shklar, "Rousseau's Images of Authority," 58 *Am. Pol. Sci. Rev.* 919 (1964).
13. His basic concern was authority (authorization) on the institutional level of the structure of the social system, not authorization as an aspect of collective decision-making. See Talcott Parsons, "Authority Legitimation, and Political Action," in *Authority* (NOMOS I) 198 (Carl J. Friedrich, editor, Cambridge: Harvard University Press, 1958).

creation of community. These are real political problems, in the solution of which representation (in its full sense) can play an important part." [14] Similarly, the important current goal of equalization of legislative districts, which purifies the "authorization" of legislators, is only a formal and not a functional goal. It may be insufficient as a sole reliance in achieving the operational goals of consensus, of disputes settlement, and of community.

In sum, from the insufficiency of Hobbes's construction flows one of the major issues of representation (and reapportionment) today: representation as (formal) *authorization* versus representation as (effective) *action*. The former is now justiciable, and judicially policed; the latter, though presumably also justiciable, is still in embryo so far as judicial policing is concerned. A modern majoritarian democrat would be shocked to be told he had anything in common with the author of the *Leviathan*. But reapportioners who argue for a purely formal entry into the political thicket—an entry to "purify authorization" by equalizing legislative district populations, without concern for curbing gerrymandering and other operational inequities—are more the heirs of Hobbes than of Madison.

LOCKE

The historian of representative democracy might expect to find himself at home with John Locke. He was both the rationalizer of the system of parliamentary supremacy which England acquired in 1688, and the spiritual ancestor of the signers of the American Declaration of Independence. The Declaration, indeed, is little more than a simplified presentation of several grand Lockeian themes: the origin of man in a state of nature, natural rights, the law of nature, the unsatisfactory state of nature because of the lack of any mode of enforcement of the natural laws' rules of self-limitation, the consensual creation of government to better preserve natural rights and enforce natural law, and the implicit right of government change (revolution) if the conditional allegiance of subject to ruler is vitiated by the ruler's deviation from his charter of preservation of natural rights. At the level, however, of setting up a legislature, arranging subelectorates, and working out effective forms of representation, Locke largely assumed the English forms of his day, in which suffrage was narrow and population was only one of several representation components. Like many seminal democratic theorists, Locke was not process-oriented, either regarding the political processes of democracy in general or the processes of legislation as influenced by the underlying apportionment and districting system. His comments on "rotten boroughs" may suggest a connection to

14. Pitkin, *supra* note 6, at 918.

the Levellers of an earlier day, but the Leveller concept of a mass electorate was totally foreign to Locke. Indeed, in Locke's day the mass electorate, which is now the basis for representative democracy and colors all
of its workings, was for England still almost 300 years away.

Although hardly a "one man-one vote" advocate in the Leveller tradition, because wealth and property had their prerogatives too, Locke's intrinsic majoritarianism did inveigh against "rotten boroughs." A no-inter-
est borough is an anomaly in a consensual system of self-rule. Therefore
he saw an obvious need to remedy situations where a place with "scarce so
much housing as a sheep-cote, or more inhabitants than a shepherd" nevertheless "sends as many representatives to the grand assembly of law-
makers as a whole county numerous in people and powerful in riches." [15]
The power of the people having been exhausted by the social compact, at
least pending a further revolution, the solution suggested is executive prerogative: "for it being the interest as well as intention of the people to
have a fair and equal representative, whoever brings it nearest to that is
an undoubted friend to and establisher of the government, and cannot
miss the consent and approbation of the community." [16]

Reading executive prerogative as judicial prerogative, we have here the
spirit and justification for *Baker* v. *Carr* in 1962! However, the functioning of a "fair and equal representative," the nature of actual voting patterns and systems, the limits, if any, on majoritarianism were never carefully delineated by Locke. Indeed, a deep probing into representation
might have involved Locke in difficulties, for his theory of social contract
and the absence of formal review devices implied "a competency to the
majority which cannot be mechanically subordinated to his previous
values." [17]

BURKE

English representation thought immediately relevant to the American scene
reached a high point a century after Locke in the work of Edmund Burke.
Nineteenth-century English thought and experience was more specialized
and took two forms: (1) the mechanism of periodic population reapportionment which followed the further expansion of the suffrage in 1884;

15. John Locke, *An Essay Concerning the True Original, Extent and End of Civil
Government* 3, 93 (New York: Oxford University Press, World's Classics Galaxy Edition, 1948).
16. *Ibid.*
17. Alfred de Grazia, *Public and Republic* 27 (New York: Knopf, 1951); Robert Luce,
Legislative Principles 460–91 (Boston: Houghton Mifflin, 1930).

(2) the devices for proportional representation popularized by Hare and Mill.[18]

Unlike most writers, Burke, as a theorist-practitioner of the arts of representation, was empirical. His thought still conditions disscussions of constituent-legislator relationships, corollary questions such as the harmonization of constituency interest with national interest, and the supposed distinction between a mere "delegate" and a statesmanlike "representative." [19]

It is in regard to these questions that we turn to Burke, rather than in regard to the question of the structure of a representation system. For on the latter question, Burke, unlike Locke, was a "virtual representer" in the seventeenth-century tradition. Indeed, he improved on the theoretical justifications for nonpopular representation formulated a century earlier in reaction to the Leveller thrust for broadened manhood suffrage and for strict constituency control of legislative decision-making.

It has become conventional to derive from Burke an either-or approach to constituency representation. The legislator figuratively is to poll his constituency before each legislative vote and faithfully record the majority feeling—the so-called delegate model of representation. Alternatively, the legislator, upon due study and reflection, is to make an independent judgment on the merits of the issue at hand, including any necessary accommodation of constituency interest and national interest, and vote accordingly—the so-called free-agent model of representation. If one must choose between these two strict Burkeian alternatives, one must opt of course for the delegate model, else there is no representative function; in grossest terms, no democracy. One might as well set up a Platonic philosopher-king.

On this basis can be explained the rise and practice for a time in England and America of a "doctrine of instructions," i.e., the doctrine that a legislator is bound by a clear expression of the will of the majority of his constituents, or a clear expression of the will of his patron in the case of an English pocket borough. The doctrine was common in early English parliamentary democracy, especially among the Levellers or radical democrats. In America it took the form of state legislative instructions to the United States Senators elected by them.[20]

The trouble with this doctrine of instructions is not that it is concep-

18. For a recent survey with a heavier stress on party practice than on representation theory, see A. H. Birch, *Representative and Responsible Government: An Essay on the British Constitution* (Toronto: University of Toronto Press, 1964).
19. Robert H. Murray, *Edmund Burke: A Biography* 238 (New York: Oxford University Press, 1931).
20. De Grazia, *supra* note 17, at 123–28.

tually bad but that it is psychologically bad. It places the stress on legislator passivity and constituency dominance. It thus denigrates the potentially creative leadership role of the legislator. Insofar as the legislator is a professional, expending more time and having more information resources at his disposal than his constituents, it also denigrates the role of intelligence in politics. Perhaps it is this factor, rather than any desire for the outright adoption of the free-agent model, which explains the appeal of the Burkeian analysis of representation even inside the robust American democratic tradition of direct legislator-constituent relationships. Leaders are needed, as well as mere recorders. The eternal ambivalence of the democrat is that by his principles he must delegate in miserly fashion but in practice he expects to receive salvation at the hands of strong, wise leaders.

The essence of Burke's theory of representation was sharply expressed in his oft-quoted speech to the electors of Bristol, explaining his conduct during his six-year term. On the issue of legislator responsiveness to the public polls he said:

> I am to look, indeed, to your opinions; but to such opinions as you and I *must* have five years hence. I was not to look to the flash of the day.[21]

Burke then defended himself against four principal criticisms of his record. His defense to the first charge, that he had not returned to Bristol often enough, was disarming. He had not come back earlier, he said, because he was in opposition to the constituents on the American and the Irish trade question; he had not come back later, because he had been proven right and did not want to gloat. The other three charges were that he had not followed constituency desire on the Irish Trade Acts, on bills to ease imprisonment of debtors, and on the Roman Catholic question. In all three instances he had favored easing the restrictions. His position was what most today might call the enlightened, the proper, view. He was facing in the direction of accommodation, tolerance, and national unity.

Burke's position has an appeal; it also has an Achilles' heel. He failed to perform an additional task which, perhaps, is the highest task of the legislator who aspires to the aura of philosopher-king and seeks to go down in history as a legislator-statesman. That task is to share his knowledge, in-

---

21. *The Works of the Right Honourable Edmund Burke* III: 13 (New York: Oxford University Press, World's Classics Edition, 1935); see also Alfred Cobban, *Edmund Burke and the Revolt Against the Eighteenth Century* 60–62 (New York: Macmillan, 1929). The question, "How can government be both rational and representative?" is explored in Harvey C. Mansfield, Jr., "Rationality and Representation in Burke's 'Bristol Speech,'" in *Rational Decision* (NOMOS VII) 197 (Carl J. Friedrich, editor, New York: Atherton Press, 1964).

sights, and purposes with his constituency and to participate in the task of building a consensus for viable policies. Burke neglected what was referred to a century later by Walter Bagehot—himself distinctly Burkeian in cast, as was the entire nineteenth-century English Establishment—as the "teaching" function of members of Parliament.[22] A remote correctness is not sufficient. Democracy has many crucibles, and the legislator who specializes in the legislative arena at the expense of maintaining consensus within his constituency may end by finding himself successful in the former but melted down in the latter.

So with Burke. Having turned his back on his constituency for six years, he returned to a divided populace.[23] After taking their pulse for a few days he bowed to their opposition, withdrew his candidacy, and never stood before a large electorate again. He pursued the balance of his illustrious parliamentary career as an M.P. from Lord Rockingham's pocket borough of Malton, free from constituency worries, from the developing intricacies of party government, and from concern for the components of fair representation. Burke's retreat from Bristol to Malton signifies not so much a switch from a principle of population representation to area representation but rather a continuance of his "natural aristocrat" philosophy, which was at once antiroyal and antimajoritarian. This philosophy remained dominant in feeling and practice until the Reform Act of 1867 and the Representation of the People Act of 1884 approached universal manhood suffrage, remade the tone of English politics, and laid the basis for strong party discipline. Walter Bagehot could still say in the latter part of the nineteenth century that the "nominal constituency was not the real constituency." [24] Aided by the English custom of deference to one's "betters," political parties and their candidates were rank-and-wealth-based; the issue put before the electorate was "which of two rich people will you choose?" [25]

From Burke, in short, we get the alternative representation constructs —free-agent model v. delegate model—which are the starting point for all serious conceptional analyses of representation. These constructs are the starting point also for recent empirical inquiry, to be discussed subsequently, which uses mathematical techniques and analyzes the voting power in legislatures of the legislator and the represented constituency.[26]

22. Walter Bagehot, *The English Constitution* 236 (New York: Oxford University Press, 1900); Cobban, *supra* note 21, at 61.
23. P. T. Underdown, "Edmund Burke, the Commissary of His Bristol Constituents, 1774–1780," 73 *English Historical Review* 252–69 (1958).
24. Bagehot, *supra* note 22, at 6.
25. *Id.* at 7.
26. John F. Banzhaf III, "Weighted Voting Doesn't Work: A Mathematical Analysis," 19 *Rutgers L. Rev.* 317 (1965); William H. Riker, "Some Ambiguities in the Notion

And it is from the delegate model, obviously, that we receive much of the impetus to equalize—and to equalize closely—the populations of legislative constituencies. Only thus, it is argued, can the people, with equal power, instruct their governors.

of Power," 58 Am. Pol. Sci. Rev. 341 (1964); L. S. Shapely and Martin Shubik, "A Method for Evaluating the Distribution of Power in a Committee System," 48 Am. Pol. Sci. Rev. 787 (1956).

III

Representation in the Grand Tradition:
Issues and Values – American

"Democracy is a form of government that is never completely
achieved."

Robert M. MacIver, *The Web of Government* (1947)

As an operating democracy America always has had "representation" implicit in its institutions. Surprisingly, however, American representative institutions constitute a virtually unanalyzed morass of logical inconsistency
and conceptual ambiguity which is ill-concealed by the simple, repetitive
rhetoric of "popular sovereignty," "political equality," and "majority
rule." This insufficiently scrutinized area includes the structure of representative institutions, the premises from which they derive, their precise
modes of operation, the supposed goals to be attained, and standards for
assessing relative success or failure in operation.

THE AMERICAN EXPERIMENT

The Spirit of 1776 itself seems to present few problems, or at least to present problems no more serious than those that exist on the face of John
Locke's work. The inalienable rights of man, natural law, and consent of
the governed, seem to present a unified and simple political philosophy
until the process of implementation begins. The concept of "consent of
the governed" implies some process of regularly ascertaining that consent.
This leads naturally to the concept of decision-making by majority rule in
a legislature or parliament which is itself the product of popular vote.

But by what process are inalienable rights to be preserved, including
preservation even against the strong feelings of a current majority? Does
majority rule imply majority infallibility? If so, the concept of "natural
rights" or of "natural law" has no place in democratic theory; voting is
sufficient. If majority infallibility is rejected, then a single rule of popular

35

voting would be able to subsume under it a preservation of *each* individual's inalienable rights *only* if a rule of unanimity is substituted for majority rule. Wholly apart from the practical consequences of inaction which such a rule would entail, a rule of unanimity also would pose the philosophic problem of elevating the power of the one or the few above the power of the many. A rule of unanimity could operate to require a majority to continue to live under a set of conditions which, however distasteful, they were powerless to change through governmental action.

At a more practical level, the implementation of the Declaration of Independence required the institution of new state governments to serve the newly freed American colonial societies, and the institution of a central government to carry on the Revolutionary War. It also brought to the fore the full richness of policy disputes on such problems as finance and taxation, trade and commerce, and debt management. It impelled the rise of interest alignments, or "factions," to promote and safeguard the developing political and economic interests. The rule of unanimity, tried in the central government under the Articles of Confederation more on grounds of necessity than on principle, proved to be a glorious failure—glorious only in that the war was won.

As a consequence, the men who assembled to create the American Constitution, and who defended it in the essays known as *The Federalist*, were men who had found the simplified democratic doctrines of John Locke and of the Declaration of Independence not so much faulty as simply inadequate to the dimensions of the task of building and operating a consensual system. Although still Lockeian in spirit, the Founding Fathers—or at least a substantial portion of them—were also Burkeian in outlook. They placed substantial stress on the importance of preserving the influence of status, wealth, and education. They feared the onslaught of those with insufficient stake in society to have a capacity for deliberate action.

Although the electorate was small by latter-day standards, recent studies which severely undercut the work of Charles A. Beard suggest that property and wealth were sufficiently diffused, at least in the Northern states, so that the electorate was far larger than that in contemporary England.[1] A concern for the power of numbers therefore was not strange. Even by its own limited standards, the new government was standing on an electorate far broader than any that had yet attempted to govern a nation-state. This attempt was to be made in the aftermath of several years of war, in the absence of national tradition, in the absence of experience

1. Robert E. Brown, *Middle Class Democracy and the Revolution in Massachusetts, 1691–1780* (Ithaca: Cornell University Press, 1955); Robert E. Brown, *Charles Beard and the Constitution* 61–72 (Princeton: Princeton University Press, 1956).

with national political associations, and in the presence of a very recent experience of discord on vital economic issues culminating in the failure of the predecessor government under the Articles. Experience under state governments in the period immediately following revolution had been so unreassuring that legislative powers, rather than executive powers, were viewed as posing the greater danger to the liberties of men. Even Jefferson could be cited, referring to the concentration of powers in the Virginia legislature, for the proposition that "173 despots should surely be as oppressive as one. An elective despotism is not the government we fought for." [2]

In the sweep of American political theory since 1787 the following elements merit brief analysis because they have had a critical role in shaping the forms and standards of legislative representation: first, the Madisonian system of the original constitution, including the subsequent distortion in Calhoun's doctrine of the concurrent majority; second, the Jacksonian-Populist return to a Lockeian majoritarianism which dominated the nineteenth century and made all-pervading the spirit, although not always the form, of direct representation; and third, twentieth-century pluralism-in-fact (though not well articulated in theory) with its proliferation of minorities. This pluralism, in interesting and quite ambivalent ways, has forced us further in the direction of political equality. At the same time it has preserved, if not heightened, the sense of tension between commitment to majority rule and concern for minority rights which characterized the original Madisonian system. Under our present pluralism, concern for minority rights has assumed a functional rather than a formal meaning. In regard to representation it seeks to provide the means for minority access to government and minority participation in the multifaceted process of decision-making. Few Americans are not now a member of at least one identifiable minority, with interests and goals sufficiently overt to have important bearing on at least some aspects of national policy. Examples include our religious groups in regard to increasingly clear-cut issues of church-state relations; union and business groups in regard to industrial relations, trade policy, and government contracts; our political party system, where the term minority party takes on new meaning as Republicanism shows increasing signs of following Whiggism into the futility of a loyal opposition and eventual reformation; attempts of political associations ranging from the well-established Americans for Democratic Action (the "know-everythings") to various right-wing groups (the "know-nothings") to fill the vacuum in public dialogue created by weakness of the

2. Thomas Jefferson, *Notes on the State of Virginia* 120 (William Peden, editor, Chapel Hill: University of North Carolina Press, 1955).

conventional party system; and innumerable subgroups covered within these very broad and shifting groupings.

MADISONIANISM

The essence of all government is the creation of a set of power relationships whereby a *part* may conclude the *whole*. Modes for formation and reformation of the conclusive *part* (it may need to be reformed with each new decision), the role of opinion and deliberation, provision for reviewability and accountability—all these are elements which in various combinations produce nondemocracy, and the variant forms and degrees of democracy. Failure to perceive, or to concede, the principle that a part may conclude the whole may flow from a misconception of the "consent of the governed" concept,[3] or from desire to safeguard nonnegotiable interests. Whatever the cause, a rejection of this vital principle of governmental action—and governments do exist to act—underlay the failure of the Articles of Confederation. It also underlay the extremism of Calhoun's doctrine of concurrent majorities, a doctrine which sought to conceal what really was an antigovernment secession principle under the more innocuous-appearing mantle of a plenary sectional veto power.[4] In fairness it must be added that, very prophetically, Calhoun was stating the *price of Union*. For the majority, the price was too high; the Civil War resulted. He was also illustrating what recent social scientists have identified as the factor of intensity with which divergent views are held.[5]

From the principle that on occasion a part necessarily must be able to conclude the whole flows also the constitutional principle that denies the existence of absolute rights. Even the near-absolute of freedom of speech has limits. These are found either in overriding social interests (e.g., no one may cry fire in a crowded theater with impunity), or in a somewhat

3. C. W. Cassinelli, *The Politics of Freedom* 86–101 (Seattle: University of Washington Press, 1961). This problem is also central to the "public interest" concept. See *The Public Interest* (*NOMOS V*) (Carl J. Friedrich, editor, New York: Atherton Press, 1962), especially the essays by Stephen K. Bailey, Brian M. Barry, Edgar Bodenheimer, Gerard Colm, Wayne A. R. Leys, and Frank J. Sorauf. See also the essay by Cassinelli at 46 note 1, and Glendon A. Schubert, *The Public Interest: A Critique of a Political Concept* (Glencoe, Ill.: Free Press, 1961).

4. John Calhoun, "A Disquisition on Civil Government," in *The Works of John C. Calhoun* I:187 (Richard K. Cralle, editor, New York: Peter Smith Press, 1864). This historically oriented statement is not meant to denigrate Calhoun's significance as a cogent expositor of a new science of self-interest politics, which leads conceptually to modern behavioral social science. This aspect of Calhoun is analyzed appreciatively in Ralph Lerner, "Calhoun's New Science of Politics," 57 *Am. Pol. Sci. Rev.* 918 (1963).

5. Robert A. Dahl, *A Preface to Democratic Theory* 90–123 (Chicago: University of Chicago Press, Phoenix edition, 1963); James M. Buchanan and Gordon Tullock, *The Calculus of Consent* 125–52 (Ann Arbor: University of Michigan Press, 1962).

less honest process of special definition (i.e., expressions of obscene nature are not free speech and hence not within any constitutional principle of protected expression).[6] This principle of legal order does not deny the possible existence of inalienable rights; it indicates that their ultimate vindication may be only by revolution, transcending the constitutional system.

The concept of "inalienable rights," at least in the socialized form of near-absolute rights inside a constitutional system, is grounded deep in the American theory and practice of government; through self-limitation, checks and balances, and judicial review it perpetually conditions the concept of "majority rule." Madisonianism, which is really the basic theory of the original constitutional system of 1787, grounds itself on this view, with an added thought that certain interests of status, education, and wealth are among the rights needing special protection against full majoritarianism.

The primary concern of 1787 was to create a viable power to govern; a corollary concern was to avoid tyranny—and to the Madisonians this meant a tyranny of the majority. The burden of the essays of Madison, Hamilton, and Jay, collected as *The Federalist*, is to articulate and defend this system.

The major outlines of the nonmajoritarian constitutional system of checks and balances, including the augmenting forms which have arisen since 1787, are familiar to all observers of American government. They constitute a rather imposing list. From the constitutional text derive the indirect election of the President and Senators and the direct election of Representatives—all three from separate constituencies; bicameralism; presidential veto power; congressional power of impeachment and removal; presidential appointing power and senatorial power of confirmation; presidential treaty negotiation and senatorial assent; differing terms for the Senate and House, and the two-year rotation of one-third of the Senate; the extraordinary majority requirements in the two-step constitutional amendment procedure; and the division of power between nation and state implicit in federalism itself.

From constitutional practice derive the institution of judicial review, the Senate filibuster, senatorial "courtesy," the seniority system for committee chairmen and their special powers, decentralized political parties, and a variety of lesser techniques formal and informal for curbing leadership. Parenthetically it may be noted that insofar as Calhoun's post-Madisonian and minority-protecting "doctrine of concurrent majority"

6. Schenck v. United States, 249 U.S. 47, 52 (1918) (O. W. Holmes, J.). Roth v. United States, 354 U.S. 476, 485 (1957).

has lived, and to a surprising extent it has, it rests primarily on such non-majoritarian constitutional practices as the broad power of committee chairmen, the "conservative" Southern monopoly of congressional committee chairmanships whenever the Democratic party is in power, the seniority system, which insulates committee rank from the current election returns, requirements of extraordinary majorities to pass certain measures, the filibuster, and the veto. State legislatures are equally affected by some of these practices and such additional factors as the pressure for unanimity in short sessions, and such suggested but empirically unexplained typologies of unanimity as custom and a disposition to avoid coercion (the consensus of the Quaker meeting).[7]

Of special relevance to representation theory is the stress on dangers of "faction" and the necessity of controlling "faction," which is central to Madison's thought. It is only because of the rise of factions that the extensive play and counterplay of separated and checked powers is necessary, for although a "dependence on the people is, no doubt, the primary control on the government," all "experience has taught mankind the necessity of auxiliary precautions." [8]

Madison's famous definition of "faction" occurs in Number 10 of *The Federalist* and treats majorities and minorities with equal suspicion:

> By a faction, I understand a number of citizens, whether amounting to a majority or a minority of the whole, who are united and actuated by some common impulse of passion, or of interests, adversed to the rights of other citizens, or to the permanent and aggregate interests of the community.[9]

Madison offered two solutions to the problem of controlling factions and averting tyranny. One was that minority factions could be controlled by the republican principle of majority rule; the other was that danger of majority factions could be minimized, and in fact was minimized in the proposed new republic, by the factor of a large, diverse electorate. Small republics, in Madison's view, would tend to be faction-ridden but, as he put it:

> Extend the sphere, and you take in a greater variety of parties and interests; you make it less probable that a majority of the whole will have a common motive to invade the rights of other citizens; or if

7. Heinz Eulau, "Logics of Rationality in Unanimous Decision-Making," in *Rational Decision* (NOMOS VII) 26 (Carl J. Friedrich, editor, New York: Atherton Press, 1964).
8. Alexander Hamilton or James Madison, *The Federalist* No. 51:354–55 (New York: Tudor Publishing Co., 1947).
9. Madison, *supra* note 8, No. 10:63.

such a common motive exists, it will be more difficult for all who feel it to discover their own strength and to act in unison with each other.[10]

As Professor Dahl has pointed out, there are a number of gaps and inconsistencies in the Madisonian system. Not the least of them is that on this crucial question of avoiding a majority "factionalism," Madison's argument really boils down to a prediction of inefficiency. In Professor Dahl's words, "because majorities are likely to be unstable and transitory in a large and pluralistic society, they are likely to be politically ineffective" [11] either for good or for evil. He sees no likelihood that extending the sphere of political activity will operate only to curtail "bad" majorities and not "good" majorities. Logically his position is impregnable.

As a matter of democratic faith, however, and perhaps also as a matter of empirical observation over the course of American history, the proposition is at least arguable that, in Madison's terms, the creation of a "common motive to invade the rights of other citizens" will be less likely to arise on a broad basis than the common motive to achieve a compromised and adjusted general good. There is a necessary interrelation in the Madisonian system between the pluralism of factions and the parceling out of power among governmental units, thus requiring a coalition of factions even for a temporary majority.

Viewed thusly, the essence of the Madisonian system, conceding its ambivalence on questions of preferred position for the educated and the wealthy, is a theory of *representation*. A primary safeguard against "factionalism," that is, against the rise of dominant interests "adversed to the rights of other citizens," is provision of channels for representation of the maximum number of interests so that policy decisions will reflect views and interests of a broad cross-section of society. If this be the goal and the faith, then the representation system should be devised to maximize the likelihood that a variety of interests, rather than a few dominant interests, will be represented formally in the processes of government: hence, the original constitutional system, with its varied provisions for direct and indirect election of the different parts of the legislature and the executive, based on overlapping but distinct electorates.

Translated into modern parlance, this key principle of representation in the Madisonian system of safeguards against "factionalism" certainly would frown on systems of apportionment and districting which predictably and continuously operate to overrepresent majorities and to underrepresent minorities. Specifically, a Madisonian theorist would tend to

10. *Id.* at 69.
11. Dahl, *supra* note 5, at 30.

view with suspicion a frequent use of "winner-take-all" systems such as apportionments into large, multimember districts, which make it difficult for minority interests, even when relatively concentrated, to elect representatives. The suspicion might extend also to the "general ticket" modification of the original electoral college system where, by direction of the state legislatures, the entire electoral vote of a state traditionally has been allocated to the candidate achieving a mere plurality in the state's popular vote. However, the single nature of the executive office makes its analysis in terms of representation theory substantially different from analysis of the legislature.

In short, from the Madisonian system derives faith in representative pluralism as a safeguard against the tyranny of majority factionalism. By a slight extension of democratic belief, there also derives faith in representative pluralism as a mechanism for identifying the common good. If one were to attempt to capture the essence of the Madisonian representation system in a label, it might aptly be called a system of *preponderant, concurrent minorities*. The Madisonian style of thought is deeply rooted and continues to have great appeal today for, as Professor Dahl also has observed, "the preponderant number of politically active Americans believe themselves to be members, at least part of the time, of one or more minorities" [12] and consequently have occasion to fear from time to time the implications of unlimited majority rule.

JACKSONIAN-POPULIST SYSTEM OF DIRECT REPRESENTATION

At the risk of rather gross oversimplification, it may be suggested that the sweep of American political thought and practice from the decline of Madisonianism in the early nineteenth century to the modern American era dating roughly from the end of World War II, may be characterized by these relatively simple elements: (1) rise of a robust but also almost childlike faith in the self-governing capactiy of the great mass of the people, embryonic in Thomas Jefferson, full-grown in Andrew Jackson; (2) consequent impatience with all forms of indirect or attenuated representation, which reached full development in Populist-backed reforms such as the direct primary, the initiative, the referendum, and the recall only after the beginning of the twentieth century; (3) continuance of a sectionalized and decentralized political party system, whose operation as a representation device always has been fundamentally different from the English system of party government; (4) concern—as a counter-development to the majoritarianism of the direct democracy movement—for enriching

12. *Ibid.*

the representation process by building into the election system specific devices to ensure some minority representation.

a. *Confidence in the People*

The resounding, variously phrased rhetoric of "popular sovereignty," "majority rule," "political equality" seldom can be taken at face value. Few "conservatives" have wanted to abolish elections; few "liberals" have wanted to go it alone without a constitution. Major differences often can be detected, however, in the degree of confidence placed in people. Differences on this issue may reveal more important distinguishing characteristics of a political philosopher than the carefully articulated logic of his system. Few elements stand out more sharply in Madisonian theory than distrust of "faction," including "majority faction."

By the time we reach the age of Jackson an almost complete reversal has occurred. The transition theorist is the ever-ambivalent but ever-quotable Jefferson. His central characteristic, perhaps explaining his ambivalence, is that he was a highly successful practising politician over a long period of colonial, revoluntionary, confederate, and national development. He was sufficiently Madisonian to be a supporter of the original constitutional system of separated and checked powers in the central government. He recognized a "natural *aristoi*" [13] and viewed that governmental form as good which enabled the *aristoi* to rise to positions of leadership. His position on breadth of franchise cannot be summarized in a word. His well-known inclination to view a nation of small farmers as the model for the good society was sometimes expressed in almost lyrical terms:

> Those who labour in the earth are the chosen people of God, if ever He had a chosen people, whose breasts He had made His peculiar deposit for substantial and genuine virtue.[14]

In a nation that *was* a nation of small farmers this is a democratic-oriented concept. But he could write as follows of the city population, which was already becoming an important force:

> The mobs of great cities add just as much to the support of pure government as sores do to the strength of the human body . . . .

> I think our governments will remain virtuous for many centuries; as long as they are chiefly agricultural; and this shall be as long as there shall be vacant lands in any part of America. When they get piled up

13. Charles E. Merriam, *A History of American Political Theories* 156 (New York: Macmillan, 1928).
14. Jefferson, *supra* note 2, at 175.

upon one another in large cities, as in Europe, they will become corrupt as in Europe.[15]

Yet the belief persists that a distinguishing characteristic of Jeffersonian democracy was faith in the political capacity of the great mass of people. As a factor distinguishing Jeffersonians from the Madison of *The Federalist* Number 10, from John Adams, and from Alexander Hamilton, the distinction is supportable. But it is not until Jacksonianism that we encounter full-blown majoritarianism.

The major elements of Jacksonianism are well known and include: extension of the suffrage so that only race and sex restrictions remained; short tenure and rotation in office; extension of popular election to judges and to administrative officials; preference for direct rather than indirect representative forms, best exemplified by transformation of presidential electors into mere party functionaries; emergence of the executive as a popular spokesman tending to dominate the legislature.[16]

Likewise the basic elements of that latter-day Jacksonianism known as Populism, whose slogan was "return government to the people," are well known and include: direct primary; initiative, referendum, and recall; nonpartisan elections; further extension of the elective principle to officeholders; curbing of judicial review.[17]

In basic spirit Jacksonianism, and its latter-day variant Populism which has been referred to as the "extremity of direct representation," [18] is a return to the untrammeled majoritarianism of John Locke. Although inspired by Locke, the men of the Revolution and of the Constitutional Convention were keenly aware that in Locke's system the rights of the individual and minority rights against government stood in uneasy potential opposition to Locke's central doctrine of majority rule. There was no formal provision for protecting the former against the latter; indeed, there was no overt recognition that a problem could exist. Add to this a lack of full trust in the great mass of the people, found not only in the leading Federalists but to a degree also in Jefferson, and we have the explanation for the tension and ambiguity that runs through Madisonian theory.

The tension vanishes with Jacksonianism and Populism. The explana-

15. Jefferson, *supra* note 2, at 179.
16. Arthur M. Schlesinger, Jr., *The Age of Jackson* (Boston: Little, Brown, 1945); Joseph L. Blau, editor, *Social Theories of Jacksonian Democracy* (New York: Liberal Arts Press, 1954); Glyndon G. Van Deusen, *The Jacksonian Era* (New York: Harper, 1959).
17. Richard E. Hofstadter, *The Age of Reform* (New York: Knopf, 1955); Austin Ranney and Willmoore Kendall, *Democracy and the American Party System* (New York: Harcourt Brace, 1956).
18. Alfred de Grazia, *Public and Republic* 146 (New York: Knopf, 1951).

tion seems to be that the leaders of these movements were able to adopt what Professor Willmoore Kendall has referred to as Locke's "latent premise" that men on the average are rational and just. Thus:

> The man who thinks he knows that the majority is rational and just can speak of the right of the majority and remain silent about the duties which attach to that right, because it follows as a matter of course from his major premise that the latter will be discharged.[19]

With the tension thus resolved, Kendall derives the four tenets of the majority-rule democrat: formal political equality, formal popular sovereignty, techniques for discovering the (unanimous or divided) popular will, reception of majority decisions as the equivalent of (though not necessarily as desirable as) unanimous ones.[20] Except for the critical problem of fitting in judicial review, these four tenets would seem to have more than a little in common with today's "one man-one vote" reapportionment majoritarianism.

Both as systems assumed to be consistent with protection of individual and minority interests, and as representation systems, Jacksonianism and Populism leave much to be explained. The openness of society, the frontier, the exuberance of Manifest Destiny, and the mere fact that the range of matters thought to be within the range of government was small, all contributed to minimization in practice of majoritarian excesses. There was a seamy side, however, which included not only such events as the hounding of the Mormons but also as Professor Arthur M. Schlesinger, Jr., has noted, a general debasement of standards of official performance. The Populist answer was simply to try to cure the ills of direct democracy by still stronger doses of direct voter impact on governmental structure and public policies. Its emotive "return government to the people" slogan assumed an ever-alert, constantly rational and substantially homogeneous community. It thus flew directly in the face of every significant population, technological, sociological, heterogeneity-producing trend of its own time. Yet such was the appeal to the intellectual of the agrarian Populist attack on bigness and on machine politics, and of its plea to institute direct citizen-government controls, that Populism, through support of intellectuals, had considerable influence on community standards for reforming government despite its slight impact on practical politics, where localized machines continued to hold sway.[21]

19. Willmoore Kendall, "John Locke and the Doctrine of Majority Rule," *Illinois Studies in the Social Sciences*, Vol. 26, No. 2, 134 (Urbana: University of Illinois Press, 1941).
20. *Id.* at 43.
21. Hofstadter, *supra* note 17.

b. *Political Parties and Representation*

From the standpoint of representation theory a central aspect of the long sweep of direct representation from Jacksonianism through Populism into the present century is the weak—indeed, largely ignored—role of political parties. Although weakness of American political parties cannot be attributed solely to the effects of the direct representation movement, because parties were weak when this movement began, it certainly is true that most of the dominant tendencies of the long direct representation period were essentially nonparty, if not antiparty.

The Madisonian system itself did not depend upon a concept of party. Rather, it was aimed at fitting into the checked and balanced governmental framework as many self-identifying groups or "factions" as possible. Madison has been criticized, perhaps unjustly, for missing the significance of political parties. But he was correct in knowing, or simply assuming, that parties of the English type had not and were not likely to arise in America. Federated America had little resemblance to unified England. There, quite cohesive political parties for a century after Burke found major support in an essentially aristocratic tradition, in salons of the patrons, in unity of the realm, and in the history and psychology of constitutional monarchy itself, which tended to polarize, but not to fragment, different political viewpoints.[22]

Political parties did arise in America soon enough to cause breakdown of the electoral college system in the third presidential election, in 1800. The result was the Twelfth Amendment and associated practices under which presidential electors became mere party ciphers and the presidency was subjected to as direct popular control as was possible without actual abolition of the electoral college.

Notwithstanding this early assertion of power, American political parties have tended ever since to remain loose leagues for capturing the presidency rather than to develop as integrated national organs of power and policy on the English model.[23] One of the original parties, the Federalist party, failed before it was well off the ground, and it took well-nigh a half-century to produce a strong replacement. The South to this day has not known a real two-party system. Federalism undoubtedly has played a

22. Although the Settlement of 1688 made party government possible in Britain, the first formal argument for party government is Burke's "Thoughts on the Causes of the Present Discontents" (1770). See Harvey C. Mansfield, Jr., "Party Government and the Settlement of 1688," 58 *Am. Pol. Sci. Rev.* 933, 935 (1964).
23. V. O. Key, *Politics, Parties, and Pressure Groups* (New York: Crowell, 1952); see also W. E. Binkley, *American Political Parties: Their Natural History* (New York: Knopf, 1943.

major role in the long-continued decentralized structure of the American political party system. Whether Federalism by itself would have prevented the rise of a relatively integrated national two-party system is now perhaps a bootless question. But certainly Jacksonian democracy, with its stress on representation through the executive,[24] and its tendency to view the legislative department with suspicion,[25] contributed little to the growth of parties as effective representation institutions. As an effective representation institution, political party activity traditionally is far more closely tied to the legislative than to the executive department. Nor was the Populist stress on direct popular action—bypassing all intermediate forms of representation, of negotiation, and of deliberation—conducive to party government and party responsibility.

When Professor Robert M. MacIver says that the principle of representation must be vitalized by conflict of parties as organizers of opposing opinions, and that when "parties flourish we have in effect passed from a pre-democratic mode of representative government to a genuinely democratic one," he has in mind primarily the process of compromise, adjustment, and decison-making in legislative halls.[26] Another writer views party as "prior to government" because it "makes" the people, i.e., the consensus, which government represents.[27]

American ambivalence about political parties is a product both of natural difficulties associated with a federal system and of a set of political principles which at best were mixed and frequently were negative regarding the representation role of a party system. This seemingly intrinsic weakness in the American party system, making it indeed a one-party system in many areas for long periods of time,[28] serves to emphasize the need to be concerned with electoral devices of apportionment and districting which will maximize the prospect of producing some meaningful opposition to the current majority party. Long periods of dominance in both national and state government, first of one party and then another, underscore this fact. Overrepresentation of the majority party flowing from our traditional districting arrangements should be a point of special attention for persons concerned, in Professor MacIver's words, with vitalizing "the principle of representation" by "the conflict of parties." [29]

24. Dahl, *supra* note 5, at 144.
25. Merriam, *supra* note 13, at 200.
26. Robert M. MacIver, *The Web of Government* 213–24 (New York: Macmillan, 1947).
27. Mansfield, *supra* note 22, at 933.
28. V. O. Key, *Southern Politics* (New York: Knopf, 1949); see also his *American State Politics* (New York: Knopf, 1956).
29. MacIver, *supra* note 26, at 209–10.

c. Minority Representation

Before coming to the present era with its pluralism-in-fact, two significant strands of thought between the Jacksonian-Populist direct representation and the present remain to be explained. They are the amorphous body of thought on representation which for lack of a better term has been called "enlightened individualism," [30] and the numerous variants of proportional representation (PR).

"Enlightened individualism" denotes a kind of latter-day rationalized Jacksonianism: Jacksonian in its stress on possible direct representation in the executive of the national majority; but rationalized to the extent of rejecting the "cult of incompetence" [31] which seemed to pervade Jacksonianism. The individualistic conception of society continues, but new concepts (and operational trends) emerge of the presidency as a representative embodiment of the nation, and the executive as director of competent government. The legislature continues, but becomes more "conciliar" than directive. Professor Charles E. Merriam records this development, and Professor Alfred de Grazia finds it significant that in Merriam's last major work, where the role of the legislature is specifically treated, Merriam refers to it as a conciliar organ,[32] thus evoking images of a royal council rather than images of direct constituency representation.

Although not advocating proportional representation expressly, Merriam's construction can be viewed as sympathetic to it. If the President is both the efficient head of state and, in himself, a major national-*majority* representative organ, the conciliar role of the legislature is itself maximized and made more "efficient" to the extent that it can operate as an organ for more detailed representation, including minority representation. In other words the legislator is to "represent"—in the sense of "presenting" the view of another—the maximum possible number of significant views bearing upon national issues.

Proportional representation per se never has found in England or the United States ground fertile enough to be commensurate with the amount of attention given to it by persons as eminent as John Stuart Mill and as recent as Professor Ferdinand A. Hermens. Thomas Hare's system, which John Stuart Mill helped to popularize,[33] utilized the concept of a transferable vote in order to get "voluntary constituencies" based on in-

30. De Grazia, *supra* note 18, at Ch. 7.
31. *Id.* at 172.
32. Charles E. Merriam, *Systematic Politics* 134–49 (Chicago: University of Chicago Press, 1947).
33. Thomas Hare, *On the Elections of Representatives, Parliamentary and Municipal* (1859); popularized by John Stuart Mill first in *Frazer's Magazine* (April 1859), then in his *Thoughts on Parliamentary Reform* (2d ed., 1860), contained in J. S. Mill, *Dissertations and Discussions* Vol. IV (New York: H. Holt, 1874).

terest groupings rather than residence groupings. In other words, by abolishing "fixed constituencies" set by district lines and by using a proportional representation formula, each significant organized interest should be able to obtain seats in the legislature proportional to its general voter strength.

The English nineteenth-century constitutional scholar, Walter Bagehot, was both intrigued and repelled by proportional representation. This kind of reaction has characterized reception of "PR" in most circles to the present day. If PR could accomplish the goals it proclaimed it would be "captivating," Bagehot felt, and would be worth working for even if it could not be achieved "till the year 1966." [34] He feared, however, that PR's overly precise interest representation would make of voluntary constituencies a "church with tenets," [35] and unduly jeopardize the vital parliamentary process of compromise and adjustment which to him was the essence of politics and governmental stability.[36] With a few exceptions, such as occasional use for city council elections, PR in its pure form has seldom been considered for America. Nevertheless, Professor Hermens, rather myopically impressed with troubles of Europe which with dubious validity he attributes largely to the fact that most European nations have had PR in some form, has made opposition to PR almost a lifework.[37]

In its pure form, PR can be subjected to an impressive list of objections. Its use of voluntary constituencies, its long ballot, its complexities by contrast with a simple district system, all raise the likelihood of confusing the voter and eroding the two-party system, thus necessitating coalitions in the legislature as a condition for getting a government majority. But in various modified forms, which for the sake of getting a rational hearing probably should not even be referred to as PR, the proportionalizing principle may emerge, at least arguably, as a beneficent democratic principle. It may be the only way short of direct mass-meeting democracy of avoiding major losses of voting power for significant numbers of the electorate; severe imbalances either of overrepresentation or of underrepresentation; the strong tendencies to one-party dominance inherent in the district system. Although PR normally is viewed as aiding smaller parties, it also helps those larger parties whose vote strength is geographically centered by averting loss of votes in large, wasteful majorities.[38]

34. Walter Bagehot, The English Constitution 217 (New York: Oxford University Press, 1900).
35. Id. at 224.
36. Id. at 216.
37. Ferdinand A. Hermens, Introduction to Modern Politics 201–7 (South Bend: University of Notre Dame Press, 1959).
38. Frank J. Sorauf, Political Parties in the American System 146 (Boston: Little, Brown, 1964).

Such PR modifications as *limited voting* and *cumulative voting*, designed to insure some minority representation, would preserve the two-party tendency of the district system but modify the system's monolithic majority party dominance characteristic.[39] Under *cumulative voting*, as successfully practised in Illinois for many decades, members of the lower house of the state legislature are elected in three-man districts, each voter possessing three transferable votes.[40] The weaker party normally cumulates its votes on one candidate. The almost universal result is that in each district the legislators are split two-to-one between the stronger and weaker parties, and each party thus has political life throughout the state. In practice the parties also have been represented in the Illinois lower house substantially in proportion to their statewide popular strength.[41] *Limited voting* may take several forms. The central feature is that the voter shall cast fewer votes than there are offices to be filled, thus preventing a majority from making a clean sweep and capturing all of the offices. By use of a limited voting system the minority Republican party in the early 1960s achieved some representation in the New York City Council, although the representation fell short by a considerable degree of representing the party's normal citywide strength.[42]

Exploration of devices for broadening the representative character of legislatures by modest modifications in traditional apportionment and districting systems, thus strengthening the "conciliar role" of the legislature while at the same time preserving the "power to govern" advantages of a two-party system, would seem to flow logically from Professor Merriam's "enlightened individualism." It would harmonize also with the Madisonian stress on maximizing the number of voices—or factions—heard from in order to avoid monolithic power of any one group. Although a strong executive lies outside the Madisonian system, such an executive is a construction of the "enlightened individualism" of Merriam and others, for which PR may be suggested as a natural corollary. A modified proportionality, leaving intact the basic two-party system, would at least be more in accord with twentieth-century pluralism than the one-party tendencies which conventional district systems exhibit when not modified by considerations of *proportional equality*.

39. W. J. M. MacKenzie, *Free Elections* 75–84 (Oxford: Clarendon Press, 1958); J. F. S. Ross, *Elections and Electors* Pts. II and III (London: Eyre & Spottiswoode, 1955).
40. George S. Blair, "Cumulative Voting," *Illinois Studies in the Social Sciences* Vol. 45 (Urbana: University of Illinois Press, 1960).
41. For a more extended discussion, see Ch. XIX.
42. For a more extended discussion, see Ch. XIX.

TWENTIETH-CENTURY PLURALISM-IN-FACT

Although John Dewey's fears concerning the possible eclipse of "the public" and its interests now seem exaggerated,[43] many may agree with Professor Wolfgang Friedmann's recent declaration that "surely one of the outstanding—perhaps the preeminent—problems of contemporary industrialized society, and most particularly in the United States, is the position of group interests between the state and the individual." [44] Analysts of the public interest find a "multiplicity of common sense publics" [45] displacing the older more localized and more homogeneous publics of a simpler era.[46]

Two leading recent commentators on representative institutions see de facto pluralism—with its numerous group controls and organically intertwined relationships, even though unrationalized in theory—as the mark of postwar American society, replacing the atomistic, individualistic credo of the nineteenth century. The richness and complexity both of individual and group life, and the current tendency of all individuals to have membership in several minorities at any given time, combine to give us a system best described in a paraphrase of Calhoun: we have a government of shifting concurrent minorities.

For example, in his work *A Preface to Democratic Theory*, Professor Dahl's seventh and last proposition bearing upon the problem of majority tyranny is as follows:

43. John Dewey, *The Public and Its Problems* (Denver: A. Swallow, 1954).
44. W. Friedmann, "The Changing Content of Public Interest: Some Comments on Harold D. Lasswell," in *The Public Interest* (NOMOS V) 84 (Carl J. Friedrich, editor, New York: Atherton Press, 1962). See also Earl Latham, *The Group Basis of Politics* (Ithaca: Cornell University Press, 1952); David Truman, *The Governmental Process* (New York: Knopf, 1955); Joseph Monsen and Mark W. Cannon, *The Makers of Public Policy: American Power Groups and Their Ideologies* (New York: McGraw-Hill, 1965); Lucy S. Dawidowicz, *Politics in a Pluralist Democracy* (New York: Institute of Human Relations Press, 1963).
45. William S. Minor, "Public Interest and Ultimate Commitment," *Public Interest, supra* note 44, at 26, 27.
46. In a way, the modern analog of Rousseau's "general will" concept, which in turn has roots in the "right of reason" of the Stoics and Cicero, is the "public interest" concept. Although all persons share some sense of public interest, few can agree on its exact dimensions. Whether the public interest is different from the sum of particular interests represented in the legislature can be contrasted with the problem of the "beautiful woman" concept. No one would deny that there is such a thing; but in the words of Professor Pennock, "no one would dream of defining a 'beautiful woman' procedurally (or 'operationally'), that is as 'one who wins a beauty contest.'" *The Public Interest, supra* note 44, at 178. But laying to one side the "beautiful woman" problem, in a democracy the "public interest" can *only* be approached "operationally," albeit there may be better and poorer systems of representation procedure.

A central guiding thread of American constitutional development has been the evolution of a political system in which all the active and legitimate groups in the population can make themselves heard at some crucial stage in the process of decision . . . .

When I say that a group is heard "effectively" I mean more than the simple fact that it makes a noise; I mean that one or more officials are not only ready to listen to the noise, but expect to suffer in some significant way if they do not placate the group, its leaders, or its most vociferous members . . . .

Thus the making of governmental decisions is not a majestic march of great majorities united upon certain matters of basic policy. It is the steady appeasement of relatively small groups. Even when these groups add up to a numerical majority at election time it is usually not useful to construe that majority as more than an arithmetic expression. For to an extent that would have pleased Madison enormously, the numerical majority is incapable of undertaking any coordinated action. It is the various components of the numerical majority that have the means for action.[47]

A call for further development of institutions of representation to better serve the needs of pluralist reality that has replaced the direct democracy excesses of past decades concludes Professor de Grazia's three-century survey in his *Public and Republic*. He suggests that consideration be given to modifications mixing conventional district representation with proportionalizing devices because: "Whatever the opinion of contemporaries to the contrary, representative devices have resulted in relatively few cases in the adequate fulfillment in demand for representation." [48]

The much-discussed recent analysis and critique of voting systems by Professors Buchanan and Tulloch,[49] although proceeding from an individualistic set of premises, is not inconsistent with this point. Their initial premise of unanimity minimizes to zero a voter's "external cost," i.e., the possibility of his being harmed by being in a minority. But the resultant cost of getting agreement is too high for effective government. Nevertheless, in their necessary retreat from unanimity it would seem to be implicit, despite their lack of treatment of institutional factors, that they remain concerned about such things as maximizing the range of political action, the range of possible participation in decision-making, the effectiveness of choices (votes). Minimization of "external costs" of voters seems to require a stress on broadening participation in the political game not merely in the sense of having a universal electorate but in the sense of

47. Dahl, *supra* note 5, at 137, 145–46.
48. De Grazia, *supra* note 18, at 257.
49. Buchanan and Tullock, *supra* note 5. See also Anthony Downs, *An Economic Theory of Democracy* (New York: Harper, 1957).

feeding the diverse interests and goals of social groups, through constituency voting, into the legislative halls: there, to paraphrase, the big "calculus of consent" can take place. With a monolithic winner-take-all majority voting system there would be no need for a "calculus of consent"; consent would come prepackaged and sterile. Similarly, Professor Downs's statement that "when the cost of voting is zero, any return whatsoever, no matter how small, makes it rational to vote and irrational to abstain," [50] may be paraphrased as follows: When no return whatsoever can be expected from voting (which is the position of sizable minorities in some district systems), it is irrational to make the effort to vote. The result is a truncation of formal representation.

Monolithic majority-exaggerating voting systems find support neither in the Madisonian system nor in most recent strands of American political thought. From quite different premises, each body of thought converges on the principle of maximizing the range of individual and group maneuver, the opportunity to play the political game meaningfully, and the opportunity to achieve results as nearly proportional to one's strength as is consistent with the basic premise of maintaining a power to govern.

CONCLUSION — PROBLEMS OF IMPLEMENTATION

Discussions of representation theory proceed on several levels. Not all are relevant to this study. At one level there is a concern for the nature of political obligation, including the creation and legitimization of governmental authority, exemplified by the irrevocable social contract of Hobbes. Although involving an interesting theory of representation in political context, the Hobbesian system's central feature of vesting plenary power in the "Leviathan state" once created, places it outside the line of disquisitions on consensual government. Within this line of development of consensual systems, discussions of representation theory have tended to take two forms: one is that concerning the nature and goals of an operating consensual system, i.e., representative democracy or a thing called by that name; the other is that concerning the formalization of representation inside a democratic system.

A pervading problem in democratic political thought has been the attempted reconciliation of popular will with individual rights, in particular the problem of majority rule and minority interests. Difficulties in reconciling the two have involved in contradictions most who have tried it, e.g., Locke, Rousseau, Madison. If Burke seemed to avoid contradiction it was only at the cost of substantially rejecting majoritarianism in favor of a tradition-based, rational aristocracy and a corollary free-agent theory of legis-

50. Downs, *supra* note 49, at 261.

lator role. Anomalously, in Burke's Bristol experience, this approach led him to favor policies more liberal than the constituency majority would support. If the buoyant Jacksonians and Populists of the nineteenth century seemed to avoid contradiction it was only at the price of elevating a majority infallibility which few minority-group-minded twentieth-century democrats can accept.

Resultant tension and ambivalence between majoritarian impulses and minoritarian fears—all the more tense because of realization that today's self-assured majority may be tomorrow's struggling minority—is evident in both English and American writers during the seed-time of modern democracy. The tension continues in thought and practice through the nineteenth century, although at a subdued level. It emerges more strongly in postwar pluralist America. The White House itself, traditionally the apex of American politics, well illustrates the point. President Johnson sometimes may seem to be the happiest of majoritarians. But the Johnson of the South and the Southwest, the Johnson who reached the White House, is the Johnson of the national consensus—almost of the concurrent majority. In an essay entitled "My Political Philosophy" a few years ago, then-Senator Johnson wrote:

> It is part—a great part—of my own philosophy that the Congress reaches a very dubious decision when its choices are made solely by head counts . . . .
> I do not believe we have arrived at an answer until we have found the national answer, the answer all reasonable men can agree upon, and our work is not done until that answer is found—even if the process requires years of our lives.[51]

And in 1965 a perceptive writer outlined in a national magazine article the operating philosophy of government by consensus of President Johnson.[52]

Actual formalization of institutions of fair and effective representation which can operate broadly enough to provide a basis for achievement of government by consensus rather than by simple majority is a never-ending task. It involves recognition of the many subtleties of political behavior as well as choices among more overt forms of organization and expression of political opinion. Only the latter can be considered in this work, but they constitute a not inconsiderable part of the iceberg of choice-identification, decision-making, execution, and popular review.

The dominant overt forms of representation tend to be the *party system*, the *legislative election process*, and *legislative action process*. Con-

51. Reported in *New York Times*, December 30, 1964, p. 8, col. 1.
52. Louis W. Koenig, "The Hard Limits of Government by Consensus," *New York Times Magazine*, March 7, 1965, p. 26.

cededly, the executive plays an important role through general leadership, veto, and party. But even such an executive enthusiast as Charles E. Merriam could write that: "The strength or weakness of the legislative agency is an index of the strength and weakness of the political community." [53]

The essence of the *party system* is that it be a system of two or more effective parties, providing both the consensus on which government rests and the choice which vitalizes political action. And yet, these two basic concepts of party purpose, in their extremity, vitiate the representation function and endanger the two-party system. Excessive stress on program (principle) makes the party an uncompromising "church with tenets." Excessive stress on consensus yields a party with overwhelming numerical power but hobbled by its lowest common denominator. The resultant problem of representative government is seen by one recent analyst "as the issue between representation and effective government: representation understood as respect for variety, and effective government understood as following a consistent program set forth by a strong leader." [54] An effective competitive party system is the foundation for both.

The *legislative election process* is the crucial nexus between parties and legislative action. Goals to be achieved are several. Most are consistent with the implications if not the express analysis of such main bodies of representation theory as Madisonianism; "enlightened individualism" of Merriam and others which succeeded the Populist excesses of direct representation; and emerging bodies of current thought either in the neo-Madisonian pluralist form outlined in Dahl's *Preface to Democratic Theory* or the neo-individualist form portrayed in the Buchanan-Tulloch *Calculus of Consent.*

A basic goal of legislative election and subsequent legislative action is maintenance of popular faith in the system. This goal is the core meaning of the slogan "consent of the people" and as one critical study has shown, its only operative meaning. A second goal is really a twofold one, affecting the crucial role of parties as opinion-organizers and candidate-selectors. In one aspect it is a goal of ensuring continual existence of a power to govern in a majority party by avoiding a splintering, multiparty development. In its other aspect it is a goal of maximizing the effectiveness of the minority party as an opposition party potentially capable of leadership, and in any event capable of representing effectively the interests whose allegiance the majority party has failed to capture. A third major goal, in part reflective of the second, is that the legislative action process shall not be a mere process of rubber-stamping previously prepared positions, but shall be a deliberative process of compromise and adjustment in which the right to

53. Merriam, *supra* note 32, at 149.
54. Mansfield, *supra* note 22, at 934.

be *heard* is preserved to all even though the right to *control* is reserved to those who can organize majority sentiment on the issue at hand.

As the vital link between parties on the one hand and legislative action ·on the other, a crucial and even determinative role is played by the legislative election process. This includes the whole range of apportionment and districting alternatives and practices. In this perspective the needs of fair and effective representation, which at bottom is what the reapportionment revolution is all about, entail a disposition to analyze critically our traditional legislative apportionment and districting practices, to assess their support of these goals, and to weigh critically in the light of these goals the merits of possible modifications or alternative devices.

Under such goals analysis, significant deficiencies may appear both in traditional American apportionment-districting practices and in its diametric opposite, pure proportional representation. The former may be seen to involve a "fixed constituency extremism" which in many respects is as unsatisfying as the "voluntary constituency extremism" of pure proportional representation.

Straight plurality election of legislators from single or multimember districts under our traditional *fixed constituency* system is causally related to such problems as the following: (a) the malapportionment-reapportionment problem of keeping districts relatively coterminous with population growth and shift; (b) the likelihood—because parties and interests are not rationally spread or rationally grouped geographically—that all apportionment-districting decisions, whether made by design or by chance, will have a crucial but arbitrary political effect on such matters as candidate availability, safe v. swing districts, homogeneous v. heterogeneous districts, and party competition; (c) the tendency to safeguard against the rise of third parties at the possible price of overrepresenting the dominant party, of strengthening one-party system tendencies, and of blocking effective representation of minority interests, including those centered in the second party; (d) the tendency to produce nonproportional and irrational relationships between the degree of party support in the electorate and the degree of actual party strength in the legislature. It may even be plausible, on careful analysis, to suggest that *some "one man-one vote" developments*, coupled with the nature of the scene on which the initial developments took place, *may operate to worsen some of the representation deficiencies of "fixed constituency extremism" unless the forces which have impelled speedy reapportionment also impose restraints on the breadth of reapportioning discretion.*

The "*voluntary constituency* extremism" of pure proportional representation on the other hand has its own deficiencies for: (a) it tends to encourage the development of a multiparty system with its instability of coalition government; (b) it minimizes the integrative process of compromise and adjustment at the citizen level which a choice confined to two parties tends to encourage, and which process by minimizing opinion extremism tends to maximize forces of allegiance and stability; (c) it tends, in short, to pursue proportionality at the price of compromise, adjustment, and agreement.

Goals analysis may open the way to an exploration of means to achieve the ultimate goal of fair and effective representation by devices combining the virtues both of fixed constituency systems and of proportional systems, while avoiding the representation deficiencies of each. The range of possibilities may run from a mere heightened sensitivity to gerrymandering, and to means of building more bipartisanship into initial apportionment-districting processes, all the way to adaptation of our traditional fixed constituency system in the direction of formal hybrid systems such as cumulative voting, limited voting, or mixed but still equal representation formulae in a bicameral system.

A final word may be added regarding the contention that minority rights are sufficiently cared for by judicial review and need no recognition in the process of legislative representation. Judicial review is well adapted to safeguarding individuals against oppression in the two primary forms of curbing freedom of expression and curbing harshness in criminal procedure. But these elements do not cover the total interests of men. Despite the one-time excesses of judicial review of substantive governmental policies, courts generally now do not, and should not, restrict the major policy choices of government. This is so even though some policy choices hang by the thread of a vote or two, and if adopted have the effect of substantially remaking large areas of American society in all of its interests— production, trade, working conditions, opportunity, politics, social practices, education, family life, welfare, and even religion. The now-rejected practice of "substantive due process" review too much colors our present thought.

Most policy choices are not constitutional choices; most policy choices which do approach the frontier of previously exercised power are legitimated when new test cases reach the Supreme Court. Only through effective representation devices can America continue to move forward on a "calculus of broad consensus" which has been our traditional model and is still the faith most widely held today. The fundamental premise of the democrat is that if means be well ordered, ends will take care of themselves; hence, the pragmatic conception of the "common good or public interest as a governmental process" [55] which was incipient in Madisonianism, explicit in Calhoun, and which guides much modern political science. The Great Society should rest on an integrated pluralism; pluralist in representation and integrated in allegiance to agreed policies.

55. Lerner, *supra* note 4, at 932.

IV

Representation Practice:
Statehood to *Baker* v. *Carr*

"When *I* use a word," Humpty Dumpty said, in a rather
scornful tone, "it means just what I choose it to mean—neither
more nor less."

"The question is," said Alice, "whether you *can* make words
mean so many different things."

"The question is," said Humpty Dumpty, "which is to be
master—that's all."

Lewis Carroll, *Through the Looking-Glass*

Discussions of representation and of reapportionment always come back
to numbers, but numbers can be tricky. It may be said that from the early
nineteenth century to the turn of the century, with a few exceptions, population has ruled in the apportionment of seats for both houses of state
legislatures. Paradoxically, it also may be said that, with a few exceptions,
anything approaching substantial equality of legislative district population
in both houses of state legislatures was never the general practice in America until after the Supreme Court's decisions of 1964.

Both statements are true, depending on one's approach to the "population" concept. The former statement requires acceptance of some district
population disparities of 2 to 1, 5 to 1, and perhaps higher, as still being
within a population principle. The latter statement assumes, in the light
of the implications of the Supreme Court's 1964 decisions, that apportionments are not population-based if districts exceed by very much a 15
percent deviation from average size, and a population variance ratio (large-
to-small district disparity) of more than 1.5 to 1. And as Supreme Court
doctrines unfold, these latter figures are being pushed steadily downward.

A. To the Turn of the Century

1. BEGINNINGS

In political philosophy the word "people" has had meanings as narrow as the baron class in King John's day and, quite recently, as broad as total populace. In apportionment usage, the term "population" has been equally slippery. Only one generalization can be made with certainty: In the long span from 1789 to 1964, "population" had no settled meaning as an apportionment concept. Disagreement encompassed both the apportionment base, e.g., use of gross population or use of narrower bodies such as qualified voters, and the required degree of equality of population in legislative districts.[1] Much enlightenment can be gleaned, however, from the formal provisions of the federal, state, and territorial constitutions and organic acts, and from a scattering of population data and comment.

a. "Representation Compromise" for Congress

As noted in the preceding chapter, the Madisonian system as embodied in the federal Constitution eschewed direct popular elections of either the President or the Senate. Concerning representation and apportionment, the famous large state-small state arrangement commonly called the "Connecticut Compromise" provided for state equality in the Senate regardless of population. For the House of Representatives, states were to be weighed in proportion to population, with each state guaranteed at least one Representative regardless of population to ensure a right to be heard. On the question of intrastate allocation of Representatives to districts, the Constitution was silent. Most states elected their Representatives in districts.[2] Detailed data have never been collected making intrastate and interstate comparisons of population inequality in congressional district formation. Whether actual disparities generally were within an upper limit of 15 percent deviation from average, or ranged with some frequency up to 50 percent or higher is unknown. For the Senate, of course, where each state has an equal voice regardless of population, representation disparities

---

1. As discussed in detail in Ch. XVII, even the relative certainty of "population" apportionment under the 1964 *Reapportionment Decisions* has encompassed deviations ranging from near zero to more than 30 percent.
2. By 1842, all but six states—New Hampshire, New Jersey, Alabama, Georgia, Mississippi, and Missouri—were electing Representatives by districts. Lawrence F. Schmeckebier, *Congressional Apportionment* 132 (Washington, D.C.: Brookings Institution, 1941).

have varied directly with differences in population of states. By the 1960 census, the population disparities among the states were such that—under one common measure of mathematical malapportionment—it could be said that approximately 16 percent of the nation's population could elect a majority of the Senate.[3]

b. The Original Thirteen

Such evidence as is available indicates that malrepresentation both in terms of sectional interest and population was endemic in the colonial legislatures, and was only partially and gradually ameliorated in the revolutionary and constitution-building eras. Of the colonial period it has been said that "Nowhere did representation bear any uniform relation to the number of electors. Here and there the factor of size had been crudely recognized." [4]

What "population" meant to the ratifiers of the federal Constitution, as revealed in the legislative apportionment formulae in their own contemporary state constitutions, defies easy generalization either in terms of announced principles of apportionment or in terms of actual population disparities in the resultant legislative districts. (See Chart No. 1 on Formal Apportionment Formulae of the Thirteen Original States as of 1790.) Two of the states, Connecticut and Rhode Island, retained the provisions of their colonial charters. These placed primary stress on local unit representation and geographic diffusion of representatives throughout the state, rather than on representation proportioned to population. The Rhode Island system continued until changed by the upheavals associated with Dorr's Rebellion in 1841 and 1842.[5] As one scans the apportionment formulae for the upper and lower houses respectively in these early state constitutions,[6] these common points emerge:

> (1) Provision for equal representation of political subdivisions regardless of population is found in five states for the upper house (Del., Ga., N.J., N.C., R.I.) and for one state in the lower house (Del.). An additional three states (Md., N.C., Va.) had county equality in their lower houses plus one representative each for

3. *Statistical Abstract of the United States 1965* 12–13 (Statistical Reports Division, Bureau of the Census, Department of Commerce).
4. Robert Luce, *Legislative Principles* 342 (Boston: Houghton Mifflin, 1930).
5. Kirk Porter, *The History of Suffrage in the United States* (Chicago: University of Chicago Press, 1918).
6. State constitutions and changing provisions therein down to 1908 may be found in Francis N. Thorpe, *American Charters, Constitutions and Organic Laws 1492–1908* (Washington, D.C.: U.S. Government Printing Office, 1909). Only those constitutions and/or provisions presenting research difficulties will be separately cited.

specified municipalities. New Jersey started with equality for the lower house, subject to legislative change.

(2) Analyzed from the slightly different perspective of guarantees of some representation to each county (or New England town) regardless of population, these figures appear: for the upper house, six states (Del., Ga., N.J., N.C., R.I., S.C.); for the lower house, all thirteen states except South Carolina.

Unless one makes arbitrary and unlikely assumptions concerning natural population distribution in these states, the necessary operating effect of apportionment formulae such as these would be to produce frequent population disparities. The disparities would be considerably in excess of any maximum deviation standard expressed in percentages as low as 10 or 15 percent, or perhaps even as "low" as 50 or 100 percent. In addition may be noted the general absence of relatively pure population formulae, with the apparent exceptions only of four states for the upper house (Mass., N.H., N.Y., Pa.) and three states for the lower house.[7]

Further clues concerning overrepresentation or underrepresentation of particular groups and sections may be gleaned from general historical writing. The struggle of Piedmont against Tidewater—of back country against coastal plain—dating from colonial times, continued.[8] Arguably this was a far more serious problem for the development of democracy and systems of fair and effective representation than the related question of voting qualifications, which tended to receive the lion's share of the attention. A most striking malrepresentation of numbers was the grossly insufficient number of seats awarded to the growing back country in the Carolinas and Virginia in both houses. In South Carolina, the "Nabob Phalanx" of

7. The Massachusetts and New Hampshire senators are only questionably included here, because of lack of empirical evidence on the unequalizing effect of apportionment by "the proportion of public taxes paid" by the said districts. Similarly, the large percentage deviations created by the lower house sliding ratio formulae for these same two states would be deemed unconstitutional under the standards of the 1960s. Arguably both Massachusetts houses are disqualified from inclusion in this list because of the ceiling of six senators per district, and the guarantee of one representative per town.
8. Jackson Turner Main, *The Antifederalists: Critics of the Constitution 1781–1788* 17–24, 28 *et seq.* (Chapel Hill: University of North Carolina Press, 1961); J. Allen Nevins, *The American States During and After the Revolution 1775–1789* 95–96, 114–15, 131–34, 174–75, 182, 193, 203 (New York: Macmillan, 1924). Nevins indicates that malrepresentation, both in terms of area and population, was endemic in the colonial legislatures, and was only partially and gradually ameliorated in the revolutionary and constitution-building era. Property qualifications played their part, but the most striking malrepresentation was in the grossly insufficient number of seats awarded to the growing back country in the Carolinas and Virginia.

Upper House (Senate)	
Delaware (1776)	Three Senators per county.
Georgia (1789)	One Senator per county.
Maryland (1776)	Fifteen Senators: nine from Western Shore; six from Eastern Shore. Chosen by electoral college-type body, the "electors" being elected similar to lower house.
Massachusetts (1780)	Forty Senators elected by districts, Provided: districts never to fall below thirteen and no district to elect more than six Senators. Apportioned as to taxes paid.
New Hampshire (1784)	Twelve Senators, apportioned as to taxes paid. Converted from multimember to single member districts, 1792.
New Jersey (1776)	One person per county to be a member of the legislative council.
New York (1777)	Senate to consist of twenty-four freeholders, elected from four districts. Reapportioned every 7 years on freeholder basis.
North Carolina (1776)	One "Representative" (Senator) for each county in the state.
Pennsylvania (1790)	Never less than one-fourth, nor greater than one-third of the number of Representatives. Chosen by districts, containing such a number of taxable inhabitants as shall be entitled to elect not more than four Senators.
South Carolina (1790)	Charleston received two Senators. All other parishes received one with the exception of eight two-parish districts having one Senator, one three-parish district having two Senators, and one three-parish district having one Senator.
Virginia (1776)	Twenty-four senatorial districts, each to elect one member. But: Each county in the district to vote separately for an actual resident, the man in the whole district having the greatest number of votes the winner.
Connecticut (1662)	Twelve Assistants to be elected annually on an at-large basis.
Rhode Island (1663)	One Assistant for each town elected annually.

Connecticut and Rhode Island retained the complex provisions of their colonial charters; primary stress was on geographic diffusion of representation throughout the state, rather than representation proportioned to population.
Sources: Benjamin P. Poore, The Federal and State Constitutions, Colonial Charters,

Chart 1 (*Continued*)

Lower House

Seven Representatives per county.

Range of two to five Representatives per county.

Four Delegates per county plus two each for Baltimore and Annapolis.

Every corporate town containing 150 ratable polls entitled to one Representative; with 225 ratable polls the mean increasing number for each additional Representative. Any town having less than 150 polls entitled to one Representative.

One Representative for every place entitled to town privileges, having 150 ratable polls; 300 such polls the mean increasing number for each additional Representative. All those with less than 150 are ordered and then take turns.

Three members of Assembly per county. Legislature may reapportion to achieve more equality.

At least seventy members elected in counties. Reapportioned every 7 years on voter basis. Possibility of losing representation.

Two Representatives per county, and one each for the towns of: Edenton, Newbern, Wilmington, Salisbury, Hillsborough, Halifax.

From sixty to one hundred, apportioned on basis of taxable inhabitants. Each county and Philadelphia to have at least one Representative.

Each parish received from one to three Representatives with Charleston receiving fifteen.

Two Representatives per county, and for the district of West-Augusta, plus one Representative for the city of Williamsburg and one for the borough of Norfolk; and one for such other cities and boroughs as established by the Legislature. As soon as any city has a population of less than one-half of any county, it shall lose its delegate.

Each town may annually send not more than two Representatives.

Not more than six Representatives for Newport, not more than four Representatives for each of Providence, Warwick, and Portsmouth; and not more than two from every other town. Elections annually.

and Other Organic Laws of the United States (1878); Francis N. Thorpe, *The Federal and State Constitutions, Colonial Charters, and Other Organic Laws of the States, Territories, and Colonies Now or Heretofore Forming the United States of America.* (1906).

Charleston, as their opponents called them, held sway aided by malapportionment. For example, in 1790 in South Carolina the eastern lowlands,
with a population entitlement of 50 seats in the lower house, had 143; the
western highlands, with a population entitlement of 186 seats, had only
93.[9]

At least four of the seven states basing representation for at least one
house largely on counties (see Chart No. 1) had significant population
ranges in 1790 between the largest and smallest counties: N.J., 2571 to
20,153; Md., 4809 to 30,791; N.C., 3071 to 15,828; Va., 951 to 22,105,[10]
which provoked a criticism from Jefferson.[11] Property qualifications for
voting also played their part, particularly by shrinking the apportionment
base for the state senates.

2. NINETEENTH-CENTURY REPRESENTATION TRENDS

Constitutional texts and apportionment practices dictate the conclusion
that the early story of the populous seaboard states is not a story of simple
population-based representation—except perhaps in a sense so general that
the Glorious Revolution of 1688 could be described as a popular movement. Similarly, a century later, in 1900, the operative constitutional practices were characterized by major deviations from population equality,
notwithstanding various population-oriented ambiguities in the apportionment clauses of the state constitutions. In many states a tendency toward
political subdivision equality in one house, commonly referred to as a
little "federal plan" patterned after the Congress, either was confirmed or
created by constitutional amendment.

There is, however, a long nineteenth-century middle period. It includes
the Northwest Ordinance's stress on population as a basis for apportionment clauses in the new Western territories, and the nationwide impact
of Jacksonianism and direct democracy on constitutional apportionment

9. Nevins, *supra* note 7, at 95–96. The district of St. Johns with 587 whites and 4705
slaves had seven lower house representatives yielding a ratio of one for every 84 whites;
Camden County with 29,400 whites and 8865 slaves had nineteen lower house delegates yielding a ratio of one for every 1547 whites. Main, *supra* note 7, at 27–28.
10. United States Advisory Commission on Intergovernmental Relations, "Apportionment of State Legislatures" 7–8 (1962). Delaware's three counties ranged only from
18,920 to 20,488.
In some of the states some additional representation was provided for certain cities
but it is not clear that these additions reduced the population disparities to narrow
limits. The statement found in the Commission survey that representation based on
counties in both houses of the legislature did not differ greatly from the distribution of the state population is surprising, unless one gives an exceedingly liberal
construction to the population concept. The same survey reports South Carolina
as a population apportionment state, but see Main's population disparity figures given
in note 9 *supra*.
11. Luce, *supra* note 4, at 352.

clauses. Influenced by these elements, some recent writers [12] have asserted that use of nonpopulation factors and the resultant malapportionment of numbers are a latter-day aberration of the past six or seven decades. The historic norm is asserted to be a population-apportionment principle which dominated the nineteenth century even though it may have lacked firm roots in the first decades of national independence. This hypothesis is supported by part of the meager empirical data available; it is rebutted by other parts.

The sweep of Jacksonianism and of the direct democracy movement which affected all governmental forms has been noted in Chapter III. The relation of these forces to representation in the sense of apportionment, however, is far less clear than their relation to the associated matter of restrictions on the suffrage. Suffrage affects apportionment only if the apportionment base be qualified voters rather than population. Suffrage restrictions, and particularly the property or tax payment requirements which in some states such as Massachusetts did have the effect of causing malapportionment in the form of narrowing the apportionment basis for the state senate, were gradually eradicated. Examples include Massachusetts in 1840; New Jersey, Connecticut, New York, and Louisiana in 1844–1845; others somewhat earlier.[13] But for the long period from the beginning of the nineteenth century almost to its end there is virtually a complete dearth of data on the role of population in actual apportionments. The story has to be pieced together from surmise and occasional nuggets in old histories.

A complete record of senate apportionment does exist for New Jersey. There an adherence to a rule of one senator per county yielded population variance ratios (ratio of largest to smallest county) which climbed upward, with one small dip in the 1830s, as follows: in 1791, 7.84 to 1; in 1852, 11.5 to 1; in 1882, 19.45 to 1; in 1922, 33.51 to 1. Thereafter the ratios declined to a figure of 19.02 to 1 on the eve of *Baker* v. *Carr*.[14] Population variance ratios only compare extremes but even an analysis in terms of the average percentage population deviation from ideal district size yields relatively high figures: In 1791, 27.7 percent; in 1858, 33.6 per-

12. See generally, Robert B. McKay, *Reapportionment: The Law and Politics of Equal Representation* 9–98 New York: Twentieth Century Fund, 1965); Gordon E. Baker, *The Reapportionment Revolution* 14–22 (New York: Random House, 1966); Royce Hanson, *The Political Thicket, Reapportionment and Constitutional Democracy* 4–17 (Englewood Cliffs, N.J.: Prentice-Hall, 1966), where the proposition continually appears as an undocumented premise.
13. Robert Luce, *Legislative Assemblies* 234 (Boston: Houghton Mifflin, 1924).
14. Ernest C. Reock, Jr., *Population Inequality Among Counties in the New Jersey Legislature 1791–1962* 22 (Bureau of Government Research, Rutgers, N.J., 1963). For the assembly, the population variance ratio fell from 7.85 to 1 in 1791, to 1.87 to 1 in 1818; thereafter it normally ranged near 1.8 to 1.

cent; in 1872, 47.0 percent; in 1902, 70.6 percent; in 1922, 80.0 percent. On the eve of *Baker* v. *Carr* the figure was 68.4 percent.[15]

Even where county equality was not the rule, the common practice of the original thirteen states of using the county (or town) as the apportionment unit continued and spread to other states, including some Northwest Ordinance states. (For the original thirteen, as of the Civil War period, see Chart 2.)

a. *Effect of Northwest Ordinance*

The effect of the Northwest Ordinance on the representation theory and the actual apportionment practice in the states formed under it is a matter of considerable uncertainty. As noted by the U.S. Advisory Commission on Intergovernmental Relations,[16] the basis of representation specified in the Ordinance does not emerge clearly from a reading of its provisions. The Ordinance specified that the "inhabitants of said territories shall always be entitled to the benefits . . . of a proportionate representation of the people in the legislature . . . ," and provided as follows in regard to actual mechanics of apportionment:

> So soon as there shall be five thousand free male inhabitants of full age, in the districts, upon giving proof thereon to the governor, they shall receive authority, with time and place, to elect representatives from their counties or townships to represent them in the general assembly: *Provided,* That for every five hundred free male inhabitants there shall be one representative, and so on, progressively, with the number of free male inhabitants, shall the right of representation increase, until the number of representatives shall amount to twenty-five; after which the number and proportion of representatives shall be regulated by the legislature . . . .[17]

In context, the purpose was to devise a plan of government for a sparsely settled territory largely devoid of political tradition, of established and traditional local units, of customary sectional subloyalties, and the multifarious other elements which complicate apportionment in a long-established society. The Ordinance devised a representation system keyed to the one readily identifiable element—an expanding population of set-

15. *Ibid.* These figures are obtained by averaging the percentage by which the districts for a given house vary from the representative ratio, i.e., the figure obtained by dividing the population of the state by the number of seats in a given house.

For the assembly, with the exception of 1791 when the average deviation was 27.6 percent, the reported figures have exceeded 16 percent only in 1821 and 1825 when they were 18.1 percent and 18.8 percent, respectively. (*Id.* at 14.)

16. U.S. Advisory Commission, *supra* note 9, at 9.

17. Charles C. Tansill, editor, *Documents Illustrative of the Formation of the Union of the United States* 51 (Washington, D.C.: U.S. Government Printing Office, 1927).

tlers grouped in natural political communities in the form of counties and townships who would be represented through these units on a population basis.

Actual apportionment experience in the five territorial legislatures— Ohio, Indiana, Illinois, Michigan, Wisconsin—which operated under the Northwest Ordinance provisions as amended periodically by Congress shows that proportionate representation meant different things in different places.[18] In apportioning, county lines were not cut. Equalization was approximated by grouping less populous counties into single districts, and by making more populous counties multimember. These two practices, coupled with a lack of egregious differences in county population, produced apportionments in which the most extreme population variance ratio seldom exceeded 2.5 to 1 and the maximum percentage deviation seldom exceeded 60 percent. But deviations near or exceeding these figures, which clearly exceed the apparent limits of tolerance which courts have derived from the 1964 Supreme Court *Reapportionment Decisions,* were not uncommon.

Two equally true but paradoxical statements can be made, therefore, concerning the implementation of the "population" concept under the Northwest Ordinance. First, under the "one man-one vote" standards of the mid-1960s, most of the territorial legislatures under the Northwest Ordinance would have been unconstitutional, even though the Ordinance and some supporting statutes of Congress were oriented toward the population principle "as near may be." [19] Second, none of the population disparities approached the ranges of the more deviant states on the eve of *Baker* v. *Carr;* rather, they were more similar to the ranges which the Supreme Court held unconstitutional in 1964 for Colorado (upper house, 3.6 to 1; lower house, 1.7 to 1).[20]

The influence of the Northwest Ordinance on the formal apportionment provisions in the original state constitutions of the five states formed entirely from Ordinance territory can be gleaned from Chart No. 3. Four states, Illinois, Indiana, Ohio, Wisconsin, are classifiable seemingly as population apportionment states for both houses of their legislature. However, Ohio amended in 1851 to insert a guarantee of one representa-

18. For the factual data in this section I have drawn upon an exploratory mimeographed memorandum, "Apportionment of Territorial Legislatures–Northwest Territory," dated February 15, 1965, and prepared by Robert L. Tienkin, legislative attorney in the Legislative Reference Service of the Library of Congress. He reports that the records are incomplete and difficult to assemble and use. Both the number of counties and the apportionment base shifted frequently, and often were coterminous neither with the dates nor data in the federal census.

19. 4 Stat. 200–201 (1827 regarding Michigan); 5 Stat. 10 (1836 regarding Wisconsin).

20. Lucas v. Colorado General Assembly, 377 U.S. 713, 727, 728.

Chart 2

APPORTIONMENT FORMULAE OF STATE LEGISLATURES—THIRTEEN ORIGINAL STATES
AS OF 1865–1870

Basis of Representation	Upper House (Senate)		Lower House	
I. Representation Based on Geographic Unit Without Regard To Population:				
(a) Equal Representation for each county.	Delaware New Jersey	(2)	Delaware	(1)
(b) Equal Representation Based on Geographic Units other than counties.	Georgia Massachusetts New York Rhode Island	(4)	Connecticut	(1)
II. Representation Based On Geographic Unit With MINOR Modifications Based On Population.[a]	Maryland Pennsylvania South Carolina Virginia	(4)		(0)
III. Representation Proportioned To Units (county or district) On Basis Of Population but with MAJOR limitations to achieve geographic diffusion which may substantially defeat population principle: e.g., (1) Minimum limits, e.g., rule that no unit may have *less* than one representative, and, or, limitation on number of units which may be combined to approximate one quota; (2) Maximum limits, e.g., rule that no unit may have *more* than a designated number of representatives; and (3) Low limit (in relation to number of counties) on maximum size of legislature when combined with minimum diffusion rules.[a]	Connecticut	(1)	Georgia Maryland New Hampshire New Jersey New York	North Carolina Pennsylvania Rhode Island South Carolina Virginia (10)
IV. Representation To Be Apportioned On Population Basis With Apparently MINOR Limitations.[b, c]	New Hampshire	(1)	Massachusetts	(1)
V. Population.[c]	North Carolina	(1)		(0)

a Some states may be classified to either II or III, depending on the weight given to special constitutional formulae. The distinction may not be vital however, because the primary thrust of both II and III is toward geographic diffusion, not representation by population.

b Some states charted in this category have special formulae not easily classifiable but weighted more to population principle than to geographic diffusion. The line between categories III and IV is designed to separate states using a strong geographic diffusion factor from states using a relatively unqualified population factor.

c Despite constitutional provisions apparently specifying apportionment by population, all states in categories IV and V have population disparities between largest and smallest district at least exceeding 25 percent, and in most cases far exceeding that figure.

Sources: Benjamin P. Poore, *The Federal and State Constitutions, Colonial Charters, and other Organic Laws of the United States* (1878); Francis N. Thorpe, *The Federal and State Constitutions, Colonial Charters, and other Organic Laws of the States, Territories, and Colonies Now or Heretofore Forming the United States of America* (1906).

Comment: States other than the original thirteen were examined for the 1865–70 period but many were not chartable for a number of reasons, e.g., lack of explicitness in formal constitutional provisions coupled with lack of information on actual implementation; frequent constitutional change; instability in the South during Reconstruction. There was little evidence of a widespread embracing of a simple population principle, there was emphasis on geographic diffusion.

tive in the lower house for each county which had at least, a half-ratio,[21] and Illinois amended in 1870 to allow a 20 percent deviation in upper house districts and a 40 percent deviation in lower house districts.[22] The fifth state, Michigan, from the outset guaranteed at least one representative to each existing county regardless of population in the lower house, and forbade dividing counties in districting for either house.

b. Mid-Century Territorial Legislatures

Experience in setting up thirteen territorial legislatures in the West in mid-century was similar to the earlier experience under the Northwest Ordinance. Congress specified population as the apportionment base.[23] Again, as under the Ordinance, the degree of legislative district equality contemplated, and actually attained, is not fully known. But it is clear that the original constitutions of the fourteen states which eventuated from these territories (fourteen rather than thirteen because the Dakota Territory was split) show some departures from a straight population apportionment principle, in regard to at least one house. In five—Idaho, Kansas, Montana, Utah, and Wyoming—there were guarantees that in one house every county should have at least one representative regardless of population; an additional three states—Colorado, North Dakota, Oregon—prohibited dividing counties in forming legislative districts. (See Chart No. 3.)

c. State Experience

The scattering of data for other states indicates that long before the end of the nineteenth century there were major state constitutional hassles over representation caused by widely differing growth rates of various parts of the state. With population shifting and localized interests developing, "struggles to secure equitable apportionments were always vigorous." [24]

21. Ohio Const. of 1851, Art XI, § 2, in Thorpe, *supra* note 6, at 4158.
22. Ill. Const. of 1870, Art. IV, § 7, *id.* at 1017.
23. Brief for Appellants, pp. 68–69 n.14, Roman v. Sincock, 377 U.S. 695 (1964). The language of the authorizing statute for Wyoming is typical: "An apportionment shall be made by the governor as nearly equal as practicable among the several counties or districts for the election of the council and house of representatives, giving to each section of the Territory representation in the ratio of their population, (excepting Indians not taxed) as nearly as may be . . . ." (15 Stat. 178, 179). See also, 12 Stat. 172, 173 (Colorado Territory), 12 Stat. 209, 210 (Nevada Territory), 12 Stat. 239, 240 (Dakota Territory), 12 Stat. 664 (New Mexico, to be modeled after Arizona at 9 Stat. 446, 448), 12 Stat. 808, 809 (Idaho Territory), 13 Stat. 85, 87 (Montana Territory), 9 Stat. 323, 324 (Oregon Territory), 9 Stat. 403, 404 (Minnesota Territory), 9 Stat. 453, 454 (Utah Territory), 10 Stat. 172, 173 (Washington Territory), 10 Stat. 277, 278 (Nebraska Territory), 10 Stat. at 284 (Kansas Territory).
24. Francis N. Thorpe, *Constitutional History of the American People 1776–1850* II:413 (Washington, D.C.: U.S. Government Printing Office, 1898).

The Louisiana Constitutional Convention of 1845 was agitated by tension of city and country. There was a desire to give some voice to each unit, and a desire to put some ceiling on the size of the delegation from New Orleans, which was "filling up with all kinds of people" and more prone than the country to "those sudden passions which pervert and carry men's minds to fearful extremities." [25] Although a federal plan was rejected, a proposal to guarantee at least one representative for each parish was accepted. New Orleans, with one-fifth of the aggregate population, received only 4 senators and 9 representatives in a legislature whose authorized size was 32 senators and from 70 to 100 representatives.

The Pennsylvania Constitution of 1838 gave Philadelphia only two senators and limited the number "permanently" to four.[26] Virginia, which had extensive representation troubles up to the Civil War, did finally provide in 1851 for apportioning the lower house on a white population or registered voters basis yielding 83 seats for the West and 69 for the East; but in the senate the East was arbitrarily awarded 30 and the West 20.[27]

Population apportionment was the object of Dorr's Rebellion in Rhode Island and was achieved in the Constitution of 1842. But the population principle was qualified by provisions that each town and city should have at least one representative and should not be divided in choice of representatives.[28] Massachusetts abandoned separate town representation in 1857,[29] which is one of the reasons it was one of the last of the states to be affected by *Baker* v. *Carr*. But Connecticut and Vermont retained separate town representation until changed by post-*Baker* reapportionment litigation.

d. *Fifty States – Original Apportionments*

Another mode of ascertaining how theories of representation were implemented in actual modes of apportionment and districting is to examine the original constitutions of each of the fifty states. These constitutions cover a wide sweep of American history from the late eighteenth century to the last state admissions in 1959.

With striking frequency the draftsmen of these original constitutions saw no inconsistency in specifying population as a major premise in legislative apportionment formulae, and in immediately qualifying it with nonpopulation provisions designed to disperse representation and guarantee a corollary right to be heard. An analysis of the text of these fifty original

25. Thorpe, *supra* note 24, I:438.
26. Thorpe, *supra* note 24, II:98.
27. Julian A. C. Chandler, *Representation in Virginia* 42–44, 68–69 (New York: Macmillan, 1896). The 1851 provisions were never implemented because of the Civil War.
28. Robert Luce, *Legislative Problems* 348 (Boston: Houghton Mifflin, 1935).
29. Luce, *supra* note 4, at 347.

Chart 3

FORMAL APPORTIONMENT FORMULAE OF STATE LEGISLATURES IN ORIGINAL CONSTITUTIONS

A. Political Subdivision or Mixed Population—Geographic Principle

Basis of Representation	Upper House	Lower House
I. Representation Based on Geographic Units without Regard to Population	Arizona Connecticut Delaware Louisiana Montana	New Jersey North Carolina Rhode Island Virginia	Connecticut Delaware New Jersey North Carolina
(a) Equal Representation for each County	Delaware Montana	New Jersey North Carolina	Delaware New Jersey North Carolina [a]
(b) Representation Based on Geographic Units other than Counties (including districts initially devised according to population but fixed in Constitution)	Connecticut Louisiana Rhode Island Virginia		Connecticut North Carolina [a]
II. Representation Based on Geographic Units with Minor Modification Based on Population [b]	Arizona Hawaii Maryland South Carolina		Georgia Maryland Vermont Virginia

III. Representation Proportioned to Units Based on Population with Major Limitations to Achieve Geographic Diffusion which may Substantially Defeat Population Principle or to Keep Political Subdivisions Intact [c]	Alabama Arkansas California Colorado Florida Idaho Iowa Kentucky Maine Massachusetts	Michigan Mississippi Missouri North Dakota Oklahoma Oregon Tennessee Texas Utah West Virginia Wyoming	Alabama Arizona Arkansas California Colorado Florida Hawaii Idaho Iowa Kansas Kentucky Maine Massachusetts	Michigan Mississippi Missouri Montana North Dakota Oklahoma Oregon Rhode Island Utah Wyoming
(a) Minimum Limits, e.g., rule that no unit may have less than one representative	Kentucky Wyoming		Alabama Arizona Arkansas Florida Hawaii Idaho Kansas Massachusetts	Michigan Mississippi Missouri Rhode Island Utah Wyoming
(b) Maximum Limits, e.g., rule that no unit may have more than designated number of representatives	Massachusetts		Maine Oklahoma Rhode Island	

Chart 3 (Continued)

B. Population Principle, Substantially Unqualified

Basis of Representation	Upper House	Lower House
(c) Contiguity Requirements, e.g., rule that counties constituting elective unit shall not be separated by county belonging to another elective unit and that no county shall be divided in forming such unit	Alabama, Arkansas, California, Colorado, Florida, Idaho, Iowa, Maine, Michigan, Mississippi, Missouri, North Dakota, Oklahoma, Oregon, Tennessee, Texas, Utah, West Virginia, Wyoming	California, Colorado, Idaho, Iowa, Montana, North Dakota, Oregon, Wyoming
(d) Low Limit on Maximum Size of Legislature (in relation to number of counties) when combined with minimum diffusion rules	Kentucky, New Hampshire, Washington, Wisconsin	Alabama, Arkansas, Florida, Hawaii, Idaho, Kansas, Kentucky, Michigan, Mississippi, Missouri, Rhode Island, Utah, West Virginia
IV. Representation to be Apportioned on Population Basis with Apparently Minor Limitations	Alaska, Minnesota, Nebraska	Alaska, Nebraska, South Carolina, West Virginia, Wisconsin

V. Representation Based on Population

Illinois	New Mexico	Illinois	New Mexico
Indiana	New York	Indiana	New York
Kansas	Ohio	Kentucky	Ohio
Nevada	South Dakota	Louisiana	Pennsylvania
		Minnesota	South Dakota
		Nevada	Tennessee
		New Hampshire	Texas
			Washington

TOTALS

14[d]	20
(32, including III(c))	(26, including III(c))

---

[a] Two representatives for each county and one representative for each town.

[b] Some states may be classified either II or III, depending on the weight given to special constitutional formulae. The distinction may not be vital, however, because the primary thrust of both II and III is toward geographic diffusion, not representation strictly by population.

[c] Some states charted in this category have special formulae not easily classifiable but weighted more to population principle than geographic diffusion.

[d] Only forty-seven upper legislative houses (thirty-three in chart A and fourteen in chart B) are listed because the first constitutions of Georgia, Pennsylvania, and Vermont provided for unicameral legislatures.
Source: Francis N. Thorpe, *The Federal and State Constitutions, Colonial Charters, and Other Organic Laws of the States, Territories, and Colonies Now or Heretofore Forming the United States of America*, 7 Vols. (1906); state codes.

75

state constitutions is instructive, bearing in mind two uncertainties: (1) the manner in which the ambiguities in some of these provisions were resolved in practice; (2) the actual legislative district population deviations which resulted when these formulae were applied to the subfactor of uneven and shifting population distribution. Some of the qualifying language could be a major or only a minor limitation on an equal population principle, depending on how the actual population was dispersed, e.g., a rule against dividing counties in creating districts. Analyzed textually with these inherent uncertainties in mind, the frequent use of a variety of nonpopulation or population-limiting apportionment considerations is striking. (See Chart No. 3.) Nonpopulation considerations are represented by such provisions as the following, relating to one or to both houses of the legislature:

(1) Equal representation for each county;

(2) Equal representation for special districts not directly or continuously related to population;

(3) Mixed geographic-population formulae with the area factor only slightly modified;

(4) Formulae using population as a major factor but modifying it with corollary subrules which frequently operated to produce substantial population disparities in district population, e.g., guarantee of at least one representative to each major political subdivision, fixed ceiling on the number of representatives from any one political unit no matter how populous, requirement that counties be treated as whole units and not be subdivided, low ceiling on the size of legislature which when combined with a guarantee of one legislative seat for each county leaves an insufficient number of seats available for allocation on a population basis.

The most difficult qualification to assess is that given in category III (c) in Chart 3 concerning preservation of local boundaries. Such a requirement would have a distorting effect unless actual county populations were fairly neat multiples of the apportionment quota. If this qualification is treated, nevertheless, as a relatively insignificant check on the population principle (and the states which would be "population" states but for this provision are counted with the states in categories IV and V), the following figures appear: 32 upper houses and 26 lower houses were apportioned originally essentially on the basis of population; states apportioning both houses on a population basis numbered 21. However, if category III (c) is deemed a significant restriction on the population principle, these figures appear: only 14 upper and 20 lower houses were on a population basis; both houses were on a population basis in only 12 states.

Strikingly different figures are reported by the United States Advisory Commission on Intergovernmental Relations and appear in Chief Justice Earl Warren's opinion for the Court in *Reynolds* v. *Sims*, the principal opinion in the 1964 *Reapportionment Decisions*. Relying on the Commission's survey, Chief Justice Warren's opinion explaining the Court's 1964 equal population ruling contained the statement that the "original constitutions of thirty-six of our states provided that representation in both houses of the state legislatures would be based completely or predominantly on population." [30] These figures have been picked up by others and cited frequently without fresh analysis. They figured prominently in the House Judiciary Committee hearings on proposals to check federal court jurisdiction in legislative apportionment in July–August 1964, and in subsequent congressional hearings and debates in 1965 and 1966 on the issue of a reapportionment constitutional amendment. The intended implication, of course, is that the *Reapportionment Decisions* are not so much ground-breaking decisions as they are a return to simple original understandings.

The tabulation published by the U.S. Advisory Commission, on which Chief Justice Warren placed his reliance, uses gross categories, is not detailed state by state, cites no sources, and reveals no standards for resolving the numerous classifications problems. The points at which it may deviate from the detailed analysis presented in Chart No. 3, and the reason for the quite substantial deviations, cannot be ascertained. Certain explanations can be suggested. One is the simple matter of textual ambiguity. Another is the uncertain effect of some of the qualifying provisions in differing population settings. These factors dictate caution in placing much reliance on attempts to classify states into groups, using overly simple categories of population states and nonpopulation states. It is unfortunate that the Supreme Court, by the manner of its reference to the Commission report, implied that accurate and agreed-upon classification was a simple matter—or even possible.

A third explanation of the marked discrepancy between the Commission's figures and the figures to be derived from Chart No. 3 relates to the "population" concept used by the Commission analyst in making his report. The Commission report was done shortly after *Baker* v. *Carr*, at a time when the coming rigidity of the population principle was not yet perceived or even widely anticipated. This was the era when a modified "federal plan" of apportionment still was thought by many to be a live

30. Reynolds v. Sims, 377 U.S. 533, 573 (1964).

option. For example, in the course of a speech made three months after his victory in *Baker* v. *Carr*, the Solicitor General of the United States said: ". . . it would not surprise me greatly if the Supreme Court were ultimately to hold that if seats in one branch of the legislature are apportioned in direct ratio to population, the allocation of seats in the upper branch may recognize historical, political and geographical subdivisions *provided that the departure from equal representation in proportion to the population is not too extreme.*"[31] One might expect therefore that a person in 1962 making an analysis of original apportionment clauses would feel that a number of provisions and ambiguities were classifiable as within the "population principle" even though they might yield some population deviations of 2 to 1, 3 to 1, or even higher. Such deviations, though major by post-1964 standards, still would be in sharp contrast to the egregious population disparities of 10 to 1, 15 to 1, 20 to 1, and even higher in some states on the eve of *Baker* v. *Carr*.

That this actually happened was indicated to the present author by the analyst who prepared the Commission's report shortly before his untimely death in 1965. He said that in the process of resolving ambiguities, estimating the actual effect of some provisions qualifying a straight population principle, and making his resultant classification, he had in mind a population concept substantially less rigid than that apparently reached by the Court in the 1964 *Reapportionment Decisions*.[32] Indeed, a population concept flexible enough to yield the conclusion that the original constitutions of 36 states placed both houses on a "population basis" also would validate, or come close to validating, the apportionments in three of the states whose legislatures were held invalid by the Supreme Court in 1964—Colorado, Virginia, and perhaps New York.

The grossly misleading character of the figure "thirty-six" is therefore to be attributed partly to pre-1964 flexibility in the population concept, and partly to those, including the Commission itself and the Supreme Court, who have misused the Commission report by assuming, sub silentio, that the loose population concept used in 1962 by the Commission analyst was also the concept of the Supreme Court in the 1964 *Reapportionment Decisions*.[33] Subsequently, Senator Paul Douglas and others, seeking ammu-

31. Archibald Cox, "Current Constitutional Issues—Reapportionment," 30 *Tenn. L. Rev.* 28 (1962); also published in 48 A.B.A.J. 711 (1962).

32. Internal evidence alone in the report indicates as much. Even making large allowances for the apparent flexibility of the population standard used, to conclude that the degree of population emphasis in state constitutions in the 1790 period and in the original constitutions of the fifty states is the conceptual equivalent of modern "substantial equality" (i.e., a rule of thumb confining deviations to 15 percent or less) comes close to what lawyers call special pleading.

33. The Commission's report and its mystic figure of "thirty-six" population states is defended in Professor McKay's recent treatment of reapportionment. But it is defended

nition rather than verifiable historical accuracy, further popularized the mystic figure "thirty-six" in their successful opposition to the proposed Dirksen (Reapportionment) amendment.

e. *Readmitted Confederate States*

A full discussion of the "original meaning" of the Fourteenth Amendment in regard to apportionment of state legislatures, to which Justice John Marshall Harlan devoted the major part of his dissenting opinion in *Reynolds* v. *Sims,* is appropriately reserved until consideration of that opinion. But the available information on the constitutional texts and actual population data in apportionments of ex-Confederate states, as of the date of readmission by Congress, is relevant at this point. Readmission of ten former Confederate states was conditional on their ratifying the Fourteenth Amendment (Tennessee was readmitted earlier).

Again, textual ambiguities impede analysis. Even persons with the mutual purpose of demonstrating that several states did *not* base both houses on a straight population apportionment principle disagree on the classification and number. Justice Harlan, in his dissenting opinion in *Reynolds* v. *Sims,* said that substantial departures from the rigidity of the population principle, held by the Court majority in *Reynolds* to be required by the Fourteenth Amendment, were found in the constitutions of six ex-Confederate states.[34] But one of the defendants' counsel listed five states,[35] and the two lists were in full agreement only in regard to four states.

Clearly, however, in approximately half the readmitted states there were significant departures in regard to at least one house of the legislature from the population apportionment principle found in *Reynolds* to be part of the meaning of the Fourteenth Amendment. These departures are substantiated by the available data on district population, and departures include at least one state (Texas) whose constitution on its face seemed to call for unqualified population apportionment. Interestingly, neither the state constitutional text analysis nor the actual district population data were successfully rebutted in the 1964 reapportionment briefs and opinions by the Court majority, by the plaintiffs' counsel, nor by the Solicitor General of the United States who operated as co-plaintiff in all of the re-

by surmise only, not by empirically verified data. Such sketchy empirical data as do exist, e.g., the discussions herein of the original thirteen states, the Northwest Ordinance states, and other states, undercut the plausibility of Professor McKay's surmise, unless the surmise really rests on the thought that population deviations considerably larger than those emerging under the 1964 *Reapportionment Decisions* are still classifiable as "population-based" systems.

34. 377 U.S. 606.
35. Brief for Appellants, pp. 57–58, Roman v. Sincock, 377 U.S. 695 (1964).

apportionment cases. Their primary response was simply that the developing meaning of the Fourteenth Amendment, as shown in the 1954 *Desegregation Decision*, made all historical evidence immaterial.

The actual population data are more significant than the often ambiguous constitutional texts. The population variance ratios of large to small districts in the state senates of six of the ten readmitted states exceeded 2 to 1: Florida, 73.7 to 1; Georgia, 5.7 to 1; Louisiana, 2.82 to 1; South Carolina, 5.2 to 1; Texas, 2.19 to 1; North Carolina, 5.2 to 1.[36]

Analyzed in terms of the electoral percentage, i.e., the minimum population of districts whose representatives would constitute a majority in the legislature, the figures for the upper and lower houses respectively were: Florida, 33 percent and 27 percent; Georgia, 36 percent and 37 percent; Louisiana, 48 percent and 40 percent; South Carolina, 36 percent and 44 percent; Virginia, 44 percent and 40 percent.[37] As Justice Harlan further noted:

> In South Carolina, Charleston, with a population of 88,863, elected two Senators; each of the other counties, with populations ranging from 10,269 to 42,486, elected one Senator. In Florida, each of the thirty-nine counties was entitled to elect one Representative; no county was entitled to more than four. These principles applied to Dade County with a population of 85 and to Alachua County and Leon County with populations of 17,328 and 15,236 respectively.[38]

As discussed in further detail subsequently, the comparable upper and lower house electoral percentages in some of the state legislatures invalidated by the Supreme Court in 1964 were: Colorado, 33.2 percent and 45.1 percent; New York, 41.8 percent and 34.7 percent; Virginia, 41.1 percent and 40.5 percent.[39]

f. Northern States Ratifying the Fourteenth

In a further effort to demonstrate the historical novelty of the tight "population apportionment" construction given to the Fourteenth Amendment by his brethren in the 1964 *Reapportionment Decisions*, Justice Harlan, dissenting, analyzed also the contemporaneous constitutions of the 23 loyal states which ratified the Amendment. He found that five, all in the Northeast, had constitutional provisions for apportionment of at least one house of their respective legislatures which wholly disregarded

36. *Id.* at 57–63 (on the basis of the 1860 census).
37. Brief for the United States as Amicus Curiae, pp. 54–56, Roman v. Sincock, 377 U.S. 695 (1964).
38. 377 U.S. 606–07.
39. Robert G. Dixon, Jr., "Reapportionment in the Supreme Court and Congress: Constitutional Struggle for Fair Representation," 63 *Mich. L. Rev.* 209, 238 (1964).

the spread of population.[40] An additional ten, including all sections of the country, had constitutional provisions which gave primary emphasis to population but which also applied other principles, such as special recognition of political subdivisions, "which were intended to favor sparsely settled areas." [41]

Although little is known of the district population differences in most states, some figures available for New York are especially interesting. It is commonly thought that the New York legislature's apportionment base did not become consciously skewed to limit New York City—"constitutionally Republican" as Al Smith later called it—until the 1894 revision of the state constitution.

Under the New York system, the legislature apportioned seats to the counties and then the county boards subdistricted into single-member districts under a constitutional provision prohibiting the subdividing of towns. Actual subdistrict populations are not known. However, an analysis of the basic apportionments to the counties (treating them for this purpose as multimember districts) indicates that the population variance ratio was 2.98 to 1 and that 40 of 128 assemblymen were elected from counties whose populations deviated by more than 15 percent from the statewide average.[42] Actual district population figures probably would reveal greater disparities because the provision against subdividing towns could aggravate the inequalities present in the basic apportionment.

g. *Summary*

Sketchier treatments of this same field have produced confident generalizations concerning the overweening dominance of the population principle for apportionment of both houses of state legislatures in the nineteenth century. One report states that "of the twenty states" joining the Union after ratification of the Constitution and prior to the Civil War "only two" (Vermont and Florida) failed to follow this principle.[43] Another states that "between 1790 and 1889 no state was admitted to the Union in which the original constitution did not provide for representation principally based on population in both houses of the legislature." [44] Such generalizations are seriously undercut by the evidence summarized here, sketchy as it is; it would seem that more complete evidence could serve only to qualify them still further.

It would be more accurate to say that population, with a few excep-

40. 377 U.S. at 602.
41. *Id.* at 603.
42. Charles Z. Lincoln, *The Constitutional History of New York* III:162–69 (New York: Lawyers Co-Operative Publishing Co., 1906).
43. U.S. Advisory Commission, *supra* note 9, at 9.
44. McKay, *supra* note 12, at 24–25.

tions, has been the starting point but not the sole consideration for apportionment formulae for both houses of the state legislatures in the first century of our history. During this period relatively few states, concentrated mainly in the Northeast, used the "federal" principle of straight county equality regardless of population differentials as the basis of representation in one legislative house. But during this same period a great many states—both old and new—mixed the population principle with provisions giving some voice to each political subdivision in at least one house of the legislature, thus yielding for allocation to the more populous political subdivisions an insufficient number of uncommitted seats to equalize their representation on a population basis.

There seems to be little basis for concluding that a "one man-one vote" equality reasonably approximating the Supreme Court's concepts of the 1960s, with something approaching a "nearly equal as possible" constitutional norm, was ever either the understood goal or the implemented goal of the nineteenth century, even in the frontier states. Rather, the population principle, to which all very naturally gave primary emphasis in the total representation pattern as the cornerstone of democracy, was always deemed to involve corollary questions of representation of differing interests and of communities expressed through political subdivisions. The total representation pattern would involve, of course, the governor as well as both houses of the legislature. The aim of the many apportionment struggles affecting not only the East and South but also such interior states as Louisiana, Kentucky, Ohio, and Illinois was to reduce population discrepancies *and* to achieve more effective sectional and class representation. A possible conflict between a right to be heard, i.e., represented, and a single-minded pursuit of an ideal of equal population districts for both houses seems never to have been an issue.

B. Twentieth-Century Apportionments

1. CONSTITUTIONAL REVISION; LITTLE FEDERAL PLANS

Uncertainties concerning the role of population in apportionments for bicameral legislatures begin to disappear by 1900. A number of states revised their constitutions to institutionalize their practice of apportioning one legislative house predominantly on the basis of political subdivisions rather than on population. A similar policy of "local unit" representation in at least one house continued, or developed, in other states even without constitutional revision. The effect was produced simply by interaction of differing population growth and inherited apportionment provisions which guaranteed each county at least one seat, and which provided an insufficient number of uncommitted seats for proportional allocation to the more populous localities.

Provisions to limit the population principle and disperse representation throughout the state became more stringent and more common in the decades following 1890. This movement may not be unrelated to the fact that 1910 was the last year in which rural America could muster a majority in the federal census. At the same time, this movement defies simple characterization as a liberal-conservative struggle. In this era, as Samuel Hofstadter has demonstrated, rural Populists and intellectual reformers frequently found common ground in opposition to the big city machines whose core of strength was organization of the urban masses. Whatever the cause, state after state revised or clarified its apportionment formulae.

Ohio, which in 1851 had guaranteed a legislative seat to each county with at least a half-ratio, i.e., half of the state average population per seat, added the Hanna amendment in 1903 which abolished this provision and guaranteed a seat to each county regardless of population. Pennsylvania, which had restricted populous cities and counties (Philadelphia) to a maximum of four senators in 1838, and had guaranteed each county a representative in the house in 1873, amended again in 1901 to provide that no more than one-sixth of the senators could come from any city or county.

New York, in 1894, achieved a similar result through a series of quite complex formulae.[45] These survived to baffle the Supreme Court in 1964 and to make difficult the attempted argument that a "rational plan" underlay New York's population disparities—disparities which actually were relatively moderate by comparison to the gross malapportionments being challenged concurrently in the defendant Southern states.

The New York Constitutional Convention of 1894 also produced some classic statements concerning balancing rural spaces and urban places in representation formulae. Defending provisions which apportioned seats to rural counties in excess of their population entitlement, Elihu Root asserted that the greater separation of interests in those areas made representation more difficult than in urban areas, and claimed that urban representatives gain effective force by speaking for a unified urban interest even though their district be but a part of the city. He went on to say:

> I insist, sir, upon the principle which has been adopted in a large
> number of the States of this Union, in almost every State which has
> had to deal with the problem of a great city within its borders, and

45. Charles Z. Lincoln, *supra* note 42; Ruth C. Silva, "The Legal Aspects of Reapportionment and Redistricting," 30 *Fordham L. Rev.* 581, 603 *et seq.* (1962).

the relations of that city to an agricultural community, that the problem which they have had to deal with shall be dealt with by us on the same principle; that the small and widely scattered communities, with their feeble power comparatively, because of their division, shall, by the distribution of representation, be put on an equal footing, so far as may be, with the concentrated power of the cities. Otherwise we can never have a truly representative and a truly republican government.[46]

This thought by the eminent Root was echoed in 1948 by another well-known figure, Governor Earl Warren of California, who said: "Many California counties are far more important in the life of the State than their population in the State. It is for this reason that I have never been in favor of restricting the representation in the senate to a strictly population basis." [47] When, as Chief Justice in 1964, Mr. Warren announced for the Court the sweeping rule of "one man-one vote," he was reminded of this earlier statement in the press and on the floor of the United States Senate.

In some states it was easier simply to stop reapportioning. A survey in 1960 showed that 12 state senates and also 12 lower houses had not been reapportioned for thirty years or more.[48] Alabama, Delaware, and Tennessee had not reapportioned since 1901, 1897, and 1901 respectively. Although 28 senates and 31 lower houses were modified in the 1950s, for some states, such as Illinois, it was the first change in decades.

This era was marked by a frequently successful appeal to the "federal" principle, i.e., county equality or something approaching it in one house, and population apportionment in the other house. This principle had been appealed to frequently, but usually unsuccessfully, in state constitutional conventional debates in the early decades of the nineteenth century.[49] Although not unknown at the state level, the "federal," or county equality, principle was relatively rare in the original constitutions of the states except in the East and South. (See Chart No. 3.) Persistent examples have been New Jersey, Delaware, and, with slight variation, Maryland.

Although now mooted by the 1964 *Supreme Court Decisions*, it is pos-

---

46. Luce, *supra* note 4, at 365–66.
47. 110 *Cong. Rec.* 16061 (July 8, 1964). Senator Roberts had read into the *Record* the editorial from the July 6, 1964, Newport News, Virginia, *Daily Press*. The *Press* quoted the statement made by Warren on October 29, 1948, which had been first reported by *U.S. News & World Report*.
48. *The Book of the States* 1960–1961 54–58 (Chicago: Council of State Governments, 1960).
49. Francis N. Thorpe, *Constitutional History of the American People 1776–1850* Vol. I:Chs. XIII–XIV, Vol. II:Ch. IV (Washington, D.C.: U.S. Government Printing Office, 1898).

sible to construct some plausible if not convincing arguments in support of a "federal" principle for one house. It would be essentially a virtue-of-consensus argument. The argument would center on the fact that, considering the executive as part of the effective legislative process, a federal plan subjects one-third, not one-half, of the representation system to a nonmajoritarian bias. However, one may suspect that something less than pure principle underlay many of the state constitutional revisions in this period.

Montana, for example, came into the Union in 1889 with a guarantee of county equality in the senate. The provision was motivated mostly by fear that otherwise both houses would be controlled by three counties containing the copper and gold boom towns of Butte, Anaconda, and Helena. By the eve of *Baker* v. *Carr* the policy of equal representation in the state senates of fixed geographic units, with insignificant modifications based on population, was part of the formal apportionment formulae in seventeen states, of which ten were Western or Midwestern states. (See Chart No. 4.)

Population disparities in state legislative apportionment since 1910 have been computed by decades for every state and reveal some interesting figures. Chart No. 5 indicates that the break point comes in regard to counties of 100,000 population. In 1910, 1930, 1950, and 1960, citizens residing in counties of less than 100,000 population were consistently overrepresented; citizens residing in counties with more than 100,000 population were consistently underrepresented. Using "100" as the average vote value, the spread of overrepresentation and underrepresentation as between citizens in counties under 25,000 and cities and counties of 500,000 and over increased from a range of 113 to 81 in 1910 to a range of 171 to 76 in 1960. Overrepresentation of the less populous areas increased to a greater degree than did underrepresentation of the more populous areas.

Motivations are not difficult to perceive for simple nonapportionment and constitutional revision in the direction of big-city limitations and geographic diffusion of representation throughout the state. Bare census figures hint at much of the story. American population growth has been phenomenal from the beginning. But rate of growth increased dramatically in the latter part of the nineteenth century and created a novel problem of absorption and institutional adjustment. Immigration played a dominant role. In the decade 1820–1830 the United States admitted approximately 140,000 people. For the decade 1880–1890 the number leaped to approximately five million and the derivation of the immigrants had shifted from Northern to Southern Europe. In the decade 1900–1910—before war and revised immigration policies reduced immigration to a trickle—almost nine million immigrants arrived.

Chart 4

APPORTIONMENT FORMULAE OF STATE LEGISLATURES AS OF JULY 1, 1961

Basis of Representation	Upper House (Senate)	Lower House
I. Representation Based On Geographic Unit Without Regard To Population: (a) Equal Representation For Each County.	Arizona, Idaho, Montana, Nevada, New Jersey, New Mexico, South Carolina (7)	(0)
(b) Equal Representation Based On Geographic Units Other Than Counties (including districts initially devised according to population but fixed in constitution, e.g., Ark., N.D., Okla.)	Arkansas, Delaware, Illinois, Michigan, North Dakota, Oklahoma (6)	Delaware, Vermont (2)
II. Representation Based On Geographic Unit With MINOR Modifications Based On Population.[a]	Hawaii, Maryland, Mississippi, Ohio (4)	(0)
III. Representation Proportioned To Units (county or district) On Basis Of Population but with MAJOR limitations to achieve geographic diffusion which may substantially defeat population principle: e.g., (1) Minimum limits, e.g., rule that no unit may have less than one representative, and, or, limitation on number of units which may be combined to approximate one quota; (2) Maximum limits, e.g., rule that no unit may have more than a designated number of representatives; and (3) Low limit (in relation to number of counties) on maximum size of legislature when combined with minimum diffusion rules.[a]	Alabama, California, Connecticut, Florida, Georgia, Iowa, Louisiana, Maine, Rhode Island, Texas, Utah, Vermont, Wyoming (13) (Low quota for first representative; much higher for additional representative.)	Alabama, Arizona, Arkansas, California, Connecticut, Florida, Georgia, Hawaii, Idaho, Iowa, Kansas, Louisiana, Maine, Maryland, Mississippi, Missouri, Montana, Nevada, New Jersey, New Mexico, New York, North Carolina, North Dakota, Ohio, Oklahoma, Pennsylvania, Rhode Island, South Carolina, Texas, Utah, West Virginia, Wyoming (32)

IV. Representation To Be Apportioned On Population Basis With Apparently MINOR Limitations.b,c

Alaska	Oregon	Alaska	Oregon
Missouri	Pennsylvania	New Hampshire	South Dakota
New Hampshire	South Dakota	(Tax basis; appears	(4)
New York	(7)	to avoid gross inequity.)	

V. Population.c

NEBRASKA

Colorado	Tennessee	Colorado	Tennessee
Indiana	Virginia	Illinois	Virginia
Kansas	Washington	Indiana	Washington
Kentucky	West Virginia	Kentucky	Wisconsin
Massachusetts	Wisconsin	Massachusetts	(12)
Minnesota	(13)	Michigan	
North Carolina		Minnesota	

a Some states may be classified to either II or III, depending on the weight given to special constitutional formulae. The distinction may not be vital however, because the primary thrust of both II and III is toward geographic diffusion, not representation by population.

b Some states charted in this category have special formulae not easily classifiable but weighted more to population principle than to geographic diffusion. The major chart division is between categories III and IV, separating states using a strong geographic diffusion factor from states using a relatively unqualified population factor.

c Despite constitutional provisions apparently specifying apportionment by population, all states in categories IV and V have population disparities between largest and smallest district at least exceeding 25 percent and in most cases far exceeding that figure.

Sources: State Constitutions; National Municipal League, Compendium on Legislative Apportionment (1962); The Book of the States (1962–63); Gordon E. Baker, State Constitutions: Reapportionment (1960).

Comment: The state constitutions themselves and the National Municipal League's Compendium are the best sources. The simple "population" classifications sometimes found in other tabulations are misleading because the qualifications on the basis of representation noted under I (b) and III in this chart are often ignored.

As significant as the sharply increased number of immigrants is the fact that the later nineteenth-century arrivals, unlike those in the early part of the century, did not come to settle the agricultural frontier. They came to seek the benefits of the industrial revolution in the large manufacturing and trading centers of which each section except the Rocky Mountain

Chart 5

VALUE OF CITIZENS' VOTES FOR THE STATE LEGISLATURES, 1910–1960
100 = Average Vote Value

Categories of Counties by Population Size	Number of Counties in Category	Total Population of Counties in Category	Percent of National Population	Vote Value
	1960			
Under 25,000	1,942	23,064,000	12.9	171
25,000– 99,999	884	41,247,000	23.1	123
100,000–499,999	238	48,542,000	27.2	81
500,000 and over	64	65,705,000	36.8	76
	1950			
Under 25,000	1,954	24,261,000	16.2	141
25,000– 99,999	901	40,757,000	27.2	114
100,000–499,999	200	40,088,000	26.7	83
500,000 and over	41	44,789,000	29.9	78
	1930			
Under 25,000	2,062	26,331,000	21.5	131
25,000– 99,999	869	37,411,000	30.6	109
100,000–499,999	142	29,911,000	24.5	84
500,000 and over	23	28,634,000	23.4	74
	1910			
Under 25,000	2,149	27,421,000	29.9	113
25,000– 99,999	796	32,203,000	35.1	103
100,000–499,999	87	17,154,000	18.7	91
500,000 and over	15	14,853,000	16.2	81

Source: Reproduced with permission from Congressional Quarterly Weekly Report, Feb. 2, 1962, p. 170, as adapted from statistics in Paul T. David & Ralph Eisenberg, Devaluation of the Urban and Suburban Vote (1961).

states had at least one. The Midwest had Milwaukee, St. Louis, Kansas City, and Des Moines, in addition to Chicago. The South had Birmingham and Atlanta in addition to the pre-Civil War center of New Orleans. Rural America recorded its last majority in the federal census in 1910.

Few states escaped the burgeoning romance of the Big City and its concurrent practical problems of political vigor, social purpose, and human needs, which cut squarely across the traditional rural-small town character of the nineteenth-century political system. A tension and a confusion of values resulted, but a sense of rural virtue remained strong. As late as 1918 a refrain like "How can you keep them down on the farm after they've seen Paree?" had a captivating and readily understood message—compounded of nostalgia for a weakening but still vital rural ethic, and new pride in urban vigor. By 1962, when *Baker v. Carr* was decided, the response would be: "Who is down on the farm?"

Unless legislative bodies were to become too large and unwieldy to be effective, which arguably has happened in regard to the national House of Representatives, many small political subdivisions faced the prospect by 1900 of seeing seats held since statehood transferred to more rapidly growing urban areas. The personal interest of incumbents was at stake as well as larger issues of community as a basis for constituency. Long-standing political alignments and elements of party structure were threatened. In more partisan terms, the prospective seat transfer, if linked reasonably closely to population trends, was from a rural-small town constituency to an urban-big city machine constituency. Even when the same political party controlled both areas—universally in the South and occasionally in the North, e.g., Pennsylvania—vitally different interests were felt to be in conflict.

a. *Federal Plan Popular Referenda*

It would be an exaggeration, however, to present the issue as one between two solid monoliths. The many constitutional revisions authorizing some nonpopulation considerations in apportionment seemed to be based on solid popular acceptance—if one accepts the basic premise that voter preference is meaningful in a democracy. Most changes had to be submitted to popular referenda. With few exceptions they received substantial endorsement throughout the state, including significant voter approval in the urban areas themselves. Further, a number of these popular referenda came rather late in our history—up to the eve of *Baker v. Carr* and even after *Baker* in some states.

In California, for example, voters in an initiative in 1926 ratified a federal plan providing for apportionment of the senate among the counties on an essentially equal basis. The plan was the product of political tensions caused by the more rapid growth of the southern part of the state. Initiative measures aimed at upsetting the plan failed in 1928, 1948, and 1960.[50] To be sure, some side issues may have been involved, particularly in 1960, but on three successive occasions it was impossible to muster a popular majority for population apportionment in both houses, even

50. Charles M. Hardin, "Issues in Legislative Reapportionment," 27 *Review of Politics* 147 (1965).

among those who were sufficiently motivated to participate in the referendum.

In Michigan the constitution also authorized the popular initiative, and in 1952 the voters were faced with two proposals regarding the state senate. They rejected one to reapportion the senate under a population principle and approved the other based on a geographic distribution principle.[51] The result, roughly speaking, was a population-based lower house and a geographically distributed upper house. Subsequently in 1963 in the course of the reapportionment upheavals induced by *Baker v. Carr*, the people of Michigan ratified a new constitutional apportionment clause leaving the house on a population basis and apportioning the senate 80 percent by population and 20 percent by area.[52]

In 1962, when *Baker v. Carr* was already several months old, the voters of both Washington[53] and Colorado[54] rejected initiative measures to redistrict the state legislature under formulae more strictly based on population than the existing system. The Colorado vote is especially interesting because, as in Michigan in 1952, the initiative was not a "take it or leave it" affair. Rather, with two plans on the ballot, the Colorado voters by a majority in every county and by a two-to-one statewide majority rejected the plan placing both houses on a population basis, and endorsed the plan placing one house essentially on a population basis and the other house on a modified population-political subdivision basis. Political factors in the Colorado 1962 reapportionment referendum are analyzed in Chapter X.

As these instances show, and as Professor Hugh A. Bone has demonstrated for the earlier period, even in the minority of states where the people may initiate constitutional change by petition, a population-based apportionment for both legislative houses could not muster widespread support.[55] In those few instances where a successful initiative petition nudged a state nearer a population-based apportionment, the plans still were a far cry from a tight "one man-one vote" principle.

Despite the announced constitutional mandate of the 1960s, the American public up to 1960 had shown something less than constancy of purpose in the direction of a fully egalitarian, fully majoritarian representation system.

51. For a recent discussion of all the states mentioned here, and others, see Edward M. Goldberg, "The People Legislate," 55 *Nat. Civ. Rev.* 82, 90 (1966), who concludes that the "appeal of the little federal plan to voters appears to have been substantial." 52. *Ibid.*
53. Thigpen v. Meyers, 211 F. Supp. 826, 832 (1962).
54. Lisco v. Love, 219 F. Supp. 922, 924, 930–31 & n. 32 (1963).
55. Hugh A. Bone, "States Attempting to Comply With Reapportionment Requirements," 17 *Law & Contemporary Problems* 387, 409–12 (1952).

2. CONGRESSIONAL DISTRICTS

The corollary question of the degree of population inequality in congressional districts in the nineteenth century has been subjected to as little scrutiny as has the question of state legislative district population inequality. Data have been assembled, however, for the period since 1900. In evaluating it one must bear in mind that the posture of congressional representation is quite different from the posture of state legislative representation. The House of Representatives is the one population-based branch of the Congress. For this reason, and because the least percentage of the population capable of electing a majority of the Senate was as low as 16 percent in 1960,[56] one might expect a compensating rigid population equality for the lower house of Congress. In practice congressional districts exceeding by 40 percent or more the population of the smallest district in the state have not been uncommon.[57]

A bill introduced in Congress in 1936 was designed to create pressure for redistricting by providing that at-large elections would be required whenever the population of the largest congressional district exceeded the smallest in a given state by more than 50 percent.[58] Although recent federal district courts have worried about congressional district population deviations of under 10 percent,[59] a Brookings Institution study as late as 1941 suggested that a 20 percent deviation from the average for all districts in the state would be "a fair and workable tolerance" arguing that: "This tolerance is large enough to allow a division between congressional districts based on the boundaries of counties and such other subordinate minor civil divisions as may be recognized by the state law and by the census." [60]

C. A Glance Abroad

1. GREAT BRITAIN

Great Britain often has been viewed as the creator and guardian of the democratic tradition of political freedom. As noted in Chapter II, politi-

56. Computed from figures given in *Statistical Abstract of the United States* 12–13 (Washington, D.C.: U.S. Government Printing Office, 1965).
57. Colegrove v. Green, 328 U.S. 549, 557–59 (1946); see generally Lawrence F. Schmeckebier, *Congressional Apportionment* (Washington, D.C.: Brookings Institution, 1941), especially tables from 182–225.
58. Schmeckebier, *supra* note 57, at 141.
59. Drum v. Seawell, 250 F. Supp. 922 (M.D.N.C. 1966).
60. Schmeckebier, *supra* note 56, at 130.

cal egalitarianism has not been an equally prominent feature of British thought and practice. Wolfgang Friedmann has observed that the ethos of British politics, unlike French and American politics, has been oriented more toward effective leadership than equality of rights. Until the latter part of the nineteenth century, British "malapportionment" in district formation was related also to a policy of suffrage restriction.

In the post-World War I era a heightened concern for population-based apportionment has been reflected in frequent parliamentary action. On the eve of World War I, population variance ratios, which had been reduced to 7 to 1 in the initial effort to distribute parliamentary seats by population in 1885, had risen to 15 to 1. By the Representation of the People Act of 1918 the ratio was reduced to 5 to 1, but agitation continued seeking further equalization and a better articulation of standards throughout the 'twenties and 'thirties. (See Chart No. 6 showing popula-

Chart 6

BRITISH POPULATION VARIANCE RATIOS: 1832–1948

For Parliament: The tabulation shows the approximate ratios between the largest and smallest electorates in territorial constituencies after each of the five major redistributions.

Year	U.K.	England only
1832	100 to 1	60 to 1
1868	150 to 1	80 to 1
1885	8 to 1	7 to 1
1918	5 to 1	3 to 1
1948	3 to 1	2 to 1

Source: D. E. Butler, The Electoral System in Britain, 1918–1951 (Oxford: Clarendon Press, 1953), p. 205.

tion variance ratios after each of five major parliamentary redistributions from 1832 to 1948.) The 1918 rule of thumb was to operate within outer ranges of 70 percent below and 170 percent above the quota; in actual result, only a handful of constituencies departed from the national average by more than one-third.[61]

The tendency of the single-member district system to fail to represent the political parties in Parliament in close approximation to their popular voting strength also gave rise to proposals to adopt a modified proportional representation system for Parliament. PR proposals were defeated by a vote of 211–112 in 1921 and again in 1923 by a vote of 240–146. Some votes on various amendments and modifications were often closer than these figures.

61. D. E. Butler, The Electoral System in Britain 1918–1951 209 (Oxford: Clarendon Press, 1953). I have relied heavily on this work for much of the material in this section.

a. *New Standards*

Something approaching a "final solution" to the redistribution of seats problem resulted from a series of measures enacted in the 1940s. A 1944 statute specified new standards and placed redistribution on a periodic basis to be handled primarily by administrative agencies known as Boundary Commissions for England, Scotland, Wales, and Northern Ireland, respectively. There was to be a 25 percent limit on population deviation, local boundaries were to be respected where possible, and permission was given to vary these rules in accord with "special geographic considerations" such as size, shape, and accessibility factors of a given constituency.

These guidelines were short-lived because of their threatened effect on the strong British tradition of identifying constituencies with communities. In the words of D. E. Butler, a leading student of British parliamentary representation, the 25 percent limitation was "far too rigid and produced results which in some instances cut right across local unities." [62] Accordingly, the 25 percent standard was abolished in 1947 and replaced with the more elastic instruction that "the electorate of any constituency shall be as near the electoral quota as is practicable," [63] having regard to pre-existing rules about respecting local boundaries. The resultant population variance ratio was 3 to 1 in 1948 (2 to 1 considering England only).

Butler's analysis finds two additional limitations on the principle of numerical equality. The first is a tradition of overrepresentation of Wales and Scotland and of underrepresentation of Northern Ireland (the latter having a parliament of its own). For example, the average electorates under the 1949 register were: England, 56,073; Wales, 50,061; Scotland, 47,465; Northern Ireland, 72,090. The second is a practice of the Boundary Commissions to treat not only remote rural areas but relatively compact rural areas more generously than urban areas.

Butler's assessment of the new British system, centering on permanent Boundary Commissions operating under parliamentary instructions, is nicely balanced. He notes that periodic reviews may check anomalies at the outset, but such local patchwork may create differences between the quotas for the various regions. Also, it may be easier to be drastic in long overdue redistribution than in frequent reviews with a handful of districts way out of line. He also noted the obvious point, seldom adequately emphasized in American discussions of the virtues of apportionment by administrative agencies, that although the "neutrality of the Boundary

62. *Id.* at 206.
63. *Ibid.*

Commissioners is beyond question . . . the consequences of redistribution are not necessarily neutral." [64]

b. *Mathematics and Community*

A continued concern for community factors, as well as a natural British distaste for running any mathematical principle into the ground, lead to a further enhancement of Boundary Commission discretion in 1958 when the Commissions were expressly directed to consider "local ties." Concurrently, the interval permitted between Commission reports was increased from seven to fifteen years. Challenges to the English Boundary Commission's discretion in implementing its elastic instructions were judicially rejected in 1954.[65] In short, the British have come far from the 150 to 1 population variance ratios of 1868, and have experimented in interesting fashion with periodic review by administrative agency. Yet a rigid "one man-one vote" policy of elevating mathematics above community would be contrary to deeply imbedded English conceptions of representation and to recent practice. The "noncommunity" policy advocated in 1954 by an American Political Science Association Committee—i.e., conscious avoidance of local unit lines in favor of creating a fresh if artificial layer of districts—would leave a British reapportioner bemused, and perhaps amused.[66]

2. WEST GERMANY

The land of Bismarck and Hitler seems an unlikely source of instructive guidance on how to operate a democratic representation system. The Weimar republic did go all the way with PR but after twelve years it "was junked by the Nazi one-party state when Hitler made his Reichstag into the hightest paid male chorus in the world." [67]

After World War II, however, West Germany was occupied by the English and Americans as well as the historically unstable French. The Anglo-American concept of districts and the Continental concept of pro-

---

64. *Id.* at 211.
65. Hammersmith Borough Council v. Boundary Commission for England, *The Times,* December 15, 1954, p. 4, cols. 1–2; Harper v. Secretary [1955] 1 Ch. 238.
66. See American Political Science Association Committee Report, *American State Legislatures* 46 (Belle Zeller, editor, 1954), which recommended "disregard of counties and other areas of local government in laying off representative districts insofar as is consistent with efficient election administration."
67. James K. Pollock, "The Electoral System of the Federal Republic of Germany— A Study in Representative Government," 46 *Am. Pol. Sci. Rev.* 1056, 1057 (1952). For the material summarized in this section I am indebted primarily to this article by Professor Pollock, and also his "A Sensible Approach," 54 *Nat. Civ. Rev.* 357 (1965).

portional representation collided. The result was to produce for the Federal Republic of Germany a mixed proportional representation and single-member district system which so far has proved to be a very healthy mongrel. Ironically, the postwar Germans may have achieved the most sophisticated, rational, and empirically workable system of representation the world has yet known.

The concept is simple. The electoral law for the *Bundestag* (lower house) dates from 1949 and its essential provision is that 60 percent of the seats are based on single-member districts of relatively equal population and 40 percent are selected by PR from party lists in the individual states (subsequently modified to be 50-50 rather than 60-40). Further, the number of legislators each party acquires by direct vote in the single-member districts is deducted from the PR compilation in order to maximize the "corrective" force of the PR feature; e.g., "corrective" in the sense that the PR feature compensates for the tendency of all single-member district systems to overrepresent the dominant parties and underrepresent the weaker parties. Interestingly enough, the leading party figures tend to be those elected from districts rather than from the PR list, despite the common lore that one of the virtues of PR is the preservation of continuity in party leadership. (The other half of the Federal Parliament, the *Bundesrat* with lesser powers, consists of representatives appointed by the "state" governments—the *Länder*.)

The electoral law specifies that constituency populations shall not vary more than $33\frac{1}{3}$ percent from the federal average. The electoral district commission which administers the law, however, has sought to stay inside a 25 percent limit. In the reallocation approved in 1963, seven of the 247 constituencies ranged between a 25 and $33\frac{1}{3}$ percent deviation; the variances of all others were within 20 percent of the federal average. In arranging districts, the commission also seeks to: follow local government boundaries as far as possible; give to every constituency as much geographical unity as possible in order to preserve the natural and economic relations within the voting district and prevent *Wahlkreisgeometrie* (gerrymandering); preserve existing constituencies as far as possible to avoid disrupting existing relationships between constituents and candidates.

A further feature of the German system is that the commission's report to the Federal Parliament includes all relevant information necessary to an informed understanding of the changes and their effect, and even indicates the prospective impact of the redistribution on party representation in the *Bundestag*. Because this system, to a far greater extent than the English or American, has in practice operated to give each party a "fair shake" in the sense of parliamentary representation roughly approximating its popular strength, the pathway to acceptance of periodic revision is markedly eased. The most recent commission report on apportionment was approved by the parliament without major change in 1963.

In short, the use of single-member districts insures intimacy of representation, minimizes party bossism, and counteracts the splintering tendency of PR. The use of a PR list system as a corrective avoids the minority party freeze-out which is a tendency of the pure district system, and has a balancing effect in the direction of representational equity.

D. Conclusion

The significance of this review of decades of constitutional history is its direct bearing on whether *Baker* v. *Carr* and *Reynolds* v. *Sims* can be viewed as a return to a lost tradition of population exclusivity in apportionment, or a significantly new concept concerning the relevance and exclusivity of population in an apportionment formula. Historical arguments have a way of counterbalancing each other, because most history, like mankind, is confused.

The supporters of a policy substantially qualifying the factor of population in apportionment point to the federal plan for Congress, the language in most state constitutions qualifying in some way a pure population apportionment principle, the considerable body of evidence concerning actual population disparities, and other practices. Supporters of a "one man-one vote" population-only principle of representation have dismissed the federal plan for Congress as an historical compromise; exalted the text of the Northwest Ordinance without, however, examining the practice; shrugged off as inconsequential the state constitutional language qualifying a pure population apportionment; and played down or ignored evidence that population spread throughout the nineteenth century was not sufficiently uniform to neutralize guarantees of individual county representation. To compound the uncertainty, the degree of support which either camp can muster from an historical analysis depends on the degree of allowable tolerance in the equality yardstick used to measure compliance with a "population" principle of apportionment.[68]

68. Part of the problem of assessing the historical record is that historians tend to write the history of *politicians*, not the history of *politics and government*. There are a number of questions on which data must be gathered before an agreed assessment can be made of the degree of use of the "population principle" in apportionment throughout American history. These questions, which could occupy a whole stable of masters and doctoral thesis writers, include the following: (1) How were the many patent ambiguities in the apportionment formulae of the original constitutions of the fifty states resolved; (2) apart from the formal formulae, what were the actual population disparities among the legislative districts for each house in each state at various

A further barrier to reasoned analysis is the fact that the purpose of the "population-only" apportionment enthusiasts was in most instances laudable. Malapportionment is not a pathway to vigorous democracy in tune with current needs and problems. And yet the historical record, sketchy as it is in many places, clearly suggests that those who seek to base "one man-one vote" on history rather than on a specific concept of the moral relation between man and government, have been more hortatory than historical. It is quite clear that the framers and amenders of state constitutions saw no inconsistency in specifying population as the major premise in legislative apportionment formulae and in immediately coupling the population factor with nonpopulation provisions designed to disperse representation geographically and use political subdivisions as building blocks for apportionment. History, of course, need not and should not rule us. But it should be possible to deviate from past practice without rewriting history to create a pretense of return to original truth.

The dichotomy that arose in the *Baker–Reynolds* period between the most vocal defenders of the status quo and the most vocal proponents of major change had one most unfortunate result. It left undefended by rational argument a possible middle position on apportionment. Such a position, intertwining the moral force of "one man-one vote" with equally moral considerations of fair representation, would be analogous to the practice in postwar democracies in Europe. England has modified the majoritarianism of equal population districts with a concern for the right to be heard of traditional local units. Germany has modified the majoritarianism of equal population districts by infusing some proportional representation elements into the apportionment system, in order to avoid a one-party monolith. Most American states by contrast have tended to move from the pathology of small-town-oriented malapportionment to the my-

time periods from 1800 to 1960; (3) was county population in general so equal in the long period from 1800 to 1890 that requirements or practices of awarding each county at least one seat produced insignificant population disparities; (4) if there were significant population disparities in the 1800 to 1890 period what interests were affected (by significant disparity is meant exceeding 15 percent); (5) if there were relatively few instances of wide disparities, did these disparities nevertheless affect a significant percentage of the population, e.g., perhaps the entire urban population of the state concentrated in one or two centers: (6) were there regional differences in such disparities as existed; (7) did the disparities produce any significant impact on the character of representation of identifiable interests, and on the character and volume of the legislative product, e.g., selecting the states typically identified as pioneering in progressive legislation in fields of social and economical concerns, were these states significantly different in use of population as a factor in apportionment and districting practices from other states; (8) were the dissatisfactions which began to arise and be recorded regarding some apportionment and districting practices directed primarily at the unequal population aspect, or was this aspect subordinate to a primary concern about gerrymandering devices designed to favor one political party—devices which were not necessarily tied to district population imbalance?

thology of "one man-one vote" extrapolations from bare census data. The 1970 census will provide the first opportunity to reassess and relate our new rather rigidly mathematical guidelines to our political realities and needs.

V

Political Thickets and Judicial Forays:
Baker v. *Carr* in Context

"Scarcely any political question arises in the United States that is
not resolved, sooner or later, into a judicial question."
De Tocqueville
Democracy in America

In *Baker* v. *Carr*, a case certain to be as historic in American constitutional history as *Marbury* v. *Madison* in February 1803, the United States
Supreme Court for the first time subjected legislative apportionment to
judicial review. This decision in March 1962 in a case challenging apportionment of the Tennessee state legislature has been characterized variously as a constitutional thunderclap, a charter of freedom, the final
absurdity of judicial activism, and as the culmination of the equality
principle in America. None of these generalizations is accurate, or wholly
inaccurate.

Baker v. *Carr* is a Janus-faced decision. It stands at the end of a long
line of judicial refusals to enter the political thicket of reapportionment,
so well and so eloquently summarized by Justice Felix Frankfurter in his
Baker dissent. As such, it evokes memories of lost battles of the past. But
the ruling that the courts could begin to entertain challenges to the unrepresentative character of legislatures under the equal protection of the
laws clause of the Fourteenth Amendment also served to inaugurate a
new era for American politics and constitutionalism. Legislative institutions, political theories of representative government, and the unique institution of judicial review are being profoundly affected.

For some the decision to make legislative apportionment a justiciable
question was a new Statue of Liberty, signaling a new majoritarianism
which would yield fresh political force for more effective approaches to
problems of city and suburbia, civil rights and liberties, social welfare, and
even international relations. For others the decision seemed to sound the

death knell on a rule of rural virtue rooted in the mystique of the settler tradition, the log cabin, and the family farm. Without knowing yet the dimensions of the change, all realized that a new order had begun. In a sense *Baker* was and is a more pregnant decision than *Brown* v. *Board of Education* in 1954 regarding school desegregation. It involved, as do the social contract philosophies of Hobbes, Locke, and Rousseau, basic choices regarding conditions of political allegiance and modes of effective expression of public will and opinion. School desegregation presents an issue as "black and white" in moral terms as in physical terms. Neither our Judaeo-Christian moral heritage nor the legal institutions derived therefrom have room for a governmental policy of conditioning public programs and benefits on grounds of race. But reapportionment involves definitions of "democracy" and arrangement of complex and sometimes unpredictable institutions of representation.

As Justice John Marshall Harlan noted in dissent, *Baker* v. *Carr* brought to the surface some still unresolved conflicts of principle concerning our traditional and expedient arrangements of election districts, majority requirements, and legislative assemblies. For example, in the fall of 1966 the Supreme Court, without a hearing and without reasons, turned aside a suit seeking an airing under "one man-one vote" principles of the constitutionality of the general ticket system of presidential election under the electoral college, whereby all of a state's electoral votes are appropriated by the mere plurality party. (See Chapter XX.) In the same period such enthusiastic backers of the new judicial activism in political matters as the *Washington Post* openly wondered whether a federal district court in Georgia may not have gone too far in interceding in the Maddox-Calloway contest for the governorship. The court nullified the provision in Georgia's constitution—analogous to a provision in the federal Constitution regarding presidential election—providing for a legislative selection of the governor if no candidate achieves a majority in the election. A divided Supreme Court reversed. (See Ch. VI, 136–37; Ch. IX, 221 n. 59.)

Although the dimensions of *Baker* and the dimensions of the reapportionment issue itself have not always been clearly perceived, a principled and thorough-going analysis of the interests in legislative representation and apportionment would require as a minimum a fresh look at: bicameralism; the single-member district system; population versus area as bases for representation; traditions of thought and political action geared to counties as historic representation units; the problem of the political artificiality of mathematically equal and frequently changing districts; voting qualifications; the extent to which a "one man-one vote" principle should be universalized in domestic political institutions as distinct from international political institutions; the area, population, and institutional bases of political parties, and conditions of effective party competition as related to apportionment and districting.

Of special significance is *Baker's* impact on our inherited doctrine of "political questions" which has long served as a sort of escape hatch to avoid court handling of issues thought to be inappropriate for judicial resolution or impossible of judicial solution. The Supreme Court's handling of the "political question" doctrine in *Baker* has potential significance far beyond the field of reapportionment itself. For this reason the nature of this doctrine, and *Baker's* modification of it, merit careful examination.

THE "POLITICAL QUESTION" CONCEPT

When the Supreme Court at the threshold of our constitutional history sanctioned judicial review, i.e., court enforcement of the Constitution against other branches of the government, it did so in uncompromising terms in the middle of a political struggle so intense that one member of the Court, Justice Samuel Chase, was thereafter impeached by the Jeffersonian House of Representatives. Had the Senate sustained his impeachment, the next in line for removal was thought to be Chief Justice John Marshall himself, author of the *Marbury v. Madison* opinion. Despite this firm beginning, and lack of any constitutional language on exceptions to judicial review, a doctrine allowing the Court to duck certain issues classified as "political questions" also dates from an early period. Its origin and scope always have been unclear. As early as 1796 the Court refused to pass on the question whether a treaty had been broken.[1] In the better known case of *Luther v. Borden*[2] in 1849, the Court refused to decide which of two governments in Rhode Island during Dorr's Rebellion was the legitimate government under the Constitution's "republican" government clause.

The "political question" concept is one of the most tantalizing of all American constitutional law principles, and by nature indefinable because it is really not a "principle" at all. Its elusiveness proceeds from the fact that it is more a rule of expediency than a rule of reason. It is designed to cover areas where judicial wisdom fails for lack of guiding standards, or judicial power is undermined by prospective inability to shape or enforce a remedy. It is a self-imposed limitation yielding judicial disengagement from an issue or an entire case.

To the cynical, aided by the Court's inability to articulate clearly the metes and bounds of the doctrine, and imbued with the American tendency to wrap judges in the robes of philosopher-kings, the "political

1. Ware v. Hylton, 3 U.S. (3 Dall.) 199 (1796).
2. 48 U.S. (7 How.) 1 (1849).

question" doctrine is an abdication of responsibility. Others, mindful of infrequent use of the doctrine, view it as a natural corollary of a system of judicial review. A practice of an enforceable Constitution periodically puts vox populi and higher law in apparent opposition, with the judiciary as uneasy mediator.[3]

For example, the Court has treated the constitutional amending process and such issues as whether a state's legislature may ratify an amendment after a prior rejection, as being judicially nonreviewable questions.[4] When Mississippi sought to enjoin the first President Johnson from enforcing Reconstruction legislation, the Court felt that discretion was a better part of valor and turned the plea aside.[5] Under a policy of not reviewing internal operations of co-ordinate branches of government, state courts have refused to police internal legislative procedure in mustering quorums and passing bills with the proper majority.[6] Matters of high policy dealing with international relations, and such interstate relations as exchange of criminals are typical examples of operation of the "political question" doctrine.[7]

CONFLICTING STRANDS

One of the most active categories of "political questions"—indeed *the* most active category in terms of number of suits—has been the general judicial disposition to reject suits questioning apportionment of seats in legislative assemblies, drawing of election district lines, and weighting of votes under electoral college or unit vote plans. Many generalizations made about judicial precedents in this category have been erroneous or misleading because of failure (1) to separate state court action from federal court action, (2) to separate state law bases for complaint from federal law bases, and (3) to separate state legislative cases from congressional districting cases.

Filing a case in state rather than federal court may directly affect the question of justiciability, i.e., whether the suit is to be treated as presenting an issue the judiciary can handle or as presenting a nonjusticiable "political question." Many state courts do not follow the federal principle of

3. See generally, Charles G. Post, *The Supreme Court and Political Questions* (Baltimore: Johns Hopkins Press, 1936); Maurice Finkelstein, "Judicial Self-Limitation," 37 *Harv. L. Rev.* 338 (1924). Also see "political question" discussion in Edmond D. Cahn, editor, *Supreme Court and Supreme Law* 36–47 (Indianapolis: University of Indiana Press, 1954).
4. Coleman v. Miller, 307 U.S. 433 (1939).
5. Mississippi v. Johnson, 71 U.S. (4 Wall.) 475 (1867).
6. Kelley v. Marron, 21 N.M. 239, 153 P. 262 (1950).
7. Oetjen v. Central Leather Co., 246 U.S. 297 (1918); Kentucky v. Dennison, 65 U.S. (24 How.) 66 (1861).

separation of powers and the corollary of restricted judicial power, and do things which would be clearly outside the "judicial function" as limited by Article III of the federal Constitution. For state courts the scope of the "judicial function" is determined by the state constitution, not the federal Constitution, unless elemental bounds of fairness are exceeded. Some state judiciaries do not shrink from acting in areas where there is no principle of right but only a bare public policy choice of the sort that could and probably should be made by normal political and legislative processes. A notable example of "nonjudicial" action by state judges is the Virginia judiciary's municipal annexation activity. In the guise of court "cases" judges order annexation of land to cities, determine boundaries, and specify financial and other conditions.[8] In those states where interpretation of the separation of powers principle conforms more closely to the federal interpretation, such unstandardized delegation of policy-making authority to courts would be unconstitutional. In the light of this too-little recognized facet of state constitutional law, some early state court cases on apportionment and districting are irrelevant to the question of scope of the "political question" doctrine in federal courts under the federal Constitution.

In addition to distinguishing state court action from federal court action it is also important to separate state law grounds for challenging legislative apportionment and districting from federal grounds. State law grounds cover a wide range of constitutional and statutory provisions, some quite discretionary but many quite clear and simple. Because uncertainty concerning possible decisional standards is one major component of the "political question" doctrine, cases which merely call for application of precise state constitutional formulae are of a different dimension from cases seeking application of the "equal protection of the laws" guarantee of the Fourteenth Amendment. Many early apportionment cases in state courts concerned such state constitutional standards as the following: fixed ceilings on size of legislature or one house, fixed ratios between size of state senate and state lower house, mandates to follow town boundaries, contiguity requirements.[9]

Adjudications of this sort under relatively narrow state law standards and normally not involving the elusive "population" concept comprise the bulk of pre-*Baker* state court apportionment litigation. Such cases are of slight relevance to the "political question" issue posed by a federal court

8. Henrico County v. City of Richmond, 106 Va. 282, 55 S.E. 683 (1906).
9. See, e.g., Caesar v. Williams, 371 P.2d 241 (Idaho, 1962); State *ex rel.* Attorney General v. Francis, 26 Kan. 724 (1882); Sandoz v. Sanders, 125 La. 396, 51 So. 436 (1910); Adams v. Forsyth and Robertson, 44 La. 130, 10 So. 622 (1898); Tishman v. Sprague, 293 N.Y. 42, 55 N.E.2d 858 (1944); Shoemaker v. Lawrence, 31 Pa. D. & C. 681 (C.P. Dauphin Cty. 1938).

challenge to an entire legislature under a generalized population equality theory derived from the Fourteenth Amendment.

There is need also to distinguish congressional districting cases from state legislative apportionment cases, both on the question of existence of a judicially ascertainable decisional standard and on the question of existence of an effective, judicially administrable remedy. Population as a classifying principle, uncomplicated by other factors, underlies federal constitutional principles concerning the House of Representatives. From decennial reapportionment of seats to the states on a population basis, it is a short step to argue that congressional districting *within* states likewise should be on a straight population basis.[10] By contrast, in constructing state legislative districts more numerous and complicated factors cloud the picture, such as area, traditional local unit boundary lines, political party impact, and bicameralism. More significantly, the possibility of an election at-large, either as threatened sanction to compel legislative redistricting or as temporary remedy for the complainants, has far greater appropriateness for congressional elections than for state legislative elections. In congressional elections, state voice in the House of Representatives is the primary representation aim and is achieved even with an at-large election in the state. But in state legislative elections, geographic diffusion within the state is needed for effective representation and to preserve political party balance. An at-large election could jeopardize these needs because of the voting power of one or two urban areas where a majority of the voters reside.

THE MYTH OF PRE-BAKER LOWER COURT ACTIVISM

Tabulations of early apportionment cases in state and federal courts have been made for the purpose of suggesting that *Baker* v. *Carr* was not such a novel case. These tabulations can be grossly misleading unless handled with care. For example, a tabulation made shortly after *Baker* was decided listed twenty-nine instances of judicial invalidation of apportionments (including three congressional district cases). However, in four instances the reported decisions were lower court decisions later overruled or decisions in a sequence of litigation ultimately culminating in failure; in two instances there was no actual holding of invalidation.[11] More critically, in

---

10. For an analysis of the historical materials bearing on the "democratic character of the House," see Joey F. Paschal, "The House of Representatives: 'Grand Depository of the Democratic Principle?' " 17 *Law & Contemp. Prob.* 276 (1952).

11. See Arthur L. Goldberg, "The Statistics of Malapportionment," 72 *Yale L. J.* 90 (1962) and cases listed therein.

For listed reapportionment or congressional redistricting decisions which actually were reversed or ineffective see: Broom v. Wood, 1 F. Supp. 134 (S.D. Miss.), *rev'd*, 287 U.S. 1 (1932); Hume v. Mahan, 1 F. Supp. 142 (E.D. Ky.), *rev'd per curiam*,

most of the other cases the court's order was unaccompanied by any order for affirmative relief. In only two instances was there an unreserved assertion of judicial authority to enjoin the holding of an election.[12]

In only two states was there remedial judicial action regarding the states' legislatures which went beyond a mere declaration of invalidity and reversion to earlier apportionments which were even more unequal than the plan invalidated.[13] The same study listed only eleven early cases in which other courts had refused to invalidate apportionments, but a check of only one early compilation reveals an additional seven.[14]

Amusing examples of loose citation of precedents may be found within the state judicial systems themselves. The highest courts of New Jersey and Maryland in 1960 and 1962 confidently asserted that "in 1938, the courts of twenty-two states had exercised the power, or had stated that they had the power, to review legislative apportionment acts upon constitutional grounds. . . ."[15] The statement was taken from a 1943 Oklahoma case which actually held that the separation of powers doctrine *barred* affirmative relief against the legislature for malapportionment. The Oklahoma Supreme Court in turn had cited the quoted statement to a 1938 article which in turn cited no authorities. By such workmanship is the web of changing law kept seamless!

Another portion of this same 1938 article stated that *no* successful cases of judicial control of legislative inaction on apportionment were found by the researcher because the separation of powers doctrine prevented courts from interfering "to force the legislature to perform a legislative duty, even if that performance is required by the constitution."[16]

EXAMPLES OF STATE COURT ACTION

Among the numerous instances of unsuccessful recourse to the courts for reapportionment are a series of cases filed in Illinois state and federal

287 U.S. 575 (1932); State *ex rel.* Winnie v. Stoddard, 62 Pac. 237 (Nev. 1900); *In re Sherrill*, 81 N.E. 124 (N.Y. 1907).

For listed litigations not culminating in any conclusive order see: State v. Heatherington, 61 N.W.2d 737 (Minn. 1953); Jones v. Freeman, 146 P.2d 564 (Okla. 1943).

12. Williams v. Wood, 162 S.W. 1031 (Ct. Civ. App. Texas 1914); State v. Cunningham, 53 N.W. 35 (Wis. 1892). See also Anthony Lewis, "Legislative Apportionment and the Federal Courts," 71 *Harv. L. Rev.* 1057, 1066–70 (1958).

13. Smith v. Bd. of Apportionment, 243 S.W.2d 755 (Ark. 1951); Pickens v. Bd. of Apportionment, 246 S.W.2d 556 (Ark. 1952); Attorney General v. Suffolk County Apportionment Commissioners, 113 N.E. 581 (Mass. 1916); Donovan v. Suffolk County Commissioners, 113 N.E. 740(Mass. 1916); Merrill v. Mitchell, 153 N.E. 562 (Mass. 1926).

14. 2 A.L.R. 1337 (1919).

15. Asbury Park Press, Inc. v. Woolley, 33 N.J. 1, 13–14, 161 A.2d 705, 711 (1960); Maryland Committee v. Tawes, 228 Md. 412, 431–32, 180 A.2d 656, 666 (1962).

16. David O. Walter, "Reapportionment and Urban Representation," 195 *Annals* 11, 13 (1938). A more extensive analysis of some of the early cases can be found here.

courts by John D. Fergus and others in the 1920s and 1930s seeking directly or indirectly to compel action by the malapportioned Illinois legislature. Unsuccessful strategies included petitions to mandamus the legislature, to restrain payment of salaries to legislators, to institute quo warranto proceedings against legislators, to bar the governor from certifying congressional elections, to avoid federal taxes pending federal enforcement of the "republican form of government" guarantee against Illinois, and to invalidate laws of the malapportioned legislature.[17] Other examples include the 1943 Oklahoma case just mentioned and a series of Massachusetts cases in 1916 which have been miscited for the opposite proposition that state courts can and have intervened in legislative districting.[18]

The Massachusetts cases illustrate the point that earlier courts normally did not reapportion even when they decided that an existing apportionment act was illegal. Their choice was to revert to a prior act, thus perhaps worsening malapportionment, or to rely hopefully on further action by the legislative body. The Massachusetts litigation involved invalidation of districts, mandamus to the county apportionment commissioners, begrudging legislative response in the form of a slightly altered plan, a second invalidation and mandamus, a second begrudging legislative response. At this point the court simply gave up. Population disparity had been reduced from a range of 1957 to 6182 per representative to a range of 2427 to 4282. The court said: "With some hesitation we are brought to the conclusion that the inequalities of voting power between the several districts . . . are not quite so great and the means for avoiding them are not quite so clear as to leave fair-minded men in no reasonable doubt that there is a grave and unnecessary inequality between the different districts. . . ."[19]

Evaluation of these precedents differs depending on whether one focuses on mere adjudication of constitutionality in the abstract which may approach the advisory opinion type of action forbidden in federal jurisprudence, or focuses on effectiveness of judicial relief where the record is rather barren. Indeed, because justiciability is not always mentioned in

17. Fergus v. Marks, 321 Ill. 510, 152 N.E. 557 (1926) (mandamus); Fergus v. Kinney, 333 Ill. 437, 164 N.E. 665 (1928), cert. denied, 279 U.S. 854 (1929) (restrain payment of salaries to legislators); People ex rel. Fergus v. Blackwell, 342 Ill. 223, 173 N.E. 750 (1930) (quo warranto); Keogh v. Horner, 8 F. Supp. 933 (S.D. Ill. 1934) (certification bar); Keogh v. Neely, 50 F.2d 685 (7th Cir. 1931) (federal tax avoidance); People v. Clardy, 334 Ill. 160, 165 N.E. 638 (1929) (invalidation of laws).
18. Oklahoma case: Jones v. Freeman, 146 P.2d 564, 570 (1943). Massachusetts cases: Attorney General v. Suffolk County Apportionment Commissioners, 113 N.E. 581 (1916); Donovan v. Suffolk County Apportionment Commissioners, 113 N.E. 740 (1916); Brophy v. Suffolk County Apportionment Commissioners, 113 N.E. 1040 (1916).
19. 113 N.E. 1040 at 1042.

the state court opinions, the frequent denial of relief in some cases loosely classified as "adjudicated" cases may well have resulted from an unspoken premise about the "political question" doctrine than from an adjudication of the merits.[20]

THE SUPREME COURT'S FIRST LOOK: 1932

Attempts to involve the United States Supreme Court in apportionment and districting matters date from 1932. Two-thirds of the states were affected by congressional reapportionment after the 1930 census. In states receiving additional seats in the House of Representatives, a state legislative failure to redistrict did not produce critical problems. The election at-large device could be used for the additional representation, leaving previous districts intact for the remaining representatives and thus ensuring continued geographic spread of representation throughout the state. The difficult problems arose in states losing representation. After the legislature had redistricted to absorb the loss, suits were filed in several of these states challenging the new districts. Four of these cases reached the Supreme Court, two from state courts, and two from federal district courts. The Supreme Court also received a state court case from a state with increased representation.

The three cases from state courts all turned on applicability of the governor's veto power to a congressional redistricting statute. As handled by the Supreme Court these cases did not involve larger issues of the existence and applicability of overriding federal *substantive* standards.

The leading veto power case was *Smiley* v. *Holm* from Minnesota [21] and the decision in it controlled the other two from Missouri and New York.[22] In *Smiley* the petitioner sought a declaration of the invalidity of the state redistricting statute and an injunction against its use on two grounds: first, that the governor's veto power applied to this matter and that the statute had not been re-enacted over his veto; second, that the statute violated standards of compactness, contiguity, and population equality in the 1911 Federal Reapportionment Act. The Minnesota Supreme Court ordered dismissal of the suit for two reasons.[23] It said that

20. E.g., People *ex rel.* Hefferman v. Carlock, 198 Ill. 150, 65 N.E. 109 (1902); Prouty v. Stover, 11 Kan. 235 (1873); Brophy v. Suffolk County Apportionment Commissioners, 225 Mass. 124, 113 N.E. 1040 (1916); State *ex rel.* Sullivan v. Schnitger, 16 Wyo. 479, 95 P. 698 (1908); State *ex rel.* Winnie v. Stoddard, 25 Nev. 452, 62 P. 237 (1900); Festler v. Brayton, 145 Ind. 71, 44 N.E. 37 (1896).
21. 285 U.S. 355 (1932).
22. Carroll v. Becker, 329 Mo. 501, 45 S.W.2d 533, *aff'd*, 285 U.S. 380 (1932); Koenig v. Flynn, 258 N.Y. 292, 179 N.E. 705, *aff'd*, 285 U.S. 375 (1932).
23. Smiley v. Holm, 184 Minn. 228, 238 N.W. 494 (1931).

in redistricting congressional seats the state legislature was exercising a special federal constitutional power rather than a normal state lawmaking power, and hence was immune to gubernatorial review and veto. It said, secondly, that the Federal Reapportionment Act of 1911 with its substantive standards on congressional districting had expired, and that even if the Act still were in existence this aspect of the case would present a nonjusticiable political question.

The United States Supreme Court on appeal managed to avoid the "political question" issue. It simply reversed the state court on the first aspect of the case because it found that the federal Constitution did not invest state redistricting with such special character as to shield the legislature from gubernatorial veto power. The Court commented that this result left Minnesota with no valid districts and that absent timely enactment of a new and valid statute the only recourse would be election at-large of Minnesota's congressional delegation.

The vital issue of the continued existence—and judicial enforceability —of the 1911 Reapportionment Act's standards against the states, left unresolved in *Smiley*, was raised by appeals from federal district courts in Mississippi and Kentucky.[24] The issue was disposed of in a single opinion in *Wood v. Broom*. The federal district courts had issued injunctions against the new state districting statutes because of noncompliance with standards in the 1911 Act. The Supreme Court concluded, however, that the 1911 Act had expired and ordered dismissal of the suits.

The Court thus was able to dispose of five congressional districting cases in 1932 on side issues without making a definitive ruling on justiciability, i.e., federal court enforceability of federal restraints on state districting discretion. The *Smiley* opinion did contain a cryptic remark inferring that recourse should be had *only* to Congress for state malfunction on congressional districting, and not to courts, unless Congress specifically directed otherwise. The Court said: "In exercising this power, the Congress may supplement these state regulations or may substitute its own. It may impose additional penalties for the violation of the state laws or provide independent sanctions. It 'has a general supervisory power over the whole subject.' "[25]

Any such inference was severely undercut by the Court's handling of the second plea in *Smiley*—alleged noncompliance with the standards of the 1911 Act. The Court said this issue was not properly before it in the light of its disposition of the case on the basis of the gubernatorial veto issue, and therefore was "wholly abstract." This latter phrase suggested

24. Wood v. Broom, 287 U.S. 1 (1932), *reversing* 1 F. Supp. 134 (S.D. Miss. 1932); Mahan v. Hume, 287 U.S. 575 (1932), *reversing* 1 F. Supp. 142 (E.D. Ky. 1932).
25. Smiley v. Holm, *supra* note 18, at 366–67.

that in a proper case the Court would *have power* to consider the matter, and might consider it appropriate to *exercise* the power.

The conflict between these inferences was not resolved in the appeals from the federal district courts in Mississippi and Kentucky. Because Chief Justice Charles Evans Hughes's opinion for the Court in *Wood v. Broom* was grounded on the conclusion that the 1911 Act had expired, one could infer that if the Act had not expired the Court might have considered the question. The inference was weakened by the fact that four remaining members of the Court—Justices Louis D. Brandeis, Harlan F. Stone, Owen J. Roberts, and Benjamin N. Cardozo—would have dismissed the suit for "want of equity." [26] The cryptic "want of equity" phrase suggests a policy of judicial self-limitation analogous to the doctrine of "political question," and probably indistinguishable in this context. It suggests that the Court normally would not *exercise* jurisdiction in this kind of case, despite noncompliance with either statutory or constitutional standards.

Failure to take account of the background of *Smiley* and the related 1932 cases, and of the specific relief requested, has produced some erroneous assertions that the federal courts had assumed jurisdiction and ordered elections at-large.[27] Such assertions create the misleading impression that federal courts, even prior to *Baker v. Carr*, had actively enforced federal substantive standards against the states in apportionment and districting matters. Actually, the issue in *Smiley* was whether the new districting statute could be saved by finding a federal exemption from the gubernatorial veto. This approach involved treating redistricting of congressional districts as a special activity not subject to normal review by the governor, analogous to the unique "federal" role of state legislatures in ratification of federal constitutional amendments. The Supreme Court, reversing the Minnesota court, could find no such exemption and treated congressional districting as an ordinary state legislative act fully subject to gubernatorial veto.

Thus by *congressional* action killing the old districts and *gubernatorial* action killing the new districts, rather than by judicial negation, no valid districts were available in Minnesota. In this situation an election at-large would be a ready way to preserve state representation in Congress and could—and did—occur without specific court order.[28] However, because

---

26. Wood v. Broom, *supra* note 19, at 8.

27. Lewis, *supra* note 12, at 1057, 1078–88; Brief for the United States as Amicus Curiae on reargument, pp. 52, 54; Baker v. Carr, 369 U.S. 186 (1962); *U.S. Commission on Civil Rights Report, Voting* I: 123, 128 (1961).

28. A state court case resting on *state* constitutional grounds did eventuate in a mandamus which was in effect an order for an election at-large of Virginia's congressional delegation in 1932. Brown v. Saunders, 159 Va. 28, 166 S.E. 105 (1932). The

there was no Supreme Court-directed order requiring an election at-large in *Smiley*, the possibility existed that a special legislative session could have produced valid districts in time to avert an election at-large, or that Minnesota simply would hold no election of congressional representatives, which would have posed a fresh series of problems.

THE ERA OF COLEGROVE *V.* GREEN

A few years later a political science professor at Northwestern University, Kenneth Colegrove, immortalized his name by serving as spokesman for a group seeking invalidation of unequal population districts used for congressional election in Illinois.

At the time of *Colegrove v. Green* [29] the population disparity between largest and smallest congressional district in Illinois was the most extreme in the nation: 914,053 to 112,116. Other states with significant population disparities included Ohio, 698,650 to 163,561; Maryland 534,568 to 195,427; Texas 528,961 to 230,010; Florida, 439,895 to 186,831. Illinois had not redistricted since 1901.

Before considering the *Colegrove* case, which dominated the "political question" field for almost twenty years, it would be well to note that potentially there were three positions which the Supreme Court could take in congressional districting cases, rather than two. First, the Court could say that Article I, Section 4 of the Constitution confers a plenary and exclusive power on Congress and that the Court has *no jurisdiction* to entertain a suit unless specifically authorized by Congress. Some language in *Smiley* supported this idea.

Second, the Court could say that any standards Congress lays down by statute in this field, or any standards of fairness and equality found in the Fourteenth Amendment's due process or equal protection of the laws clauses, are self-executing as are most federal standards. This could mean that federal courts would have *jurisdiction* under the general grant of judical power to entertain suits whenever a federal standard found either in a statute or the Constitution was violated. Further, the courts could proceed to *exercise* this jurisdiction.

Third, the rule could be that federal courts have *jurisdiction*, but may

Virginia legislature redistricted after its congressional delegation was reduced from ten to nine but the governor refused to sign the bill. In the ensuing litigation Brown and others sought and obtained a mandamus to compel the Secretary of the Commonwealth to accept their filings as candidates at-large. The court based its decision on a Virginia provision, not generally found in state constitutions, that congressional districts be "composed of contiguous and compact territory, and containing as nearly as practicable an equal number of inhabitants."
29. 328 U.S. 549 (1946).

refuse to exercise jurisdiction on grounds of *policy.* A policy of not exercising jurisdiction constitutionally possessed could be explained by such phrases as "want of equity" or "political question." It could be a broad and consistent "hands-off" policy such as nonreview of constitutional amendments, or it could be a narrow, discretionary policy turning on such special conditions as imminence of the next election and resultant impossibility of shaping a timely remedy. Such a policy would be—and for many years actually was—a policy of judicial self-restraint derived from a particular assessment of the proper limits of the Court's role as guardian of public morals in our political system.

Of all the precedent cases, *Colegrove* v. *Green* cast the longest shadow over the *Baker* v. *Carr* litigation. In *Colegrove* a seven-man Supreme Court split 4-3 in dismissing a suit seeking to restrain further use of Illinois congressional districts on the ground that inequality in population violated the Fourteenth Amendment. But the Court split 3-3-1 in its reasoning.

Justice Frankfurter's plurality opinion for the Court, in which only two others concurred, is not easy to characterize. It is one of those opinions that say all things to all men, and was even cited by some ingenious lower court judges in support of judicial review where state legislative districts, rather than congressional districts, were at issue.[30]

Justice Frankfurter may have put the dismissal of the suit under the first of the positions delineated above—that is, lack of jurisdiction. He relied in part on Article I, Section 4, of the Constitution and *Smiley* v. *Holm* for the proposition that the Court lacked power (i.e., jurisdiction) to proceed because the matter was exclusively committed to Congress. But he also talked about the inadvisability of courts' deciding "party contests," which is language more appropriate to position three.

"It is hostile to a democratic system," he said, "to involve the judiciary in the politics of the people." The courts "ought not to enter this political thicket."[31] There also was language phrased in terms of such alternative grounds for dismissal as lack of standing to sue, doctrine of "political questions," delicacy of federal-state relations, unsuitability of the only readily available remedy—i.e., an election at-large.

Justice Wiley B. Rutledge joined the Frankfurter contingent to achieve the 4-3 vote to dismiss, but clearly put his vote under position three. For Rutledge there was jurisdiction per se, but for policy reasons it should *not* be exercised. The policy reasons which Justice Rutledge had in mind are not crystal clear. He indicated preference for the view that the Constitu-

---

30. E.g., Magraw v. Donovan, 159 F. Supp. 901 (D. Minn. 1958); Dyer v. Kazuhisa Abe, 138 F. Supp. 220 (D. Hawaii 1956); Latting v. Cordell, 197 Okla. 369, 172 P.2d 397 (1946) (dissenting opinion).
31. Colegrove v. Green, *supra* note 29, at 553–54, 556.

tion itself, in its sections dealing with Congress, had removed congressional districting from judicial cognizance but felt that *Smiley* v. *Holm* had made the "no jurisdiction" view untenable. He also noted the shortness of time remaining before election and the insufficiency of election at-large as a remedy. He feared that the "cure sought may be worse than the disease," and said that there "could not be, except abstractly, a right of absolute equality in voting." [32] Justices Hugo L. Black, William O. Douglas, and Frank Murphy dissented and adopted position two—there is judicial power (constitutional jurisdiction) in this field and it should be exercised.

Two years later the Supreme Court handled a second Illinois "political thicket" case, an outgrowth of the tragi-comic 1948 presidential campaign of Progressive party nominees Henry A. Wallace and Glen H. Taylor. Wallace had missed the presidency by being replaced in 1944 as Democratic nominee for vice-president by Harry S. Truman; Taylor was best known as the "singing cowboy" senator from Idaho. The Progressive party sought to set aside an Illinois law requiring a petition containing at least 200 signatures from each of 50 of the state's 102 countries as a precondition of placing nominees of a new political party on the ballot. The federal district court in one breath upheld the constitutionality of the law and in the next breath denied it had jurisdiction.[33] In an unsigned opinion, the Supreme Court affirmed. Because the Court both discussed some constitutional issues and cited the *Colegrove* precedent, there was much uncertainty whether the ruling rested on a finding of nonjusticiability or on an adjudication of the merits. The effect was judicial nonintervention. In any event the Illinois geographic diffusion rule on nomination petitions did not involve issues as thorny and frought with discretion as apportionment and districting.

Any thought that the Progressive party case had weakened the *Colegrove* "political thicket" precedent was terminated in 1950. A full bench with only two dissents refused to litigate the constitutionality of Georgia's county-unit system of vote-weighting in filling such statewide offices as governor and U.S. Senator.[34] (Under the system, which was analogous to the federal electoral college, victory went to the candidate who prevailed in the total county-unit vote, which was allocated in each county to the candidate with the popular vote plurality in that county. In the basic allocation of "unit votes" the more populous counties were discriminated against.) With only Justices Douglas and Black dissenting, the Court said: "Federal courts consistently refuse to exercise their equity powers in

32. *Id.* at 566.
33. MacDougall v. Green, 80 F. Supp. 725 (1948), *aff'd*, 335 U.S. 281 (1948).
34. South v. Peters, 339 U.S. 276 (1950).

cases posing political issues arising from a state's geographical distribution of electoral strength among its political subdivision." [35] Both the *Colegrove* case and the Progressive party case of 1948 were cited.

The negative view on federal court action on apportionment and districting matters stemming from *Colegrove*, the 1948 Progressive party case, and the 1950 Georgia county-unit case was reinforced by a series of Supreme Court per curiam (summary) dismissals of appeals in attempted federal district court suits in several states, e.g., Oklahoma, Pennsylvania, Illinois, and Georgia. Concurrently the early disposition of some state courts to assume even a modest advisory opinion or declaratory judgment jurisdiction was considerably diminished in the fifteen-year period prior to *Baker v. Carr*. Although *Colegrove* was not binding on state courts regarding state law remedies for malapportionment, the Supreme Court's admonition in *Colegrove* that courts should stay out of the "political thicket" had obvious influence. Between *Colegrove* in 1946 and *Baker* in 1962 reapportionment litigants suffered frequent rebuff in state courts, e.g., Wisconsin, Oklahoma, Alabama, Tennessee, Pennsylvania, Michigan, and Mississippi. [36] Seeming exceptions in Wisconsin, Washington, and Florida turned on narrow fact situations and accomplished little or nothing. [37] In short, attempts to invalidate state laws apportioning political influence among prescribed state subdivisions—involving such matters as congressional districts, state legislative apportionment, nomination require-

---

35. *Id.* at 277.

36. State *ex rel.* Broughton v. Zimmerman, 261 Wis. 398, 52 N.W.2d 903 (1952); State *ex rel.* Martin v. Zimmerman, 249 Wis. 101, 23 N.W.2d 601 (1946), both citing Colegrove v. Green. Romang v. Cordell, 200 Okla. 369, 243 P.2d 677 (1952); Latting v. Cordell, 197 Okla. 369, 172 P.2d 397 (1946). Waid v. Pool, 255 Ala. 441, 51 So.2d 869 (1951). Kidd v. McCanless, 200 Tenn. 273, 292 S.W.2d 40 *appeal dismissed*, 352 U.S. 920 (1956).

The last-named case was a forerunner of Baker v. Carr and turned on a narrow point. The chancery court had "simply made a declaration that [Tennessee has] no valid reapportionment statute and then fell back on the de facto doctrine in order to avoid the otherwise necessary conclusion that . . . [Tennessee] would no longer have any lawfully elected members of the General Assembly." *Id.* at 279, 292 S.W.2d at 43. The Tennessee Supreme Court reversed, finding the doctrine inapplicable, and hence, judicial intervention unthinkable.

See also Butcher v. Rice, 397 Pa. 158, 153 A.2d 869 (1959); Costello v. Rice, 397 Pa. 198, 153 A.2d 888 (1959); Scholle v. Hare, 360 Mich. 1, 104 N.W.2d 63 (1960), *vacated and remanded* (in light of Baker v. Carr), 369 U.S. 429 (1962); Barnes v. Barnett, 241 Miss. 206, 129 So.2d 938 (1961), dictum, citing Colegrove v. Green.

37. State *ex rel.* Thomson v. Zimmerman, 264 Wis. 644, 60 N.W.2d 416 (1953). The court voided, on procedural grounds, a constitutional amendment on which a new apportionment act was based, thus reinstating the apportionment act of 1951. The constitutional amendment was in violation of the provision that multiple amendments must be voted on separately. State v. Myers, 51 Wash. 2d 454, 319 P.2d 828 (1957). The court left undisturbed a 1957 legislative modification of a 1956 initiative approved by the voters regarding apportionment. Brewer v. Gray, 86 So.2d 799 (Fla. 1956).

ments, local legislatures, and county-unit voting—were before the Supreme Court fifteen times from 1932 to 1962, all unsuccessfully.[38]

SOME RESTIVE COURTS

Exceptions to the *Colegrove*-influenced negative response to attempts to involve the judiciary in policing apportionment and related matters occurred in three cases much discussed in *Baker* v. *Carr*. Two courts—one state and one federal—assumed jurisdiction of state legislative apportionment cases and then postponed decision on the merits to give the legislature opportunity to act.[39] The courts warned that continued legislative inaction would result in invalidation of existing districts and judicial relief in unspecified ways. In the third case, the Hawaiian territorial district court reached the merits and announced orally that it would grant relief without detailing the manner of contemplated relief.[40] Although this judicial activity was disparaged in *Baker* v. *Carr* by Justice Tom C. Clark as a form of judicial "blackjacking," [41] and by Justice Frankfurter as "*in terrorem* pronouncements*," it did achieve results in the form of legislative action in all three cases.

a. *The Hawaiian Case*

The litigation in Hawaii, properly viewed, was not of direct relevance to the *Baker* v. *Carr* case because it involved action by a territorial court. Territorial courts, unlike the regular United States District Courts and United States Courts of Appeals in the continental United States (customarily called "constitutional" or "Article III" courts) are not bound by the fairly stringent limitations on the judicial function deemed to flow from Article III of the Constitution.

Challenge to the Hawaiian territorial legislature was founded on fifty years of noncompliance with the congressional mandate to reapportion from "time to time." Because the suit involved a territorial rather than a

---

38. Mathews v. Handley, 361 U.S. 127 (1959); Hartsfield v. Sloan, 357 U.S. 916 (1958); Radford v. Gary, 352 U.S. 991 (1957); Kidd v. McCanless, 352 U.S. 920 (1956); Anderson v. Jordan, 343 U.S. 912 (1952); Cox v. Peters, 342 U.S. 936 (1952); Remmey v. Smith, 342 U.S. 916 (1952); Tedesco v. Board of Supervisors, 339 U.S. 940 (1950); South v. Peters, 339 U.S. 276 (1950); MacDougall v. Green, 335 U.S. 281 (1948); Colegrove v. Barrett, 330 U.S. 804 (1946); Cook v. Fortson, (Turman v. Duckworth), 329 U.S. 675 (1946); Colegrove v. Green, 328 U.S. 549 (1946); Wood v. Broom, 287 U.S. 1 (1932); Mahan v. Hume, 287 U.S. 575 (1932).
39. Magraw v. Donovan, 163 F. Supp. 184 (D. Minn. 1958); Asbury Park Press, Inc. v. Wooley, 33 N.J. 1,161 A.2d 705 (1960).
40. Dyer v. Kazuhisa Abe, 138 F. Supp. 220 (D. Hawaii 1956), *reversed on other grounds*, 256 F.2d 728 (9th Cir. 1958).
41. Baker v. Carr, 369 U.S. 186, 260 (1962).

state legislature, the territorial district court felt that *Colegrove*, with its overtones of delicacy in federal-state relations, posed no barrier to enforcement of the plaintiff's request for a reapportionment order.

On remedies the court was more indefinite. It talked in strong terms of a power to "order affirmative action to readjust legislative districts to population needs." [42] But it also spoke of wiping out districts in an election at-large. However, having scaled the mountain of judicial activism, the court found no enemy to repel. Shortly after the court announced it was prepared to grant relief, Congress mooted the matter. By amendment to the Organic Act, Congress redistricted and shifted authority for future reapportionment to the governor, subject to judicial control, a reapportionment device which Hawaii retained in her first state constitution.[43]

b. *The Minnesota Case*

Three years before *Baker*, a federal district court in Minnesota ruled on a petition seeking to use the equal protection of the laws clause of the Fourteenth Amendment as the lever to achieve reapportionment of the legislature. The strategem was successful but the case left unexplored the crucial question of the substantive meaning of equal protection because the court never had to decide the merits of the case. The court dallied but retained jurisdiction and said: "It is obvious that substantial inequality exists." [44] This warning was sufficient to induce action at the next session of the Minnesota legislature. The *Colegrove* precedent was essentially ignored rather than distinguished.

c. *The New Jersey Case*

The New Jersey suit in 1960 was filed in a state court, thus avoiding the "case and controversy" limitations imposed by Article III of the federal Constitution for federal courts. On the issue of standards also the New Jersey case was simpler than the Minnesota case. Instead of relying on the uncertain contours of the Fourteenth Amendment, plaintiffs relied on the legislature's mandatory duty under the state constitution to reapportion every ten years. Plaintiffs here, as in the Minnesota case, sought to avoid the appearance of proceeding directly against the legislature by requesting only a declaration that the existing apportionment statute was invalid and an order against its continued use. Despite the simplicity and exactness of the standard, and the clear violation of the state constitution, the New Jersey court did not decide the merits. It chose simply to retain jurisdiction

---

42. Dyer v. Kazuhisa Abe, *supra* note 40, at 235.
43. Constitution of Hawaii, Art. III, §4.
44. Magraw v. Donovan, *supra* note 39, at 187.

and to give the legislature an opportunity to reapportion once the new 1960 census figures were available.[45] The legislature acted.[46]

THE TUSKEGEE RACIAL GERRYMANDER CASE

In 1960 in *Gomillion* v. *Lightfoot*,[47] the Supreme Court rendered an opinion voiding an Alabama racial gerrymander. The state had detached and excluded from the town of Tuskegee most of the territory in which the Negro voters resided. Although the case has little relationship to the issues involved in state legislative reapportionment, in retrospect it may have been a straw in the wind regarding *Baker* v. *Carr*, even though it most certainly did not dictate the result in *Baker*.

Gomillion is an example of plenary state legislative power, still retained under some state constitutions, to incorporate municipalities and to alter municipal boundaries by annexing or detaching territory. The distinctive feature of the case was the racial allegation. In motivation and effect, complainants argued, the statute which detached from Tuskegee a 28-sided, jigsaw-shaped piece of territory resembling a stylized seahorse, was aimed at the political influence of Tuskegee Institute, one of the well-known Southern Negro colleges. By placing the Institute and all but a handful of Negro voters outside the municipal boundaries white control of the city would be assured. Of course, Negro voters, unless retarded by other factors, could continue to participate in county, state, and national elections.

The result of the Supreme Court's review in this case was foreordained. The suit challenged state action obviously geared to race, a kind of action which has been virtually a per se violation of the Fourteenth Amendment ever since a Negro jury exclusion case in 1880, and most certainly since the school desegregation decision of 1954.[48] Further, an easily administrable

45. Asbury Park Press, Inc. v. Wooley, *supra* note 39; and see *New York Times*, Feb. 2, 1961, p. 1, col. 2; p. 16, col. 2.

46. A more dramatic example of judicial activism regarding apportionment occurred in Oregon in 1961 when the state supreme court invalidated a reapportionment plan and directed the Oregon Secretary of State to draft a reapportionment in compliance with the state constitution. *In re* Review of Chapter 482, Oregon Laws 1961, 228 Ore. 562, 364 P.2d 1004 (1961); *In re* Apportionment of Senators and Representatives, 228 Ore. 575, 365 P.2d 1042 (1961). To place this case in proper context it must be noted, first, that the state constitution contained detailed mathematical formulae and, second, that the state constitution provided that if the legislature failed to reapportion, it should be done by the Secretary of State. Judicial review was specifically authorized.

47. 364 U.S. 339 (1960). The background and the flavor of the oral argument in the Supreme Court are portrayed in Bernard Taper, *Gomillion versus Lightfoot: The Tuskegee Gerrymander Case* (New York: McGraw-Hill, 1962).

48. Strauder v. West Virginia, 100 U.S. 303 (1880); Brown v. Board of Education, 347 U.S. 483 (1954).

judicial remedy was available in the form of an injunction to restore previous boundaries.

More interesting were the Court's opinions explaining nullification of the Alabama statutory gerrymander. The Court's opinion was written by Justice Frankfurter, author of the then-unreversed plurality opinion in *Colegrove*, warning the courts to avoid the "political thicket." In a manful effort to preserve in full force the *Colegrove* precedent, and perhaps with an eye on the rising tide of state legislative reapportionment suits in the lower courts, Justice Frankfurter turned his back on the equal protection clause of the Fourteenth Amendment. He chose to rest the decision solely on the Fifteenth Amendment's mandate that neither state nor federal governments may restrict voting rights on grounds of race.

The trouble with such an approach is that it does not fit the facts. Negro voters affected by shrinking of Tuskegee's boundaries could still vote in all elections except city elections. Their noneligibility to vote in city elections stemmed from the fact that they were no longer city residents. They were the victims of a racially motivated action and were, of course, aggrieved. But their generic complaint was not that there was an impairment of "voting rights" in the conventional sense of the term. Rather, they were being *excluded from the city* by state action impermissibly grounded on race. "Voting" was only one facet of their changed status. At issue was a violation not of the Fifteenth Amendment but of the equal protection of the laws clause of the Fourteenth Amendment— the clause on which Justice Charles E. Whittaker grounded his concurring opinion. The complaint concerned an obvious racial classification. As such, even if grounded properly on the equal protection of the laws clause of the Fourteenth Amendment, it would not by itself have undercut the *Colegrove* precedent that general nonracial malapportionment lay outside the range of cases and controversies as authorized by the federal Constitution.

STATE OF THE LAW ON THE EVE OF BAKER V. CARR

This review of state and federal court action on apportionment and districting matters prior to *Baker v. Carr* yields several generalizations.

In addition to the fact that state judiciaries are not bound by the federal separation of powers doctrine and federal precepts of justiciability, there had been little discussion of standing and justiciability in the state cases. The older breed of rough-and-ready state judges tended to ignore these niceties of advanced jurisprudence. Even where state courts acted, they were weak in formulating remedies and rarely did more than invalidate legislative action, often under relatively precise state constitutional standards. In the 1960 case in New Jersey, where a suit successfully impelled legislative action, the state court was never compelled to show its hand.

Federal courts had consistently adopted a hands-off attitude, particularly since the *Colegrove* decision in 1946. In two exceptions in Hawaii and Minnesota the federal district courts, like the New Jersey state court in 1960, did not have to reach a decision under a broad substantive standard or shape a remedy. Influenced by the *Colegrove* example, the later state trend seemed to be away from an earlier disposition to assume a "remediless jurisdiction."

No court, federal or state, had ordered an election at-large as remedy for malapportionment of state legislatures. Election at-large of a state's entire congressional delegation had resulted from failure to pass valid redistricting statutes after state apportionments were changed by congressional action. It had not resulted from judicial imposition of *substantive* federal standards, with one exception in 1932 in which the standard was statutory. Even there the Supreme Court reversed the lower court after the congressional election had been held.[49] Further, in a precise sense, federal courts had not *ordered* elections at-large.

The dramatic about-face in both federal and state courts impelled by *Baker* v. *Carr* cannot be minimized by citing an occasional variant straw in the wind. Unlike the 1954 *School Desegregation Decisions*, it was not well signaled by a series of cases in the Supreme Court, or any other courts. What *Baker* v. *Carr* represents is an agony of democracy. The Supreme Court, without precedent, finally concluded that some judicial participation in the politics of the people—to an undetermined degree—was a precondition to there *being* any effective politics.

49. Hume v. Mahan, 1 F. Supp. 142 (E.D. Ky. 1932), *rev'd per curiam*, 287 U.S. 575 (1932) on authority of Wood v. Broom, 287 U.S. 1 (1932).

VI

Baker v. Carr: Preserving the "Politics of the People"

> "It is hostile to a democratic system to involve the judiciary in the politics of the people."
> Justice Felix Frankfurter, *Colegrove v. Green*

> ". . . Governments long established should not be changed for light and transient causes, but. . . ."
> Declaration of Independence

When extraordinary problems call forth extraordinary remedies, results may outrun logic. *Baker v. Carr* is such a case. In few recent cases can one make such a sharp distinction between the *holding* of the Court, widely acclaimed, widely accepted, and productive of dramatic change, and the indistinct—almost casuistic—level of the supporting *reasoning*.

It has been said that "it is precisely in the identification of values and the explanation of reasons that our judiciary finds its most distinctive and significant role in the law-making process." Despite the half-dozen years and many further opinions since *Baker*, this "most distinctive" judicial role in the apportionment field has yet to be played. The political map of America has been remade, pending of course the 1970 census and further major upheavals. But the scope and rationale for judicial policing of the politics of the people, and also the precise substantive content of "one man-one vote" values, remain largely open-ended questions. We are at best at the threshold of a common law process of developing a jurisprudence of democratic norms to mark the boundaries of political free choice. Well-articulated reasons may lag behind decisions in this area; and overly simple formulae may be traps for the future.

BAKER COMPLAINT AND FACTUAL SETTING

The Supreme Court decision in *Baker v. Carr*[1] in 1962 can be described as a three-legged stool with a crucial fourth leg left for future construc-

1. 369 U.S. 186 (1962).

tion. The Court found that federal district courts had *jurisdiction* of claims that state legislative apportionments violate the Fourteenth Amendment. It found that the plaintiffs had *standing* as resident voters to assert such a claim. It held that such claims were *justiciable* despite previous "political question" precedents. It then remanded without reaching the *merits* and without giving the district court any guidance on the possible nature or dimensions of a federal restriction on state discretion in apportionments. In sharply delineating these four elements which are present in all cases whether separately considered or not, the opinion of Court written by Justice William J. Brennan, Jr., not only clarified these precepts in the context of *Baker* but also sought to clarify the general heading of "cases and controversies" subject to federal judicial review.

Unlike many state constitutions, where apportionment formulae phrased in terms of a population principle are engulfed by exceptions designed to achieve geographic diffusion of political power, the Tennessee Constitution's apportionment formula at issue in *Baker* put few qualifications on its rule of numerical equality for both houses of legislature. The basic formula for each house was apportionment "among the several counties or districts, according to the number of qualified voters in each." In practice, population disparities among Tennessee legislative districts presented the same sorry picture as in most other states. Counties having but 37 percent of the population elected 20 of the 33 members of the state senate. Senatorial district population varied from 131,971 to 25,190. Counties having 40 percent of the population elected 63 of the 99 members of the lower house. The number of voters in the representative districts varied from 42,298 to 2340.[2]

Political pressures and an abortive state court suit in 1956[3] had alike proven ineffective either to impel the legislature to act or to accomplish reapportionment directly by constitutional amendment. Tennessee had no provision for popular initiative. The legislature had not acted, nor could it be expected to act, either to submit constitutional amendments on reapportionment to popular vote or to include reapportionment in the call for a constitutional convention.

Against this background the plaintiffs—registered voters in overpopulated and allegedly underrepresented districts—asserted a federal right under both the due process and equal protection of the laws clauses of the Fourteenth Amendment to legislative districts of equal population. They sought an injunction against further use of the 1901 Reapportionment

---

2. Record, pp. 25–31, Baker v. Carr, *ibid.*
3. Kidd v. McCanless, 200 Tenn. 273, 292 S.W. 2d 40, *appeal dismissed*, 352 U.S. 920 (1956).

Act and requested a court order for election of the legislature at-large pending equalization of the districts by legislative action.

JURISDICTION AND STANDING

The term "jurisdiction" denotes the kinds of cases that a particular court is empowered to hear. The term "standing" is a much more flexible and tricky concept. It denotes the range of persons who have a sufficiently individualized interest to be permitted to raise a given legal claim, in contrast to "self-appointed champions of a particular theory of law." Neither jurisdiction nor standing posed a serious problem for the court majority in *Baker*.

On the question of jurisdiction it was sufficient for Justice Brennan that the complaint was based on the Constitution and was within a statutory provision vesting jurisdiction of certain federal civil rights claims in United States District Courts.

In short, a bare allegation of violation of the Fourteenth Amendment surmounts the jurisdiction hurdle unless the claim is "so attenuated and unsubstantial as to be absolutely devoid of merit." [4]

Only Justice John Marshall Harlan had difficulty with this threshold question of jurisdiction. He argued that until it first be decided that the Fourteenth Amendment does impose *some* restraint on apportionments of state legislatures, there cannot even be a colorable federal claim, and hence no basis for jurisdiction in a federal court. Justice Harlan's argument has plausibility if one bears in mind that in previous Supreme Court cases there had not been the slightest intimation that the Fourteenth Amendment applied to apportionment. But it really is a sort of chicken-and-egg argument. The Constitution is a dynamic thing. From time to time claims will be asserted which will not even be colorable federal claims until after the Court adds the needed unprecedented meaning to the Constitution by accepting and deciding the case. Should this process of constitutional development and refinement take place at the "jurisdictional" level as Justice Harlan apparently would have it, or at the level of trial on the "merits" as the Court would have it? The tidier approach would seem to be that of the Court; otherwise there would be something like a pre-jurisdictional trial of the essence of the case.

Perhaps the only simple aspect of *Baker*, and one on which the entire Bench seemed to agree, was the question of plaintiff's standing to litigate the alleged unconstitutionality of Tennessee's legislative districts under the Fourteenth Amendment. As Professor Louis L. Jaffe has noted, a direct

4. Baker v. Carr, *supra* note 1, at 199.

interference with a citizen's franchise has been actionable as a private wrong since 1703. Under the assumption—which is a necessary assumption for the purpose of determining standing—that Tennessee's districts were producing a federally cognizable injury, the registered-voter plaintiffs in *Baker* who resided in overpopulated districts were among those who had sustained such injury.

The only troublesome prior Supreme Court language on the standing issue was the comment in Justice Felix Frankfurter's plurality opinion in *Colegrove* v. *Green*, in which he said inter alia that the "basis for the suit is not a private wrong, but a wrong exercised by Illinois as a polity." [5] However, the force of this language was undercut within the *Colegrove* opinion itself, because Justice Frankfurter also discussed justiciability, which logically could not have been reached if there were no plaintiffs entitled to address the Court.

JUSTICIABILITY

Yes! There is a temptation to let this vital heading go with that one word. If there is some merit in Justice Tom C. Clark's flip observation that Justice Frankfurter's words "go through so much and conclude with so little," [6] there is equivalent merit in an observation that the majority's words "go through so little and conclude with so much." Whether or not one agrees with Justice Frankfurter's negative conclusion on justiciability —and the writer feels that he must disagree—Justice Frankfurter's lengthy opinion in this landmark case, not marked by equally landmark majority opinions, bears out his accolade of "scholar on the Bench."

The general approach of the full opinions on the majority side—Justice Brennan for the Court, Justice William O. Douglas, and Justice Clark— was to distinguish and explain away the apparent contrary decisions or dicta of the past rather than overrule them. But if past cases really were so inconclusive and uncontrolling on the issue before the Court in *Baker* v. *Carr*, then a great many commentators, lawyers and laymen alike, had been led to needless worry and idle speculation. Wholly lacking from *Baker* is the stark simplicity and brevity of Chief Justice Earl Warren's statement in *Brown* v. *Board of Education* that "We cannot turn the clock back . . . we must consider public education in the light of its full development and its present place in American life throughout the Nation." [7] The lack of articulation in *Baker* of the "necessity-changing

5. 328 U.S. 549 at 552 (1946).
6. Baker v. Carr, *supra* note 1, at 251.
7. 347 U.S. 483, 492–93 (1954).

times" principle is all the more surprising in view of the major reversal of very recent precedent which the decision represented.

a. *Brennan for the Court*

The tone of Justice Brennan's section on justiciability was set in his first paragraph where he not only stated that apportionment presented no non-justiciable political questions but also asserted that "cited cases do not hold the contrary." [8] The district court had "misinterpreted" the decisions of the Supreme Court, including *Colegrove v. Green.*

Justice Brennan analyzed the political question doctrine under several headings, especially its relation to the separation of powers doctrine. He traced its past developement vis-à-vis such problem areas as foreign relations, dates of hostilities, review of constitutional amendment procedures, Indian tribes. He attempted to state the essence of the political question doctrine as follows:

> Prominent on the surface of any case held to involve a political question is found a textually demonstrable constitutional commitment of the issue to a coordinate political department; or a lack of judicially discoverable and manageable standards for resolving it; or the impossibility of deciding without an initial policy determination of a kind clearly for nonjudicial discretion; or the impossibility of a court's undertaking independent resolution without expressing lack of the respect due coordinate branches of government; or an unusual need for unquestioning adherence to a political decision already made; or the potentiality of embarrassment from multifarious pronouncements by various departments on one question.[9]

He devoted several pages to a refutation of the argument that the Tennessee apportionment case was analogous to the line of cases under a clause in Article IV of the Constitution known as the "guarantee clause," whereby the United States is to guarantee to each state a "republican form of government." Issues under that clause traditionally have been classified as presenting political questions. Central to his discussion of this clause was his review of the famous old case of *Luther* v. *Borden.*[10] This case arose out of the suffrage rebellion in Rhode Island in 1841–1842, which was aimed at liberalizing the old colonial charter which Rhode Island was still using. The rebellion produced two governments and a contest for legitimacy. The dispute reached the Supreme Court in the form of a case in which—depending on the issue of legitimacy—the defendants

8. Baker v. Carr, *supra* note 1, at 209.
9. *Id.* at 217.
10. 17 U.S. (7 How.) 1 (1848).

either would be "officers" and thus entitled to arrest the plaintiff, or mere trespassers and thus liable to him for monetary damages. The Supreme Court avoided the issue by allocating to Congress the determination of state government legitimacy under the "guarantee clause"—a determination which Congress was deemed to have made when it continued to seat the representatives of the old or "charter" government.

Justice Brennan quoted extensively from Chief Justice Roger B. Taney's opinion giving the Court's reasons for treating guarantee clause claims as nonjusticiable. Much of Taney's opinion rested on now-repudiated pre-Civil War conceptions of state sovereignty. However, given the traditional nonjusticiability of guarantee clause claims—which Justice Brennan accepted—it would have been helpful if Justice Brennan had devoted an equal amount of space to explaining why apportionment cases should not likewise be classified as political questions. The guarantee clause area is after all only a political question subheading. Therefore, a conclusion that apportionment does not fall inside the guarantee clause does not prove that apportionments are justiciable causes rather than political questions. As one commentator noted: ". . . The net conclusion of his opinion seems to be that the issue presented in *Baker* v. *Carr* is justiciable when presented under the equal protection clause but non-justiciable when presented under the guarantee clause. This seems rather incongruous." [11]

Concerning *Baker* and the political question doctrine in the context of apportionment, Justice Brennan gave hurried treatment to the prior federal precedents relied on by the district court. He mis-characterized *Smiley* v. *Holm* and the other 1932 cases as having "settled the issue in favor of justiciability of questions of congressional redistricting." [12] Actually as noted earlier these cases only "settled the issue" in favor of justiciability of *one* type of question concerning congressional redistricting, and a very narrow one at that. The *Smiley* case concerned the applicability of the governor's *veto power* to a state redistricting statute. It did not raise at all the question of a *substantive* federal restraint on future weighting of voting strength among counties or districts.

Justice Brennan then concluded in favor of justiciability without reaching two crucial factors which in historical context are perhaps the true explanation for political question dismissals: lack of clear federal substantive standards for decision; doubt concerning the availability of effective and enforceable remedies. Such factors, more than abstractions about separation of powers, have provided the impetus for the political question doc-

---

11. Arthur E. Bonfield, "Baker v. Carr: New Light on the Constitutional Guarantee of Republican Government," 50 *Calif. L. Rev.* 245, 252 (1962).
12. Baker v. Carr, *supra* note 1, at 232. See discussion of *Smiley,* 285 U.S. 355, Ch. V, notes 21 and 27.

trine. One cannot help but feel that it was the majority's lack of a searching analysis of possibilities and problems regarding federal standards and remedies, as much as the actual decision, that upset Justices Frankfurter and Harlan.

b. *Douglas Concurring*

Justice Douglas already had spoken on the basic issue in his dissent to *Colegrove* v. *Green* and later cases, and he hewed to his previous line. He made no pretense of arguing that the present majority result was what the Court had intended all along, except for a cryptic footnote endorsing in general Justice Brennan's historical review. The main thrust of his opinion was to document the idea that in numerous past cases federal courts had intervened to safeguard voting rights of individuals against violence at the polls, discrimination on racial grounds, or slippery election practices.[13] With these cases few persons would disagree, and certainly not Justice Frankfurter, who had voted with the majority in the key voting rights cases and written the majority opinion in the Tuskegee "racial gerrymander" case. But these precedents concerning judicial action on particularized pleas of individual voters had little or no relevance concerning weighting through apportionment of votes freely cast and counted (some weighting being intrinsic to all districting systems) unless an emotive righteousness, rather than reason, is to become the touchstone of judicial action.

c. *Clark Concurring*

Justice Clark was the only majority justice who tried to come to grips with the standard-remedy problem, on which ultimately political question issues should turn rather than on Justice Brennan's separation of powers abstractions. His discussion of the substantive standard problem merits separate treatment below. Regarding justiciability, Justice Clark was content to rely largely on his understanding of the old Progressive party case of 1948, *MacDougall* v. *Green*.[14] Reading it for all it was worth, and quite a bit more, he concluded that the Court actually had adjudicated an equal protection attack on the Illinois election statute. The vagaries of the majority opinion in *MacDougall*, the fact that the Court simply left the Illinois practice undisturbed, and the crucial fact that the law involved conditions for forming a new political party rather than apportionment did not disturb him.

13. E.g., United States v. Classic, 313 U.S. 299 (1941).
14. 335 U.S. 281 (1948). See discussion in Ch. V, note 33 and accompanying text.

d. *Stewart Concurring*

Justice Potter Stewart did not write a full opinion but did feel moved to write a brief cautionary note on what the Court had done and left undone. It would have been a helpful prefix to the opinion of the Court. He wanted to make it clear that in bringing forth its roaring mouse of justiciability, the Court had left a little mountain of uncertainty concerning the merits and the remedy.

FRANKFURTER'S LAST TOUR DE FORCE

It was to be expected that the Court's paramount scholar would produce an exhaustive analysis commensurate with the landmark dimensions of the case. He gave full measure. He did not deign to analyze the cavils and quiddities by which counsel had sought to distinguish some of the precedent cases. But he felt that no amount of paralogy would serve to distinguish two earlier and conflicting Supreme Court precedents. One was *Colegrove* v. *Barrett*,[15] an unsuccessful challenge initiated in federal district court to Illinois state legislature districts which was on "all fours" with *Baker*. The other was *Kidd* v. *McCanless*,[16] an unsuccessful challenge initiated in a state court which was a "precisely similar attack" on the Tennessee state legislative districts at issue in *Baker*. He then embarked on a review of the general nature of "political questions," as revealed in American judicial history over several decades.

In professorial manner he chided those who fail to note "the danger of conceptions of 'justiciability' derived from talk and not from the effective decision in a case." [17] He found that judicial use of the political question label as a ground for nonintervention had been the product of several converging considerations: a spirit of caution where "standards meet for judicial judgment" are lacking; reluctance to "interfere with matters of state government" unless an unquestionable constitutional mandate, such as the one against racial discrimination, is present; unwillingness to make courts "arbiters of the broad issues of political organization historically committed to other institutions and for whose adjustment the judicial process is ill-adapted." [18] All of these considerations explained the consistent line of past decisions holding nonjusticiable claims based on the guarantee clause.

In *Luther* v. *Borden*, for example, there was concern about the delicacy

15. 330 U.S. 804 (1948).
16. 352 U.S. 920 (1956).
17. E.g., Smiley v. Holm, 285 U.S. 355 (1932), and related cases, discussed in Ch. IV.
18. Baker v. Carr, *supra* note 1, at 289.

of judicial intervention into the very structure of state government. But the critical aspect was absence of any guiding standard for judgment: " . . . the question whether the Dorr constitution had been rightfully adopted depended, in part, upon the extent of the franchise to be recognized—the very point of contention over which rebellion had been fought." [19]

The relevance of this background to the case before him was that *Baker* involved all of the elements that traditionally had been taken to make guarantee clause cases nonjusticiable. In effect, *Baker* is "a Guarantee Clause claim masquerading under a different label." [20] Further, he insisted, the fact that the equal protection label now was being used did not strengthen one whit the case for justiciability.

The equal protection label fails to help despite the fact that at first blush a charge of discrimination gives "the appearance of more private, less impersonal claim, than the assertion that the frame of government is askew." [21] The reason is that resolution of a so-called equal protection challenge to legislative apportionment ultimately and unavoidably necessitates a choice among competing theories of political philosophy.

> What, then, is this question of legislative apportionment? Appellants invoke the right to vote and to have their votes counted. But they are permitted to vote and their votes are counted. They go to the polls, they cast their ballots, they send their representatives to the state councils. Their complaint is simply that the representatives are not sufficiently numerous or powerful—in short, that Tennessee has adopted a basis of representation over which they are dissatisfied. Talk of "debasement" or "dilution" is circular talk. One cannot speak of "debasement" or "dilution" of the value of a vote until there is first defined a standard of reference as to what a vote should be worth. What is actually asked of the Court in this case is to choose among competing bases of representation—ultimately, really, among competing theories of political philosophy—in order to establish an appropriate frame of government for the State of Tennessee and thereby for all the States of the Union.[22]

Justice Frankfurter then proceeded to place the claim in historical perspective by surveying actual apportionment and districting practices in Great Britain, the colonies, states at the time of the formation of the

19. *Id.* at 295.
20. *Id.* at 297. Bonfield, *supra* note 11, expressing the contrary view, seems to place undue weight on the distinction between those schemes of "malapportionment" which are sanctioned by state law and those—as in *Baker*—which are contrary to state law. He classifies the former as being within the guarantee clause, and the latter as being outside the clause.
21. Baker v. Carr, *supra* note 1, at 298–99.
22. *Id.* at 299–300.

Constitution, states during the nineteenth century, including apportionment practices at the time of ratification of the Fourteenth Amendment, and the contemporary scene. A paradox emerges from his lengthy survey. Concern has often been expressed over apportionments grossly malproportioned to population. But the generally prevailing feature—if any one feature can be singled out from the numerous widely varying principles and practices—"is geographic inequality in relation to the population standard." [23]

Justice Frankfurter concluded his sixty-three page dissent by brushing aside the assertion that courts could ease the problem of lack of an adequate federal guiding standard—and thus avoid one traditional basis for nonjusticiability—simply by putting the force of the Fourteenth Amendment behind the particular apportionment formulae specified in the Tennessee State Constitution. This proposition rested, he said, on a false conception of what "state law" means in the context of federal constitutional adjudication. Federal courts take state law as they find it in current practice. As the Court had said much earlier: "Settled state practice . . . can establish what is state law. . . . Deeply embedded traditional ways of carrying out state policy, such as those of which petitioner complains, are often tougher and truer law than the dead words of the written text." [24] A state cannot escape censure for a federally forbidden practice merely by showing that its state constitution likewise forbids the practice.

Conversely, although state action or inaction may shape the nature of federal law violation, it does not form the content of the federal standard. In short, from the standpoint of a federal constitutional plea in *Baker*, the "law" of Tennessee is the actual practice of the past sixty years, not the long-ignored formal commands of the Tennessee Constitution. So the question remained, given the clear and easily proven "law-practice" of Tennessee regarding reapportionment, did it violate any identifiable federal standard?

In demolishing the assertion that violation of a state constitution also constitutes a violation of the Fourteenth Amendment, Justice Frankfurter highlighted one sharp distinction between the counsel on the plaintiffs' side of the case. This rejected assertion was central to the plaintiffs' position as presented by Charles S. Rhyne, former president of the American Bar Association, who argued the case twice for the plaintiffs in the Supreme Court. [25] The main burden of presenting to the Court the ulti-

---

23. *Id.* at 321.
24. *Id.* at 326, quoting from Nashville, C. & St. L. R. Co. v. Browning, 310 U.S. 362, 369 (1940).
25. The plaintiffs' basic theory was stated thusly: "The complaining voters are not charging inequality of representation under the Fourteenth Amendment . . . . On the contrary, they claim equality of voting rights as provided by the Constitution of Tennessee, and charge that the legislative attempt (successful so far) to deny that equality

mately victorious theory that Tennessee's current apportionment practice constituted a violation of a federal right—whatever the nature of the state constitution—was borne by the Solicitor General of the United States, Archibald Cox, who as amicus curiae supported the plaintiffs' complaint. Although Mr. Rhyne was widely credited with bringing the courts into the political thicket in *Baker* v. *Carr*, one might wonder whether the outcome would have been the same without the amicus brief and argument of the Solicitor General. This initial plaintiff theory, analyzed away by Justice Frankfurter, and deemed "manifestly untenable" by Justice Harlan, was ignored by the Court majority.

One commentator noted that this state law violation theory of equal protection has considerable appeal. It would obviate the onerous task of finding substantive standards in the Fourteenth Amendment itself. He concluded, however, that the implications of such a novel doctrine with respect to the relations between federal and state law are too extreme to permit its serious consideration: the "acceptance of such a doctrine would go far toward substituting federal for State courts in the administration of all State law involving official action." [26]

In short, it never has been the law that violation by a state of its own constitution—even though such violation frequently could have differential impact on the state's citizenry—gives rise to a federal question unless the same state conduct or nonaction is, independently, a violation of some identifiable right embedded in the federal Constitution. Further, if *Baker* had rested on the theory suggested by the plaintiffs, the anomalous result would have been that a federally policed "one man-one vote" doctrine would apply *only* in the minority of states whose own state constitutions then called for straight equal population apportionment. By state constitutional amendment this might well have been a rapidly vanishing minority!

a. *Harlan Also Dissenting*

Justice Harlan concurred in Justice Frankfurter's exhaustive treatment of the justiciability issue and in turn was joined by Justice Frankfurter in his

results in a violation of equal protection of the laws. This is an important distinction, which reflects the manner in which the Fourteenth Amendment operates. *It does not in itself decree equality in voting rights.* It says that *if* the state policy is to afford equal voting rights (expressed here by the people of Tennessee in their organic law), the attempt by state officers, under color of law, to deny such equality to *some* of the citizens is a denial of equal protection." (Emphasis added) Reply to Appellees' Statement in Opposition and Motion to Dismiss, p. 2, Baker v. Carr, 369 U.S. 196 (1962).

See Jurisdictional Statement, pp. 3, 9, 12–13, 14–15; Brief for Appellants, pp. 4, 23–26, Baker v. Carr, 369 U.S. 196 (1962). Also Phil C. Neal, "Baker v. Carr: Politics in Search of Law," 1962 *Supreme Court Review* 252, 291–300 (Chicago: University of Chicago Press, 1962).

26. Neal, *supra* note 25, at 299.

separate dissenting opinion. The separate Harlan opinion, like the opinion of Justice Clark on the majority side, was devoted primarily to the standard-remedy question. It was clear to him that the equal protection clause did not require that "each vote cast in state legislative elections be given approximately equal weight." [27] Short of that, he was satisfied that the Tennessee apportionment did not offend equal protection by being "so unreasonable as to amount to an arbitrary and capricious act of classification." [28] He also put his finger on what emerges ever more clearly as the nub of the matter, the more one reads the opinions in *Baker*. The underlying and largely unexpressed premise of the majority and concurring opinions was a sort of broad democratic necessity principle:

> The fact that the appellants have been unable to obtain political redress of their asserted grievances appears to be regarded as a matter which should lead the Court to stretch to find some basis for judicial intervention. While the Equal Protection Clause is invoked, the opinion for the Court notably eschews, explaining how, consonant with past decisions, the undisputed facts in this case can be considered to show a violation of that constitutional provision.[29]

SHADOWS FORWARD

As Justice Stewart noted in his concurring opinion, the Court technically had ruled only on justiciability. It had not touched the merits of the claim of violation of the Fourteenth Amendment by Tennessee's existing apportionment system. Intimations in several of the opinions made clear, however, what the major issues would be as lower courts proceeded to grapple with judicial review of legislative apportionment on a case-by-case basis. Few persons thought the Court had authorized entry into the political thicket of reapportionment only to say, when the merits were reached, that there was after all no federal limitation on state legislative discretion in selecting apportionment factors, and in drawing district lines in the light of these factors.

a. *Standards of Constitutional Apportionment*

In his opinion for the Court, Justice Brennan achieved a masterpiece of overstatement when he asserted:

> Nor need the appellants, in order to succeed in this action, ask the Court to enter upon policy determinations for which judicially manageable standards are lacking. *Judicial standards under the Equal Pro-*

27. Baker v. Carr, *supra* note 1, at 332.
28. *Ibid.*
29. *Id.* at 339.

tection Clause are well developed and familiar, and it has been open to courts since the enactment of the Fourteenth Amendment to determine, if on the particular facts they must, that a discrimination reflects *no* policy, but simply arbitrary and capricious action.[30]

Despite this blithe assertion, few clauses in the Constitution have had more uncertain meaning than the equal protection clause of the Fourteenth Amendment, except in its racial applications. Although the clause seems to imply exactness, or equality, in the relationship between two classes or categories, the one clear touchstone has been that mathematical exactness in governmental classifications and treatment of persons was *not* required. Lower courts in the period from *Baker* v. *Carr* to the Court's pronouncement on state legislative reapportionment in mid-1964 found the relevant standards to be something less than "well developed and familiar." They differed widely in their approaches toward restrictions on legislative discretion in the apportionment field. A thorough review of the intrinsic conceptual difficulties in the equal protection clause, and the special development of this clause in the apportionment field, will be undertaken in the next chapter. For now it will suffice to bear in mind the following oft-quoted rule—repeated approvingly as recently as 1959—for construing and applying the equal protection clause to governmental action, other than action conditioned on racial classification: "A classification having some reasonable basis does not offend against that clause merely because it is not made with mathematical nicety or because in practice it results in some inequality." [31]

b. *Justice Clark and the "Rational Plan" Idea*

Alone among the *Baker* v. *Carr* majority (at least overtly), Justice Clark was prepared to decide the merits on the basis of the undisputed facts in the record and to conclude that "the Tennessee apportionment statute offends the Equal Protection clause." [32] Indeed, he suggested that the majority had so held, "at least *sub silentio,*" [33] and thought it was unfortunate that there was a remand to the district court "for it to make what is certain to be that formal determination." [34] He was clairvoyant on the result, but not on the content and sweep of the federal substantive standard announced two years later in 1964.

30. *Id.* at 226. (Emphasis added)
31. Lindsley v. Natural Carbonic Gas Co., 220 U.S. 61, 78–79 (1911), quoted approvingly in Morey v. Doud, 354 U.S. 457, 463–64 (1959). Because civil rights-equal protection cases are notable in their failure to discuss equal protection at length, other areas must be appealed to for guidance regarding the standard created by the clause.
32. Baker v. Carr, *supra* note 1, at 258.
33. *Id.* at 261.
34. *Ibid.*

The exact content of Justice Clark's federal standard, which Tennessee in his view had violated, is not easily deduced from his opinion. However, because it would have left room for preservation of the so-called federal plan of apportionment (population as the base for one house; political subdivisions as the base for the other), and because it had great influence in subsequent lower court cases, it merits elaboration.

It was clear, as he himself stated, that he rejected the idea that "numerical equality of representation throughout a State is constitutionally required." [35] It was *not* clear that he found a constitutional mandate to recognize population factors in devising apportionment formulae for either house of the legislature. He discussed Tennessee county population figures extensively in his opinion but his purpose was not to evaluate compliance with some federal mandate phrased in population terms. Rather, he was exploring one possible basis for concluding that the arrangement of state legislative districts did comply with a federal mandate that state *classification* for any given governmental activity or function be done under an *identifiable and intelligent principle*—whether formally announced or not—*consistently applied*. Because Tennessee's state constitution itself called for an apportionment formula primarily based on population, and because numerical equality of representation was the only apparent principle that Tennessee may have tried to follow, he did not have to reveal his thoughts on the constitutionality of a nonpopulation county equality principle, consistently followed, for one or both houses of the legislature.

The essence of his position in this case seemed to be that "invidious discrimination," i.e., discrimination of the kind constitutionally forbidden, exists when two factors are shown: first, that a "classification" pattern exists in regard to a particular governmental activity or function, whether formally announced or not; and second, that the classification pattern has no underlying rational, ordering principle, consistently followed. He did not clearly identify the "class" in Tennessee's pattern of classification but he seemed to be thinking of the county as the building block in the state's apportionment system. Some counties, grouped into legislative districts, had more than one representative. Others, similarly grouped, had a fractional representative. But there seemed to be no rational principle, in terms of population size or any other factor, which determined that one county was in a "class" having a fractional representative, while another county was in a "class" having more than one representative.

He spoke of Tennessee's apportionment as "a topsy-turvical of gigantic

35. *Id.* at 260.

proportions" [36] and as "a crazy quilt without rational basis." [37] The evidence did not even show a conscious "attempt to effect a rural-urban political balance" [38] by underrepresenting all urban counties and overrepresenting all rural counties. Taking a population of 10,000 as a break point, tabulations showed that among "rural" counties of less than 10,000 population there were significant disparities in representation. Similarly, among "urban" counties of more than 10,000 population there were significant disparities.

Justice Clark's equal protection standard as formulated for this case had the appeal of simplicity. It provided a basis for deciding the case—setting aside for the moment the question of remedy—and left maximum room for state discretion in deciding what "rational" policy consistently to follow. Close scrutiny reveals, however, that it was an incomplete, if not defective, formulation of an equal protection standard. The general thrust of his opinion, and his use of the terms "topsy-turvical" and "crazy quilt without a rational basis," indicated that he was using the term "rational" simply in the sense of "intelligible."

What, then, of a case where there was a rational—in the sense of intelligible—ordering principle, consistently followed, but which principle was in itself intrinsically *unreasonable?* That, precisely, was *Brown* v. *Board of Education,*[39] and the Court held unconstitutional the resultant racial segregation in the public schools. Perhaps Justice Clark's formulation of the equal protection standard could have been rounded out and perfected simply by adding the additional factor that the rational policy, consistently followed in setting up the classification pattern, must also be "reasonable." Because "reasonableness" is the language of due process this proviso would have linked the two clauses—due process and equal protection—and provided two levels of unconstitutionality: first, where there is no "rational" plan at all; second, where the rationalizing or ordering principle offends a fundamental sense of fairness, decency, and justice, i.e., "unreasonable" in the constitutional sense.

In thus formulating possible outlines of a constitutional standard for apportionment, Justice Clark inadvertently touched on a crucial issue which consistently has played a vital role in apportionment litigation—the question of burden of proof. It is obvious that if the fundamental standard was one turning on the "reasonableness" of state apportionment policy—viewed as a test going beyond the "rationality" in the sense of inter-

36. *Id.* at 254.
37. *Ibid.*
38. *Id.* at 255.
39. 347 U.S. 483 (1954).

nal consistency—then the ultimate determination would be influenced greatly by the manner in which the *burden of proof* on this issue was allocated, and by the manner in which presumptions were handled. These are the factors which seem to explain the split in *Baker* v. *Carr* between two justices—Justices Clark and Harlan—who joined each other two years later in dissent from the Court's eventual standard.

At the time of *Baker*, both justices started from the premise that the Constitution does not require the "one man-one vote" principle. Justice Clark then took the obvious mathematical disparity between urban counties of similar size, inter se, and rural counties of similar size, inter se, as justifying imposing a burden on the *state* to show that the disparity resulted from a rational and perhaps intrinsically reasonable classifying principle. In other words, there was not even a consistent pro-rural, anti-urban policy. Justice Harlan looked at the same figures but avoided a conclusion of unconstitutionality by the manner of his burden of proof allocation. He placed on *plaintiffs* the burden of showing that the obvious population disparity was not simply the product of "all other factors justifying a legislative determination of the sort involved in devising a proper apportionment of State Legislatures." [40]

c. *The Presumptions—Burden of Proof Game*

Regarding this vital question of burden of proof, so strikingly illustrated in the contrasting approaches of Justices Clark and Harlan, it is instructive to compare *Baker* with the "all-white jury" cases where presumptions also played a major role. The premise in the latter cases that "all-white juries" are not illegal per se, and hence are not grounds in themselves for reversal of convictions of Negro defendants, is analogous to the Clark-Harlan premise that absolute numerical equality of representation throughout a state is not constitutionally required. The premise in the jury cases is qualified by the rule that continued existence of all-white juries over a time period creates a presumption that absence of Negroes does not result solely from operation of legitimate—i.e., racially neutral—selection factors. This qualifying rule has its analogy in Justice Clark's view, not shared by Justice Harlan, that continued population disparities raise a presumption that an illegitimate classifying factor is operating. The effect of the presumption in either instance is to put the burden on the state to show absence of improper classification factors.

But the analogy is incomplete. Racial motivation is the illegitimate hidden factor in the jury cases, which the Court reaches by means of a presumption after proof of absence of Negroes in the jury panel. What was the illegitimate hidden factor in the Tennessee apportionment case, which

40. Baker v. Carr, *supra* note 1, at 341.

Justice Clark (and later the Court itself) would reach by means of a presumption after proof of population disparities among districts? " . . . aye, there's the rub," as Justice Frankfurter exclaimed.

Race not being involved, there remained two other possible illegitimate hidden factors in the apportionment situation. First, the Court could move from *Baker* to create a basic rule, as a matter of constitutional law, that the constitution requires numerical equality in district formation (which may or may not lead to equality in "representation"), unless intrinsically reasonable and consistently used grounds for deviation can be shown. Second, the Court could move from *Baker* to create a constitutional rule that apportionment must be done under some intelligible and consistently used formula, perhaps related to a developed theory of representation, without pre-judging at all the question of the role that population or other factors should play. Although the general thrust of Justice Clark's opinion seemed to point toward the second of these two approaches, his closing peroration on population inequalities suggested identification with the first approach.

It was with such uncertain guidance from the Supreme Court that lower courts after *Baker* attempted to traverse the political thicket.

AN ALTERNATIVE RATIONALE FOR BAKER

Although both the due process and equal protection clauses of the Fourteenth Amendment were mentioned in the early course of the *Baker* v. *Carr* litigation,[41] due process rather quickly dropped out. The views of the Supreme Court, as articulated by Justice Brennan, were explicitly geared to the equal protection clause in regard both to justiciability and to a possible federal constitutional standard for state legislative apportionment. In retrospect it is unfortunate that the Court's entry into the political thicket was not made under one or another of two other constitutional banners which would have been more relevant to the nature of reapportionment. Most relevant would have been the clause in Article IV of the Constitution under which the federal government guarantees to each state a "republican form of government." Next most appropriate would have been the due process clause of the Fourteenth Amendment. Either clause would permit invalidation of apportionment systems under which districts containing a majority of the population of the state—typically urban and suburban districts—could be shown not to have majority control of either house of the legislature. On such a record it could be argued that the "republican guarantee" clause was violated because whatever this clause may mean it certainly would seem to require a con-

41. See note 39, *supra*, and accompanying text.

sensual system of government. On such a record it could be argued also that the due process clause was violated because in common understanding minority process is not due process in governmental decision-making.

In the ultimate configuration Justice Frankfurter undoubtedly was correct when he said that apportionment plaintiffs asked the Court to be willing to make a choice "among competing theories of political philosophy" and to make "an inquiry into the theoretic base of representation in an acceptably republican state." [42] But, one may ask, difficult though the articulation may be, what is wrong with a court commitment to a "democratic political philosophy"?

Approaching the matter from the standpoint of the republican guarantee clause or the due process clause would have permitted—indeed, required—a focus on the realities of political representation. It would have avoided the rather barren numbers game, focusing on raw population data, which tended to result from stress on the equal protection clause. Apportionment cases do involve voting, but their scope transcends the personal right to vote of a given voter-plaintiff. Motivation for the litigation did not arise from denials of a right to vote, or failure to count votes as cast. The complaint was that voting which did occur did not fairly express the popular will, or wills, in the state because of the distorting effect of the apportionment and districting system.

Plaintiffs from the outset thus were concerned with *voting results* in the sense of *representation results,* not with the voting process per se. In addition to personal voter interest which can be articulated, apportionment also involves governmental structure, i.e., formulae for composition of the legislative branch.

The republican guarantee clause would dictate a constitutional litigation focus encompassing necessarily a concern for representation results. The due process clause through its stress on ground rules of substantial reasonableness would yield the same breadth of focus. By contrast, grounding apportionment litigation on the equal protection clause tended to lead to a near-exclusive focus *not* on representation results and *not* on considerations of equal treatment of voter-plaintiffs, but rather on concern simply for equality in the total population masses encompassed in legislative districts—a concern in short for physical form and not for political substance.

The insufficiency of the equal protection clause as a guide to widely held "one man-one vote" values, was demonstrated strikingly in the Georgia governorship litigation in 1966. Because "one man-one vote" values had been identified solely with the equal protection clause ever since *Baker* v. *Carr* in 1962, both sets of complaining parties used that clause. It

42. Baker v. Carr, *supra* note 1, at 300, 301.

was the ground for their plea that the Georgia state legislature should not be permitted to perform a state constitutional duty of resolving the deadlock between candidates Howard H. "Bo" Callaway and Lester G. Maddox—neither having achieved a popular majority as the state constitution required. (The case did not turn on the status of legislative apportionment. Although the Georgia legislature had not completed the process of reapportionment, it had been substantially reapportioned and provisionally approved as the constitutional legislature of the state by the United States Supreme Court itself at the time of the dispute over the governorship election.)

Conceding there may be a "one man-one vote" problem in having the legislature resolve popular vote deadlocks for executive office, it cannot be reached intelligently by talking about the equal protection of the laws. A majority of the Court so held.[43] By contrast the issue could be approached intelligently from the standpoint of the republican guarantee clause or the due process clause. The question would be whether legislative resolution of a "no-majority" result in the popular vote for governor was consistent with the former clause's stress on consensual governmental forms, and the latter clause's stress on avoidance of unreasonable or arbitrary governmental action.

In the area of legislative apportionment a focus on equal protection, defined as a concern solely for equality in legislative district population, does provide a seemingly simple and easily administrable standard for testing constitutionality. It does so, however, at the cost of excluding, or tending to exclude, consideration of corollary problems of effective representation as an end result of the voting-apportionment processes. Reapportionment litigation under the republican guarantee clause or the due process clause would face these problems, and admittedly would be more difficult. Litigation under the equal protection clause has tended to be relatively easy only because the realistic questions, by definition, seem to become irrelevant.

CONCLUSION

Laying aside the question of the appropriate constitutional clause on which to ground and develop constitutional restrictions on the reapportionment process, *Baker* v. *Carr did* open up the political thicket to some judicial policing—in the case of such states as Tennessee, some long-needed judicial policing.

Baker v. *Carr* rests on a principle of judicial necessity to act to preserve the very essence of the democratic process. Its novelty is not to be mini-

43. Fortson v. Morris, 385 U.S. 231 (1966); and see Ch. IX, 221 n. 59; Ch. XVI, 423.

mized by distortion of earlier and generally negative precedents. It was, and remains, a very large step in the direction of close judicial scrutiny of the politics of the people. As "an eminently realistic body of men," it is difficult to suppose that the Court was uninfluenced by the fact of exhaustion of nonjudicial modes of relief over a period of several decades.

For the urban majority the decision evoked memory of the famous lines of the Declaration of Independence that prudence "will dictate that Governments long established should not be changed for light and transient causes," but that a duty to act arises from "a long train of abuses and usurpations, pursuing invariably the same object . . . ." The Declaration led to a new political order. *Baker* v. *Carr* likewise led to a new political order in some states, although the full character of the political power shift destined to flow from *Baker* v. *Carr* will not be known for years. On the eve of the 1970 census it is clear that federal constitutional standards of apportionment need further elaboration.

One of the most striking aspects of *Baker* v. *Carr* was the rapidity with which, within a year or two, extensive reapportionment was accomplished through judicial pressure and accepted, even though disliked intensely by some. If this seemed surprising, it may be because there was a tendency to equate *Baker* v. *Carr* with the bitter and tedious aftermath of *Brown* v. *Board of Education*, forgetting the uniqueness of racial tension against a Southern background of de jure slavery and a Southern foreground of de facto serfdom. But De Tocqueville would understand the decision, because to him the thrust for equality was both the mark of American history and the touchstone of modern history.

VII

The Reapportionment Revolution Unfolds

"Room continues to be allowed for weighting. This of course implies that geography, economics, urban-rural conflict, and all the other non-legal factors which have throughout our history entered into political districting are to some extent not to be ruled out in the undefined vista now opened up by review in the federal courts of state reapportionments. To some extent— aye, there's the rub."

Justice Felix Frankfurter, commenting on *Baker* v. *Carr's* guidance to the lower courts.

For many decades reapportionment, like Pandora's Box, was felt to be so full of intricate political factors that courts, particularly federal courts, should sit on the lid and never look inside. As Justice Felix Frankfurter had said in the *Colegrove* congressional districting suit in 1946, courts should not enter the "political thicket" because it would be "hostile to a democratic system to involve the judiciary in the politics of the people." [1] In a series of cases down to 1962, this thought became the touchstone also for state legislature apportionment. *Baker* v. *Carr* made the Frankfurter touchstone an epitaph. Courts not only entered the thicket, they proceeded to occupy it.

The strength of pent-up pressure for reapportionment was indicated dramatically by the volume of reapportionment activity which had occurred by the end of 1963—the first full year of legislative sessions after the *Baker* decision. Under impetus of *Baker*, reapportionment was on the agenda of most of the forty-seven state legislatures in session that year. Cases were before federal courts in thirty-one states, before state courts in nineteen states, and before both federal and state courts in eleven states. At least one house of twenty-four state legislatures had either been declared unconstitutional, or declared suspect with the court reserving final

1. Colegrove v. Green, 328 U.S. 549, 554 (1946).

139

judgment to allow time for legislative action. Twenty-six states had approved reapportionment plans or state constitutional amendments designed to reduce population disparities in legislative districts—some applying only to one house, some to both houses.[2]

In most instances validity of so-called federal plans (one house based on equal population districts, the other primarily on political subdivisions or areas) either was not at issue or had been left open, but there were important exceptions.

For decisional standards lower courts had only the assurance of Justice William J. Brennan, Jr., that standards of equal protection were "well developed and familiar," or Justice William O. Douglas's statement that the traditional test was "invidious discrimination," or Justice Tom C. Clark's "rational plan" idea, i.e., internal logical consistency of the state's apportionment system.[3]

Intimations and sometimes express statements in opinions of lower courts grappling with the reapportionment problem suggest the earlier comment of Justice Robert H. Jackson in another murky area: "I give up. Now I realize fully what Mark Twain meant when he said, 'The more you explain it, the more I don't understand it.' "[4] To appreciate the extent of the quandary of lower courts in attempting to discharge the mission assigned by the Supreme Court, some review of traditional substantive standards under the equal protection of the laws clause of the Fourteenth Amendment is essential. *Baker* v. *Carr* and its progeny unsettled and then reshaped both "equal protection" and the state legislatures.

A. Past Guidance on Equal Protection

1. RACIAL CASES

In motivation and initial understanding, the Thirteenth, Fourteenth, and Fifteenth Amendments were racial amendments. They were designed to conclude slavery and the Civil War by opening the door to full integration into American society of the several million new Negro citizens. As Justice Samuel F. Miller wrote in 1873, "[t]he one pervading purpose" of the Amendments was to secure "the freedom of the slave race" and to protect "the newly-made freeman and citizen."[5]

2. 21 *Cong. Quart. Weekly Report*, 2258 (1963).
3. Baker v. Carr, 369 U.S. 186, 226—Brennan, 244—Douglas, 258—Clark (1962).
4. SEC v. Chenery Corp., 332 U.S. 194, 214 (1947).
5. The Slaughterhouse Cases, 83 U.S. (16 Wall.) 36, 71 (1873).

One of the earliest of the racial cases, *Strauder v. West Virginia*,[6] dealt with jury discrimination and proceeded squarely on the assumption that these Civil War amendments made race a forbidden category for governmental policies of exclusion or classification. The "separate but equal" qualification, permitting the rise of official racial segregation systems—the so-called Black Codes—did not enter the law until 1896, in *Plessy v. Ferguson*.[7] Even during the "separate but equal" era ordinances designed to segregate white and colored homes were nullified.[8] But not until 1948 were private restrictive covenants on sales of housing deemed unenforceable in state courts either directly against Negroes or through damage suits against white signers who breached the covenant by selling to a non-Caucasian.[9] After a long detour, the Court returned to the *Strauder* principles in the 1954 school desegregation decisions, *Brown v. Board of Education*.[10] Abolishing the separate but equal formula, the Court held that equal protection required elimination of separate Negro and white public schools. And the courts have since required elimination of race as a classification factor in setting up and running public programs in general.[11] So far as race is concerned, the message of the old *Strauder* case and the recent *Brown* case is that the equal protection clause requires an absolute equality.

a. *Other Personal Characteristic Cases*

The underlying but not always expressed principle of the race cases is really a status principle. Official classifications and resulting disabilities and benefits may not be keyed to personal characteristics which individuals cannot change, or should not be required to change. This principle has been invoked most frequently and most rigidly regarding race, but there are other examples. Alienage is one, and most assuredly religion would be another under this facet of equal protection if the First Amendment did not exist to serve the same function. Discrimination or onerous classifications aimed at aliens have not met the absolute barrier which equal protection erects against racial classifications. Some distinctions be-

6. 100 U.S. 303 (1880).
7. 163 U.S. 537 (1896).
8. Buchanan v. Warley, 245 U.S. 60 (1917).
9. Shelley v. Kraemer, 334 U.S. 1 (1948); Barrows v. Jackson, 346 U.S. 249 (1953).
10. 347 U.S. 483 (1954).
11. Mayor of Baltimore v. Dawson, 350 U.S. 877 (1955) (public beaches and bathhouses); Holmes v. City of Atlanta, 350 U.S. 879 (1955) (municipal golf courses); State Athletic Commission v. Dorsey, 359 U.S. 533 (1959) (statute forbidding integrated athletic contests); Johnson v. Virginia, 373 U.S. 61 (1963) (courtroom seating). See also Robert G. Dixon, Jr., "Transportation: Desegregation and Government Initiative, 1887-1964" in *Legal Aspects of the Civil Rights Movement* 103 (Donald B. King and Charles W. Quick, editors, Detroit: Wayne State University Press, 1965).

tween citizens and aliens have been conceded, e.g., the special interest of the state in reserving to citizens such things as wild game, employment on state public works, and licenses for pool halls.[12] The pool hall restriction does, however, seem to rest on the questionable premise that aliens as a class are more criminally associated than are citizens. But unless special justification can be shown, state laws restricting aliens (laws sometimes tinged also with racial bias against Orientals) normally have fared poorly in the Supreme Court. Invalidations include an Arizona law restricting aliens to 20 percent of an employer's work force,[13] and California laws barring aliens "ineligible to citizenship" (primary impact on resident-alien Japanese) from obtaining commercial fishing licenses or from obtaining agricultural land as owner or occupier.[14] In the famous Chinese laundry case, constitutional restraint was extended beyond a law fair on its face to reach discriminatory administration. In that instance a law requiring licensing of all wooden laundries, which was valid as a fire-protection measure, was enforced against some 200 Chinese laundrymen but not against 80 others who were not Chinese subjects.[15]

2. NONRACIAL EQUAL PROTECTION

Once the precedents concerning application of the equal protection clause to state-supported or state-permitted racial discrimination (or discrimination based on other personal characteristics) are laid aside—and *Baker* v. *Carr* is not a race discrimination case—the meaning of equal protection becomes quite elusive. Justice Oliver Wendell Holmes, Jr., with an aptness decreasing in relevance today, once said the clause was "the usual last resort of constitutional arguments." [16]

Nonracial applications of the equal protection clause prior to *Baker* v. *Carr*, as identified in a work by Professor Robert J. Harris, can be grouped under five major headings: (1) barrier to state economic legislation, i.e., regulation or taxation; (2) restraint on legislative discriminations in favor of or against women; (3) restraint on certain political processes including alleged malapportionment; (4) device to mitigate the handicap of poverty in appealing criminal convictions; (5) some miscellaneous mat-

12. Patsone v. Pennsylvania, 232 U.S. 138 (1914) (wild game); Heim v. McCall, 239 U.S. 175 (1915) and Crane v. New York, 239 U.S. 195 (1915) (employment); Ohio *ex rel.* Clarke v. Deckebach, 274 U.S. 392 (1927) (pool rooms).
13. Truax v. Raich, 239 U.S. 33 (1915).
14. Takahashi v. Fish and Game Commission, 334 U.S. 410 (1948) (fishing licenses); Oyama v. California, 332 U.S. 633 (1948) (owning land).
15. Yick Wo v. Hopkins, 118 U.S. 356 (1886).
16. Buck v. Bell, 274 U.S. 200, 208 (1927).

ters of no general import.[17] *Baker* v. *Carr* invigorated the "political processes" category in this list. The Court's reaction to cases in the other categories, with the notable exception of criminal pauper appeals and allied
issues, has been mixed or negative.

Three categories—economic legislation (which had produced three-
fourths of the cases as of the 1950s), criminal appeals, and political processes, contain possibly significant sources for enlightenment in handling
the equal protection plea in reapportionment and merit special treatment
below. The remaining categories yield small cases, often mixed with
humor.

It has always been difficult for law to take seriously the claims of
women for equality. There was a fifty-year gap, which some might dub a
cultural lag, between the Fifteenth Amendment and the Nineteenth
Amendment regarding voting by Negro men, and by women, respectively.
Among judges, as revealed by the case law, Professor Harris finds "an almost josephic aversion to women." [18] In a relatively recent pronouncement sustaining a Michigan statute forbidding licensing of female bar-
tenders, with exception of wives or daughters of male bar owners, Justice
Frankfurter recalled "the alewife, sprightly and ribald, in Shakespeare,"
and said:

> The fact that women now have achieved virtues that men have long
> claimed as their prerogatives and now indulge in vices that men have
> long practiced, does not preclude the states from drawing a sharp line
> between the sexes, certainly in such matters as the regulation of the
> liquor traffic.[19]

Miscellaneous other equal protection cases touched on such matters as
evidence, legal procedure, regulation of secret societies.[20] Perhaps the best
known of these miscellaneous cases, although in a class by itself, is *Skin-
ner* v. *Oklahoma*,[21] which invalidated a statute authorizing sterilization of
certain habitual criminals who had committed offenses "involving moral
turpitude," and exempted others. Although in a case which produced the
famous Holmesian line about "three generations of imbeciles" [22] being
enough the Court had upheld compulsory sterilization of incurable mental defectives, the Court held the Oklahoma statute unconstitutional on
classification grounds. General larceny was covered, but not the white-

17. Robert J. Harris, *The Quest for Equality* Ch. III (Baton Rouge: Louisiana State
University Press, 1960).
18. *Id.* at 73.
19. Goesaert v. Cleary, 335 U.S. 464, 465–66 (1948).
20. Harris, *supra* note 17, at 80.
21. 316 U.S. 535 (1942).
22. Buck v. Bell, 274 U.S. 200, 208 (1927).

collar offense of embezzlement. The Court could find no reasonable distinction between auto thieves and a cashier with his hand in the till—at least not a constitutional distinction justifying sterilization of one and not the other. The question whether a compulsory sterilization statute applicable to all habitual felons would be valid was not reached.

3. CRIMINAL PAUPER APPEALS

Rules regarding criminal pauper appeals developed since 1956 represent one of the newer frontiers of the law. But it is not clear whether the rules are properly classifiable as a frontier of equal protection, as the Court seems to have done, or as a frontier of due process, which Justice John Marshall Harlan in dissent in the landmark case, *Griffin* v. *Illinois*,[23] would have thought more logical. In *Griffin* the Court reversed, 5–4, an Illinois conviction of two armed robbers who had been unable to appeal because they lacked money for a trial transcript and could not qualify under two free transcript provisos.

The components of the alleged inequity are quite different, however, in the *Griffin* line of cases and in legislative apportionment. Apportionment involves alleged *state*-created inequities in "weighting" of votes. In criminal pauper appeals the question is the extent to which states are under an affirmative obligation to shape their rules so as to minimize the effect of such *natural* differences as wealth or family connections. *Griffin* conveys the idea that states are under a constitutional duty to ensure that poverty —itself not a state-created differentiating condition—does not become in practice a differentiating condition affecting a person's capacity to take advantage of the privilege of obtaining review of a criminal conviction. But *Griffin* did not articulate a principle to measure the sweep of the new equal protection rule regarding poverty. If mere poverty-influenced differences in capacity to enjoy opportunities offered by the state render a state program unconstitutional, then tuition would have to be abolished in state universities and necessitous public school students would have to be provided with state sustenance so that they could complete their education. Is not the social interest in education as deep as the social interest in equitable criminal procedures?

Griffin's relevance to legislative apportionment is this: it illustrates a recent tendency to decide equal protection cases without ever identifying

23. 351 U.S. 12 1956).

Beyond the scope of this discussion is the recent expansion of the *Griffin* "equalization" principle in other aspects of criminal law and procedure. See, e.g., Douglas v. California, 372 U.S. 353 (1963) regarding indigents' right to assigned (free) counsel on appeal. Extension of the principle to the field of bail requirements is a likely next step.

clearly the aspect of the particular discriminatory effect which makes it also "unreasonable," "invidious," and hence unconstitutional. Differential effects are legion. The essence, therefore, of a successful equal protection plea, outside the field of race, must be a showing not merely of "discrimination" or differential treatment, but a showing that the discrimination or differential treatment derives from an *unreasonable* classification.

Griffin's vagueness on the substantive meaning of equal protection troubled Justice Harlan. His reaction presaged his later opinion in *Baker v. Carr*, where he and Justice Clark were the only ones to try to illuminate the essential meaning of equal protection. Dissenting in *Griffin*, Justice Harlan felt that a simplistic equal protection approach, focused essentially on the differentiating factor of poverty, ignored the real issue. Why should poverty be an impermissible conditioning factor in criminal appeals but—for the present at least—a permissible conditioning factor in access to a state university? He did not see how poverty as a classifying factor could have one meaning in certain equal protection cases and a different meaning in another. The solution he felt would be to handle *Griffin* not as an equal protection case but as a due process case involving a particular, identifiable, and relatively narrow concept of fundamental fairness regarding criminal appeals. He said:

> . . . the issue here is not the typical equal protection question of reasonableness of a "classification" on the basis of which the State has *imposed* legal disabilities, but rather the reasonableness of the State's failure to *remove* natural disabilities. The Court holds that the failure of the State to do so is constitutionally unreasonable in this case although it might not be in others. I submit that the basis for that holding is simply an unarticulated conclusion that it violates "fundamental fairness" for a State which provides for appellate review, and thus apparently considers such review necessary to assure justice, not to see to it that such appeals are in fact available to those it would imprison for serious crimes. That of course is the traditional language of due process . . . and I see no reason to import new substance into the concept of equal protection to dispose of the case, especially when to do so gives rise to the all-too-easy opportunity to ignore the real issue and solve the problems simply by labelling the Illinois practice as invidious "discrimination." [24]

A prime virtue of the due process approach is that it allows the Court to police the outer boundaries of governmental action, correcting particularly egregious conduct and legislative excrescences, without getting into

24. *Id.* at 35–36 (emphasis added).

the detailed process of attempting to equate group with group in areas where full functional equality is an impossibility.

4. EQUAL PROTECTION AND POLITICAL PROCESSES

Prior to *Baker* v. *Carr*, the *Colegrove* nonjusticiability precedent ruled the legislative apportionment field. There was one case, however, which bore significantly on the question of the application of the equal protection clause to alleged malapportionment. And this case—neither reversed, clearly modified, nor clarified in the welter of reapportionment litigation —still raises the pertinent conceptual questions which must be clarified if equal protection is to become a meaningful decisional formula and not an incantation.

In *Snowden* v. *Hughes* the Court stated the basic premise that it takes more than a denial of a right conferred by state law to constitute a violation of equal protection, "even though the denial of the right to one person may operate to confer it on another." [25] It then stated the following oft-quoted rule:

> The unlawful administration by state officers of a state statute fair on its face, resulting in its unequal application to those who are entitled to be treated alike, is not a denial of equal protection unless there is shown to be present in it an *element of intentional or purposeful discrimination*. This may appear on the face of the action taken with respect to a particular class or person . . . or it may only be shown by extrinsic evidence showing a discriminatory design to favor one individual or class over another not to be inferred from the action itself. . . . But a discriminatory purpose is not presumed. . . . there must be a showing of "clear and intentional discrimination.[26]

As applied to the facts this meant that the action was dismissed for failure to state a cause of action. Petitioner Snowden did not allege that what was done to him—refusal to certify him as a nominee for the Illinois legislature even though he had received sufficient votes—was done so that *somebody else* could obtain the nomination, or that somebody else in fact did obtain the nomination to the particular office. Two nominations were to be made, under a prior political party agreement; Snowden ran second, and therefore was entitled to one of them. The fact that the candidate who ran first was certified by the Canvassing Board as one of the nominees was immaterial because his relationship was to a different "office" than the one improperly denied to Snowden.

25. 321 U.S. 1, 8 (1944).
26. *Ibid.*

Other language of the Court in this case leaves uncertain the essence of an equal protection claim, and what must be alleged to constitute a cause of action. It is clear that a person, A, does not show an equal protection cause of action merely by showing wrongful treatment of himself at the hands of the state. Would it be sufficient for A to allege, additionally, that the injurious treatment of him was motivated by a desire to render different treatment, in relation to the same matter, to B, which desire was effectuated? Would this constitute, in the Court's words, "intentional or purposeful discrimination"? In particular, in the *Snowden* situation, would the defect in the complaint have been cured merely by adding that the nomination was given, instead, to Mr. X? If Snowden were rejected and X certified on the ground that Snowden, unlike X, was a member of a disfavored racial or religious minority, all might agree that this stated a good cause of action. But suppose Snowden and X were both white Presbyterians and the Canvassing Board's action was allegedly motivated by (a) personal animosity, or (b) a feeling that Snowden, unlike X, was a party wrecker, or (c) a feeling that Snowden was too old and ill and would not live out the term, or (d) a feeling that Snowden, unlike X, was too uneducated for the position. Assuming each of these actions to be wrongful, would they create also an equal protection claim in light of the Court's admonition in *Snowden* that a "construction of the Equal Protection clause which would find a violation of a federal right in every departure by state officers from state law is not to be favored"? [27]

Related to legislative apportionment, *Snowden* at least seems to indicate that there should be a showing not merely of population disparity among districts, but also proof of a conscious scheme to have disparity of a particular kind, e.g., urban-rural, and accomplishment of that scheme in that Group A actually received what Group B was entitled to. But there is still further complexity in building from *Snowden*—or the *Snowden* dicta as to what would constitute a good equal protection cause of action—to legislative apportionment.

Suppose that A alleges different treatment of himself and B in relation to the same matter, but neither mode of treatment taken by itself is a violation of state law, unlike the *Snowden* situation. The typical legislative apportionment case would seem to fall in this category because there always are some differences in district population. Does mere difference in treatment, in some situations, constitute a violation of equal protection? The Court in *Snowden* spoke of "unequal application to those who are entitled to be treated alike," [28] as being a component of the claim, although not enough in itself. But who are entitled to equal treatment?

27. *Id.* at 11–12.
28. *Id.* at 8.

And what constitutes "equal" treatment? Are these independent federal questions?

The foregoing analysis suggests that at bottom the *content* of state action is the crucial thing. What is required is not just a showing of differential treatment, but the making of a distinction between permissible and impermissible governmental purposes. And this seems to sound more in due process than equal protection. At this point has the Court, not clearly and perhaps unwittingly, opened a new door to judicial reevaluation of substantive legislative purposes? Are we recreating the broad judicial discretion which figured so prominently in the actions of the pre-1937 Court in measuring state economic legislation by judicial concepts of due process?

5. STATE REGULATION AND TAXATION

Such life and verve as this category possessed largely expired with the 1930s, although cases continue to arise. In the economic field the test had become not the *existence* of discrimination but the *reasonableness* of the statutory scheme of classification. The "rules," as codified by Justice Willis Van Devanter in 1910 and oft-repeated since, are: [29] (1) equal protection permits classification, i.e., discrimination, if the classification is reasonable and not purely arbitrary; (2) an apparently reasonable classification is not invalidated because lacking in mathematical nicety or productive of some inequality; (3) if facts making a classification reasonable can be conceived, their existence at the time of enactment must be assumed; (4) the one who challenges a classification formula has the burden of showing it has no reasonable basis and is essentially arbitrary.

Aided doubtless by the fourth rule, allocating burden of proof to the challenger of economic legislation, the Court frequently rejected the attack. But a presumption of constitutionality does not serve to explain cases where the Court agreed with the challenger. If one searches the cases for elucidation of principles as to the limits of the presumption of constitutionality he will meet only disappointment. Recently in *Morey* v. *Doud*,[30] for example, the Court split 6–3 against constitutionality of an Illinois statute requiring all firms issuing and selling money orders to obtain a license, but exempting the American Express Company.

Neither the reason for decision nor the cause of the split in the Court was well explained. It is hardly satisfying to revert to the second rule listed above and simply say that equal protection is not a matter of mathematical nicety so that the Court has what Justice Holmes called "sover-

29. Lindsley v. Natural Carbonic Gas Co., 220 U.S. 61, 78–79 (1911).
30. 354 U.S. 457 (1959).

eign prerogative of choice." With such vagueness should not statutes be sustained under a normal judicial review postulate of a presumption of constitutionality? Or should the facts rule, yielding varying sets of presumptions? For example, should the presumption of constitutionality be balanced with a presumption of unconstitutionality where, as in *Morey*, it is alleged that the statute favors the big company against small companies? Opinions in the cases indicate that the game of presumptions— made all the more interesting by keeping the presumptions hidden—can be played on an especially rich field in regard to equal protection. Possibilities include a presumption for an open and competitive market, a presumption for small as against big business, or a presumption for a national concern against favored local concerns.

6. SUMMARY

The Court has taken quite different approaches to different equal protection pleas. In the largest categories, racial cases and cases involving economic or welfare legislation, diametrically opposing trends emerged: an absolute equality for racial matters; a strong disposition to accept legislative classifications for the latter. Classifications regarding aliens have been frowned on but not eliminated. Rights of political equality, though commonly thought to be basic, fared ill under equal protection in *Colegrove* and in *Snowden*, but poverty has been taken into account regarding availability of criminal appeals. Where reapportionment should be fitted into this mixed heritage—to determine such crucial matters as burden of proof and presumptions of constitutionality—was the question opened up once *Baker* declared that reapportionment was no longer a nonjusticiable question.

Although there have been suggestions to the contrary, any effort to group all of these cases into two simple categories, economic cases and "basic rights of man" cases, with reapportionment neatly falling in the latter, is too gross to be supportable.[31]

Racial equality must be an absolute because it is an *end* in itself as a matter of human dignity. Apportionment and districting are *intermediate* steps in an election process where, by definition, full proportionate equality of political influence is impossible short of a shift to proportional representation forms. The extent to which reapportionment should be handled in terms of a relatively rigid equality concept must find its rationale not in a mystic "basic rights of man" assertion but rather in terms of the relation of particular apportionment systems to fair representation goals,

31. See Robert B. McKay, "Political Thickets and Crazy Quilts: Reapportionment and Equal Protection," 61 *Mich. L. Rev.* 645, 660–77 (1963).

the nature of the alternatives, and the results, empirically analyzed.

Three primary aspects of equal protection of the laws clause do emerge from this brief review. *First,* in regard to racial matters, at least since *Brown* v. *Board of Education,* the school desegregation decision of 1954, the clause has supported a constitutional absolute of color-blind official action. (Subsequently, questions concerning the permissibility of preferred treatment of Negroes to ameliorate the effects of past slavery and repression have arisen but this development lies outside the present discussion.) *Second,* in regard to nonracial matters, the clause has been one focusing on *relationships.* The burden is on the complaining party not only to show differential status between two clearly identifiable groups, but also to show that the differential status is the product of purposeful official discrimination. *Third,* even a showing of differential official treatment, i.e., classification, of persons may not warrant a holding of unconstitutionality unless the classification categories are "unreasonable." In this latter aspect equal protection would seem to merge with due process.

The equal protection clause in truth is paradoxical. If taken to signify little more than a restraint on unreasonable and arbitrary governmental action, it safeguards a field already protected by due process. If taken more literally as commanding a flat equality in governmental dealings with citizens, it proves far too much and erodes the necessary distinctions and rewards for special performance which flow from competitive vigor safeguarded both by liberty and by justice, in the Aristotelian sense of "distributive justice." And something more than a mere erosion may occur if the frequently mooted concept of *affirmative* governmental obligations under the Fourteenth Amendment be accepted and keyed to literal and simplistic equality concepts. The equal protection of the laws clause thus has within it the seeds of all the conflicts and issues stemming from the grand philosophic concepts of liberty, equality, and justice.

B. Lower Courts Muddle Through

1. CONTINUING QUESTIONS OF STANDING AND JUSTICIABILITY

Despite *Baker* v. *Carr's* explicit focus on jurisdiction, standing to sue, and justiciability, some lingering problems remained for resolution by lower courts, particularly in regard to standing. *Baker* made it clear that voter-plaintiffs had standing if they resided in overpopulated and thus allegedly underrepresented districts. What other persons could litigate the reapportionment issue—the state itself, a corporation, voters in underpopulated and thus allegedly overrepresented districts, unincorporated associations? Courts generally have pursued a permissive policy concerning standing, partly because conventional plaintiffs (i.e., resident voters in overpopulated districts) were always available and could be added.

A federal district court in Wisconsin held that the state, in its sovereign capacity, could not be an apportionment plaintiff.[32] But private plaintiffs were allowed to intervene, thus enabling the state to acquire parens patriae status and continue in the suit as spokesmen for the resident-voter intervenors. The state Attorney General continued to dominate plaintiffs' side of the case both as state representative and as counsel for the private plaintiffs. The nominal defendant was the Secretary of State.

A federal district court in Nebraska denied standing to the League of Municipalities, the AFL-CIO, and mayors in their official capacity, but accorded standing to mayors as individuals.[33] A federal district court in Connecticut in a state senate suit expressed concern because the plaintiff was overrepresented in the state senate (i.e., a resident of an underpopulated district), and underrepresented only in the house. The court noted that in any event additional parties could easily be added.

However, when Los Angeles attorney Phill Silver—better known to sports fans as the one who mounted a citizen suit to try to keep the ex-Brooklyn Dodgers out of Chavez Ravine—attempted to litigate reapportionment without widespread support or the backing of either political party, he encountered some difficulties.[34] One of his several suits, filed in his own behalf, was dismissed for lack of standing because he was a resident of an underpopulated district. Thereafter he added a relative from an overpopulated district as plaintiff and the suit did go forward under the same name.

In a Mississippi reapportionment suit in 1966, the defendants requested that the Mississippi Freedom Democratic party, most of whose attorneys were Northern civil rights lawyers, be dismissed from the suit as party plaintiff. The federal district court expressed grave doubts whether this unincorporated association had standing because "deprivation of Constitutional rights is more properly to be asserted by persons, not organizations which merely claim to speak for persons . . . ."[35] But because there were other conventional plaintiffs, the dismissal of the Freedom Democratic party would not affect the litigation and the court decided to allow this group to remain active as plaintiffs.

Much more questionable is the judicial permissiveness which allowed

32. State of Wisconsin v. Zimmerman, 205 F. Supp. 673 (W.D. Wis. 1962).
33. League of Nebraska Municipalities v. Marsh, 209 F. Supp. 189 (D. Neb. 1962).
34. Silver v. Jordan, 241 F. Supp. 576 (S.D. Cal. 1964).
35. Connor v. Jackson, 256 F. Supp. 962 (S.D. Miss. 1966).

Radio Station WMCA in New York City not only to remain as plaintiff in the long sequence of New York state reapportionment litigation but to gain substantial advertising value by affixing its name to the title of the case.[36] The station was owned by long-time Democratic party activist R. Peter Straus. Because funds supporting reapportionment litigation customarily came from a variety of sources—personal, labor union, and corporate contributions, donated time, etc.—it would be unrealistic to question WMCA's active participation so far as the financing of the suit was concerned. It would seem, however, to be a most serious breach of the proprieties to allow a private profit-making corporation such as WMCA to gain incalculable benefit through free advertising by being allowed to lend its name to a wholly public law suit grounded on personal voter rights under the Fourteenth Amendment.

The nominal defendants in virtually all suits were state election officials charged with the duty of conducting the next election under the existing state apportionment law. The question whether the governor and attorney general of a state were necessary defendants was raised in Virginia; a federal district court allowed dismissal of these officers because they had no "special relation" to the elections in question.[37]

2. BREAKDOWN OF THE ADVERSARY METHOD

More important than some continuing problems of standing in *Baker*-inspired apportionment legislation has been the problem of breakdown, in many suits, of the traditional common law requirement of adversity. The theory of the Anglo-American adversary method of litigation has been that courts are neutral, impartial decision-makers, to which the opposing parties bring the "facts" of their dispute and legal arguments and conclusions relevant to the facts. Adversity between parties is essential, therefore, in order to maximize the likelihood that the court, which does not itself research or investigate, will receive all relevant factual and legal data. As one commentator has observed, "The adversary system is a sort of legal personification of the principle that all is fair in love and war."[38] Thus, no stone is left unturned.

Unfortunately there has been a breakdown of this adversary method in some apportionment cases. It is important to remember that primary defendants in apportionment cases are executive branch officials who conduct elections. Minimum relief sought is a declaration of invalidity of ex-

36. WMCA v. Simon, 196 F. Supp. 758 (1961).
37. Mann v. Davis, 213 F. Supp. 577 (E.D. Va. 1962) (governor and Attorney General dismissed because they had no "special relation" to the elections in suit).
38. Harry D. Nims, "The Cost of Justice," 28 *Conn. B.J.* 1, 2 (1954).

isting apportionment statutes and an injunction against their continued use. But in some states, such as Oklahoma, where the governor had campaigned repeatedly for reapportionment, the executive branch defendants already favored reapportionment.[39] The Michigan defendants—the Secretary of State and Attorney General—began to argue for reapportionment as soon as the issue of justiciability was removed.[40] In effect this yielded two sets of "plaintiffs" asserting unconstitutionality of the state apportionment system. Defense was left to such additional defendants as may have been allowed to intervene earlier in the litigation, or who were allowed to intervene at the last minute when it became apparent that the nominal defendants in the executive branch were going to be complaisant. Surprisingly enough, the federal district court in Oklahoma only begrudgingly allowed some state senators to intervene, even though without them a major and exceptionally murky federal constitutional issue would have been decided without opportunity for argument, in an essentially ex parte proceeding.

In the Delaware litigation the adversary process was cramped because certain defendants who were members of the Boards of Canvass and also judges in the state court system felt that "as judicial officers serving in ministerial capacities" it would be "inappropriate to take a position on the merits of this law suit . . . ."[41] This eventuality illustrates the oft-mentioned separation of powers principle concerning the extreme inadvisability of imposing nonjudicial responsibilities on judges.

The time may come, in fields such as apportionment, when judges who are alert to avoid imposition on judicial process by friendly parties may have to give fresh consideration to the matter of adequately informing the court. The problem is not novel but has been aggravated both by heightened judicial awareness of the polycentric nature of legal problems and by steady proliferation of social complexities resulting from advances in technology. In broad areas of law, particularly public law, a litigant's problems and conceptions are not coterminous, except fortuitously, with public policy dimensions of the issue.

Public intervenor statutes, designed for situations where public laws are under limited private attack and authorizing the government to intervene, by their nature offer no solution in those apportionment cases where

39. Moss v. Burkhart, 207 F. Supp. 885, 888–90 (W.D. Okla. 1962). For an illuminating discussion of the parties, their positions and judicial attitude, see Jurisdictional Statement of the Intervenors (state senators and Oklahomans for Local Government), Price v. Moss, Supreme Court of the United States No. 688, 1962 Term). A Motion to Stay and Supersede was denied by Justice White, *Oklahoma City Times*, March 7, 1963, p. 1, col. 8.

40. Scholle v. Hare, 367 Mich. 176, 116 N.W. 2d 350 (1962), following remand from the United States Supreme Court, 369 U.S. 429 (1962).

41. Sincock v. Terry, 210 F. Supp. 396, 399 n. 1 (D. Del. 1962).

government in effect is attacking itself. The equitable device of appointing a master may be better adapted to problems requiring extensive value-weighing along with detailed "fact" finding. The master device has virtues of close relationship to the court and adaptability to research techniques. Alternatively the amicus curiae device has acquired great flexibility, but often rests on private initiative. More recently, it has undergone transformation from advisor to advocate, and this transformation has affected also the role of the federal Solicitor General.[42] Both in *Baker* v. *Carr* and in *Gray* v. *Sanders*,[43] the Georgia county-unit case a year later, the Solicitor was essentially a vigorous co-plaintiff, and not above warping precedent to the desired end, in traditional appellate advocacy style. Of course, an awareness, or concern, regarding the nonadversary nature of some apportionment litigation may be minimal in states following the tradition of popular election of judges, whether on partisan or nominally nonpartisan tickets.

Equally distressing was the unsatisfactory quality in some apportionment briefs and apportionment opinions after *Baker*. This was attributable in part to intrinsic complexities in apportionment, in part to deficiencies in the adversary method for this kind of litigation, and in part to unpaid status of some counsel.

The problems of lack of adequate adversity, and lack of adequate coverage of a public law-oriented dispute by the particular parties who bring it to court, is especially keen in apportionment although not unique to this field. In the administrative law field there is concern for an analogous problem of inadequate representation of the "public interest." Some administrative and regulatory agencies have employed "public counsel" to represent interests of the using or consuming public. A "Public Counsel Section" was established in the Antitrust Division of the Department of Justice in 1961 to "represent the public interest in competition and in preservation of a free competitive economy." [44]

A continuing urgent need, well illustrated by the course of apportionment litigation, will be to be ever alert to frequent deficiencies in the adversary method as a device to elicit the full spectrum of data, and to illuminate the full range of conceptual choices, relevant to large public law

---

42. See, e.g., Brief for the United States as Amicus Curiae on Reargument, pp. 52, 54, Baker v. Carr, 369 U.S. 186 (1962). The brief treats Smiley v. Holm, 285 U.S. 355 (1962), so as to create in the mind of one unfamiliar with the facts of the case the misleading impressions that the Court had held that substantive federal standards on congressional districting by state legislatures were justiciable, and that the Court had ordered an election at-large. These misleading impressions are copied and magnified in *U.S. Commission on Civil Rights Report, Voting* I: 123, 128 (1961).
43. 372 U.S. 368 (1963).
44. Antitrust Division, Department of Justice, Directive No. 17, Nov. 2, 1961.

issues. Some might suggest that the need could be met by a formal process of "representing" the public interest through a special governmental office allied to or apart from the court system.[45] Hardly encouraging, however, is the transformation of the amicus or "friend of court" role of the Solicitor General of the United States into a position of near-advocacy of one party's cause of action.

The most fruitful approach, and most flexible, may be simply a judicial policy of relatively free intervention in public law suits stemming from awareness of the breadth of the issue, the differential impact of possible remedies, and the necessarily narrow focus of any one litigant. In the post-*Baker* era such awareness was perhaps best exemplified in the closely analogous field of congressional redistricting by the three-judge Maryland federal district court, led by retired Chief Judge Simon E. Sobeloff of the Fourth Circuit. The court held special hearings both at the Supreme Court building in Washington and in Baltimore to accommodate numerous interested parties, including the affected Congressmen themselves.

3. THE MERITS: "RATIONALITY" *v.* "REASONABLENESS"

Sharp differences between lower courts in substantive rulings on reapportionment standards in the interim between the Supreme Court's *Baker* pronouncement and the Court's pronouncement in its 1964 *Reapportionment Decisions* were grounded on the intrinsic ambiguity of the equal protection clause. As already noted, the clause has its "absolute" side in racial cases and its "relative" side in most other past cases. The issue was: to which line of precedents should legislative apportionment be allocated?

Perhaps the most relevant recent rule for guidance of the lower courts was the Supreme Court's 1961 holding in the packet of Sunday Closing cases, in which equal protection was one of the featured issues.[46] Exemptions of certain kinds of businesses and commodities from the Sunday Closing rule were challenged as constituting invidiously discriminatory classifications in violation of the equal protection clause. The Court up-

45. Senator Kefauver and a bipartisan group of 21 other Senators introduced a bill in 1961 to create a Department of Consumers to secure more effective federal representation of economic interests of consumers and to co-ordinate the administration of consumer services now scattered through the Department of Health, Education, and Welfare and the Department of Labor.

Following a Presidential Message to Congress on March 15, 1962, a Consumer Advisory Council was created informally in the Council of Economic Advisors. See Presidential Message, H.R. Doc. No. 364, 87th Cong., 2d Sess. (1962); White House Press Release for July 18, 1962; Council of Economic Advisors Press Releases for September 14, 1962, January 31, 1963, March 20, 1963, and March 25, 1963.

46. McGowan v. Maryland, 366 U.S. 420 (1961). See also Two Guys from Harrison-Allentown v. McGinley, 366 U.S. 582 (1961); Gallagher v. Crown Kosher Market, 366 U.S. 617 (1961); Braunfeld v. Brown, 366 U.S. 599 (1961).

held the classifications, finding twin purposes of avoiding interruption of health service and promoting the recreational atmosphere of the day. But whether health or recreation were in themselves valid legislative purposes, and thus supportive of the classifications, was simply assumed without discussion. Although health obviously may be conceded as a valid legislative purpose, only a small fraction of the statutory exemptions could be sustained on that ground alone. Under one state's law, Massachusetts, Sunday clamming was permitted but going after oysters was prohibited. To be honest about it, the Sunday Closing laws are essentially a legislative undergirding to what one commentator has called the "transformation of Sunday from a religious into a civil holiday" [47] for rest and relaxation. In the process, some Orthodox Jewish merchants and other Sabbatarians faced a cutback to a five-day week if they obeyed the commands both of their state and their religion. Nevertheless, Sunday Closing laws were sustained on the theory that classifications used did relate reasonably to valid governmental purposes of a health-recreation nature.

If the equal protection approach of the Sunday Closing cases were to be applied to apportionment, the formula would require an identification of the valid legislative purposes which the particularized and detailed apportionment rules (classifications) supported. In this process, if the underlying purposes in the apportionment classification systems were not self-evident—as health and recreation were thought to be in the Sunday Closing cases—which party should have the burden of proving their existence or nonexistence? And if plausible purposes could be shown, which party should bear the burden of showing whether the classifications are themselves reasonable, and reasonably related to the underlying reasonable purposes? Chief Justice Earl Warren's opinion in the leading Sunday Closing case, *McGowan v. Maryland*,[48] like the statements in other cases cited by him, speaks of a presumption that legislatures have acted within their constitutional power. If taken as the touchstone for apportionment litigation—and for a time some lower courts did take such an approach—the Warren formulation would seem to place upon the apportionment plaintiffs the burden of showing that particular apportionment rules could not be relevant to any conceivable valid legislative purpose. As Chief Justice Warren had phrased it: "A statutory discrimination will not be set aside if any state of facts reasonably may be conceived to justify it." [49]

As reapportionment litigation developed, however, the equal protection formulation of *McGowan* and other cases was "stood on its head." Some

47. Paul G. Kauper, *Civil Liberties and the Constitution*, 22 (Ann Arbor: University of Michigan Press, 1962).
48. 366 U.S. 420 (1961).
49. *Id.* at 426.

lower courts, and eventually the Supreme Court, reversed the formula just quoted from Chief Justice Warren and made most state apportionments prima facie *invalid* rather than prima facie *valid*.

The Michigan litigation provides a good example of this important shift in approach toward the restraint the equal protection clause imposes on state legislative discretion. Following *Baker* v. *Carr*, the Michigan Supreme Court invalidated the state senate and intervening legislators appealed to the United States Supreme Court. The Michigan Attorney General, nominally a defendant, opposed the appeal and asserted the unconstitutionality of his own state constitution's senate apportionment formula—a good example of the problem discussed earlier in this chapter of the problem of maintaining adversity in reapportionment litigation. His legal argument went as follows. He properly stated that a statute whose discriminations are so unreasonable that no conceivable fact situation could justify them must be nullified under the equal protection clause. He also stated the corollary rule that in all other instances the burden is on the *challenger* "to affirmatively demonstrate that in the actual state of facts which surround its operation" [50] the classification is unreasonable. He then asserted that Michigan's senate apportionment fell in the first category, i.e., it was so "patently without reason" [51] that the challenger did not have to bear a heavy burden of proof in order to overcome the presumption of constitutionality normally attaching to a state statute. For this last proposition, he relied on the concurring opinion in *McGowan* of Justice Felix Frankfurter.

This approach is a significant mischaracterization of Justice Frankfurter's position, as revealed by Frankfurter's actual *decision* in the Sunday Closing cases. It brings us right to the heart of the problem of equal protection as a constitutional standard in apportionment cases. The Sunday Closing laws were sustained despite obvious illogical differences in the exemption formulae, and differential impact on substantially similar commodities and types of business. They were sustained also even though, like apportionment cases, they border on civil rights, and thus are not readily allocable to the line of business regulation-equal protection cases in which the Court has looked kindly on legislative experimentation in economic affairs. The essence of Justice Frankfurter's position, which amplified but did not conflict with Chief Justice Warren's opinion for the Court in *McGowan*, is that "neither the Due Process nor the Equal Protection Clause demands *logical tidiness*. . . . It is enough to satisfy the Constitution that in drawing [lines of distinction] the *principle of reason* has not

50. Brief for James M. Hare, Secretary of State of the State of Michigan, Respondent, In Opposition, p. 21, Beadle v. Scholle and Hare, No. 517.
51. *Id.* at 28.

been disregarded." [52] With such elusiveness of principle, he also felt that evidence of divergent state practice is quite relevant in deciding where to draw the line of constitutional reasonableness.

The point at which the Michigan Attorney General, like Justice Clark in *Baker* itself, departed sharply from the main line of nonracial equal protection precedents exemplified by the Sunday Closing decisions was in confusing the concept of *rationality* with the principle of *reasonableness*. Although the departure is a sharp one, it apparently was unwitting because it was not and indeed never has been adequately rationalized.

It is true that Justice Frankfurter in his *McGowan* opinion did switch back and forth between ideas of "reasonableness" and of "rationality." But if one pushes beyond semantics to his core of meaning, it is obvious that he is talking about reasonableness of impact rather than strict logic or rational consistency in legislative distinctions and classifications.

An "irrational plan," i.e., illogical, unprincipled, possessed of internal inconsistencies, may have an effect that is not unreasonable. That is all the Constitution traditionally has required at the level of judicial review of public choice. This distinction between *constitutional reasonableness* and *logical rationality* (internal consistency in classification systems) is vital to an understanding of judicial handling of past equal protection cases like Sunday Closing law cases and others. In the immediate post-*Baker* period, courts which felt the distinction to be equally relevant to the intricate factual and conceptual difficulties involved in the theory and practice of representative government allowed more reapportionment freedom, including freedom to adopt a federal plan, than did those courts who followed a formulation like that suggested by Michigan's Attorney General.

Additional support for the proposition that burden of proof should be shifted to defenders of existing apportionment statutes was sought by suggesting an analogy to civil liberties and civil rights cases. Although there still is a dispute whether the "firstness of the First Amendment" requires a reversed presumption, i.e., a presumption of unconstitutionality of alleged governmental infringements on freedom, it is true that governmental restraints in this area receive little judicial support. For example, in one of the several cases in which states sought disclosure of the membership lists of the National Association for the Advancement of Colored People, the Court said that where "there is a significant encroachment upon personal liberty, the State may prevail only upon showing a subordinating interest which is compelling." [53]

The application of this statement to apportionment is not immediately

52. McGowan v. Maryland, 366 U.S. at 524 (emphasis added).
53. Bates v. Little Rock, 361 U.S. 516, 524 (1960).

obvious. The basic constitutional right—freedom of association—which underlay this NAACP case was already established. Also the "fact" that compelling disclosure would deter this freedom was deemed to be established by evidence submitted by the NAACP. The evidence showed that NAACP membership was harassed, restive, or declining. Only then did the burden of proof shift to the state to justify the disclosure requirement.

By contrast, in the apportionment cases after *Baker* (which had merely opened the courthouse doors), the nature and dimensions of a basic constitutional right in regard to representative government were not yet established. Alternatives, each requiring a supporting constitutional rationale, included the following: a right to strict numerical equality in district population for both legislative houses; a right to strict numerical equality in district population for one legislative house; a right to a minimum relation of gross population to representation in at least one house; a right to a formula in which population is the predominant factor in regard to both houses; a right to a minimum relation of party vote to party representation in at least one house; a right to some freedom of experimentation in apportionment formulae provided the formulae were subject to popular referendum and to revision by popular initiative. Given these varied alternatives, and the large corollary questions of representation theory and party-voter relation to party government which these alternatives suggest, it seemed appropriate to some lower courts [54] that the plaintiff articulate his theory of federal right and adduce proof in conventional terms, as in *McGowan*, to support his articulated theory.

4. RELEVANCE OR IRRELEVANCE OF POPULAR REFERENDA

"One man-one vote" is most closely achieved in statewide popular referenda on such things as proposed constitutional amendments—including possible new apportionment formulae. Assuming a common desire for apportionment systems which will produce a representative expression of popular will in such fashion as to approximate a direct expression of the popular will, these referenda would seem to have high evidentiary value, even if not dispositive of the constitutional issue. But in states where

54. In WMCA v. Lomenzo, 208 F. Supp. 368, 373 (S.D. N.Y. 1962), the court, in refusing to invalidate New York apportionment formulae, said: "The principle that there is a presumption in favor of the constitutionality of a statute and the principle that a violation must be clear before a federal court of equity will lend its power to the disruption of the state election process . . . have been re-enunciated in apportionment decisions rendered since the Baker v. Carr determination." The court cited Caesar v. Williams, 371 P. 2d 241 (Idaho 1962) *id.* at 373, Maryland Committee for Fair Representation v. Tawes, Md. Cir. Ct., Anne Arundel County, May 24, 1962, *ibid.*, and Toombs v. Fortson, 205 F. Supp. 248 (N.D. Ga. 1962).

such votes occurred they were not always viewed as weighty evidence in apportionment litigation. Michigan voters in 1952 were faced with two proposals regarding the state senate. They *rejected* one to reapportion the senate under a population principle; they *approved* one based on geographic distribution principle. Despite this background, the Michigan Supreme Court in 1962 invalidated the composition of the state senate.[55] In 1963, the voters then approved a new state constitution which again sought to continue some recognition of area in the state senate.

In Washington, a federal district court in December 1962, invalidated apportionment of the state legislature even though the voters, a month earlier, had rejected a new formula based more strictly on population. Referring to the defeat of the initiative measure, the court said it had no way of knowing whether people did not understand it, whether its opponents were better organized, whether the majority really did not desire reapportionment, or whether the majority did not approve the proposed method. But this line of speculation by the court turned out to be shadowboxing because the court went on to say: "It makes no difference. The inalienable constitutional right of equal protection cannot be made to depend upon the will of the majority." [56] By contrast, a federal district court in New York in 1962 refused to hold unconstitutional the state legislature, placing considerable stress on the fact that reapportionment had been made a major issue by Governor W. Averell Harriman in the unsuccessful 1957 referendum on the question of calling a constitutional convention.[57]

Post-*Baker* popular referenda in several other states frequently supported modified rather than absolutistic approaches to "one man-one vote"—e.g., Tennessee, Colorado, California, Oregon, and Nebraska. After the United States Supreme Court decision in *Baker*, the Tennessee legislature in special session made a tinker with the apportionment formula, which the federal district court then held inadequate and unconstitutional under the Fourteenth Amendment. The legislature received a grace period to June 1963 to make a further modification.[58] Concurrently, however, the legislature had put on the November 1962 ballot a proposal for a 1965 constitutional convention, delegates to be chosen on the same basis as legislators. The avowed aim was to have this convention propose a constitutional amendment to abolish the population formulae of the 1901 Tennessee Constitution (never implemented) and to substitute a federal plan of population emphasis in one house, political subdivision emphasis

55. Scholle v. Hare, 367 Mich. 176, 116 N.W. 2d 350 (1962).
56. Thigpen v. Meyers, 211 F. Supp. 826, 832 (W.D. Wash. 1962).
57. WMCA, Inc. v. Simon, 208 F. Supp. 368 (S.D. N.Y. 1962).
58. Baker v. Carr, 206 F. Supp. 341 (M.D. Tenn. 1962).

in the other house. The people approved the call of such a convention, 216,966–206,390.[59]

Colorado voters on November 6, 1962, had a choice of two reapportionment initiative measures. By substantial margins they approved a federal plan reapportionment, 305,700–172,725, and rejected a plan basing both houses on a population basis, 149,822–311,749.[60] California voters on November 6, 1962, rejected an initiative measure to abandon the federal plan and provide more representation for Los Angeles and other heavily populated counties, 2,181,758–2,495,440.[61] Oregon, by contrast, has had a population formula for apportionment of both houses since a successful 1952 initiative measure. On November 6, 1962, voters rejected a new initiative measure, 197,322–352,182, which would have kept population as the sole standard for the senate but added area to the lower house apportionment formula.[62] In Nebraska in 1962 the voters ratified a constitutional amendment designed to abandon the pure population principle for the unicameral legislature and substituted a formula in which area was to be weighed a minimum of 20 percent and a maximum of 30 percent.[63]

5. EMERGING LARGER REPRESENTATION ISSUES

Baker v. Carr thus did open a Pandora's Box concerning the requirements of democratic representation. As lower courts grappled with the problem, several large constitutional issues emerged.

Could there be room in republican concepts of American federalism for multiple concepts of representation?

Would popular referenda on apportionment questions, or relatively easy procedures for popular revision of apportionment formulae (which was not the case in Tennessee before *Baker*), either be controlling or of high evidentiary value?

Might there be a theory focused almost exclusively on population (as in Oregon) and co-existing a "federal plan" theory (as in California), focused mainly on political subdivisions? A federal plan operates, of course, not so much to diffuse political initiative as to create a partial minority veto, thus necessitating a broader base as a precondition of affirmative governmental action. It thus raises the issue of majoritarianism versus consensus as bases for public policy development.

Not all these questions were made academic by the Supreme Court's

59. 21 *Cong. Quart. Weekly Report* 429 (1963).
60. *Id.* at 425.
61. *Ibid.*
62. *Id.* at 427.
63. League of Nebraska Municipalities v. Marsh, 232 F. Supp. 411 (D. Neb. 1964).

1964 "one man-one vote" ruling. If new apportionment-districting systems, as reformed by "one man-one vote" judicial pressure, allow the minority party with some frequency to capture a *majority* of the seats, there would seem to be some deficiencies in the constitutional formulae used. Just such results did occur in the 1966 elections in some states. (See p. 462.)

6. VARIED PATTERNS OF ACTION

At least eight major patterns of action quickly emerged in lower court apportionment litigation in the first year or so after *Baker* v. *Carr.*

First, a small minority of courts refrained from ruling existing apportionment plans invalid on the ground that federal constitutional standards for a valid apportionment had not yet been clarified.[64] Because the only way to clarify federal constitutional standards is through litigation, these courts were in effect inviting courts in other states to be more adventurous and attempt to hew out guidelines for subsequent United States Supreme Court approval or rejection.

Far more common were the decisions conceding the invalidity of the existing apportionment systems but differing sharply on the scope of the invalidity and on the appropriate remedy. The essence of the problem for many courts was simply this. Deviations from mathematical equality in district population frequently were so great as to be invalid even under a fairly flexible constitutional standard. But it is one thing to invalidate "obvious" malapportionment districts; it is much more difficult to indicate what kinds of districts would be constitutionally valid. On this point there was no agreement even among the majority of courts who were disposed to take some action against the existing apportionment pattern.[65]

A *second* major pattern of action, therefore, and an appropriate one in view of the nature of this unique constitutional area, was to attempt to "pass the buck" back to the state legislatures under a mandate to act. In many cases the court declared the existing plan invalid because population deviations were too "extreme," without articulating the constitutional standard very clearly. It then retained jurisdiction and declared that it would consider the matter further unless the legislature enacted a reap-

---

64. *In re* Legislative Reapportionment, 374 P. 2d 66 (Colo. 1962); State *ex rel.* Lein v. Sathre, 113 N.W. 2d 679 (N.D. 1962); Mikell v. Rousseau, 183 A. 2d 817 (Vt. 1962).

65. Moss v. Burkhart, 220 F. Supp. 149 (W.D. Okla. 1963); Maryland Committee for Fair Representation v. Tawes, 180 A. 2d 656 (Md. 1962); 184 A.2d 715 (Md. 1962); Fortner v. Barnett, No. 59, 965 (Ch. Ct., 1st Jud. Dist., Hinds Co., Miss. 1962) (opinion set forth in 1 National Municipal League, *Court Decisions on Legislative Apportionment* (New York, 1962).

portionment plan within a reasonable period.[66] This approach had the seeming virtue of flexibility. However, without a clearer guideline than a command to avoid "extreme" deviations, some legislatures either deadlocked or made only modest changes in pre-existing apportionment patterns.

Third, some courts put greater pressure on the legislature by enjoining further use of existing apportionment formulae. With a few exceptions, however, courts were disinclined to enjoin use of existing apportionment patterns on the eve of an election even if the apportionment was felt to be unconstitutional.[67]

A *fourth* device, of limited utility because it rests on special circumstances, was for the court to construct an apportionment formula by using parts of different plans enacted by the legislature. The Alabama case, which subsequently became the leading case when the United States Supreme Court reached the merits in 1964, was handled in this fashion. The federal district court disapproved two reapportionment plans enacted by the legislature—one in statutory form, the other as a constitutional amendment. However, in order to reapportion Alabama in time for the November 1962 election the court then issued an interim reapportionment order. It modeled one house of the legislature on one of the two legislatively enacted plans, and the other house on the other plan. When Justice Hugo L. Black denied a stay pending appeal to the Supreme Court, the court's plan went into effect at once.[68]

Denial of a stay pending appeal in a reapportionment suit, it may be noted, obviously has a more serious impact on the issues than denial of a stay in ordinary litigation. Once a legislature has been elected under a revised apportionment plan, new forces arise which make it as impossible to restore the status quo ante as to unscramble eggs.

Fifth, courts have split sharply—in the immediate post-*Baker* period and also down to the present day—on the question whether a declaration of invalidity should be accompanied by specific directions to the legislatures. At least one court,[69] and by inference the Solicitor General of the United States, expressed the feeling that detailed directions would be in-

66. E.g., Baker v. Carr, 206 F. Supp. 341 (M.D. Tenn. 1962); Moss v. Burkhart, 207 F. Supp. 885 (W.D. Okla. 1962); Thigpen v. Meyers, 211 F. Supp. 826 (W.D. Wash. 1962); Sweeney v. Notte, 183 A. 2d 296 (R.I. 1962).
67. See e.g., Baker v. Carr, 206 F. Supp. 341 (M.D. Tenn. 1962); Moss v. Burkhart, 207 F. Supp. 885 (W.D. Okla. 1962); Thigpen v. Meyers, 211 F. Supp. 826 (W.D. Wash. 1962); Sweeney v. Notte, 183 A. 2d 296 (R.I. 1962). But see also Mann v. Davis, 213 F. Supp. 577 (E.D. Va. 1962).
68. Sims v. Frink, 208 F. Supp. 431 (M.D. Ala. 1962). Justice Black's stay of Sept. 25, 1962, was noted in Reynolds v. Sims, 377 U.S. 533, 553 (1964).
69. Mikell v. Rousseau, 183 A. 2d 817 (Vt. 1962).

appropriate. As the Solicitor General said in a brief: "To adjudicate the constitutionality of a specific plan that the legislature has not adopted would seem to run the risk of interference in the political process and to have many of the dangers of an advisory opinion." [70]

In several states, however, both federal and state courts have given detailed guidelines. Although the advisability of this practice may be questioned, as indicated above, giving guidance on permissible constitutional standards provides the outer boundaries within which legislative compromises and adjustments may operate. Firm guidelines invariably produce speedier legislative action. In California, for example, after many long months of reapportionment deliberation, the legislature in 1965 reapportioned within a month after the court fixed mathematical outer boundaries of a plan it would accept. The court specified that no district exceed the average size district by more than 15 percent, and that the electoral percentage be at least 48 percent.[71] (The electoral percentage, a fictional figure, is computed by ranking the districts for a given legislative house in order of size and then cumulating the population and the seats from the smallest districts upward until one-half plus one of the seats have been accounted for. See further discussion of reapportionment mathematics in Chapter XVII.)

This California case occurred after the Supreme Court in 1964 had indicated that the "one man-one vote" concept was a fairly rigid one in regard to legislative reapportionment. In the two-year period between *Baker* and the Supreme Court's pronouncement in 1964, almost no court thought the constitutional mandate should be this stringent. An exception was the federal district court in Oklahoma which in 1962 favored a "general principle of substantial numerical equality" [72] for both houses. More typically the Michigan Supreme Court, ruling on the state senate, felt population should be the basis but would allow deviations up to 100 percent, i.e., 2 to 1 disparity.[73] Many states felt that differential treatment of the two houses was permissible and in accord with traditional understandings about a bicameral legislative system. The federal district court in Delaware, for example, felt that if one house were on a fairly strict population basis, the population basis could be qualified somewhat in the other

70. Brief for the United States as Amicus Curiae, p. 62, Gray v. Sanders, 372 U.S. 368 (1963).
71. Silver v. Brown, 46 Cal. Reptr. 308, 405 P. 2d 132 (1965).
72. Moss v. Burkhart, 207 F. Supp. 885, 898 (W.D. Okla. 1962).
73. Scholle v. Hare, 367 Mich. 176, 116 N.W. 2d 350 (1962). The less-than-lucid opinion of the court can be interpreted as resting the 2 to 1 ratio on a state law ground, after first holding the then-existing formula invalid under the Fourteenth Amendment.

house.[74] In many states the courts approved, or indicated that they would approve, a pure or modified federal plan.[75]

Sixth, at least one court, again in Oklahoma, and before the Supreme Court in 1964 clarified the constitutional standards, itself imposed a reapportionment plan. The court had first entered a rather freewheeling "advisory order" to the legislature. The court removed the constitutional ceiling of seven legislators per county on lower house membership and said that Oklahoma and Tulsa Counties would be entitled to nineteen and fifteen house seats, respectively. But, without explaining why, it indicated it should respect the state constitution's limit on the size of the senate. When this advisory order failed to produce the desired response, the court in 1963 judicially reapportioned both houses on a population basis, the first post-*Baker* court to take such action.[76]

Seventh, although a judicial order for an election at-large of one or both legislative houses was often suggested as a remedy for malapportionment, it never eventuated. The single instance of an at-large election—the Illinois lower house in 1964—resulted not from a judicial order based on the federal Constitution but from a unique provision in the Illinois state constitution discussed in detail in Chapter XII.

Persons who have championed elections at-large of state legislatures have not thought through the problem of representative government. A shift to elections at-large abandons any pretense of representation, at least where state legislatures are concerned. It would be tossing the representation baby out with the equal protection bath. Every legislator would have the same statewide constituency as the governor, and a single large city could dominate. Proponents have sometimes said that a request for a judicial order for an at-large election is intended only as a device to pressure the legislature to reapportion—with no expectation that such an election actually be held. The defense fails for two reasons: an at-large election is too deficient a representation device even to flirt with as a sanction; an equally effective sanction, and one that would not destroy representation, would be a threat of judicial revision of the existing districts. Such a threat, explicit or implicit, underlay the action of a great many courts through the reapportionment litigation of the early and mid-1960s.

Explicit rejections of election at-large proposals occurred in at least a half-dozen states in the immediate post-*Baker* period. As one court said,

74. Sincock v. Duffy, 215 F. Supp. 169 (D. Del. 1963).
75. Toombs v. Fortson, 205 F. Supp. 248 (N.D. Ga. 1962); Baker v. Carr, 206 F. Supp. 341 (M.D. Tenn. 1962); Fortner v. Barnett, Ch. Ct., 1st Judic. Dist. Miss. 1962, reported in full in 1 National Municipal League, *Court Decisions on Legislative Apportionment* (New York, 1962); Sweeney v. Notte, 183 A. 2d 296 (R.I. 1962).
76. Moss v. Burkhart, 207 F. Supp. 885 (W.D. Okla. 1962); See Ch. XII.

such a reapportionment "would only cause chaos and confusion," and "would defeat the very object of this suit." [77] Although normally viewed as an advantage to the urban area, an election at-large could be adverse to the interest of an underrepresented urban section of the state if that section were not large or influential enough to control the election. For this reason the attorneys for the northern Virginia plaintiffs in the Virginia legislature case backed away from the election at-large remedy in their amended plea for judicial action. They feared the possibility that in an at-large election, liberal-oriented northern Virginia would have not merely inadequate representation but no representation.[78]

Use of elections at-large as a remedial device for state legislative malapportionment must be distinguished sharply from use of this device as a remedy for unequal congressional districts. Election at-large of a state's congressional delegation poses less serious representation issues, is authorized by Congress, and has occurred in the past.[79] An important representation function would remain, because each state would be represented in Congress through its entire delegation. The proper analogy at the national level to election of a state legislature at-large would be to elect *all* Congressmen at-large in the nation, ignoring state lines.

Eighth, weighted voting as a device for remedying state legislative malapportionment seldom received serious consideration although it was occasionally mentioned.[80] Under weighted voting a legislator would cast a vote in proportion to the size of his constituency. However, as discussed in detail in Chapter XIX, weighted voting in one form or another as a temporary or permanent measure was implemented for some county boards of supervisors in New York State. It was a means of complying

77. Fortner v. Barnett (Miss. 1962), reported in 1 National Municipal League, *Court Decisions on Legislative Apportionment* (New York, 1962).
See also *In re* Legislative Reapportionment, 374 P. 2d 66 (Colo. 1962); Opinion to the Governor, 185 A. 2d 111 (R.I. 1962); State v. Gage, 377 P. 2d 299 (Wyo. 1963); League of Nebraska Municipalities v. Marsh, 209 F. Supp. 189 (D. Neb. 1962); Brown v. State Election Board, 369 P. 2d 140 (Okla. 1962); Moss v. Burkhart, 207 F. Supp. 885, 891–92 (W.D. Okla. 1962).
78. Mann v. Davis, 213 F. Supp. 577 (E.D. Va. 1962). See Complaint, Plaintiffs' Trial Brief, pp. 2, 19, and letter to author from E. A. Pritchard, Fairfax, Virginia (Plaintiffs' Counsel; with Edmund D. Campbell, Washington, D.C.), March 6, 1963.
79. 2 U.S.C. § 2(c)(5) (1964): "Until a State is redistricted . . . (5) if there is a decrease in the number of Representatives and the number of districts in such State exceeds such number of Representatives, they shall be elected from the State at large."
E.g., Brown v. Saunders, 159 Va. 28, 166 S.E. 105 (1932); Smiley v. Holm, 285 U.S. 335 (1932). See discussion of these cases and others in Robert G. Dixon, Jr., "Legislative Apportionment and the Federal Constitution," 27 *Law and Contemporary Problems* 330, 340–47 (1962); Anthony Lewis, "Legislative Apportionment and the Federal Courts," 71 *Harv. L. Rev.* 1057, 1087–90 (1958).
80. Maryland Committee for Fair Representation v. Tawes, 228 Md. 412, 180 A. 2d 656 (1962).

with the "one man-one vote" requirement while at the same time preserving substantially intact the pre-existing ward and township representation districts. In one sense weighted voting is analogous to a multimember district system with the added requirement that the district delegation to a legislature act in unison.

In review, it may be noted that a flexible approach toward reapportionment mathematics, and the continued validity of a federal plan of apportionment, underlay several of the patterns of action summarized here. All were consistent with understandings of the meaning of *Baker* set forth in Justice Clark's concurring opinion—the only opinion to discuss reapportionment standards. This fact goes a long way toward explaining the surprise with which most observers greeted the Supreme Court's rather stringent pronouncement concerning the constitutional standards of apportionment in 1964.

7. APPORTIONMENT LITIGATION—THE "ACTIVIST" FORMULATION

Because minority process is commonly conceived not to be democratic process, all persons would agree that population merits a prominent place in a representation formula. This thought has been the proper starting point for many briefs and opinions on constitutional standards for apportionment. It is easy, however, to move from this starting point to a decisional formula deceptive in its simplicity under which all of the intricate and realistic aspects of apportionment and redistricting magically disappear. It was just such a formula that did tend to dominate reapportionment litigation up to and including the Supreme Court's basic pronouncement in the 1964 *Reapportionment Decisions.*

a. *The Numbers Game*

The decisional formula, slightly generalized, went as follows. Plaintiffs, using census data, made the following demonstrations: that numerical disparities existed in the population of districts having the same representation in the legislature; that the urban-suburban parts of the state did not have legislative seats proportionate to their population; that it would be theoretically possible for districts with a minority of a state's population to control a majority of seats in one or both houses.

This latter statistic, sometimes called the "electoral percentage," is obtained as already mentioned by ranking districts in order of population and by cumulating district population and seats from the least populous districts upward until a bare majority (one-half plus one) of legislative seats is accounted for. Thus, this measure, which is a kind of raw population measure and *not* an *electoral control* measure, ignores such factors as multiple candidacies, use of multimember and mixed districting systems rather than single-member districts, actual party deviations in each district, and the like—in short, the essence of representation.

Even as a bare mathematical "index of representativeness," with all the vital stuff of politics set aside, this approach must be used with great care. On this scale a 50 percent index is not just half-way home; it is a near-perfect score. Even with equal population districts the "minimum population-majority of seats" figure can never rise much above 50 percent unless there are only a handful of districts. For example, in a tiny legislature based on four single-member districts of 10,000 population each, the minimum population necessary to control a majority of seats (3) would be 30,000, yielding an index figure of 75 percent. But the figures are quite different if one assumes a conventional size legislature consisting for example of 100 single-member districts governing a 1,000,000 population area in which the "ideal" district size would be 10,000 (obtained simply by dividing the number of districts into the total population). If all districts were this size, the minimum population required to elect 51 legislators, a bare majority, would be 510,000 population, yielding an index figure of 51 percent. But since perfect equality in district population is neither possible nor required, it is instructive to compute the index figure for certain assumed population deviation standards. If each district's population varied by 25 percent (50 districts of 12,500 and 50 of 7,500), the index would be 38.8 percent. If each district varied by 5 percent (50 districts of 10,500 and 50 districts of 9,500) the index would be 48.55 percent. The index figures computed the same way for deviation maximums of 15 percent and 10 percent would be, respectively, 43.65 and 46.1.

It takes only a little thought and imagination to perceive that under this measure of rank-ordering districts by gross population to get an "electoral" percentage, every large American legislature has in the past been "elected" by a minority of the population. Most will continue to be "elected" by a minority of the population even if the maximum district population disparities be held to 5 percent.

Further, in a perfectly apportioned system with two parties of near-equal strength in all districts, the minimum effective legislative *control* percentage, in terms of voter behavior, never would be much more than 25 percent. In other words, assuming single-member districts and only two candidates, a party which gained one-half plus one of the popular *vote* in one-half plus one of the *districts* could control the legislature.

b. *Burden of Proof—"Rational Plan"*

In actual apportionment litigation courts nevertheless tended to take at face value the plaintiffs' simple mathematical proof in terms of numerical disparities and so-called "electoral" percentages. At least one house of virtually every state legislature in the nation showed substantial "minority" influence, if defined in terms of such arithmetic abstractions. Given this showing of population data by the plaintiffs, the typical court then stated that numerical disparities would be taken to prove invidious discrimination unless they could be explained as part of a "rational plan" of representation taking account of various nonpopulation factors. The influence of Justice Clark's concurring opinion in *Baker* is obvious. Next, and this was the critical point, the court shifted the burden of proof to the defenders of the apportionment to show a "rational plan." This the defenders had great difficulty in doing, and quite understandably. This approach to the burden of proof issue, reversing the presumption of constitutionality, was inconsistent with the burden of proof allocation discussed above in most past equal protection cases including the recent Sunday Closing cases.

Apart from burden of proof, a further question may be raised about this formulation. Is it feasible in regard to apportionment and districting to insist on a "rational plan"? By this term the courts seemingly have in mind a plan which is internally consistent with, and proceeds logically from, a set of identifiable and clear principles.

But how can there be a rational plan for the political process of compromise and adjustment, particularly in regard to an apportionment law which structures the very institution which is the focus of community conflict, and which law itself is a product of that institution? Legislation, unlike adjudication, is intrinsically "irrational" in the philosophic sense of the term, as students of government and jurisprudence know. Legislation is designedly a compromise process and therefore is "unprincipled" in not being logically derived from identifiable premises. It is impossible, and sometimes impolitic, to explain all of the "reasons" for the nature and wording of each item included and excluded from a bill, or to explain the reasons for rejection of major alternatives, or to explain the reasons for the Yes or No votes of each member and the reasons for his active or passive role at each stage of a measure. Judicial insistence on "rational plans" of apportionment confuses the reasoned process of adjudication where decisions are justified in written opinions—with the intricate process of multilateral negotiated settlements which characterize the political-legislative arena. Dean Phil C. Neal of the University of Chicago Law School was moved to characterize this combined burden of proof-"rational plan" approach as "mere sophistry" bordering on "winning without actually cheating." [81] Nevertheless, it was the dominant and winning formulation in the first years of the reapportionment revolution.

81. Phil C. Neal, "Baker v. Carr: Politics in Search of Law," 1962 *Supreme Court Review* 252, 287 (Chicago: University of Chicago Press, 1962).

8. THE PRE-REYNOLDS POSTURE IN THE LOWER COURTS: SUMMARY

During the interim period between *Baker* v. *Carr* in 1962 and the *Reapportionment Decisions* of June 1964, a wave of reapportionment litigation in both federal and state courts, affecting virtually every state, had begun to remake the political map of America. "Stand-patters" were few. The dominant pattern was the development of an equal population premise, i.e., that the districts for at least one legislative house should be of equal population. To win their cases, plaintiffs in many instances needed only to show district population inequalities. Then, as indicated above, a heavy burden of proof devolved on the state to rationalize all deviations from the equal population premise.

At least three crucial issues remained to be settled. One was the relation of the developing equal population premise to bicameralism. Did the Constitution require each house to be substantially a carbon copy of the other? Another issue was the relation of the equal population premise to popular referenda. Could popular approval in a statewide "one man-one vote" referendum supply the needed rationalization or justification for some departures from the equal population premise? A third issue concerned the definition of the equal population premise itself—i.e., how "equal" is "equal"? No one believed that absolute district population equality was feasible but there was little discussion of the breadth of this core concept of "equal" population districts.

Such questions were intertwined with the larger issue of balancing two conflicting elements in our heritage of democratic thought and practice, that is, the problem of adjusting the conflicting modes and values of majoritarian democracy with those of consensus democracy. In subsequent arguments before the Supreme Court, this larger question was pinpointed by contrasting statements of opposing counsel. Arguing for the plaintiffs in the Alabama case, Charles Morgan, Jr., said:

> The one standard that is measurable, leaving less room for doubt, is population. . . . This country's dream says the people should govern themselves. The courts are there to protect the minority from the majority, but surely the majority should have power in both branches of the legislature.[82]

Presenting the views of fifteen states, the First Assistant Attorney General of New Jersey, Theodore I. Botter, responded:

82. Quoted by James E. Clayton, "The Reapportionment Riddle," *The Reporter*, Feb. 27, 1964, p. 35.

Our view is that an intentional check on majority rule in both houses of a bicameral government is a rational objective for a state. Majority rule in both houses does not provide adequate protection for minorities. The minority should have bargaining power in one house.[83]

Also a part of this picture, though never given adequate analysis and recognition, is a third power center—the office of governor—which is concededly and properly majoritarian. In a state with traditional gubernatorial legislative leadership, the Botter position of asking that majoritarianism be tempered in one house really was a request for a check on a third, not a half, of the policy-forming process.

The dispute concerning the relation of the equal population premise to our conflicting heritages of majoritarian democracy and consensus democracy can be seen also as coinciding with an historic shift in popular conception of the role of government. The wave of the future, with a strong assist from the judiciary, may well be majoritarian. Slow, consensus democracy can perpetuate evils, and make a virtue of nonaction, as well as check precipitate action. Nevertheless, the past American tradition has been oriented strongly toward slow, consensus-creating arrangements designed to give minorities a defensive or bargaining position, or even veto power against bare numerical majorities. As of 1961, on the eve of *Baker v. Carr*, the formal apportionment formulae for thirty of the state senates and for thirty-four of the lower houses were based on factors other than a straight population principle. [See Chart No. 4, Chapter IV, pp. 86–87.]

They were oriented toward geographic diffusion, or a mixed population–political subdivision arrangement, accomplished through rules placing minimum or maximum limits on the number of representatives per county, coupled with fixed ceilings on the size of the legislature, and other special provisos. Whether or not Mr. Morgan was right about the "country's dream" for a straight population principle, the actual formulae embedded in state organic law, and thus representing a kind of policy choice, were much more complex.

83. *Id.* at 35–36.

VIII

The Court Invokes "One Man-One Vote"

"The conception of political equality from the Declaration of
Independence, to Lincoln's Gettysburg Address, to the Fifteenth,
Seventeenth, and Nineteenth Amendments can mean only one
thing—one person, one vote."

Justice William O. Douglas in *Gray* v. *Sanders*

". . . by focusing exclusively on numbers in disregard of the area
and shape of a congressional district as well as party affiliations
within the district, the Court deals in abstractions which will be
recognized even by the politically unsophisticated to have little
relevance to the realities of political life."

Justice John Marshall Harlan in *Wesberry* v. *Sanders*

"COUNTY UNITS" IN THE SUPREME COURT: GRAY *v.* SANDERS

In its most elemental connotation, the "one man-one vote" idea denotes simply the principle of *majority rule* in the filling of a *given* office
in a *given constituency*. In modern times the idea goes back at least to
Jeremy Bentham's maxim that "Each must count as one." [1] In these
five words the intrinsic difficulty in applying equality to legislative representation is subtly revealed; for the key word is "count." Although a minority should not rule, does it even "count" when its representatives are
too few to be heard, or are nonexistent? Does a voter "count as one"
when equal population districts—whether contrived carefully or casually

1. Consistent with his "greatest happiness of the greatest number" principle, Jeremy
Bentham, although writing before the broadening of English suffrage and consequent
rise of modern politics, strongly espoused what can be classified as a single-member,
equal population district principle, resting on universal suffrage. Writing also before
the rise of proportional representation concepts—although such concepts may be a
logical *practical* derivative of his "greatest happiness" principle—he had little to say
about effective political or minority representation. He did favor giving consideration to
the boundaries of pre-existing communities (e.g., counties, parishes) in devising legislative districts *unless* the resultant population inequalities would be "in an adequate
degree considerable." *The Works of Jeremy Bentham* III: 582, IX: 107, 109 (published
under the superintendence of his executor, John Bowring, New York: Russell & Russell,
1962).

—operate to convert bare pluralities into smashing victories sweeping nearly all seats? These difficult representation issues were not present, however, in the first case decided on "one man-one vote" grounds.

After *Baker v. Carr* [2] opened up the political thicket, the first United States Supreme Court invalidation of a state law because of conflict with an announced "one man-one vote" principle occurred in the Georgia "county-unit" case, *Gray v. Sanders*.[3] Attorney General Robert F. Kennedy made his debut before the Supreme Court in this case in March 1963. It was a major social event, the Kennedys in the courtroom outnumbering the Bench, 13 to 9. At the end of argument made by other counsel concerning constitutional issues, Mr. Kennedy appeared as amicus curiae to lend the weight of the government's prestige to the plaintiff's side of the case. He confined himself mainly to facts, leaving law and philosophy to others. But on the facts he gave a virtuoso performance, reciting columns of statistics from memory.

a. *The Electoral College Analogy*

The Georgia "county-unit" system, unsuccessfully challenged on four previous occasions,[4] was essentially a device for weighting votes for nomination of *statewide* officers, e.g., governor and United States Senators.[5] Its operation was roughly analogous to the electoral college system for weighting of votes by "state units" in presidential elections. For the presidency a

2. 369 U.S. 186 (1962).
3. 372 U.S. 368 (1963).
4. Cook v. Fortson, 329 U.S. 675 (1946); South v. Peters, 339 U.S. 276 (1950); Cox v. Peters, 342 U.S. 936 (1952) (appeal dismissed "for want of a substantial federal question"—Justices Black and Douglas dissenting); Hartsfield v. Sloan, 357 U.S. 916 (1958) (motion for leave to file petition for writ of mandamus denied—Chief Justice Warren and Justices Black, Douglas, and Brennan dissenting). The addition of the Chief Justice and Justice Brennan to the list of dissenters indicated the trend toward intervention.
5. The system of weighting voter strength by county units began with Georgia's first constitution in 1777 even before it became a state. The Neill Primary Act of 1917 made the plan applicable to all statewide political party primaries. Congressional elections in multicounty districts were brought in later. Ga. Code of 1933, Secs. 34-3212-34-3217 as modified, Acts of 1944, Ex. Sess. pp. 2 & 4. For a discussion of the system's operation, see Albert B. Saye, "Georgia's County Unit System of Election," 18 *Journal of Politics* 93 (1950).
The first attack on the system, Cook v. Fortson, 68 F. Supp. 624 (N.D. Ga., 1946), was by a plaintiff who had won the popular vote but not a majority of the unit votes in the fifth congressional district Democratic primary. An injunction against certifying his opponent's nomination was denied on the basis of Colegrove v. Green. See Brief for United States as Amicus Curiae, Gray v. Sanders, 372 U.S. 368 (1963), Appendix B.
A similar suit was brought regarding nomination of a governor by the candidate who had gained a plurality of the popular vote but lost the county-unit vote. Again, certification of the unit vote winner was allowed. Turman v. Duckworth, 68 F. Supp. 744 (N.D. Ga. 1946).

state's entire electoral vote is awarded under a "winner-take-all" custom to the candidate who obtains a popular vote plurality in the state. Similarly, to be elected governor of Georgia a candidate would have to capture a majority of the county-unit vote, each county's total unit vote being awarded on a winner-take-all basis to the candidate with a popular vote plurality in the county.

Any unit vote (winner-take-all) system can have a distorting effect because narrow popular vote pluralities can be magnified into clean sweeps of the crucial unit vote. But the distortion may be magnified considerably if the basic allocation of unit votes is not proportioned to population. Such a malapportionment of unit votes is a feature both of the state-unit electoral college system and Georgia's former county-unit system, but is less serious in the former. The electoral college system is population-based insofar as one electoral vote is allocated to a state for each seat in the population-based House of Representatives. Malapportionment results in two ways: first, a state receives a House seat, and a corresponding electoral vote, even though its population is below the national quota for a House seat; second, each state, no matter how small, has two Senators and two corresponding electoral votes.

In Georgia's county-unit system, however, there was a dramatic disparity between a county's population and the number of unit votes allocated to a county. At the time of *Gray*, the difference in Georgia between the weight of a citizen's vote in the most populous county (Fulton—556,226 population, 6 unit votes), and the weight of a citizen vote in the least populous county (Echols—1,876 population, 2 unit votes) was 99 to 1. By contrast, in the electoral college at that time, the equivalent disparity between a New York voter (16,782,304 population, 43 electoral votes) and an Alaska voter (226,167 population, 3 electoral votes) was 5 to 1.

In *Gray* the United States Supreme Court affirmed the federal district court's nullification of Georgia's county-unit system on the ground that it violated the equal protection of the laws clause of the Fourteenth Amendment. It rejected the unusual mathematical yardstick used by the district court—a yardstick made in Wonderland for Alice. In an effort to get a "judicially manageable standard," in the words of Justice William J. Brennan, Jr., in *Baker*,[6] the district court had suggested that no population-based allocation of voting power should be deemed unconstitutional if the disparity against any county was "not in excess of the disparity that exists against any state in the most recent electoral college allocation."[7] Such a rule would outlaw the 99 to 1 disparity which the district court

6. 369 U.S. 186, 217 (1962).
7. Sanders v. Gray, 203 F. Supp. 158, 170 (N.D. Ga. 1962).

faced in the *Gray* case but would permit disparities up to the electoral college disparity of 5 to 1.

As applied to congressional districts such a 5 to 1 ratio, based on electoral college disparities, would mean that citizens in a 1,000,000 population district would have no constitutional grounds for complaint if smaller districts were not less than 200,000. But prospects for relief would be considerably improved if there were a population boom in the smallest state, thus decreasing the electoral college 5 to 1 disparity!

In the United States Supreme Court, the district court's authorization of vote weighting up to the 5 to 1 electoral college ratio was replaced by a total prohibition on devices for weighting votes in a single constituency with a single office at stake. The Court did not merely require that the unit vote be properly proportionalized. It required total abolition of the unit vote practice and substitution of a simple state-at-large plurality rule. As explained in a footnote by Justice William O. Douglas:

> The county unit system, even in its amended form . . . would allow the candidate winning the popular vote in the county to have the entire unit vote of that county. Hence the weighting of votes would continue, even if unit votes were allocated strictly in proportion to population. Thus if a candidate won 6,000 of 10,000 votes in a particular county, he would get the entire unit vote, the 4,000 other votes for a different candidate being worth nothing and being counted only for the purpose of being discarded.

Given the nature of the issue in *Gray* v. *Sanders*, the Supreme Court's decision was eminently proper. *Gray* involved *not* legislative representation but a system whereby a popular vote winner could lose if he failed to capture enough counties to yield a majority of the county-unit vote—the unit votes themselves having been allocated to counties on a nonpopulation basis to exaggerate the strength of less populous counties. The opinion of the Court by Justice Douglas points out that the case "did not have anything to do with composition of the state or federal legislature." [8] The Court's focus was on the single-constituency nature of the *Gray* case and the essence of the ruling is captured in this sentence in the Douglas opinion:

> Once the *geographical unit for which a representative is to be chosen* is designated, all who participate in the election are to have an equal vote—whatever their race, whatever their sex, whatever their occupa-

8. Gray v. Sanders, 372 U.S. 368, 378 (1963).

tion, whatever their income, and wherever their home may be in that geographical unit.[9]

In this context, one person, one vote was to be the rule.

b. *The Political Theory of Gray*

The political theory of *Gray* is simply the theory of popular control of governmental officers. The prize of office in a given constituency should go to the man who has a majority or a plurality in the equally weighted votes cast by politically equal citizens in the constituency to be served. Put another way, the case raised the question whether an officeholder should be the most popular man in the entire constituency or the man with maximum appeal to the maximum number of artificially weighted geographical units within the constituency. The Court answered that the election should be simply a popularity contest, not a mystic search for a lowest common denominator of *statewide* acceptance. The continuance of a "unit vote" weighting device in the electoral college was alluded to by the Court. But it felt that "this conception of political equality belongs to a bygone day"; its validation for the presidency, by being specifically included in the Constitution, provided no measure of state duty under subsequently enacted constitutional amendments which yield the new conception of "one person, one vote." [10]

The Georgia county-unit case was an especially convenient case in which to announce the "one person, one vote" rule, not only because the case involved the simplest kind of election issue but because Georgia was the only errant state. The Maryland unit rule device, which likewise fell by force of the Court's ruling, applied only to the Democratic party nominations.[11]

Justice John Marshall Harlan dissented, finding the record inadequate, and would remand for proof of the invidious effect alleged to flow from the county-unit system, saying:

> I do not understand how, on the basis of these mere numbers, unilluminated as they are by any of the complex and subtle political factors involved, a court of law can say, except by judicial fiat, that these disparities are in themselves constitutionally invidious.[12]

9. *Id.* at 379 (emphasis added).
10. *Id.* at 377, n. 8.
11. Maryland Committee for Fair Representation v. Tawes (consolidated with Culotta v. Rinehart), D. Md., No. 14, 452, May 10, 1963, unreported. Order was by agreement of parties, under rule of Gray v. Sanders. For a discussion of the operation of the system, see Robert S. Friedman, "The Maryland County Unit System and Urban-Rural Politics," Bureau of Government Research Pamphlet (College Park: University of Maryland, 1957).
12. 372 U.S. at 388 (Harlan, J., dissenting)

This comment may be appropriate in the context of *legislative representation* because of the complexities of districting and the ease with which districts even of equal population can be arranged to exaggerate the partisan strength of one group and minimize the strength of another. But it is difficult to see what enlightenment could flow from further proof in a nonrepresentation case like *Gray v. Sanders.*

Although the catch-phrase "right to vote" has on occasion been abused by the Court in legislative representation cases as a way of concealing the "subtle political factors involved," *Gray* was very close to being a simple "right to vote" case and hence the true home of a "one person, one vote" slogan. In a contest for a single office, why should not the front-runner in the popular vote win? This is all that was involved in *Gray v. Sanders.* In the American democratic tradition the customary answer has been that the front-runner should win because of the impossibility of ever getting unanimity, and the likelihood that control of the many by the few could result from more complicated choice systems.

THE SOLICITOR GENERAL'S ROLE IN BAKER AND IN GRAY

No review of the development of the "one man-one vote" principle in the Supreme Court from *Baker v. Carr* through *Reynolds v. Sims* would be complete without recognizing the role played by the Solicitor General of the United States, Archibold Cox. His briefs and participation in oral argument as amicus curiae tended to shape the Court's perception of the issues and indeed to dominate the litigation at certain stages.

a. Baker v. Carr

In *Baker v. Carr*, as noted earlier in Chapter VI, it was the Solicitor General, rather than the plaintiffs of record and their counsel, who helped the Supreme Court to conceptualize the basis of a federal constitutional right to challenge state apportionment systems. Whereas the plaintiffs relied on a novel and never accepted theory that a violation of a population apportionment principle stated in a state's own constitution somehow also constituted a violation of the Fourteenth Amendment, the Solicitor General largely ignored the state constitution. He focused on Tennessee's actual practice of population malapportionment, and asserted a basic Fourteenth Amendment right to be "free from gross discrimination in the selection of a state legislature." This approach—the approach accepted by the Court —envisions a uniform federal yardstick applicable to all states.

The basic premise of the Solicitor General's *Baker* brief was that "surely the starting point must be *per capita* equality of representation." [13]

13. Brief for the United States as Amicus Curiae on Reargument, Baker v. Carr, p. 26.

And yet the Solicitor General in 1961 seemingly contemplated the continuation of a quite large degree of local apportionment discretion within the initial premise of per-capita equality—a range of discretion which the Solicitor General progressively narrowed in devising arguments against the constitutionality of less egregious plans in subsequent cases. Tennessee's apportionment at issue in *Baker* deviated so markedly from a population basis, and was so marked by irrational treatment of seemingly similar districts, that even a loose equality concept could achieve the result of invalidation.

The Solicitor General therefore could suggest the following rather flexible approach in *Baker*—an approach he altered considerably in arguing later against Colorado's apportionment plan, in which population deviations were relatively small, and in which a statewide popular majority had approved the plan and could modify it at will by state initiative process: "The Fourteenth Amendment reaches at least those *egregious* cases in which geographical or other discrimination *imposed by a minority* lacks a rational foundation." [14] In similar vein, he suggested a number of criteria which could justify some population inequality in apportionment, such as a concern for political subdivision representation, which also automatically serves the "interest in geographical distribution of political power." [15] "Constitutional statecraft," he said, "often involves a degree of protection for minorities which limits the principle of majority rule." [16] This is a fundamental reason for not electing an entire state legislature at-large.

Indeed, the Solicitor General's championing in his *Baker* brief of the possible continuation of much state apportionment discretion provided one of the more amusing aspects of the crucial "one man-one vote" decisions of 1964. Justice Stewart, dissenting in the Colorado and New York cases in 1964, was able with a straight face and in all good conscience to feature in his dissent a long quotation from the Solicitor General's *Baker* brief on the virtues of some limitation on the principles of majority rule, including even some reduction of the weight of votes in great cities so that they would not become political monoliths totally dominating a 30 percent rural minority.

In short, in his *Baker v. Carr* brief, the Solicitor General discussed not only the basic issue of justiciability but also the possible content of appropriate constitutional standards. The general tone of his brief was reassuring, suggesting that a reapportionment judicial bath would not be so bad after all where apportionments like those at issue in Tennessee were pre-

14. *Id.* at 44 (emphasis added).
15. *Id.* at 29.
16. *Ibid.*

sented. Undue thwarting of majority feeling and of urban interests—particularly in Southern legislatures—was long overdue for correction. And there still could be much play in the joints for arrangements, perhaps even including a federal plan, which might serve to give geographic or other minorities a voice beyond their numbers in one part of the total legislative process.

b. Gray v. Sanders

Once *Baker* v. *Carr* had terminated the political question doctrine in state legislative apportionment, the invalidation of Georgia's county-unit system for nomination and election to statewide office was a foregone conclusion. The simple issue in the Georgia county-unit case was whether or not the majority principle should control nominations for such statewide offices as governor and United States Senator or whether the state should be allowed to continue the practice of allocating much greater weight to some votes than to others. Because the suit involved only voter equality inside a single constituency, and not legislative representation of voters divided into many constituencies, the suit had no necessary relation—indeed, no *logical* relation—to the issue of legislative apportionment.

Gray was a suffrage case, not a representation case. Nevertheless the Solicitor General in his *Gray* v. *Sanders* amicus brief, in fusing and confusing the two issues by inadvertence or design, did lay a foundation for his future, more stringent amicus briefs on legislative apportionment. He said:

> In addition, they [Georgia's county-unit rules for statewide office] bear upon the distinct, but related, problem of the standards which should govern in determining whether the malapportionment of seats in legislative bodies is valid under the Fourteenth Amendment. Thus, this case involves issues of great importance to millions of American citizens seeking full and fair participation in their federal and state governments.[17]

There were some corollary inconsistencies in the shaping of his argument in the *Gray* brief. In *Baker* the Solicitor General had said that "recognition of geographic and other minority interest is also a comprehensible reason for reducing the weight of votes in great cities."[18] He also had said that "constitutional statecraft often involves some limitation on the principle of majority rule"[19] for the protection of minorities.

By contrast, in *Gray*, where he conceded that the county-unit system proceeded from an "intelligible plan" in discriminating against voters in

17. Brief for the United States as Amicus Curiae, Gray v. Sanders, pp. 3–4.
18. Brief for the United States as Amicus Curiae on Reargument, Baker v. Carr, p. 30.
19. *Id.* at 29.

the larger and more populous counties, he argued for unconstitutionality under the absolute principle that *any* plan which reduces the weight of some votes in order to protect minorities by limiting the principle of majority rule is intrinsically unconstitutional:

> The fundamental answer is that our basic democratic ideals forbid the notion that any particular "community of interest" should be accorded greater voting strength than the number of people comprising the community warrants.[20]

This new stress on straight nose-counting is clearly inconsistent with the proposition in the Solicitor General's *Baker* brief that "constitutional statecraft" involves some vote weighting to protect minorities. The inconsistency is all the more apparent in the light of the Solicitor General's insistence that the county-unit issue was closely related to the state legislative apportionment issue.

Of course, there is no inconsistency *if* the one statement is related solely to those problems of fair representation and of minority representation which complicate *legislative apportionment,* and if the other statement is related solely to the issue of *county-unit weighting* in a statewide election. On the facts of *Gray* it does make sense to insist that no "community of interest" should be accorded weighted votes in excess of its numbers because such a practice would denigrate majority rule in its most simple context and open the way to election of a minority governor. The explanation for commingling these two diametrically opposed concepts is either that the Solicitor General did not perceive that *Baker* v. *Carr* was a representation case and that *Gray* v. *Sanders* was merely an election-to-office case, or that the muddled brief in *Gray* was designed to lay a foundation for abandoning his earlier moderate statements in the *Baker* brief on voter equality in legislative apportionment.

Some parts of the Solicitor General's *Gray* v. *Sanders* brief make sense solely in the context of legislative apportionment, e.g., his discussion of the "inevitable lack of mathematical precision," [21] under the equal protection and due process clauses. Treating as one matter both "legislative apportionment" and the "electoral process" (the latter term encompassing Georgia's county-unit system), he suggested for the Court two minimal principles of unconstitutionality: any apportionment or electoral system should be deemed unconstitutional (1) if it produced divergence in voting power "defying any intelligible explanation" or (2) had the effect of imposing "an extreme and invidious discrimination against any class of voters." [22] Whatever merit these two rules may have in regard to state

20. Brief for the United States as Amicus Curiae, Gray v. Sanders, p. 18.
21. *Id.* at 39.
22. *Id.* at 40–41.

legislative apportionment, they are highly inapropos as applied to the electoral system (i.e., Georgia's county-unit system). They clearly suggest that vote weighting *is* permissible even in a single constituency election for a single office if the vote weighting is not "extreme" or has an "intelligible explanation"!

The anomalous nature of the Solicitor General's brief in *Gray*—nominally arguing *county-unit* but seemingly using the case as a vehicle to instruct the Court and the country on possible standards of fair *legislative apportionment*—emerges starkly when his brief is contrasted with that filed in the Supreme Court on behalf of the plaintiffs. Appealing from their defeat in the district court, the plaintiffs perceptively characterized their case as one involving the "franchise, not legislative representation." Representation, they noted, is "a shared right," [23] whereas voting is a "personal right." Their suit, they said, involved *only* voting and *not* representation. Their sharp distinction of representation as a flexible shared right and voting as an absolute personal right, in contrast to the Solicitor General's intermixture of the two in the loose phrase "legislative apportionment and the electoral system," was phrased thusly:

> A Court seeking to apply Equal Protection standards to *representation cases* must perforce fashion standards and other possible but reasonable criteria. There is no other way except to decree the end of all districts and to require state-wide elections.
>
> No such difficulties are presented in *franchise* cases. The relief prayed in such a case is simple: Abolish or forbid the utilization of the contrived step by which the *normal* popular tabulations are converted into a weighted and distorted result.[24]

In these few lines is condensed the central conceptual issue which has bedeviled legislative apportionment litigation since *Baker v. Carr*. In *franchise cases*, a voter has an absolute right to equality. *Representation cases* are not franchise cases. But the instinctive inclination in many briefs and opinions to treat the two as one fostered a strong tendency to import the absolute equality principle, which is necessary as a democratic postulate in the franchise cases, into the quite different field of representation cases. As the litigation developed, the Court needed help on this crucial distinction but little help was forthcoming either in the parties' briefs or in the briefs of the nominal friend of court—the Solicitor General. A confusion of franchise issues and representation issues continued also despite the concurring opinion in *Gray v. Sanders* filed by Justices Potter Stewart and Tom C. Clark, amplifying the Douglas opinion, in which they prop-

23. Brief for Appellee, Gray v. Sanders, pp. 8–10.
24. *Id.* at 10.

erly characterized the issue and stated the narrow rule of the case thusly: "*Within a given constituency* there can be room for but a single constitutional rule—one voter, one vote." [25]

CONGRESSIONAL DISTRICTS IN THE SUPREME COURT: WESBERRY *V.* SANDERS

After *Gray* v. *Sanders* "one man-one vote" was well on its way, and little notice was taken of the fact that *Gray* did not involve any of the fair representation problems associated with legislative apportionment and districting. The second application of the "one man-one vote" principle to invalidate a state law occurred in another Georgia case, *Wesberry* v. *Sanders*.[26] Because the issue was congressional districting, the range of issues, both in terms of representation theory and districting practice, was again simpler than the full range of issues posed in state legislative reapportionment. "One man-one vote" again triumphed. Despite Justice Harlan's cogent dissent it is again difficult to conceive of any more appropriate decision, assuming that the issue was to be treated as justiciable, and assuming that "one man-one vote" was to mean an equal population *premise* as in modern Great Britain and postwar Germany, and not an equal population *absolute*.

In *Wesberry* the plaintiffs were voters in a congressional district encompassing Atlanta which at that time was the second most underrepresented congressional district in the nation. (The most underrepresented was the Dallas district, where Texas Democrats had bottled up almost a million people—with a Republican majority—in one district.) The Atlanta district (823,680) was not only three times larger than Georgia's smallest district (272,154) but was more than double the quota (394,312) for an "ideal" or average district. It contained approximately one-fifth of Georgia's population but had only one-tenth of the Congressmen.

Plaintiffs had entered the federal district court relying both on the Fourteenth Amendment's equal protection clause and on Article I, Section 2, which provides that Representatives shall be elected "by the People" and shall be apportioned among the states "according to their respective Numbers," i.e., population. Their primary reliance, however, was on the equal protection clause as enlivened by *Baker* v. *Carr* and by *Gray* in which the same federal district court had just invalidated Georgia's county-unit system.[27]

25. 372 U.S. 368, 382 (1963) (Stewart, J., concurring) (emphasis added).
26. 376 U.S. 1 (1964).
27. Sanders v. Gray, 203 F. Supp. 158 (N.D. Ga. 1962) (Bell, Circuit Judge for the Court, joined by Tuttle, Circuit Judge and Hooper, District Judge); Wesberry v. Vandiver, 206 F. Supp. 276 (N.D. Ga. 1962) (Bell, Circuit Judge for the court,

The *Wesberry* plaintiffs, unlike the *Gray* plaintiffs, suffered an immediate dismissal. But the court's opinion was so confusing that in the subsequent appeal to the United States Supreme Court the plaintiffs, the defendants, and the Solicitor General as amicus curiae had three separate theories of what had happened in the district court, and what kind of relief the Supreme Court should consider. More striking is the fact that the clause on which the Supreme Court relied exclusively for its ruling applying "one man-one vote" to congressional districts—Article I, Section 2—was barely mentioned by the district court, was treated but not exhaustively in the appeal briefs of plaintiff, was ignored by the defendant and Solicitor, and was not elaborated in oral argument. What had been litigated primarily as a Fourteenth Amendment case became exclusively an Article I, Section 2 case in the Supreme Court conference room. In view of the novelty of reliance on Article I, Section 2, it would have been well to re-schedule the case for briefing and oral argument on this issue. To the extent a court reaches a decision on facts or constitutional principles not adequately aired by the parties the adversary method, and perhaps even the "right to be heard," is weakened.

The confusion in the district court's *Wesberry* opinion is a product of *Colegrove* v. *Green's* [28] complexities, which *Baker* of course left untouched because *Baker* dealt only with state legislative apportionment and not congressional districting. In *Colegrove*, it will be recalled, four members of a seven-man Bench agreed on dismissal. But Justice Wiley B. Rutledge's crucial vote rested apparently on a theory of temporary "want of equity," and Justice Felix Frankfurter's opinion for himself and two others was internally ambiguous. Frankfurter suggested both a total lack of judicial jurisdiction (exclusive constitutional commitment of congressional districting to Congress), and a theory of nonjusticiability (judicial self-restraint in entering the "political thicket" even though the Court had power to enter if it wished).

The district court voted 2 to 1 to dismiss for "want of equity" the challenge to Georgia's congressional districts but produced a very odd opinion. The court neither made clear its conception of "want of equity" nor refrained from discussing the merits in some detail. On the merits, the district court made the factual observation that in population terms Georgia's districts were "grossly out of balance." Without analyzing the substantive meaning of either the equal protection clause of the Fourteenth Amendment, or the chosen "by the People" language of Article I, Section 2, the court referred in offhand fashion to "fundamental political concepts

joined in by Morgan, District Judge, with Tuttle, Circuit Judge, concurring in part and dissenting in part).
28. 328 U.S. 549 (1946).

inherent in a republican form of government." [29] However, as a legal matter it said it would not find "proscribed invidiousness" [30] because timely relief might come through statutory redistricting now that *Baker v. Carr* was shaking up the Georgia legislature. The court then slid into a muddled discussion of *Colegrove*, stressed the point that Congress' concurrent authority to redistrict made the matter politically delicate, repeated the point that timely relief might soon be forthcoming from political channels, and dismissed because "no cognizable constitutional claim is presented under these facts." [31] Small wonder that this welter of conflicting statements left all parties puzzled. The talk of political delicacy smacked of intrinsic nonjusticiability. But the stress on prospects for alternative relief from political organs smacked of "want of equity" in the sense of temporary judicial abstention.[32]

a. *Oral Argument*

On appeal to the Supreme Court the plaintiffs sought a reversal of the district court's "want of equity" dismissal of their suit *and* an immediate order barring further use of the existing districts. Plaintiffs argued that the district court's actual discussion of the facts obviated any need for further hearing. The state attorney general naturally supported the district court's dismissal, and his brief provided a clearer rationale for this position than did the federal district court's opinion. The state stressed "Georgia's new political climate" [33] and asked for judicial abstention, at least for the time being. The third viewpoint was provided by the United States Solicitor General as amicus. He alone took the position that the district court had not effectively reached the merits, and suggested merely a remand to the district court with direction to proceed to a determination of the merits. His brief therefore did not continue his dialogue with the Court on "one man-one vote" theory which he had begun in *Baker* and continued in *Gray*. As a consequence his assistant who argued the case had a difficult time in oral argument because the Court—impelled by agreement of both plaintiff and defendant that the district court had in effect reached the merits—desired to reach the merits too.

The resulting dialogue between an insistent Supreme Court Bench and an assistant who desperately needed further guidance from the Solicitor General on how far to get into the merits, provided one of the more

---

29. 206 F. Supp. at 282.
30. *Ibid.*
31. *Id.* at 286.
32. For the most detailed and provocative discussion of *Wesberry*, see Note, "Wesberry v. Sanders: Deep in the Thicket," 32 *Geo. Wash. L. Rev.* 1076 (1964).
33. Brief for Appellees, Wesberry v. Sanders, p. 35.

amusing sequences in the course of the "one man-one vote" oral arguments. At least three members of the Bench—Justice Harlan, followed by Justice Hugo L. Black and Chief Justice Earl Warren—wanted to know whether or not Congress itself would have power to provide *directly* for unequal population congressional districts. The inference was that if the answer were "yes," one way Congress could exercise such power was to allow the states to set up unequal districts. Not wanting to say "no" and leave no reserve power in Congress, or say "yes" and undercut the plaintiff's case on the merits, the Solicitor's spokesman had a difficult time. He finally sought protective cover under the principle that the Solicitor General usually defends, rather than attacks, the constitutionality of congressional statutes!

The Court's interrogation was directly relevant, of course, to the question of whether a congressional statute allowing a specified percentage deviation in congressional district population—e.g., 10 or 15 percent—would be conclusive on the constitutional issue. Although such bills were introduced in Congress immediately after the decision in *Wesberry*, final action was delayed. The post-*Wesberry* judicially impelled equalization of the nation's congressional districts proceeded therefore without guidance or hindrance from Congress—and the Court did not have to face the issue it wondered about in the *Wesberry* oral argument.

b. *The Constitutional Text and the Alternatives*

In *Wesberry* the Supreme Court had to take as a "given" the fact that the apportionment of Congress is clearly fixed in the Constitution. The Constitution provides for a federal plan of weighting states equally in the Senate (Article I, Section 3) and even places the Senate formula beyond reach of the amending process by providing in Article V that "no state, without its consent, shall be deprived of its equal suffrage in the Senate." It also provides (Article I, Section 2) for state representation in proportion to population in the House of Representatives, qualified by a guarantee to each state of a minimum of one seat. The question of differential apportionment bases for the two houses of a bicameral legislature, therefore, was not at issue in *Wesberry* and seemingly could not be. The narrow issue that was left open, and one on which the Constitution was silent, was whether the *intrastate districting* of House seats had to be on a fairly tight equal population basis.

The two constitutional clauses primarily relevant to the issue are on the surface relatively simple. Article I, Section 2 provides for an apportionment of Representatives to the states on a modified population basis, adding three-fifths of the slaves and guaranteeing each state at least one seat. It also provides for popular election of Representatives by the same electorate the state uses for election of the larger body of its state legislature. It reads in pertinent part as follows:

> Section 2. The House of Representatives shall be composed of Members chosen every second Year by the People of the several States, and the Electors in each State shall have the Qualifications requisite for Electors of the most numerous Branch of the State Legislatures . . . . Representatives and direct Taxes shall be apportioned among the several States which may be included in this Union, according to their respective Numbers, which shall be determined by adding to the whole Number of free Persons, including those bound to Service for a Term of Years, and excluding Indians not taxed, three fifths of all other Persons . . . . The Number of Representatives shall not exceed one for every thirty Thousand, but each State shall have at Least one Representative. . . .

Article I, Section 4 vests power over election regulations in the states, subject to an overriding supervisory power in Congress. It reads as follows:

> Section 4. The Times, Places and Manner of holding Elections for Senators and Representatives, shall be prescribed in each State by the Legislature thereof; but the Congress may at any time by Law make or alter such Regulations, except as to the Places of chusing Senators.

In addition Section 5 provides that each house "shall be the Judge of the Elections, Returns and Qualifications of its own Members. . . . "

Apart from the Constitution, and viewed simply as a "1964 political theory issue," the decision in favor of an equal population rule for intrastate congressional districting has much appeal. The Senate half of Congress is apportioned on a nonpopulation, political subdivision basis, coupled with an at-large election system. The other half, the House of Representatives, is apportioned substantially on a population basis except for the guarantee of one seat to each state regardless of population. Traditionally, with minor exceptions, Congressmen are elected by districts rather than at-large. In this context is it not reasonable to relate the districts closely to population, so that the House delegation perhaps may better represent the various views in the state and better reflect the breadth of support for these views?

One might attempt to rationalize such a flat equal population districting requirement by finding that such was the clear historical intent of the framers. Alternatively, one might attempt to deduce it logically from supposed purposes to be served by the basic mandate that seats be apportioned to the states in the first instance on a "numbers" basis, subject to the qualifications noted.

c. *Justice Black—Historian for the Court*

Justice Black, in keeping with his preference for "clear meanings" and constitutional absolutes, attempted the first course in his opinion for a majority of six. In the view of at least one well-recognized historical scholar, Professor Alfred H. Kelly, he succeeded only at the price of substantially rewriting history.[34] It is not at all clear that the framers Black quotes were thinking of intrastate districting which was the sole issue in *Wesberry*. It *is* clear that most of the framers' discussion concerned the large issue of equal state weight in the Senate and state weight by population in the House. And even the Great Compromise which led to the use of population as the measure for apportioning House seats among the several states was qualified. As Justice Harlan noted in his dissent, the pure population principle was limited not only by the guarantee of one Representative per state but also by the decision to add three-fifths of the slaves to each Southern state's population. The latter provision made every Southern citizen's vote worth more than the vote of every Northern citizen until 1860.

The historical basis for Justice Black's opinion—the only basis offered by Black—has been characterized as follows by Professor Kelly:

> To put the matter bluntly, Mr. Justice Black, in order to prove his point, mangled constitutional history. The quotations from the debates of the Convention on which he builds—Mason, Madison, Wilson, Paterson, Franklin, Sherman, C. C. Pinckney, and so on—are all real enough, but they have to do with the great debate in the Convention between the proponents of state equality in the legislature and the advocates of what Madison called "proportionate representation" as between the states. They have nothing at all to do with the question of representation within the states . . . .
>
> As if to compound his historical felony, Mr. Justice Black then proceeded to identify "people" as used in the theoretical compact sense . . . with the notion of a pure democratic electorate—a compounding of the confusion that Madison undoubtedly would have greeted with equal parts of astonishment and laughter. Having thus rewritten constitutional history to his own satisfaction and thereby established a new historical myth with respect to the aboriginal meaning, Mr. Justice Black was able to maintain something of the concept of constitutional continuity even while quietly consigning *Colegrove* and other embarrassing apportionment precedents to the trash barrel of dead constitutional law. Perhaps a constitutional historian may be forgiven

34. Alfred H. Kelly, "Clio and the Court: An Illicit Love Affair," in *1965 Supreme Court Review* 119 (Philip B. Kurland, editor, Chicago: University of Chicago Press, 1965).

if he views the entire performance with some astonishment, not un-
mixed with admiration for the Court's creative historical imagination.[35]

In short, to muster historical evidence from the records of the Philadelphia Convention Justice Black had to distort and take out of context
various comments.[36] And yet Max Farrand has indicated that the basic
records themselves are subject to serious question because of inaccurate
and incomplete recordation of the three primary sources of information:
the notes of James Madison, the notes of Robert Yates, and the *Journal
of the Convention*. The matter has been summarized as follows:

35. *Id.* at 135–36. Professor Kelly some years ago had tried to help Thurgood Marshall
(later Solicitor General under President Lyndon Johnson and then an Associate Justice
of the United States Supreme Court) find an historical basis for the NAACP's school
desegregation litigation which finally achieved victory in 1954 in Brown v. Board of
Education. In a let-your-hair-down speech at the American Historical Association's
1962 annual meeting Professor Kelly subsequently admitted having more than a few
doubts about his reconstruction of the "original meaning" of the Fourteenth Amendment in reference to schools for the purpose of the NAACP suit. He said:

> I am very much afraid that for the next few days I ceased to
> function as a historian, and instead took up the practice of law
> without a license. The problem we faced was not the historian's
> discovery of truth, the whole truth and nothing but the truth;
> the problem instead was the formulation of an adequate gloss on
> the fateful events of 1866 sufficient to convince the court that
> we had something of a historical case . . . . It is not that we
> were engaged in formulating lies; there was nothing as crude and
> naive as that. But we were using facts, emphasizing facts, bearing
> down on facts, sliding off facts, quietly ignoring facts, and
> above all interpreting facts in a way to do what Marshall said we
> had to do—"get by those boys down there."

"A Historian Reports on the Drafting of the 1954 NAACP School Brief," *The Sunday
Star*, January 21, 1962, p. C 3, cols. 1–7.

36. See the following comment on Justice Black's opinion by W. Theodore Pierson,
Jr., and Alvin Capp in their Note, "Wesberry v. Sanders: Deep in the Thicket," *supra*
note 32, at 1094 n. 123:

> To summarize his interpretation of Art. I, § 2, Justice Black
> quoted from William Samuel Johnson's statement that "in *one*
> branch the *people* ought to be represented; in the *other*, the
> *States*." 376 U.S. at 13. But the Court neglected to place the
> quote in its context. It was made during debate over whether
> members of the House of Representatives should be chosen by
> members of the state legislature or by the persons qualified under
> state law to vote for members of the state legislature. In this
> context it is impossible to conclude with any certainty that John-
> son was concerned with *how* the states should determine which
> people were to vote or the method by which they would be rep-
> resented.

James Madison's comment on Johnson's position suggests similar ambiguities. Farrand,
I: 461–62 (quoting Madison's notes).

Though Madison's notes traditionally have been considered the most authoritative, his own correspondence indicates that he revised them after publication of the *Journal*, partly in order to conform them to the *Journal* and Yates' notes. This "might be merely of antiquarian interest, were it not for the fact that the printed *Journal* is itself unreliable." The ability and trustworthiness of the original *Journal* reporter has been doubted. Furthermore, after the Convention, the reporter destroyed "all the loose scraps of paper which he evidently thought unimportant"; the remaining notes eventually were turned over to the Department of State. It was not until 1818 that Congress ordered the Convention record to be printed from the surviving notes. This arduous task was given to Secretary of State John Quincy Adams, who declared that the papers "were no better than the daily minutes from which the regular *Journal* ought to have been, but never was, made out." Thus Adams was forced to take the remaining rough notes and attempt to compile an accurate record of the Constitutional Convention, which he had not attended and of which neither he nor the reporter had sufficient memory. Similarly, Yates' notes appear to be of questionable reliability. His entries cease on July 5, 1787, *prior* to the conclusion of the debates arising over the Great Compromise. Although Madison "condemned [them] severely, as being a 'very erroneous edition,'" he made more than fifty changes in his own notes on the strength of Yates' notes.[37]

Less subject to challenge on grounds of historical accuracy, but also much less relevant as proof of the *general* original understanding, is Justice Black's use of two comments made *after* the Convention by James Madison and James Wilson. Madison in No. 57 of *The Federalist* papers indicated his understanding that a state's congressional delegation was to be elected in districts rather than at-large in the state, and that the districts would consist of relatively equal population. In terms of the electorate, he speculated that each Representative "will be elected by five or six thousand citizens,"[38] and speaking specifically of Pennsylvania he assumed districts of equal population as follows:

Some of her counties which elect her State's representatives are almost as large as her districts will be by which her Federal Representatives will be elected. The City of Philadelphia is supposed to contain between fifty and sixty thousand souls. It will therefore form nearly two districts for the choice of Federal Representatives.[39]

37. See Note, *supra* note 32, at 1095–96 (footnotes omitted).
38. James Madison, *The Federalist* No. 52: 389, 393 (New York, Tudor Publishing Company, 1947).
39. *Id.* at 394.

For at least three reasons Madison's statement, though relevant, cannot be taken to establish Justice Black's thesis. The comment came after the Convention. It also came after six of the nine states required for ratification had acted affirmatively. And the comment is undercut by the historical fact that for many decades in our early history several states did not use districts at all but elected their congressional delegation at-large under the nonrepresentative winner-take-all formula.

Views similar to Madison's were expressed by James Wilson in a series of lectures in Philadelphia in the following terms:

> [A]ll elections ought to be equal. Elections are equal when a given number of citizens, in one part of the state, choose as many representatives, as are chosen by the same number of citizens, in any other part of the state. In this manner, the proportion of the representatives and of the constituents will remain invariably the same.[40]

But these comments were not made until after the Constitution had been adopted, and relate not to the original understanding but to what "ought" to be; they are relevant to be sure, but hardly conclusive.

Justice Black also included a reference to Article I, Section 4's authorization of general supervisory power in Congress, which presumably could include congressional districting. It perhaps was one of his stronger points, *if* one may import to a clause which in plenary terms authorizes *congressional* supervision a concurrent, sub silentio grant of power for *judicial* supervision. At the Philadelphia Convention Madison did advert inferentially to the clause as a safeguard against gerrymandering of congressional districts, but no discussion ensued.[41] There was more discussion in the ratifying conventions. But the focus was whether or not to entrust Congress with such an open-ended supervisory power, which might, as Luther Martin of Maryland had suggested, lead to the "utter extinction and abolition of all State Government." [42]

d. *"Better" Arguments*

An alternative line of argument, eschewing a "forced history" approach, would have been textual analysis. Article I, Section 2 specifies apportionment of Representatives to the states "according to their respective Numbers," and it could have been asserted that it is only a small jump from numbers in apportionment to numbers in intrastate districting. The difficulty with the textual approach is that one must consider the entire text, and thus encounter the further provision in this same section that the

40. The Works of James Wilson II: 15 (Andrews, editor, Chicago: Callaghan Press, 1896), quoted by the Court in *Wesberry*, 376 U.S. 1, 17.
41. Farrand, *supra* note 36, at II:241.
42. *Elliot's Debates* I:361 (Philadelphia: J. B. Lippincott, 1888).

states shall control the franchise, i.e., that "the Electors in each State shall have the Qualifications requisite for Electors of the most numerous Branch of the State Legislature." In other words, although the states are to be *weighted* in the lower House by their *population*, rather than equally as in the Senate, the delegation thus assigned shall be *elected* by an electorate as broad or as narrow as the state chooses to use. There is no assurance obviously that such voting qualifications as the state selects will be uniformly distributed in the state's population. Hence, an interest in "equal representation" in the sense of *voter equality* has no necessary relation to a district system based on equal masses of raw *population*.

Hence, there is a logical non sequitur in the following statement in a Brookings Institution monograph on this point. After suggesting that the logic of Article I, Section 2's "numbers" apportionment calls for intrastate districting on the same "numbers" (total population) basis, and noting the qualifying effect of state power over voting qualifications the writer said:

> But this rule [state power over suffrage] simply narrowed the electorate, or the number of "People" recognized as effective citizens. The presumption remains that *all of these effective citizens*, whether a small or large proportion of the total adult population of a state, should have votes of equal weight in electing representatives.[43]

To achieve "votes of equal weight" would require not an *equal population* district system, but an *equal registered voters* district system—a refinement clearly beyond the contemplation of the times.

At best then, not to put too fine a point on it, there is an obvious "halo" effect or implication that population apportionment of the House contemplates some sort of population-related, or at least voter-related equality in intrastate electorate arrangements. But it is still a forced march, at least in terms of *historical and textual analysis* of original meaning, to a tight equal population district system in 1964.

In many instances a "purpose analysis" is a more certain guide to constitutional meaning than textual grammaticism or an historical collation of debaters' statements. It is clear that despite the qualifications noted, the framers' purpose was to make population the dominant factor in the construction of the House of Representatives. Although the question of districting was not highlighted, and the text contains no mandate to use districts rather than at-large voting for intrastate congressional elections, there was apparently some expectation of districting. As brought out more clearly in Justice Harlan's dissenting opinion, the fear of unequal district-

43. Andrew Hacker, *Congressional Districting* 7 (Washington, D.C.: Brookings Institution, 1963) (emphasis added).

ing apparently was one of the motivations for conferring a supervisory power on Congress (Article I, Section 4) regarding the "manner" of holding elections. More importantly, it could be argued that a natural corollary of weighting states by population in the House would be population-based districting inside the states in order to maximize the responsiveness of the House to the various segments of the "people."

e. *Justice Harlan Dissenting*

Justice Harlan's dissent rested on several of the historical and textual elements suggested in the foregoing review and critique of Justice Black's *Wesberry* opinion. Both Justices Clark and Stewart concurred with Harlan in totally rejecting Black's attempt to deduce an equal population district mandate from the debates at the Philadelphia Convention. But unlike Harlan, Clark and Stewart would have held congressional districting to present a justiciable issue, thus leaving the way open for judicial scrutiny under other parts of the Constitution, e.g., the equal protection clause of the Fourteenth Amendment.

After noting some difficulties in implementing the new nearly-equal-as-practicable rule, Justice Harlan moved to a textual analysis, then to an historical analysis, and concluded that the Court majority was not only undertaking to exercise a power reserved exclusively to Congress but was overruling congressional judgment. He pointed out that far from being inactive, Congress had regulated congressional elections since 1842. From 1872 through 1911 the decennial congressional apportionment acts had specified that Congressmen be elected from districts of equal population. After the congressional deadlock of 1920, when no apportionment occurred, the equal population requirement was dropped in the 1929 Act and never restored, despite repeated requests to re-enact it. Because the omission was deliberate, although the floor debates do not make the reason clear, Justice Harlan argued that court action would not merely fill a "gap" but supersede the expressed will of Congress.

Regarding implementation of the new rule, Justice Harlan asked questions which still continue to trouble redistricters and courts. Whose "equality" is at issue—that of "voters" or of total "inhabitants"? [44] Should the mathematical measure of allowable deviation be keyed to the "greatest disparity," comparing only the two extremes, or the "average departure from the average population per district"? In representation terms, what of such factors as area or natural boundaries "which are plainly relevant to the practicability of effective representation"? What of "party affiliations within the district"? Would an occasional variation for

44. The quotations in this paragraph are taken from 376 U.S. 1, 21 n. 4, 25.

a special purpose be more permissible in a large state than in a state with only a few districts? Feeling that a "nearly equal as practicable" standard provided no criteria at all for answering such questions, he twitted his brethren for a "whole-hearted but heavy-footed entrance into the political arena" and for dealing in abstractions with "little relevance to the realities of political life."

But in pointing to some real problems of implementation Justice Harlan did not suggest any mediative formula which would have admitted some federal judicial purview, case by case, on philosophically and politically sounder grounds than "one man-one vote." He thus offered no middle ground between nonaction and the majority's absolutism.

Textual and historical analysis of Article I, Sections 2 and 4 convinced Justice Harlan (1) that a "population" principle was contemplated only for apportionment to the states; (2) that even as to apportionment of seats to the states any supposed equal population premise was seriously derogated by the three-fifths clause regarding slaves and by the minimum guarantee to each state of one seat; (3) that the states had been given near-plenary discretion in arranging popular election of Congressmen, including use of at-large or winner-take-all elections instead of districts, and including also a power to have a large or small electorate; and (4) that to Congress was granted a plenary and exclusive power to alter state regulations for the conduct of congressional elections. That this last-named power would give Congress authority to regulate intrastate districting and impose some kind of equal population rule was no warrant, Harlan thought, for judicial creation of an equality standard as a matter of fixed constitutional law.

Here, as in *Baker*, Harlan's dissent served to bring into sharp forcus the recurring dispute between judicial activism and judicial restraint. In reapportionment and redistricting the issue becomes especially tense because judicial nonaction may merely throw the matter back to a political process already indisposed to act because so intertwined with the very evil at issue—malapportionment and maldistricting. Harlan phrased the "unstated premise" underlying the majority's activism this way:

> The unstated premise of the Court's conclusion quite obviously is that the Congress had not dealt, and the Court believes it will not deal, with the problem of congressional apportionment in accordance with what the Court believes to be sound political principles. Laying aside for the moment the validity of such a consideration as a factor in constitutional interpretation, it becomes relevant to examine the history of congressional action under Art. I, Sec. 4. This history reveals that the Court is not simply undertaking to exercise a power

which the Constitution reserves to the Congress; it is also overruling congressional judgment.[45]

But is Harlan's answer satisfactory? Was the "congressional judgment" to which he referred a free and informed judgment? Or was it merely a congenial consensus among common beneficiaries of a congressional districting system overly skewed to factors of incumbency and special interest?

However rationalized, the Court's *Wesberry* ruling clearly mandated a population basis for intrastate arrangements for congressional districts. Left open was the question of "how equal is equal?" Although equality was said to be the "fundamental goal," Justice Black spoke of the impossibility of "mathematical precision" and phrased the new guideline in these terms: "As nearly as is practicable, one man's vote in a congressional election is to be worth as much as another's." [46]

With no better guideline than this, and with no principled discussion in the opinion of the Court of permissible representation factors in the context either of political theory or political realities (see Chapters II, III, IV), it was to be expected that bare population equality would become the operating rule. And in practice, as noted in Chapter VII, lower courts did have difficulty in avoiding the "safe" transition from an equal population premise to an equal population absolute—a transition which, whatever else it did, would produce an order immune to reversal on appeal.

The *Wesberry* decision was rendered in February 1964 and the Georgia legislature redistricted in time for the 1964 election. Thus the question whether a judicially impelled at-large election would be a better representation device than the existing districts was averted. The *Wesberry* case did not touch therefore on the ultimate configurations of a federal fair representation standard. Counsel for the state, Assistant Attorney General Paul Rodgers, in the course of oral argument in the Supreme Court, had suggested that if the Court were to enter the political thicket of congressional districting it would be logically necessary to consider the inequities which result from gerrymandering and at-large elections, as well as those which result from population inequality in a district system. In partial rebuttal a plaintiff's counsel, Frank T. Cash, indicated he had no qualms about use of an at-large election on the ground that intrastate districting, although traditional, is of secondary importance compared to averting the "deprivation of a constitutional right." [47]

Thus was posed almost inadvertently a basic constitutional and philosophical question regarding democratic representation; and it was left

45. *Id.* at 42.
46. *Id.* at 7–8.
47. Author's court notes.

unanswered. If constitutional purpose, and representation needs, be fully served wherever there is a mathematical one-to-one relation of citizens to a given office, then an at-large election is unobjectionable; it does guarantee a one-to-one relation of each citizen to the state's congressional delegation. But if "representation" connotes a system for eliciting and representing the maximum possible breadth of viewpoint, then a continuance of districting by judicial order if necessary, and not an at-large election, would be the *only* appropriate remedy to terminate the "deprivation of a constitutional right."

IX

The "Big Six": Framing the Issues in State Legislative Reapportionment–I

"The one standard that is measurable, leaving less room for doubt, is population."

Charles Morgan, Jr. (Alabama case)

"The minority should have bargaining power in one house."

Theodore I. Botter (14 states, amici curiae)

"If we get a majority we'll be as nice to them as they were to us."

Alfred L. Scanlan (Maryland case)

A. The Setting

From the *Wesberry* v. *Sanders*[1] decision of February 1964 mandating equal population districts for elections for the lower house of Congress, it was only a short four-month step to the package of *Reapportionment Decisions*[2] of June 1964 mandating equal population districts for both

1. 376 U.S. 1 (1964).
2. The cases decided with full opinions after oral argument were the Alabama cases, Reynolds v. Sims, Vann v. Baggett, McConnell v. Baggett, 377 U.S. 533 (1964); the New York case, WMCA, Inc. v. Lomenzo, 377 U.S. 633 (1964); the Maryland case, Maryland Commission for Fair Representation v. Tawes, 377 U.S. 656 (1964); the Virginia case, Davis v. Mann, 377 U.S. 678 (1964); the Delaware case, Roman v. Sincock, 377 U.S. 695 (1964); and the Colorado case, Lucas v. Colorado General Assembly, 377 U.S. 713 (1964).
The following week the Court, using the same principles, disposed of reapportionment cases from the following states in memorandum decisions: the Michigan cases, Beadle v. Scholle, 377 U.S. 990 (1964), and Marshall v. Hare, 378 U.S. 561 (1964); the Washington case, Meyers v. Thigpen, 378 U.S. 554 (1964); the Oklahoma case, Williams v. Moss, 378 U.S. 558 (1964); the Illinois case, Germano v. Kerner, 378 U.S. 560 (1964); the Idaho case, Hearne v. Smylie, 378 U.S. 563 (1964); the Connecticut case, Pinney v. Butterworth, 378 U.S. 564 (1964); the Florida case, Swann v. Adams,

houses of bicameral state legislatures. But the "big six" cases which produced the Court's major reapportionment opinion in *Reynolds* v. *Sims*, with amplifying opinions in the other cases, had been two years and in some instances three years in the making. Therefore the issues and record in many of them had been shaped at the trial level without benefit of either the Court's *Wesberry* ruling or the "one man-one vote" ruling in *Gray* v. *Sanders*[3] mandating a straight popular plurality rule for election of statewide officials. The generally skimpy character of the records in these cases, the uncertain articulation of the issues, and the generally narrow approach toward the reapportionment problem was due in no small part to the novelty and suddenness of the reapportionment revolution. Three conceptually distinct problems tended to become an indistinguishable mass: election of statewide officials by popular majorities (or pluralities); election of the lower house of Congress on a population apportionment basis while the Senate remains on a state equality basis; and constituting a bicameral representation system for state legislatures. All were approached under a simple and appealing "one man-one vote" slogan, using the most elementary mathematical analysis, and there was no consideration of the political realities and complexities of achieving democratic representation through a system of district elections.

The Constitutional Convention of 1787 has been called a "reform caucus in action,"[4] a term which helps to emphasize the well-known point that the Constitutional Convention was not so much an open, public outpouring of popular will as it was a closed-door planning session by a brilliant activist minority. They hoped to carry the country with them on their final product, although detailed point-by-point consideration might have been fatal. They succeeded, and to the extent they succeeded they created a unified nation, not a mere confederation. Neither a true open convention nor a "reform caucus" has been attempted since.

The sequence of reapportionment litigation from 1962-1964 and since is also a striking example of constitutional revision by a process other than an open convention process. It is a commonplace, except perhaps in the mystic chambers of Justice Hugo L. Black, that the Supreme Court always has and always will—as long as judicial review continues—"make new constitutional law." It does so not merely by logical extrapolations from existing text, but by finding unprecedented and *originally un*contemplated meaning in the language of the document we call our "Constitution."

Some Court "amendments" to the Constitution, to use a term which

378 U.S. 553 (1964); the Ohio case, Nolan v. Rhodes, 378 U.S. 556 (1964); the Iowa case, Hill v. Davis, 378 U.S. 565 (1964).
3. 372 U.S. 368 (1963).
4. John P. Roche, "The Founding Fathers: A Reform Caucus in Action," 55 *Am. Pol. Sci. Rev.* 799 (1961).

both Justices Hugo L. Black and John Marshall Harlan on occasion have embraced, are more dramatic than others. Some represent sharper cleavages with the past, more obvious breaking of new legal ground regarding basic policy choices and elemental understandings of our public law system. Tested by this criterion, the famous public school desegregation decision of 1964, *Brown* v. *Board of Education*,[5] was really *not* a constitutional "amendment" by the Court. It was rather a first payment on a long-due promissory note. Clearly the Civil War Amendments were Negro-oriented, clearly their goal was integration of the slave into the mainstream of American life, clearly it was a goal not expected to be accomplished overnight. The *Brown* case made the "immanent" equality of the Negro under the Fourteenth Amendment an "imminent" equality a century later.

By contrast, reapportionment is a means to a democratic representation system; it is the basic element in structuring a democratic society. It is therefore a "constitutive" act in the generic sense; it restructures government at the core. In short, the reapportionment litigation of 1962-1964, and its continuing unfolding and refinement as we move toward the 1970 census, is perhaps the most dramatic example in our history of the unique American custom of constitution-making by judicial action.

From this perspective the six major cases brought together for Supreme Court resolution in June 1964 take on special meaning. Who were the actors in this new version of the "reform caucus in action"? What were their personal interests? How broad was their perception? What range of issues was articulated? How adequate were the data used to illuminate and verify the policy choices available? What range of alternatives was considered? What unproven assumptions were made and generally accepted? Who were leaders and who were followers in the sequence of litigation?

Detailed analysis of multiple suits in nearly 50 states would present a tedious if not insuperable task. However, careful scrutiny of the six major cases chosen by the Supreme Court for plenary review not only serves to round out the portrayal in Chapter VII of the nationwide explosion of reapportionment litigation touched off by *Baker* v. *Carr*, but also shows parties in particular cases in battle array. These six cases offer a fair sampling not only of issues and parties but also of the content and calibre of briefs and oral arguments by counsel. And because they were argued orally before the full Supreme Court Bench, they thus have the added virtue of providing glimpses of the mental process of the "reform caucus" as it was making up its mind and moving toward its epochal decisions.

5. 347 U.S. 483 (1954).

B. Note on the Actors and on the Crucial Role of the U.S. Solicitor General

Perhaps the most striking aspect of the "big six" reapportionment cases is their superficial, politically aseptic quality. From listening to oral arguments in many of these cases, and reading briefs and opinions in these and other post-*Baker* cases, a foreigner unversed in ways of American politics might get the impression that the dispute was a minor one of primary interest to clerks in the Bureau of the Census. Gross populations of various legislative districts were compared assiduously. Occasionally a major frustration arose from the fact that census tract lines, by which census data are reported, and legislative district lines did not coincide, thus necessitating informed guesswork and creating some margin of error.

Below the surface, however, a wholly different sort of battle was being waged. It is common to label the contest as one between urban interests and rural interests. But in many states such as New York and Maryland, and perhaps in most states, the rise of populous suburbs had created a third interest with uncertain relation to city and small town. None of these three interests identified uniformly with political party labels. Outside the one-party South and border South states, suburbs were often politically mixed. Whereas large urban centers were Democratic party monoliths, farmers in many states were not uniformly Republican but were in significant degree anti-city Democrats of early twentieth-century Populist lineage. But legislatures are organized and run by political parties, not by loose interest groups. Hence, all reapportionment litigation was motivated by plaintiffs' calculus in regard to prospects for shifting political party control of the legislature, or for "reforming" a political party by changing its power base through reapportionment, or both.

Almost without exception plaintiffs either were front-men for a political party, or were politically active and politically ambitious citizens loosely classifiable as liberal Democrats and liberal Republicans. In "constitutionally Republican" New York, for example, the moving forces on the plaintiffs' side were primarily downstate Democratic party liberals. In Alabama the plaintiffs included urban-centered anti-red-necks of both parties. When the case reached the Supreme Court the nominal defendant—striving for a middle position—was Attorney General Richmond M. Flowers, widely known in many quarters as the "Negroes' white hope in Alabama."

In Maryland a leading reapportionment proponent, Royce Hanson, was an American University political science professor with his eye on a congressional seat who subsequently did run for Congress in 1964 and 1966. The key Maryland reapportionment attorney, Alfred L. Scanlan, was to become increasingly active in Democratic politics serving as a campaign aide to United States Senator Joseph D. Tydings. And he might have become attorney general of Maryland in 1967 had not ex-Congressman Carlton R. Sickles's campaign for the governorship been derailed in the Democratic primary by the Wallace-type "Your home is your castle" campaign of Baltimore building contractor, George P. Mahoney.

In Delaware, plaintiffs included liberal Wilmington Republicans. In an amusing twist, after plaintiffs' efforts succeeded in compelling the Democratic legislature to reapportion, the result was so distasteful to the Republican segment of the plaintiffs that this segment went to court again, and were again successful, crying "gerrymander." [6] An analogous situation occurred in Iowa, where some urban Republicans who had been among the backers of the initial suit awoke to discover that they had conferred reapportionment power on a "Goldwaterized" Iowa legislature. Both houses shifted to Democratic control in the Republican debacle of November 1964. The ensuing reapportionment featured at-large elections in the populous counties, thus raising the prospect of submerging rural and suburban Republican votes.[7] It should be noted that in both Delaware and Iowa the court managed to find fresh mathematical grounds for outlawing reapportioned districts in the renewed litigation and did not rest invalidation squarely on a gerrymandering principle.

In Virginia the moving spirits for reapportionment were primarily northern Virginia liberal Democrats in Washington suburbs. They were opposed to the Byrd machine which had ruled Virginia and the Democratic party for decades. In Colorado, Denver-based labor union leaders and Democratic liberals were prominent in the reapportionment struggle. In Michigan, where the United Auto Workers and the Democratic party are not easily separated, the most insistent reapportionment proponents were primarily Detroit-based UAW and Democratic liberals.

Characteristically, where some Republicans joined the reapportionment movement they usually did so in regard to congressional districts, and in regard to one house of the legislature. But they often split with Democrats on the issue of preserving a federal plan, or some modified arrangement short of straight population apportionment for the second house. In

6. Sincock v. Gately, 262 F. Supp. 739 (D. Del. 1967).
7. Kruidenier v. McCulloch, 142 N.W. 2d 355 (Iowa 1966), *cert. denied*, 385 U.S. 851 (1966).

short, in no state was reapportionment a mere mathematical exercise by political innocents.

a. *The U.S. Solicitor General*

Next to the Supreme Court itself perhaps the most important factor in the sequence of reapportionment litigation, viewed as a "reform caucus in action," was the Solicitor General of the United States, Archibald Cox. His leading role in *Baker* v. *Carr* has already been noted. In the "big six" state legislative reapportionment cases, his role as chief theoretician and chief coordinator for the plaintiff is perhaps the highlight of the story. His cleverness in shaping litigation tactics to match apparent judicial predilections (an aspect of constitutional law development upon which too little research has been done) suggests that the creative aspects of the decision-making process in the Supreme Court are only half revealed when attention is confined to judicial votes and written opinions. The Solicitor's role cannot be fully appreciated, however, until one has in mind the factual sequence to which he was reacting, and the calibre of counsel directly serving the parties. For this reason an articulation of the Solicitor General's role, despite its importance, is reserved until the end of the analysis of the "big six" cases.

C. New York: "Accessibility" and a Touch of Representation Theory

The New York case, *WMCA* v. *Lomenzo*,[8] came up from a three-judge federal district court which before *Baker* had dismissed the suit on political question grounds and after *Baker* had unanimously dismissed again.[9] The district court's rationale was that the apportionment formula fixed in New York's 1894 Constitution, though not based "solely on population," was not "irrational" under their understanding of the *Baker* guidelines.[10] The court was impressed with the apportionment formula's historic focus on the county as the "classic unit of governmental organization and administration." It also noted such factors as "accessibility of legislative representatives to the electors," [11] and "proper diffusion of political initiative

8. 377 U.S. 633 (1964).
9. WMCA v. Simon, 202 F. Supp. 741 (S.D. N.Y. Jan. 11, 1962); 208 F. Supp. 368 (S.D. N.Y. Aug. 16, 1962).
10. 208 F. Supp. at 384 (Ryan, J., concurring).
11. *Id.* at 324.

as between a state's thinly populated counties and those having concentrated masses." [12]

Taking a general representation approach, rather than an individual voter equality approach, the district court noted that New York City with 46 percent of the state's population under the 1960 census controlled 43.3 percent of the assembly and 43.1 percent under the still-existing 1953 apportionment. But it did not mention that under the forthcoming 1960 census reapportionment these figures would drop to 37.3 percent and 36.8 percent respectively. Focusing on the urban areas encompassing the ten most heavily populated counties—New York City and environs, Buffalo, Rochester, and Syracuse—the court went on to note that after reapportionment on the basis of the 1960 census these ten counties with 73.5 percent of the citizen population would control 64.9 percent and 61.3 percent of the senate and house respectively.[13]

Hence the district court had ruled that New York's regressive population apportionment formulae [14] did not cause invidious discrimination.

12. *Id.* at 379.

13. *Id.* at 378–79; Plaintiff's Trial Brief, Appendix C, pp. 6–7; Gus Tyler and David I. Wells, "New York: Constitutionally Republican" in *The Politics of Reapportionment* 221, 236 (Malcolm E. Jewell, editor, New York: Atherton Press, 1962).

14. New York's "1894" formula may be summarized as follows:

Senate. The state's citizen population is divided by 50, yielding the first ratio. All counties having between three and four times this ratio are given three seats; those with between four and five ratios receive five seats, etc. If this apportionment accords to a county more seats than it had in 1894, the senate membership is increased by a like number. Next, the counties having less than three ratios are accorded the remaining seats, including the newly created ones. This is done by dividing the number of remaining seats by the citizen population of these counties. The remaining seats are then distributed on the basis of this second ratio.

Assembly. First every county (except Hamilton) is given one seat. Next, every county having in excess of one percent of the state's population is given a second seat. Finally, the remaining seats are divided among those counties having more than one and one-third percent of the state's citizen population.

In the senate there are six "first ratio" counties apportioned 26 senators and having 9,519,000 people. The "second ratio" counties are represented by 31 senators but have a population of only 6,721,000. Thus, a minority of the citizen population (41 percent) is able to elect a majority of the senate (54 percent). The real inequity lies in the fact that the "first ratio" counties do not receive the full benefit of their population increase. Whereas the "first ratio" counties may receive more seats than accorded in 1894, the increased benefit is in part transferred to the "second ratio" counties in that the senate is increased by the same number of seats that are accorded to "first ratio" counties above their 1894 allotment.

Since the state constitution limits the number of seats in the assembly to 150, giving one seat to every county takes up 61 seats—or 41 percent of the total available—without any regard to population. Quite obviously, giving an additional seat to all counties having more than one percent of the state total prejudices those having a population greatly in excess of one percent and favors those with a population just over the requirement. Thus, the heavily populated counties receive an assemblyman for every 130,000 population, the medium-sized "two-assemblyman" counties receive one for every 110,000, and the "one seat" counties receive one for every 63,000 citizens. See

Although concededly operating to overrepresent smaller counties, the formula did not give them significant control or jeopardize rule by the urban majority.

But what is *significant control*, what is *majority rule*, and *which grouping* of urban counties is the appropriate measure of urban interest? Plaintiffs, for example, found it to their advantage to suggest a limited, downstate six-county analysis based on their residences. This grouping—encompassing Long Island, including the rural eastern end; New York City minus Staten Island; and excluding adjacent, populous Westchester County—had 56.2 percent of the 1960 citizen population of the state, but under the reapportionment then due would have only 45.6 percent and 46.0 percent control of the senate and assembly respectively.[15] An alternative six-county analysis, focusing on largest or "first ratio" counties and thus encompassing Buffalo, New York City minus Staten Island, and Nassau County on Long Island, yields 58.6 percent of the 1960 citizen population, and 46 percent and 51.3 percent of the senate and assembly respectively.[16]

Political data on the beneficial effect of the regressive apportionment formula to the Republican party were not formally considered at the district court level (though there were some conclusionary allegations in plaintiffs' trial brief) despite the fact that this consideration was a prime motivation of plaintiffs' case. The suit was dominated by R. Peter Straus, president of WMCA radio station that was allowed to lend its name to the case, and who was frequently mentioned as possible Democratic nominee for the United States Senate. However, statistics comparing the Republican and Democratic party vote cast for legislative seats with seats actually captured were included in briefs subsequently filed by both sides in the Supreme Court. The data indicated that Republicans on occasion could capture a majority of seats with a minority of the statewide legislative vote. The data were not alluded to in oral argument or mentioned in the Supreme Court's opinion, despite the fact that in the New York case this was the real issue for most people.[17]

Several offers of proof by the plaintiffs were rejected by the district court. One, which would have required exploration of grant-in-aid theory and the philosophic question of the extent to which urban areas with a richer economic base should help rural areas with a poorer economic

generally Ruth C. Silva, "Apportionment in New York," 30 *Fordham L. Rev.* 581 (1962) and "Apportionment of the New York Assembly," 31 *Fordham L. Rev.* 1 (1962).
15. Plaintiffs' Trial Brief, generally, and Transcript of Record; see also Motion to Dismiss or Affirm, p. 4, WMCA v. Lomenzo.
16. Computed from 208 F. Supp. 380 and Brief for the Appellants, pp. 28, 120–22.
17. Brief for the Appellants, p. 36.

base,[18] was that regressive apportionment had led to the state's short-changing New York City financially. "For every dollar the Legislature bestows on a school child upstate," the brief said, "it can spare only 63 cents for a school in New York City." [19] Another proof rejected was that the 1894 Constitution apportionment formula had been devised with the deliberate intent of underrepresenting the urban areas.

A third category of proof rejected was expert testimony on apportionment practice and theory. This ruling limited both sides. The state could not present expert political scientist testimony on apportionment theory and on the importance of counties as "units of government and administration" and as "communities of interest" from Professor Alfred deGrazia of New York University, Professor Spencer D. Parratt and Dr. Michael O. Sawyer of Syracuse University, and Dr. Hollister Kent, Syracuse regional planner.[20] The plaintiffs could not present political scientist testimony on "one man-one vote" as a sole apportionment standard.[21] Oddly, this aspect of plaintiffs' case indirectly was gotten in through the state's cross-examination of plaintiffs' political scientist-statistician, Professor Ruth C. Silva of Pennsylvania State University. The colloquy went as follows:

> Q. In your tabular presentations and in your writings on New York apportionment, you referred to the Fordham Law Review and material of that sort. Have you used the term "equitable representation" or "equal representation"?
>
> A. Yes, sir, I have.
>
> Q. Would you tell us exactly what you mean by those terms?
>
> A. That one man equals one vote, that a popular vote cast for a State Senator in any one county has equal weight with one popular vote cast in any other county.
>
> Q. There are other theories of equal representation known to the science of political science, well recognized ones?
>
> A. Not that I know of. Historically there have been other theories. But I do not believe political science accepts other theories.

18. The Supreme Court bypassed this question in Baker v. Carr and has never had occasion to return to it. The "one man-one vote" theory embraced in Reynolds v. Sims makes irrelevant the question of "discriminatory" effects in tax and expenditure matters of apportionment formulae not based solely on population. In *Baker* in bypassing such "proofs" the Court said: "Whether, when the issue to be decided is one of the constitutional adequacy of this particular apportionment, taxation arguments and exhibits as now presented add anything, *or whether they could add anything however presented*, is for the District Court in the first instance to decide." Baker v. Carr, 369 U.S. 186, 195 n. 15 (1962) (emphasis added).

19. Transcript of Record, Affidavit of R. Peter Straus, pp. 250, 253–54. Similar allegations were made in the Maryland case, but were not noticed either by the state courts or the Supreme Court on appeal.

20. *Id.* at 182.

21. *Id.* at 129 *et seq.*

Q. Other theories than the theory of one man, one vote?

A. Yes.

Q. I take it that all these charts and statistics that you have presented here, and all these references you have made in your writings in the Fordham Law Review and elsewhere to the apportionment system of New York are valid only to the extent that the doctrine of equal representation, which you have just explained, is valid?

A. I would assume so, sir.[22]

a. *Plaintiffs' Case on Appeal*

On appeal to the Supreme Court, plaintiffs' case was shaped by a focus on the "weight" of the individual voter, and on district-by-district population comparisons—all aided by shift of the burden of proof to the state to justify all district population deviations. As a hedge against the possibility that the Supreme Court might deem "accessibility" and "diffusion of political initiative" to be relevant apportionment factors, plaintiffs also argued that it should not be necessary to qualify the population principle in *both* houses to promote these interests. Plaintiffs also tried to turn the "accessibility" argument around to favor themselves by suggesting that it is easier for a rural legislator to be "visible" and known—to advise his constituents and to be advised by them—than for an urban legislator. The reason given was that greater publicity is possible in small community media—papers and radio stations—than in densely populated areas where there are more competitors for public attention.[23]

Although in a sense population was a factor in apportionment formulae for both houses, plaintiffs could show many qualifications—called "opaque intricacies" in Chief Justice Earl Warren's opinion invalidating the plan in 1964. Analogous to the graduated income tax principle, as a county's population increased it received progressively less net gain in terms of additional seats.[24]

b. *State's Case on Appeal*

Of all the briefs filed with the Supreme Court on behalf of the defendant states in the "big six" apportionment cases of 1963–1964, the New York brief was the most effective in trying to break out of the "per capita" equality straitjacket, which points to a single-factor, population-equality apportionment formula. Assistant Attorney General Irving Galt, without resting simply on the "federal analogy," tried to raise questions concerning the interrelationships of population districting and effective representation, the propriety of "apportioning" some requirements of consensus

22. *Id.* at 164–65.
23. Brief for the Appellants, p. 43.
24. See note 14 *supra*.

into the representation system as a qualifier on simple majority power, the propriety of some overrepresentation for underpopulated areas to ensure their having a "voice" but not affirmative power to rule. His effort was not eminently successful, and failed utterly on oral argument. New York's case, although better prepared than most, was not thought through sufficiently. In any event the Court was not ready in 1964 for the "representation" side of "equal representation"—a side highlighted by the still-continuing flow of apportionment cases raising representation issues not amenable to resolution under rigid district population equality theory—e.g., multimember districting, weighted voting, fractional voting, gerrymandering both racial and political, at-large voting, floterial districting, minority representation.

In his brief in the Supreme Court, Assistant Attorney General Galt urged the Court not to adopt plaintiffs' per-capita apportionment standard and to focus on the "problem of assuring that legislatures be responsive to the popular will." [25] But by "popular will" he meant not full power in a bare numerical majority, but a generalized, common denominator will, which expressed a consensus. As reasonable means to achieve such an undefined "consensus will" he listed three elements in New York's apportionment system: (1) guarantee of some representation for each county; (2) limitation on district physical size to preserve accessibility; (3) anti-concentration rules so that "no one small group of counties can control the legislature and ignore the needs of the rest of the state." [26] He buttressed the anti-concentration idea by pointing out that New York was one of only two states in which metropolitan central cities could elect a majority of each house.[27] He also reverted to the comment in Solicitor General Cox's amicus brief in *Baker* v. *Carr* that in a state with a dominant central city it might be reasonable to underrepresent the city to avoid "the danger of total neglect" of rural areas.[28]

His central point, however, and one which if accepted would have yielded maximum flexibility in justifying various population deviations, was the factor of accessibility, articulated as follows:

> If a per capita standard resulted in the creation of *overly large* districts in sparsely populated areas, a voter in such a district would be *disadvantaged in two ways*: (1) he would not have the intimate contact with his legislator possessed by a voter in a heavily populated district covering a relatively few city blocks—distance might prevent the

25. Brief for Appellees Secretary of State and Attorney General, p. 23.
26. *Id.* at 38–50.
27. *Id.* at 46. See United States Advisory Commission on Intergovernmental Relations, *Apportionment of State Legislatures* 44 (1962).
28. Brief for Appellees, pp. 46–47. See Amicus Brief for the United States, Baker v. Carr, 369 U.S. 186 (1962), pp. 29–30.

voter from expressing his views to the legislator and the legislator from consulting his electorate; (2) a voter in an overly large district would be likely to lose one of the most important benefits of a single-member district system—representation in a district which has some modicum of shared problems, enabling the legislator to become a spokesman for views which might otherwise not be heard. If a district spans too large an area, there may well be no such community of interest among its voters, and one of the most important links between a citizen and the legislative process will have disappeared.[29]

Size and distance aspects of the accessibility argument are easily rebutted, of course, by appeal to modern techniques of communication. This second aspect—shared problems and community of interest—is not easily rebutted. It goes to basics of representation theory and involves a number of value choices, e.g., homogeneity versus heterogeneity in district formation, safe versus swing districts, importance of ensuring that communities be "heard" in at least one house, and the like.

Plausible as some of these means might be for adducing the various components of a generalized "popular will," they all rest on acceptance of an initial premise of consensus as the goal. But this premise was simply thrust forward. There was no adequate over-all rationalizing theory based on goals, practices, and operating complexities in the American system where we hope to achieve "fair representation" through the chance pyramiding of legislative district pluralities.

c. *Oral Argument*

In oral argument, when "accessibility" was the sole answer to the penetrating questions of the Bench on various population deviations, Mr. Galt had a difficult time. Justice Arthur J. Goldberg noted that New York "repeatedly used 'accessibility' as a justification for discrimination" and asked what it meant. In response Mr. Galt was unable to avoid the implication of minority rule by articulating a theory of limited *defensive power* in a minority to ensure being heard effectively. He never could link-up "access" considerations with legislative control considerations in a way that did not scare the majority. Part of the problem, of course, was that New York, like all of the defendant states, was trying to hang on to too much. Even under a more sophisticated representation theory than they were able to articulate, the defendants could not readily have explained the population deviations which so often existed even between seemingly similar areas and communities of interest.

It was to this point, at least indirectly, that some of the questions asked of plaintiffs' counsel by Justices Harlan and Potter Stewart were directed.

29. Brief for Appellees, p. 44.

They wanted to know how equal protection, concededly applicable to civil rights of voters per se, also applied to legislative apportionment and districting. If applicable, they also wanted to know with what rigidity the clause should be interpreted in legislative apportionment, having in mind perhaps the Court's winking at logical inconsistencies in the Sunday Closing law cases decided under very flexible equal protection principles of general reasonableness. Justice Harlan opened the questioning from the Bench by observing that in reapportionment cases "the problem is distribution of power, not discrimination in personal voting rights" such as racial discrimination. He asked Leonard B. Sand, plaintiffs' counsel, for a discussion of constitutional standards relevant to this question.

Justice Stewart talked of political party realities and the relevance of such factors as the "meaningful representation," in terms of legislative operation, which a political party majority in one district provides for its members who are only a minority in another district. He suggested that the "problems in these cases are more subtle than suggested in the briefs and cannot be solved by eighth grade arithmetic." (In his subsequent written opinion this was reduced to "sixth grade" arithmetic!)

To such questions, the response of Mr. Sand, and of Solicitor General Cox as amicus for the plaintiffs, was essentially to ignore them. They reasserted their own characterization of the issue as centering simply on an individual civil right to cast an equally weighted vote, which was to be achieved by per-capita population apportionment and nothing more. They were not pursued.

To Justice Harlan's question about the relation of equal protection to apportionment, Solicitor General Cox did make the oblique response of neatly extending *Gray* v. *Sanders* to legislative apportionment. (*Gray*, of course, had abolished "county units" and required a state at-large election for governor with no vote weighting.) The Solicitor pointed out that one possible mode for electing a legislature was a state election at-large, in which he presumed no one would wish to permit any vote weighting. Hence, there should be no "vote weighting" when the legislature is elected instead from districts. This response seems more cute than relevant. It makes an interesting contrast with the Court's approval of a shift from "one man-one vote" to "something else" when it allowed the gubernatorial election in Georgia in 1966 to shift from ballot box resolution to legislative resolution, where second-runner Lester G. Maddox prevailed.

d. *Unconstitutional, 6 to 3*

With the Supreme Court's acceptance of the per-capita apportionment principle as the only proper formula for apportioning both houses of state legislatures, the case became much simpler. By this standard the mathematics of New York's apportionment system were not impressive, and therefore other matters did not need to be considered. The reapportionment then due under the 1960 census would yield the following figures if the 1894 formula continued in force: the population variance ratio and the electoral percentage for the assembly would be 12.7 to 1 and 37.5 percent; the same figures for the senate would be 2.61 to 1 and 38.1 percent. These figures were deemed to be too deviant to be constitutionally sustainable.

Taking note of the effect of New York's formula the Court's opinion also expressed a pro-urban concern by speaking of the "undervaluation of the weight of the votes" of persons living in "populous areas." [30] The Court found a "built-in bias against voters living in the State's more populous counties. And the legislative representation accorded to the urban and suburban areas becomes proportionately less as the population of those areas increases." [31]

D. Alabama: "Kicking and Screaming" (or, Send in Flowers)

Most paradoxical of the reapportionment cases resolved by the Supreme Court in 1964 was *Reynolds* v. *Sims*,[32] the one selected by the Court to bear the principal opinion. It came from Alabama, home of the Confederacy and the only Deep South state represented in the 1964 cases (other than the Florida case,[33] which was given summary treatment). Thus the case came up from a federal judiciary impatient with Southern recalcitrance on school desegregation and which with some exceptions was the most liberal and vigorous in the nation—particularly where legislative nonaction was involved.

The pre-*Baker* malapportionment in Alabama was egregious, with population variance ratios in the senate and house respectively of 41 to 1 and 16 to 1 and electoral percentages respectively of 25.1 percent and 25.7 percent. One 13,462 population county had two house seats whereas Mobile (314,301) had only three and Jefferson County (634,864) had only seven. Urban underrepresentation was asserted to cause legislative inattention to modern issues, albeit the continued "one man-one vote" election of Wallace-type governors warned against asserting a close correlation.

Reapportionment litigation in Alabama followed swiftly on the heels of

30. WMCA v. Lomenzo, 377 U.S. 633, 653 (1964).
31. *Id.* at 654.
32. 377 U.S. 533 (1964).
33. Swann v. Adams, 378 U.S. 553 (1964).

Baker v. *Carr* and by midsummer an Alabama federal district court was the first in the nation to accomplish legislative reapportionment by direct judicial order.[34] In doing so it created a pattern which was followed by many other courts in ensuing years: (1) devise a court plan by combining the best features of plans made available by the legislature or the parties, or adopt in toto the "best" of several plans available; (2) order the plan into effect on a temporary basis pending further action by the legislature or by constitutional amendment procedure. A court thus can avoid getting into the highly political business of drawing fresh district lines, conceding of course that a political effect is unavoidably present in simply choosing from different plans already prepared. And a court can avoid the drastic but unrepresentative remedy of election at-large—a remedy never yet ordered under the Fourteenth Amendment for a state legislature, despite an occasional judicial threat.

For Alabama the court combined the best features of two plans newly enacted under judicial pressure in special legislative session, taking the house plan from a new statute and the senate plan from a proposed constitutional amendment. As a result population disparities were reduced so that population variance ratios in senate and house respectively became 4.7 to 1 and 20 to 1, and the electoral percentages 27.6 percent and 43 percent. This was the order appealed from, Justice Black having denied a stay[35] and an election having been held under the new plan in the meantime. This judicial vigor prompted one of the plaintiffs' attorneys to comment:

> More rapid remedial results seem to have been reached in the Southern Federal Courts than in those of other sections. My personal belief is that the United States District Judges in the South, having been faced with cantankerous legislatures and general vilification since Brown v. Board of Education, seem less fearful of seemingly drastic remedies than do others. Many of the judges of the Fifth Judicial Circuit have had to fashion decrees with the knowledge that at least the United States Army would be necessary to carry them out.[36]

34. Sims v. Frink, 208 F. Supp. 431 (M.D. Ala. 1962).
35. *New York Times*, Aug. 26, 1962, p. 42, col. 3. Dean Phil C. Neal of the University of Chicago Law School finds an "apex of irony" in the following statement attributed to Justice Black, giving his reasons for not staying the primary under the *court-ordered* plan: "All preparations for this primary appear to have been made. No facts are alleged or shown which in my judgment would support a stay that would so drastically disrupt the state's primary plan." Phil C. Neal, "Baker v. Carr: Politics in Search of Law," 1962 *Supreme Court Review* 252, 315 n. 176 (Chicago: University of Chicago Press, 1962).
36. Letter to author from Charles M. Morgan, Jr., Birmingham, Alabama, February 2, 1963.

It is easier to characterize what the federal district court did, its action being essentially declaratory and unrationalized, than to sort out subsequent developments in the Supreme Court appeal. From a melange of parties and briefs the following four-way breakdown emerges.

a. *The Four-Ring Circus*

First, the primary defendants' brief was filed not on behalf of the state but on behalf of certain probate judges.[37] The brief was prepared by Thomas G. Gayle, McLean Pitts, and Joseph E. Wilkinson, Jr., of Selma, Alabama, and Rankin Fite of Hamilton, Alabama. It was these parties, and not the "state" through the Attorney General, who had unsuccessfully sought the stay from Justice Black to forestall election under the new plan in 1962. Because of their ministerial duties in connection with elections, the probate judges had been included in a long list of initial defendants which was headed by the Secretary of State and the Attorney General and ended with some petty officials.

This brief, however, may well have expressed the feelings of a considerable part of the legislature, if not the state. In tone it verged on a plea to raise again the Confederate flag over Montgomery. In specific request it asked the Supreme Court to reverse *Baker* v. *Carr*, restore the rule of nonjusticiability, and leave the political thicket alone. In short, unless the Court could have been persuaded to turn back, and there never was any indication that such was likely, this brief was not responsive to any of the issues on which the Court wanted and needed enlightenment. In its own perverse way it probably strengthened the vigor and simplicity of the "one man-one vote" slogan, thus achieving the opposite of the effect intended. Indeed, the real explanation for Chief Justice Warren's opinion in *Reynolds*, which became the basic reapportionment opinion, may be that it was an impatient response to this brief written in Selma, Alabama, and filed on behalf of Probate Judge B. A. Reynolds and associates.

Second, a brief (hereafter called Vann Brief) was filed on behalf of one set of intervening plaintiffs who appealed from their district court "victory" seeking more.[38] They said that by allowing retention of the guarantee of at least one seat for each county in the house (which still allowed a fairly high and respectable electoral percentage of 45 percent) the district court had exhausted "such latitude as may exist for non-population appor-

37. Brief for Appellants, B. A. Reynolds *et al.*, filed in No. 23, Reynolds v. Sims.
38. Brief of Appellants, Vann v. Frink (No. 27). The brief was prepared by David J. Vann, Robert S. Vance, and C. H. Erskine Smith. The first two occupied the dual role of being intervening plaintiffs and of serving as counsel for themselves and some other intervening plaintiffs.

tionment"[39] and should have placed the senate on a strict population basis. Hence, although in historic context the district court had acted in almost revolutionary fashion, it was accused of having imposed minority rule on Alabama. " 'Pernicious and destructive' minority rule," they said, "has now been imposed on the people of Alabama in the name of the United States Constitution by a United States District Court."[40]

This Vann Brief reasserted the theory of relief relied on in district court, i.e., that the Alabama Constitution of 1901, properly construed, itself required a population apportionment of the senate, and that the district court should adopt it as the federal standard. The twin difficulties of this theory were that the proposed interpretation of the Alabama Constitution was tenuous almost to the point of being specious,[41] and the Supreme Court in *Baker* v. *Carr* had already refused to follow a plaintiff invitation to make state constitutional command the measure of federal equal protection. As already noted, the Court in *Baker* preferred the Solicitor General's theory of articulating an independent right of "equal representation" under the Fourteenth Amendment.

Third, a set of original plaintiffs, who had shared the attempt in district court simply to rest on a "population principle" interpretation of the Alabama Constitution, filed a brief (hereafter called Morgan Brief) commending the district court's provisional apportionment order. They only asked dismissal of the appeals and remand to the district court "to finish the job."[42] They were the only parties to take this position, other than the Attorney General, who occupied an anomalous lone wolf role. All other parties in this case either were appellants asking the Court to get out of the thicket (two probate judge defendants) or were appellants asking the Court to order a strict "one man-one vote" principle (two sets of intervening plaintiffs).

The very short Morgan Brief was noteworthy mainly for dissociating the original plaintiffs from the attack being made on the district court in the Vann Brief by one set of intervening plaintiffs. Accusing the latter of "impatience," the Morgan Brief referred to the district court as "the only institution to which freedom in Alabama has been entrusted."[43]

Fourth, another set of intervening plaintiffs filed the only brief (hereafter called McConnell Brief) on either side which attempted to discuss

39. *Id.* at 25.
40. *Id.* at 24.
41. See discussion in Brief for the Appellants, McConnell v. Frink (No. 41), pp. 19–21.
42. Brief for Appellees, M. O. Sims *et al.*, Reynolds v. Sims (No. 23), p. 11. The brief was prepared by Charles Morgan, Jr., and George Peach Taylor who occupied the dual role of being original plaintiffs and of serving as counsel for themselves and other original plaintiffs.
43. *Id.* at 11.

representation theory and representation realities, the one issue really relevant on appeal.[44] It sought to articulate a federal right to strict population equality under the Fourteenth Amendment. But it also sought to take account of objections based on concern for minorities and the checks and balances principle. Its flavor is well indicated by the following excerpts:

> The concept of one person, one vote, permits no deviation, no dilution and is merely a matter of numbers, of the ratio 1:1 . . . .[45]

> Restrictions on the majority, such as the requirement of extraordinary majorities for the enactment or adoption of certain laws or the requirement that certain types of legislation become effective only after certain time limitations or even after approval by more than one session of the legislature, although not derogating from the principle of majority rule, may be a means of insuring against precipitate action and of allowing for greater deliberation upon proposed legislation. It is through such methods, and not by means of unequal representation in, or minority control over, the legislative process, that the state may assure a proper diffusion of political initiative or control as between the various elements of its population.[46]

Fifth, and last, was a short, almost apologetic brief filed rather late by Richmond M. Flowers, successor to Attorney General MacDonald Gallion who was named in the original action. For his stand on the apportionment issue, and on issues of racial desegregation, Mr. Flowers soon became portrayed in the Northern press as the voice of moderation in the New South. He was to lose to Mrs. George C. Wallace, however, in the Alabama Democratic gubernatorial primary in 1966.

As a constitutional state officer and named defendant, Attorney General Flowers felt he should not ignore the matter. But he could join neither the standpat defense of pre-*Baker* apportionment nor the all-out plea for rigid "one man-one vote." He finally sided with the district court and its apparent principle that "representation according to population *to some extent* must be required in both Houses to avoid invidious discrimination." [47] And he gently reminded the Court of its past statements in equal protection cases, suggesting that the clause does not demand "rigid

44. Brief for the Appellants, McConnell *et al.* v. Frink (No. 41), p. 20. This brief was prepared by John W. McConnell, Jr., for himself and some other intervening plaintiffs. It abandoned reliance on the ambiguous Alabama Constitution. Compare with Brief of Appellants, Vann v. Frink, pp. 14–16.
45. McConnell Brief, p. 26.
46. *Id.* at 28–29.
47. Brief for Appellee Richmond M. Flowers as Attorney General, Reynolds v. Sims (No. 23), Vann v. Frink (No. 27), McConnell v. Frink (No. 41), p. 5.

equality," [48] that "proper diffusion of political initiative" throughout the state is a legitimate objective [49] and that only "invidious discrimination" is prohibited.[50] There being as yet no permanent apportionment plan he asked that the matter be returned to Alabama for further action by district court or legislature under these population-oriented but somewhat flexible guidelines.

b. *Oral Argument*

Oral argument in the Alabama case was opened by McLean Pitts, who had filed the brief on behalf of the two probate judge defendants asking the Court in effect to reverse *Baker v. Carr.* He opened by noting the uniqueness of apportionment litigation, which involves not merely a judicial negation of state action in traditional fashion but a "judicial transfer of political power." [51] However, instead of proceeding from this thought to a discussion of possible federal standards in the light of the unavoidably political effect which any court apportionment order would have, he shifted to a fruitless attack on *Baker v. Carr.* Chief Justice Warren asked, "How long can we wait?" noting that Alabama had no reapportionment from 1901 to the federal district court's action in 1962.

When counsel tried to suggest that there might be a federal power to declare a right but no power to enforce it, Justice Harlan intervened: "If Alabama's apportionment did violate the federal Constitution, a federal court would have power to act would it not?" Justice Harlan obviously was trying to warn Mr. Pitts away from attacking the principle of federal supremacy itself and to focus on the basic question of what state legislative apportionment standards, if any, can be derived from the Fourteenth Amendment. But the effort was fruitless, for Mr. Pitts skipped to a barebones state sovereignty argument, asserting in conclusion that states "would lose the last vestige of sovereignty if federal courts can reapportion."

Mr. Pitts was followed by Attorney General Flowers, who freely conceded that Alabama needed federal judicial pressure in order to achieve reapportionment. Like so many Southern attorneys general before the Supreme Court in reapportionment and civil rights cases in recent years, he played a losing hand pleasantly and well. The 1901 apportionment, because of population changes, is now "unfair, unjust, and approaches the ridiculous," he conceded. At the same time he felt that a call for a general

---

48. McGowan v. Maryland, 366 U.S. 420 (1961). Brief, p. 4.
49. MacDougal v. Green, 335 U.S. 281 (1948). Brief, p. 4.
50. Williamson v. Lee Optical, 348 U.S. 483 (1955). Brief, p. 4.
51. The thought was quoted from the present author's article "Apportionment Standards and Judicial Power," 38 *Notre Dame Lawyer* 367 (1963).

federal standard was unsound. He requested in effect an advisory opinion from the Supreme Court stating that the 1901 Alabama Constitution could be the basis for an apportionment valid under the Fourteenth Amendment; to be followed by federal court action to force the legislature to reapportion under the 1901 Constitution. However, as Justices William J. Brennan, Jr., and Byron R. White noted, this would be to ask the Court to render an advisory opinion on an abstract question because of the discretionary features of the 1901 Alabama apportionment provisions, and because of uncertainty concerning the true meaning of the 1901 Constitution.

Similar to the Flowers argument was the one made by David J. Vann. He wanted the Supreme Court to construe and modify the Alabama state constitution, and then declare it as modified to be in accord with the Fourteenth Amendment. This he thought would lead to effective legislative action. But it is not the function of federal courts to construe and modify state law on constitutional questions. It is the function of federal courts to take state laws as clarified and implemented by *state practice* and ascertain whether or not the "living law" of the state is in accord with federal constitutional standards.

The argument of Charles Morgan, Jr., agreed with Attorney General Flowers on the basic proposition of leaving future developments to the federal district court, but disagreed on the proposition that an apportionment complying with the 1901 Alabama Constitution would be adequate. Going considerably beyond the position taken in his brief, he now argued for concentration on population as the sole relevant standard for apportionment. At the risk of considerable oversimplification he asserted that a population standard was not only constitutionally correct but also workable and easily achieved in practice.

Just as the brief by John W. McConnell, Jr., for some intervening plaintiffs was the only one to probe representation theory and practice, so the McConnell oral argument was by far the most interesting in the Alabama sequence. It also was the one where Justice Harlan by his silence indicated that he had given up on attempts to dissuade the Court from a simple equal population rule. McConnell was sensitive to the problem of minority representation but also absolutely rigid on a mathematical approach toward district equalization to achieve "one man-one vote." There might be experimentation in regard to the *unit* of representation, he said, but there should be absolute per-capita equality in assigning representatives to the selected units. He apparently meant to leave room for proportional representation where, in effect, the political party becomes the *unit* of representation and its actual representation in the legislature is proportioned mathematically according to its percentage of popular support. The thought was not picked up by the Court, however. There was no real discussion of the problem of minority representation and the corollary problem of overrepresentation of the dominant party, which so frequently accompanies multimember district systems and is possible too in single-member district systems whenever the dominant party's voting strength is fortuitously spread.

Alternatively, as had been mentioned in the McConnell Brief, some check on bare majority power without disturbing a rigid per-capita equalization of districts, could be provided by requiring an extraordinary majority in the legislature to pass certain kinds of measures. Solicitor General Cox was asked by Justice Byron R. White to comment on this thought. He was inclined to agree that if both houses were apportioned on a population basis it would be concurrently permissible to require both houses to operate by extraordinary majorities, even though this might yield an extraordinarily "negative government."

Elaborating on his response, the Solicitor suggested that some balancing of interests should still be permissible in legislative apportionment, so long as it did not create preferred political classes. Realistically, however, as Justice Goldberg noted, any system of population deviations in districting whether "rational" or capricious *does* tend to create preferences between classes which often can be loosely dubbed "rural" and "urban." For example, a federal plan—a plan which Solicitor General Cox felt was not squarely at issue and whose constitutionality could be avoided—has the conscious purpose and effect of minimizing the per-capita representation which the more populous areas otherwise would obtain in order to achieve corollary interests of providing some representation for political subdivisions as such, without regard to their relative population.

c. Unconstitutional, 8 to 1

By an eight-to-one vote the Supreme Court affirmed the district court's reapportionment actions.[52] And certainly if the equal protection clause were to be construed to check "invidious discrimination" in apportionment, Alabama qualified for federal restraint. Neither in fact nor legal theory did the case offer any basis for staying the federal hand, unless *Baker* v. *Carr* itself were to be reversed. Hence, the sole dissent by Justice Harlan was devoted to the proposition that *Baker* had no foundation, because the Fourteenth Amendment, construed in historical context, created no federal cause of action against state legislative apportionment discretion.

52. Reynolds v. Sims, 377 U.S. 533 (1964).

E. Maryland: "Federal Plan, Almost"

Yet another Southern case in the 1963–1964 Supreme Court Term sequence of reapportionment appeals came from Maryland—*Maryland Committee for Fair Representation* v. *Tawes*.[53] Maryland has been an odd state, caught on the "wrong side" of Washington during the Civil War. Its politics have been torn between the dominant antebellum slavery spirit of southern Maryland and the Eastern Shore (across Chesapeake Bay), and the Northern-oriented, family-farm spirit of the Upland and Appalachian western portion. Its port city of Baltimore, an uneasy mixture of North and South, was always allied politically by Democratic party ties more to the Eastern Shore than to the Upland West.

The pre-*Baker* malapportionment was egregious, in typical Southern fashion, in both houses.[54] Maryland was also one of two states, the other being Delaware, in which the state constitution froze apportionment of *both* houses of the legislature. In the house and senate respectively the population variance ratios were 12 to 1 and 32 to 1 and the electoral percentages respectively were 24.7 percent and 14.1 percent. In more meaningful terms of actual regional politics, it could be noted that in the house the four populous suburban counties plus Baltimore City, containing 75.3 percent of the state's population, had less than half of the house seats—60 of the total of 123. In the senate these same five units had only 10 of a total of 29 senators. Of the ten urban-suburban senators, six were allocated to Baltimore City with a 1960 population of 939,024, while the four largest counties with a combined population of 1,397,385 had only one senator apiece. Thus there was a real threat of minority rule because of egregious population deviations in both houses. There was also a "crazy-quilt" allocation of urban area senators.

The Maryland plaintiffs, who first filed their suit in mid-1960, chose the state courts rather than the federal district court as their reapportionment battle-ground. In a ruling by the state's highest court, the Court of Appeals, they met partial success so that Maryland was one of the first states

53. 377 U.S. 656 (1964).
54. See table of pre-*Baker* apportionment figures, Appendix A. With the exception of a few large and sparsely populated Western states such as Nevada and Idaho, and the state of Connecticut in New England, the egregious underrepresentation of population in both houses is more a Southern than Northern characteristic. The outstanding exception in the South was, of course, Virginia which had always been remarkably well apportioned by pre-*Baker* standards.

to achieve a post-*Baker* v. *Carr* reapportionment of part of its legislature. *Baker* was decided on March 26, 1962. The Maryland Court of Appeals on April 25, 1962, reversed a lower court which had tossed out a reapportionment suit and remanded for trial. The Court of Appeals intimated (1) that if plaintiffs' allegations of mathematical deviations were proven, the Maryland legislature would be unconstitutional, (2) that in that event appropriate relief would be to give the governor opportunity to call an extraordinary reapportionment session.[55] On May 24, 1962, the lower court did invalidate Maryland's lower house but not the senate. One day later Governor J. Millard Tawes called a special session which reapportioned the lower house on May 31, 1962, but not until Governor Tawes, in what the *Washington Post* called the "first open display of executive anger at the Legislature during his four years in office," had sent a sharp message. The interim reapportionment produced by the governor's message added nineteen additional house seats, and for the first time gave the 75 percent of the population in urban areas a majority (55 percent) of the seats in the lower house.

Until the governor's message arrived, legislators from southern Maryland and the Eastern Shore, with an odd persistence bred from generations of comfortable overrepresentation, were laboring to bring forth a bill which actually could have worsened the urban position in the long run.[56] The tone of Maryland legislative politics for generations was reflected in this refrain from a song which Eastern Shore legislators were wont to sing while resting from their day's labors:

> . . . we don't give a damn
> For the whole state of Maryland,
> We are from the
> E a s t e r n   S h o r e !

The appeal to the United States Supreme Court in the Maryland case was from the split decision of the Maryland Court of Appeals in *Maryland Committee for Fair Representation* v. *Tawes*[57] on September 25, 1962, which had held that *Baker* v. *Carr* had not touched federal plans. The Maryland court felt that Maryland's senate, despite the representation bulge in favor of declining Baltimore City (one senator per county but six for Baltimore City which was not part of any county) could be upheld as part of a valid federal plan in view of the court-forced interim reapportionment of the lower house which consisted of adding nineteen seats to be elected at-large in the larger units. The interim plan had

55. Maryland Committee for Fair Representation v. Tawes, 228 Md. 412, 180 A. 2d 656 (1962).
56. *Washington Post*, June 1, 1962, p. 1, col. 8, p. 9, col. 1.
57. 229 Md. 406, 184 A. 2d 715 (1962).

changed the lower house population variance ratio and electoral percentage from 12 to 1 to 6 to 1 and from 24.7 percent to 35.6 percent.

a. *Plaintiff's Case on Appeal*

Technically, plaintiffs were appealing only the Maryland Court of Appeals holding that the senate could continue on a one-senator-per-county basis, with six senators for Baltimore City. But Alfred L. Scanlan (who shepherded all of Maryland's legislative apportionment, county-unit, congressional districting litigation to successful conclusion) also developed and asserted a theory that a legislature's representativeness must be viewed as a whole. This theory, eventually embraced by the Supreme Court, had special appeal in the Maryland situation for two reasons. First, it is a premise of the federal plan argument itself that the "population" house should follow population not just to a degree but rigidly. Second, the Maryland Court of Appeals decision leaving the senate undisturbed apparently was premised on the thought that the legislature could finish the job of putting the lower house on a population basis. But no further reapportionment action had occurred and it seemed unlikely that without further judicial pressure the legislature would replace the 1962 interim reapportionment of the lower house with a plan more exactly based on population.

Plaintiffs' brief in the Supreme Court was noteworthy for including two lines of proof (or conclusionary factual allegations) which had been rejected at the trial level in the New York reapportionment case. These were (1) a compilation of statements from political scientists and others on the adverse consequences of malapportionment (not based, however, on empirical studies), and (2) some data showing that revenue collections in more populous areas of the state exceeded in percentage terms both return of funds to those areas and the percent of representation of populous areas in the legislature.[58] This latter material however was unaccompanied by any discussion of grant-in-aid or "share-the-wealth" theory. The Supreme Court has yet to hold that lack of correspondence between amount of tax revenue raised in an area and amount of tax revenue spent in an area presents a constitutional question, or is relevant to the issue of constitutionality of a given apportionment plan. Indeed, such a ruling would end the "war on poverty." The brief also gave some post-1962 instances where measures passed by the partially reapportioned Maryland lower house had been defeated in the Maryland senate, e.g., proposal to abolish the county-unit system for nominations in Maryland, a nonpopulation house reapportionment measure passed by the senate in 1963 but rejected by the house, senate rejection of increased financial aid to the

58. Brief for Appellants, pp. 8–9, 34–41.

state school system, and measures concerning small loans and conservation.

The primary reliance of the Maryland plaintiffs on appeal was to demonstrate continued major population disparities, to rebut the federal plan defense by showing that Maryland did not in truth have a federal plan, and to assert that in any event even a true federal plan would not comply with the Fourteenth Amendment.

b. *State's Case on Appeal*

The obvious strategy for the state was to push to the fore one argument available only in the Maryland case and unavailable in the other cases receiving plenary consideration: that is, that a federal plan was both a traditional and reasonable apportionment device, and that Maryland now was operating under a federal plan. However, the state entered the fray with one hand tied behind his back. Legislative recalcitrance—in part induced by the Supreme Court's deliberate withholding of standards in the *Baker v. Carr* opinions—had prevented the state in the 1963 legislative session from eliminating disparity of treatment between Baltimore City and large suburban counties in the senate, or from replacing the 1962 interim reapportionment of the house with a straight population plan.

In retrospect it is possible to see a plausible basis for recriminations on each side. The legislature—indeed, legislatures in general in this situation —could say that *Baker* gave legislators no specific target to shoot at, and contained no intimation that the Court eventually would adopt so strict a standard as to invalidate virtually each house in each legislature in the nation. On the other hand it could be said on behalf of the Supreme Court that the basic problem of legislative malapportionment being one of legislative nonaction, evidence of continued nonaction or niggardly action in the immediate post-*Baker* period would justify vigorous judicial response. The Court could feel that little change would be accomplished unless a fairly strict and simple population equality standard were imposed across the board.

At a higher level of critique it may be suggested that this kind of polarization of positions, with no possibility of communication in between, exemplifies the deficiency of the adversary method of litigation as the mode for accomplishing major alterations in governmental principles, policies, and structure. Litigation, by forcing both polarization and lack of communication, forecloses meaningful consideration of middle-ground positions which may be more sound both in principle and in operation. If ever a constitutional convention has utility it would seem to have utility to a unique degree in regard to the standards and process of legislative apportionment for the simple reason that apportionment is a constitutive act of government.[59]

The most telling argument for the state (which would have been more plausible had Maryland had as good a reapportionment record as Virginia) was to attempt to put the burden of proof of invidious discrimination back on the plaintiff, and to call for empirical evidence rather than gross census tract comparisons. Plaintiffs, for example, had treated as a unity the 75 percent of the population residing in Baltimore City and in four large suburban counties, and had found them to be underrepresented. The state noted the forced-marriage nature of such a statistic, combining as it does the "have nots" of the Negro ghettos of Baltimore City and the white middle-class "haves" of Baltimore County and other counties. As Professor Alexander M. Bickel had said:

> All we have been given are plays on words, plays on statistics, and meaningless figures arbitrarily picked out of thin air . . . . What does it mean to juggle ratios or to bewail the fact that 20 per cent of a state's population can elect a majority of its legislature, X per cent of the population of the United States can elect the President, and X − 10 per cent can elect the Senate? These are not facts; such things never happen.[60]

On the basic issue of validity of state use of a federal plan the state relied on Professor Bickel's question whether we are "to believe that our federal government lacks a feature that is 'basic to the successful operation of a democracy'?—that, indeed, it contains an inconsistent feature, and is therefore not a successfully operating democracy?" [61] It added the similar comment of Professor Israel:

> . . . it would be anomalous to hold that the Constitution condemns a state's adoption of a bicameral legislature with one house appor-

59. A case which sharply illustrates the point that not all "one man-one vote" issues are simple civil right to vote issues is the disputed Georgia gubernatorial election case, Fortson v. Morris, 385 U.S. 231 (1967). The majority in that case felt that since there would be no apparent constitutional basis for denying a state the option of adopting the parliamentary system (legislative selection of the executive head), there likewise should be no constitutional objection to Georgia's half-way house system of legislative selection of the governor from the top two candidates in the event no candidate achieved a popular vote majority. However, the supposed spirit of "one man-one vote" induced three members of the Supreme Court to express the view that Georgia should neither be allowed to pursue her existing policy of using legislative selection of a governor as a backstop for the popular election process nor be permitted to make a complete substitution of the parliamentary system for the traditional American system of popular election of the executive head. See Ch. VI, pp. 136–37; Ch. XVI, p. 423.
60. Alexander M. Bickel, "Reapportionment and Liberal Myths," 35 *Commentary* 483, 490–91 (June 1963).
61. *Id.* at 487.

tioned essentially on the basis of population and the other apportioned with reference to the representation of political subdivisions when that same Constitution adopted just such a legislative system, with substantial numerical inequality of representation in the Federal Senate, which has been accepted without question since ratification. . . . the question has been raised as to how an institutional scheme may be rational if it is the product of compromise between equal forces and arbitrary when it results from a grant made within the discretion of the granting body.[62]

c. The 14-State Amici Brief for the Federal Plan

The Maryland case also evoked the only "united front" amici brief on behalf of the states in the course of reapportionment litigation in the Supreme Court. The brief, confined to the federal plan issue, was filed by the Attorney General of New Jersey and signed by attorneys general of the following additional states: Arizona, Colorado, Hawaii, Idaho, Indiana, Kansas, Louisiana, North Carolina, North Dakota, Pennsylvania, Rhode Island, South Dakota, Vermont.[63] This amici brief, like the appendix to the United States Solicitor General's amicus brief also filed in the Maryland case, contains an interesting collection of materials on the principles of representative government expressed in the federal Constitutional Convention of 1787 and immediately thereafter. But the issue was Fourteenth Amendment restriction on state legislative discretion in apportionment and districting matters. And the Court already had signaled in Brown v. Board of Education its distaste for historical objections to creative constitutionalism, and its preference for functional analyses.[64] It would seem therefore that a disquisition on the reasonableness of a federal plan arrangement in the context of democratic representation theories and operating political realities would have had greater relevance. However, to this question were devoted only eight pages of the seventy-two page amici brief filed on behalf of the fourteen states and only five pages of the one hundred and eighteen page appendix filed by the United States Solicitor General.

Impressions derived from a perusal of the "history" in these briefs are several. "People" and "population" are as elusive terms in these historical

62. Jerold H. Israel, "On Charting a Course Through the Mathematical Quagmire: The Future of Baker v. Carr," 61 Mich. L. Rev. 107, 121–22 (1963).
63. Brief for Attorneys General of the States as Amici Curiae, Maryland Committee for Fair Representation v. Tawes, 39–40.
64. At the time these briefs were filed, the anomalous history-stretching opinion of Mr. Justice Black justifying the equal population district principle for congressional districts in Wesberry v. Sanders had not yet been issued. See discussion in Chapter VIII, supra.

materials as in state constitutions. A speaker or a draftsman may refer to
"population basis" as the foundation of democratic government. But it
makes a world of difference whether the intended connotation is rigid
equalization within a range of 5 to 10 percent, or occasional variations up
to a ratio of 2 to 1. Another impression is that the record is skimpy indeed
on the proposition that the Founding Fathers contemplated a constitutional rule placing all three legislation-influencing organs—governor,
upper house, lower house—on a rigid population equality basis. A third
impression is that representation concepts throughout our history and into
the modern era have always found room for a federal plan, or something
approaching a federal plan. Although not mentioned in the brief filed on
behalf of fourteen states, a recognition of constituent units *as units* frequently has been a precondition of city-county consolidation or of other
arrangements designed to coalesce local units into a more effective metropolitan area government. Solicitor General Cox himself in his Maryland
brief had said that if one house of a bicameral legislature is apportioned
substantially according to population there may be "considerable room" [65]
for recognition of other considerations in the second house.

d. *Oral Argument*

A highlight of the Maryland oral argument, and of all the oral arguments,
was the vigorous presentation for the plaintiffs by Alfred L. Scanlan. A
lawyer's lawyer and a politician's lawyer, he subsequently played a major
role in Joseph D. Tydings's successful candidacy for the United States
Senate. At one point he was asked by Justice Goldberg why Baltimore
City—which had been separated from Baltimore County years before and,
therefore, had acquired quasi-county status of its own—had been given
more senate representation than was accorded to counties. "They tell me
it is because Baltimore is unique, your Honor," Scanlan replied, "and I
find this to be irrefutable. Ask anyone who has been there." In more serious vein, he went on to say that population was the apparent basis for
Baltimore City's extra senators, and equal treatment now required that
the larger suburban counties with a similar population bulge likewise receive extra senators.

Mr. Scanlan's inclusion in his listing of harmful effects of malapportionment of such effects as legislative stalemate and use of nonpopulation
factors in the so-called "equalization formula" for sharing certain state tax
revenues prompted Justice Stewart to wonder whether the "Court is to
weigh the goodness and badness of these effects," and particularly the pol-

65. Brief of the United States as Amicus Curiae, Maryland Committee for Fair Representation v. Tawes, p. 47.

icy of having "more money go to the impoverished areas of the state."
In a closing peroration Mr. Scanlan countered the state's argument
about fear of "tyranny of the majority" with the assurance that "if we get
a majority we'll be as nice to them as they were to us."

The case for the state was virtually derailed at the outset of oral argument when Assistant Attorney General Robert S. Bourbon brought a new
development to the Court's attention. He noted that a lower state court,
operating under a state constitutional provision but also mentioning the
equal protection clause, had voided state legislature districts *inside* Baltimore City because of population inequalities.[66] Perhaps his purpose was
to show good faith on the part of the state judiciary; that it could be
trusted to act on reapportionment without detailed supervision from the
United States Supreme Court. But the immediate result was to invite a
devastating question from Chief Justice Warren: "How can you distinguish between the constitutional rule regarding Baltimore City and the
rules applicable to the rest of the state?"

After a further detour into Maryland geography and the historic tradition of county representation, the argument was finally refocused on basic
questions of representation theory and apportionment standards. The
state's strongest points were to focus on the complexities of representation, on politics and compromise, on the "total responsiveness of government"—in short, to stress the proposition that the operating tradition of
the American system was more one of consensus government than of inci-
sive majoritarianism. But the state's hands were not sufficiently clean to
make the most of this line of argument. As Justice White pointed out,
the population disparities in both houses were not counterbalancing, but
tended to favor the same people. And in response to a question from
Chief Justice Warren, it was conceded that there was no nonjudicial remedy in the state for malapportionment. In 1950 a substantial popular majority had called for a constitutional convention, but the legislature refused to call a convention.[67] Under the Maryland state constitution the
needed majority is a majority of all those at the polls and not just a majority of those voting on the question.

Throughout the proceedings the state insisted that only the constitutionality of the senate was before the Supreme Court and not the lower
house. It relied on the 1962 sequence of litigation in Maryland courts, and

66. Culotta v. D'Alesandro (Circuit Court for Baltimore City, October 31, 1963).
The intra-Baltimore state legislative districts were realigned in special session of the
legislature in March 1964 but no other reapportionment action was taken.
67. Jurisdictional Statement, Maryland Committee for Fair Representation v. Tawes,
p. 11.

on the flat statement of the Maryland Court of Appeals in its opinion invalidating the state senate that: "No question is presented as to the validity of the 'stop-gap' legislation or the reapportionment of the House of Delegates." [68]

Part of the state's time was yielded to Assistant Attorney General Theodore I. Botter of New Jersey who spoke on behalf of the fourteen states who had filed the above-noted amici brief supporting the federal plan concept. He was the only counsel to try to revive the guarantee clause of Article IV (guarantee to every state of a republican form of government) as the touchstone of reapportionment litigation rather than the equal protection of the laws clause. What was guaranteed, he suggested, was the existing form of government of the states, which was not "one man-one vote government"; thus, a state without violating this clause could choose any other "republican" form. In response to a question from Justice White he suggested that if the guarantee clause were thought to give the states too much latitude it could be deemed modified, but not entirely replaced, by the subsequently enacted equal protection clause of the Fourteenth Amendment. "Majority rule in both houses does not provide adequate protection for minorities," he said; "the minority should have bargaining power in one house."

e. *Unconstitutional, 7 to 2*

Rejecting the federal plan argument of the state, and of the attorneys general of fourteen other states, the Supreme Court invalidated the Maryland senate. Adopting the plaintiffs' view that the issue under the Fourteenth Amendment always should be the "combined total representation" of a legislature, the Court also reached and invalidated Maryland's lower house saying:

> Regardless of possible concessions made by the parties and the scope of the consideration of the courts below, in reviewing a state legislative apportionment case this Court must of necessity consider the challenged scheme as a whole in determining whether the particular State's apportionment plan, in its entirety, meets federal constitutional requisites. It is simply impossible to decide upon the validity of the apportionment of one house of a bicameral legislature in the abstract, without also evaluating the actual scheme of representation employed with respect to the other house. Rather, the proper, and indeed indispensable, subject for judical focus in the legislative appor-

68. Maryland Committee for Fair Representation v. Tawes, 229 Md. 406, 410, 184 A. 2d 715, 716 (1962).

tionment controversy is the *overall representation* accorded to the State's voters, *in both houses of a bicameral state legislature.*[69]

The Court's use of an "overall representation" concept as delineated in this quotation reveals some conceptual confusion and may indeed be inconsistent with the basic "right to vote" thrust of its opinions in the other cases. If the central theory is a personal civil right to vote, measured solely in terms of district population equality, there is no basis for treating one house differently from the other. The quoted statement, however, with its talk of "the challenged scheme as a whole" and "overall representation" seemed to infer that an equalization-in-toto concept may counterbalance some inequalities inside a given legislative house.

In other words, if a given area is underrepresented in the lower house, but correspondingly overrepresented in the senate, the plan might be upheld. Such a conclusion would require a judgment—if our concern really is representation and not bare population mechanics—that the two houses are sufficiently equal so that a "voice" loss in one can be equalized by a corresponding "voice" gain in the other. Yet it is common knowledge that differences in regard to size of a house, seniority, age, leadership, talent, length of term, power to initiate certain bills, and so forth, normally make one house far more important to a given constituency than the other house. Smaller units of government (the underpopulated towns and counties), and the more localized political or social interests, either obtain a "voice" in the larger legislative house by having their own districts or have no effective voice at all. In the smaller house (normally the senate), such interests are submerged components of large multitown, multicounty districts. Therefore, a mathematical (and actual) underrepresentation in a lower house of a localized area *cannot* be counterbalanced in true *representation* terms in the senate by giving greater weight to the large senate district of which the local area is merely a component part. Although the senate district as a whole will have more weight, the local sub-area within it often will share little of it.

On analysis, therefore, the quoted statement from the Court's opinion in the Maryland case, which the Court repeated and expanded in the Colorado case, as noted below, is anomalous and reveals either a deficient or an inconsistent constitutional theory of apportionment. A better course for the Supreme Court to have taken to reach and invalidate Maryland's lower house, assuming the Court felt plaintiffs had sufficiently preserved their "standing" in this regard, would have been simply to take judicial notice that lower house figures were in the record and that they were too deviant.

69. Maryland Committee for Fair Representation v. Tawes, 377 U.S. 656, 673 (1964) (emphasis added).

F. Virginia: Population Rectitude; Military Personnel; Federal Abstention

The Virginia case, *Davis* v. *Mann*,[70] came to the Supreme Court from a state which had consistently reapportioned itself after each federal census as required by the state constitution, and which at the time of *Baker* was the eighth best apportioned state in the nation as measured by the fictional electoral percentage. The top seven were Oregon, Massachusetts, New Hampshire, West Virginia, Maine, Wisconsin, and Alaska, none of which were involved in the reapportionment appeals from 15 states decided by the Court in June 1964. The electoral percentage figures for Virginia were for the senate 41.1 percent and for the house 40.5 percent; and the respective population variance ratios were 2.65 to 1 and 4.36 to 1. Among the plaintiff attorneys in the various state apportionment appeals to the Supreme Court the Virginia case therefore was viewed as one of the "tough ones" despite the fact that a federal district court had invalidated the plan by a 2 to 1 vote in 1962 after *Baker* v. *Carr*.

The federal district court majority in an opinion by Judge Bryan had used the fairly common post-*Baker* approach of presuming unconstitutionality on the basis of population disparities alone and shifting the burden of proof to the state to show a "rational basis" for the disparities. The court was impressed with the pattern of discrimination against Norfolk and against the more populous northern Virginia counties adjacent to Washington which had ballooned in the war and postwar period. For example, Fairfax County had three rather than its mathematical entitlement of seven lower house delegates, two rather than three senators. In the lower house, 27 districts (of a total of 70) had more than three times the representation of Fairfax. The defendant's "federal plan" argument was deemed irrelevant because Virginia had purported to apportion both houses on the same basis. An alternative argument that the disparities would not look so bad if military personnel were subtracted was properly treated as an afterthought for at least two reasons: (1) some military personnel had qualified to vote in Virginia; (2) the state had not consciously adjusted its statewide apportionment base by subtracting military personnel (later approved for Hawaii by the Supreme Court in 1966).[71] Vir-

---

70. 377 U.S. 678 (1964). For the "Virginia story" down to 1965 see Ralph Eisenberg, "Legislative Reapportionment and Congressional Redistricting in Virginia," 23 *Wash. & Lee L. Rev.* 295 (1966).
71. Burns v. Richardson, 384 U.S. 81 (1966).

ginia appeared to have operated "ad hoc and by hunch" in cutting back apportionments in certain areas.

District Judge Hoffman, dissenting, had objected to deciding the major constitutional issue of "invidious discrimination" [72] on the basis solely of mathematical evidence and presumptions. Not only might such an approach fall short of elucidating the complexities of apportionment; it would invite continuous litigation over population percentage points.

a. Federal Abstention

In the Virginia case, as in several of the other reapportionment cases between *Baker* and *Reynolds*, the defendants and the dissenting district judge made much of the doctrine of federal abstention. (However, among the "big six" reapportionment cases of June 1964 only the Virginia case included the federal abstention issue.)

In this delicate field, it was argued, more time should be allowed for legislative reaction. And federal district courts should stay their hand where state courts have not yet been utilized. To this the plaintiffs responded that the abstention doctrine has only limited application to civil rights cases—characterizing their suit as simply a right to vote case—in the absence of exceptional circumstances.[73]

The abstention dispute really turned on one major point. Plaintiffs would confine federal abstention to the area of state law ambiguity. Defendants and Judge Hoffman thought the doctrine should extend also to areas like reapportionment where constitutional standards, even if known, would still leave broad discretion in implementation, and where state court knowledge of the local scene might be especially pertinent. Interestingly enough, while the appeal to the Supreme Court from the federal district court's invalidation of Virginia's apportionment was still pending, another suit was filed in a Virginia state court. It held the apportionment constitutional. Some persons saw in this effort an attempt—which failed —to get the litigation established in state courts and thus stave off or influence action by the Supreme Court.

Basically, "federal abstention," like "standing" and "justiciability," is more a matter of finding some place to hide when faced with a difficult issue than a matter of clear principle. The narrow exception is where an ambiguous state law which is crucial to the decision has not yet been in-

72. Mann v. Davis, 213 F. Supp. 577, 586 (E.D. Va. 1962) (Hoffman, D.J., dissenting).
73. Plaintiffs' Reply and Supplemental Trial Brief, pp. 7–18. See also Defendant's Brief, pp. 16–42.
Musical chairs occurred in North Dakota; the federal court abstained, but then the state court invoked comity and put the federal court back in the hot seat again. State v. Meier, 127 N.W. 2d 665 (N.D. 1964).

terpreted by the state's own courts. The abstention doctrine played no significant role in the reapportionment field despite the attempt of some journalists to read into some cryptic Supreme Court reapportionment orders in 1965 a preference for state court resolution of the reapportionment muddle.

b. Oral Argument

In the oral argument in the Supreme Court the state strategy was to stress the point that the population disparities in Virginia's apportionment were far smaller than in any other case then before the Court, and that if military personnel be excluded the population variance ratios would be further reduced. Seemingly unimpressed by the military exclusion argument Justice Black pressed counsel for any other "rational" ground for urban underrepresentation. Without mentioning the Byrd machine by name, Henry E. Howell, Jr., of Norfolk enlivened a politically aseptic argument by responding that the "politically-manageable counties were favored— *that* was the classification device."

d. Unconstitutional, 8 to 1

The Supreme Court, voting 8 to 1 with special concurrences by Justices Tom C. Clark and Potter Stewart, sustained the district court's invalidation of Virginia's apportionment as not being apportioned "sufficiently on a population basis to be constitutionally sustainable." The Court also implied that even if military population were excluded (which it would not concede as proper on this record) the resulting population variance ratios of 2.22 to 1 and 3.53 to 1 in the senate and house respectively still would be too great.

G. Delaware: "Let's Reverse *Brown* v. *Board of Education*"

Of the six cases accepted for plenary review, the population deviations at issue in the Delaware case, *Roman* v. *Sincock*,[74] were the most extreme. And Delaware, like Maryland, had a strong Southern orientation. Under a 1963 apportionment proposed under judicial pressure the population variance ratio would have been reduced from 35 to 1 to 12 to 1 in the lower house but would have remained 15 to 1 in the senate. The electoral percentage in each house would still be miniscule—18.5 percent and 22 percent in the house and senate, respectively. It is a mystery why such a sim-

74. 377 U.S. 695 (1964).

ple case as Delaware presented was brought on for plenary review. It raised no issues not also raised, or better raised, in the other five plenary review cases. Conversely, there were issues among the nine additional cases retained for summary review which merited full airing and which were not represented in the cases granted full review, e.g., the interrelation of the bipartisan apportionment commission and the state supreme court in Michigan,[75] and in Ohio the pure federal plan.[76]

The Delaware case came up from a federal district court which had invalidated both the pre-existing apportionment dating from 1897 and the proposed 1963 reapportionment constitutional amendment. The court felt that population must be the starting point for apportionment of both houses, and intimated that maximum deviations of under 50 percent might be tolerable. One judge dissented, feeling that a federal plan was permissible for one house. In contrast to the New York case, where the federal district court had refused to admit social science testimony on the ground that it would be merely an opinion on a legal issue, the Delaware court heard opinion testimony by political scientists and others. It is unclear what weight was given to the testimony, although the court did note that the social scientists unanimously favored placing at least one house on a population equality principle.[77] As might be expected, given the egregious population disparities in Delaware's apportionment, the court placed special stress on the importance of assuring the majority an affirmative power of action so that "major legislation desired by the great majority of electors of Delaware" may not be blocked. "Effecting the will of the majority of the people of the State," the court said, "must be deemed to be the foundation of any apportionment plan." [78]

a. *State's Case on Appeal*

If lower courts agreed on anything in the interim between *Baker* and *Reynolds*, it was the irrelevance of history and "original meaning" as guides to the scope of the equal protection clause. Judges obviously were influenced by *Brown* v. *Board of Education*, the basic desegregation decision of 1954. There the Supreme Court, although nominally giving some consideration to history and finding no conclusive mandate to desegregate education, had moved to impregnable higher ground by embracing developmental constitutionalism and saying "we cannot turn the clock back to 1868 when the Amendment was adopted, or even to 1896 when Plessy v. Ferguson [separate but equal doctrine] was written." [79]

75. Beadle v. Scholle, 377 U.S. 990 (1964).
76. Nolan v. Rhodes, 378 U.S. 556 (1964).
77. Roman v. Sincock, 215 F. Supp. 169, 185 (D. Del. 1963).
78. *Id.* at 190.
79. Brown v. Board of Education, 347 U.S. 483, 492 (1954).

Nevertheless, the Delaware appeal was centered on history and the original meaning of the Fourteenth Amendment. It was an attack therefore on the current constitutional posture of the Court and, inferentially, on *Brown* itself. At oral argument the state's special counsel, Frederick Bernays Wiener, was asked at least twice if the logic of his position did not entail reversing *Baker*, if not *Brown* itself.

If one concentrates on history and evidence of contemporary understanding as guides to original meaning, there is much to be said for the basic Wiener argument for Delaware, even though it captured the fancy of only one justice—Justice Harlan. But it would need to be handled more carefully than was done in the Delaware brief in order not to scare off the Court by appearing to make a frontal assault on *Brown*. The first step, which the brief omitted, would be to reinterpret and distinguish *Brown*.

The starting point of such a reinterpretation would be to point out that *Brown* is a Negro case; and that the Fourteenth Amendment is concededly a Negro-centered amendment, even if not confined to racial matters. Therefore, it could be urged, the Amendment needs to be expansively interpreted in order to accomplish its central purpose of integrating the freed slave into American society. Concededly when the starting point is slavery, integration is not easy. Hence, the argument would continue, a plausible interpretation of the Fourteenth Amendment in relation to segregated educaton would be to read it as prohibiting racial classification in governmental matters "as soon as feasible." Such a reading would explain away the historical proof that desegregation was not immediately pressed by the men who had brought into being the Fourteenth Amendment. The integrative purpose of the Fourteenth Amendment would remain intact—and overdue for fulfillment in 1954. The second step in such a cautious historical argument would be to note that apportionment is not a racial matter. Thus apportionment is outside the trend of expansive interpretation of the Fourteenth, a trend concededly necessary to accomplish its integrative purpose in racial matters.

The final step, the only one detailed in the state's brief, is to show by rather solid evidence that neither voting nor apportionment matters were contemplated as being within the scope of the Fourteenth Amendment. And it also could be shown that "malapportionment" (as measured by the then *relatively* strict new post-*Baker* standards of the Delaware federal district court—by which no district in either house could deviate by more than 50 percent) was endemic in the legislatures which ratified the Amendment, and in legislatures of subsequently admitted states.

Vigorous stress on this third step in Delaware's brief, without adequate attention to the other two, created the aura of an attack on *Brown* itself.

Also, even if a separation of segregation and apportionment could be made in regard to original meaning of the Fourteenth, appellants faced the likelihood that the Court would be disinclined anyway to do anything which might be misconstrued as undercutting *Brown*. It is a fair question therefore whether this Delaware line of argument, offered as virtually the sole defense, was advisable. Counsel and state had the satisfaction of bringing home to the Court that it was really amending the Constitution —as Justice Harlan subsequently charged—*if* we grant the state its version of original meaning. But if the purpose of litigation is to win cases, or at least to compromise them on the least onerous terms possible, an "all eggs in one basket" argument is unduly chancy. Like an experimental high-fashion bathing suit, it leaves no second line of defense.

The state did offer two other points, both greatly overshadowed by the historical argument. One was that the Court's previous and now discarded experience with "erecting economic philosophies into constitutional absolutes under the Due Process Clause stands as a solemn warning against now erecting political philosophies into similar constitutional absolutes under the Equal Protection Clause." [80] The other was that the interpretation of equal protection in nonracial matters traditionally had been flexible rather than rigid, as in the Sunday Closing cases. Each of these points was related in the brief to a plea in favor of state discretion. Neither point was sufficiently related to representation theory and practice which was, and still is, the central issue.

b. *Plaintiff's Case on Appeal*

Plaintiffs had gained one of the tighter judicial orders issued in the interim between *Baker* and *Reynolds*. They simply sought to hold on to their victory by dissuading the Court from following the path back to the original meaning of the Fourteenth Amendment indicated by Mr. Wiener for the state. Their brief reiterated the customary arguments about a burden of justification being placed on the state when mathematical disparities are proven—an especially forceful argument in the light of the egregious population inequalities in both houses in Delaware. And they sought to push apportionment under the umbrella of the *Brown* decision.

c. *Oral Argument*

A month elapsed between the oral arguments in the Alabama, Maryland, New York, and Virginia cases and the Delaware oral argument. The Colorado argument was not due for three months, until March of 1964. But the questioning from the Bench in the Delaware case suggested that

80. Brief for Appellants, Roman v. Sincock, p. 78.

several members of the Court were beginning to test out some logical lines of progression from certain premises. Both Chief Justice Warren and Justice Douglas, for example, asked Mr. Wiener why the apparent *Baker* v. *Carr* principle of disallowing invidious discrimination should not apply equally to both houses. The answer was to refer to Justice Holmes's statement that most rights are qualified and suggest that it is all too easy to slip from a qualified right in the premise to an unqualified right in the conclusion.[81]

d. *Unconstitutional, 8 to 1*

Delaware's apportionment was no better, and in some respects worse, than Tennessee's apportionment which in *Baker* v. *Carr* was found to present a justiciable question. One may surmise, therefore, that the Delaware case was the easiest to decide of the six given plenary treatment. And one may wonder, again, why it was granted plenary review. Perhaps the Court simply wanted to have one rock-bottom Tennessee-type case available in the event it should decide to take a step-at-a-time, rather than a sweeping across-the-board approach to the meaning of equal protection in state legislative apportionment.

81. American Bank & Trust Co. v. Federal Reserve Bank of Atlanta, 256 U.S. 350, 358 (1921).

X

The "Big Six": Framing the Issues in State Legislative Reapportionment–II

"The contention that the voters have discriminated against themselves appalls rather than convinces. . . . [A] proper recognition of the judicial function precludes a court from holding that the free choice of the voters between two conflicting theories of apportionment is irrational or the result arbitrary."

Circuit Judge Jean S. Breitenstein (Colorado case)

"The Government is not prepared to reject the rule of 'per capita' equality, but it does not presently urge it. Such an interpretation would press the Equal Protection Clause to an extreme, as applied to State legislative apportionment, would require radical changes in three-quarters of the State governments, and would eliminate the opportunities for local variation."

Solicitor General's Brief (Colorado case)

"The rights which are here asserted are the rights of the individual plaintiffs to have their votes counted equally with those of other voters."

District Judge William E. Doyle (Colorado case)

H. Colorado: "The People Have Spoken"

The Colorado case, *Lucas* v. *Colorado General Assembly*,[1] was a "majorities in conflict" case. It thus posed a supreme test for "one man-one vote" theory and was by far the most important of the "big six" cases. By popular initiative the voters of Colorado in November 1962 were offered a choice of legislative apportionment plans in a "one man-one vote" statewide referendum. Under proposed Amendment No. 8 both houses were to be apportioned substantially on a population basis. Under proposed Amendment No. 7, one house was to reflect population and the other was to be apportioned on a basis combining population with such other fac-

1. 377 U.S. 713 (1964).

tors as topography, economic interest, and customary political alignments.

a. Reapportionment by Initiative-Referendum

The two plans had not been hastily formulated or presented.[2] In addition
to many individuals interested in the comparative "weight" of their vote,
labor unions, voters' leagues, farm and ranching groups, education associations, and other politically attuned groups had been jockeying for position
and influence for several years. Similar apportionment plans had been rejected in popular referenda in 1954 and 1956. The victorious Democratic
candidate for governor in 1956, Stephen McNichols, appointed a distinguished 45-member bipartisan reapportionment committee which held
extensive hearings and compiled six volumes of material. Although the
committee settled little, much energy was expended and demands for immediate action subsided.

When the 1960 census figures were released reapportionment debate
was renewed. Under the census figures the electoral percentages for the
senate and house, respectively, were 29.8 percent and 32.1 percent, with a
population variance ratio of approximately 8 to 1 in each instance. Denver
and three adjacent suburban counties, containing almost one-half of the
state's total 1960 population of 1,753,947, had 11 of the 35 seats in the
senate and 23 of the 65 seats in the house under the existing apportionment of 1953.

The Opposing Parties. In the agitation leading up to the two popular
initiative reapportionment plans in 1962, the leading interest groups held
firm to positions they had already expressed before Governor McNickols's
Reapportionment Committee. The modified Federal Plan (Amendment
7) was backed by such groups as the Colorado Farm Bureau, the Colorado
Cattlemen's Association, and the Chamber of Commerce. Their position
had been characterized by a Farm Bureau spokesman as follows: "We are
for the 'Federal Plan' because it makes the same compromise between
area and population, between urban and rural, in the same way as was
made in 1789 at the Constitutional Convention where the Constitution
of the United States was written."

The "Voter" or "Equal Representation" proposal (Amendment 8) was
backed by such groups as the Colorado League of Women Voters, State
Council of the AFL-CIO, and the Colorado Education Association. Their
view was that "representatives of labor and the administration of the City

2. Material in this and the following subsection has been adapted from Robert G.
Dixon, Jr., "Colorado Apportionment: 'One Man-One Vote' and the Elusive Majority,"
in *Cases in American National Government and Politics* 195 (Rocco J. Tresolini and
Richard T. Frost, editors, Englewood Cliffs, N.J.: Prentice-Hall, 1966).

of Denver feel that, because both houses are not apportioned on the basis of population, rural interests dominate to the detriment of the people of the state as a whole." Conflict soon developed along political party lines. Individual Republican candidates endorsed the Federal Plan, while some Democrats and especially organized labor supported the "Equal Representation Plan." However, Edwin C. Johnson, three times Democratic governor and three times Senator—who was unofficially regarded as Colorado's elder statesman—campaigned vigorously for the Federal Plan. He stressed Colorado's historical diversity and its tradition of balanced representation among the four distinct geographic sections of the state.

The Federal Plan was overwhelmingly endorsed and the Equal Representation Plan resoundingly defeated in the November election, the statewide margin of victory for the Federal Plan being 2 to 1 (305,700 to 172,725). The Equal Representation Plan was defeated in every county of the state and also in Denver, the statewide margin of defeat likewise being 2 to 1 (311,749 to 149,982). Former-Governor Johnson issued this statement:

> It is very unusual in the annals of Colorado politics that any proposal or candidate receive a plurality in each and every county of this diverse state. I believe the principal reason for the character of the vote on Amendment No. 7 is that the issues were very clearly defined . . . . in short, in these campaigns, the people were intensely interested, fully informed, and voted accordingly.

A somewhat different appraisal came from the *Colorado Democrat*, which asserted editorially:

> What the voters voted for is reapportionment and what they got turned out to be a strict Republican interpretation of the best way to hang on to a majority in the state legislature.

The Subdistricting Issue. A factor of uncertain dimension was the difference between the two plans in regard to manner of election of senators and representatives from the City and County of Denver, and from any county entitled to more than one seat in either house.[3] Under the existing system, all legislators in multimember counties—for Denver 8 senators and 17 representatives—were elected at-large rather than from subdistricts within the county. Because of their winner-take-all feature such elections tend to freeze out the minority party; the larger the multimember district the more serious is the freeze-out in terms of impact on representation. Such elections also may result in lack of intimacy between legisla-

3. Several years ago Denver became a separated city-county, with the official names of City and County of Denver.

tor and constituent, and there may be voter confusion stemming from the long ballot.

However, in the November 1962 election there was no way for a voter to express a preference both for straight population apportionment and for subdistricting. The Federal Plan required that the at-large election practice—which tended to be disliked by Republicans and by non-Denver Democrats—be terminated; all legislators were to be elected from single-member districts. The Equal Representation Plan permitted continuation of at-large elections in multimember counties and in Denver. The labor interests in Denver were strongly in favor both of this plan's application of the population principle to both houses, and its retention of at-large voting for all of Denver's legislative delegation. Those voters who would have preferred a plan combining the feature of population apportionment for both houses with a general requirement of single-member districts found no such plan on the ballot. Thus, it is doubtful that the Federal Plan would have had such strong support without the subdistricting issue; it is equally doubtful that enough votes would have shifted to change the outcome if both plans had required subdistricting.[4]

b. *District Court Challenge*

In spite of *Baker* v. *Carr*, two residents of the Denver metropolitan area filed suit in the federal district court seeking an immediate reapportionment order. Because of the imminence of the 1962 election, the court decided to defer conclusive action until after the election, but did say that population disparities shown by the plaintiffs were of "sufficient magnitude to make out a *prima facie* case of invidious discrimination," and that this could be rebutted only if there were some "rational basis" for disparities. The court took judicial notice of Colorado's size and sectionalism, the metropolitan population concentration of the past 20 years, traditional patterns of apportionment, and varied economic interests. It also issued this warning:

> These matters of general knowledge may justify disparities in legislative districts. They do not, of themselves, sustain the rationality of the legislative districts as they now exist. Reliance on generalities is

4. Popular preference for a mixed representation system rather than straight population apportionment of both houses has been a marked feature of popular referenda in many states, e.g., the series of referenda supporting the federal plan in California in 1928, 1948, and 1960 (Charles M. Hardin, "Issues in Legislative Reapportionment," 27 *Review of Politics* 147, 152 [1965]); the Michigan referendum of 1952; the New York vote on the call of a convention in 1958 (reapportionment being publicized as a major reason for the call); and the Washington referendum in 1956.

misplaced when a case must be decided on the basis of specific situations.[5]

Following the 1962 election, plaintiffs amended their complaints and directed their attack against the newly adopted Amendment No. 7—the Federal Plan. The same three-judge court now found itself in a different situation. Those who thought that the court's warnings in its ruling of August 10, 1962, presaged invalidation of the nonpopulation-based senate under the new plan were due for a surprise.

In regard to the population-based lower house, the court obviously was impressed with reduction of the population variance ratio from 8 to 1 to 1.7 to 1. In regard to the senate, plaintiffs, continuing to rely solely on census data, had offered several kinds of mathematical proof, pointing out that the three metropolitan areas—Denver, Colorado Springs, and Pueblo —with 67 percent of the state's population had only 20 of the 39 senate seats.[6] The Denver metropolitan area, which elected 16, had 52.99 percent of the population. The population variance ratio between most populated and least populated senate district was 3.6 to 1. Under the fictional electoral percentage measure 33.2 percent of the population theoretically could control a majority of seats.

Majority View. The court, however, seemed to be impressed with what it felt was a reasonable and balanced treatment in the senate of the four principal regions of the state, which were also assumed to represent identifiable and different economic interests. These were the western region (west of the Continental Divide and part of the eastern Rockies) with 13 percent of the population, 45.47 percent of the area, and 20.5 percent of the senators; the eastern region (Great Plains area) with 8.1 percent of the population, 26.21 percent of the area, and 12.8 percent of the senators; the south central region (the impoverished Rio Grande area) with 3.8 percent of the population, 13.99 percent of the area, and 7.7 percent of the senators; and the east slope region (a rich strip north and south of Denver) with 75.1 percent of the population, 14.33 percent of the area, and 59 percent of the senators.

But the principal reasons the two concurring judges gave for upholding the constitutionality of Amendment 7 were (1) that Colorado had a liberal initiative process which would enable popular change of the apportionment if the people became disenchanted with it; (2) that the plan had been approved in every county and by an overwhelming statewide

5. Lisco v. McNichols, 208 F. Supp. 471, 478 (D. Colo. 1962).
6. Lisco v. Love, 219 F. Supp. 922, 938 (D. Colo. 1963).
Under the United States Census Bureau's designation of "Standard Metropolitan Areas," the Denver area consisted of Denver, the surrounding counties of Adams, Arapahoe, Jefferson, and the adjacent county of Boulder. The two other areas designated as metropolitan were Colorado Springs (El Paso County) and Pueblo (Pueblo County).

majority; (3) that contrary to the apparent view of the Supreme Court in *Baker* v. *Carr*, reapportionment should be approached as a problem of effective representation of divergent interests, as well as a matter of reacting to census population data.

Circuit Judge Jean S. Breitenstein, supported by District Judge Alfred A. Arraj, saw the case as one turning partially on the concept of majority rule:

> With full operation of the one-man, one-vote principle, the Colorado electorate by an overwhelming majority approved a constitutional amendment creating a Senate, the membership of which is not apportioned on a strict population basis. By a majority process the voters have said that minority process in the Senate is what they want. A rejection of their choice is a denial of the will of the majority. If the majority becomes dissatisfied with that which it has created, it can make a change at an election in which each vote counts the same as every other vote.[7]

And in a more legalistic vein the court concluded that:

> The contention that the voters have discriminated against themselves appalls rather than convinces. Difficult as it may be at times to understand mass behavior of human beings, a proper recognition of the judicial function precludes a court from holding that the free choice of the voters between two conflicting theories of apportionment is irrational or the result arbitrary . . . .
>
> We believe that no constitutional question arises as to the actual, substantive nature of apportionment if the popular will has expressed itself.[8]

Key Issues Ignored. Although the state as defendant had submitted much proof on regional economic factors through a battery of "expert" witnesses, one line of evidence was notably lacking. It perhaps could have affected the eventual outcome of this case, and even the sweep of the Supreme Court's other reapportionment rulings of June 15, 1964. There was no inquiry into realities of political representation in the legislature. There was no inquiry into the possibly tricky relationship between arrangement of legislative *districts* and achievement of fair and effective *representation* in the voting done through these districts. In short, there was no exploration of the question: Could the practice of electing legislators from districts confined to a *particular* part of the state—whether or not on a "one man-one vote" basis—be relied on to produce effective representation of viewpoints *shared* by persons residing in *different* parts of the state?

7. *Id.* at 926–27.
8. *Id.* at 933.

A related and even more important issue also was left unventilated: What interpretations were possible in regard to the 1962 referendum? Even the populous areas, including Denver and its suburbs, had voted against putting both houses on a straight population basis. They preferred to keep the senate on a mixed basis even though the effect was to give Denver fewer seats than it would have had on a straight population system. Could this have been caused by a fear, a fear shared by a statewide majority—including a majority in Denver itself—of Denver's dominating the state?

Could the referendum result be attributed to Colorado's "central city" politics and an appreciation of "balance of power" factors? In operational terms, was there a particularized fear that organized labor and associated interests—a statewide minority holding a possible balance of power position within the Democratic party of Denver—could have exaggerated influence under a population apportionment formula? A controlling or balance of power minority within the dominant political party of an urban center with half the state's population may be in a position to parlay its strength in state legislative politics far beyond the influence it could have in a statewide popular vote on the particular policy issues. The out-of-court record of Colorado's opposing interest groups and political parties during the reapportionment struggle in the 'fifties and early 'sixties lends more than a little credence to this hypothesis as an explanation of the 2 to 1 majority in 1962 in favor of the Federal Plan. However, these subtleties (or are they the true realities?) lay beyond the scope of the issues delineated by the parties in the court action. (See Chart 7 for a diagrammatic presentation of the hypothesis suggested here—a hypothesis given much support by many leaders interviewed by the author in Colorado in 1965.)

Dissenting View. Federal District Judge William E. Doyle, reacting to the same data which Circuit Judge Breitenstein and District Judge Arraj had considered, entered a vigorous dissent. Like the majority, he eschewed political analysis, although political gain and avoidance of political loss was the aim of the parties to the suit. In his dissent he turned his back to Justice Clark's opinion in *Baker,* and also to the line of cases treating "equal protection" as a rule of general fairness. Instead, he hewed to the line of substantial mathematical equality. Viewing arrangement of census population into equal legislative districts as mandated by a rule of equality, Judge Doyle saw no basis for applying that rule differently to one house than to the other. There was much logic in this position—granted the judge's implicit premise that the core of an apportionment case is the civil right of a voter to have some kind of personal equality in the election of legislators. If only a personal civil right is involved, it is indeed difficult to explain why it should have different breadth in regard to different parts of the governmental process.

CHART 7

"MAJORITY RULE" IN A ONE-CITY STATE *

State Pop.:   1,000,000

Central City and Suburbs	Rest of State
550,000	450,000
If Split	If Split
D 290,000	R 275,000
R 260,000	D 175,000

Then statewide total would be D 465,000 and R 535,000

In this situation one could expect that a proposal to apportion both legislative houses on a "one man-one vote" equal population district principle would be defeated in a "one man-one vote" statewide referendum. The R party members in both parts of the state could be expected to prefer some population imbalance in favor of the area outside the central city and suburbs in order to obtain "political equity" for R party in the legislature as a whole.

* *Source:* Robert G. Dixon, Jr., "Congress and Reapportionment," *Regional American Assembly Report on the Congress and America's Future* (Washington, D.C.: George Washington University, 1965), p. 12.

Judge Doyle, without discussing the problems posed by political party affiliations and interest group affiliations, also assumed that arrangement of districts into substantially equal masses of *population* would give the *voters* an "equal" and "effective" vote. Speaking of voters, he said:

> The rights which are here asserted are the rights of the individual plaintiffs to have their votes counted equally with those of other voters. . . . It is impossible to justify substantial differences between voting rights accorded to voters who live in the mountains, for example, as opposed to those who reside in the cities, and any attempts to rationalize on the basis of geography, sociology, or economics will, as has been shown above, necessarily rest upon the subjective evaluation of the minds which attempt the rationalization. . . . [F]airness requires that every individual be guaranteed the right to cast an effective vote.[9]

c. *Plaintiffs' Case on Appeal*

Apart from a fundamental mis-citation of *Gray* v. *Sanders*,[10] plaintiffs filed an effective brief designed to counter the defeat they had suffered in

9. *Id.* at 944, 941.
10. Plaintiffs quoted and stressed the comment in the *Gray* opinion that "Once the geographical unit for which a representative is to be chosen is designated, all who participate in the election are to have an equal vote." *Gray* at 808; Appellant's Brief, Lucas v. Colorado General Assembly, p. 51. They did not realize or, for the purposes of their case, chose not to recognize the fact that the context of this statement was a case concerning a statewide election with the entire state as a constituency; whereas their own case concerned legislative representation through multiple constituencies.

the federal district court. Plaintiffs tried to rebut the district court's reliance on the 1962 popular referendum, to assert that there were evils associated with Colorado's existing apportionment, and to show that despite Colorado's peculiar geography and population distribution it was not "statistically or practically difficult to establish rational districts" without cutting county lines and staying within a maximum population deviation of 26.6 percent.[11]

On the crucial popular referendum issue, the plaintiffs' primary reliance was to assert that fair legislative representation involved a civil rights issue no different from racial segregation, and hence was not subject to any consideration of popular will. Thus baldly stated there was an anomaly in the plaintiffs' position because fair legislative representation normally is thought to have some relation to the question of popular will. However, this anomaly was crucial to the plaintiffs' case and indeed to the subsequent Supreme Court opinion.

In the Colorado case, as in the other reapportionment cases, there was no empirical proof of the consequences of population malapportionment. Indeed, in the Colorado case there could not have been such proof because the new apportionment approved in the 1962 popular referendum had not yet acquired an experience record. Plaintiffs instead invited judicial notice of urban-rural conflict and obliquely suggested that the 1962 referendum was tainted because of the publicity and campaign techniques employed. They said:

> Minority interests, faced with the actuality of majority controls, have, however, discovered that a sudden divorce of the Senate from the population nexus will result in control of the Senate by those minority economic interests which desire to preserve control as against the urban and suburban population. It has been found that techniques of referendum salesmanship can persuade variant population groups, for a variety of reasons, to coalesce in support of a particular amendment.[12]

Plaintiffs also included in their brief a table demonstrating that "without offending either the principles of geography or population," i.e., by

11. Appellants' Brief at 63–65, Appendix C. By way of hindsight, it is interesting to note that plaintiffs' goals in the reapportionment litigation were far more modest than the equal population principle came to be through court interpretation in 1967. In their brief, the plaintiffs' hypothetical plan was thought not to have "any serious aberrations from a true population standard," although the maximum deviation was 26.6 percent. Similarly, plaintiffs in Maryland accepted a 36 percent deviation in 1966. By 1967, however, the Supreme Court was invalidating 18 percent variations and was intimating that no deviation would be permissible unless explained. See Swann v. Adams, 385 U.S. 440 (1967).

12. Appellants' Brief at 62.

grouping physically proximate counties together, it would be possible to apportion the senate as well as the house on a fairly close population basis.[13] Under their arrangement the Denver area (excluding Boulder) with 49 percent of the population would have 47.7 percent of the senate, which the plaintiffs characterized as "almost as close as practicable to mathematical exactness."[14] The Denver area plus Boulder, Pueblo, and El Paso, containing 63 percent of the state's population, would have 68.5 percent of the senate. The population variance ratio and the maximum percentage deviation from ideal district under the plaintiffs' suggested senate plan would be respectively 1.67 to 1 and 26.6 percent.[15]

d. State's Case on Appeal

The state properly noted that the Colorado case was quite unlike the five state legislative apportionment cases already argued. Because of the initiative and referendum process there was no "rural stranglehold" to be broken. The people had recently given overwhelming approval to the plan at issue. The population disparities were minimal in the lower house and modifiable by further popular action in the senate. In the senate the populous counties though underrepresented, did have by various measures a majority of the votes.[16] Using the plaintiffs' own identification of "urban interest," which coincides with the counties designated by the United States Bureau of the Census as comprising Colorado's three "Standard Metropolitan Areas," 20 of the 39 senators would come from Denver and its surrounding counties of Adams, Arapahoe, and Jefferson, plus Boulder, Pueblo, and El Paso.[17] An independent examination of the range of county populations in Colorado reveals a major breakpoint at the population figure of 72,000. Computing on this basis would add two additional senators yielding an "urban" majority control of the senate figure of 22 senators out of 39.[18] Below this figure, which accounts for eight of Colorado's 63 counties, there are two counties in the 50,000 range, 10 counties in the 20,000 range and all the rest are below 20,000.[19]

Despite the several promising elements in the facts of the Colorado case, and the state's victory in the district court, the state's brief on the whole was weak. Likewise, the large report of the Denver Research Insti-

13. *Id.* at Appendix C.
14. *Id.* at 98.
15. *Id.* at 65, 98.
16. Brief for Appellees, pp. 37–42.
17. Appellants' Brief, p. 98.
18. Appendix to Briefs of Appellees, pp. 227–28. The county of Weld would be included in the "metropolitan" grouping. Weld, as the other seven in this group, is part of the "east slope" region.
19. *Ibid.*

tute attached as an appendix to the brief was nonresponsive to the basic issues in the case. The Institute's report, designed to present data on possible apportionment factors other than population, was strong on economics, socio-economics, and economic geography; but it specifically excluded "political and legislative interests." [20]

Neither in this report nor in the state's brief was the real basis for the 2 to 1 popular referendum majorities in 1962 discussed and related to supporting theories of political representation. As noted above, a major factor, and in the eyes of many observers a dominant factor, in the 1962 referendum was the feeling of a majority of Colorado voters that urban pressure groups (particularly in Denver), although a minority in the state as a whole, would be able to achieve exaggerated statewide influence through their balance of power control of elections in the urban districts. If such a possibility could be demonstrated, the real issue for the Supreme Court in the Colorado case would be whether or not it is permissible for a statewide popular majority to use a balanced representation system, departing somewhat in one house from "one man-one vote" standards as a "majoritarian" check on the balance of power influence of cohesive minorities in urban centers. The state's brief had nothing to offer on this fascinating issue, which poses a question of democratic theory closely analogous to the issue subsequently raised in 1967 concerning the constitutionality of the California popular referendum repealing fair housing laws and reasserting property owners' common law right to deal with whom they please and to discriminate racially if they wish. Anomalously, the United States Solicitor General's brief in the California fair housing case in 1967 contains some of the thoughts which the state of Colorado sorely needed in 1963.[21]

A second brief in support of the 1962 popular referendum apportionment plan was filed by a bipartisan group of intervenors—former-Governor Edwin C. Johnson and others—which included some of the original backers of Amendment No. 7. In addition to reasserting that under Colorado's new plan the three major metropolitan areas of Denver, Colorado Springs, and Pueblo would have proportionate representation in the house

20. Denver Research Institute, Industrial Economics Division, University of Denver, "Economic Analysis of State Senatorial Districts in Colorado," p. viii (1963).
21. The problem, in one perspective suggested by the Solicitor General, was this: Is it unconstitutional to embed a "private right to discriminate" in a state constitution, whence it may be removed only by another statewide referendum? Doing this deprives the Negro minority of the opportunity it otherwise would have of achieving its ends statutorily through other forms of political action, such as utilizing balance of power tactics in key election districts and in the legislature. In short, what is democratic political action? See Brief for the United States as Amicus Curiae, Mulkey v. Reitman, 387 U.S. 369 (1967). The Supreme Court voided the state anti-fair housing constitutional amendment.

and a majority of 20 of the 39 senators, two new points were pressed. One was that extensive adoption of home rule in Colorado had placed 56 percent of the people, numbering most of the metropolitan area residents, under local home rule, whereby many of their needs could be met without resort to the state legislature. The other was that the policy of balancing Denver's 8 senators with 8 for the surrounding counties, although not strictly reflecting population, was consciously designed to ease conflict over Denver's annexation policy.[22]

e. Oral Argument

The oral argument in the crucial Colorado case was seriously imbalanced. It was opened by George Louis Creamer for the plaintiff-appellants who gave a colorful and forceful presentation and was allowed to proceed with few interruptions from the Bench. "Geography, topography, and history, like a Greek chorus" run through this record, he said, as part of his opponents' attempt to justify the mixed apportionment basis for the senate. He rang the changes on the rotten-borough theme, and described as "mythical" the state's stress on approaching representation in terms of the four distinctive regions of Colorado. He also asserted that defenders of any degree of nonpopulation apportionment really impugned urban virtue—despite the fact that Denver and its suburban metropolitan counties had supported by substantial majorities in the 1962 referendum the very senate plan he was attacking.[23] Times have changed, he noted, making us a dynamic urban civilization in which Cabinet members ski in Colorado on weekends and are back at their desks on Mondays.

He skillfully avoided the real issue. The Achilles' heel of the plaintiffs' position was that the apportionment system approved in the 1962 referendum appealed to many—indeed, a majority—as a way of checking the balance of power influence of Denver activists. He attributed the 1962 referendum results to dislike of multimember districting, rather than to dislike of population as the sole apportionment factor. His basic theme, however, was to dismiss political factors as not being "fruitful," and to direct the Court's attention elsewhere.

He left unanswered two questions of Justices Arthur J. Goldberg and Byron R. White. The former wondered whether it was enough to rebut a current popular preference for the federal plan simply by pointing out that the historical derivation of the plan in the "compromise on Con-

22. Brief of Appellees, pp. 34–35.
23. The 1962 vote in the City and County of Denver and its surrounding counties supporting the mixed representation system Amendment No. 7) was as follows: Denver: 75,877 to 61,183; Arapahoe: 18,193 to 12,351; Jefferson: 24,815 to 17,597. In nearby Boulder County, situs of the University of Colorado, the vote was 12,654 to 9636. Appendix to Briefs of Appellees, pp. 229–31.

gress" of 1787 was inapplicable—as an historic compromise—to the states. Justice White wondered if the two houses did not produce different results and if that was not what the people wanted. In rebuttal Mr. Creamer's co-counsel, Charles Ginsberg, almost gave the case away by overstatement, and by opening up the issue of political realities, when he asserted that the Constitution "tries to give equal weight to all voters on every issue." This sparked sharp questioning by Justice Stewart as to where in the Constitution he found any such principle; but the implication of proportional representation implicit in Mr. Ginsberg's statement was not explored.

The Solicitor General's Half-Way House. Solicitor General Archibald Cox's argument in the Colorado case, like his brief, was an on-again off-again sort of thing, responsive, at least to a degree, to the conceptual and practical complexities of the Colorado case. He did not ask for an across-the-board "one man-one vote" rule. He suggested that the Court recognize that some reasons for population deviations in apportionment are permissible, e.g., following county lines; and that others are impermissible, e.g., recognition of economic interests as such without any regard for numbers, or arrangements based on the proposition that urban people are worth less than rural people. He recognized that "equal representation," unlike simple civil right's matters, is a "shared right," and that a holding for the plaintiffs in the Colorado case would force on a majority something they had rejected (unless special reasons could be found for the 1962 referendum vote).

Nevertheless, he urged a decision on the merits in favor of the plaintiffs on the ground that even within a principle allowing some deviations from population equality the actual deviations for the Colorado senate were too great and could be modified easily. He pointed out that a slight tinker in regard to two districts would free two senators for transfer to the El Paso and Denver areas. This slight change, he pointed out, would raise the fictional electoral percentage for the senate from 33.2 percent to 40 percent and improve the representation of 39 percent of the people.

Significantly, however, Mr. Cox also argued that if the Court could not adopt his "half-way house" position on population equality it should dismiss the case and let the apportionment approved in the 1962 popular referendum go into effect. He argued that the plaintiffs' proposition that the Fourteenth Amendment required straight population equality in both houses was (on this record) "so balanced by want of equity factors," that the Court should stay its hand.

Last Chance for the States. The primary argument on behalf of the state in this sixth and last of the reapportionment cases was presented by Anthony F. Zarlengo, a Denver private practitioner who served as Special

Assistant Attorney General for Colorado for this matter. He was subjected to a withering cross-fire from the Bench and his argument never got off the ground. He did attribute Colorado's mixed apportionment plan to a purpose to ensure that each view be heard. But he did not develop the crucial issue of effective representation of the statewide majority, and the fascinating corollary problem of ascertaining a "majority" in the context of Colorado's "central city" politics.

Precious time was lost when Chief Justice Earl Warren led Mr. Zarlengo into an irrelevant discussion of apportionment provisions in the Colorado constitution going all the way back to the nineteenth century. Perhaps the questions were inspired by Mr. Creamer's hurried summary of Colorado history. The Creamer summary had been designed apparently to show that Colorado had tended to follow population as an apportionment principle in the past, and that a Fourteenth Amendment-based court order forcing Colorado to follow population now would not be an order forcing the state to adopt a policy contrary to her past traditions. Justice Hugo L. Black rescued Mr. Zarlengo from this blind alley and put the case back on the track by pointing out that the sole question before the Court was whether or not Colorado's presently adopted apportionment plan violated the *federal* Constitution.

Justice Black also cautioned counsel against spending too much time developing the point that Colorado's initiative process prevented freezing any apportionment plan into the constitution, on the ground that that too was "not the issue." By this comment Justice Black was forecasting his own vote in the case. The initiative aspect would be relevant to the posture in which the Solicitor General had approached the case. In other words, if the starting premise be that *some* population deviations are permissible for one house, then the fact of lack of experience under the proposed plan, the fact of the availability of the initiative process for change, and the difficulty of judging what deviation is "too much" all *would be* relevant in guiding a court to a decision either to invalidate the plan or to stay its hand.

At several points in response to questioning from the Bench Mr. Zarlengo had an opportunity to develop the legal rationale for the apportionment plan in the referendum vote in terms of Colorado's "central city" politics, and the inappropriateness of defining "majority" in other than realistic political terms. But the state did not have the wit to develop the representation issue, even though the bipartisan nature of the support for Amendment No. 7, and the 2 to 1 vote with at least a plurality in every county of the state, clearly made the issue something other than a naked Republican party versus Democratic party fight. Further, the concept of "population" and the concept of "people" was never separated. The Colorado system concededly did not represent "population" equally; it may have represented "people" well.

Defining the Issue. Toward the end of the state's argument, Chief Justice Warren flatly asked, "What is the issue?" He suggested that the issue should be simply "whether the plaintiffs have proper representation as individuals," regardless of "liberal-conservative" factors, "rural-urban" factors, labor factors, and so on. Mr. Zarlengo murmured an assent, thus making an admission fatal to his case. This opened the way for Warren to add rhetorically that if there was no rule of per-capita equality, based nakedly on population as such, then "who has the right to say that some will have less representation or less equal protection than others?"

At this point it seemed that no one on the Bench was inclined to view the apportionment litigation as presenting a political *representation issue.* Or at least none seemed so inclined unless state counsel developed a rationale to counter plaintiffs' persistent portrayal of apportionment litigation as posing only a simple, personal, civil right to vote issue. Justice John Marshall Harlan, silent through nearly two hours of oral argument, could contain himself no longer. He pointed out that if all sides conceded that the Fourteenth Amendment required "equal representation," defined solely in terms of arrangement of districts in equal population clusters, then the argument was over. He gently, but sharply, criticized Mr. Zarlengo, and state counsel in all of the reapportionment cases, for not discussing the basic issue of political representation and legislative operation in a democracy where all political and party feeling is channeled through the popular pluralities of particular election districts.

So, near the end of the last of the six major state legislative apportionment arguments, with the Solicitor General wavering and hinting at dismissal as a not inappropriate solution for the case at hand, the basic legal-philosophic-political issue was finally out. However, the clarity of the Harlan characterization of the issue was immediately undercut by Justice Potter Stewart's reversion to the thought that "rationality" in the sense of logical consistency in district layout was relevant too. Instead of accepting Justice Harlan's invitation to discuss the issue of democratic representation, Mr. Zarlengo fell into the trap laid by Justice Stewart. The state's remaining time dribbled away in a series of futile interchanges between Mr. Zarlengo and Justice White (and also Chief Justice Warren, who seemed particularly intrigued by this approach) on details of certain Colorado districts and the "rationality" of particular lines.

The issue of the ends and means of democratic representation remained lost during the ensuing and final argument on behalf of the state, presented by Stephen H. Hart, counsel for a bipartisan group of intervenors on the state's side in behalf of the plan approved in the 1962 referendum.

The discussion did not separate the personal right to vote from broader issues of representation theory and practice, nor did it discuss standards. One of Mr. Hart's stronger points was to revert to the dubiety expressed by the Solicitor General and to suggest that the matter was de minimis if, as the Solicitor General had seemed to suggest, the mere combining of two districts and freeing of two senators for transfer to El Paso and to Denver would satisfy whatever restraints the Fourteenth Amendment imposed. His concluding point was that the right to vote, which he viewed as having been vindicated in *Baker* v. *Carr*, would be "of little avail if the integrity of the vote when cast on a 'one-man one-vote' basis is not respected."

Here we have in a nutshell the central issue of the Colorado case, majoritarian principles in conflict, as expressed on the one hand in the popularly initiated popular referendum, and on the other hand in the asserted equal population theory of the plaintiffs. But the reasons for these two expressions of the "majority principle," their operating effects, and ways of harmonizing them were never discussed.

The crowning irony of the Colorado case, particularly in its oral presentation to the Supreme Court, is that only the Solicitor General—who was arguing for the plaintiffs—and not the counsel arguing on behalf of the state, was able to give the Court any intellectual basis for upholding the plan, or at least withholding a finding of unconstitutionality until a better record was prepared. The Solicitor General's position was more moderate even in oral argument than in his brief, although doubts about a rigorous equal population standard for both houses of a bicameral legislature—reflecting some thoughts expressed in his initial *Baker* v. *Carr* brief—were evident in both.

f. *Unconstitutional, 6 to 3*

Although finding that the lower house was "at least arguably apportioned substantially on a population basis" [24] and that the whole scheme had been "adopted by a majority vote of the Colorado electorate," [25] the Court, with dissents by Justices Harlan, Clark, and Stewart, nullified the apportionment plan because the population deviations in the senate were "too extreme" and there was no indication in the Colorado plan that the house apportionment was severable from the senate apportionment.[26]

The Court got around the 2 to 1 popular approval of the apportionment plan by saying: "An individual's constitutionally protected right to cast an equally weighted vote cannot be denied even by a vote of a major-

24. Lucas v. Colorado General Assembly, 377 U.S. 713, 730 (1964).
25. *Ibid.*
26. *Id.* at 734–35.

ity of a State's electorate." [27] Thus the Court characterized the apportionment issue as involving not representation but a personal civil right to vote, confirming the intimations in oral argument when Justice Goldberg had thought it relevant to point out that a majority could not by popular vote establish a church, and to ask rhetorically whether the Fourteenth Amendment racial cases were not on the same constitutional footing as reapportionment cases.

As in the Maryland case, the Court also considered the possibility that population deviations in one house might be saved constitutionally by counter-balancing population deviations in the other house. The Court said: "Deviations from a strict population basis, so long as rationally justifiable, may be utilized to balance a slight over-representation of that area in the other house." [28] As already noted in the foregoing discussion of the Court's decision in the Maryland case, such a concept of counterbalancing population disparities is quite inconsistent, both conceptually and practically, with the Court's basic premise that apportionment cases are personal right to vote cases.

Justice Stewart in dissent noted that "Colorado is not an economically or geographically homogeneous unit," [29] and that the state contains mountainous areas, agricultural areas, and areas economically depressed because of water scarcity, along with metropolitan areas. Given these entirely different regions, he felt that in regard to one house, "it was not irrational to conclude . . . that planned departures from a strict per capita standard of representation were a desirable way of assuring some representation of distinct localities whose needs and problems might have passed unnoticed if districts had been drawn solely on a per capita basis." [30]

I. Solicitor General—Co-Ordinator for the Plaintiffs

With the aid of the Solicitor General, nominally amicus curiae but more nearly plaintiffs' mentor and chief advocate, plaintiffs had an easy time in the "big six" reapportionment appeals. Plaintiffs also had held a planning session to learn each other's cases and to guard against shooting each other down in the course of making a point for their own state.

On the defendants' side there was no planning session, no detailed knowledge of each other's cases, no able co-ordinator of constitutional

27. *Id.* at 736.
28. *Id.* at 735.
29. *Id.* at 755.
30. *Id.* at 756.

theory analogous to the Solicitor General on the plaintiffs' side. Too many of the defendants' counsel wasted many of their precious hours of oral argument. They dwelt on the varied topography and geography of their states, sounding like a misplaced chamber of commerce commercial; or they stressed history, which, to a Court that had decided the desegregation case on broad principles of developing constitutionalism, was like trying to get Bertrand Russell to take Holy Communion; or they simply fell into the trap Justice Clark had constructed more neatly than he knew in *Baker*, by trying to establish how *every* interdistrict population disparity could be shown to be the result of some clear and "rational" formula, which is almost always an impossibility.

None of the defendant states seemed to realize that what they needed was not just a lawyer—a young assistant attorney general as in the case of Maryland, or a private law practitioner as in the case of Colorado—but a constitutional law specialist. Many experienced constitutional law professors in the law schools of the country would have been more useful to the defendant states in constructing a plausible argument than the talent relied on from the attorney general offices or the general practicing bar. Broader concessions would have been made, but total defeat may have been avoided. Supreme Court practice is a very different kind of practice, and when it focuses on broad constitutional questions—divorced from the lucrative public law fields of business regulation—it touches on issues which the average practitioner encounters once in a lifetime, if then. On behalf of the states there was, to be sure, an amicus brief on the defendants' side signed by the attorneys general of 14 states but it was limited to a defense of the federal plan.[31]

a. *On the Merits–4 Propositions*

The Solicitor General's technique in clinching victory for the plaintiffs was to offer the Court a sequence of alternative standards, presented in a tightly written main brief,[32] and then to refuse to be drawn into a discussion of the practical implications of his standards, or their relation to representation theory. Had Justice Felix Frankfurter lived, oral argument on these terms might well have been a tense affair. But the subsequent Bench seemed at times to be almost putty in the Solicitor's hands, and

31. Brief and Appendix for the Attorneys General of the States as Amici Curiae, Maryland Committee for Fair Representation v. Tawes.

32. The Solicitor General's basic constitutional posture regarding reapportionment and representation are presented in his Brief for the United States as Amicus Curiae, Maryland Committee for Fair Representation v. Tawes, pp. 22–50. Only half of this brief is devoted to a specific discussion of the Maryland case. The Solicitor General's separate briefs in the other five cases from Alabama, Colorado, Delaware, New York, and Virginia relate the general propositions to the facts of the particular suits. This sequence of six Solicitor General amicus curiae briefs totaled 530 pages.

this was never more apparent than in the reapportionment field. Justice Harlan to some extent and Justice Stewart with vigor pressed unsuccessfully for broader discussion of the source and reach of the constitutional standards. The latter seemed to foresee the second level of reapportionment litigation beginning in 1965 and reaching first fruit in the *Local Apportionment Decisions* of 1967,[33] when the simple conceptions and simple mathematics of the plaintiffs' arguments would not only be irresponsive to fair representation issues but actually impede an adequate airing of them.

The Solicitor General argued that all six state apportionments receiving plenary consideration by the Court were unconstitutional. His basic four point list of guiding propositions went as follows:

1. The basic standard of comparison is the representation accorded qualified voters per capita.
2. The equal protection clause is violated by an apportionment that creates gross inequalities in representation without rhyme or reason.
3. The equal protection clause is violated by a discriminatory apportionment based upon criteria which are contrary to express constitutional limitations or otherwise invidious or irrelevant.
4. The equal protection clause is violated by an apportionment which subordinates the principle of popular representation to the representation of political subdivisions to such a degree as to create gross inequalities in the representation of voters and give control of the legislature to small minorities of the people.[34]

The Solicitor's *first standard*—population equality with the burden of proof on the defender to justify all departures—is rooted squarely on the unchallengeable democratic proposition that population is the starting point for constructing a consensual government. But is the implied associated premise true, i.e., that deviation from a population principle necessarily makes the government nonconsensual? Is our national government nonconsensual, and hence "undemocratic," because of state equality in the Senate, or the guarantee of one seat in the House to each state no matter how small its population? As stated by the Solicitor, the basic standard—applicable to both houses—would limit bicameral structure to differences of term and district size.

---

33. In a startling reversal of form, the Supreme Court in May 1967 approved a system of electing city councilmen at-large from grossly unequal candidate residence districts, ranging in population from 733 to 29,048. Dusch v. Davis, 387 U.S. 112 (1967), discussed in Ch. XX, *infra* with the other three local apportionment cases: Bd. of Supervisors of Suffolk County v. Bianchi, Sailors v. Bd. of Education of County of Kent, Michigan, Moody v. Flowers, 387 U.S. 97, 105, 97 (1967).

34. Brief for the United States as Amicus Curiae, Maryland Committee for Fair Representation v. Tawes, pp. 29–49.

If we insist on consensus as a vital component of democratic government, is it necessary to state the starting premise for bicameral apportionment in the Solicitor's terms? Is it necessary to start with any single-factor premise, other than a firm commitment against minority rule *and* against permanent minority obstruction of majority wishes? Also, should all elements of fair and effective representation, and of operating political realities, be excluded from the initial premise?

A simple population equality premise normally will safeguard majority interests, but may not do much for minorities. Nor are all minority interests taken care of adequately through the Bill of Rights and the court system, without need to involve the representation system, as plaintiffs often argued. A minority group's political and economic interests, if not reflected in the representation system, may go unrecognized because such interests are not suited to "Bill of Rights" adjudication. They raise broad policy questions which, despite *Baker* v. *Carr*, are still nonjusticiable. For example, the claim of "Black Power" is not for access to courts, but for better access to the legislative arena, where are made the crucial decisions concerning governmental policy and expenditure of money. Civil rights and civil liberties litigation is supremely irrelevant to these kinds of minority group interests.

The Solicitor's *second standard*—the "crazy-quilt" argument derived from Justice Clark's *Baker* opinion—would deem unconstitutional all significant departures from arithmetic equality which did not follow a rational plan, i.e., which treated similar areas or counties differently. In the cases before the Court, he saw "crazy-quilt" inconsistencies in the districting patterns in Alabama and Virginia for both houses, and in Maryland for the senate. Although in Maryland there was a "rational" (consistent) pattern of one senator per county regardless of population, the award of six senators rather than one to the separated City of Baltimore made the plan irrational. Some of the suburban counties had populations comparable to Baltimore City, which for most governmental purposes is treated by Maryland as a county. Undercutting his initial premise of per-capita representation in both houses, the Solicitor did suggest, however, that so long as a crazy quilt did not result, "representation of historical political subdivisions having an identity and significance of their own might be, within limits, a permissible basis of representation under some circumstances and may be blended with representation by population." [35]

The Solicitor General's *third standard*, an awkward circumlocution, seems to say this: in addition to being "rational" in the sense of being internally consistent, the apportionment plan also must conform to some objective standard of "reasonableness." Where a nonpopulation factor is

35. *Id.* at 38.

DEMOCRATIC REPRESENTATION

used consistently, and creates population inequalities, he suggested two subsidiary tests to get at the question of "reasonableness." First, the Court should consider whether the factor is "relevant for purposes of governmental organization or the election process." [36] This test calls for analysis of representation theory but the Solicitor held back, suggesting only that a political subdivision basis for representation would be "relevant" even though it caused population inequality, while a farmer-banker basis would not be appropriate. Second, the Court should consider whether the "objective" achieved by the governmentally "relevant" non-population factor is sufficiently important to "justify the inequalities actually resulting." [37] This, of course, is the "balancing" process of constitutional adjudication. The answer turns not only on the qualitative importance of the nonpopulation objective, but also on the degree of adverse impact on the initial premise of per-capita equality. In the current cases the only "rational" and "relevant" nonpopulation factor at issue in the Solicitor's view was use of political subdivisions to qualify straight population.

The Solicitor General's so-called *fourth standard* was designed merely to provide guidance on the question left open by his third standard, i.e., the issue of the *extent to which* political subdivisions could be considered along with population in apportioning and districting a state. At this point he seemed to make a major retreat from his initial per-capita equality premise. His fourth standard is this: if one house is based on population, then *established* political subdivisions (but not specially created areas having no "independent significance") may to some extent be used in the other house *provided* the over-all result is not minority rule or a likely possibility of minority rule. His stress on using only established political subdivisions having "independent significance, coherence and sense of identity," [38] was dictated apparently by two considerations. One was the "representative" function in terms of community of interest and of ensuring a voice to particular interests and areas. The other was the desire to confine the exception. He wanted to prevent watering down of per-capita equality through creation of artificial "area" districts. Referring to Michigan, whose appeal was pending but not receiving plenary consideration, he asserted that the senate districts specially created on an area basis in 1952 (and by implication the proposed 80 percent population-20 percent area formula authorized by a 1963 constitutional convention) would not qualify for the exception. It is not clear why they would not qualify. There is a more obvious special representativeness function when the

36. *Id.* at 44.
37. *Ibid.*
38. *Id.* at 47.

"nonpopulation" district is an independent political subdivision such as a county or township. But is this function entirely lost when a number of rural political subdivisions or substantial parts of them are "artificially" grouped into a district? The artificiality caused by grouping is also one way of reducing the population deviation; and if the grouped units were all of the same type there would not be a total loss of "sense of identity."

In its application to the litigation before the Court these four approaches pointed toward plaintiff victory in each case. Although the New York and Virginia apportionments were not as egregious on a population basis as plans in some other states, Virginia's pattern had crazy-quilt elements and New York's pattern designedly and impermissibly overrepresented less populous areas in both houses. In addition to violating Propositions Two and Three respectively, New York's plan, more deviant on a population basis than Virginia's, was thought to raise the minority control factor covered by Proposition Four. Maryland's senate apportionment violated the crazy-quilt standard of Proposition Two because of differential treatment of populous Baltimore City (six senators) and equally populous suburban counties (one senator apiece). Delaware's plan seemed to fail on all counts. Both of the revisions suggested by the Alabama legislature were thought to be insufficient to avoid the danger of minority rule, and in addition, one was a crazy quilt.

b. Solicitor's Colorado Brief

There remained the sixth case, *Lucas* v. *Colorado General Assembly*,[39] which was not brought to the stage of briefing until after completion of arguments in the other five cases. Although the Solicitor General's approach professed to rest on the principles discussed above, there were subtle differences in his Colorado brief. What in his other briefs were possible narrow exceptions to the equal population premise for both houses became major themes, and the equal population premise suddenly was watered down. Colorado's apportionment plan had been approved in every unit of the state including Denver and by a statewide popular referendum plurality of 2 to 1. The population deviations were comparatively modest, considering the two houses together.

Conceding that the issue was "far more closely balanced than in the other cases"[40] the Solicitor General nevertheless argued for unconstitutionality. He got around the popular referendum matter by characterizing the issue as one of personal civil rights—the right to vote—and hence not subject to popular referendum. On the merits, he saw minority rule as a

39. 377 U.S. 713 (1964).
40. Brief for the United States as Amicus Curiae, Lucas v. Colorado General Assembly, p. 20.

mathematical possibility. He argued further that the senate apportionment, not based solely on population, was also not based on any other factor relevant to permissible "representation" objectives. The senate formula seemed to be clearly designed to put a check on Denver.

At the same time the Solicitor stayed short of espousing the principle the Court eventually was to adopt, i.e., population equality as nearly as practicable for both houses. He expressed his "wait and see" attitude as follows:

> One of the grounds for asserted relief appears to be the claim that the Equal Protection Clause requires seats in both houses of a State legislature to be apportioned as nearly as practicable in proportion to population. The argument would exclude from consideration the claims of geography, history, and established political subdivisions, such as our briefs in the prior cases assumed "arguendo" to be constitutionally permissible considerations. The Government is not prepared to reject the rule of "per capita" equality, but it does not presently urge it. Such an interpretation would press the Equal Protection Clause to an extreme, as applied to State legislative apportionment, would require radical changes in three-quarters of the State governments, and would eliminate the opportunities for local variation. On the other hand, to reject the interpretation at this early stage of the development under *Baker* v. *Carr*, would prematurely close an important line of constitutional evolution.[41]

In expressing such unease the Solicitor was less than consistent within his own formulation. His theory for getting around the Colorado popular referendum was that a simple civil right to vote was involved, and nothing more. Now, voting by a qualified voter does seem to be that kind of civil right which is an absolute and which cannot be "balanced" and limited by other considerations. It seems more like the absolutist guarantee against compulsory self-incrimination than like the freedoms of expression where balancing, despite Justice Black's opposition, is part of the definition of the right. (One has a right of free speech, but this does not include the right to cry "Fire!" in a crowded theater, etc.) Therefore, the Solicitor's theory for treating as irrelevant the popular referendum also made irrelevant his expressions of unease. And it made anomalous his inference that the "right to vote," which somehow overcomes all popular referendum problems, somehow also has a different reach in regard to one house than in regard to the other house of a bicameral legislature.

In candor too it may be suggested that the four propositions he already had submitted to the Court as guidelines left little room for his newfound unease about a rigid population principle. For example, the crazy-

41. *Id.* at 32.

quilt argument alone is an almost insurmountable obstacle to population deviations because legislation generally is an "irrational" process—a compromise and adjustment process—and can hardly be expected to be otherwise in as difficult and inherently politicized a field as apportionment and districting. "Rationality" in the sense of internal, logical consistency is never expected and seldom achieved in the legislative arena, e.g., tax legislation, exemptions of certain businesses from Sunday Closing laws, traffic and speed laws, even general business regulation.

Another inflexibility resulted from the Solicitor's mathematical approach to the possible danger of minority rule. His sole measure was the fictional electoral percentage, not empirical data concerning actual legislative operation or concerning popular reactions. Under the fictional electoral percentage a perfect score is not 100 percent but near 50 percent, i.e., if all districts were equalized one-half plus one of the legislators would come from districts encompassing one-half of the state's population *plus* the population of one additional district.

At oral argument much interest was shown in this so-called electoral percentage but the questions indicated little perception of its computation or meaning. Under 10 percent, 15 percent, and 20 percent maximum population deviations (the last-named still being below the recent British and German practice of 25 percent maximum deviation) the lowest possible electoral percentages of a 100-seat house would be 46.1, 43.65, and 41.2 percent, respectively.

c. "S.G.'s" Briefs Analyzed Tactically

It is part of the lore of the Supreme Court that briefs for it, at least by its experienced practitioners, are written for particular justices who can be anticipated to be "swing" justices in the case being presented. In the Office of the Solicitor General of the United States this art has been brought to a particularly high level. The art is not so easily practised in other appellate tribunals, including the U.S. Courts of Appeals, which sit under a shifting panel system. But the composition of the Supreme Court Bench is fixed. Therefore, on any given public law issue with a past Supreme Court experience record, the votes of more than half the Bench often are predictable with near certainty. The Solicitor General's briefs may thus be aimed at two or three justices.

In reapportionment it is apparent that some of the Solicitor's arguments were designed to extract the maximum support from a Bench which had partially tipped its hand in its several opinions in *Baker* v. *Carr*. Justices Black and William O. Douglas, having fought ever since their dissents in *Colegrove* v. *Green* for justiciability and a simplistic "right to vote" approach toward apportionment and districting could be counted as too committed to this approach to turn back, at least in the ordinary case. Justice William J. Brennan, Jr., naturally having a certain amount of pride of authorship, could be expected to follow through vigorously on his historic opinion for the Court in *Baker*.[42] Chief Justice Warren, who had not written opinions in the *Baker* and *Gray* cases, had frequently espoused similar constitutional values in cases where Black, Douglas, and Brennan could agree. The newest appointee and Frankfurter's replacement, Justice Goldberg had not been present for *Baker*. However, in his short period on the Court he had distinguished himself for ultra-liberalism. And on an issue such as apportionment where the interests of his labor union background could be shown to march in tandem with democratic theory, it was inconceivable that he would not embrace "one man-one vote" as a basic premise.

By this count there were five votes already for an absolutist "one man-one vote" principle; the plaintiffs' cases were won. However, no case is a "sure thing" until it is won. For example, Justice Black was soon to shock some of his civil libertarian worshippers by voting and writing vigorously against certain kinds of civil rights demonstrations.[43] Justice Harlan, despite his reservations about free trial transcripts for indigents seeking to appeal,[44] had written the majority opinion in the leading NAACP case which had established the new constitutional right of freedom of association as a derivative from the First Amendment.[45] In a series of congressional investigatory power cases Justice Stewart had gotten himself into a swing position and pulled the Court away from First Amendment constitutional issues, although still ruling for the defendants, by a rigid factual analysis.[46] Justice Douglas once provided the crucial vote supporting public financing of parochial school transportaton, and also supported "released time" to provide a captive audience for religious teachers.[47] But he

42. At times during the course of oral argument, Justice Brennan almost seemed to bounce on the bench when counsels' statements seemed to undercut *Baker* or give it a restrictive reading. But he was also one of the most astute, once his "*Baker* baby" was placed out of harm's way by the 1964 *Reapportionment Cases*. It was Justice Brennan, not Chief Justice Warren, who wrote the opinions in 1965 and 1966 in the Georgia and Hawaii cases which seemed to recognize a federal cause of action to challenge invidious racial or political discrimination resulting from multimember district systems (or, by inference, gerrymandered single-member district systems). See discussion in Ch. XVIII *infra*.
43. Adderly v. Florida, 385 U.S. 39 (1966); Brown v. Louisiana, 383 U.S. 131 (1966); Cox v. Louisiana, 379 U.S. 536 (1965).
44. Douglas v. California, 372 U.S. 353 (1963); Griffin v. Illinois, 351 U.S. 12 (1956).
45. NAACP v. Alabama, 357 U.S. 449 (1958).
46. Deutch v. United States, 367 U.S. 456 (1961); Wilkinson v. United States, 365 U.S. 399 (1961).
47. Everson v. Bd. of Education, 330 U.S. 1 (1947), decided 5 to 4; Zorach v. Clauson, 343 U.S. 306 (1952), decided 6 to 3, with Justice Douglas writing the majority opinion.

later recanted and took a strong church-state separation position.[48]

The task, therefore, for a careful advocate for the plaintiffs in the reapportionment cases was not to count five justices and stop. Against the ever-present chance of vote miscalculation, the Solicitor naturally desired to find an additional vote or two to guarantee an eventual winning margin. These could come only from Justices White, Clark, Stewart, and Harlan, in descending order of likelihood. Unlike the flamboyant liberalism of Justice Goldberg, whose appointment dated from the same month as Justice White's, White had distinguished himself as a calm and careful reasoner, with a passion for intellectual honesty.[49] He was perhaps the one justice who by careful appeal to his reason could be persuaded to cast a vote one step short of his heart. He also had distinguished himself as a justice not much given to absolutes; one disinclined, as Justice Cardozo once put it, to "push every principle to the limit of its logic." [50] Justice White might find appealing, therefore, a formula with some alternatives, one which fell short of saying that "one man-one vote" solves all problems and entails no problems of its own.

Justice Clark was already on record in his *Baker* opinion as opposing internal inconsistencies in apportionment—the "crazy-quilt" theory—but as favoring retention of much state discretion, including, inferentially, a federal plan. Insofar as a crazy-quilt theory alone would invalidate some of the plans before the Court, Clark's partial support, at least, was in view. If it could be suggested that a federal plan was not necessarily invalid, but that none of the plans before the Court qualified as a federal plan, then Clark might be counted on for all except the Colorado case. Of the Solicitor's four propositions, Proposition Two, along with elements of Propositions Three and Four on the relevance of political subdivisions, seems aimed at Clark.

Justice Stewart, by his vote in *Baker* to enter the political thicket and his vote for majority rule in *Gray*, seemingly could be counted on for a minimal check at least on state districting discretion, and could be counted on in all cases where minority rule was in prospect. Proposition Four therefore seems especially to be aimed at Stewart, and perhaps Justice Harlan too, if Harlan were to abandon his nonjusticiability position. As it turned out the prospective majority of five held firm and Jus-

---

48. School District v. Schempp, 374 U.S. 203, 229 (1963); Engel v. Vitale, 370 U.S. 421, 443 (1962).
49. Gibson v. Florida Legislative Investigation Committee, 372 U.S. 539 (1963). Compare the opinion of the Court written by Justice Goldberg with the dissenting opinion of Justice White.
50. Benjamin N. Cardozo, "Jurisprudence" (Address before the New York State Bar Association, Hotel Astor, January 22, 1932) in *Selected Writings of Benjamin Nathan Cardozo* 7, 31 (Margaret E. Hall, editor, New York: Fallon Publications, 1947).

tice White, without articulating his reasons in a separate opinion, chose to join them. In addition, Justices Clark and Stewart joined the majority to make three of the six cases (Alabama, Delaware, Virginia) 8 to 1 decisions on grounds, alternatively, of the crazy-quilt theory and of endangering majority rule.

Conversely, the only hope the defendants had of holding Justices Harlan, Stewart, and Clark, adding Justice White, *and* picking up one vote from the bloc of Justices Black, Douglas, Brennan, Warren, and Goldberg was in fundamentally recasting the issue away from a simple "right to vote" characterization and toward a rather sophisticated "fair representation" characterization. Such an approach probably could not, and should not, have "saved" the egregious malapportionment records in Alabama, Delaware, and Maryland. The Colorado, Virginia, and New York cases, in that order, would have become much more difficult; remand might have been needed to get evidence on the largely unargued, unbriefed, and unilluminated issue of whether or not effective representation and effective majority rule were being jeopardized. Mere recitation of the concededly fictional electoral percentage would not have been enough.

But the defendants, with the exception of New York, not understanding the larger implications of their own cases, were unable even to make the attempt to refocus the issue. There was no Solicitor General to coordinate the weaker side, strengthen it by concessions, and make plausible what remained. Perhaps even that would not have been effective to stay the judicial hand, but it would have raised the intellectual level of the discussion considerably.

In summary, the Solicitor General did a superlative job of co-ordinating the plaintiffs' cases, appealing to known quantities on the Bench, formulating rationalizing themes which superficially seemed to be many-faceted rather than monolithic, demonstrating the paucity of plausible arguments by the defendants (except for the pure federal plan idea), and transforming the issue into a simple civil rights issue. His argument was an excellent example of the art of advocacy. But it was so well done that it acquired a momentum extending perhaps beyond his intent—certainly well beyond his *Baker* v. *Carr* position. It was not slowed by the caveats inserted in his Colorado brief. He did not give the Court any well-reasoned basis for viewing the issue as a *voting-plus* issue—i.e., an issue encompassing the *politics of representation* as well as the *mathematics of equal-sized districts*. Thus, he gave the Court no basis for balancing, for a multifaceted approach, for proceeding slowly—for avoiding, in short, a simple, wholly mathematical approach toward democratic representation.

XI

The "Equal Population" Mandate for State Legislative Apportionment: *Reynolds* and Companion Cases—1964

"Legislators represent people, not trees or acres. Legislators are elected by voters, not farms or cities or economic interests."
Chief Justice Earl Warren, *Reynolds v. Sims*

"But legislators do not represent faceless numbers. They represent people, or, more accurately, a majority of the voters in their districts—people with identifiable needs and interests."
Justice Potter Stewart,
Lucas v. Colorado General Assembly

THE COURT VOTES

Major restructuring of state legislatures followed swiftly on the heels of the *Baker* v. *Carr* decision, as noted in Chapter VII, even though the Supreme Court had yet to articulate the scope of possible federal constitutional restrictions on state discretion in apportionment matters. A significant number of lower courts had shifted the burden of proof to defendants, and with the aid of very simple population mathematics had nullified traditional patterns for composition of state legislatures. Although splitting on some issues, these courts had been developing an equal population premise, at least for districts for one legislative house. Against this background, and with the aid of a large shelf of briefs and almost 20 hours of oral argument—of sorts—the Supreme Court approached its landmark decisions of June 1964 in state legislative reapportionment cases from 15 states.

Despite major changes already impelled by lower courts in 1962-1964, the Supreme Court's ruling was not destined to be an anti-climax. True, few persons doubted that the developing equal population premise, which the Supreme Court had already endorsed in the Georgia "county-unit" case, *Gray v. Sanders*,[1] and the Georgia congressional districting case, *Wesberry v. Sanders*,[2] would be carried forward in some degree to state legislative apportionment. There would have been little point in going through the agony of reversing major "political question" rulings and creating justiciability in *Baker v. Carr* if the Court subsequently were to hold that the Fourteenth Amendment did not impose any population-oriented restraint after all. Nevertheless, few persons were prepared for the full sweep of the Court's one man-one vote rulings of June 1964 which had the effect of nullifying at least one legislative house in every state, and both houses in most states. Neither the degree of population equality apparently required, nor its flat application to both state legislative houses, nor the complete disregard of the factor of popular approval of apportionment plans, were anticipated.

As Supreme Court reporter Anthony Lewis reported in the *New York Times* a few days after the decisions: "Even some liberal-minded persons, admirers of the modern Supreme Court, found themselves stunned by last Monday." [3] Such columnists as Walter Lippmann and Max Freedman were sober and restrained in their praise, hesitating not so much over the need for reapportionment of state legislatures as the sweep of the decisions. On reflection some time later one of the victorious plaintiffs' counsel commented that "we would have been satisfied with less than we got." [4]

Of 15 reapportionment rulings reviewed at this time, cases from six states had received full consideration and were decided with written opinions after oral argument: Alabama, New York, Maryland, Virginia, Delaware, and Colorado.[5] Cases from nine other states were disposed of with brief statements a week later: Michigan, Washington, Oklahoma, Illinois, Idaho, Connecticut, Florida, Ohio, Iowa.[6]

Continuing the "made in the South" label for the reapportionment

1. 372 U.S. 368 (1963).
2. 376 U.S. 1 (1964).
3. *New York Times*, June 21, 1964, Section 4, p. 3, col. 8.
4. *Washington Post*, June 12, 1966, p. E4, col. 1.
5. Alabama cases—Reynolds v. Sims, Vann v. Baggett, McConnell v. Baggett, 377 U.S. 533 (1964); New York case—WMCA v. Lomenzo, 377 U.S. 633 (1964); Maryland Commission for Fair Representation v. Tawes, 377 U.S. 656 (1964); Virginia case— Davis v. Mann, 377 U.S. 678 (1964); Delaware case—Roman v. Sincock, 377 U.S. 695 (1964); Lucas v. Colorado Gen. Assembly, 377 U.S. 713 (1964).
6. Michigan—Beadle v. Scholle, 377 U.S. 990 (1964) and Marshall v. Hare, 378 U.S. 561 (1964); Washington—Meyers v. Thigpen, 378 U.S. 554 (1964); Oklahoma— Williams v. Moss, 378 U.S. 558 (1964); Illinois—Germano v. Kerner, 378 U.S. 560 (1964); Idaho—Hearne v. Smylie, 378 U.S. 563 (1964); Connecticut—Pinney v. Butterworth, 378 U.S. 564 (1964); Florida—Swann v. Adams, 378 U.S. 553 (1964); Ohio—Nolan v. Rhodes, 378 U.S. 556 (1964); Iowa—Hill v. Davis, 378 U.S. 565 (1964).

revolution, the Court chose the Alabama case, *Reynolds v. Sims*,[7] as the vehicle for the principal opinion in the *Reapportionment Decisions*. Some subtleties may have impelled this choice. Past population disparities in Alabama were egregious; urban-suburban interests by common knowledge had not received effective representation; the reputed "backwardness" of the state on the national scene was relatively easily related to population malapportionment and the Southern rural vote. By contrast such states as New York and California commonly had been accorded the accolade of being exceptionally progressive despite a practice of some malapportionment affecting both houses (New York) or astounding malapportionment in one house (California senate). In the course of oral argument in the Supreme Court in the earlier Georgia congressional districting case, *Wesberry v. Sanders*, one of the counsel openly had invited the Court to consider political results—referring to the record of the partially reapportioned Georgia legislature as ushering in a "new Georgia" era. A possible "new Alabama" result may well have undergirded the Court's thinking in *Reynolds*. But a "new New York" or a "new California" theme would have had a strange ring.

Significantly, of the "big six" reapportionment cases decided in June 1964, four were from the South—Alabama, Virginia, Maryland, and Delaware. Justice John Marshall Harlan dissented on historical grounds in all six cases, but only the two Northern cases from Colorado and New York produced major dissents from Justices Tom C. Clark and Potter Stewart. It is a fair question whether without the South, which has forced the "making" of so much constitutional law for the nation in the last two decades, the reapportionment rulings would have come when they did or have been handled in such sweeping fashion.

In *Reynolds*, and more particularly in the accompanying Maryland senate case, *Maryland Committee v. Tawes*,[8] the Court settled the first uncertainty which had divided lower courts by laying down a simple rule that the equal protection clause of the Fourteenth Amendment requires both houses of a bicameral legislature to be elected from districts of substantially equal population.

In *Lucas v. Colorado General Assembly*,[9] the Court settled the second uncertainty, the role of popular referenda. The Court treated as irrelevant the fact that the people of Colorado, by statewide majorities of 2 to 1 and at least a bare majority in every county, had voted down a straight equal population plan and had approved a mixed representation formula under which one house deviated from the equal population principle.

7. 377 U.S. 533 (1964).
8. 377 U.S. 656 (1964).
9. 377 U.S. 713 (1964).

The third uncertainty which ran through the cases—How equal is equal?—was covered only with a formula of "substantial equality" and thus has remained to plague legislators and courts. None of the cases reviewed in 1964 had population deviations so narrow as to force the Court to respond in more precise terms than "substantial equality." More significantly, none of the cases involved racial or political gerrymandering, use of special representation forms, at-large voting with its "winner-take-all" feature, or other subtleties which are not well resolved by a bare substantial equality concept and which might have forced the Court into more sophisticated inquiry, in the words of Justice Felix Frankfurter in *Baker*, "into the theoretic base of representation in an acceptably republican state." [10]

As a generalization it can be said that the *Reapportionment Decisions* proceed from surprisingly simple premises and highlights can be summarized rather readily. The principal opinion of the Court was delivered by Chief Justice Earl Warren in the Alabama case (decided 8 to 1), with brief but consistent elaborations and separate opinions in the other five cases. As a basic test, the Court espoused an equal population apportionment principle for both houses of a bicameral legislature, thus invalidating at least one legislative house in virtually every state and in most instances both houses. The new rule was variously expressed in such phrases as "substantial equality of population among the various districts" [11] and "as nearly of equal population as is practicable." [12] Added as a secondary test (perhaps to glean the votes of Justices Clark and Stewart for some of the cases) was a prohibition against "crazy quilts, completely lacking in rationality." [13] (For a succinct summary of the population disparities in the 15 state plans ruled on in June 1964, see Chart 8.)

The whole tone of Chief Justice Warren's opinion was flatly inconsistent with a statement he had made earlier as governor of California. And because one's past always rises to haunt one, it was to be expected he would be reminded of this in the public press and on the floor of Congress. In 1948 speaking in opposition to a flat "population equality" rule he had said:

> Many California counties are far more important in the life of the State than their population of the State. It is for this reason that I have never been in favor of restricting the representation in the senate to a strictly population basis.[14]

10. 369 U.S. 186, 301 (1962).
11. 377 U.S. at 559.
12. Id. at 577.
13. Id. at 568.
14. From speech at Merced, California, on October 29, 1948, as excerpted in *U.S. News & World Report*, July 6, 1964, p. 34. The then-Governor Warren in this speech

Justice Stewart, who produced the principal dissents, was the only justice to try to come to grips with the philosophic and practical complexity of the concept of representation in a large, polycentric society. Not willing to have the Court try to do everything, but not wanting the Court to do nothing, he agreed with the *decision* in three of the six cases (Alabama, Delaware, and Virginia), but with the *rationale* in none. He would have remanded the Maryland case for further proof. In sharp dissent from the majority he would have approved existing apportionments in two cases— Colorado and New York.

His vote to remand the Maryland senate case for further hearing explains well his two guiding principles. His narrower principle, the easier to apply, is that crazy quilts, i.e., patterns of apportionment defying rational explanation, are bad. Because the Maryland senate was based on a fairly consistent political subdivision principle, it passed muster for Justice Stewart under this crazy-quilt test. But, because of lack of sufficient data, the constitutionality of the Maryland senate was not then determinable under his broader and more difficult principle; i.e., that apportionments that systematically "prevent ultimate effective majority rule" [15] are unconstitutional. It may be noted in passing that both of these tests find their juristic home more naturally under the due process clause or guarantee of a "republican form of government" clause. But it is the equal protection clause which has come to dominate and narrow the Court's handling of apportionment matters.

Justice Harlan, in lonely isolation, wrote a fitting epilogue to Justice Frankfurter's monumental dissenting opinion in *Baker*. He would have gone back to pre-*Baker* times by dismissing all of the cases as "an experiment in venturesome constitutionalism." [16] He could find no original understanding that the Fourteenth Amendment was to apply to voting or apportionment. His historical and textual argument is overpowering, all the more so because not rebutted by Chief Justice Warren's opinions for the Court. But like the history he used, his opinion seems destined to become history, unless it eventually has influence in recurring proposals for constitutional amendments to authorize limited use of nonpopulation factors in reapportioning one house of the legislature, i.e., the modified local

continued as follows: "It is the same reason that the Founding Fathers of our country gave balanced representation to the States of the Union—equal representation in one house and proportionate representation based on population in the other. Moves have been made to upset the balanced representation in our state, even though it has served us well and is strictly in accord with American tradition and the pattern of our National Government . . . . Our State has made almost unbelievable progress under our present system of legislative representation. I believe we should keep it."
15. 377 U.S. at 677.
16. 377 U.S. at 625.

CHART 8

STATISTICAL MEASURES OF "MALAPPORTIONMENT" IN THE FIFTEEN STATE
LEGISLATURES HELD UNCONSTITUTIONAL BY THE UNITED STATES
SUPREME COURT, JUNE 15 AND JUNE 22, 1964

State	Minimum population theoretically able to control a majority of the seats		Population variance ratio	
	Senate	House	Senate	House
Alabama				
Existing apport.	25.1%	25.7%	41-1	16-1
67 Senator Amendmt.	19.4%	43.0%	59-1	4.7-1
Crawford-Webb Act	27.6%	37.0%	20-1	5-1
Colorado				
Existing apport.				
(Amendmt. No. 7)	33.2%	45.1%	3.6-1	1.7-1
Prior apport.	29.8%	32.1%	8-1	8-1
Delaware				
Existing apport.				
(1963 Amendmt.)	21.0%	28.0%	15-1	12-1
Prior apport.	22.0%	18.5%	15-1	35-1
Maryland				
Existing apport.				
(1962 revision of				
lower house)	14.1%	35.6%	32-1	6-1
Prior apport.	14.1%	24.7%	32-1	12-1
New York				
Existing apport.	41.8%	34.7%	3.9-1	21-1
Projected apport. under				
revision due by 1966 (under				
state constit. standards.)	38.1%	37.5%	2.6-1	12.7-1
Virginia	41.1%	40.5%	2.65-1	4.36-1
Connecticut	32.0%	12.0%	8.1-1	424.6-1
Florida	14.1%	22.9%	38.1-1	23.3-1
Idaho	16.6%	32.7%	102.2-1	17.0-1
Illinois	28.7%	39.9%	10.6-1	4.9-1
Iowa	35.2%	26.9%	8.9-1	16.8-1
Michigan	29.0%	44.0%	12.4-1	3.9-1
Ohio	41.0%	30.3%	1.9-1	9.4-1
Oklahoma	24.5%	29.5%	26.4-1	13.9-1
Washington	33.9%	35.3%	7.3-1	4.6-1

Source: The figures for the first six states listed, Alabama through Virginia, are taken
from the Supreme Court opinions as reported in 377 U.S. 533 *et seq.* (1964). The
figures for the last nine states, Connecticut through Washington, are taken from National Municipal League, *Compendium on Legislative Apportionment,* 1963 Supplemental Chart.

Note: The first six cases were decided with full opinions after oral argument. The last
nine were noted as memorandum decisions without oral argument.

option "federal plan" proposal of Senator Everett M. Dirksen and others.

Justice Clark, beyond joining in the basic opinion of Justice Stewart in the New York and Colorado cases, simply adhered to his "crazy-quilt" theory as expressed in his *Baker* opinion. He would accept nonpopulation factors in one house if the other were based substantially on population. The Clark position, and of course Harlan's too, would have permitted continuance of a federal plan analogous to Congress, with one house based on population and the other on nonpopulation factors, *provided* (for Clark) the factors were "rational." Stewart was not ready to reject or embrace a federal plan without more evidence on the question whether it would prevent effective majority rule; hence his vote to remand the Maryland senate case for further hearings.

In terms of basic rationale, therefore, the Court split 6–2–1. There were six justices for a fairly tight equal population district system; two (Stewart and Clark) in favor of more flexible, case-by-case standards inside the outer boundaries of preservation of majority rule and avoidance of crazy quilts; and one (Harlan) for a hands-off approach.

CONSTITUTIONAL THEORY OF THE WARREN (MAJORITY) OPINIONS

Several distinctive approaches fixed the frame of reference for the Supreme Court's decisions of 1964 articulating federal constitutional standards governing apportionment of state legislatures. First, the issue was to be approached essentially as a relatively simple "right to vote" issue. Second, the constitutional clause used was to be the equal protection of the laws clause of the Fourteenth Amendment, rather than the due process clause or the guarantee of a "republican form of government" clause. Third, the equal protection of the laws clause itself was to be interpreted in fairly absolute, arithmetic terms.

a. *Premises*

Regarding the first point, the "suffrage" or "right to vote" approach excluded any serious analysis of "representation" as a many-faceted concept within the democratic tradition. Attention was shifted away from representation in the functional sense and away from such operational elements as the demographic features of constituency composition and the political realities in the electoral and legislative process. As corollary points, the "right to vote": (a) was deemed protected when gross constituency population was equalized (or proportionalized if multimember districts were used); (b) was not related to any consideration of proportionalizing a party's legislative seats to its share of the electorate; (c) was not related to any measures of effectiveness and fairness of representation in the actual process of legislative decision-making.

The second approach, i.e., using the equal protection clause as the vehicle for change, was foreshadowed by *Baker* v. *Carr* and impelled perhaps by failure of counsel and judges in all of the cases to consider the possible greater relevance of the guarantee clause or the due process clause. Reapportionment really is a right to vote *plus* issue. The "plus" encompasses some of the basic policy choices suggested in Chapters II and III on representation theory. It encompasses also the self-evident but oft-ignored proposition that a near-infinite number of equal population districting plans can be devised, many of which however have a dramatically different *effect* on "representation" despite their one common feature of deviating minimally if at all from arithmetic equality.

The third approach, i.e., an absolutist interpretation of equal protection, has been delineated in Chapter VII. It accords with the relatively absolute concept of equality developed in the race cases, but not with the loose "reasonable classification" concept exemplified by Chief Justice Warren's opinion in the Sunday Closing cases [17] and by the main line of nonracial cases under this clause.

It is far too late, of course, to attempt to shift reapportionment litigation from the equal protection clause to the due process clause or the guarantee clause. In the nature of things, plaintiffs would always prefer the equal protection clause because *if* geared simply to population and *if* applied with a degree of rigidity, it would yield maximum change with minimum burden of proof so far as plaintiffs were concerned. Because parties shape any law case, only the Court could have shifted attention from equal protection to one of the other two clauses. It would have had to deny relief on equal protection grounds and thus force consideration of the issue in broader context under one of the other two clauses. Although cases would have been no easier to solve under the due process or republican guarantee clauses, difficult questions concerning majoritarianism and representative democracy would have been faced rather than skirted. In particular, either of the other two clauses would have been far better adapted to intelligent consideration of the kinds of issues which arise in the second stage of the reapportionment revolution—i.e., the "malrepresentation of interests" issue which persists after the egregious "malapportionment of people" issue has been resolved.

The Court majority's adherence to a relatively absolute equal protection concept in the *Reapportionment Decisions* automatically resolved one issue on which lower courts were split, i.e., whether the equal population premise should apply to both houses or only to one house. Characterizing

17. McGowan v. Maryland, 366 U.S. 420 (1961).

rights involved as being "individual and personal in nature," [18] and impelled by a rigid equality principle, the Court had no choice but to invalidate apportionment plans which sought to authorize a mixed factor basis or nonpopulation basis for apportionment of one house. For how could a voter's constitutionally guaranteed right to equal protection in apportionment have one "equality" dimension regarding one legislative house and a different "equality" dimension in regard to a second legislative house? Where equal protection applies it necessarily applies to all governmental acts.

The so-called federal plan, although continued for Congress because of antecedent constitutional grant, automatically became unconstitutional for states under the Fourteenth Amendment by the very nature of the Court's characterization and perception of the reapportionment issue. Only an approach to reapportionment from the standpoint of the "republican form of government" guarantee clause—or possibly the due process clause, with its core meaning of general fairness and reasonableness— would have given room for differing bases of representation in the two houses of a bicameral legislature.

b. *Equal Numbers and "Equal Representation"*

In addition to grounding complexities of state legislative reapportionment on a simple "right to vote" concept, undergirded by a relatively absolute equality principle, a further key element of the majority's constitutional theory was the equating of *districting* based on "equal numbers of people" with an *operating result* of "equal representation." It was assumed unquestioningly that "equal representation" magically arises from creating districts of equal population. The term *"equal population districts"* denotes a verifiable objective concept. But *"equal representation"* is a highly subjective term connoting a hoped-for result. The result may be promoted or defeated by a congeries of factors, some objective, like "equal population districts," and some subjective, like gerrymandering. The Court's equating of the two concepts is a classic example of moving from an objective concept to a highly subjective concept without noting the shift. Though a good debater's trick it is hardly worthy of constitutional adjudication.

This easy equating of the objective and the subjective is the central inadequacy of the majority's constitutional theory in the 1964 *Reapportionment Decisions*. This approach has hemmed in plaintiffs (usually racial or political minorities) in the post-1694 "second level" of the reapportionment revolution. The new issues, which require a more sophisticated approach, include permissible districting patterns, placement of particular

18. 377 U.S. at 565.

district lines, use of at-large voting methods, outright gerrymandering of "equal" districts, and the like. Because semantics so often shapes our perceptions, it would be well by general agreement to repeal the term "equal representation" and to substitute, whenever *representation* is discussed, some term such as "fair representation" or "political equity."

This linking of two quite separate concepts first appeared in Justice Hugo L. Black's opinion in the Georgia congressional districting case, *Wesberry* v. *Sanders*, when he referred to the Constitution's plain objective "of making equal representation for equal numbers of people the fundamental goal. . . ." [19] It was quoted and elaborated by Chief Justice Warren in *Reynolds*. But though "representation" may be fair, with effective representation in the legislature of various views and interests, such as urban interests, in approximate proportion to their statewide strength, it never can be "equal." In any district system the pyramiding of regional pluralities creates winners and losers *disproportionate* to actual votes cast. If there *were* a constitutional goal of "equal representation," then some system of proportional representation would be constitutionally mandated. Only through a proportional representation system of election are winner-take-all pluralities minimized, and the possibility maximized that parties and groups actually will gain representation equal (i.e., proportional) to their voting strength.

This Black-Warren formulation is perhaps an unwitting inversion of a perfectly proper statement of James Wilson of Pennsylvania during the Constitutional Convention of 1787. As quoted by Justice Black in his *Wesberry* opinion, Wilson was summarizing the House of Representatives' apportionment principle as follows: "Equal numbers of people ought to have an equal no. of representatives. . . ." [20] This is a perfectly legitimate concept. Wilson was saying that for half of Congress, the House of Representatives, seats should be allocated equal to (i.e., proportional to) the population of the constituencies (i.e., *states*) to be served. Intrastate districting was a separate matter. Whether such an apportionment formula in the many contexts in which it might appear would also achieve the goal of equal representation lay beyond the scope of the Wilson comment.

A narrow "numbers game" focus for reapportionment was perhaps not a necessary result of the Black-Warren formulation. There were some conflicting statements elsewhere in the Warren opinion in *Reynolds*. In point of fact, however, subsequent judges and reapportioners, comforted and aided by this formulation, did put on blinders in regard to reapportionment subtleties. Corollary factors supporting the narrow approach

19. 376 U.S. 1, 18 (1964).
20. *Id.* at 11.

seemingly sanctified by the Black-Warren formulation were the exigencies of judicially imposed time pressure in the ensuing months and years, the appealing simplicity of a bare population standard, the standard's seeming capacity to yield an apportionment impregnable on appeal, and the esoteric nature of political and racial gerrymandering.

c. *Puzzling Caveats*

Although Chief Justice Warren indicated that constitutional rectitude in legislative apportionment was to be achieved by an equal population principle in districting, he did insert at several points some puzzling caveats. For example, he said:

> We realize that it is a practical impossibility to arrange legislative districts so that each one has an identical number of residents or citizens or voters. Mathematical exactness or precision is hardly a workable constitutional requirement.[21]

Yet it would seem that it *is* possible to achieve something approximating mathematical precision in districting simply by abolishing all or many traditional lines and making a fresh start. Some lower courts after *Reynolds* did take this approach in regard both to state legislative apportionment (Michigan) [22] and to congressional districting (Missouri).[23]

Whether or not mathematical precision is "practicable" (to use the Court's own word) as well as mechanically "possible" would seem to depend upon whether or not continued use of some nonpopulation considerations is permissible. In a left-handed sort of way the Court did speak in one section of the *Reynolds* opinion of several possibly legitimate nonpopulation considerations: "insuring some voice to political subdivisions, as subdivisions"; "according political subdivisions some independent representation in at least one body of the state legislature"; following principles of compactness and contiguity in districting; achieve "some flexibility by creating multimember or floterial districts"; "effectuation of a rational state policy." [24]

Perhaps the Court's clearest expression in *Reynolds* of a consideration that might not make it "practicable" to achieve mathematical exactness in districting was this statement:

21. 377 U.S. at 577.
22. E.g., Michigan—*In re* Apportionment of Michigan State Legislature, 128 N.W. 2d 721, 722 (Mich. 1964); Oklahoma—Reynolds v. State Election Board, 233 F. Supp. 323 (W. D. Okla. 1964); Missouri—Jones v. Hearnes, 236 F. Supp. 699 (W. D. Mo. 1964).
23. E.g., Missouri—Preisler v. Secretary of State, 257 F. Supp. 953 (W. D. Mo. 1966); North Carolina—Drum v. Seawell, 250 F. Supp. 922 (M. D. N.C. 1966).
24. 377 U.S. 533, 577–81.

. . . [I]ndiscriminate districting without any regard for political subdivision or natural or historical boundary lines, may be little more than an open invitation to partisan gerrymandering.[25]

Apart from considerations of this sort, there would seem to be no *merely logical* reason why an "as nearly of equal population as is possible" standard should not lead to near mathematical exactness in districting.

In addition to these puzzling caveats about "mathematical exactness" and "indiscriminate districting," Chief Justice Warren at one point phrased the ultimate goal to be sought in legislative reapportionment in more sophisticated terms, terms inconsistent with a simple "equal numbers yield equal representation" assertion. At one point he characterized the goal as being "full and *effective participation* by *all* citizens in state government." [26] A few lines further on he stated even more clearly that "fair and *effective representation* for *all* citizens is concededly the basic aim of legislative apportionment." [27] (Emphasis added.) Quotations such as these could have been the foundation of a long-needed fresh dialogue on the nature of representation in a dynamic democratic order which is only partially organized by political parties and is disordered by strongly held and sometimes overlapping interest group alignments, by rapid population shifts, and other factors. However, the "equal numbers" overlay which dominated the Court's approach has in practice operated to discourage such a dialogue. And Chief Justice Warren in a later part of his opinion seemed expressly to reject consideration of the group dynamics of American politics by saying that neither "economic or other sorts of group interests" [28] are relevant factors in devising a representation system.

Under analysis even Chief Justice Warren's famous line that "legislators represent people, not trees or acres" undercuts the thought that "equal numbers" guarantees "equal representation." The distinctive thing about people, in contrast to trees or acres, is that *people* are *not fungible*. Failure to perceive this leads to the "identity of interest" fallacy which underlies such simple arithmetic measures as the electoral percentage (Dauer-Kelsay measure), and which is the central fallacy of a rigid, simplistic "one man-one vote" theory. Although legislators are elected "by voters," as Chief Justice Warren said, they are elected by voters who have interests which lead them to organize for group political action. The struggle for legislative control is a group struggle; the method is to seek popular pluralities in a majority of districts. It is not struggle by voters operating, in Justice Stewart's words, as "faceless numbers." How the group

25. *Id.* at 578–79.
26. *Id.* at 565.
27. *Id.* at 565–66.
28. *Id.* at 579–80.

fares in the electoral struggle and its prospects for achieving a "fair share of the seats" may be more important questions from the standpoint of representation than the question whether district population has been equalized within a minimal percentage point spread of 10 percent rather than 15 percent. These questions, which lie at the heart of democratic representation, are largely foreign to the main thrust of the constitutional theory of the majority in the 1964 *Reapportionment Decisions* with the occasional exception noted.

The essence of *Reynolds* may be its simplistic, narrow, humorless quality. Although it has been said to be Chief Justice Warren's most prideful opinion, it has no trace of pragmatism which also has been said to be his pre-eminent quality.[29] And, anomalously, when in a frankly pragmatic and even inconsistent ruling the Court in 1967 cut back considerably on the "one man-one vote" constitutional cliché in order to leave more room for experimentation with representation forms at the local government level, it was one of the Court's nominal absolutists, Justice Douglas, who wrote the opinions.[30] Opinions can and must be categorized; but those who categorize justices do so at their peril.

CONSTITUTIONAL THEORY OF THE STEWART PARTIAL DISSENTS

Justice Stewart dissented wholly from the Court's invalidation of New York and Colorado apportionments, although for different reasons. He gave limited concurrence to the Court's invalidation of Alabama, Delaware, and Virginia apportionments because population disparities and differential treatment of some counties similarly situated were not shown to have any "rational basis." [31] But Maryland's system of representing each county equally in the state senate (with six seats awarded to the separated city of Baltimore) was deemed by him to be based on an intelligible principle; hence he could not invalidate it as "completely lacking in rationality." [32] Also, there was no basis in the record for finding—nor had any court made a finding—that Maryland's system operated "systematically to prevent ultimate effective majority rule." [33] He would have remanded the case to the Maryland Court of Appeals for full consideration of this issue.

---

29. Fred Rodell, "It Is the Earl Warren Court," *New York Times Magazine,* March 13, 1966, p. 28. Referring to the Chief Justice as "unbookish" and "no scholar," Professor Rodell did credit him with a "result-minded pragmatism."
30. Moody v. Flowers, 387 U.S. 97 (1967); Sailors v. Board of Education, 387 U.S. 105 (1967); Dusch v. Davis, 387 U.S. 112 (1967).
31. 377 U.S. at 588.
32. *Id.* at 676–77.
33. *Id.* at 677.

Justice Stewart's twin principles emerged, therefore, as (1) concern for preservation of effective majority rule, and (2) use of a "rational basis" in making classifications of constituencies which reapportionment necessarily entails. The second principle flows naturally from the equal protection clause's concern for reasonableness for all classifications. The first principle obviously would be grounded more appropriately on either the due process clause or republican guarantee clause. As phrased by Professor Robert G. McCloskey, it is directed to the central question of "whether ultimate constituent power was being allowed an opportunity to express itself." [34]

Justice Stewart's more elaborate explanations of his two constitutional standards—avoidance of irrational plans and avoidance of frustration of majority rule—occur in his opinion explaining why he would have held constitutional the apportionment plans in force in New York and Colorado. After noting that the issue in reapportionment is not "impairment of any person's right to vote" [35] per se or "the 'weighting' or 'diluting' of votes cast within any electoral unit," [36] he characterizes the issue in legislative reapportionment as being one of achieving "effective and balanced representation of all substantial interests, without sacrificing the principle of effective majority rule." [37] The essence of his approach is well captured in this paragraph:

> Representative government is a process of accommodating group interests through democratic institutional arrangements. Its function is to channel the numerous opinions, interests, and abilities of the people of a State into the making of the State's public policy. Appropriate legislative apportionment, therefore, should ideally be designed to insure effective representation in the State's legislature, in cooperation with other organs of political power, of the various groups and interests making up the electorate. In practice, of course, this ideal is approximated in the particular apportionment system of any State by a realistic accommodation of the diverse and often conflicting political forces operating within the State.[38]

a. Colorado Case

Applying his principles to the facts of the Colorado case, it was easy to conclude—indeed, necessary to conclude—that there had been no showing of systematic denigration of majority rule. The Colorado case pre-

34. Robert G. McCloskey, "Foreword: The Reapportionment Case," 76 *Harv. L. Rev.* 54, 71 (1962).
35. 377 U.S. at 744.
36. *Ibid.*
37. *Id.* at 751.
38. *Id.* at 749.

sented an apportionment plan placing one house on a population basis and the other on a modified population basis which had been approved by every county in Colorado in a popular referendum. In the same "one man-one vote" statewide referendum an alternative plan placing both houses on a population basis had been resoundingly rejected. None of the five other cases decided on June 15—Alabama, Delaware, Maryland, New York, Virginia—nor any of nine additional apportionment cases disposed of briefly a week later, involved this popular referendum feature.

Compliance of the Colorado plan with Justice Stewart's other constitutional reapportionment principle, i.e., a "rational basis" for grouping counties and constructing constituencies, was more assumed than explicitly analyzed. He seems to have been so impressed by the popular referendum feature that fine details of constituency comparison became unimportant. He further bolstered his preservation-of-majority-rule thesis by pointing out that the metropolitan areas of Denver, Pueblo, and Colorado Springs elected a majority of the Colorado senate. The senate could not be controlled by any possible combination of senators from rural districts, even assuming they would vote as a bloc. On this basis he chose to ignore, perhaps on a de minimis theory, the fact brought out in oral argument under questioning by Justice Byron R. White that apportionment disparities among seemingly comparable counties did not follow a consistent pattern throughout the state.

It would seem that Justice Stewart's central principle was preservation of majority rule, not "rationality" to the "nth" degree. From this standpoint, if the goal be to insure that the legislature shall achieve a representative expression of popular will, how better can this be ascertained than through a popular referendum among the "represented" people themselves—a referendum itself called by process of popular initiative and subject to change in future popularly initiated referenda?

b. *New York and Virginia Cases*

The New York and Virginia cases presented closer questions for Justice Stewart. He managed to join the majority in its invalidation of the Virginia apportionment but split from the majority to uphold New York's reapportionment. In purely mathematical terms his separation of the two cases is puzzling. The population theoretically able to control a majority of the seats (fictional electoral percentage) in the two states was similar —and Virginia had the better figures. Indeed, by this measure Virginia was the eighth best apportioned state in the nation. The respective senate and house figures were for Virginia 41.1 percent and 40.5 percent, and for New York 38.1 percent and 37.5 percent. The distinction, for Justice Stewart, is that while there was no proof or logical inference that either

New York's or Virginia's apportionment systematically denigrated majority rule, Virginia's plan unlike New York's was "irrational."

In Virginia the disparities appeared to be ad hoc and not the result of any statewide policy consistently applied of providing effective voice for the smaller units. However, in New York he could explain apportionment disparities among various counties as being the result of an apportionment formula, albeit somewhat complicated, designed to guarantee minimum representation to each county. The formula provided "that each county [with one exception] shall have at least one representative in the Assembly, that the smaller counties shall have somewhat greater representation in the legislature than representation based solely on numbers would accord, and that some limits be placed on the representation of the largest counties in order to prevent one megalopolis from completely dominating the legislature." [39]

Of course, it should be noted that insofar as smaller units in New York tended to be Republican, the New York policy, coupled with a ceiling on New York City's representation, tended to avoid a straight population apportionment which would have placed the central cities in control of both houses of the legislature. But it did so, as Al Smith expressed it, only at the price of making New York's legislature "constitutionally Republican." Important as balance of party representation may be in total context of representative democracy, none of the 1964 reapportionment cases as they came to the Court focused on this issue.

The constitutional theory of Justice Stewart on the merits of reapportionment is really the constitutional theory which Solicitor General Archibald Cox had used in 1961 to induce the Court to embark on the task of policing legislative reapportionment! Although in 1963 and 1964 the Solicitor General had argued against the constitutionality of *all* reapportionment plans before the Court, he had in 1961 expressed a constitutional view seemingly supportive of the kinds of reapportionment plans that were at issue in 1964 in the Colorado, New York, and perhaps Virginia cases. The Solicitor General had said:

> Constitutional statecraft often involves a degree of protection for minorities which limits the principle of majority rule. . . . Due recognition of geographic and other minority interests is also a comprehensible reason for reducing the weight of votes in great cities. If seventy percent of a State's population lived in a single city and the remainder was scattered over wide country areas and small towns, it might be reasonable to give the city voters somewhat smaller representation than that to which they would be entitled by a strictly

39. *Id.* at 760–61.

numerical apportionment in order to reduce the danger of total neglect of the needs and wishes of rural areas.[40]

CONSTITUTIONAL THEORY OF THE HARLAN TOTAL DISSENT

Justice Harlan, who had been unable to agree with the Court majority in *Baker, Gray,* and *Wesberry,* entered a total dissent to the 1964 *Reapportionment Decisions.* As in *Wesberry* his approach was historical, seeking to ascertain the intended "original meaning" of the Constitution in congressional redistricting and legislative reapportionment matters. His review of sources convinced him that neither framers nor ratifiers of the Fourteenth Amendment ever contemplated its application to legislative apportionment or even to the narrower question of franchise (voting qualifications). But, alas, there was no dialogue, because the majority opinions of Chief Justice Warren ignored rather than rebutted the Harlan research.

a. *Majority's Avoidance of History*

Except for one brief reference concerning the supposed "federal analogy," Chief Justice Warren's opinions for the majority in the 1964 reapportionment cases ignored the question of "original understandings." This tactic contrasts sharply with Justice Black's approach a few months earlier in *Wesberry* v. *Sanders* when, speaking for the Court, he purported to find in Article I, Section 2's original meaning a self-sufficient basis for requiring congressional districts to be of equal population.

The one historical reference in the Warren opinions in reapportionment cases was, interestingly enough, not to supposed Fourteenth Amendment "original understandings" but to supposed "original understandings" of 1787. Technically, of course, a Fourteenth Amendment designed to restrict state legislative discretion in apportionment would make irrelevant any impressions of the Founding Fathers. The Chief Justice's reversion to 1787, therefore, was a silent admission that the Fourteenth Amendment did not clearly cover apportionment, either as written or as amplified by clear legislative history.

The argument the Chief Justice was seeking to rebut by his 1787 reference was one commonly known as the "federal analogy." The argument is that the general language of the Fourteenth Amendment, which does not mention apportionment, should not be interpreted to prohibit state use of the bicameral system sanctioned for Congress in the Great Compromise in the Constitutional Convention of 1787. Chief Justice Warren quite appropriately rejected any thought that the agreed pattern of congressional

40. *Id.* at 759–60.

apportionment conferred on states any *right* to have a similar pattern. But the true question is whether the federal pattern nevertheless would be a reasonable and appropriate option within the range of constitutionally permissible state discretion.

The closest the Chief Justice came to discussing this issue was to revert to supposed "original understandings" of 1787 concerning state legislative apportionment. His primary evidence for concluding that the Founding Fathers rejected the federal pattern for state legislatures was that the Northwest Ordinance adopted in 1787 by the last Congress under the Articles of Confederation specified population as the basis for apportionment in territorial legislatures. However, the Ordinance applied only to a handful of legislatures and, as noted in Chapter IV, its supposed "population" mandate was in practice never understood to require stringent arithmetic equality.

Chief Justice Warren's reliance on the Northwest Ordinance has been viewed as "nothing short of astonishing" [41] by a well-known student of constitutional history for the further reason that the Confederation Congress and Philadelphia Convention were two distinct bodies whose deliberations had nothing in common. Further, if contemporary political practice be a necessary component of ascertaining "original understandings," there is one piece of evidence far more important than the Northwest Ordinance. Each state legislature that sent delegates to the Philadelphia Convention deviated grossly from any "one man-one vote" standard, and the subsequent ratifying conventions in each state—called for by the Philadelphia Convention itself as a way of getting the highest possible sanction for the new instrument—were apportioned on the same basis as the state legislature.[42]

b. *Justice Harlan's History*

Justice Harlan's negative approach to judicial review of state legislative reapportionment was a logical extension and elaboration of his *Baker* dissent. In *Baker* he had intimated that if the Fourteenth Amendment has no possible application to legislative apportionment the Court simply could dismiss for lack of "jurisdiction" (no federal cause of action), and not reach questions of standing and justiciability. His detailed historical review in *Reynolds* convinced him that this was the case.

41. Alfred M. Kelly, "Clio and the Court: An Illicit Love Affair," in 1965 *Supreme Court Review* 119, 136 (Philip B. Kurland, editor, Chicago: University of Chicago Press, 1965).
42. The portion of the Warren opinion dealing with the readmission of the Confederate states and admission of new states is aimed not so much at "original understandings" as at the proposition that *if* there be a constitutional right, Congressional action cannot whittle it down. See Reynolds v. Sims, 377 U.S. 533, 582 (1964).

There has been a plethora of literature concerning "original understandings" of the Fourteenth Amendment in various contexts.[43] The various contexts encompass a large proportion of major issues of constitutional law in the past twenty years. For example, in the "state action" dispute the question is whether framers of the Fourteenth Amendment intended to reach only governmental action in the pure sense, or also to reach private discriminatory acts linked to the state by such elements as financial aid, licenses, mere access to the courts. Regarding "segregation," the question is whether framers contemplated full integration or merely an "equal but separate" principle. Regarding "incorporation," the question is whether the Fourteenth Amendment incorporated by shorthand process, and hence nationalized at one sweep, the entire Bill of Rights.

In *Reynolds* the new question—controlling question for Justice Harlan —was whether framers understood the equal protection clause of the Fourteenth Amendment to deal with the right to vote, and to create national power over state legislative apportionment. For him the answer was a forceful and unequivocal "No":

> The history of the adoption of the Fourteenth Amendment provides conclusive evidence that neither those who proposed nor those who ratified the Amendment believed that the Equal Protection Clause limited the power of the States to apportion their legislatures as they saw fit. Moreover, the history demonstrates that the intention to leave this power undisturbed was deliberate and was widely believed to be essential to the adoption of the Amendment.[44]

Interestingly enough, the Harlan conclusion is squarely supported by an article written long before the reapportionment decisions in which the authors were seeking to extract the maximum "original understandings" from the equal protection clause by combining the understandings of congressional initiation in 1866, state ratification in 1868, and of the full Reconstruction decade down to the Civil Rights Act of 1875. Using this approach John P. Frank and Robert F. Munro could assert in 1950 that the original understanding was to create a broad congressional power to ensure racial equality in business enterprises, property ownership, civil and criminal justice and public accommodations without regard to whether the inequality was the product of state action or state inaction. But they added that "the clause was meant to have no bearing on the right to vote." [45]

43. See Kelly, note 41 *supra* and authorities cited therein.
44. 377 U.S. 595 (1964) (Harlan, J., dissenting).
45. John P. Frank, and Robert F. Munro, "The Original Understanding of 'Equal Protection of the Laws,'" 50 *Colum. L. Rev.* 131 (1950). Subsequently, however, when Mr. Frank had occasion to review a book on *Reynolds* v. *Sims*, he carefully

Several elements contributed to the Harlan formulation. First, he insisted on reading the Fourteenth Amendment as a "single text" and thus giving full effect to Section 2 in ascertaining the intended scope of Section 1. Although the two Sections originated in different bills, they were discussed and ratified as a unit, a proposal to submit them separately to the states having been rejected by the Senate. In this way, and on grammatical basis alone he could suggest that the second Section, which provides a sanction for state abridgment of the right to vote in the form of proportionate reduction of the states' basis of representation in Congress, obviously confirms an *initial* power in states to control voting and voting qualifications. The relevant clause in Section 1 of the Fourteenth Amendment states that no state shall "deny to any person within its jurisdiction the equal protection of the laws." The relevant portion of Section 2 provides:

> But when the right to vote at any election . . . is denied to any of the male inhabitants of such State, being twenty-one years of age, and citizens of the United States, or in any way abridged, except for participation in rebellion, or other crime, the basis of representation therein shall be reduced in the proportion which the number of such male citizens shall bear to the whole number of male citizens twenty-one years of age in such State.

Second, Justice Harlan finds support in various comments made during congressional debates for the proposition that Section 1 of the Fourteenth Amendment was understood to leave authority over voting and voting qualifications with the states, subject of course to the penalty provision in Section 2. The following series of comments by Congressman John A. Bingham of Ohio, who had drafted and vigorously supported the first Section of the Fourteenth Amendment, were thought to be particularly pertinent:

> Allow me, Mr. Speaker, in passing, to say that this amendment takes from no State any right that ever pertained to it. No State ever had the right, under the forms of law or otherwise, to deny to any freeman the equal protection of the laws or to abridge the privileges or immunities of any citizen of the Republic, although many of them have assumed and exercised the power, and that without remedy. *The amendment does not give, as the second section shows, the power to Congress of regulating suffrage in the several States.*

avoided discussion of the constitutional theory of the *Reapportionment Decisions*, or the merits of the Harlan dissent as a work of historical scholarship. See Frank, Review of Robert B. McKay, *Reapportionment: The Law and Politics of Equal Representation* (New York: Twentieth Century Fund, 1965), 41 N.Y.U. L. Rev. 847 (1966).

The second section excludes the conclusion that by the first section suffrage is subjected to congressional law; save, indeed, with this exception, that as the right in the people of each State to a republican government and to choose their Representatives in Congress is [one] of the guarantees of the Constitution, by this amendment a remedy might be given directly for a case supposed by Madison, where treason might change a State government from a republican to a despotic government, and thereby deny suffrage to the people.

To be sure we all agree, and the great body of the people of this country agree, and the committee thus far in reporting measures of reconstruction agree, that *the exercise of the elective franchise, though it be one of the privileges of a citizen of the Republic, is exclusively under the control of the States.*[46]   (Emphasis added.)

Similarly, in the other house of Congress, Senator Jacob M. Howard of Michigan, who reported the Fourteenth Amendment to the Senate in 1866 from the Joint Committee on Reconstruction, stated forthrightly that the first Section of the proposed Amendment does not give to either of these classes [white or black] the right of voting. He expressed regret concerning the limited scope of the Amendment in this respect, as had Congressman Thaddeus Stevens of Pennsylvania who had introduced debate in the House, and justified the limited scope of the Amendment as a necessary concession to political realities affecting prospects for ratification:

But, sir, it is not the question here what will we do; it is not the question what you, or I, or half a dozen other members of the Senate may prefer in respect to colored suffrage; it is not entirely the question what measure we can pass through the two Houses; but the question really is, what will the Legislatures of the various States to whom these amendments are to be submitted do in the premises; what is it likely will meet the general approbation of the people who are to elect the Legislatures, three fourths of whom must ratify our propositions before they have the force of constitutional provisions?

The committee were of opinion that the States are not yet prepared to sanction so fundamental a change as would be the concession of the right of suffrage to the colored race. We may as well state it plainly and fairly, so that there shall be no misunderstanding on the subject. It was our opinion that three fourths of the States of this Union could not be induced to vote to grant the right of suffrage, even in any degree or under any restriction, to the colored race . . . . *The second section leaves the right to regulate the elective franchise*

46. *Cong. Globe,* 39th Cong., 1st Sess. 2542 (1866) (hereafter cited as *Globe*).

still with the States, and does not meddle with that right.[47] (Emphasis added.)

From his combination of textual analysis and legislative history, Justice Harlan concluded that state power over voting and voting qualifications was expressly considered in the course of drafting the Fourteenth Amendment and that framers "deliberately chose not to interfere with the States' plenary power in this regard" because Congress "believed that if such restrictions were included, the Amendment would not be adopted."[48]

It was a "nice argument" as Professor Alfred H. Kelly has noted[49] but it was oriented to the issue of state control over the voting *franchise*, whereas *Reynolds* involved the different issue of *apportionment* of seats in legislative bodies. The link-up can be made in two ways, and Justice Harlan seems to have assumed the first and then gone on to discuss the second. The first link-up, strangely ignored by some critics of the Harlan "historical dissent," is simply to note the opinion from which Harlan was dissenting. The essential theory of the majority in the reapportionment cases, rightly or wrongly, was to view reapportionment disputes as simply one more round of "right to vote" cases, i.e., *franchise* cases, substantially divorced from those considerations of representation and group political dynamics which have been suggested in this work as necessary corollaries of a "voting rights" approach to legislative apportionment. It may be conceded that on the precise issue of the application of the Fourteenth Amendment to *malapportionment* the congressional debates were scanty to the point of being irrelevant. But on the implicit and explicit understandings regarding the application of the Fourteenth Amendment to state power over *suffrage* there was much in the *Congressional Globe* which seemed to undercut the right to vote dogma which is the core constitutional theory of the Warren reapportionment opinions.

The second way to connect "original understanding" concerning the Fourteenth Amendment with legislative apportionment is to examine actual legislative apportionments (1) in "loyal" states which ratified the Fourteenth Amendment, (2) in ten "reconstructed" states which were required to ratify the Amendment as a condition of readmission, and (3) in states generally, including, after 1868, newly admitted Western states. Justice Harlan's data on this point, extended by some additional sources, have been summarized in Chapter IV as part of the nineteenth-century history of apportionment. Nonexistence of a rigid "one man-one vote" concept in the nineteenth century before, during, and after ratification of the Fourteenth Amendment is irrefutable.

47. *Id.* at 2766.
48. 377 U.S. at 607–8.
49. Kelly, *supra*, note 41 at 127.

c. The True "Original Understanding"

How has Justice Harlan's dissent fared at the hands of critics on or off the Bench? His brethren on the Bench not only chose to ignore his historical analysis of the Fourteenth Amendment in the reapportionment cases but continued to ignore Harlan's similar "historical dissents" in a subsequent series of pure "right to vote" cases. In this series (military voting,[50] poll tax,[51] literacy tests,[52]) state franchise restrictions were invalidated under the Fourteenth Amendment over Harlan's continued argument that the Amendment does not relate to suffrage matters and that the national government was given suffrage control over states only in regard to racial matters under the Fifteenth Amendment. By the Court's continued silence, as one commentator noted, "the majority seems tacitly to have conceded the argument, if not the vote." [53]

Voluminous debates in the *Congressional Globe* have been re-culled by Professors Alfred Avins and William W. Van Alstyne in lengthy articles with many additional quotations, some tending to support and some tending to rebut the Harlan position.[54] Individual Congressmen, e.g., Congressman Bingham, can be shown to have made inconsistent statements, explainable perhaps by a tendency to play down the intended scope of the Fourteenth Amendment *prior* to enactment in order to quiet fears, and to read broadly the Fourteenth Amendment *after* enactment in order to find a foundation for the Radical Republicans' vigorous policy of Reconstruction and Negro enfranchisement as a hedge against a restored Southern white electorate.[55]

Although Professors Avins and Van Alstyne write nominally from op-

50. Carrington v. Rash, 380 U.S. 89, 97 (1965) (Harlan, J., dissenting).
51. Harper v. Virginia State Bd. of Elections, 383 U.S. 663, 680 (1966) (Harlan, J., dissenting).
52. United States v. Mississippi, 380 U.S. 128, 144 (1965) (Harlan, J., dissenting); Louisiana v. United States, 380 U.S. 145, 156 (1965) (Harlan, J., dissenting). And see Katzenbach v. Morgan, Cardona v. Power, 384 U.S. 641, 672 (1966) (Harlan, J., dissenting).
53. William W. Van Alstyne, "The Fourteenth Amendment, the 'Right' to Vote, and the Understanding of the Thirty-Ninth Congress," in 1965 *Supreme Court Review* 33, 36 (Philip B. Kurland, editor, Chicago: University of Chicago Press, 1965).
54. *Ibid.* See also Alfred Avins, "Literacy Tests and the Fourteenth Amendment: The Contemporary Understanding," 30 *Albany L. Rev.* 229 (1966), especially at 237-38. For a detailed collation of the relevant material in the *Congressional Globe* see Alfred Avins, editor, *The Reconstruction Amendment Debates* (Richmond, Va.: Virginia Commission on Constitutional Government, 1967).
55. See statements of Rep. Bingham (*Globe*, 39th Cong., 1st Sess. 431-32, 2542 [1866]). These are quoted in Van Alstyne, *supra* note 53, at 51-53, 61-63. Van Alstyne comments that the "inconsistency is puzzling" (at 63). See also Avins, *supra* note 54, at 237-38 where Bingham's inconsistencies are attacked vigorously by Garfield on the House floor.

posing camps, a careful scrutiny of their work suggests that both—Avins wholeheartedly and Van Alstyne grudgingly—support the substantial accuracy of Justice Harlan's approach to the "original meaning" of the Fourteenth Amendment at least in regard to *voting qualifications*. Indeed, Professor Van Alstyne suggests that Justice Harlan's historical review in *Reynolds* "raises a fair question respecting the historical integrity of the Court's willingness to entertain *Carrington* v. *Rash* [concerning Texas' denial of voting rights to a resident soldier whose original home was outside Texas] strictly as an equal protection case, since here state voter qualifications were themselves in issue." [56] Because *Reynolds* was an apportionment case rather than a "voter qualification" case, Van Alstyne went on to suggest that Harlan wrote the " 'right' dissent in the 'wrong' case." [57] Professor Van Alstyne, it turns out, is not contesting Justice Harlan's historical scholarship so much as he is arguing: (1) that the Harlan dissent does not make a case against national control over state legislative apportionment, although it may make an historical case against national control over state nonracial voter qualifications under the Fourteenth Amendment; (2) that "original understanding" approaches are a treacherous guide to constitutional meaning. The latter point, of course, significantly changes the terms of the debate. Both points merit brief elaboration.

Concededly, Harlan's historical analysis is not as illuminating regarding national power over legislative election districts as it is concerning national power over personal voting qualifications. The answer to the objection that Harlan uses *suffrage* quotations from the *Congressional Globe* to resolve the quite separate issue of legislative *apportionment* is that the two topics are not wholly separate. There is at least an analogy between national power over state suffrage and national power over state apportionments. And, as noted above, the central approach of the Court majority in the reapportionment cases was to treat them *simply* as right of suffrage cases. Strong support for Justice Harlan's negative conclusion about the relevance of the equal protection clause to reapportionment is found also in his data showing general acceptance of malapportionment by state legislatures and Congress itself. Even if Section 2 of the Fourteenth Amendment is interpreted not to limit the equal protection clause of the first Section, and even if no other expressed or intimated limitation on the equal protection clause itself is found, widespread contemporary practice of malapportionment would alone be enough to raise doubts— from the standpoint of *historical* analysis—concerning propriety of using the equal protection clause as the vehicle for national supervision of state apportionments.

56. Van Alstyne, *supra* note 53, at 85.
57. *Ibid*.

d. *The Relevance of History*

The best answer to the Harlan dissent is not to try to fault his historical scholarship, which may have been the most reliable on the contemporary Supreme Court Bench. It is rather to question the relevance of "original understandings" in constitutional interpretation. Short of that it can be suggested that the process of getting at "original understandings" may properly encompass matters going beyond statements of debaters and contemporary political practices. This approach, of course, is not so much to answer the Harlan dissent as to sidestep it and recast terms of discussion and basic theories of judicial power.

At this point a rigorous intellectual honesty is called for. In breaking beyond confines of "original understandings" the Court *does* update the Constitution. By treating the loose terms of the great constitutional clauses as "principles" rather than as "definitions," the Court enables a constant flow of new meaning. A narrow historicism always fares ill at the hands of those seeking a "just" result. "Justice" concepts have a way of advancing and calling for unprecedented judicial action in pursuit of new goals of "freedom," "equality," "fairness." An historical approach to constitutional text and to apparent understandings of drafters in the setting of their own times almost never supports either broad new goals or judicial activism. As Justice Benjamin N. Cardozo has noted, historicism is only one of several accepted and commonly used American approaches to elaboration of legal principle, others being logical progression (method of philosophy), community custom (method of tradition), mores of the day (method of sociology).[58]

What the Court should never do, however, is to engage in devious and tortuous rewriting of history in order to justify dramatic new constitutional rules under a *pretended* original meaning. This approach, which did underlie Justice Black's opinion for the Court in the congressional districting case, *Wesberry* v. *Sanders*,[59] was lacking except for one lapse in the

---

58. Benjamin N. Cardozo, *Nature of the Judicial Process*, 30–31, 51 (New York: Fallon Publications, 1921).

In the constitutional field especially, an exploration into the *meaning* and *purpose* of constitutional clauses frequently is more productive than a search for original intent. It normally will provide a more plausible basis for a new rule, and better describes the reasoning process used by the Court, whatever be the articulated reasons for the result. See Harris L. Wofford, Jr., "The Blinding Light: The Uses of History in Constitutional Interpretation," 31 *U. Chi. L. Rev.* 502, 510 (1964).

59. Justice Black has been chided by a long line of eminent critics (many of whom did agree with the end sought) for his penchant for rewriting history to serve his own purposes, e.g., his assertion that the Fourteenth Amendment was clearly intended to incorporate the whole Bill of Rights, his assertion that the clear meaning of the First Amendment bars prescribed prayer in the public schools, his assertion that a state's duty to provide counsel for indigents is part of the original meaning of "right to counsel," and the *Wesberry* opinion itself. See Charles Fairman, "Does the Fourteenth

Chief Justice Warren opinions in the reapportionment cases. In reapportionment cases, as in Chief Justice Warren's opinion for a unanimous Court in the basic desegregation decision of 1954, *Brown* v. *Board of Education*, the ruling is grounded more on a conceded developmental approach toward the scope of American concepts of equality than on a pretended finding of an original Garden of Eden truth which may now be restored after being overlaid for decades by sinful error.

FOOTNOTE TO AN APPARENT GUIDEPOST
FOR THE REYNOLDS MAJORITY OPINION

Shortly after *Baker* v. *Carr* was decided a strange little leaflet—strange, considering its source—was issued by the Twentieth Century Fund entitled "One Man-One Vote." Billed as conclusions of a Fund-sponsored conference of political scientists and research scholars, but with the Fund responsible for particular phraseology, the statement unqualifiedly endorsed a simple equal population basis for representation for both houses of bicameral legislatures. It also said that no other basis was defensible in 1962. Foreshadowing one line of Justice Black's subsequent opinion in *Wesberry* v. *Sanders*, the statement said that congressional districts should be "as nearly equal in population as practicable." [60] Foreshadowing one oft-quoted line of Chief Justice Warren's subsequent opinion in *Reynolds* v. *Sims*, the statement said that "acres do not vote; nor do trees." [61]

In retrospect, this leaflet may have been as influential as all of the briefs and arguments in the Supreme Court in the "big six" cases. Interestingly, there was no counter-document, issued by a foundation of differing orientation and based on conclusions of other scholars, seeking to set forth counter-views. Possible counter-views could include the role of consensus in representation theory, the de minimis nature of an occasional deviant district to give a separated community a voice, the possible viability of a modified federal plan, or even an argument for proportional representation as the only logical answer to "one man-one vote."

Amendment Incorporate the Bill of Rights? The Original Understanding," 2 *Stan. L. Rev.* 5 (1949); Paul Murphy, "Time to Reclaim: The Current Challenge of American Constitutional History," 69 *Am. Hist. Rev.* 64 (1963); Kelly, *supra* note 41, at 119; Yale Kamisar, "A Dissent From the Miranda Dissents: Some Comments on the 'New' Fifth Amendment and the Old 'Voluntariness' Test," 65 *Mich. L. Rev.* 59, 63 (1966). See also Wallace Mendelson, *Justices Black and Frankfurter, Conflict in the Court* (Chicago: University of Chicago Press, 1961).

60. "One Man-One Vote" 17 (New York: Twentieth Century Fund, 1962). The fifteen signers consisted of ten political scientists in the academic profession, one journalist, one trade union official, one representative from the National Municipal League, one representative from the Ford Foundation, and one free-lance researcher. (Hereafter cited as *Leaflet*.)

61. *Id.* at 5.

Morris L. Ernst has wondered, for example, "if the Bar has been sufficiently inventive to design a course of conduct somewhere in between the workable but undemocratic provision in the Federal Constitution and the mathematical absolutism of one man, one vote." [62] For newly formed nations he suggests that minority parties be assured of one-third of the legislative votes for "spokesman" purposes. One may wonder whether foundation activity along these lines would raise any question of jeopardizing tax-exempt status because of using foundation funds to further political advocacy on a particular issue, or to influence pending public policy litigation.

Of the sixteen persons invited to the conference, only one refused to sign the statement. On the central issue before the conference the one dissenter said that "it is *completely erroneous in fact and principle* to say there is no justification in our democratic heritage, in logic, or in practical requirements of government" for constructing representation systems which include more elements than population.[63] His dissent also alluded, at least indirectly, to the problem of foundation role, and the distinction between a foundation's subsidizing research designed to illuminate a public policy field, and pronouncing a policy conclusion. On this issue he said:

> There are, besides, no suggestions for research of this subject, which was one of the reasons for calling the Conference. More importantly, the statement does not envision what I should regard as a task precisely suited to the history and character of the Twentieth Century Fund, namely the study of a new system of representation for the new America. Lacking this larger and more significant vision, the statement becomes less useful and might be unfortunately construed as intended to fit the needs of current political controversy.[64]

62. Morris L. Ernst, Letter to Editor on "The Right to be Heard vs. The Right to Vote," 51 *Am. Bar Assoc. J.* 508 (1965).

63. *Leaflet* at 19 (emphasis in the original).
Questions of tax deductibility for donors to foundations, and tax exemption for a foundation's own income, present interesting and touchy questions related not to the "goodness" or "badness" of foundation activities but to the statutory question of whether a "substantial part" of the foundation's activities are directed to influencing "legislation." Int. Rev. Code Sec. 501 (c)(3). The Twentieth Century Fund lost tax deductibility status briefly in 1935 when representatives appeared before congressional committees. F. Emerson Andrews, *Philanthropic Foundations* 332 (New York: Russell Sage Foundation, 1956). A better-known recent example is the conservation-oriented Sierra Club. Int. Rev. Serv. Fact Sheet, Dec. 19, 1966.

64. *Leaflet, supra* note 60, at 20.
A vigorous defense of the 1962 leaflet was published by the Twentieth Century Fund in 1965. But it has been said to give insufficient attention to representation theory, counter-views, and the intricacies of equal population districting in relation to fair representation and legislative outcomes. See Robert B. McKay, *Reapportionment:*

It is precisely just this lack of the larger and politically realistic vision which makes the Chief Justice Warren opinion an unsatisfying document and explains its own internal ambiguities between a pounding stress on population equalization as the only relevant consideration, and an occasional mention of the much more difficult question of "effective representation." It explains the uncertain caveats inserted here and there about the importance of using pre-existing political subdivision lines as guards against promiscuous gerrymandering, and the denial that absolute equality is the goal. And it explains the difficulty the Court encountered subsequently in representation cases from Georgia and Hawaii in 1965 and 1966, and the local government cases of 1967 which raised issues impelled by, but also transcending, a "one man-one vote" population-equalizing reapportionment.[65]

THE COURT'S GUIDELINES FOR THE REAPPORTIONMENT REVOLUTION: SUMMARY

The *Reapportionment Decisions* of June 1964 marked the second stage of the reapportionment revolution. The Supreme Court's pronouncements in *Baker* v. *Carr* in 1962 putting the courts into the "political thicket" of reapportionment had been followed by two years of groping in the lower courts for federal standards of proper apportionment and districting.

In the second stage marked by the Supreme Court's pronouncements in *Reynolds* v. *Sims* and companion cases, a strong majoritarian standard was embraced. Although Chief Justice Warren touched on many things in the course of his opinions for the Court in the six major cases, the recurring message was twofold. One aspect, given more by implication than by express statement, was that questions of political and interest representation, and evidence concerning the operating results in the legislature of a given apportionment system, were secondary if not irrelevant. The other aspect, stated loudly, clearly, and repetitively, was that an apportionment system in which equal population districts elected equal numbers of legislators would be presumptively constitutional. Further, the relevant mathematical measures were simple, centering on the population variance ratio which compares the two extreme districts and the fictional electoral percentage which is easily computed but which concededly measures no percentage of legislative control known to the real world of district pluralities and legislative politics.

Thus as the lower courts moved into the third stage of the reapportion-

The Law and Politics of Equal Representation (New York: Twentieth Century Fund, 1965); reviewed by Kent Greenawalt in 19 Stan. L. Rev. 1151 (1967).
65. Discussed infra, Chs. XVIII–XX.

ment revolution, implementing the Supreme Court's "one man-one vote" standard, the formula for change was crystal clear—*equalize*. The capacity of an equalization policy to achieve sound *representation* results was taken on faith. Clearly the "rural stranglehold" on one or both houses of the legislature in many states maintained by the old policy of gross population malapportionment was dead. Legislatures would be more *timely* in their policy discussions now that the larger population clusters where are centered the pressing governmental problems of the twentieth century were guaranteed spokesmen proportionate to their numbers. This change was a signal achievement and served to clarify lines of responsibility for "progressive" or "unprogressive" government. Any continued nonenactment of measures sought by various urban and suburban groups would now be a *political* failure and serve to focus attention on the relevant complexities and divisions of popular feeling rather than an *institutional* failure guaranteed by the structure of the system.

However, this new equality standard of the Court geared solely to gross population was not a standard responsive to finer aspects of representation centering on political parties and interest groups, which after all are the nominators of candidates and the organizers of legislatures. Nor is a gross population standard responsive to problems of winner-take-all districting and to various devices designed to achieve an over-all goal of *fair representation* by ensuring adequate minority representation. A representative democracy must be sufficiently majoritarian to guarantee majority, rather than minority, rule; but, an excess of the majoritarian principle may rob the system of its representative character and may yield action without accommodation.

As the third stage of the reapportionment revolution unfolded in the lower courts after *Reynolds* v. *Sims*, a new conflict emerged. It centered on the tension between the *Reynolds* principle defining "one man-one vote" in terms of numbers only, and the more sophisticated democratic theory defining "one man-one vote" as a component of a representation system designed to build into the legislative assembly both majority rule and a proportionate voice for all major political elements.

XII

Implementing "One Man-One Vote": Some State Vignettes–I

"I certainly did [consider political realities]; it's a necessary part of trying to work out a fair and balanced set of districts from the standpoint of the interests of each political party, but there is crucial difference between considering political factors in an attempt to do justice to each party in regard to provision of safe and swing districts, and a one-sided partisan political gerrymander for the advantage of one party alone."

Chief Judge William J. Campbell
United States District Court (Illinois)

"No one, bent other than on pretense, can deny the pressures and counter-pressures of politics to which this Court has been subjected . . . . Even the baited subject of *amount of salary, to be paid in the future to Supreme Court Justices*, appeared in a measure which was proposed in and passed by the senate during the current legislative session, and then was held up by the house." (Emphasis in the original)

Justice Eugene F. Black
Michigan Supreme Court

The effect of *Reynolds* v. *Sims* on the fifty states is a rich topic for analysis and requires some organizing themes. There are many points of interest: the degree and manner of judicial activism, the range of data considered, the opportunities for effective appeal and review, the *appearance* of fairness in the procedures used, the *actual* fairness in their result (political equity), the transferability of a given procedure from one state to another, the mixture of judicial and nonjudicial techniques.

The judiciary continued to play a prominent and indeed dominant role in the post-*Reynolds* period. *Reynolds* made virtually all houses in all states unconstitutional but did not provide self-evident standards. Therefore, in all states the judiciary were involved in final approval of "one man-one vote" apportionment plans, whatever their source. Frequently the

judiciary had to act creatively and in effect become the state's apportioners when deadlock prevented effective and timely action by the normal political agencies. Patterns of interaction between the judiciary and
the political agencies were so varied that neat classification between pure
judge-made plans and "nonjudicial" apportionment is not possible. Continued uncertainty in Fourteenth Amendment standards for state legislative apportionment suggests that judicial approval, if not outright manu-
facture, will be a feature of the American reapportionment scene in the
1970s and thereafter under successive revisions reflecting the decennial
census or a more frequent special census.

As organizing themes for the immediate post-*Reynolds* apportionment
developments, something more precise than the above list of points of interest is needed. Concededly, the complexity of apportionment in fifty
states with widely varying types of party systems and interest group elements prevents neat categories without overlap or qualification. The following themes are suggested as meriting special consideration, and they
have been utilized where appropriate in organizing the material in this
chapter: (1) the political nature and effect of apportionment must be
admitted, whatever may be the apportioning agency; (2) the task should
be performed, therefore, under circumstances giving an impression of fairness and partisan balance; (3) bipartisan procedures in many instances
will be a strong guarantee both of the appearance and the effect of fairness; (4) among the many routes to bipartisan fairness in procedure and
effect, the pre-trial process used imaginatively and successfully by federal
district Chief Judge William J. Campbell in Illinois, and New Jersey's
new Bipartisan Commission with tie breaker, merit special attention.

It is also worth stressing that the fact that reapportionment is done by
the legislature does not necessarily guarantee bipartisan fairness; nor does
the fact that apportionment is handled by a nonlegislative agency necessarily exclude bipartisanship.

A. Contrasting Styles of Judicial Activism

In the third stage of the reapportionment revolution in lower courts after
the *Reapportionment Decisions* of June 1964 the most striking examples
of tension between "one man-one vote" defined solely in terms of population equality, and "one man-one vote" defined in terms of fair representation occurred in Oklahoma and Illinois. The court in the former state
pursued equality; the court in the latter state pursued fair representation.

The sharp difference in approach reflected perhaps the fact that Illinois has been a vigorous two-party state while Oklahoma has been essentially a one-party Democratic state. Although Oklahoma acquired its first Republican governor since statehood in 1962, both houses of the legislature remained monolithically Democratic. Even recognizing these political factors, the difference in approach runs deep and expresses more a fundamental difference in conception of reapportionment than a difference in the current political makeup of the two states.

1. OKLAHOMA: CHIEF JUDGE MURRAH, UNITED STATES COURT OF APPEALS [1]

Like many states Oklahoma had a long and tedious record of unsuccessful reapportionment efforts, including disinclination of the state judiciary to deal with the matter. This may explain in part the vigor, bordering on impatience, of the federal court. In the immediate pre-*Baker* period, two reapportionment measures presented to the voters were defeated, even though both were voted on in special elections to ease the majority requirement. One of the measures, favored by Governor J. Howard Edmondson and designed to achieve automatic mathematical reapportionment through an ex officio commission, was defeated by a majority of nearly 2 to 1. Another, sponsored by the lower house and pertaining only to it, was defeated by more than 3 to 1. A senate bill on apportionment also failed in 1961.

After *Baker* v. *Carr* another reapportionment measure was presented by popular initiative process in 1962. It would have created an administrative commission and removed the reapportionment function from the legislature. The commission was to apply regularly the apportionment provisions of the Oklahoma state constitution which, though falling short of "one man-one vote" standards as later developed by the United States Supreme Court, would still have significantly increased the number of urban seats. Proponents' desire to have this measure presented in a special election was frustrated by prolonged litigation and the measure was placed on the ballot at the regular November 1962 election. However, Governor Edmondson designated the vote on the initiative measure as a "special election" falling on the same day as the regular election in an attempt to come under the lower majority requirement. The measure did receive a majority of those voting on it, but not a majority of those voting at the general election. The following month the Oklahoma Supreme Court nullified the initiative measure. It rejected the governor's designation of the initia-

1. Where not otherwise indicated the material in this section is based on author interviews in 1965 in Oklahoma and Washington with all major actors in the Oklahoma drama.

tive vote as a "special election" and adhered to its earlier rule that the required majority is a majority of all those voting in the election.[2]

a. *Preliminaries*

Meanwhile in a class action suit filed by a voter a three-judge federal district court in June 1962, with Chief Judge Alfred P. Murrah of the Tenth
Circuit Court of Appeals presiding,[3] had declared the Oklahoma apportionment statutes "prospectively null and void, and inoperative for all future elections," thus presumably requiring reapportionment prior to the
November 1962 election.[4] According to the Capitol grapevine, United
States Senator Robert S. Kerr of Oklahoma then flew to Oklahoma City
to try to talk to the judges concerning the speed of the remedy. On
August 3 a modified order was entered fixing March 8, 1963 as the deadline for reapportionment "on the general principle of substantial numerical equality.[5] Judge Ross Rizley dissented from the modification, saying
that the majority "has backed away . . . and is now taking a position
where they sanction that which they condemned." [6] Judge Rizley argued
that it was the "unqualified duty" of the court to reapportion at once,
which would have made Oklahoma the only state in the nation, other
than Alabama, to have a judge-made apportionment of both houses in
effect within seven months of *Baker* v. *Carr*. (Alabama's interim reapportionment of both houses for the November 1962 election was by judicial
marriage of parts of two plans proposed by the legislature.[7])

The legislature did reapportion by the March 1963 deadline, United
States Supreme Court Justice Bryon R. White who handled such matters
for the Tenth Circuit which included Oklahoma having denied a stay of
the district court's order.[8]

However, the legislature's work was declared unconstitutional by the
federal district court in mid-1963 because the electoral percentage for the
house was still only 30.2 percent and the population variance ratio for the
senate was 4.73 to 1. The court, finding the legislature "unable or unwill-

2. Allen v. Burkhart, 377 P.2d 821 (Okla. 1962); see also George J. Mauer, "Resumé
of Legislative Apportionment in Oklahoma 1961–1963," Bureau of Government Research Pamphlet, University of Oklahoma (Norman) (1963).
3. As a sidelight it may be noted that in Oklahoma reapportionment litigation in the
1950s, Judge Murrah had denied a request to reappraise the "political question" precedent of *Colegrove* v. *Green* in the light of the Supreme Court's school desegregation
cases of 1954 on the ground that it was not the function of the lower courts to
"psychoanalyze the Justices of the Supreme Court in order to divine the trend of
decisions." Radford v. Gary, 145 F. Supp. 541, 544 (W.D. Okla. 1956).
4. Moss v. Burkhart, 207 F. Supp. 885, 898 (W.D. Okla. 1962).
5. *Id.* at 898–99.
6. *Id.* at 903.
7. Sims v. Frink, 208 F. Supp. 431 (M.D. Ala. 1962).
8. *Oklahoma City Times*, March 7, 1963, p. 1, col. 8.

ing to reapportion itself," then itself apportioned both houses on a population basis, relying on a plan submitted by the Bureau of Government Research, University of Oklahoma.[9] It was the first court in the nation to take such sweeping action affecting both houses. Saying that "if apportionment is to be our lot, we should not stop short of the ideal," [10] the court adopted a plan which transferred several seats to the two largest counties, Oklahoma and Tulsa, raising the former to 8 senators and 19 house members and the latter to 7 and 15 members, respectively. Formerly each had had only one senator and seven house members.

However, the ingenuity of reapportionment defendants and intervenors was not yet exhausted and this federal court-ordered plan never went into effect. Further litigation in the state supreme court culminated in January 1964 [11] in a modification of the plan which had been enacted by the legislature in March 1963 and rejected by the federal district court. On this basis Justice White was prevailed upon to grant a stay of the federal district court's own apportionment plan.[12]

The spring 1964 primaries and run-off primaries were conducted under the legislature's plan as modified by the state court. It was a bootless act. In June 1964 the Supreme Court finally announced standards for legislative apportionment and affirmed the federal district court's 1963 action on Oklahoma apportionment [13]—one of nine state cases handled summarily following pronouncements of standards in the "big six" apportionment opinions.

b. *Instant Reapportionment*

On remand from the United States Supreme Court, the Oklahoma federal district court made a fresh start. Although not elaborated in the district court's reported opinions and orders of August 1964 ordering a fresh reapportionment for Oklahoma,[14] the major events yield a fascinating story. After the district court reconvened, several parties proposed alternative reapportionment plans. Time was of the essence because of need for new primaries, but confusion developed because of divergences among the plans presented. At this point Attorney General Charles Nesbitt, nominally a defendant, brought matters to a head by devising and submitting to the court fresh apportionment plans for both houses. Using counties as basic units and crossing a few county lines for the house but not for the senate, he followed the equal population principle closely by

9. Moss v. Burkhart, 220 F. Supp. 149, 155 (1963).
10. *Id.* at 156.
11. Davis v. McCarty, 388 P.2d 480 (Okla. 1964) and 386 P.2d 993 (Okla. 1963).
12. Stay granted in chambers, Feb. 6, 1964, unreported.
13. Williams v. Moss, 378 U.S. 558 (1964).
14. 233 F. Supp. 323 (W.D. Okla. 1964).

grouping underpopulated counties and assigning multiple seats to populous counties. Impressions varied as to whether his purpose was to accomplish immediate reapportionment, or whether his purpose was to give an example of the blockbuster effect on existing political arrangements— including pitting incumbents against each other—which could result from a quickie approach based on simple mathematics with eyes closed to all other types of information. The latter purpose would have pointed toward a court order yielding more time for orderly reapportionment by legislative process now that the Supreme Court finally had announced standards—standards far more stringent than had been expected.

In any event, on submission to the court the Attorney General's plan was approved forthwith. The court obviously both desired to terminate the case promptly and, politically, to "get off the hook." The Attorney General's plan was an ideal vehicle for accomplishing both these objectives because, as the court noted, it was submitted by the chief legal officer of the state (albeit acting wholly on his own). However, the federal district court construed the new "one man-one vote" principle of *Reynolds* v. *Sims* to be violated by use of large multimember districts. The Attorney General's plan therefore was deemed incomplete because it provided no subdistricts for multimember counties—the two largest being Oklahoma and Tulsa with 19 and 15 house seats, respectively.

"Petticoat Districting." At this point Circuit Chief Judge Murrah, presiding member of the three-judge district court, in keeping with the haste and informality of the proceeding informally requested aid from Mrs. Trimble B. Latting, former chairman of the state reapportionment committee of the League of Women Voters with an advanced degree in statistics, who was present in the courtroom. She had been active in Oklahoma's long and frustrating reapportionment struggle, through such organizations as the League and the PTA and earlier she had been a witness for the plaintiffs. Although not officially appointed master or aide to the court, her mission was to follow the equal population principle in drawing subdistrict lines for multimember counties and to report back within five days.

Only in an essentially one-party state could such a technique have been considered, or allowed to pass unchallenged and unappealed. In such states as New York or Illinois or even maverick California the procedure would have been utterly incredulous. In reapportionment as in so many things, however, the South is sui generis. And in political style the "South" encompasses not merely the eleven states of the Confederacy but all border states and most of the Southwest as well. Although the court was apparently oblivious to the inevitable policy choices which it was calling on Mrs. Latting to make, whether or not by conscious design, some of the parties were very much aware of the total impossibility of wholly "neutral" districting. Mrs. Latting herself, a very intelligent woman, was painfully aware of the delicacy of her task.

The event caused quite a stir in some quarters and was referred to by some as the "petticoat apportionment" or "coffee table apportionment" of Oklahoma. Assessments varied as to actual political neutrality of the eventual plan. The saving grace was that in Oklahoma the primary political conflict was not along political party lines, or even urban-suburban, but urban-rural. Thus, in whatever manner the details of apportionment and districting were worked out, the equal population principle itself required major shift of seats from rural areas to urban areas.

Seeking to be scrupulously fair, Mrs. Latting asked for all plans and did entertain requests from such delegations as visited her. However, as a predictable consequence of informality it was reported later that at least one group did not see Mrs. Latting. When they arrived at her home they found their opposite numbers already present, and so departed.[15] The *raison d'être* of due process requirements of notice and hearing is to avoid this very contingency so that the decision-making process will not only have the appearance of fairness, and thus quell rumor, but the substance of fairness, and thus ensure just results.

One major consideration in subdistricting, particularly in urban areas, is whether to provide some safe seats for minorities, such as the Negro minority, or to spread a minority's votes over several districts. Under the latter tactic the minority may through a balance of power factor have influence on several seats, but have certain control of no seat. Another consideration is whether to keep suburban communities together as homogenous districts, or to link them with downtown districts to create heterogenous districts. In addition there are many particular considerations, all consistent with bare equality of numbers, such as shifting the line to preserve the seat of an incumbent or to strengthen the hand in a given locality of a political party or interest group.

In the case of the informal subdistricting of Oklahoma, the first two considerations entered into the decision-making process but special dispensations requested by various visitors to Mrs. Latting were not incorporated as a primary principle. A strong desire was expressed to keep suburban communities together as homogenous units and this was adopted as one subdistricting principle insofar as consistent with maintenance of population equality. The advisability of attempting to create some safe Negro districts also was given favorable considerations not so much be-

15. Some defendants charged that plaintiffs' attorneys were using "the judges' chambers and Mrs. Latting's house." There probably is some hyperbole here but the point is that the procedure used by the court invited suspicion and speculation.

cause of any official or unofficial requests but because of a particular assessment of the meaning of fair representation, and a desire to broaden the base of support for the plan. An earlier reapportionment plan had aroused ire by seemingly splitting the Negro community and there had seemed to be a judicial sympathy for the desire of the Negro community to achieve its own representation.[16]

Within the time provided, Mrs. Latting was able to subdistrict the largest counties: Democratic-leaning Oklahoma County (containing Oklahoma City) and Republican-leaning Tulsa County with 19 and 15 house seats, respectively, and Comanche County with 4 house seats. Although later there were Democratic murmurs that the Oklahoma County map bore a strange resemblance to a Republican map submitted at an earlier stage of the prolonged litigation, the matter did not become a major issue. Mrs. Latting's subdistricts were promptly adopted without hearing, in the conventional sense of the term. Their actual mathematics were unknown because insofar as they did not follow census tract lines they rested on estimated rather than actual population data. All assumed, however, that they were quite "equal."

At this point, on suggestion of plaintiff's attorney Norman E. Reynolds, Jr., the court made an order allowing at-large elections in the remaining multimember districts. But on the Attorney General's motion this was changed to allow the Attorney General to subdistrict the remaining multimember units.[17]

Absence of Review. The Attorney General completed the subdistricting process using in some instances a "town and country" rule, i.e., where two counties formed one district and there was only one large town, the town

16. In the litigation culminating in the initial but never effected judicial reapportionment of Oklahoma in July 1963, four Negro voters had intervened as plaintiffs and asserted that Negro voters were discriminated against in the districting of Tulsa and Oklahoma City under the legislature's proposed reapportionment. By voiding the plan on other grounds, the court did not have to reach the issue. Moss v. Burkhart, 220 F. Supp. 149, 154 (W.D. Okla. 1963).

17. All were converted into single-member districts with the exception, over the Attorney General's objection, of a handful of districts whose boundaries had not been changed by the court's new reapportionment order. Temporarily excepting them made it unnecessary for the nominees in those districts to run in a special September 1964 primary after having won in the May primary. After requiring new primaries for the rest of the state, the court said, however: "[W]e do not indicate approval of at-large elections and do not mean to hold that such elections would necessarily comport with constitutional requirements of equal protection of citizens under other circumstances." 233 F. Supp. at 364.

Pursuant to the court's direction, the new legislature subdistricted these "excepted" districts into single-member districts in the spring of 1965; and there were rumors that some legislators went to the federal district court for unofficial "approval" regarding the subdistricting of their counties. The same bill also incorporated the court-ordered apportionment of 1964.

area would receive one seat and the remaining area the other seat or seats. When reported, these too were adopted on the spot without hearing. Thus neither on the report of Mrs. Latting's subdistricting nor on the report of Attorney General Nesbitt's completion of the process was there any prolonged briefing, argument, consideration of the policy choices implicitly adopted, or consideration of alternative policy choices on such issues as safe seats for minorities or homogeneous seats for suburbs. Although there were no exact mathematical figures because of the cutting of census tracts, the estimated population variance ratios for the house and senate respectively were 1.2 to 1 and 1.5 to 1.

The plan was ordered into immediate effect by the federal district court and was not successfully appealed. Plaintiffs were happy. The nominal official defendant on the state's side, the Attorney General, who had devised most of the plan except for that part of the subdistricting done by Mrs. Latting, was hardly in a position to appeal. This left as possible appellants the intervening senators and one or two other groups. Their intervention had been permitted only reluctantly in 1962 by the federal district court even though without them the customary adversary process of litigation could not have functioned. At that time one intervenor's attorney had received a tongue-lashing from Chief Judge Murrah, charging obstruction.[18]

Intervenors sought an immediate stay of the new court-ordered primary scheduled for September from United States Supreme Court Justice White. When he denied a stay on August 26, 1964, and the September primary and general election of November 1964 were held, the intervenors gave up on the theory that the "eggs had become too scrambled" to permit any effective review or relief. Earlier, the defendants in Alabama similarly found the posture of their case markedly changed after Justice Black's denial of a stay had permitted the November 1962 election to proceed on the basis of the federal court's interim reapportionment of the legislature. Whatever one's view may be of the merits of a given reapportionment and the need for speed, it is a simple fact that the process of Supreme Court review of federal constitutional issues breaks down whenever a denial of a stay permits an election to be held under an appealed reapportionment order.

Denial of a stay effectively completed the apportionment process in Oklahoma, satisfying some and irking others, in general along urban-rural lines of conflict. Intervenors felt that whenever there were two Old Guard senators in geographic proximity the reapportioners had thrown them into

18. Record, Moss v. Burkhart, No. 9130, on the injunction hearing of July 31, 1962; Jurisdictional Statement in the United States Supreme Court, pp. 6–9; author's correspondence and interviews on both sides of the case.

one district to compete against each other—a policy which they charged was carried out "with precision—a work of art." Control of the senate did shift from a rural Old Guard orientation to a liberal-moderate coalition with a modern orientation. By general agreement, however, the first session of the legislature under the new apportionment in 1965 was not marked by startling changes, even though there were more new senators than at any time since statehood.

In general the Oklahoma reapportionment does not seem to have been bitterly resisted—certainly not on a statewide basis. This is testimony in favor of the fairness of the Attorney General's apportionment plan and the subdistricts worked out by him and by Mrs. Latting, augmented perhaps by the simple fact that Oklahoma was getting tired of its endless reapportionment struggle, which long antedated *Baker v. Carr*. Most importantly, Oklahoma was not a conventional two-party state. In retrospect, however, one is left almost breathless by the casual decision-making process judicially employed in Oklahoma and the federal district court's apparent assumption that all that was involved was a simple exercise in equal population mathematics, which any good-hearted and proficient statistician could accomplish.

From the standpoint of the country as a whole, and the nationwide interest in clarification of Fourteenth Amendment standards for state legislative apportionment, the denial of the stay in the Oklahoma case—and hence the effective abolition of appeal—had one unfortunate effect. It prevented a prompt airing in the United States Supreme Court of the question whether in principle the Fourteenth Amendment either requires single-member districts or at least is violated by use of large multimember districts running to 10, 15 or 20 members or more. Oklahoma's subdistricting was judicially required under the federal district court's premise that the "one man-one vote" principle announced in June 1964 by the United States Supreme Court is inconsistent with use of large multi-member districts. Under a ruling which the United States Supreme Court finally made in a case from Hawaii in 1966 (see discussion in Chapter XVIII) the Fourteenth Amendment does *not* empower a court to require use of single-member districts absent a showing of special circumstance. Hence much of Oklahoma's 1964 reapportionment was accomplished by federal court order under a false constitutional premise made unappealable by Justice White's denial of a stay!

The real conundrum of the Oklahoma case is this: If "equal population" is a self-evident and simple constitutional rule for state legislative apportionment, why should the federal district court have felt any compulsion to subdistrict? Under the mathematical measures of *Reynolds v. Sims* large multimember districts can have just as much proportionate equality as small single-member or two-man districts. To be sure, multi-member districts may not provide as effective a basis for fair *representation* of diverse groups as single-member districts. But if the district court were concerned about *representation* as a facet of "one man-one vote" along with equality, then it could hardly have taken such a casual approach to the subdistricting process as to pretend that it is just a matter of arranging gross population into equal clusters.

The fact that interests and party strength are not spread evenly by residence is the single most important fact in all apportionment and districting. And it simply begs the issue to suggest that a person is not required to reside in a given place. Also, even if interests and party strength be spread evenly by residence in a given area the difficulty of achieving a just representation system continues, for under ordinary districting the slight majority then would always get all the seats and the slight minority would get none.

2. ILLINOIS: CHIEF JUDGE CAMPBELL, UNITED STATES DISTRICT COURT

In Illinois, state of *Colegrove* v. *Green*,[19] *MacDougall* v. *Green*,[20] and myriad other apportionment cases, the post-*Reynolds* development reached its peak of judicial vigor, political sophistication, and political equity along with numbers equality. It stands in refreshing contrast to the Oklahoma federal district court's action, which at times smacked of Star Chamber proceedings in pursuit of quick results. Although the story is not widely known, Illinois finally provided one reapportionment model for the nation. But it first wandered in a morass and had the "inglorious distinction," as the *New York Times* put it, of holding the only at-large state legislative election in American history.[21]

a. *Backdrop for Crisis*

Technically we should begin with the reapportionment finally accomplished by constitutional amendment in 1954, but detailed elaboration of all pertinent events from that date to 1966 would be a book in itself. Illinois' original state constitution was one of the few to provide for decennial population apportionment of both houses. (See Chart 3, Chapter IV.) The provision caused deadlock after the 1910 census and thereafter

19. 328 U.S. 549 (1946).
20. 335 U.S. 281 (1948). See Chapter V for discussion of some of the pre-1954 Illinois cases.
21. *New York Times*, Oct. 17, 1965, p. 84, col. 1.

because it would have given Cook County, containing Chicago, control of both houses of the legislature.

In 1954 deadlock was broken when a divided legislature and downstate Republican Governor William G. Stratton reached agreement on a proposed "federal plan" constitutional amendment which was ratified by 80 percent of the voters (87 percent in Cook County). The support of Governor Stratton was crucial in the successful campaign for this 1954 reapportionment amendment. He received early endorsement from the Republican State Convention, and held reluctant downstate Republicans in line by patronage. Downstate Democratic legislators, fearing loss of party control to the Richard J. Daley machine in Chicago-Cook County, were the major opponents. All major statewide organizations supported the "federal plan" theory of the amendment with the exception of the political extremes—the Illinois Association of Manufacturers who did not want a straight population basis for either house, and the CIO which wanted an immediate "one man-one vote" formula for both houses.[22]

For the lower house the amendment created a 177-member house to be districted by the legislature in 1955, 1963, and decennially thereafter "as nearly as practicable" according to population, with maximum deviation of 20 percent from an average size district. The 177 members were to be elected from 59 three-man districts, each district voter to have three transferable votes, thus preserving Illinois' system of cumulative voting dating from 1870. Under the cumulative voting system each three-man district tends to be split 2 to 1 between dominant and weaker party, thus ensuring minority party representation. Prior to 1954 lower house and senate districts were coterminous, i.e., three lower house members were elected at-large in each senate district. Because senators felt the coterminous feature allowed assemblymen to groom themselves to run against senate incumbents, this feature was not continued in the 1954 amendment; rather the senate was fixed at 58 rather than an even one-third of the 177-member lower house, thus necessitating some noncoterminous districts.

In the event of legislative failure to reapportion the lower house regularly, apportionment was to be accomplished by a ten-man Bipartisan Reapportionment Commission appointed by the governor from names submitted by the state central committee of each of the two major parties. If the Commission deadlocked, the constitutional amendment provided that the lower house should be elected at-large.

22. See John E. Juergensmeyer, "The Campaign for the Illinois Reapportionment Amendment" (Urbana: Institute of Government for Public Affairs Pamphlet, University of Illinois, 1957). See also Gilbert Y. Steiner, Samuel K. Gove, *Legislative Politics in Illinois* (Urbana: University of Illinois Press, 1960).

Regarding the senate, the 1954 constitutional amendment directed the legislature in 1955 to create 58 single-member senator districts utilizing area as "the prime consideration." In the event of legislative nonaction concerning the senate in 1955, districting was to be accomplished by the Bipartisan Commission. The clear meaning of the amendment, although subsequently disputed, seems to be that no further revision of senate districts was contemplated except by constitutional amendment. For purposes of senate apportionment, the amendment also recognized three distinct areas of the state—city of Chicago, Cook County excluding the city of Chicago, remainder of the state.

b. At-Large Election of Lower House, 1964

A common misunderstanding is to view Illinois' unique at-large election of its lower house by "bed-sheet" ballot in 1964 as a by-product of the United States Supreme Court's "one man-one vote" revolution. In truth this unique event resulted from the mandatory equal population district policy of the 1954 amendment to the Illinois Constitution. The first deadlock in 1963 in the attempt to again reapportion the lower house as specified by the Constitution occurred between the Democratic governor and Republicans, who controlled the senate 35 to 23 and lower house 90 to 86. Proposed reapportionment plans ran into difficulty because two of Chicago's house districts (6 seats) appeared destined to be lost by virtue of Chicago's relative decline in population. Mayor Daley proposed that Chicago keep control of its existing number of seats by extending six of its districts into the suburbs sufficiently far to meet the 1954 amendment's 20 percent maximum deviation requirement. Republicans countered with a 1955 state attorney general's opinion that the state constitution forbade crossing city lines. Neither side yielded and Democratic Governor Otto Kerner—in accord with the general impression that Democrats were less fearful of at-large election than Republicans—vetoed in the meantime a house apportionment enacted by the Republican-controlled legislature.

A Bipartisan Commission was subsequently created under terms of the 1954 amendment. It deadlocked 5 to 5 on virtually every vote taken during the four-month existence allotted to it by the Constitution. Expiration of the four-month period brought into force, as provided by the 1954 amendment, the "sanction"—or "remedy," depending upon how one views the matter—of election at-large for the lower house.[23]

After Governor Kerner called a special legislative session for January 1964 to map plans for holding the unique at-large election, the Democratic Attorney General ruled that state senators as well as representatives

23. See Twiley W. Barker, Jr., "A Long, Long Ballot," 53 *Nat. Civ. Rev.* 170 (1964).

would have to run at-large under his interpretation of the 1954 amendment. The Republican-controlled state supreme court, with a dissent by Justice Schaefer, rejected the Attorney General's interpretation.[24]

Two thoughts dominated the special session of the legislature. One was the possible winner-take-all result of the forthcoming at-large election which would have had a blockbuster effect on representative government; another was the practical consideration that incumbent legislators who chose to run for re-election might be lost in a general "bed-sheet" ballot. Responding to both considerations the major parties, the legislature, and the governor agreed on a statute providing that no party could make nomination for more than two-thirds of the legislative seats (118 of the total of 177), *and* providing for nominations in party primaries held in the existing legislative districts. Districts generally reported renominated incumbents' names first so that they would appear first on the general election ballot. Each party chose to nominate the full permissible number of 118, resulting in a total of 236 candidates who were listed on separate orange ballots three and a half feet long for the November election. With the aid of the "Goldwater debacle" in the presidential race, the Democrats swept to victory, resulting in a lower house with 118 Democrats and 59 Republicans.

This Illinois so-called at-large election has few messages for other states. It tells little about the generic nature of an at-large election, because of the way the parties had structured it by restricting nominations and by basing nominations on traditional districts. A study of voting patterns and results showed, as might be expected, that endorsements by newspapers and organizations guided many voters. The house elected on this "guided" at-large basis "almost perfectly represented the divisions of population between metropolitan and non-metropolitan areas, between northern and southern areas of the state outside major cities, and between Cook County and downstate."[25] The majority party's advantage, however, which in three sessions since the 1955 apportionment had been 5, 1, 3, jumped to 59.

24. People *ex rel.* Giannis v. Carpentier, 195 N.E. 2d 655 (Ill. 1964). See also further discussion, with the same division in the court, in People *ex rel.* Engle v. Kerner, 205 N.E. 2d 33 (Ill. 1965). Party division aside, an independent analysis of the 1954 amendment seems to confirm the Illinois Supreme Court's ruling that the Illinois senate was intended to be exempt from decennial apportionment and the at-large election proviso once it had been created under the terms of the amendment in 1955. The amendment is quite clear on the composition of the senate and house (Art. 4, Secs. 6 and 7); and the ambiguity, on which the state attorney general and Justice Schaefer rested their views, occurs in a separate section on implementation (Sec. 8) that is caused only by an attempt to be brief.

25. James H. Andrews, "Illinois' At-Large Vote," 55 *Nat. Civ. Rev.* 253, 257 (1966).

c. *Illinois Senate and "One Man-One Vote"*

A week after the basic *Reapportionment Decisions* of June 1964 the Supreme Court reversed a federal district court ruling of 1963, which had held constitutional Illinois' federal plan apportionment under the 1954 amendment, and remanded under a mandate to apportion both houses on an equal population basis.

Unlike quickie actions of courts in a few states immediately after the June 1964 *Reapportionment Decisions* in order to accomplish reapportionment in time for the November elections, [26] the Illinois federal district court panel, with District Court Judge Campbell as one of its members, did not act on the Supreme Court's mandate in the senate apportionment case until after election. In addition to being more politically sophisticated than courts in many states, the Illinois three-judge panel may well have thought that Illinois' capacity to absorb governmental upheaval already was being tested sufficiently by at-large election of the lower house.

Events from remand in 1964 of the Illinois senate case to final accomplishment of reapportionment in late 1965 involved virtually every element of Illinois' legislative, executive, and judicial structure. It also involved the federal district court and, informally, the United States Supreme Court. The first step in January 1965 was for the reassembled federal district court to formally invalidate the "area" basis of the Illinois senate and to direct the Illinois legislature to submit a revised senate apportionment to the federal district court for approval or face a judicially ordered at-large election for all state senate seats in the 1966 election.[27]

The next step was for the Illinois Supreme Court to become active on Senate reapportionment in a fashion subsequently criticized by the federal district court. In February 1965 the Illinois Supreme Court acted on a long-pending state senate case. This case had been filed prior to the Supreme Court's articulation of the "one man-one vote" theory in the 1964 *Reapportionment Decisions* by Robert H. Engle, a former high school civics teacher and non-lawyer acting without an attorney. His suit attacked the apportionment of the senate under *Baker v. Carr* and also raised a number of interesting but somewhat technical questions concerning the state constitutional provisions for senate apportionment. At the appellate level, with the aid of the *Reynolds* ruling, the equal population issue more clearly emerged. Equally important from the standpoint of achieving a

26. E.g., Reynolds v. State Election Board. 233 F. Supp. 323 (W.D. Okla. 1964); Sincock v. Roman, 233 F. Supp. 615 (D. Del. 1964); Robertson v. Hatcher, 135 S.E. 2d 675 (W. Va. 1964) (judicially impelled reapportionment not challenged).

27. The order of Jan. 22, 1965 is set forth in the subsequent opinion in Germano v. Kerner, 241 F. Supp. 715, 717 (N.D. Ill. 1965).

satisfactory and realistic resolution of this necessarily political question was the entry into the lists of attorney Don H. Reuben representing State Treasurer William J. Scott (a member of the Electoral Board and the only "Republican defendant") and Attorney General William G. Clark representing the "Democratic defendants," i.e., all other members of the Electoral Board including the governor.

Those who were clairvoyant could have perceived here the seed of the statesmanlike bipartisan apportionment that Illinois, with the aid of both courts, was eventually to achieve. At the moment, however, the effect of the renewed activity of the Illinois Supreme Court was to establish a basis for jurisdiction in the state court system as a hedge against vigorous action of the federal district court and uncertainty on the crucial issue of what that court would deem to be a constitutionally "satisfactory" senate apportionment. Although denying Mr. Engle's technical claims, the Illinois Supreme Court retained jurisdiction on request of State Treasurer William J. Scott and asserted general supervision over senate apportionment in the following terms:

> As the final forum available in this State, it is our responsibility to construe and apply provisions of our State and the Federal constitutions as related to the problems of legislative reapportionment. We conceive it to be the responsibility of the State of Illinois to establish its own constitutionally selected legislative body and the State agencies, both historically and logically, are the proper forum for resolution of the problems therein, consonant with the Federal constitutional interpretations relating to equality of representation.[28]

Attorneys for State Treasurer Scott and other intervening defendants then requested the federal district court to reconsider and vacate its January order in deference to the state court's assertion of jurisdiction. The federal district court was unimpressed; indeed, it was piqued. In May it reaffirmed its January order, characterized the request for deference to the Illinois Supreme Court as a cavalier suggestion, referred to the state court's assertion of final authority in regard to federal constitutional law (see quotation above) as a "slight oversight if indeed not sheer presumption," and twitted the state court for its late-coming to the Fourteenth Amendment issue by the device of remaking the *Engle* case on appeal—a case which the federal district court said raised issues only of state law.[29]

The federal district court's orders were interpreted by defendants not only as requiring the legislature to reapportion under threat of an at-large election but more crucially as precluding any other state agency, including the Illinois Supreme Court, from devising a constitutionally valid appor-

28. People *ex rel.* Engle v. Kerner, 203 N.E. 2d 33, 40–41 (1965).
29. Germano v. Kerner, 241 F. Supp. 715, 722 (N.D. Ill. 1965).

tionment plan in event of legislative failure. The orders also were interpreted as specifying an election at-large as the sole *judicial* remedy, thus also precluding judicial creation of revised districts in event of legislative failure. Speaking of the at-large election remedy, the federal district court had said:

> Reapportionment or apportionment *per se* is not a necessary prerequisite to having a valid election scheme. If a state legislature does not want an apportioned election system *we question the authority of any court to order such a legislature to form election districts*. Absent any apportionment scheme, a state would have the best legally (if not necessarily practically) perfect realization of the mathematical "one man-one vote principle". . . . The essence of such relief is found in the realization that one of the cures of malapportionment is nonapportionment—for that matter it is mathematically the only perfect solution.[30]

Preclusion was the central issue presented in the appeal to the United States Supreme Court by State Treasurer Scott and his attorneys. Although counsel for the initial plaintiff asserted that the federal district court's order was not intended to "preclude" action by any state court, the "preclusion" interpretation was not disputed by the Attorney General.[31] The United States Supreme Court in June 1965 in an unsigned opinion directed the federal district court in effect to defer to agencies of the state. The district court was to retain jurisdiction and set a timetable but there was to be no preclusion and the agencies of the state were the ones to accomplish reapportionment. The Supreme Court said:

> The power of the judiciary of a State to require valid reapportionment or to formulate a valid redistricting plan has not only been recognized by this Court but appropriate action by the States in such cases has been specifically encouraged. . . . The case is remanded with directions that the District Court enter an order fixing a reasonable time within which the appropriate agencies of the State of Illinois, including its Supreme Court, may validly redistrict the Illinois State Senate. . . .[32]

d. *Failure in the Legislature*

While reapportionment litigation was being jockeyed back and forth between federal and state courts, a tense drama was unfolding in the Illinois

30. *Id.* at 719 (emphasis added).
31. Jurisdictional Statement in the United States Supreme Court, Germano v. Kerner (typescript), pp. 2, 7; Motion to Dismiss Or, In the Alternative to Affirm (filed for the initial plaintiffs by Bernard Kleiman, General Counsel of the United Steelworkers of America), p. 18; Motion to Affirm (filed by Attorney General William G. Clark), p. 6.
32. Scott v. Germano, 381 U.S. 407 (1965).

legislature regarding senate reapportionment. With more diligence than success, the legislature in the spring of 1965 had been laboring to effect reapportionment of the senate in order to avoid the uncertainties of judicial apportionment, or the spectre of another election at-large. Although the at-large election in 1964—with the aid of the Goldwater candidacy—had shifted lower house control to the Democrats, and the governor was a Democrat, a basis for deadlock on apportionment matters continued because of Republican retention of control in the senate.

The situation was tight politically, and negotiating room correspondingly narrow, because party forecasts of voter strength in state elections indicated possibility of a near tie. Every seat became crucial. One issue was the proper proportionate allocation of 58 senate seats among the three distinct areas of the state contemplated by the 1954 amendment to the state constitution, i.e., Chicago, Cook County excluding Chicago, and "downstate." Because the population of these three areas did not make an even division into the total population of the state, the issue here turned on whether to allocate the so-called "fractional seat" to the downstate area or to Chicago. Nine seats were conceded for suburban Cook County but for the other two areas the Democrats insisted on 21 districts for Chicago, 28 for downstate; the Republicans insisted on 29 for downstate, 20 for the city.[33]

Equally critical was the problem of political data and political forecasting, that is, the problem of getting agreement on what was a "safe" or "swing" district for one party or the other. Even after agreements were achieved on party seat ratios, negotiations often broke down at the district mapping stage because of disputes over which past elections and what other data were relevant in deciding whether a given proposed district was a "safe" or "swing" district for one party or the other. Interests of incumbents further clouded the matter. But even without the much-maligned incumbency factor, and even with agreement on basic principles of seat allocation proportionate to party strength, such political data disagreements made difficult the task of negotiating a plan "fair" to each party in the light of the party "strength."

Further variables bearing directly on the task of constructing a set of districts providing a "fair" basis for party competition in the state as a whole were: (1) the problem of how to handle wasted votes (excess votes for one party in an overly safe district) in constructing an over-all state profile of party strength; (2) the problem of getting agreement on the per-

33. See Twiley W. Barker, Jr., "Illinois Tries Again," 54 Nat. Civ. Rev. 417 (1965), as amplified considerably by the author's interviews in August 1965. The interviews are also a primary basis for the subsequent section on federal pre-trial resolution of the matter.

centage of party strength needed to create a "safe" district. In regard to the latter point, because a dominant party's voter registration figures tend to exceed its actual strength at the polls, the party may need a 52 percent registration edge in a given district in order to classify it as "safe." As a consequence, each side on occasion could charge that "we are getting one thing at the bargaining table" from our opponents, "and something else by map."

The federal district court's reiteration in May 1965 of its assertion of jurisdiction, and its threat of an election at-large, pleased Democrats who felt confident of their prospects in an at-large election in view of their sweep of the lower house at-large election in 1964. It scared a number of downstate Republicans. As a consequence there were rumors that the Democrats had "bought" a sufficient number of downstate Republican votes, on promises of taking care of incumbents, to push the Democratic reapportionment plan through the Republican-controlled senate. Before a conclusive vote could be taken, however, the federal district court's order was appealed to the United States Supreme Court by attorneys for Republican State Treasurer Scott. The Court's prompt announcement that it would consider the case restored Republican unity. Even so, near-agreement was reached late in June, but jockeying for position had taken too long and any prospects for final legislative agreement were cut off by the mandatory termination date of the legislative session, after which, under the state constitution, a two-thirds majority would have been required to pass measures on an "emergency basis." A factor of uncertain dimensions which perhaps still would have prevented agreement, unless Republican senate apportionment wishes were honored, was the fact that of the justices of the Illinois Supreme Court at that time four were Republicans and two were Democrats (with one vacancy).

Thus the legislature was under heavy pressure from many sides to accomplish reapportionment. In addition to party pressures, a bipartisan Citizens Reapportionment Committee co-chaired by Chicago attorney George T. Bogert and Roger T. Kelley, vice president of Caterpillar Tractor Co. was active. Although agreement reportedly was very nearly reached, the legislature adjourned in June without having enacted any senate apportionment plan for submission for judicial approval. Adjournment placed the matter back in judicial hands with the state supreme court being in lead position by virtue of the United States Supreme Court's June 1 order.

e. *The Illinois Supreme Court's Tactics*

The Illinois Supreme Court for a variety of reasons was understandably loath to grasp the nettle of reapportionment. It was Republican by a 4 to

2 margin, the federal district court panel was Democratic by a 2 to 1 margin. And as in Michigan there had been so much in the press about the political complexion of the courts, that some lawyers—more conversant with traditional judicial ethics than with the intrinsic political nature of the new reapportionment cases—had grown concerned. But the Illinois Supreme Court was in an especially delicate position. Earlier a Republican legislator reportedly had seen judges in chambers and had made embarrassing statements about what that court might do, and had stated that he might fare better in an Illinois Supreme Court-controlled apportionment than in one bargained-out with the Democratic governor and the Democratic-controlled lower house.

The Illinois Supreme Court's order after legislative adjournment directing litigants "to submit suggestions for a judicially constructed senatorial reapportionment plan" was followed a few days later by another order. Perhaps as a pressure device, or perhaps to lend protective coloring to a judicially supervised reapportionment, the court appointed Deans Russell N. Sullivan of the University of Illinois College of Law, John Ritchie of the Northwestern University School of Law, and Phil C. Neal of the University of Chicago Law School as amici curiae for the purpose of preparing and submitting a reapportionment plan for the court's approval.[34] As one wag quipped, we will escape a pig-in-the-poke judicial apportionment only by receiving a three-blind-mice apportionment. The three deans never functioned, however, because relief was soon forthcoming from other quarters for them, for the state supreme court, and for the parties in general.

The propriety of appointing the deans or any similar group is subject to question unless the appointment was merely a sanction or was a protective coloration device. The action may have been rested on the persistently held dual myths that nonpartisans exist and that a nonpartisan apportionment is possible. The facts are that party sympathies are generally known or at least thought to be known, and that "equal" line-drawing involves just as many discretionary political choices as unequal line-drawing, even when done by computer. Also, the deans themselves noted possible conflicts of interest on the part of the Dean of the University of Illinois College of Law who was dependent upon the legislature for his budget, and on the part of the Dean of the Law School of the University of Chicago which, although a private university, necessarily had a variety of relationships with Mayor Daley's city administration, including urban renewal matters. The appointments were accepted with reluctance. Had the deans been forced to face the task of actually preparing a reapportionment plan for submission to the court, at least one of them, although keenly aware

34. People *ex rel.* Engle v. Kerner, 205 N.E.2d 33 (1965).

of the "unneutral" nature of every district line, was prepared to seek protective coloration in a wholly mathematical "nonpolitical" computerized solution.

f. Reapportionment by Federal Pre-Trial Conference [35]

At this critical juncture the federal district court and more particularly District Chief Judge William J. Campbell, a member of the three-judge district court panel handling the case, moved back into the picture most creatively and most successfully. He appreciated the explosive nature of the situation from the standpoint of the two courts, federal and state. Although the United States Supreme Court's June 1965 ruling had placed the state supreme court in the forefront, it had specified also that the federal district court had a "retained jurisdiction" of the matter. Thus was created the likelihood that whatever might happen by action of the three law school deans, or of the Illinois Supreme Court, the matter would be brought before the federal district court again by some aggrieved party.

This would have presented the odd spectacle of a federal district court with "retained jurisdiction" of a reapportionment matter sitting in review over a state supreme court. This not only would put the two courts back into conflict again but also raise the additional possibility of a concurrent review petition direct to the United States Supreme Court from the state supreme court. Further, if the federal district court, by this route, should be commissioned to itself perform the task of reapportioning, there then would be the possibility of a long three-judge hearing with tedious battles over mathematics and admissibility of political evidence. The makeup of the three-judge panel might have made such a trial an interesting affair from the standpoint of the spectator, because one of Chief Campbell's colleagues was the former Republican speaker of the Illinois house, now a federal court of appeals judge, and the other was by background a staunch Chicago organization Democrat.

Chief Judge Campbell found in the device of off-the-record pre-trial conference before a single judge, as authorized by the Federal Rules of Civil Procedure, a ready-made device for avoiding further exacerbation of an issue which had grown increasingly difficult and emotional despite the fact that the two major political parties had managed to come very close to agreement before the legislature adjourned. Success of the plan depended on getting agreement not only from the other members of the three-judge federal panel but also from the parties and, most importantly, from the Illinois Supreme Court.

It is a tribute to Chief Judge Campbell's astuteness and reputation for

35. The material in this section is based primarily on author's interviews in Chicago in August 1965, and subsequent correspondence and interviews in Washington.

fairness that the needed agreements were achieved so that pre-trial could go forward. An important stage was re-establishing friendly relations with the state supreme court. Some help was forthcoming here through the good offices of a United States Supreme Court justice who was alerted to the potentially explosive situation between the two courts in Illinois under the June order. The parade of horribles which all other reapportionment alternatives seemed to conjure up undoubtedly played a role in moving all parties to agree to pre-trial.

The central premise was that the parties were close to agreement and that with further work they could reach near 90 percent agreement. Conditions of pre-trial were frankly outlined in advance by Chief Judge Campbell. They were that this further work would take place as part of the pre-trial conference and that the anticipated final disagreement on 10 or 15 percent of the districts would be resolved by informed judicial fiat in the light of the pre-trial evidence, considering all factors and especially the political factors, and being as fair to each side as possible. There would be an explicit attempt to achieve racial and political equity. And all parties would be expected to support the order thus devised.

On this basis the parties moved into pre-trial. The Democrats negotiated through Democratic Attorney General Clark and particularly First Assistant Attorney General Richard E. Friedman, serving as counsel to Democratic members of the State Electoral Board. Republicans negotiated through Don H. Reuben, serving as counsel to Republican State Treasurer Scott, also a member of the State Electoral Board. Negotiators were given a 5 percent maximum population deviation limit in the thought that with such a goal the parties would at least be inside a 10 percent deviation which was thought to be sufficient to satisfy apparent standards of the United States Supreme Court as announced in the 1964 *Reapportionment Decisions*. Negotiation proceeded on a consciously political basis, and thus a highly informed basis, directly relevant to the realities of legislative election and legislative representation.

There was some experimentation with computers but it had no effect on the outcome other than to make all negotiators disenchanted with use of computers in this context. Only State Treasurer Scott, who had almost derailed the pre-trial plan on its eve by announcing that the whole job could be done easily by a computer, was a strong supporter of this method. In practice, the parties reported that "precinct leader-type political data," and a desk calculator, were much better suited to the shifting negotiation process. A computer, after three or four hours of programing, could produce within thirty seconds the answer to a suggestion which had already been found by hand and discarded.

An example of the danger of relying blindly on a single-factor approach like population for speedy districting is that the original plan of Mayor Daley for the districts inside Chicago would not have worked out to produce a single safe Negro district. Some were provided in the final plan. Republican negotiators noticed the matter and brought it to the attention of the court, perhaps motivated not so much by a desire to create a bitterly anti-Republican seat as by a wish to avoid any factor which could cause the whole delicate process to blow up and thus jeopardize other interests. The decision to maintain the 1954 amendment's three-way division of senate seats among Chicago, suburban Cook County, and downstate, with no overlapping districts, created a problem of a "fractional seat." Although the downstate area had the largest fraction of the three areas, Cook County and Chicago taken together had a still larger fraction and the fractional seat was awarded in pre-trial to Chicago, yielding 21 senators for the city, 9 for suburban Cook County, and 28 for downstate.

The parties neared full agreement, Chief Judge Campbell did resolve in "informed chancellor" fashion the final areas of disagreement, and the resultant plan was accepted by all parties. Estimates of which political party had gotten the edge in districting of safe versus swing seats varied, but neither party was noticeably upset. There was some criticism for the record, some downstate Democrats feeling that their Chicago brethren had not protected them sufficiently. But there was not widespread dissatisfaction and there was no appeal. In mathematical terms the maximum percentage deviation above and below the average size district was $+7.7$ and -7.0 and the electoral percentage was 50.4 percent.[36] Chief Judge Campbell's pre-trial memorandum of August 25 announcing the agreed senate reapportionment stated his belief that "the plan constitutes a fair compromise between the divergent proposals submitted by the parties." [37]

Chief Judge Campbell's central premise, building out really from Justice Felix Frankfurter's dissenting opinion in *Baker* v. *Carr*, seems to be this: Reapportionment is generically a political matter; but having made the crucial decision to enter the political thicket, judges must act as statesmen-politicians, within the safeguards of bipartisan pre-trial conference, in order to do an honest job of reapportionment. At the press conference a reporter noted there had been some comments that Judge Campbell had considered political factors in arranging some districts. The Judge's response was forthright and clear:

> I certainly did; it's a necessary part of trying to work out a fair and balanced set of districts, from the standpoint of the interests of each political party. But there is crucial difference between considering political factors in an attempt to do justice to each party in regard to

36. Germano v. Kerner, 247 F. Supp. 141, 144, 147, 155 (N.D. Ill. 1965).
37. *Id.* at 142.

provision of safe and swing districts, and a one-sided *partisan* political gerrymander for the advantage of one party alone.[38]

In general accord with this statement is the comment of Associate Justice Horace W. Wilkie of the Wisconsin Supreme Court. That court on the eve of *Reynolds* v. *Sims* was the first in the country to perform the task of reapportionment of both houses of a state legislature by the process of itself working out some adjustments rather than by simply adopting in toto a plan prepared by an outside group. It is not always sound, he indicated, to resolve differences concerning award of seats and placement of district lines simply on a population percentage-point basis, although concededly such other factors as community of interest, incumbency and continuity of representation, traditional political subdivision lines, and party equity are difficult to pin down.[39] With pre-trial process, however, these difficulties may be minimized.

In sum, the pre-trial technique devised and successfully used by District Chief Judge Campbell may be one model for the nation, at least in those states where there is no formal and effective provision for a bipartisan commission with a tie breaker as recently created in New Jersey. It may be especially appropriate in the forthcoming reapportionments of the 1970s when, with egregious population deviations already minimized, attention can be expected to focus upon the more sophisticated political aspects of a fair and effective representation system. In some situations of course it may be necessary to take a broad view in regard to intervenors in order to establish the necessary adversity to provide a basis for political party negotiation through pre-trial. Operating within very narrow bounds of constitutionality in terms of mathematical standards, the Campbell pre-trial technique nevertheless places a premium on reaching agreement through normal political processes and on recognition of political realities. Because no legislative district line can be "neutral," a pre-trial method also insures that judicial resolution of remaining differences will be equitable rather than blind.[40]

38. As related in interview with author, Washington, D.C., September 1965.
39. Interview with author, Madison, Wisconsin, August 1965. The Wisconsin Supreme Court had called for plans from parties to the litigation. After devising its own plan, it allowed six days for filing of objections and requested changes. At the expiration of the six-day period, without a hearing, it denied all requested changes and made its plan final.
40. The creative pre-trial process which reapportioned Illinois' senate also indirectly opened the way for breaking the deadlock of the Reapportionment Commission with regard to house districts. On November 30, 1965, the Commission reapportioned the house, adopting for Cook County the same 30 districts used for senators and creating 29 downstate house districts. (There being only 28 senate districts the some districts could not be used for senate and house downstate.)
Congressional redistricting also was accomplished by the same pre-trial process and joint agreement of the federal district court and the Illinois Supreme Court. People

B. Michigan: Bipartisan Commission and Judicial Backstop

Analogous to the Illinois experience, Michigan in a referendum in the 1950s, which carried in the state as a whole but lost in Detroit, had achieved a federal plan-type reapportionment (locally called the "balanced legislature" amendment). The amendment placed a 110 member lower house on a decennially revised population basis and the senate on a fixed area basis. From this point the reapportionment stories of the two states diverged sharply.

The 1952 "balanced legislature" amendment was overlaid by a constitutional convention in 1961–1962 in which the key issue was legislative reapportionment. The deliberations of the convention in turn were overshadowed by the *Baker* v. *Carr* decision, decided while it was sitting. The *Baker* decision told the Republican majority in the convention that their new modified "federal plan" proposal would be subject to judicial review under federal standards yet to be announced. It stiffened the will of the Democratic delegates in the direction of a stringent population-based apportionment because of the heightened prospect of future judicial support.[41]

a. The 1963 Constitution

The convention did produce a new constitution and a new reapportionment provision which was adopted by a narrow margin by Michigan voters on April 1, 1963. The new constitution continued apportionment of the lower house on a population basis. Seats were to be allocated under a method of equal proportions, subject to the qualification that any county or group of counties with .7 percent of the state's population could receive a seat (whereas the normal quota per seat was fixed at .91 percent). For a 38-member senate the delegates created an 80-20 formula with population accounting for 80 percent and land area for 20 percent in determining senate representation. For both houses there were prohibitions on

ex rel. Scott v. Kerner, 211 N.E. 2d 736 (1965) and Kirby v. Illinois State Electoral Board, 251 F. Supp. 908 (N.D. Ill.).

41. For a discussion of Michigan apportionment to 1963 with special stress on the reapportionment plan devised by the constitutional convention in 1962, see Karl A. Lamb, William J. Pierce, and John P. White, *Apportionment and Representative Institutions: The Michigan Experience* (Washington: Institute for Social Science Research, 1963), especially the chapters by White and Lamb.

dividing local political subdivisions in district formation, and prohibitions on multimember districts.[42]

More importantly, the new constitution transferred responsibility for decennial apportionment of both houses from the legislature to a Bipartisan Apportionment Commission consisting of eight members "selected by the state organizations of each of the two political parties" whose gubernatorial candidates received the highest vote at the last general election. Discretion of the Bipartisan Apportionment Commission was intended to be narrowly channelized by several criteria in addition to the precise mathematical formulae. The first apportionment step was to apportion seats to single counties or to counties as necessarily grouped to qualify for a minimum apportionment quota. Counties were to be grouped into senatorial districts that were "compact, convenient and contiguous by land, as rectangular in shape as possible." In the subdistricting process the following additional "anti-gerrymandering" rules were to be used: (a) members of both houses were to be elected from single-member districts which for the house were not to cross county, city, or township boundaries, and for the senate were not to cross county boundaries and were also to follow city and township boundaries "to the extent possible"; (b) districts for both houses were to be composed of "compact" and "contiguous" territories which for the senate were to be "as nearly uniform in shape as possible" and for the house "as nearly square in shape as possible"; (c) pre-existing senatorial districts were not to be altered unless clearly in noncompliance with the new standards; (d) members of both senate and house were to be selected from single-member districts, and in subdividing multimember "representative areas" (counties or groups of counties) the districts were not to deviate by more than 25 percent from the average size for that representative area.

In event of deadlock in the Bipartisan Apportionment Commission the new constitution authorized the state supreme court to order into effect an apportionment plan subject to subsequent review on voter petition. The court was not to devise its own apportionment plan. Rather it was to review plans submitted to it by individual members of the deadlocked Commission, "determine which plan complies most accurately with the constitutional requirements," and adopt that plan subject to review on petition of "any elector" filed within sixty days.

These provisions, of course, did not entirely eliminate discretion in the Bipartisan Commission in drawing district boundaries in multiseat counties. As one commentator noted, however: "The issue here would be between the parties, not between metropolitan and out-state areas, since the

42. The reapportionment provisions are set forth in Art. IV, §§ 2–6 of the 1963 Constitution.

Commission will have no discretion in deciding the number of seats a given metropolitan county will have." [43] The primary defense of course against an intracounty partisan gerrymander lay in the bipartisan nature of the Commission itself.

b. First Commission Failure

Against a backdrop of reapportionment litigation in both state and federal courts in Michigan seeking to invalidate under the Fourteenth Amendment first the old reapportionment plan [44] and then the new "80-20" plan for the senate, the Bipartisan Commission sought to perform its task of devising an initial apportionment to implement the 1963 Constitution. In the pending federal district court suit the Democratic attack extended to the composition of the Bipartisan Commission itself, appointed as specified in the 1963 Constitution by the political parties from four unequal population quadrants of the state. The quadrant plan provisions were federally unconstitutional, the argument went, because they "establish a legislative apportionment agency *totally* on an 'area' basis of representation, and thereby give 8 percent of the persons in Michigan representation equivalent to that of the remaining 92 percent." [45] (Subsequently when the proceedings operated to reapportion the state under a Democratic-devised plan this objection was dropped, and the Republicans did not pick it up in their own attack on the proceedings in 1965.)

Disputes arose as soon as the Commission convened in late 1963 over interpretation of the new formulae and over substantive issues of implementation. Democratic plans were met by a charge of gerrymandering by Commission Chairman Wilbur Brucker, former governor of Michigan and Secretary of the Army in the Eisenhower Administration. Democrats asserted that there was a built-in gerrymander in the Constitution itself in favor of Republicans on two counts: that 80-20 virtually guaranteed a Republican senate; and that guaranteeing a house seat to units with .7 percent of the state population (moiety clause) when a proper quota would be .91 percent favored Republican areas. After fruitless hassles the Com-

---

43. Comment by John P. White in Lamb, Pierce, and White, *supra* note 41, at 242.
44. In a pre-*Baker* decision in 1960 the Michigan Supreme Court refused to invalidate the 1952 senate reapportionment plan. Scholle v. Hare, 360 Mich. 1, 104 N.W.2d 63 (1960). The United States Supreme Court vacated and remanded for further consideration in light of Baker v. Carr. 369 U.S. 429 (1962). On remand the Michigan Supreme Court nullified the senate apportionment (with population disparities of 12 to 1) holding that the equal protection clauses of both the state and federal Constitutions prevented population disparities greater than 2 to 1. 367 Mich. 176, 116 N.W.2d 350 (1962). Justice Stewart granted a stay pending United States Supreme Court review. 20 *Congressional Quarterly Weekly Report* 1302–4 (August 3, 1962).
45. Trial Brief of Plaintiffs, p. 75 (typescript), Marshall v. Hare, 227 F. Supp. 989 (E.D. Mich. 1964).

mission's allotted 180-day work period expired in February 1964 with the Commission firmly deadlocked.

Among several plans devised by individual Commissioners, which together made a stack several inches high, two plans merit special mention, the Hanna Plan and the Austin-Kleiner Plan. The former was devised by a Muskegon attorney, William F. Hanna, who had been chairman of the crucial Committee on Legislative Organization in the constitutional convention. In the complicated spectrum of Michigan politics he could be classified as a moderate and somewhat maverick Republican. The Hanna Plan sought to implement all of the apportionment criteria in the new constitution. The Austin-Kleiner Plan was devised by two Democratic members of the Commission, closely identified with the United Auto Workers core of the party, A. Robert Kleiner and Richard Austin. Unlike the Republican plans and plans submitted by the two other Democratic commissioners, which followed all elements of the 1963 Constitution, the Austin-Kleiner Plan was a step toward an equal population district plan for both houses, ignoring the 80-20 formula for the senate on the assumption that it was federally unconstitutional. However it did seek to preserve city and township boundaries, which caused some population disparities. Introduced late, after the Commission at its last official session at the end of January found itself irrevocably deadlocked, the plan was not approved. It was so novel in its modifications of the state constitution that it was thought by the opposition to be a "can of worms," and received no serious consideration. Opponents viewed the plan as a "partisan equality" plan, i.e., a plan devised with the aid of UAW and Democratic political researchers with the aim of yielding the maximum number of Democratic seats and close population equality except as limited by use of city and township boundaries.

In March 1964 the Michigan apportionment muddle was back in court, both federal and state. A federal district court panel in a 2 to 1 decision in *Marshall v. Hare* held the apportionment provisions of the 1963 Constitution valid under the Fourteenth Amendment.[46] The Michigan Supreme Court, Democratic 5 to 3, in a proceeding labeled *In re Apportionment of the Michigan Legislature* assumed its duties as backstop for the deadlocked Commission under the constitutional clause directing the court to select from the individual commissioner plans that one which best complied with Michigan constitutional apportionment provisions. An immediate and critical issue, which continued to plague the court after the Commission's power revived and failed again in 1965–1966, was the scope of the court's power in this special apportionment proceeding. One view was that the state supreme court could *not* consider the federal con-

46. 227 F. Supp. 989 (E.D. Mich. 1964).

stitutionality of the Michigan apportionment formulae because it was exercising a sort of quasi-administrative power to round out the Commission's work under the state apportionment formulae. The other view, which was never fully acted on, was that the proceeding was sufficiently "general" and "judicial" to permit the court to consider federal constitutional issues, and perhaps even to assume a general creative apportionment power superseding those parts of the Michigan Constitution thought to be inconsistent with the federal Constitution.[47]

The Michigan Supreme Court temporized in its first ruling in March 1964, preferring not to discharge its "backstop" function for the deadlocked Bipartisan Commission until the United States Supreme Court reached decision on federal apportionment standards in the several state reapportionment appeals. In dicta some justices indicated they felt the state standards were constitutional under the Fourteenth Amendment on a modified federal plan theory; others had reservations.[48] April came with the United States Supreme Court still sitting on the state legislative apportionment appeals, and the state supreme court postponed action again.[49] Commissioners Austin and Kleiner were granted permission early in May to file with the court an extensively revised version of the Austin-Kleiner Plan (equal population plan) which they had introduced after the Bipartisan Commission had deadlocked in January. This Alternate Austin-Kleiner Plan ignored all of the 1963 Constitution's apportionment formulae, cut some local political subdivision lines, and reduced population disparities to a minuscule variation.

With the time for party primaries for the November 1964 elections rapidly approaching, and with the United States Supreme Court still silent, the Michigan Supreme Court decided that it could defer action no longer. Accordingly on May 26, 1964, it selected the Hanna Plan as the one which complied most accurately with the requirements of the new state constitution.[50] Because the state supreme court was Democratic-controlled and the Hanna Plan was one submitted by a Republican

47. The grant of power to the Michigan Supreme Court reads as follows: "If a majority of the commission cannot agree on a plan, each member of the commission, individually or jointly with other members, may submit a proposed plan to the Supreme Court. The Supreme Court shall determine which plan complies most accurately with the constitutional requirements and shall direct that it be adopted by the commission and published as provided in this section." Mich. Const., Art. IV, Sec. 6, parag. 7.
48. In re Apportionment of Michigan State Legislature, 372 Mich. 418, 441, 126 N.W. 2d 731, 744 (1964) (Dethmers, J., for the court); id. at 127 N.W.2d 862, 866 (1964) (O'Hara, J., concurring); contra, 127 N.W.2d at 863 (1964) (Souris, J., for the court).
49. In re Apportionment of Michigan State Legislature, 127 N.W.2d 862, 866 (1964).
50. In re Apportionment of Michigan State Legislature, 128 N.W.2d 350 (1964).

Commissioner, this decision was politically astute. It was well designed to neutralize each political party and to quell the talk about the political affiliations of the judges. In Michigan, as in Illinois, one hazard of judicial entry into the political thicket was the rise of much scrutiny and speculation concerning political affiliations of judges charged with the unwelcome task of redistributing political power by judicial order.[51]

The state court's order of May 26, 1964, adopting the Hanna Plan had a life of less than one month. On June 15, 1964, the United States Supreme Court made its epochal "one man-one vote" ruling in *Reynolds* v. *Sims* and the companion "big six" cases, mandating an equal population rule for legislative districts in both houses of state legislatures. The Michigan Supreme Court reconvened at once on June 17, and it withdrew its approval of the Hanna Plan without waiting for the United States Supreme Court's formal application of "one man-one vote" to Michigan by a short per curiam ruling on June 22, 1964.[52] Thus all the labors of the Bipartisan Commission and the deliberations of the state supreme court itself in the winter and spring of 1964 were for naught. The basic premise of all the action had been destroyed by the United States Supreme Court ruling. Up to this point all parties, except Commissioners Austin and Kleiner, who had ignored the senate 80-20 formula in their first plan and followed strict mathematical equality in their second plan, had been seeking to implement the apportionment standards of the new Michigan Constitution, which the federal district court in March had held valid and which were now held federally invalid, at least in their mathematical aspects.

c. *Instant Judicial Apportionment by Default*

The Michigan Supreme Court's reaction to this brand new "apportionment ball game" with the ground rules drastically changed was astounding. Its haste in forcing an immediate reapportionment with no time for adequate deliberation either by the Commission or by the court itself was even speedier than Chief Judge Murrah's "instant reapportionment" of Oklahoma through a three-judge district court action in this same period. The Michigan court's June 17 order gave the Commission two days (until 5:00 p.m., June 19) to devise and adopt a new

---

51. The political affiliations of the federal district judges who handled the Michigan congressional districting suit also did not pass without notice when they voted, two Democrats to one Republican, to void the new districts which had a largest to smallest ratio 1.6 to 1 and an average deviation of 9.2 percent. Calkins v. Hare, 228 F. Supp. 824 (E.D. Mich. 1964). See comment in 22 *Congressional Quarterly Weekly Report* 670 (April 3, 1964).
52. Marshall v. Scholle, 377 U.S. 990 (1964); Beadle v. Hare, 378 U.S. 561 (1964).

apportionment of both houses under the federal standard—spread through 233 pages of just-received United States Supreme Court opinions—as interpreted by the Michigan Supreme Court.[53]

The state supreme court's interpretation differed in one marked respect from the apparent federal standard as announced in Chief Justice Earl Warren's opinions in the six cases. Chief Justice Warren had used a "substantial equality" concept and suggested many qualifications including the possibility of following local political subdivision lines wherever possible in order to avoid an "open invitation to partisan gerrymandering," but the Michigan Supreme Court specified simply that the new districts shall be "as nearly as practicable on an equal population basis." There is a considerable difference—or so a majority of lower courts thought until the Supreme Court spoke again in mathematical terms in 1967[54]—between a "substantial equality" concept taken in the light of Chief Justice Warren's several caveats, and the focus of the Michigan Supreme Court. The Michigan court in effect ordered the Commission to seek perfect mathematical equality and to ignore considerations which would retard this goal. Tactically, of course, a strict equality mandate may be the greatest possible boon to partisan gerrymanderers because it provides a basis for ignoring the traditional restraints on districting freedom. The most common and perhaps most important restraints are prohibitions against crossing the traditional political subdivision lines which tend to contain communities of party and social interest.

The Michigan Supreme Court order found the Democratic commissioners with their statistics in readiness by virtue of the Second Austin-Kleiner Plan, which now seemed to be an act of sheer clairvoyance. But the GOP elephants were caught with their trunks down even though led by an astute moderate. The Republican commissioners who had been following the Michigan Constitution in their previous planning, neither had a plan available which seemed to be tight enough mathematically to satisfy the Michigan Supreme Court's interpretation of the new "one man-one vote" standard, nor a plan which like the new Austin-Kleiner Plan sought to combine strict equality with a goal of producing the maximum number of seats for their own party. When the Michigan Supreme Court's deadline expired, the Austin-Kleiner Plan was still the most "equal" plan available and was adopted as Michigan's new reapportionment.

Let us suppose that with more clairvoyance on the Republican side there had been available an equally "equal" Republican plan based on different districts devised with an eye on Republican election results and

53. 128 N.W.2d 721 (1964).
54. Swann v. Adams, 385 U.S. 440 (1967), discussed in Ch. XVII *infra*.

other relevant political data. With no distinction between the two plans in terms of the single federal standard of mathematical "equality as nearly as practicable," on what basis could the Michigan Supreme Court have chosen between the two plans? Conceivably one plan might have deviated slightly less from the state constitution by cutting fewer county or township lines than the other, but this would have been a slender and unsatisfying basis for distinction—unsatisfying both intellectually and politically. Likewise, considerations of compactness and contiguity, except in egregious instances, are too uncertain to provide judicial shelter in such a situation. Clearly then, had the Republicans had a mathematical counterpart of Austin-Kleiner to submit to the Michigan Supreme Court, that court would not merely have been deep in the political thicket; it would have been trapped, with no honorable escape route in terms of the premises on which all parties were operating.

The Austin-Kleiner Plan gave Michigan not only the earliest post-*Reynolds* v. *Sims* reapportionment in the nation, but also by far the tightest reapportionment in terms of the single consideration of mathematical equality. For the house the population variance ratio was 1.17 to 1, the maximum deviation was 2.8 percent, and the electoral percentage was 50.6. For the senate these same figures were, respectively, 1.01 to 1, 0.58 percent, and 52.5 percent. The Democratic party did capture both houses of the Michigan legislature in the first use of the Austin-Kleiner Plan in 1964, its house and senate majorities being respectively 72 to 38 and 23 to 15. Expressed more meaningfully in percentage terms, the Democrats under Austin-Kleiner in 1964 with 58 percent of the statewide vote for legislative offices captured 65 percent of the house, yielding an eight-seat "bonus." With the same 58 percent of the popular vote they captured 61 percent of the senate, yielding only a one-seat "bonus." It is virtually impossible to separate the portion of the election result which may have been due to the Austin-Kleiner Plan and the portion of the cause which must be attributed to the Goldwater presidential candidacy which had a blockbuster effect on state legislative elections in 1964 and, nationally, cost the Republicans more than 500 seats.

d. *Second Commission Failure*

Reapportionment litigation continued in the Michigan Supreme Court after the adoption of the Austin-Kleiner Plan under the state constitution's authorization of a limited review procedure on petition of "any elector." [55] The moving parties, primarily Republican electors, sought to challenge the state supreme court's adoption of the Austin-Kleiner Plan on

55. *In re* Apportionment of Michigan Legislature, 137 N.W.2d 495 (November 2, 1965); *id.*, 138 N.W.2d 16 (November 20, 1965).

several grounds, the major ones being: (1) that the hurried procedure in adoption of the plan violated due process requirements of a fair hearing; (2) that the plan deviated from the Michigan Constitution's apportionment standards far more than necessary to reach the United States Supreme Court's standard of "substantial equality," i.e., the "severability" issue; (3) that the plan was a gerrymander, being drawn for the purpose of minimizing the effectiveness of the votes of one party and maximizing the effectiveness of the votes of the other party; (4) that the plan contained localized racial gerrymanders.[56] Thus the renewed Michigan litigation raised in one fashion or another most of the interesting and crucial issues posed by the United States Supreme Court's new posture in *Reynolds v. Sims.*

The Problem of Data and Standards. Obviously the extent to which various pre-existing apportionment standards in state constitutions may coexist with "one man-one vote" is directly determined by the degree of mathematical rigidity required. Maximum deviation rules of thumb of one percent, 10 percent, or 15 percent will have widely differing effect on the one question which has recurred most frequently in post-*Reynolds* reapportionments, i.e., the extent to which city lines, county lines, and similar lines may continue to be followed in district creation. The Michigan litigation also encompassed the issue of breadth of hearing which must precede a judicial apportionment order, and the extent to which political data may be considered in devising equal district lines and the corollary question of the extent to which disclosure of use of such data in devising a particular submitted plan must be made.

However, these germinal questions and others which logically derived from them were being raised at the wrong time and in the wrong forum. These are questions better suited to airing at the trial court level at the stage of *devising* an *initial* judicial apportionment after default of the political arms of government. On remand of the federal case *Marshall v. Hare*[57] from the United States Supreme Court an attempt was made to raise some of these points in the course of a continued proceeding in federal district court, where the apparent inhibitions on the breadth of the state court review proceeding would not apply. A number of motions and pleadings were filed in the fall of 1964 but the matter dribbled away, with no final officially reported opinion. A voter petition had been filed in August to review the Austin-Kleiner Plan in the special proceeding authorized in the Michigan Supreme Court, and that court continued in

56. Brief of Petitioners, *In re* Apportionment of Michigan Legislature, Michigan Supreme Court, No. 50,999; Reply Brief of Petitioners, *id.* Jurisdictional Statement, *In re* Apportionment of Michigan State Legislature, United States Supreme Court, October Term, 1966, No. 505; Petition for Rehearing, *id.*
57. 227 F. Supp. 989 (E.D. Mich. 1964), *rev'd and remanded*, 378 U.S. 561 (1964).

dominant position. Even had the state proceeding not stood in the way, challengers faced a heavy burden of proof in the continued but aborted federal district court proceeding. They were in the position of arguing, with some subtlety, the key issue of "severability," i.e., that a *less* equal plan could still satisfy the "substantial equality" federal test and at the same time permit far closer adherence to such state constitutional policies as cutting as few county lines as possible.[58] In response the defenders of Austin-Kleiner, with considerable appeal, albeit with more wit than wisdom, could suggest the anomaly of arguing under the new federal "one man-one vote" slogan that any plan was "too equal." [59]

These central and germinal questions go deeply into representation theory and into the representation purposes to be served by the new federal equality standard. Although some challengers sought to raise them, they were not well suited to exploration in the context of the special original proceeding in the Michigan Supreme Court, serving as a limited backstop to the Bipartisan Commission. Nor were they well suited to the continued but limited "review" proceeding.[60] Technically that court's task in this 1963 Constitution proceeding was only to choose that Commission plan which was "best" in terms of state law, in event of deadlock, and to provide only limited review thereafter. Recognizing this, one of the crucial requests of plaintiff-electors in the reopening of the litigation was for an order of discovery to reopen also the matter for factual proof.

The renewed litigation did lead to a reconvening of the Bipartisan Reapportionment Commission. But within three weeks the court split 4-4 on

58. See the following papers filed in *Marshall* v. *Hare* in September-December 1964 by intervening defendants Beadle *et al.*: Motion for Summary Judgment; Brief in Support of Motion; Reply Brief.

59. As Michigan Supreme Court Justice Theodore Souris phrased it at the conclusion of the reopened proceeding in the state court: "The thrust of the challenge against the alternate Austin-Kleiner plan is that it accomplishes greater equality than the Federal Constitution's equality clause requires at the expense of surviving State standards." *In re* Apportionment of Michigan Legislature, 140 N.W. 2d 436, 457 (1966). See also various post-remand papers of plaintiffs in both federal and state court proceedings: *federal* (Marshall v. Hare)—Memorandum in Support of Motion for Settlement of Judgment, Supplemental and Reply Brief; *state* (where plaintiffs were now in the position of defending Austin-Kleiner)—Brief of Intervening Defendants in Michigan Supreme Court, Motion of Intervenors-Appellees to Dismiss or Affirm in the United States Supreme Court.

60. The grant of power to the Michigan Supreme Court to act as backstop for a deadlocked Bipartisan Commission and pick the "best" of the plans, under state constitutional standards, is quoted in note 47, *supra*. The limited review procedure is expressed as follows: "Upon the application of any elector filed not later than 60 days after final publication of the plan, the Supreme Court, in the exercise of original jurisdiction, shall direct the Secretary of State or the apportionment commission to perform their duties, may review any final plan adopted by the commission, and shall remand such plan to the commission for further action if it fails to comply with the requirements of this constitution." Mich. Const., Art. IV, Sec. 6, parag. 7.

what the Commission was to do and on the scope of the court's retained jurisdiction to review further Commission work.[61] To an outsider, and perhaps to an insider there seem to have been many latent ambiguities in this part of the 1963 Michigan Constitution. These included the definition of a "final" plan, the lack of express provision for an election under an interim plan, and ambiguities on the scope of Bipartisan Commission power and of court power in the special review procedure. The Republican members of the reconvened Commission sought to operate on the basis of a maximum 5 percent deviation rule, minimize cutting of county lines, and, presumably, take account of such political data as illuminated their party's status under various alternative districts. Otherwise there would be no realism, no basis for informed negotiation between parties, indeed no reason to use a bipartisan commission. Although there was some negotiation on a 5 percent deviation basis, the Democratic commissioners' primary strategy was to hold to the Austin-Kleiner Plan with which they were well satisfied.[62] The Commission's allotted sixty days expired at the end of the year with no agreement either to "un-adopt" Austin-Kleiner or to submit a substitute, and the matter returned to the state supreme court in January 1966.

The Court's Role. The Commission's fruitless deliberations were followed by an apparent deadlocking in the Michigan Supreme Court itself. The matter had been reopened by a temporary one-vote majority of the Michigan Supreme Court on the apparent theory that the Austin-Kleiner Plan adopted by the court in June 1964 should be viewed only as a temporary plan because the Commission had had insufficient time to react to the *Reynolds* v. *Sims* description of federal standards.[63] The reconvened Bipartisan Commission should now proceed with more deliberation to make a final plan.

A careful reading of the plethora of individual opinions produced by the justices of the state supreme court on successive dates after the Com-

61. *In re* Apportionment of Michigan Legislature, 137 N.W.2d 495 (1965); 138 N.W.2d 16 (1965).
62. They did introduce, perhaps "just for kicks," a senate plan which crossed a few more subdivision lines and had a difference of only 627 persons from smallest to largest district out of more than 205,000 persons in each district. *New York Times,* January 2, 1966, p. 52, col. 3.
63. Justice Paul L. Adams, who supported remand to the Commison, but who differed with the remand majority on the ultimately crucial issue of the scope of retained jurisdiction in the court itself, said: "The four Democratic members of the commission had foreseen the overriding guideline in Reynolds v. Sims and had . . . submitted . . . the alternate Austin-Kleiner plan based upon the formula of one man-one vote. The four Republican members of the commission apparently had not foreseen this development. . . . During the brief time allowed . . . Republican members were unable to devise a plan that met the Federal standard."
In re Apportionment of Michigan Legislature, 137 N.W. 2d 495, 513 (1965).

mission had met and again deadlocked [64] suggest that on the merits of the Austin-Kleiner Plan in contrast with the new 5 percent maximum deviation plan of the Republican commissioners, the court was deadlocked 4-4. The confused sequence is perhaps best delineated in the successive memorandum opinions of Justice Eugene F. Black,[65] who seems to have modified his views after he initially supported adoption of Austin-Kleiner in June 1964. He was one of those who criticized the Austin-Kleiner Plan substantively and preferred the new 5 percent maximum deviation plan of the Republican commissioners—although he apparently stopped short of reaching the question whether the Austin-Kleiner Plan was unconstitutional under the 1963 Michigan Constitution.[66] However, the 5 percent plan was not before the court, he felt, because the new Commission deliberations were not merely a continuation of the pre-*Reynolds* v. *Sims* sessions, and of the truncated session of June 1964 with power in individual commissioners to submit individual plans. Rather, he said, the new proceeding was under a different paragraph of the 1963 Constitution, the Commission being under a duty to submit a "final plan" and the Supreme Court under a mandate to enforce the Commission's duty. Therefore, there could be no further process of commissioner submission of plans and judicial selection of that plan which "best" satisfied the surviving apportionment standards of the new constitution.

Justice Black's January 1966 memorandum capturing the political flavor of this tense period, charging bad faith on and off the court (twitting Justice Theodore Souris in particular), and suggesting that the Michigan Supreme Court break the Commission deadlock by ousting one commissioner by a drawing of lots merits extensive quotation:

> As the Court, by inaction, releases this particular commission from duty forever, some citizens surely (the writer being one) will find themselves giving a wry salute to the four Democratic divinators of the commission. The prescience that foursome has shown is wondrously uncommon. How the four could have been so confident, in those waning days of December, that five members of the Supreme Court of Michigan would not enforce what the five ordered the commission to do, back in early November, can be attributed only to occult power; a power given to few mortals. These gentlemen, by standing firm for the *status quo* through every painful hour of that sixty day period, predictably have saved the presently districted legislature, probably for all currently foreseeable time. Their spiritual (not political of course) rewards should be of high order.

64. *In re* Apportionment of Michigan Legislature, 140 N.W.2d 436 (1966), reporting several memoranda and opinions from January to March 1966.
65. *Id.* at 436, 439, 440.
66. *Id.* at 441, 466.

Our mandatory writ should issue forthwith, requiring that the secretary of the commission proceed promptly to insert, say in a jury box borrowed from a nearby circuit court, eight uniformly folded white slips of paper bearing respectively the names of the eight members of the commission; that he then close the box and shake it up as county clerks are wont to do upon jury selection; that he then, with discreetly averted gaze, draw out seven of the slips one after the other, and that he announce after each withdrawal the name appearing on the withdrawn slip.

A separate and simultaneously issued writ should direct that the first seven members of the commission, identified thus by the seven withdrawn slips, shall "proceed to district and apportion the senate and house of representatives" within an allotted number of days, say 30, and should provide for prompt review of the action of the seven commissioners upon petition filed in the present proceeding by any elector; all in pursuance of paragraph 8 of said section 6 and paragraph 2 of our said order of November 2.

No one need despair, or flee to the hills should such an order issue. Whatever the result of any such 7 man commission action, that result would be subject to constitutional test pursuant to said paragraph 8. And even though such mandated procedure might, the time element again being critical, leave the Austin-Kleiner plan intact for the elections of 1966, this Court would be able to say that it had performed manfully the duty said paragraph 8 has imposed upon it. "Drest" only as we are "in a little brief authority," it might even be said of us some day that such was *our* finest hour. (emphasis in the original) [67]

The Austin-Kleiner Plan thus survived again. Again it was more by default—or " 'decision' by impasse," [68] as Justice Black pointed out—and by intricate involutions in the Michigan Supreme Court than by a full and fresh airing of Michigan reapportionment alternatives. Subsequently in March 1966, Justice Black, his suggestions not having been adopted, referred to the outcome as one "just about anyone, having a near or distant connection with the Capitol's moccasin telegraph, could have predicted." [69]

An attempted review in the United States Supreme Court failed in November 1966, that Court without opinion granting a motion to dismiss the appeal.[70] The many issues raised and thus left unresolved in the continued Michigan apportionment litigation are analyzed in the context of the total range of post-*Reynolds* apportionment litigation in Chapter XVIII. As there indicated, there has been a strong tendency in the United States Supreme Court since 1964 to avoid close involvement in

67. *Id.* at 438–39.
68. *Id.* at 440.
69. *Ibid.*
70. 385 U.S. 114 (1966).

reapportionment litigation, even though the natural result of this policy has been to permit more widely varying apportionments among the several states than the public or the Court itself seemed to realize.

Gerrymandering Issue. Because political gerrymandering was one of the grounds for the Michigan appeal which the United States Supreme Court refused to hear on November 21, 1966, it is interesting to note that in the November election just two weeks earlier the Republicans in Michigan's second Austin-Kleiner Plan legislative election substantially recouped the losses they had suffered in 1964. They gained a 55-55 tie in the house, while polling 53.2 percent of the popular vote for the lower house. They captured the senate by 20 to 18, while polling 51.4 percent of the senate vote.

The re-election of Republican Governor George Romney by an overwhelming majority, like the Goldwater debacle in 1964, complicates efforts to assess the "political fairness" in 1966 of the Austin-Kleiner districts. Even more important perhaps is the fact that in a state such as Michigan where the Democrats have large pluralities and hence "wasted votes" in one section of the state (Detroit area), it may be impossible to follow county lines and not virtually guarantee a Republican legislature. A similar residence distribution pattern in the state of Washington has tended to have a reverse party effect, hurting the Republicans and helping the Democrats. In other words, it may require a "benevolent gerrymander" to create a district system that will correct the "wasted votes" problem. Such a "gerrymander" may be a precondition of creating a system under which the parties will gain legislative seats in rough proportion to their division of the statewide legislative vote (i.e., vote for legislators as distinguished from the gubernatorial vote).

e. Deficiencies in Michigan's Commission Plan

Several states other than Michigan have experimented with bipartisan reapportionment commissions, the next best known example being the Illinois Commission, whose failure led to the 1964 at-large election of the Illinois legislature. Michigan, rather than Illinois, may be a better example of the bipartisan commission approach because the Michigan system, unlike that of Illinois, was designed to *ensure* an *actual* reapportionment. The Illinois system is fundamentally deficient in concept in its three-step progression from legislative default to reapportionment commission default to at-large election as the final step authorized by the Illinois Constitution. The Illinois system, instead of putting pressure on the legislature, gives the legislature the "out" of buckpassing to the Commission; and when the Commission achieves a not-unexpected deadlock, an at-large election is triggered. Because an at-large election itself undermines representative democracy, it should be contemplated as a *direct* sanction on the legislature uncomplicated by intervention of a commission or any other device for legislative buckpassing.

The Michigan Bipartisan Apportionment Commission device, in contrast to that of Illinois, does create judicial responsibility, albeit channelized, to order reapportioned districts and thus preserve the representative function. In turn, however, the Michigan Reapportionment Commission device is itself fundamentally deficient in concept and operation as demonstrated by the unfolding of events in Michigan from 1963 to 1966. Like the federal pre-trial conference device finally worked out for Illinois by Chief Judge Campbell as a fresh reapportionment approach, the Michigan Bipartisan Commission device does serve to marshal political data. To that extent it ensures a realistic and politically informed approach toward an earnestly political issue. The term "reapportionment" should always conjure up the substitute phrase "redistribution of political power." However, in the event of Commission deadlock, the ultimate reapportioner in Michigan's system is the Michigan Supreme Court. And the *fatal* defect of the Michigan Constitution at this final court action stage lies in not authorizing the carrying forward of the political data marshaled in the Bipartisan Commission's deliberations to the deliberations of the final decisional body.

Indeed, the so-called bipartisan approach of Michigan actually *guarantees* that a *partisan* plan rather than bipartisan plan will eventually be adopted in the event of Commission deadlock. The state constitution authorizes the Michigan Supreme Court only to order into effect in toto one of the plans submitted by the partisan Commissioners individually. It gives the court no power to combine or adjust two or more plans to achieve a balanced and equitable result. It thus contrasts sharply and unfavorably with the pre-trial process worked out by Chief Judge Campbell in Illinois. There, after the parties had reached near-total agreement under strong judicial pressure the court—having participated throughout the process—could resolve the final disagreements in an informed fashion. Michigan's system contrasts sharply and unfavorably also with New Jersey's newly authorized system (discussed in Chapter XIII) which combines a bipartisan commission plan with provision for appointment of a tie breaker by the state chief justice.

XIII

Implementing "One Man-One Vote":
Some State Vignettes–II

"The result of the decision now being made is that a court of one sovereign authority has directed the New York Secretary of State to prepare an election in 1965 and the court of another sovereign authority has prohibited him from doing just that."

Judge Francis Bergan (Dissenting)
Glinski v. *Lomenzo*, 1965

"Reapportionment is one of those fields where there are no non-partisans—just noncombatants."

State Senator R. R. "Bob" Greive
Democratic Majority Leader
Washington Senate, 1965

C. Other Bipartisan Approaches to Reapportionment

For the purpose of Chapters XII–XIV on state "vignettes," as noted in the introduction to Chapter XII, reapportionment goals have been defined preliminarily as centering on a combination of mathematical equity and political realism to produce a politically equitable set of equal population districts. Bipartisan procedures have been identified as a frequently helpful route toward these goals. It is worth repeating that working out a reapportionment in the legislature does not necessarily guarantee its bipartisan character, nor does reapportionment by a nonlegislative agency necessarily exclude bipartisanship. A legislature both houses of which are controlled even narrowly by one party will not exercise much bipartisan fairness in reapportioning, unless the governor with his veto power is of the other party. And a nonlegislative agency charged with the reapportionment function may be bipartisan in varying degrees, or simply blind to political realities and the unavoidably political impact of its work—this last euphemistically being called "nonpartisan" by the uninformed or disingenuous.

The gross concept of "reapportionment by nonlegislative agency" is not a helpful classification device although frequently encountered, because it is not an operational concept.[1] On the eve of *Baker* v. *Carr*, the *Book of the States* listed fourteen states whose constitutions authorized reapportionment by administrative process for at least one house of the legislature.[2] But in terms of the interest at stake in reapportionment the classification is meaningless, if not misleading. It indiscriminately groups together pure bipartisan agencies, pseudo-bipartisan agencies, partisan ex officio agencies, and various hybrid devices—agencies which would have a vastly different kind of influence on reapportionment policy and future state political control. Pursuing the functional theme of this work, special apportionment commissions or boards in several states of a distinctly partisan nature which attracted attention in the post-*Baker* and post-*Reynolds* period must be excluded from a "bipartisan fairness" analysis, e.g., in Arkansas, Ohio, and Minnesota.

Within the functional concept of bipartisan approaches to reapportionment, several states deserve mention in addition to Illinois and Michigan, already discussed at length (Chapter XII). Further examples of the *official* bipartisan commission approach are Missouri and New Jersey. These states make an interesting contrast because one is a one-party state (or at best a one and one-half party state) and the other is a vigorous two-party state. *Unofficial* bipartisan apportionment by party agreement was achieved in several states, including Connecticut, Washington, and Minnesota (this last following a fruitless commission effort). And in at least one state, New York, after a prolonged and complicated struggle, something approaching a bipartisan apportionment was achieved by the device of a special ad hoc judicial commission appointed by the state's highest court.

1. *Book of the States* 1962–1963, pp. 58–62 (1962).
2. See tabulation, Council of State Governments, *Book of the States* 1962–1963, pp. 58–62 (1962). The fourteen were: Alaska (1956), Arizona, lower house only (1958), California (1961), Hawaii (1959), Illinois (1955), Michigan, lower house only (1953), Missouri, lower house only (1961), New Jersey, lower house only (1961), North Dakota, lower house only (1961), Ohio (1961), Oregon (1961), South Dakota (1961), Texas (1961).
   For judicial action under these provisions, see Anthony Lewis, "Legislative Apportionment and the Federal Courts," 71 *Harv. L. Rev.* 1057, 1090 (1958). See also Jefferson B. Fordham, *The State Legislative Institution* 46–47 (1959); American Political Science Association, *American State Legislatures* 41–44 (Belle Zeller, editor, New York: Crowell, 1954); American Political Science Association, "Report of Committee on Apportionment of Congress," 45 *Am. Pol. Sci. Rev.* 153–57 (1951).

1. ADDITIONAL BIPARTISAN COMMISSIONS

a. *Missouri: Bipartisanship in a One and One-Half Party State*

Missouri, home of the so-called Missouri Plan for nonpartisan selection of judges, was also one of the few states to create, long before *Baker* v. *Carr*, a special device for apportionment by a bipartisan nonlegislative agency. Since 1945 Missouri has used for apportionment of the senate a 10-member bipartisan commission appointed by the governor from lists submitted by the state central committees of the Democratic and Republican parties.[3] However, some degree of bipartisanship is lost at this initial stage for two reasons. One is that the governor possesses at least a slight degree of discretion to "rig" the commission because each party submits ten names from which the governor selects the five Democratic and the five Republican commissioners. By contrast Michigan's 1963 Constitution vests full appointing power in the respective state party committees, as does the Illinois Constitution. Second, because Missouri is not a true two-party state, the five Republican commissioners have not always been a cohesive opposition group. The weak Republican party derives some of its "strength" from state laws which require bipartisan appointment to such agencies as state college boards of regents and the state highway board. This combination of circumstances has led to the rise of a number of "nominal" Republicans. This factor may provide the primary explanation for the interesting fact that in nominally bipartisan Missouri the mandatory bipartisan senate apportionment commission has never deadlocked.

Except for congressional districting [4] Missouri was not caught up in the reapportionment revolution until after *Reynolds* v. *Sims* because its 25 percent maximum deviation standard was mild compared to the apportionment traditions in most other states. When a federal district court held that a 25 percent deviation was excessive and unconstitutional under the new federal "one man-one vote" standard,[5] the senate was reapportioned again in September 1965 by a 10-member bipartisan commission. Population deviations from average or ideal were reduced from near 26 percent to 4.6 percent, ignoring a state constitutional provision against crossing county lines. However, the anomalous character of bipartisanship

3. Mo. Const., Art. III, § 7.
4. Preisler v. Hearnes, 362 S.W. 2d 552 (Mo. 1962), holding before the United States Supreme Court's ruling in Wesberry v. Sanders, that population deviations ranging from −13 percent to +17 percent were constitutional.
   Subsequently a federal district court held that population deviations of −9.7 percent and +9.9 percent were excessive for congressional districts and in 1967 the Supreme Court affirmed. 385 U.S. 450 (1967).
5. Jonas v. Hearnes, 236 F. Supp. 699 (W.D. Mo. 1964).

in a one and one-half party state is dramatized by the fact that the resulting senate apportionment was criticized as being an anti-Republican gerrymander not only by Political Science Professor David Leuthold of the University of Missouri but also by State Republican Chairman Ethan H. Campbell, who called it a "flagrant gerrymander." [6] It would seem this 10-member commission must have possessed a special brand of bipartisanship, not commonly found outside the South or border-South states.

After this senate reapportionment a battle ensued between those who wished the legislature to retain control of house reapportionment and those who wished to bring it too under bipartisan commission dispensation. Rejection by the voters of a house-enacted reapportionment in 1965 did lead to the creation by constitutional amendment, ratified in January 1966, of a new 20-member bipartisan commission for house apportionment.[7] The decision to create a new kind of commission rather than extend the competence of the 10-member senate bipartisan commission to include house apportionment reflected an intra-Democratic party dispute, not wholly along urban-rural lines, between the governor and a faction who wanted to retain house apportionment as a legislative function. The five Democratic members of the senate apportionment commission had tended to be handpicked by the governor because of his influence in the state central committee. As a compromise to curb this influence the new amendment provided that the 20-member bipartisan house apportionment commission would consist of persons nominated by the ten congressional district committees of each party, which were deemed to be less subject to gubernatorial control than the state central committee. Again, however, some discretion was continued in the governor by virtue of the fact that

6. *The Sunday Missourian*, Dec. 12, 1965, p. 7, col. 5. See also the series of page one stories in *St. Louis Post-Dispatch*, Sept. 24, 1965, Oct. 22, 1965, and in *Columbia Tribune*, Dec. 20, 1965.

An intervention brief in the federal district court suit, and also a separate state court action, were filed by Republicans charging that the new senate districts were not compact and contiguous, that they crossed county lines, and that they were deliberately shaped for partisan political advantage. They cited sharp disparities between the percentage of popular vote polled by Republicans and the percentage of seats gained. The federal district court approved the senate (and subsequent house) reapportionment in July 1966. *St. Louis Post-Dispatch*, July 13, 1966, edit. page. The state court suit was still dormant in mid-1967, Republicans apparently waiting first to see how the alleged gerrymander worked out in the November 1966 elections and then to see the results of the 1967 legislative session.

7. Mo. Const., Art. III, § 2. For the sequence of events related in this section, the author has been aided materially by University of Missouri Political Science Professor Robert F. Karsch's notes for his panel remarks at the annual meeting of the National Municipal League in Boston, November 14, 1966, and correspondence with him and with Professor David A. Leuthold, also of the University of Missouri Department of Political Science. Information has been provided also by Dewey Schade, LL.B. George Washington University Law School, 1967.

each party committee submitted two names for each party seat, the governor to select one.

The 20-member house apportionment commission avoided deadlock, like the senate commission, and achieved reapportionment in March 1966. No great outcries were forthcoming, and the most deviant reapportioned district was 10 percent from average size.[8]

The Missouri system does provide a backstop for both bipartisan commissions in the event of a deadlock, but it has never been used. However, the backstop agency—i.e., the six Missouri Supreme Court Commissioners, three Democrats and three Republicans, appointed by the Missouri Supreme Court—is itself by statute a bipartisan group and there seems to be no guarantee of achieving apportionment should this group deadlock. A Missouri "Supreme Court Commissioner" is a unique hybrid attached to the 7-member nominally nonpartisan Missouri Supreme Court.[9] A possibly prescient observation on the Missouri system, in the event the state's politics become more truly bipartisan, is Michigan Supreme Court Justice Eugene F. Black's comments chiding his Michigan brethren for not taking stronger action to break the Michigan Bipartisan Commission's deadlock in 1966:

> Now what will the Missouri supreme court do should the six commissioners of that Court arrive at a deadlock? Follow our inaction as a precedent? Come now, Brothers.[10]

b. *New Jersey: Bipartisan Model for a Two-Party State*

Except for an aborted attempt to use weighted voting as a temporary reapportionment device for the New Jersey senate, major interest in New Jersey's reapportionment sequence centers on a truly startling record of bipartisan negotiation (except in regard to her congressional districts). Because New Jersey's lower house by pre-*Reynolds* standards had traditionally reflected population more or less, the primary attack was on the senate, apportioned on a county equality basis. After the United States Supreme Court's "one man-one vote" ruling, the New Jersey Supreme Court in November 1964 reversed its 1963 validation of the state senate on a federal plan theory and voided both houses.[11] The New Jersey sen-

8. *Supra*, note 7, Professor Leuthold computations.

9. Like a judge in pay but like a law clerk in function and responsibility, the commissioners sit with the judges and prepare tentative opinions for acceptance or rejection by the state supreme court. *Official Manual of Missouri*—1965–1966, p. 233.

10. *In re* Apportionment of the Michigan Legislature, 140 N.W.2d 436, 438 n.6 (1966).

11. Jackman v. Bodine, 188 A.2d 642 (N.J. 1963); Jackman v. Bodine, 205 A.2d 713 (N.J. 1964). As of 1963 the most deviant lower house district was 51.2 percent smaller than the ideal size, but the average relative population deviation, a measure which considers all districts and not just the two extremes, was 20.2 percent. See

ate promptly enacted a new senate rule instituting weighted voting, and providing that each senator's voting power should be commensurate with the population of his county, thus preserving Republican voices if not votes. For example, a senator from Essex County with the state's largest population of 923,545 would be entitled to 19 votes while the senator from the smallest county, Sussex, 49,255, would be entitled to one vote. The state attorney general moved for a declaration that the resolution was invalid under the state and federal Constitutions. Without reaching constitutional issues the New Jersey Supreme Court vetoed the plan on the state law ground that "the vote necessary for the adoption of legislation may not be fixed by an internal rule or regulation of one branch of the legislature." [12]

Backdrop for the Constitutional Convention. Concurrently at the end of 1964, the political parties reached agreement on a special bipartisan 12-member commission set up by legislative resolution to aid in drafting reapportionment legislation for submission to the legislature.[13] Long deliberation and deadlock stemming primarily from collision between the Republican-dominated legislature and the Democratic governor, culminated in agreement on a temporary apportionment plan in April 1965, pending creation of a permanent plan by a constitutional convention which by court direction was itself to be apportioned on an equal population basis. The federal district court gave its sanction to the temporary arrangement under which the maximum district population deviations in the house and senate were 51.2 and 27.3 percent, respectively.[14]

Mathematical flexibility permitted by the temporary nature of the plan, coupled with decisions not to seek re-election made by several senators who had seen the handwriting on the wall, enabled negotiators by dexterous maneuvering and an increase in senate size to find a place for every incumbent senator who wished to run again. Said Senator William E. Ozzard, Republican leader and principal author of the plan: "We thought this out down to the last Democrat and the last Republican." [15]

Bipartisanship continued in the contemporaneous authorization of a constitutional convention to meet in the spring of 1966 and prepare a permanent apportionment plan for submission to the voters in the No-

Ernest C. Reock, Jr., "Population Inequality Among Counties in the New Jersey Legislature, 1791–1962," Rutgers University Bureau of Government Research Pamphlet (1963), p. 15.
12. Jackman v. Bodine, 205 A.2d 735 (N.J. 1964).
13. *New York Times*, December 11, 1964, p. 42, col. 1.
14. For the senate see Jackman v. Bodine, 209 A.2d 825, 827 (N.J. 1965). The interim reapportionment was new for the senate only; the court allowed continued temporary use of the 1962 house plan under which the smallest and largest districts were 48,555 and 143,913, respectively, and the "ideal" or average was 101,113.
15. *New York Times*, April 12, 1965, p. 25, col. 1.

vember election.[16] Each party received one-half of the delegates, 63 for each party, and each contingent cast 56 votes. Delegates exceeded votes because the attempt to elect the convention from counties on an equal population basis and also to divide strength evenly between the parties necessitated adding a delegate to each county with an odd number of convention votes, thus creating some fractional vote delegates.

The principal features of the permanent apportionment plan created by the convention were: (1) a 40-member senate, primarily from multimember districts, apportioned by the method of equal proportions among counties; (2) senate districts to be composed of single counties, or if not "practicable" from contiguous counties without crossing county lines; (3) an 80-member assembly elected from two-man districts (rather than county-at-large as formerly) created by subdistricting the multimember senate districts and by simply adopting the single-member senate districts; (4) assembly districts to be contiguous and compact and also within a statewide maximum deviation of 20 percent, and as nearly equal "as possible"—this last requirement apparently directed to assembly district equality inside the respective senate districts; (5) transfer of the reapportionment function from the legislature to a bipartisan Apportionment Commission with provision for tie breaker appointed by the Chief Justice of the New Jersey Supreme Court.

Pending further revision after the 1970 census, the convention created 15 senate districts on the basis of counties or groups of counties, a majority of which were multimember districts electing two to six senators at-large. Only three of the 40 senators were in single-member districts. The same 15 districts were allocated 80 house members, all to be elected from two-member districts to be drawn by the bipartisan commission. Apart from philosophical questions pro and con on single versus multimember districting, it is almost always to the advantage of the weaker party to insist on single-member districts—or no larger than two-member districts—for each house. In the convention the Republicans lost on this issue in regard to the senate, despite the even split of party votes in the convention, because one or two Republican leaders with an eye more to personal and local short-term gains than to statewide party advantage joined with the Democrats in putting much of the senate on a multimember at-large basis.

16. For a helpful summary of the pre-convention sequence of events, see the background pamphlet published by the New Jersey Taxpayers Association entitled "One Man-One Vote: Background for Constitutional Reapportionment in New Jersey" (1966), hereafter cited as *Background Pamphlet*.

For a more general discussion of reapportionment by constitutional revision with special reference to New Jersey, see Arthur J. Sills and Alan B. Handler, "The Imbroglio of Constitutional Revision—Another By-Product of Reapportionment," 20 *Rutgers L. Rev.* 1 (1965).

Bipartisan Commission and Tie Breaker. Under the convention's proposed new apportionment plan, which was approved by the people of New Jersey in November 1966, initial subdistricting of the lower house (the convention itself having provided initial senate districts), was vested in the bipartisan Apportionment Commission. All future modification of senate districts and their subdividing into two-member districts for house members was also to be done by the bipartisan commission.

As in Michigan, and unlike Missouri, the New Jersey governor has no discretionary power to influence composition of the bipartisan commission. It consists of five members from each of the two major parties appointed by the state chairmen. In the event of deadlock, ties are to be broken by an eleventh member appointed by the Chief Justice of the New Jersey Supreme Court. The commission has one month after appointment of the eleventh member to reach a decision, thus allowing the new man time for adequate briefing on all mathematical, political, and other information relevant to the apportionment process.

A survey by the Bureau of Government Research of Rutgers State University on pre-convention attitudes of individual delegates on the question of vesting apportionment power in a nonlegislative agency showed that the proposal was favored by 74 percent of Republican nonlegislator delegates; by 53 percent of Democratic nonlegislator delegates; by 47 percent of Republican legislator delegates; and by only 33 percent of Democratic legislator delegates.[17] The attitude of Democratic legislators undoubtedly was influenced by the fact that they had won a sweeping victory in the November 1965 election—the first held under the temporary bipartisan reapportionment agreement—and were in control of both houses of the legislature for the first time since 1914. Democratic majorities were 19 to 10 in the senate and 41 to 19 in the assembly. Convinced that they were the majority party in the state, it was natural for them to advocate reapportionment by the legislature. Republicans on the other hand had just taken their second bad beating in two years. Feeling that they were becoming the minority party in the state, they naturally sought refuge in the idea of a nonlegislative agency reapportionment.

At the convention an agreement for a bipartisan apportionment agency was hammered out between the party leaderships. Democratic legislator delegates, opposed both by the Republicans and by their own Democratic nonlegislator delegates, quietly backed off from advocacy of reapportionment by the legislature. A further attitude survey by the Bureau of Government Research (see Chart 9) revealed that the delegates most satisfied with the decision to transfer the reapportionment function to a bipartisan

17. Address by Professor Ernest C. Reock, Jr., 72nd National Conference on Government, National Municipal League, Boston, Massachusetts, November 14, 1966.

Chart 9
POST-CONVENTION ATTITUDES OF DELEGATES TOWARD PROPOSED NONLEGISLATIVE REAPPORTIONMENT AGENCY
NEW JERSEY, 1966

	Republicans	Democrats	Total
Legis-lators *	SA: 59% × 10.0 = 590 A: 41% × 6.7 = 275 D: 0% × 3.3 = 0 SD: 0% × 0 = 0 865 (N = 22)	SA: 8% × 10.0 = 80 A: 62% × 6.7 = 415 D: 23% × 3.3 = 76 SD: 8% × 0 = 0 571 (N = 13)	SA: 40% × 10.0 = 400 A: 49% × 6.7 = 328 D: 9% × 3.3 = 30 SD: 3% × 0 = 0 758 (N = 35)
Non-legis-lators	SA: 29% × 10.0 = 290 A: 62% × 6.7 = 415 D: 0% × 3.3 = 0 SD: 10% × 0 = 0 705 (N = 21)	SA: 23% × 10.0 = 230 A: 72% × 6.7 = 482 D: 6% × 3.3 = 20 SD: 0% × 0 = 0 732 (N = 31)	SA: 25% × 10.0 = 250 A: 67% × 6.7 = 449 D: 4% × 3.3 = 13 SD: 4% × 0 = 0 712 (N = 52)
Total	SA: 44% × 10.0 = 440 A: 51% × 6.7 = 342 D: 0% × 3.3 = 0 SD: 5% × 0 = 0 782 (N = 43)	SA: 18% × 10.0 = 180 A: 68% × 6.7 = 456 D: 11% × 3.3 = 36 SD: 2% × 0 = 0 672 (N = 44)	SA: 31% × 10.0 = 310 A: 60% × 6.7 = 402 D: 6% × 3.3 = 20 SD: 3% × 0 = 0 732 (N = 87)

* And former legislators
NOTE: Count is of delegates, not of votes; some delegates authorized to cast only ½ votes.
SA: means "strongly agree" with Proposal
A: means "agree" with Proposal
D: means "disagree" with Proposal
SD: means "strongly disagree" with Proposal
Source: Stephen A. Decter, Judson L. James, Ernest C. Reock, Jr., study in process, Bureau of Government Research, Rutgers University.

commission were Republican legislator delegates. They were followed in descending order by Democratic nonlegislator delegates, Republican non-legislator delegates, and lastly Democratic legislator delegates.

Rise of Republican legislator delegates to top position in the "satisfaction" index can be attributed not only to their feeling that they were now the minority party, but also to confirmation of their fears in the form of an "unfriendly" revision of congressional districts by the new Democratic-controlled legislature which was sitting concurrently. The new congressional districts were an especially bitter pill for the Republicans to swallow because of the events in the preceding spring of 1965 when they still controlled both houses. Then the Democratic governor, who was negotiating with the Republicans on a temporary state legislative apportionment plan, had taken a strong stand against any congressional redistricting by the Republican-controlled legislature and had threatened to veto any plan using revised congressional districts as the basis for senatorial districts.[18] The new Democratic legislature had enacted a congressional redistricting plan which was viewed by many as a conscious gerrymander designed to preserve seats of Democratic freshmen Congressmen elected in 1964 with the aid of the Goldwater candidacy. Indeed in the summer of 1966 the new congressional districts were promptly nullified by the New Jersey Supreme Court—although one-time use in 1966 was permitted—nominally on mathematical grounds but actually on quasi-gerrymandering grounds.[19]

As matters worked out in New Jersey in the spring of 1967, the bipartisan commission did deadlock, Professor Marver H. Bernstein, Dean of the Woodrow Wilson School of Public and International Affairs of Princeton University, was appointed tie breaker by the Chief Justice of the New Jersey Supreme Court, and a reapportionment was announced. Professor Bernstein's compromise plan trading off two of the larger counties between the two parties was adopted by an 8 to 3 vote of the full commission.[20] Seven of the 15 senate districts, in which 17 of the 40 senators were to be elected, exceeded a 10 percent deviation from average or "ideal," the range being +13.5 percent to −13.8 percent. Fourteen of the 40 assembly districts, in which 38 of the 80 assemblymen were to be elected, exceeded a 10 percent deviation, the range being +13.6 percent to −17.2 percent. Three assembly districts exceeded a 15 percent deviation. The electoral percentages and population variance ratios for the senate and house respectively were 49.1 percent and 1.3 to 1, and 47.3 percent and 1.37 to 1.

Although the state leadership of neither political party felt the plan was an egregious inroad on its major interest, the effectuation of the plan was immediately threatened by several suits. One was filed by two dissident Republican members of the commission who objected to the final compromise on certain assembly districts. Another was filed by a Democratic assemblyman who was attorney for the original plaintiffs. In an odd twist of "one man-one vote" theory, he now sought elimination of the two-man subdistricts for the lower house and broader use of at-large voting, which could have produced lower house multimember districts ranging from two-man districts up to a twelve-man district. The state supreme court re-

18. *Background Pamphlet*, pp. 14–15.
19. See more extensive discussion of this gerrymandering story in Ch. XVIII.
20. See "Representation News Analysis," 56 *Nat. Civ. Rev.* 352 (1967); also see Report of the Bipartisan Commission, March 8, 1967.

quired some minor alterations—extracting some from the bipartisan commission on remand and making others itself—and then allowed interim use of the plan in 1967.[21] Some of the alterations were so nit-picking as to be almost stultifying in absence of proof as to whose ox was saved or gored. And in the eyes of some observers the symmetrical bipartisan commission plan became a patchwork through court tinkering. Such casual upsetting of bipartisan plans could be avoided by amending New Jersey's new procedure and requiring challengers to show invidious political or racial effect—and not merely a way to shave a few population percentage points in one corner of the state.

In the initial, November 1967 election under the bipartisan commission court-tinkered plan, a near 2 to 1 Democratic control of both houses was transformed into a near 3 to 1 Republican control. Significantly, there were no charges that the bipartisan commission plan was a gerrymander. Rather, the result can be attributed to several causes, none related to the commission: (1) Vietnam; (2) white backlash from the Newark riot; (3) school busing policy announced by new education Commissioner to achieve racial intermixture, and expanded parochial busing; (4) the tendency of any plurality-rule district system, in contrast to cumulative voting or proportional representation, to exaggerate the dominant party's strength, sometimes excessively so.

The Superiority of New Jersey's System. New Jersey's bipartisan commission approach to legislative apportionment, backstopped by appointment of a tie breaker by the Chief Justice of the state supreme court has strong claims to be a near-model bipartisan apportionment system. Functionally viewed it is more closely analogous to the pre-trial apportionment process worked out by Chief Judge Campbell for Illinois than to the bipartisan commission procedures of either Missouri or Michigan. It is superior to the latter two bipartisan commission systems. The New Jersey bipartisan commission-plus-tie breaker process, like the Illinois pre-trial process, guarantees that reapportionment will be achieved and also guarantees that it will be achieved on as informed a basis as possible. By contrast, in the Missouri plan there is no backstop in the event of ultimate deadlock. The purported backstop in the Michigan plan mandates that the state supreme court shall pick the best of the *partisan* plans rather than make a final, informed, and fair adjustment. Even the pre-trial process of apportionment, which did work satisfactorily in Illinois, requires co-

21. Jackman v. Bodine, 231 A.2d 193, 232 A.2d 419 (1967). An ordered senate district change left one 13.8 percent deviation untouched but rearranged counties in a politically sensitive area elsewhere to reduce another 13.8 percent deviation to 6.1 percent. The change raised the senate electoral percentage from 49.1 percent to 50.2 percent. The bipartisan commission must reassess all assembly districts before the 1969 election.

operation of the parties and some imaginative judicial leadership; it therefore may be a somewhat "chancy" device to rely on.

Thus, a way to regularize the advantages of Chief Judge Campbell's experimentation with pre-trial apportionment in Illinois and to ensure accomplishment of reapportionment on an informed and realistic basis, is to adopt the New Jersey system. The New Jersey system, of course, entirely precludes legislative action, differing in this way from the pre-trial process which only occurred after legislative failure on senate apportionment in Illinois. However, in those states in which there is a strong desire to retain the legislature as the primary apportionment organ, the New Jersey system could still be used merely by modifying the role of the bipartisan commission so that its function begins only after legislative failure, not at once after each decennial census.

2. INFORMAL BIPARTISAN APPORTIONMENT

In a number of states informal bipartisan apportionment procedures occurred which were the functional equivalent of the more formal and more certain procedures exemplified by bipartisan commission operation in such states as Michigan and New Jersey.

a. *Connecticut: Party Agreement*

Connecticut is one of a handful of states [22] in which interim or final apportionment was devised by direct negotiation between the major parties without the panoply formally of setting up a bipartisan commission. In Connecticut an interim apportionment by party agreement became permanent, without significant substantive change, by virtue of the action of a constitutional convention which also was created on a bipartisan basis, and whose work was ratified by Connecticut voters in December 1965.[23]

Undoubtedly a major factor in producing reapportionment by bipartisan negotiation was the vigor of the federal district court in Connecticut and the sanctions it designed and clearly intended to use in event of breakdown in negotiations between the Democratic state senate and the Republican lower house. A contributing factor also may have been the stark fact that Connecticut's egregious lower house malapportionment concededly required such major ousting of incumbents that the minority Republican party was left with little bargaining power. It had control of the lower house of the Connecticut legislature only by virtue of a town

22. In New Jersey, as already noted, the final and formal bipartisan commission operation in 1967 was itself antedated by an informal bipartisan process, resting on divided state government, which produced an interim reapportionment of the senate in 1965.
23. "News in Review," 55 *Nat. Civ. Rev.* 90 (1966).

system of apportionment not materially changed since the Fundamental Orders of 1638.

Prior to *Reynolds* v. *Sims* a federal district court already had nullified Connecticut's version of the "federal plan" system of representation [24] despite the fact, especially poignant to some residents of the Nutmeg State, that the 1787 Connecticut General Assembly had been used as the model for the two different bases of representation in the United States Senate and House of Representatives. Thus had been derived the famous "Connecticut Compromise" by which the conflict between the large and small states was resolved in the federal Constitutional Convention. When the United States Supreme Court affirmed the federal district court's ruling a week after *Reynolds* v. *Sims* in June 1964,[25] the federal district court on remand laid down strict marching orders for re-establishing constitutional rectitude in Connecticut.[26]

The politically divided legislature was to convene in special session by August 3, 1964, and was to produce by September 10, 1964, two enactments. One would temporarily reapportion the state. The other would provide for creation of a constitutional convention which would convene by November 5, 1964, and complete its work by March 1, 1965, for submission of this reapportionment amendment to the voters by April 5, 1965. The legislature was stripped of power to perform general legislative functions until the reapportionment task was completed. An election at-large was threatened in the event of reapportionment failure.

When the first deadline for legislative action expired with the parties reportedly near agreement, the court without relenting on its sanctions devised a new timetable.[27] It canceled the November 1964 state legislative election. It then extended the terms of sitting legislators to 1966 *provided* a reconvened special session (in mid-November after the furor of the presidential election had died down) accomplished by January 30, 1965 a temporary apportionment of the legislature and authorization for a constitutional convention. A new sanction added was the appointment of Dr. Morris S. Davis, director of the Yale University Computer Center, as special master to assist the court in the event of legislative failure. He was to give consideration "to the feasibility and advisability of utilizing an appropriate electronic computer technique to minimize partisanship in redistricting . . . ." [28]

24. Butterworth v. Dempsey, 229 F. Supp. 754 (D. Conn. 1964).
25. Pinney v. Butterworth, 378 U.S. 564 (1964).
26. Butterworth v. Dempsey, 237 F. Supp. 302 (D. Conn. 1964).
27. *Id.* at 305 (*Memorandum re* Further Amendment to Judgment, Sept. 24, 1964).
28 *Id.* at 313 (Order That Special Master Be Appointed, Oct. 29, 1964). An analysis of the role of computers in apportionment and districting is reserved for Ch. XIX on continuing reapportionment issues.

This sequence of events in Connecticut in 1964 was not without its humor. Republican State Chairman A. Searle Pinney, perhaps with one eye on the faltering presidential campaign of Senator Barry Goldwater, announced that the courts had reached "a very sensible conclusion" in deciding to postpone the November 1964 election. Democratic State Chairman John Bailey forthrightly asserted that the Republicans were "afraid" to run with Goldwater.[29]

Both parties, realizing that all district lines are partisan whether drawn blindly or otherwise, were quite upset over the prospect of a "pig in the poke" computer reapportionment if they failed to reach agreement among themselves. When the second special session convened in November, the legislators were warned by Democratic Governor John N. Dempsey that if they wasted this final opportunity to reapportion, their "human judgment" would be supplanted by "mechanized leveling techniques of electronic age computers."[30] He received applause from both sides of the aisle when he repeated his previously stated objections to a special master.

Thus led, pushed, and hemmed in, the political party leaders were able to reach agreement within the January 1965 deadline on a bipartisan apportionment plan which was subsequently undergirded by constitutional convention process. The population variance ratio for the senate was reduced from 8 to 1 to 1.52 to 1 and the maximum district deviation was reduced from 226.8 percent to 23.0 percent. The electoral percentage was raised from 31.9 percent to 47.9 percent. For the lower house, heretofore based on a town representation formula of one representative for each town below 5000 and two representatives for each town above 5000, the change was even more dramatic. The house was reduced from 294 members to 177 members and the electoral percentage which at 11.9 percent had been one of the lowest in the nation was raised to 43.8 percent. The population variance ratio was reduced from 424.6 to 1 to 2.1 to 1 and the maximum deviation percentage was reduced to 38.6 (from 840 percent).

Had the parties in Connecticut been more closely balanced in popular strength, as in Illinois, with future control of the legislature hinging perhaps on allocation of a single disputed district line, settlement of the reapportionment issue by party agreement may well have been impossible despite the prospective perils of judicially arranged apportionment. Therefore, although Connecticut did achieve a peaceful bipartisan apportionment which was deemed by most observers to be as fair to both parties of the state as could be expected, Connecticut provided no "method"

29. *New York Times*, September 25, 1964, pp. 1, 31, cols. 7, 6.
30. *New York Times*, November 11, 1964, p. 32, col. 1.

for export to other states or even a method for future use in Connecticut with any certainty of producing a reapportionment agreement.

b. Washington: Governor-Legislature Tug of War

Whenever the fortuitous event occurs of divided state government, i.e., a governor of one party and a legislature at least one house of which is controlled by the other party, the possibility of bipartisan negotiation and agreement on reapportionment exists. There exists also of course the possibility of eventual deadlock, necessitating judicial intervention and resolution. But at least the party balance avoids or minimizes the prospect of outright gerrymander which normally occurs whenever there is a unified government with one party controlling both houses and the governorship. Paradoxically, the situation which minimizes reapportionment problems and guarantees a ready accomplishment of the reapportionment task— the existence of unified state government under one party—is also the situation least likely to produce a fair representation system equitable to both major parties and competing interest groups. Alleged gerrymanders perpetrated in reapportionments produced by party-unified state governments, and problems of judicial review thereof, are discussed in Chapter XVIII.

The Washington reapportionment case, Meyers v. Thigpen,[31] was one of those remanded by the United States Supreme Court in June 1964 after its decisions in the "big six" apportionment cases. After an aborted judicial proposal to utilize weighted voting as a mode of immediate interim relief, the federal district court decided to give the legislature an opportunity to reapportion itself under the new federal standards. As a sanction to ensure reapportionment agreement the court imposed stringent restraints exceeded only by the Connecticut federal district court.

31. 378 U.S. 554 (1964).
The lineup of parties in the Washington reapportionment litigation is a story in itself. The initial plaintiff, James Thigpen, was a justice of the peace who faced re-election in an enlarged district, and some saw in his Baker-inspired suit a way of becoming better known. The initial attack being on a 1962 reapportionment initiative petition, the League of Women Voters came in as defendant-intervenor to protect the initiative. But when the initiative failed, the League switched to a plaintiff-intervenor role, joining Thigpen's attorney, M. L. Borawick. After enactment of the bipartisan compromise plan in February 1965, the League joined the Attorney General's side in defending the act as a satisfactory apportionment, and Borawick only raised token opposition concerning a few parts of the plan.

The Attorney General himself, nominally a defendant, had dismayed some legislators after the Reynolds decision. He had suggested a strict January 1965 reapportionment timetable to the federal district court as a quid pro quo for allowing the November 1964 election in the old districts and thus avoiding a special session which could have embarrassed Governor Rosellini on a side issue of an item veto.

The incoming legislature in January 1965 was prohibited from enacting any legislation except the minimum necessary for continuance of state government until reapportionment was accomplished.[32]

In the November 1964 election the Democrats with the aid of the Goldwater presidential candidacy polled 52 percent of the lower house popular vote which yielded—with the aid of a Democratic-devised district system of some years' standing [33]—60 percent of the house seats. (In 1962 these same districts produced a Democratic house majority of 51 to 48 despite an actual loss of the popular vote—47.3 percent Democratic and 52.7 percent Republican.) The senate also went Democratic in 1964. But, bucking the anti-Goldwater tide in 1964, Republican Daniel J. Evans defeated incumbent Democratic Governor Albert D. Rosellini.

In the opening days of January 1965 a humorous little political farce was enacted when the Democrats attempted to take advantage of the short period of time in which there would be an overlap between a newly sworn-in Democratic legislature and a lame-duck Democratic governor with a few hours of his term left. But the opportunity came to nought even though the Democrats controlled both houses by increased margins of 60 to 39 in the house and 32 to 17 in the senate. A "Democratic" reapportionment of the Washington legislature was averted by the same split in the Democratic party between its western Seattle-Tacoma elements and its eastern rural-Spokane elements which had prevented reapportionment when the Democrats controlled the state in 1962–1964. Indeed, because of this split there had been a bloc of eight dissident Democrats in the 1963–1964 house, one of whom had been elected Speaker with Republican support and who in return had appointed a Republican as chairman of the key committee on apportionment. However, because the eventual stringency of the Reynolds "one man-one vote" rule was not anticipated, any plan approved by the Democratic legislature in the 1963–1964 period probably would not have been "equal" enough to withstand a post-Reynolds challenge.

The swearing-in of Governor Evans created an officially divided government. A reapportionment impasse resulted despite the federal court's prohibition of handling general legislative business until reapportionment was accomplished. For the Biblical period of 40 days and 40 nights, and a few

32. Thigpen v. Meyers, 231 F. Supp. 938 (W.D. Wash. 1964); order stayed (W.D. Wash., October 5, 1964), 12 National Municipal League, Court Decisions on Legislative Apportionment 170 (thus allowing 1964 elections in old districts and withdrawing weighted voting idea); stay modified (W.D. Wash., October 21, 1964), id. at 173 (and sanctions added to ensure early 1965 reapportionment).

33. In 1957 the Washington legislature had almost totally emasculated a successful 1956 initiative which had reapportioned on a more nearly equal population basis, although like all pre-Reynolds "population" concepts, it fell far short of a rigid "one man-one vote" equalization.

more, the Democratic legislature enacted and the Republican governor vetoed. Despite the expected journalistic comments about the sad spectacle thus presented of democracy in operation and the ignoring of the "people's interest," whatever that may be, this spectacle was the price of avoiding a partisan gerrymander. And a gerrymander, it must be remembered, may not only tilt governmental control in one direction unfairly for a legislative term or so, but frequently for years to come.

Reapportionment negotiations were not at all aided by Washington's blanket ballot version of the "open primary" system. Under it there are no party registration figures such as exist in closed primary states and also no requirement that the voter at least stay inside one party ballot on primary day. The blanket ballot system in effect makes each "office" a separate primary and permits the voter to shift from party to party, i.e., from primary to primary, as he goes through his ballot. Party cohesion is weakened and it thus is more difficult to "read" a district or proposed district than in closed primary states, and therefore it is more difficult to test for conscious gerrymanders or to determine whether a gerrymander has occurred inadvertently. Party votes for statewide office or Congressmen were used as a substitute index of party strength, but this gave rise to new disputes. Republicans claimed that such indices were unreliable and should be discounted by up to six percentage points to take account of the fact that Republicans tended to run better in such races than in local legislative contests.

Another issue, complicated also by incumbency interests, concerned "swing" districts and "safe" districts. Republicans, with some edge in campaign contributions and attractiveness of recent candidates, preferred creation of swing districts. The strategy was dictated also by their residence pattern, which was not widely enough spread. Democrats, with more widely spread strength but a less reliable electorate in terms of voter turnout, favored a policy of balancing safe districts.[34]

The perseverance of the legislature and the tenacity of the governor— and the expectation that neither the people nor the federal district court would remain patient forever—finally created the basis for a compromise

34. A before-and-after comparison of the districts of the two leading reapportionment negotiators is instructive. The existing district of Democratic Majority Leader R.R. "Bob" Greive was 57,059, almost perfect under the state "ideal" or average figure of 57,636. However, the 1965 reapportionment boosted it to 66,885 making it, with a 16 percent deviation, one of the more deviant districts in the senate. The inference was inescapable, and was not missed by Capitol observers, that a goodly portion of the 9000 added population were deemed to be reliable Democrats. Republican House Minority Leader Slade Gordon's pre-1965 district had a population of 33,669, exceeding by 18 percent the state average for the house of 28,527. The 1965 reapportionment, and the need for Republicans to better distribute their strength, brought it down to an almost perfect figure of 28,989.

bipartisan reapportionment in late February. It was promptly approved by the federal district court in March 1965 and regular legislative business was finally resumed.[35] In mathematical terms the resulting districts stayed inside an approximate 20 percent maximum deviation which was a common figure in many of the immediate post-*Reynolds* reapportionments. More importantly in political terms, it was viewed by leaders of both political parties as a reasonably fair apportionment, one providing a basis for maintenance of effective two-party competition in Washington. Both parties being satisfied no appeal was taken to the Supreme Court.[36]

Although none presumed Divine Guidance in the eventual plans, despite the Biblical parallel in the long deadlock, a visitor to Olympia in the spring of 1965 shortly after the reapportionment struggle was resolved might see some preternatural influence in the damage caused by an earthquake which occurred shortly after the legislature had finalized reapportionment and resumed regular legislative business. While the legislators went about their task below, the Capitol dome perched precariously above, shorn of supports and needing only a further earthquake to make the reapportionment question academic so far as incumbents were concerned.

A fair bipartisan reapportionment in Washington was accomplished by virtue of the fortuitous combination of divided government and a restrictive court order against other legislative business. In general perspective, however, the Washington procedure, like that in Connecticut, provides neither an exportable method for other states nor a method which can be relied on to recur and produce a reapportionment result in Washington in the future.

c. *Minnesota Governor-Legislature Tug of War*

Another state in which a bipartisan apportionment was achieved because of the happenstance of divided government was Minnesota. The Democratic governor and the "nonpartisan legislature" provided one of the more politically astute examples of bipartisan negotiation, including political profile tests with the aid of computers in regard to the various alternative plans submitted. There was more than a little irony in this development because the Minnesota legislature, like that of Nebraska, is nom-

35. Thigpen v. Kramer (W.D. Wash., March 9, 1965), 17 National Municipal League, Court Decisions on Legislative Apportionment 136.

Primary architects of the reapportionment in addition to Senator Greive and Representative Gordon (see note 34 *supra*), were on the Democratic side Representative Gary Grant and on the Republican side Governor Evans.

36. Based on political profile data from past elections, the initial Democratic plan which Governor Evans vetoed would have produced 65 safe Democratic seats in the 99-member house. The bill finally enacted had predicted Democratic seats ranging from 47 to 58, depending on whose figures were used.

inally "nonpartisan," the candidates running without official party designation. In practice, however, for many of the races there is an informal party endorsement system, distribution of sample ballots, and identification at least indirectly through billboard advertising. The minority party in a given area will tend to conceal its true identity and to stress the nonpartisan label.

Internally the Minnesota legislature organized itself into a Conservative caucus and a Liberal caucus, the former being dominantly Republican in its leadership and the latter being dominantly Democratic-Farmer-Labor (DFL) in its leadership. The Minnesota system dates from an anti-party-machine revolt in 1913 sparked by an alliance between liquor interests and opponents of prohibition.[37] Although the statewide Republican and Democratic parties are the primary rallying points in Minnesota, some local observers see something approaching a four-party political system consisting of an old and conservative Republican faction, a young and liberal Republican faction, a labor group which atypically tends to be conservative, and a Democratic party wing made up of liberals and university people.

Building political profiles to test out alternative apportionment plans thus becomes a somewhat complicated and uncertain procedure. An added difficulty stems from Minnesota's use of some multimember districts. Assessment of party strength in multimember districts is always difficult. Even if one party captures all seats the popular vote may vary for different winning candidates in the same district. One of the better indices for political profile building in a state such as Minnesota is the outcome of congressional district elections. Governorship elections also have been used as an index of party strength, but may cause distortion because of the frequency with which the gubernatorial vote departs from the legislative vote in Minnesota as elsewhere. Because of the complexities, computers are an obvious aid (Chapter XIX), and were used.[38]

Despite the uncertainties caused by nominal nonpartisanship, the key to the bipartisan apportionment of Minnesota was negotiation between the Republican-oriented legislature (under the "nonpartisan" label of

37. For a short discussion of the "nonpartisan" systems of Minnesota and Nebraska see G. Theodore Mitau, *State and Local Government: Politics and Processes* 855 *et seq.* (New York: Charles Scribner's Sons, 1966).
38. Professor Mitau, *supra* note 37, finds that over the years there has been a closer identification between the Liberal caucus and the Democratic-Farmer-Labor party than between the Conservative caucus and the Republican party, at least in regard to total membership of each caucus. Over the years the Conservative caucus has held the allegiance of a fair number of rural and small town legislators who are not active in Republican party affairs otherwise. However, the leadership of the Conservative and Liberal caucuses tend to be oriented quite clearly toward the Republican and Democratic-Farmer-Labor parties, respectively.

Conservative caucus) and Democratic Governor Carl F. Rolvaag whose trump card was the veto power. Confusingly, one of the ploys on the governor's side was his appointment of a commission picked by him from members of both parties which filed a report early in 1965, a month after the federal district court [39] had ordered reapportionment of both houses of the Minnesota legislature. Although functionally the Commission was the governor's partisan commission, it assumed the title of "Governor's Bipartisan Reapportionment Commission." Although no one on the inside was fooled, the title may have caused confusion among the public both inside and outside Minnesota.[40]

One area of reapportionment disagreement concerned the necessary transfer of seats from rural to suburban-urban areas to comply with the new "one man-one vote" standard. The DFL hoped to have each party lose *equally*, though they were the minority party by a 2 to 1 margin in the legislature. The Conservatives wanted *proportional* transfer or loss on a 2 to 1 basis, in accord with the then-existing balance between Conservatives and Liberals in the legislature. Another area of disagreement concerned the desire of the Conservatives to retain the practice of at-large election in two-man house districts in urban areas, and the practice of single-member house districts in rural areas. The DFL, being the minority party in legislative politics, preferred a general use of single-member districts.

In May 1965 a Conservative caucus (essentially Republican) apportionment plan was blocked by exercise of the governor's veto power and again in early May 1966. In the meantime the federal district court had modified its order to permit more time for legislative action.[41] In the one year interval between vetoes the press had been filled with charges and countercharges of gerrymander and bad faith. Behind the scenes there had been computer runs and endless calculation of political profiles under various alternative plans. By the time the second veto occurred, with little time remaining to comply with the court's order to reapportion before the November 1966 election, all parties were so thoroughly familiar with each other's positions that it was possible to reach agreement on a final compromise measure within two weeks.[42]

The "realistic" rather than mathematical character of the concessions extracted by the governor as a condition of signing the revised reapportionment measure are indicated by the fact that the vetoed measure was

39. Honsey v. Donovan, 236 F. Supp. 8 (D. Minn. 1964).
40. "Report of the Governor's Bipartisan Reapportionment Commission, January 15, 1965," 49 *Minn. L. Rev.* 367 (1964).
41. Honsey v. Donovan, 249 F. Supp. 987 (D. Minn. 1966).
42. *Washington Post*, May 12, 1966, p. A7, col. 5; May 22, 1966, p. A5, col. 1.

somewhat tighter mathematically than the revised measure eventually signed. Under the vetoed measure only one senate seat and three house seats exceeded a 13 percent deviation from average and the electoral percentages for the senate and house, respectively, were 48.35 percent and 47.23 percent. By contrast, in the measure eventually signed, one senate district and four house districts exceeded a 15 percent deviation from average and the senate and house electoral percentages, respectively, were 48.11 percent and 47.22 percent.

Although each side claimed victory, each side probably viewed the measure as being as "fair" an apportionment as could be devised, and certainly far more fair than would have been devised had Minnesota government been unified under the control of either party. The final plan retained some multimember districts but contained concessions in certain areas insisted on by Governor Rolvaag.

3. NEW YORK'S "BIPARTISAN" APPORTIONMENT BY AD HOC JUDICIAL COMMISSION

Although New York was included in the "big six" reapportionment cases decided by the Supreme Court in June 1964 it was not until the spring of 1966 that New York at last accomplished a "permanent" reapportionment. It was a more or less bipartisan apportionment worked out by the device of an ad hoc Judicial Commission on Apportionment appointed by the state's highest court, thus bringing to a close one of the longer and more complicated "state apportionment stories" in the nation. New York's role in the "big six" apportionment cases has already been summarized. Gerrymandering aspects of New York's state legislative apportionment and congressional districting are analyzed in Chapter XVIII dealing with continuing apportionment issues. Beginning in 1965, New York has had more local apportionment litigation by far than any other state in the nation; highlights, including New York's experimentation with weighted voting for local legislatures, are summarized in Chapter XIX.

In this chapter the focus is confined to those highlights of New York's post-1964 developments which illustrate two facets of reapportionment method: (1) the attempt of legislators to "talk" to the court on the question of standards; (2) the bipartisan struggle to avoid partisan dominance of the reapportionment process. On this latter issue the New York story stands in sharp contrast to that of the current second largest state, California. There a Democratic legislature and a Democratic governor were not effectively restrained from partisan exercise of apportionment power.

In the immediate flurry of activity in New York in the summer of 1964 immediately after the United States Supreme Court's nullification of the New York apportionment in *WMCA, Inc.* v. *Lomenzo* [43] the strategy of the Republicans, who controlled the governorship and both houses, and who at this point were not fearful of the November 1964 election, was to seek delay so that reapportionment could be handled in "orderly" fashion in early 1965. The strategy of the Democrats, who wished to taste some of the fruits of the victory they had seemingly won in the Court's "one man-one vote" decision, was to press in federal district court for an immediate reapportionment—even suggesting immediate adoption of a weighted voting system, i.e., weighting legislators' votes by the population of the district represented.[44] Concurrently in early July, Governor Nelson A. Rockefeller appointed a Citizens' Committee on Reapportionment. Under the chairmanship of Dean William Hughes Mulligan of the Fordham University Law School the Committee was to file a report after the November 1964 election on methodology and standards for a new apportionment system.

The federal district court set up a timetable calling for reapportionment by the spring of 1965 but allowed use of the old districts for the November 1964 elections for one-year terms. However, Republicans in New York as elsewhere discovered that, with a Barry Goldwater loose in the political thicket,

> The best laid schemes o'mice and men
> Gang aft a'gley;
> An' lea'e us nought but grief and pain,
> For promis'd joy.[45]

In the November elections in the unconstitutional districts the Democrats—even without any reapportionment—demonstrated that the New York legislature, which many-termed Democratic Governor Alfred E. Smith had said was "constitutionally Republican," turned out to be not even "unconstitutionally Republican" under *some* conditions. Democrats captured both houses of the legislature (the governorship was not at stake and Governor Rockefeller continued in office until 1966 when he won re-election for a third four-year term).

The position of the parties reversed almost as soon as the last ballot was counted. Democrats now pressed to defer any action on reapportionment until convening of the new Democratic-controlled legislature in January 1965. Republicans proceeded to call a special lame-duck session of

43. 377 U.S. 633 (1964).
44. Notice of Proposed Order of Plaintiff, WMCA v. Lomenzo (Appendix A) (July 24, 1964). Brief in Support of Defendants, WMCA v. Lomenzo (Appendix A) (July 27, 1964).
45. Robert Burns, "To A Mouse," stanza 7.

the legislature to receive the report of the Governor's Citizens' Committee on Reapportionment, which reported on December 1, and to accomplish a speedy reapportionment while New York still had a party-unified government. The legislature, however, was immediately plunged into deep uncertainty by the vagueness of the United States Supreme Court's "substantial equality" standard for legislative reapportionment. In this regard the New York legislature shared the uncertainty of reapportioners generally, including lower courts throughout the land. But the stakes were higher in New York. The temporary Republican legislature could not rely on the "ping pong" process of legislative offer and judicial response, which was used in other states to gradually define the scope of legislative discretion which could co-exist with a "one man-one vote" principle. If the legislature's December 1964 apportionment failed to survive judicial scrutiny the legislature as an institution might well get a second chance to apportion, but the Democrats would control that chance, subject of course to the condition of negotiating with a Republican governor.

a. *"Talking" to the Court Through Enactment of Alternative Plans*

The partisanship surrounding this sequence of events obscured for the press, and therefore for the country, the wisdom of the special tactic chosen by the legislature to cope with this situation. Partisan matters aside, it is a tactic of general applicability and is the only way to preserve the maximum number of apportionment options while attempting to refine vague federal apportionment standards through the awkward process of conventional adjudication. The tactic was simply this: the legislature proceeded to enact not one reapportionment plan but four plans—A, B, C, and D.[46]

The Four Plans. Plan D was nearest the legislature's desire. It would have had the least impact on New York's traditional alignments even though on mathematical grounds it was tighter by far than many apportionments approved by lower courts in other states in the post-*Reynolds* period. For the senate the electoral percentage was 49.4 percent and the maximum deviation from average district size was 8 percent; for the house the electoral percentage was 48.6 percent and the maximum deviation from average district size was 19.1 percent. Distinctive features of this plan were use of the 1962 popular vote for governor as the apportionment base, and use of a fractional vote system in the lower house for some

46. Report of the Joint Legislative Committee on Reapportionment, Leg. Doc. No. 76 (December 15, 1964). For a summarization of the salient statistics of the four plans, see Supplemental Report of the Joint Legislative Committee on Reapportionment, Leg. Doc. No. 76-A (December 30, 1964).

352   DEMOCRATIC REPRESENTATION

districts. The purpose of fractional voting was to preserve a separate *voice* (but not a whole *vote*) for all counties except two. Fractional votes ranged from one-sixth to three-quarters. Use of 1962 voter population as the apportionment base in this plan had the effect, of course, of rewarding politically active high-voting areas at the expense of areas such as Harlem, where a combination of controlled machine politics and Negro apathy reduced voter turnout.

Plan B was also based on 1962 voter population but did not use fractional voting. Its electoral percentages for the senate and lower house were 49.4 percent and 48.9 percent respectively, and the maximum percentage deviation was 13 percent.

Plans C and A were both based on 1960 citizen population. They had the same senate apportionment, producing an electoral percentage of 49.4 percent and a maximum deviation from average district size of 7.9 percent. For the lower house Plan C unlike Plan A utilized fractional voting, with the result that for Plan C the electoral percentage was 48 percent and the most deviant district was 24 percent from average size. In Plan A the electoral percentage was 49.3 percent and the most deviant district was 10.8 percent from average size district.

Evaluating the Tactic. The press had a field day with this new Republican version of alphabet soup, *The Reporter* magazine (in what actually was one of the more responsible interpretative stories) titling an article "A+B+C+D=N.Y.?" [47] As a journalistic ploy such coverage was understandable. But singling out this feature of New York's reapportionment struggle for humorous emphasis contributed little to understanding the reapportionment game and the difficulty of playing the game with no better ground rules from the Supreme Court than "substantial equality" and the accompanying puzzling caveats in the opinions of Chief Justice Warren. Laying aside the political ethics of lame-duck apportionment, and the imbalance that always surrounds reapportionment by party-unified state government, this New York tactic was one of the more imaginative used in the post-*Reynolds* period. It was copied on a smaller scale in some other states where legislatures enacted more than one plan and hopefully indicated their 'druthers. [48]

Tactically, given an uncertain constitutional standard and a time-restricted legislative session, and given also the functional impossibility of true legislative "conversations" with the judges, the New York tactic actually enhances the prospect for rationality in the apportionment process. It is applicable in any area with emergent but only vaguely articulated con-

47. *The Reporter* magazine, Dec. 2, 1965, p. 32.
48. See, e.g., Hughes v. Maryland Committee for Fair Representation, 217 A.2d 273, 275 (1966); Stout v. Bottorf, 249 F. Supp. 488 (S.D. Ind. 1965).

stitutional standards. It is the only way the legislature can experiment a bit. More importantly, it also is the only way within the conventional process of adjudication in which a court itself can be given a basis for reflection and choice on the content of the "substantial equality" standard in the setting of a particular state. It is the only way in which there can be an exploration of the various ways to juxtapose mathematical "equality" (inside some assumed outer boundary of federal constitutionality such as 5, 10, or 15 percent) and achievement of other representation goals touched on in the reapportionment opinions of Chief Justice Warren.

b. Ping Pong Litigation

Throughout 1965 in New York reapportionment events tumbled one after another in bewildering profusion. Actors in the drama included both federal and state courts in New York, the United States Supreme Court, party leaders, and various citizen groups. In late January 1965 a three-judge federal district court panel, with Circuit Judge Sterry R. Waterman presiding, nullified all plans which used fractional voting or which based apportionment on 1962 voter population, leaving Plan A as the sole surviving plan.[49]

The inconsistency of the court's ruling, which was based on the proposition that "Reynolds v. Sims concerned arithmetic and not geometry,"[50] is explored in Chapter XVIII on continuing reapportionment issues. The quoted touchstone from Judge Waterman's opinion—"arithmetic," not "geometry"—could explain the court's feeling that certain gerrymandering complaints of the challengers raised nonarithmetic issues and hence lay outside the assumed Reynolds principle. But such a focus would not explain the court's use of nonarithmetic considerations to rule against fractional voting on the ground that "voting . . . [is not] . . . the only important function of a legislator."[51] Whatever one may think of fractional voting on functional grounds, under the standards of Reynolds v. Sims it is one way of equalizing with mathematical precision the weight of various districts in final legislative votes.

A month and a half later in March, surviving Plan A was nullified by a lower state court.[52] The single judge, Justice Matthew M. Levy, discussed gerrymandering issues at some length but rested his ruling on the narrow ground that the state constitutional clause fixing the size of the lower house at 150 had survived the United States Supreme Court's

---

49. WMCA v. Lomenzo, 238 F. Supp. 916 (S.D. N.Y. 1965).
50. Id. at 926.
51. Id. at 923.
52. In re Orans Petition, 257 N.Y.S.2d 839 (Sup. Ct. 1965).

"one man-one vote" ruling. Hence Plan A was "unconstitutional as a matter of law" [53] under this surviving section of the state constitution because it created a 165-member lower house. New York's highest court, the Court of Appeals, affirmed a month later, finding it unnecessary to reach the gerrymandering claims.[54] The stage was now set—with the aid of reapportionment fumbling and deadlock within the Democratic-controlled legislature itself—for sharply worded federal-state court conflict.

When the Democratic legislature failed to produce a timely alternative by the court-imposed May 5 deadline the federal district court in May 1965 again approved Plan A as the basis for a special legislative election in November.[55] Republicans were joyous. The *New York Times* reported that some Democratic members of the lower house—primarily Reform Democrats, Negroes, and Puerto Ricans—were privately pleased because their chances would be better under the district lines of Republican Plan A than under the plan which Democratic leaders had been trying to enact before the deadline expired. According to the *Times*:

> One Democrat who was happy about the court decision said smiling: "The leaders were too slick; they outsmarted themselves. They didn't please anybody—they didn't please our party, they didn't please the court, they didn't help themselves. I'm rather amused by it." [56]

The federal court's order contemplated creating an interim reapportioned legislature, with terms restricted to one year, whose mission would be to prepare a plan consistent with both federal and state Constitutions as the basis for a further legislative election in November 1966 under a "permanent" reapportionment plan. Dissenting Judge Richard J. Levet would have preferred a temporary conversion to weighted voting under the pre-existing reapportionment system rather than a special election to create a one-year legislature under Plan A, but his view did not prevail.

53. *Id.* at 875.

Justice Levy's opinion had something of the quality of Chief Justice John Marshall's famous "political opinion" in Marbury v. Madison. There Marshall, despite a finding of lack of jurisdiction in the Supreme Court as the actual basis for dismissing the case, nevertheless in a long dictum discussed the merits of the case and castigated President Thomas Jefferson's refusal to give Marbury the commission to which he was by law "entitled." Similarly, Justice Levy, although voiding Plan A on a technical state law ground, extensively discussed plaintiff's gerrymandering claims and indicated they had made a prima facie case for a factual hearing on their claims, were it not for the declaration of unconstitutionality as a matter of law on the question of change in the size of the lower house. See my arguments for recognizing political gerrymandering as a vital and justiciable issue and allocating the burden of proof to the defenders of a reapportionment plan in Ch. XVIII.

54. *In re* Orans, 258 N.Y.S.2d 825 (1965).

55. WMCA v. Lomenzo, 246 F. Supp. 953, 956 (S.D. N.Y. 1965).

56. *New York Times*, May 11, 1965, p. 1, cols. 6–7.

R. Peter Straus, a Reform Democrat and president of radio station WMCA, and his attorney, Leonard Sands, who had played a major role in directing the New York reapportionment litigation since 1962, were willing to accept the federal district court's order. This was so even though the order clearly opened the prospect that the Republicans in the forthcoming special election, no longer burdened with the Goldwater presidential candidacy, would recapture control of the state senate but probably not the lower house. At this point the Democratic legislative leaders and their attorney, former Federal District Judge Simon H. Rifkind, presumably not wholly uninfluenced by such political calculations, were allowed to intervene. They sought a stay of the order for a special election under Plan A from Justice Harlan who had jurisdiction over such matters from the Second Judicial Circuit. After a hearing in which suspension of the federal district court's order was opposed both by the state and by Mr. Straus,[57] Justice Harlan referred the matter to the full Bench.

Courts in Conflict. The United States Supreme Court, acting on Justice Harlan's referral, on June 1 denied a stay of enforcement of the federal district court's order, and also a motion to accelerate the appeal on the substantive issues.[58] Justice Harlan dissented sharply from both denials on the ground that these matters deserved "plenary consideration and reasoned explication" because they "bristle with difficult and important questions that touch the nerve centers of the sound operation of our federal and state judicial and political systems." He correctly noted that denial of a stay on the eve of a court-ordered election—other examples being denials of stays by Justices Black and White in similar circumstances in Alabama and Oklahoma in 1962 and 1964 respectively—makes an appeal on the substantive issues virtually moot and thus denies effective appellate review:

> By denying a stay and refusing to accelerate this appeal, the Court, instead, has in effect decided them not only summarily but also *sub silentio.* For while the denial of a stay does not technically moot the appeal, it is manifest that such is the practical effect of the Court's

57. *New York Times*, May 28, 1965, p. 1, col. 8, p. 18, col. 3; June 2, 1965, p. 1, col. 8, p. 35, cols. 5–8.

After being allowed to intervene after the district court's reinstatement of Plan A the Democratic legislators in late May had first tried to get the district court to withdraw its Plan A election order. They wanted the court to adopt the interim weighted voting plan suggested by dissenting Judge Levet, which had since been passed by the Democratic legislature, and authorize further relief in the form of a bipartisan commission and a constitutional convention under two other last-minute legislature bills. Governor Rockefeller had vetoed all but the convention bill. The district court had held firm, resulting in the stay petition to Justice Harlan.

58. Travia v. Lomenzo, 381 U.S. 431 (1965).

action, since in normal course the appeal will not even be heard until after the presently ordered November election has taken place.[59]

Despite Justice Harlan's remonstrance the Court in the main has continued to play a very inactive role in the rapid developments impelled by *Reynolds* v. *Sims*. And this path has been adhered to despite the fact that many of the substantive issues of implementing "one man-one vote" are more thorny and intellectually challenging than the basic equal population premise on which *Reynolds* rests.

A few days after the United States Supreme Court denied a stay, New York's highest state court, the Court of Appeals, acted again. In a 4-3 vote on July 9 on a petition from a state senator and a law professor it enjoined state officials from proceeding to hold a special election under Plan A, Chief Judge Charles S. Desmond saying: "As we have not hesitated to do in the past . . . we must now perform our sworn duty by preventing the holding of an election that violates our state constitution." [60] He and his supporting majority cushioned the apparent conflict with the federal district court by finding or pretending to find no "final and binding orders" from the federal court that the state proceed to hold a special election under Plan A. However, three dissenting state justices saw no absence of finality in the federal district court's May order which the United States Supreme Court had let stand in June. Deploring their brethren's action as one which would serve "only to further compound a most unfortunate and confused situation," they said:

> The result of the decision now being made is that a court of one sovereign authority has directed the New York Secretary of State to prepare an election in 1965 and the court of another sovereign authority has prohibited him from doing just that.[61]

Four days later the federal district court, having read the opinions of the New York Court of Appeals "with great respect and no little concern," and with much surprise flatly stated that they had intended their May order to be final and binding.[62]

Persisting still, the Democratic legislative leaders then went again to Justice Harlan seeking a stay of the election order, which was denied three

59. *Id.* at 434–35.
60. Glinski v. Lomenzo, 209 N.E.2d 277 (1965).
    The order resulted from a new petition filed by Frank J. Glinsky, referred to by the *New York Times* (July 12, 1965, p. 12, col. 4) as a "relatively obscure state senator," and Robert B. Fleming, a professor of law at the State University of New York at Buffalo.
61. *Id.* at 279.
62. WMCA v. Lomenzo, 246 F. Supp. 953, 954 (S.D. N.Y. 1965).

days later. Because the Supreme Court had concluded its term, Justice Harlan could not refer the matter to the full Bench as he had done with the application a few weeks earlier. And he felt that the stay which the full Bench had already denied on June 1 covered the new situation, so that it would be inappropriate to ask the Chief Justice to convene the Court in special session. Justice Harlan felt bound by the June 1 denial, even though he had himself dissented from it, on the ground that the substantive issues should be resolved before the eggs were again scrambled in a new election. He again called on his brethren "to act in a sensitive and not heavy-handed manner in this novel and delicate constitutional field." [63] However, when the Supreme Court reconvened in October 1965 on the eve of the special "Plan A" legislative election for one-year terms it simply approved Justice Harlan's denial of this second stay petition.[64] In the meantime a lower state court in August 1965 had fixed February 1, 1966, as the final deadline for the reapportionment by legislative action, a ruling affirmed by an intermediate appellate state court in December.[65]

c. Final Deadlock and Resolution

In the November 1965 election Plan A produced a divided legislature, Democrats retaining control of the lower house and the Republicans recapturing the senate. The stage was thus set for deadlock and consequent bipartisan negotiation on reapportionment issues. Of course, such a bipartisan negotiation conceivably could have occurred between the Democratic legislature and the Republican governor in the spring of 1965. But then the Democrats were unable to get their own legislative house in order, and attention still was focused too much on jockeying for position in the federal and state courts.

The divided legislature impelled by further court pressure worked through a number of cliff-hanging near agreements early in 1966. But the court-fixed deadline of February 1, 1966, even though extended for three additional weeks of feverish activity, expired with no agreed reapportionment plan. Each party, however, had developed rather refined reapportionment plans, issues had become clear, and negotiating points had become highlighted. A primary Democratic plan, also called the "professors' plan," was one prepared for the Democrats by a six-man advisory council, all from New York City, which included three political science professors. Although they had started with high hopes, an announced blindness to political data, and a computer, the end product was hand-drawn. The

63. Travia v. Lomenzo, 381 U.S. 431, 435 (1965).
64. 382 U.S. 4 (1965).
65. Orans v. Village Independent Democrats, 262 N.Y.S.2d 893 (1965), aff'd, 265 N.Y.S.2d 49 (1965).

computer did such things as draw districts straight across Manhattan, paying no attention to Central Park.[66]

The Special Judicial Commission. At this point the New York Court of Appeals adopted the device of a special Judicial Commission to accomplish what was widely regarded as a bipartisan apportionment of the state although not labeled expressly as such. The Judicial Commission was composed of two Republicans, two Democrats, and one "neutral." The members were a former Republican state party chairman, the Democratic associate counsel of the Joint Legislative Committee on Reapportionment, two former Court of Appeals judges one a Democrat and the other a Republican, and the president-elect of the American Bar Association.[67] The Commission had access to all the records and staff work of the Joint Legislative Committee on Reapportionment. Consistent with its understanding of the outer boundaries fixed by federal mathematical standards, and the state Court of Appeals' direction to preserve counties as apportionment units insofar as possible, the Commission proceeded to work out a compromise between the Republican plan and the Democratic plan. The Commission's task in the critical area of subdistricting was considerably eased by bipartisan compromises in several counties submitted to it by the local Republican and Democratic organizations.

Under the final reapportionment plan as submitted by the Judicial Commission, and accepted by the Court of Appeals in March 1966 after denying all requests for alteration except one technical one,[68] the maximum deviations from average of the senate districts were from +9.40 percent to −6.24 percent and of the house districts from +8.84 percent to −10.31 percent. For the senate and house the electoral percentages were respectively 49.08 percent and 49.19 percent and the population variance ratios were 1.17 to 1 and 1.21 to 1.

Although both the political parties and the press deemed the court-approved Commission plan to be fair, and Democratic Assembly Speaker

66. *New York Times*, Dec. 27, 1965, p. 1, col. 3. Members of the advisory council were Associate Dean Robert B. McKay of New York University Law School, William J. D. Boyd, senior associate of the National Municipal League, Arthur M. Grant, Manhattan lawyer, and the following political science professors: Arthur W. MacMahon (retired), Columbia University; Harvey C. Mansfield, Columbia University; Ralph A. Straetz, New York University.

67. Listed in the order identified in the text they were Edwin F. Jaeckle, Robert D. Brady, former Court of Appeals Judges Bruce Bromley and Charles W. Froessel, and Orison S. Marden. Of Mr. Marden, the crucial fifth man who also was a former president of the New York state and city bar associations, the *New York Times* said: "A minimal financial contributor to both major parties, he is said by intimates to shun political discussion" (February 24, 1966, p. 25, col. 1).

See also, "Report of Judicial Commission," filed March 14, 1966, with Court of Appeals; and Calvin B. T. Lee, *One Man, One Vote* (New York: Scribner's, 1967).

68. *In re* Orans, 17 N.Y. 2d 721, 269 N.Y.S. 2d 671, 216 N.E. 2d 311 (1966).

Anthony J. Travia attempted to have the lower house approve it to put it on a firmer foundation, there was some dissatisfaction among some factional elements, particularly on the Democratic side.[69] The November 1966 election under the Judicial Commission reapportionment plan, as had been predicted, continued the party division in the legislature. Republicans and Democrats, respectively captured majorities in the senate and house. With 51 percent of the statewide senate vote Republicans gained 54.4 percent of the senate and with 51 percent of the statewide assembly vote Democrats gained 52.7 percent of the assembly. Concurrently Republicans re-elected Governor Rockefeller by a large margin to a third four-year term, but lost in the important battle to elect a majority of the 1967 state constitutional convention which would deal further with reapportionment.

Functionally it might appear that there is little difference between this unofficial bipartisan apportionment of New York, and the bipartisan commission and tie breaker approach specified in New Jersey's 1966 Constitution as discussed above. In each case there is a commission evenly divided between the two political parties with an additional member appointed by the state's highest court to serve as a tie breaker. Such differences as stem from the fact that in New York the entire Court of Appeals had to appoint the entire Judicial Commission, whereas in New Jersey the judicial hand is confined to the appointment of a tie breaker only by the Chief Justice of the state supreme court acting alone, do not seem to have major impact on the end result. But there is an obvious advantage in having a *regularized* process for bipartisan reapportionment with a guarantee of a tie breaker, if necessary, as under the New Jersey system. New York probably could have achieved reapportionment at least a year earlier had the state constitution already contained a bipartisan commission–tie breaker system on the New Jersey model.

There may be some grounds for difference of view on such secondary issues as whether the crucial appointment of the tie breaker should be made by all the members of the state's highest court, as was the case in New York's ad hoc approach, or by the court's Chief Justice acting alone, as provided in New Jersey. Action by the full bench would provide protective coloration for all of the members. It would diffuse the unavoidably political onus of the task of appointing a tie breaker. On the other hand full bench action could serve to dramatize externally the political complexion of the entire bench and internally to exacerbate personal feelings

69. See *New York Times*, March 23, 1966, p. 1, col. 8; March 24, 1966, p. 38, col. 4; March 25, 1966, p. 36, col. 1; March 29, 1966, p. 27, col. 4. Most unrest centered in the Reform Democrats in New York City but they also disagreed among themselves.

among the justices. Just this danger seems to have occurred in the course of the Michigan Supreme Court's long bout with the reapportionment issue.

Reapportionment in the 1967 New York Constitutional Convention. Revision of the New York reapportionment revisions had top billing along with the church-state issue, in the New York Constitutional Convention of 1967. At the outset of the Democratic-controlled convention there was no agreement between the major parties on the appropriate method for state reapportionment. In a surprise maneuver in mid-convention both parties, the Republicans somewhat reluctantly, agreed on a bipartisan commission proposal patterned fairly closely after the new New Jersey bipartisan commission.[70]

The similarities and differences were as follows: (1) the New York bipartisan commission was to consist of five men at all times, unlike New Jersey's ten with an eleventh added as tie breaker if needed; (2) the four partisans on the New York commission were to be nonlegislators appointed by the majority and minority leaders of each legislative house, rather than by the state party chairmen as in New Jersey; (3) the fifth member (chairman and tie breaker) was to be appointed by the entire bench of the highest state court rather than by the chief judge alone.

In the New York convention proposal the state's dominant practice of single-member districting was continued. Additionally, population was to be as "equal as practicable"; pre-existing political subdivision boundaries and natural geographic boundaries were to be followed "wherever practicable"; city blocks were not to be divided; the hoary terms "contiguous and compact" were continued. Rather vacuously—or piously—the draft also said that "gerrymandering for any purpose is prohibited." However, this provision would make gerrymandering a justiciable state law issue, even if it were not deemed so under the *federal* equal protection clause (Chapter XVIII).

The convention rejected a last-minute effort by Governor Rockefeller to modify the commission formula. He wanted to create a role for the governor, and to enlarge the commission so that the legislative leaders would not appoint a majority (to avoid a "legislative cabal"). His proposal would have increased the commission to nine, the additional five being appointed either by the governor alone, or divided with the governor appointing two and the Court of Appeals appointing three.[71] Not to be lightly ignored is the role of the governor in reapportionment as a source of statewide viewpoint when a commission is to be constructed, and as a

70. Convention Proposal No. 1365-H, approved September 12, 1967. The bipartisan commission also was to perform the task of congressional redistricting.
71. *New York Times*, Sept. 13, 1967, p. 1, col. 7.

check on partisan gerrymandering through his veto power when the legislature apportions itself.[72]

Unfortunately all of the convention's work was for nought. The draft constitution was submitted to the voters with no provisions for voting separately on the major sections, and was wholly rejected in a nationally publicized referendum in November 1967 largely because of a church-state separation issue. The single vote requirement—insisted on by Anthony J. Travia, Democratic legislative leader and convention chairman, and strongly backed by Francis Cardinal Spellman—was designed to ensure acceptance of a draft constitution clause written to aid parochial schools by modifying the existing strict church-state separation clause.[73]

New York has yet to create a permanent apportionment system. It is worth noting however that at the outset and throughout the convention the leaders and delegates of the two major parties, with few exceptions, were in agreement in rejecting proposals for so-called "nonpartisan" commissions to handle the reapportionment function. One such proposal was put forth by a group called Committee on Constitutional Issues. It was co-chaired by R. Peter Straus, erstwhile Democratic activist, and Robert B. McKay, Associate Dean and subsequently Dean of the New York University Law School. Its releases were identified as "a public affairs service of Station WMCA." The Committee proposed that the nonpartisan commission be composed of individuals "such as the presidents of New York's universities, the deans of the state's major law schools, and the heads of New York's most significant bar associations." [74] A refined version of this proposal was introduced by Delegate Leonard B. Sand, who also was counsel to the Committee and chairman of the Convention Subcommittee on Apportionment. From a panel of 36 nominees (six university presidents each to nominate six persons not holding public or party office) the four majority and minority legislative leaders each would select one, and the four so selected would choose a fifth member who would also be commission chairman.[75]

Whatever the outcome of state constitutional revision in New York or elsewhere on the question of nonlegislative apportioning agencies, the present writer at several points has clearly indicated his rejection of a

72. In a minority report of the Convention's Committee on the Legislature (Aug. 1, 1967, p. 17) Mr. Sand pointed out that for 64 years in New York's recent history when one party controlled both legislative houses, the opposition party controlled the governorship during 23 years. In 1966–1967 in 16 of the 42 states in which one party controls both houses the opposition party holds the governorship.

73. For interpretative comments see New York Times, Oct. 1, 1967, p. 12, col. 2; Nov. 13, p. 46, col. 1. Fear of higher governmental costs apparently induced some negative votes too.

74. Committee on Constitutional Issues, Briefing Paper No. II, Feb. 20, 1967, p. 8.

75. Convention Proposal No. 452, introduced May 23, 1967.

quest for "nonpartisanship." All evidence suggests that true "nonpartisanship" in this area is an impossibility, that even if a "nonpartisan" body could be imagined its work would not be as satisfactory as the informed deliberations of a bipartisan commission plus tie breaker as authorized in the New Jersey state constitution. Suggestions for reapportionment by nonpartisan commission devices are delusive and ill-advised. Despite recurring popularity of nonpartisanship suggestions in the press [76] and among some academicians—groups which themselves are not known for nonpartisanship despite their widespread and deserved popular respect—nonpartisan politics is a contradiction in terms.

76. The *New York Times* has been on both sides of this issue, editorializing for bipartisanship shortly after the 1964 *Reapportionment Decisions* (June 29, 1964, p. 26, col. 1), and for a "nonpartisan" bevy of platonic "guardians" in 1967 (July 26, 1967, p. 34, col. 2; Oct. 16, p. 42, col. 2).

As Professor Richard Lehne has said: "No criteria . . . will be without political implications, but use of a non-partisan commission means that these implications will not be carefully evaluated." Paper on "Preliminary Report on the Impact of Reapportionment in New York," p. 8, National Municipal League annual meeting, Milwaukee, Nov. 14, 1967.

XIV

Implementing "One Man-One Vote": Some State Vignettes–III

"As the Senator from this county for the past two years, I have had great success with all the legislation which I have carried on behalf of Los Angeles County and the cities of this county. There was no group of 'willful rural Senators' determined to hold up legislation which would be important to the 6.7 million citizens of Los Angeles County."

Senator Thomas M. Rees, Sole Pre-Reapportionment
State Senator from Los Angeles County

"When the Governor feels a sneeze coming on, the legislature opens its mouth in anticipation."

Legislator Comment on Alaska's
Strong-Governor Constitution

D. Alternative Routes for Muddling Through on Reapportionment

1. SPECIAL AGENCIES, NEITHER BIPARTISAN NOR NONPARTISAN

A *Book of the States* tabulation compiled in 1963 indicated that eight states had removed the apportionment function completely from the legislature.[1] In three of the states—Arizona, Delaware, and Hawaii—the nominal nonlegislative apportionment provisions were either inoperative or wholly ineffective in the reapportionment revolution inspired by the *Baker-Reynolds* decisions.[2]

1. Alaska, Arizona, Arkansas, Delaware, Hawaii, Michigan, Missouri, Ohio. See *The Book of the States, 1964–1965* (Chicago: Council of State Governments, 1964), pp. 62–66. This is the last volume in which this material appears.

The descriptions in the following two footnotes are based on the summaries in *The Book of the States.*

2. *Arizona:* the Secretary of State apportions seats among the counties and the county boards of supervisors then apportion this allocation within the county.

Delaware: The apportionment is accomplished by an Apportionment Commission

Michigan and Missouri are the only states in the list of eight which operate with bipartisan commissions. As already discussed, the Michigan system lacks a provision for an informed tie breaker, and the Missouri system has avoided deadlock only by virtue of the questionable bipartisan character of the so-called bipartisan commission. As a byproduct of the reapportionment revolution, however, New Jersey in 1966 created what may be taken to be the prototype for bipartisan commission operations in the future.

There remain three states—Ohio, Arkansas, and Alaska—whose provisions merit brief description. All are examples of nonlegislative apportionment provisions which normally would operate to vest apportionment power in a partisan body. An additional list of eight states providing a backstop in event of legislative failure does not merit extensive elaboration because none of the provisions played a major role in the reapportionment revolution of the 'sixties with the exception, already noted, of attempted use in Illinois of a bipartisan commission without tie breaker and in Washington of the initiative.[3]

a. Ohio: Partisan Apportionment Board in a Two-Party State

The more interesting major aspects of Ohio's reapportionment story center on a dispute on districting policies between the political parties and inside each political party. The dispute concerned the alleged gerrymander effect both racial and political which could flow from continuance of Ohio's multimember districting in the large counties, especially the coun-

consisting of the Governor, Senate Majority and Minority Leaders, the President of the University of Delaware, and the President of the Farmers Bank of the state of Delaware.

Hawaii: The Governor apportions the state.

3. *California:* After legislative failure, a reapportionment commission consisting of the Lieutenant Governor, Controller, Attorney General, Secretary of State, and Superintendent of Public Instruction. In either case, the apportionment is subject to referendum.

Illinois: After legislative failure, a reapportionment commission appointed by the Governor.

Maine: After legislative failure, the supreme judicial court.

North Dakota: After legislative failure, a special board consisting of the Chief Justice of the state supreme court, Attorney General, Secretary of State, and the Majority and Minority Leaders of the House. This body may apportion the House only.

Oregon: After legislative failure, the Secretary of State. In either case, the apportionment is expressly subject to review by the state supreme court. See Ch. V, n. 46.

South Dakota: After legislative failure, a board consisting of the Governor, Superintendent of Public Instruction, Presiding Judge of the supreme court, Attorney General, and Secretary of State.

Texas: After legislative failure, a Legislative Redistricting Board consisting of the Lieutenant Governor, Speaker of the House, Attorney General, Comptroller of Public Accounts, and the Commissioner of the General Land Office.

Washington: After legislative failure, apportionment may be had through an initiative.

ties containing Cleveland and Columbus. Elements of both parties, and particularly the Republican party, wanted to convert to a uniform single-member district system. These matters are reserved for the reapportionment issues discussed in Chapters XVIII and XIX.

Procedurally, however, Ohio did achieve an interim reapportionment in 1965 by virtue of the operation of a constitutionally named ex-officio reapportionment commission consisting of governor, auditor, and secretary of state. Operation of the commission not only removed the onus of reapportionment from the judiciary but also "saved" the Republican party from the possible perils of a court-created reapportionment because all three of these offices were held at the time by Republicans.

Ohio's case was one of those remanded in June of 1964 as an aftermath of the "big six" *Reapportionment Decisions*, the Supreme Court reversing the federal district court, which in 1963 had upheld Ohio's apportionment as a permissible example of a "federal plan." [4] When the matter returned to the lower court it deferred further action until after the November 1964 election to give the Ohio legislature opportunity to submit a proposed constitutional amendment on reapportionment or take other appropriate action. Because the Democrats gained a tie in the senate in the November election with the aid of the Goldwater presidential candidacy while the Republicans retained control of the lower house by a reduced majority, Republican Governor James A. Rhodes called a special session immediately after the election. This lame-duck and still Republican-controlled session proposed a constitutional amendment on reapportionment.[5]

The Republican-proposed amendment would have modified Ohio's system of county-at-large election of members of the lower house by providing that in counties containing more than one congressional district the state lower house members should run at-large in the congressional district rather than in the county as a whole. The measure was supported by both Negro members of the lower house.[6] Generally, urban Democrats and organized labor viewed this modified subdistricting provision as a threat to Democratic dominance of the 17-member Cuyahoga (Cleveland) delegation. They had a general opposition to any departure from the winner-take-all custom, and were additionally concerned because the congres-

---

4. Nolan v. Rhodes, 218 F. Supp. 953 (S.D. Ohio 1963), *rev'd per curiam*, 378 U.S. 556 (1964).
5. "Representation and Reapportionment," Political Studies Number 2 (Myron Q. Hale, Project Director, Department of Political Science, Ohio State University, March 1965), 58–59, and n. 7.
6. One was David D. Albritton (R) of Dayton. The other was Carl B. Stokes (D) of Cleveland, who failed by only 2143 votes to be elected mayor of Cleveland in 1965. He became mayor in 1967.

sional districts themselves were viewed as gerrymandered to favor the Republicans. This subdistricting provision, even though falling far short of a single-member district requirement, became a dominant issue in the ratification campaign and the constitutional amendment was defeated in May 1965.[7] From the standpoint of representation theory a far sounder tactic for the minority party in a state such as Ohio would be to seek a statewide cumulative voting system, as used in Illinois, rather than to attempt to counterbalance its defeats in small town, rural, single-member districts with a winner-take-all windfall in a few urban centers.

After defeat of the constitutional amendment, Ohio's divided government—divided to the extent that the Democrats held a 16 to 16 tie in the senate—fumbled unsuccessfully with the reapportionment issue through the summer months while various parties planned additional court action. When the legislature adjourned without taking further action on reapportionment, the federal district court in September ordered parties to submit plans for reapportionment of both houses to it by mid-October 1965.

At this point the ex-officio Apportioning Board named in the state constitution and consisting of the governor, auditor, and secretary of state (all Republicans) undertook to submit an apportionment plan to the court on the theory that the Board had survived judicial invalidation of other parts of Ohio's constitutional formulae for apportionment. Arguing that only a system of single-member districts would be safe from subsequent federal constitutional attack, and that such districts would provide the most adequate representation to the citizens of Ohio, the Apportioning Board's plan subdistricted almost every multimember county into single-member districts. Because each senate district contained three house districts, the plan would have been readily adaptable to conversion to the Illinois system of cumulative voting for the lower house. Such an arrangement would have better ensured minority representation than use of single-member districts, even though the use of single-member districts would avoid the previous winner-take-all result of Ohio's traditional use of multimember districts.

Noting that no district under the Apportioning Board's plan deviated from average district size by more than 15 percent, the federal district court expressly took note of the "official" source of the plan, stated that "any action taken by a properly constituted governmental agency is entitled to a presumption of validity," and put the plan into effect on a temporary basis.[8] The issue of whether the Apportioning Board had acted in accor-

7. *Washington Post*, May 5, 1965, p. A3, col. 5; May 9, 1965, p. A5, col. 1. See also *New York Times*, May 2, 1965, p. 57, col. 1.
8. 251 F. Supp. 584, 587 (S.D. Ohio 1965).

dance with its intended role under the Ohio constitution was left for resolution in state court litigation. The court further provided that in event of invalidation under state law the plan of the Apportioning Board still would continue in effect for the 1966 election until replaced by some other lawful plan. The United States Supreme Court without opinion affirmed the lower court's action early in 1966.[9]

In the ensuing November 1966 election the general Republican electoral tide, and the new single-member districts, produced Republican house and senate majorities of 62 to 37 and 23 to 10. Negro representation increased significantly, from 2 to 9 in the house (even though house size was cut from 137 to 99), and from 0 to 3 in the senate. Interestingly these gains produced the same percentage of Negro legislators—10 percent—as the Negro percentage of Ohio's total population.

Defeat of Bipartisanship. Ohio thus did achieve a fairly speedy, albeit temporary, reapportionment by virtue of a nonlegislative agency which was in composition a partisan agency. In sharp contrast to the bipartisan outcome in such states as Washington and New York, the existence of a partisan apportioning board as a backstop for the divided legislature *prevented* the achievement of a bipartisan apportionment in Ohio under court pressure or supervision. Further, the partisan agency also made a dramatic change in Ohio's traditional apportionment pattern, shifting from a mixed multimember system to single-member districts. Whatever the merits of use of single-member districts in this situation—and they do find strong support in representation theory—it is unlikely that the "Ohio method" of apportionment will commend itself to other states, or perhaps even to Ohio in the long run. Under this "method," as in vesting apportionment exclusively in the legislature itself, far too much depends on the fortuitous factor of which political party controls the apportioning machinery at the critical point when apportionment must be accomplished under federal constitutional mandate.

So long as Ohio's legislature, like New York's, was "constitutionally Republican" by virtue of the traditional apportionment formulae, the Apportioning Board did little more than administer a formula which would tend to produce a Republican legislature in any event. Now that this built-in bias toward Republican dominance in Ohio has been eroded by the federal "one man-one vote" principle, it would seem unlikely that either political party would continue to favor vesting broad discretion in such an ex-officio apportioning agency.[10] Democratic and organized labor

9. Nolan v. Rhodes, 383 U.S. 104 (1966).
10. In subsequent developments, Ohio voters in May 1967 rejected a new constitutional amendment. It would have continued single-member districts and enlarged the Apportionment Board (adding the attorney general and state treasurer), with a provision that if all five members of the Board were of the same party the treasurer should be

forces saw their May 1965 referendum defeat of the modified single-member district proposal become a Pyrrhic victory when the federal district court a few months later approved the Apportioning Board's proposal for a uniform single-member district system. On the other hand, Republicans may remember that the Democratic party in Ohio frequently has controlled the statewide offices which make up a majority of the Apportioning Board, thus raising the vision of a future "Democratic" apportionment by such a board.

b. *Arkansas: Partisan Apportionment Board in a One-Party State*

Strikingly similar to Ohio's initial post-*Reynolds* apportionment, but without the interesting backdrop of the two-party system, is Arkansas' post-*Reynolds* apportionment achieved by operation of its all-Democratic ex-officio Apportioning Board consisting of the governor, attorney general, and secretary of state. Because the apportionment plan was the work of an official agency, and because the mathematical aspects were within the mathematical rules of thumb then being used, the plan was approved promptly by both the federal district court and by the United States Supreme Court on appeal.[11] Because Arkansas is a one-party state (despite the unusual election in November 1966 of Winthrop Rockefeller as the state's first Republican governor) the appeal to the Supreme Court was not motivated by party conflict. Rather it stemmed from the unhappiness of some rural areas at being placed allegedly under the dominance of more populous areas, by virtue of the use of large multimember districts rather than single-member districts.

The Arkansas reapportionment system, like all systems resting on ex-officio boards, was essentially a device for a one-party state; or, as noted in the Ohio discussion, a state where the apportionment formulae effectively elevate one party to controlling position. Also despite the capture of the governorship by Winthrop Rockefeller in 1966 which, after the fact, gave Republicans one seat on the Apportioning Board, the Arkansas system does not seem to be a device to enhance the prospects of growth of a two-

replaced by the nominee of the other party for that post. See "Representation News," 56 *Nat. Civ. Rev.* 351 (1967).

Rejection of the amendment reportedly was caused not so much by dissatisfaction with its terms as by the fact that it was associated on the ballot with an unpopular proposal to authorize issuance of bonds for public improvements subject only to legislative veto.

Thereafter on June 30, 1967, the Ohio Supreme Court validated the 1965 Apportionment Board's reapportionment under the surviving parts of the Ohio constitution. State *ex rel.* King v. Rhodes, 11 Ohio St. 2d 95, 228 N.E. 2d 653 (1967). Agitation continued for a new constitutional provision for apportionment, and an amendment was ratified in November 1967. See Appendix A.

11. Yancey v. Faubus, 251 F. Supp. 998 (E.D. Ark. 1965), *aff'd per curiam*, 383 U.S. 271 (1966).

party system. To have influence through this vehicle it would be necessary for the minority party to win two of the three statewide offices which comprise the apportioning agency. Although there are no empirical studies of the matter, it may be suggested, however, that in one-party states like Arkansas one virtue of transferring the apportionment function from the legislature to a nonlegislative apportioning agency is to enhance the hand of the populous areas in the apportionment process. All three apportioners have statewide constituencies.

c. Alaska: Big Daddy Syndrome; All Power to the Governor

Analogous to the partisan apportioning agencies which accomplished post-*Reynolds* revision in Ohio and Arkansas, with the governor as the key figure, is the gubernatorial monopoly of reapportionment authority authorized by the constitution of America's newest state, Alaska. The governor derives his authority from a strong-governor constitution which, as one Alaskan newspaper editor once expressed it, "would make a saber tooth out of Dagwood Bumstead." [12] The system has led one Republican legislator to remark that "when the Governor feels a sneeze coming on, the legislature opens its mouth in anticipation." [13] Among other powers, the governor controls all state financial records without an independent audit, appoints the attorney general who in turn appoints the state district attorneys, and appoints judges at both trial and appellate levels. The governor also controls the size and area of lower house election districts.[14]

At the time of *Reynolds* v. *Sims*, Alaska had population disparities of 2.5 to 1 in the house and 19 to 1 in the senate. The governor, without judicial pressure, reapportioned the senate and thereby reduced population disparities to 1.56 to 1. The lower house was allowed to stand for the time being.

The Alaska Supreme Court upheld the governor's action, overruling a complaint that his action exceeded his authority under the state constitution.[15] The question arose because the governor has express reapportionment power only in regard to the lower house, where he may accept, reject, or modify plans submitted by a four-man advisory board. The Alaska Constitution provides for a "frozen" senate apportionment based on area, modifiable only by constitutional amendment. In endorsing the governor's creativity in proceeding to reapportion the senate anyway, the state supreme court indulged in a bit of psychiatric "what if" jurisprudence. What if the Alaska constitutional convention had had foreknowledge of

12. Murray Morgan, "The Most Powerful Governor in the U.S.A.," *Harper's Magazine* 98 (October 1965).
13. *Id.* at 98–99.
14. Alaska Const., Art. VI, Sec. 3.
15. Wade v. Nolan, 414 P.2d 698 (1966).

the United States Supreme Court's 1964 "one man-one vote" concept? Would the convention have given the governor the same periodic reapportionment power for the senate as for the house? The court answered the question in the affirmative, saying:

> . . . we have concluded that it is more reasonable and logical to imply that had the Convention been able to anticipate the need to reapportion the Senate on an interim or any other basis, it would have specifically given the Governor the same power to reapportion the Senate as it gave him to reapportion the House. . . .
>
> An enlightened construction of Article VI which permits realization of its fundamental purpose, that reapportionment not be dependent in any manner on legislative initiative and that effective means of enforcement be readily available to any voter, is that its remaining constitutional provisions provide the implied power in the Governor and the Reapportionment Board to reapportion the Senate on an interim basis. . . .[16]

Functionally viewed, there seems to be little distinction between accomplishing reapportionment by the device of a partisan commission in which the governor is the dominant figure, as in Ohio and Arkansas, and vesting exclusive power in the governor. None of these systems commend themselves to one concerned with maintaining bases for effective two-party competition as well as accomplishing a periodic apportionment.

2. GUIDELINES IN CALIFORNIA: PRECONDITION OF PROMPT LEGISLATIVE ACTION

California, unique as always, was the only major industrial state in which neither major party was an early and persistent backer of reapportionment litigation.[17] California was the true home of the "federal plan," with the lower house on a population basis (at least by the standards of the time), and the senate on a county equality basis with one minor exception. On several occasions in recent decades, the last being in 1961, California voters by referendum reaffirmed their preference for a federal plan apportionment.[18] Indeed, because of the huge and growing population concentration in southern California some persons viewed the federal plan as a

16. *Id.* at 698, 699.
17. Much of the material in this section is based on extensive author interviews with numerous legislators and other officials and observers in Sacramento in the spring of 1965, and on subsequent correspondence.
18. Charles M. Hardin, "Issues in Legislative Reapportionment," 27 *The Review of Politics* 147, 152–53 (1965). See also Don A. Allen, Sr., and Associates, *Legislative Sourcebook* (Sacramento: California State Assembly, 1965), Ch. 1 (hereafter cited as *Sourcebook*); Eugene C. Lee, "Senate Reapportionment—A Problem of Balance," *Public Affairs Report Bulletin*, University of California, Berkeley, August 1960.

precondition to California's continuation as a unified and more or less harmonious state. During the peak of the "one man-one vote" battle a bipartisan group of 25 northern California senators even introduced bills in the legislature to split the state into two states along the Tehachapi Mountains north of Los Angeles.[19]

The federal plan, of course, did yield for California one of the most "malapportioned" legislative houses in the nation. The California senate had a population variance ratio of 422.5 to 1 between Los Angeles County with 6,380,711 population and three "cow" counties with a combined population of 14,294 which were linked in one senatorial district. (This ratio was exceeded only in the town-based lower houses of Vermont and Connecticut with ratios respectively of 827.5 to 1 and 424.6 to 1.) But Californians liked the federal plan. Despite the malapportioned senate they prided themselves on having one of the most progressive, urban-affairs-conscious legislatures in the nation.

a. *Reapportionment in Slow Motion*

Reapportionment matters moved slowly in California and the state was represented neither in the "big six" reapportionment cases of June 1964 nor in the additional package of cases from nine states decided contemporaneously with short per curiam orders. Loose party alignments contributed to the blurring of reapportionment as a clear-cut partisan issue in California. The California senate tended to be dominated by rural senators, but in significant number their party allegiance was Democratic. The most instrumental issue in California politics year in and year out, on which so much else depended, was the position and power of Los Angeles. It was Democratic-dominated, not closely attuned to the northern Democrats either rural or urban, and adjacent to Republican or conservative-Democratic suburbs.

It is especially significant that the League of California Cities, serving as the spokesman for many California cities but not Los Angeles which is sui generis, defended the "federal plan" senate. It issued a statement designed to show that California municipal legislation tended to fare better in the "malapportioned" California senate than in the population-apportioned lower house. Supported by a summary of legislative sessions from 1933 to 1963 the statement said that "almost all bills which would infringe on the right of cities to control their own internal affairs originate in the Assembly," and are then "defeated in the Senate where there is a

19. In jest some suggested "Superior California" and "Disneyland" as names for the new states. See Karl A. Lamb, "One Man, One Vote: Previewing the Aftermath," paper delivered at annual meeting of National Municipal League, San Francisco, November 1964.

much greater recognition of the rights of city councils to control their own internal operations." The statement quoted approvingly this 1961 comment of the executive director of the League of California Cities:

> Both offensively and defensively the so-called rural Senate and its committees showed more understanding of and sympathy toward bills of interest to cities than did the urban Assembly. Contrary to popular belief this is not unusual. This year, more than ever before, the Assembly showed an alarming disregard for the principles of home rule and the needs of cities. This is not true of all Assemblymen nor is the outstanding Senate record true as to all Senators but it is a completely accurate statement as to a majority of the members of each house.[20]

The Democratic senator from Los Angeles County, Thomas M. Rees, himself had some kind words to say about the California federal plan and supported the so-called Dirksen amendment introduced by Senator Everett M. Dirksen, Illinois, designed to amend the federal Constitution to permit continuance of a federal plan by local option. By virtue of his status he possessed the largest office staff in Sacramento of any California legislator, and he prided himself on his capacity to represent Los Angeles County effectively in the legislature. Under a "one man-one vote" rearrangement he would face sharing his power with 14 or 15 other Los Angeles senators. After the Supreme Court's equal population ruling of June 1964 he issued the following statement:

> My own feeling is that the effect of the court's decision will not be too great, as in recent years Los Angeles County has fared well in both houses of the Legislature. One reason for this might be the better understanding in the Senate of problems existing in metropolitan areas such as rapid transit and air pollution.
>
> There is also the factor that with 31 Assemblymen from Los Angeles County, there was enough deterrent power in the Assembly to protect the interests of Los Angeles County in the Senate.
>
> As the Senator from this county for the past two years, I have had great success with all the legislation which I have carried on behalf of Los Angeles County and the cities of this county. There was no group of "willful rural Senators" determined to hold up legislation which

20. Statement entitled "The California Senate Record on Urban Legislation," submitted by League General Counsel Richard Carpenter to legislature shortly after the June 1964 *Reapportionment Decisions*.

Of course as one close observer of California politics has pointed out there may be a distinction between sympathy to the interests of cities as cities, and sympathy to urban interests and classes which live in cities, particularly the few large cities. Correspondence, 1964, with Acting Director Eugene C. Lee of the University of California Institute of Governmental Studies, Berkeley. And to further complicate the problem of analysis, the California senate was more heavily Democratic than the assembly in the immediate pre-reapportionment years.

would be important to the 6.7 million citizens of Los Angeles County.[21]

Similarly, Democratic Speaker of the Assembly Jesse M. Unruh, also from Los Angeles but perhaps with a potential statewide constituency in mind, tempered his approach to "one man-one vote" by pointing to the need to retain an adequate number of representatives, regardless of population, for large geographic areas which by their nature were difficult to represent.[22] Also Democratic Governor Edmund G. "Pat" Brown forthrightly favored the Dirksen amendment to permit continuance of a federal plan by local option.

Against this complicated backdrop of issues and forces, reapportionment litigation and legislative action to overhaul California's oft-approved "federal plan" apportionment system proceeded at a snail's pace, championed by no major political leader in the state of either party.[23] A persistent litigant but more as a solo performer than as a spokesman for a political interest was Phill Silver, Los Angeles attorney known for espousing "pro bono publico" type law suits. He was perhaps best known both inside and outside Los Angeles as the man who had attempted by law suit to block the conversion of Chavez Ravine to use by the transferred Brooklyn Dodgers. At one stage of the reapportionment activity when one of his several suits was cast in shadow by the fact that his own residence district was overrepresented, he intervened a relative to satisfy the procedural hurdle of lack of personal standing.[24] It was not until December 1964 that a court in California finally ruled that the California senate must be altered to comply with the Supreme Court's "one man-one vote" edict, fixing a deadline of July 1, 1965.[25] Some suits on lower

21. *Sacramento Bee,* June 23, 1964, p. 4, as summarized in *Sourcebook* 43.
22. *Los Angeles Times,* September 24, 1964, p. I-4, as summarized in *Sourcebook* 44.
23. For a study of the frequent lack of lines of clear partisanship in California politics see William Buchanan, *Legislative Partisanship: The Deviant Case of California* (Berkeley: University of California Press, 1963). He notes that from "Governor Warren's inauguration in 1943 through Speaker Lincoln's in 1955 was the period of purest non-partisanship outside the legislature;" inside the legislature, "competition for the speakership was not a contest between parties but a contest between bipartisan factions." *Id.* at 66.
24. The several "Silver" suits and the "standing" problem are noted in *Sourcebook* 40, 46, 57–58. See also the unsuccessful suits in the California state courts brought by Mayor Samuel W. Yorty of Los Angeles and dismissed without reaching the merits. One was dismissed because of naming the wrong party as defendant (Yorty v. Anderson, 384 P.2d 417 (Calif. 1963); another because a requested mandamus order to bar the November 1964 election apparently was thought to be too drastic (Yorty v. Jordan, Sac. No. 7543, review denied, 379 U.S. 8 (1964); still another because the legislature had not had time to react to *Reynolds* v. *Sims* (Yorty v. Jordan, Sac. No. 7582). They are discussed in *Sourcebook* 41 and 241 F. Supp. 576 (1965).
25. Silver v. Jordan, 241 F. Supp. 576 (1964), *aff'd* 381 U.S. 415 (June 1, 1965).

house apportionment were filed early in 1965 but remained inactive or were dismissed.[26]

b. "We'd Rather Fight than Switch"

The spring of 1965 did finally find the California legislature busily engaged in reapportionment activity. There was little friendship between the senate and the assembly even though both were Democratic-dominated. The rural Democratic senators who controlled the senate had much more in common with their Republican counterparts than with their fellow partisans from Los Angeles who played a dominant role in the assembly. In the reapportionment planning for the Los Angeles area, which presented the major problem, a not insignificant issue was the question of overlap between assembly districts and the several new senate districts which were to be constructed. Some assemblymen who had viewed themselves as natural heirs to the new senate seats wanted "noncoterminus" districts, fearing that otherwise the assembly districts would be political training grounds to groom challengers to run against the new senators.

To an observer from east of the Sierra Nevadas the truly strange aspect of reapportionment activity in the California legislature in the spring of 1965 was the fact that there seemed to be just as much activity—and certainly far more enthusiasm in some quarters—in the direction of averting reapportionment as in the direction of accomplishing it. This effort was the outgrowth of an unusual two-day strategy conference of the state senate in San Francisco in December 1964 to map both "battle and capitulation plans." Senator Stephen P. Teale, chairman of the senate reapportionment subcommittee, announced that the senators had agreed:

(1) To exhaust all possible remedies to allow us to keep the bicameral legislative system as we have known it.

(2) That the Senate must comply with court orders on reapportionment "without playing any games."

(3) That attorneys for the Senate should determine if they can appeal the federal court order. They were instructed to file an appeal if legally permissible.

(4) Finally, the Senate determined to press for a constitutional convention of the states, as well as for congressional action on a constitutional amendment to overturn the Supreme Court decision.[27]

Many members of both parties in the California senate threw themselves energetically into the battle in support of a federal reapportionment amendment. The "Dirksen amendment" on which attention tended to

26. *Sourcebook* 57–58.
27. *Oakland Tribune*, Dec. 21, 1964, p. 4, as summarized in *Sourcebook* 47.

focus had several varying elements over the lengthy time period it was before the Congress. But its eventual essence, and also the essence of similar amendments introduced by Democratic Senator Frank Church of Idaho and Republican Senator Jacob K. Javits of New York, was a partial modification of the Supreme Court's "one man-one vote" ruling to permit a deviation from the equal population district principle in one house, provided the deviation were approved by local referendum in the affected state. (See Chapter XV for detailed discussion of congressional reaction to the "one man-one vote" revolution.)

"Flying truth squads" were dispatched from Sacramento to various parts of the country to encourage other legislatures to memorialize Congressmen to support the Dirksen, Church, or Javits proposals. From the perspective of the East Coast the project seemed foredoomed to failure, at least in terms of the likelihood of the amendment's ever being ratified by three-fourths of the states even if it should pass in the Senate and should surmount the firm roadblock of Judiciary Committee Chairman Emanuel Celler in the House. And yet a frontier sense of optimism prevailed in Sacramento throughout the spring of 1965 and right up to Senator Dirksen's near-miss in mustering a two-thirds majority for Senate initiation of the amendment in August 1965. In view of the past referendum record of California, the California senators did have a reasonable basis for their feeling that if a federal amendment allowing continuation of the federal plan by local option became effective, a popular majority of California voters would have supported continuation of the federal plan. A poll in January 1965 indicated that on the question of seeking an "optional federal plan" amendment to the federal Constitution, 49 percent of Californians favored the idea, 21 percent were opposed, and 30 percent had no opinion. An April 1965 poll asked whether "population" or "geography" was favored as the basis for apportioning the senate. "Population" was favored by 49 percent on a statewide basis, by 61 percent in southern California, but only by 33 percent in northern California.[28]

Until the vote in the United States Senate dashed the hopes of the California senators, it is doubtful that any outside pressure would have forced reapportionment to an agreed vote in the senate and the assembly. This is not to say that effective reapportionment planning and political profile research was not being done. To the contrary, against the possibility of being forced to the wall on reapportionment, the opposing groups each had a chartroom in the California capitol. Political profile analyses as sophisticated as any in the nation were being devised with the aid of computer process, particularly for the Los Angeles area. The interests and prospects of all incumbents were being delineated in great detail. Both senate and

28. Mervyn D. Field's California Poll as reported in *Sourcebook* 47, 59.

assembly committees were active, and the latter may have had more influence on the final outcome because not tied up with the incumbency problem. Most equalization plans could not avoid forcing incumbent senators to share a district—one proposed district being shared by three incumbents. Nor were the assemblymen disinterested personally. In the Los Angeles area especially, with 14 new senate seats to be created, they saw pathways to the senate for themselves.

However, relative weakness and division in central party structures in California, unlike in New York, made this effort more one centering around power factions in the legislature than around statewide party leaders. Indeed, one of the most "lost-appearing" men on the capitol scene was an emissary from the Republican so-called State Central Committee, who wandered in one May afternoon in 1965 to inquire plaintively whether he could borrow the data cards worked up by the hard-nosed planners on the senate side.

Rejection by the United States Senate on August 4, 1965 of the proposed amendment allowing local option "federal plans" brought reapportionment matters quickly to a head in California. The federal district court, whose July 1, 1965 deadline had come and gone without reapportionment's being accomplished, then cleared the way for state action. In an August 16 order the court deferred further hearings until the fall after noting that the United States Supreme Court had yet to pass on the constitutionality of the existing apportionment, and that the federal court was "fully convinced" that the state court could be counted on to act "at its earliest opportunity." [29]

c. Judicial Guidelines and Prompt Compliance

Responding quickly, the California Supreme Court on September 1, 1965 —less than a month after the failure of the Dirksen reapportionment amendment—acted, as one observer commented, to rescue "everybody from anarchy in a fantastically rapid development." [30] It not only ordered the California legislature to produce a reapportionment for both senate and lower house by the end of the year, under pain of a threatened judicial apportionment under a detailed plan attached to the order, but it also laid down specific reapportionment guidelines.[31] The guidelines were ex-

29. Silver v. Jordan, No. 62–953 MC, United States District Court of the Southern District of California, Central Division, August 16, 1965.
30. From author's correspondence with Dean Edward L. Barrett, Jr., of the University of California, Davis, who had served as special consultant to the Assembly Committee on Elections and Reapportionment.
31. Silver v. Brown, 46 Cal. Rptr. 308, 405 P.2d 132 (Calif. 1965). The court acted in one of Phill Silver's suits and another filed by San Francisco attorneys Philip Adams, Edward Napier, and Roland Adicker.

pressed in simple mathematical terms more specific and detailed than any others announced by courts in the nation. No district in either house could deviate by more than 15 percent from average size districts, the court said, and the electoral percentage in each house must be at least 48 percent. Announcement of guidelines, coupled with uncertainty concerning the effect of judicially arranged apportionment, had a magical effect on the California senate. In a month and a half rather than the allotted three months time a reapportionment was produced, albeit accompanied by cries of gerrymandering from Republicans and some Democrats.[32] Los Angeles County's senate representation jumped from one to 14½, the 15th being shared with Orange County.

The importance of mathematical guidelines in forcing reapportionment by reluctant bodies cannot be exaggerated. If the rule be simply "substantial equality," with no fixed mathematical boundary, plans keep coming unstuck and votes keep slipping away. One incumbent after another suggests that his seat can be saved merely by nudging a line this way or that, and thereby increasing the population disparity by only a handful of percentage points. The reapportionment map remains perpetually fluid; compromises and adjustments have a way of evaporating almost as soon as they are made. By contrast, fixed mathematical guidelines sharply limit this kind of uncontrolled and uncontrollable "guesstimation," the range of permissible negotiable issues is revealed, and a basis for firm bargaining and decision-making emerges.

The United States Supreme Court by its substantial equality formula undoubtedly hoped to preserve some "play in the joints" in the keenly political area of legislative apportionment. But the effect in most instances, both in one-party states and two-party states, was to shroud the reapportionment negotiation process in uncertainty and to make the pursuit of "substantial equality" substantially ineffective, short of rather severe external pressure.

This denouement of California's unique reapportionment struggle had one further humorous twist. Almost as soon as the bill was signed by the governor mis-descriptions and other errors due to haste were discovered. A corrective measure was vetoed because it was coupled with a special pension plan designed to alleviate the distress of legislators adversely affected by reapportionment. The governor and both houses then petitioned the state supreme court to correctively "construe," i.e., rewrite the enacted measure, and the petition was honored. After making several modifications to make the enacted measure conform more to obvious legislative intent—e.g., construing "northwesterly" to mean "easterly and northerly,"

32. New York Times, Oct. 22, 1965, p. 27, col. 1; Oct. 24, 1965, p. 57, col. 1.

and thus shifting the whole city of Oakland (378,000) from one district to two others (!)—the court approved the thus-modified enactment.[33]

With the aid of the state court's guidelines California reapportionment was promptly achieved. It was not, however, a bipartisan reapportionment.[34] Although there were significant factional splits which contributed to Governor Brown's defeat in the ensuing November 1966 election by Ronald Reagan, both houses were in Democratic hands. Under the resulting reapportionment the districts were so drawn that even with a majority of the statewide *legislative* popular vote in November 1966, as well as a landslide victory in the governorship contest, Republicans were not able to capture control of either house of the California legislature. Democratic and Republican popular vote totals for senate and assembly, respectively, were 3,330,318 to 3,403,582 and 2,835,175 to 3,294,210, yielding Democratic majorities of 21 to 19 in the senate and 42 to 38 in the assembly. Thus, firm court guidelines produced prompt reapportionment in the Golden State; and the adventitious factor of unified government presented a golden opportunity, which no party ever can resist, to engage in partisan line drawing. Functionally viewed, California's first experience with the reapportionment revolution was a partisan one, as in Ohio and Michigan, rather than bipartisan as in New York, New Jersey, and Illinois.

3. TRENDS AND COUNTER-TRENDS IN JUDICIAL MATHEMATICS NATIONALLY

In most other states not specially mentioned above, post-*Reynolds* reapportionments were worked out through a give-and-take process of "political adjudication" set in motion by *Baker* and *Reynolds*. There was a pattern of judicially imposed deadlines, legislative action, and judicial

33. Silver v. Brown, 409 P.2d 689 (Calif. 1966); and see Respondent Edmund Brown's Application for Approval, p. 12 and attached affadavit of Harry K. Grafe, pp. 6–8. As mis-described (but not as mapped), Oakland's district was 87 percent larger than average, which was itself an indication of draftsman error.

Apart from the Republican charges of gerrymandering which raises a more enduring issue, one immediate corollary of the shift in control from northern to southern California was a shift of influence from Democratic Governor Brown, to Democratic House Speaker Unruh.

34. A major intention of the California senate in the 1965 reapportionment was to save incumbents and increase "safe" party seats, according to Professor Alvin D. Sokolow of the state legislature study project, University of California, Davis, who also states: "Districts considered safe for Republican senators, with Republican party registrations of 50% or more, were increased from two to six. Districts considered safe for Democrats, with Democratic party registrations of 65% and over, were increased from six to fifteen . . . . In the process . . . the Democrats gained more than the Republicans." Letter to author, November 30, 1967.

response. The restrictive nature of adjudication as a device for working out detailed apportionment questions under the iffy "substantial equality" concept has already been noted. The adjudication method tended to produce an inflexible take-it-or-leave-it process of reapportionment, just the opposite probably of the process anticipated by the Supreme Court in its 1964 *Reapportionment Decisions*. The attempt of the New York legislature to explore constitutional alternatives and "reason with the court" by enacting multiple plans for judicial examination was rare.

Lower court treatment of each state would have been far more equal had the Court by dictum or other intimation indicated that by "substantial equality" it was talking in terms of an absolute population variance ratio of 1.5 to 1 (or even 2 to 1) between the largest and smallest district, with most districts falling well within a 25 percent deviation from the average (analogous to the contemporary British system) or 15 percent if the Court preferred. And the change from the past would have been just as dramatic. *All states but four* on the eve of *Baker* v. *Carr* had population variance ratios between largest and smallest districts for at least one house exceeding 5 to 1.[35] In twenty-four states the largest-smallest districts in *both* houses exceed a 5 to 1 variance ratio. By contrast, under a commonly mentioned but never consistently applied post-*Reynolds* 15 percent maximum deviation rule, the population variance ratio would not exceed 1.35 to 1.

With more explicit arithmetic standards, the path to compliance also would have been eased immeasurably. Clearer guidelines—as illustrated by the California reapportionment story—by confining and channeling apportionment discretion of both legislatures and courts, would have enabled the reapportioning agency to proceed more expeditiously and more speedily through the negotiations and decisional process.

Against this background of understandable lower court uncertainty concerning the new federal standards and their impact on various elements of state apportionment formulae and customs, the process of reapportionment unfolded by means of "political adjudication" in those states not using special apportionment devices. Because the data were not well analyzed or well reported, few judges knew what national pattern was being developed by the action of their brethren in other states, nor did the United States Supreme Court itself. As a consequence, parties in some states were denied apportionment features which were approved without question in some sister states, as discussed in greater detail in Chapter XVI.

35. The figures for all states as of January 1962 are contained in the 50-state mathematical summary in Appendix A.

E. Conclusion: The Relevance of Bipartisanship

Because apportionment and districting lie at the power center of an operating democracy, a keen struggle over reapportionment can be one of the marks of a healthy democracy. Remarkably peaceful reapportionment by partisan process can be testimony to little more than the political weakness of a one-party system. Because states vary so much among themselves, and over time periods, there can be no "final solution" to the delicate reapportionment problem. It is possible and advisable, however, to build bipartisanship into the reapportionment process.

To be avoided at all costs is the bemused idea that "nonpartisan" apportionments are possible, as noted in the conclusion to Chapter XIII. Even if the actual *apportioners* be conceived as nonpartisan (a concept akin to the idea of the "Second Coming" itself), every line drawn wittingly or unwittingly will have an *apportionment political effect* different from another line which is equally "equal" and equally available. Balanced, bipartisan apportioners are the best guarantors of balanced and fair apportionments.

A major drawback of vesting all reapportionment authority in the legislature, subject only to the governor's veto power, is that a bipartisan reapportionment can never then eventuate except through the unpredictable circumstance of divided government, i.e., possession either of one house or of the governorship by the opposition party. Without such divided government, which was the pathway to bipartisan reapportionment in Connecticut, Washington, and Minnesota as already noted, a strict partisan apportionment can be expected. Even if there is a divided government, when the time comes to perform the reapportionment function, there is no guarantee of speedy accomplishment of reapportionment. If divided government produces deadlock rather than a negotiated bipartisan apportionment, the way will be opened to unpredictable judicial action on apportionment. Judicial action may range from ordering an at-large election to judicial performance of the reapportionment function with such aid as the court may be able to muster. In that event the reapportioners, whether judges or judicially appointed masters,[36] normally will lack the knowledge and background to create a bipartisan apportionment. If the judicial apportioners work only with mathematics, guesswork, and good

36. This is the defect in the 1967 Rhode Island Constitutional Convention's plan, to be submitted to popular referendum in April 1968, which specifies that the state supreme court should apportion if the legislature fails.

faith, with no political profile data, they inadvertently may create a major gerrymander.

Reapportionment need not be left to such chancy resolution. The novel Illinois pre-trial process of judicially shepherded bipartisan apportionment, as discussed in Chapter XII, worked well in the special circumstances of that state in 1965. It is too dependent, however, on the personality and perception of the judges on the scene at the moment to be deemed a reliable instrument for achieving a fair and bipartisan apportionment. The same observation may be applied to New York's ad hoc Judicial Commission in 1966, discussed in the previous chapter. Technically, of course, neither the Illinois pre-trial process of achieving a bipartisan apportionment nor the New York use of an ad hoc judicial commission in 1966 can be viewed as an independent method. A precondition of both is the existence of a politically divided government, a condition which did exist in both states. Under party-unified government an immediate partisan apportionment normally would result with no opportunity to use bipartisan devices.

Transfer of the reapportionment function from the legislature to a bipartisan commission as authorized for the lower house in the 1954 Illinois constitutional amendment and for both houses in the 1963 Michigan Constitution (see Chapter XII) might appear at first glance to be a satisfactory mode for achieving bipartisan apportionment. But the commission plan in each of these states has been shown to be fatally defective in operation. In Illinois there is no provision for a tie breaker in event of commission deadlock. In Michigan in event of deadlock individual partisan commissioners can forward plans to the state supreme court to select the one which "best" comports with the state apportionment formulae. However, political data are not carried forward and the court is not empowered to modify an individual commissioner plan to achieve a balanced result. Michigan's system guarantees therefore that in event of commission deadlock a partisan plan, rather than a bipartisan plan, will be adopted by court action.

A more perfect and more enduring form for guaranteeing completion of the apportionment function in fair fashion may be the device of a bipartisan commission with tie breaker appointed by the state's highest court, which New Jersey adopted by constitutional amendment and used in 1967 (Chapter XIII). Although providing a basic model, the New Jersey system could be altered in various ways. The tie breaker should not be ex officio, but he could be appointed by the entire bench rather than by the Chief Justice himself as in New Jersey. Also, the state constitution could provide for use of a bipartisan commission and tie breaker only after legislative failure, rather than displacement of the legislature entirely as in New Jersey. In that event, however, there probably would be a bipartisan apportionment only if the government were divided, causing a deadlock. Under a party-unified government a partisan apportionment normally would result and the bipartisan device would not be called into play.

New Jersey's example has sparked interest in bipartisan apportionment commissions in other recent state constitutional conventions. The New York draft constitution—rejected by the voters in November 1967 primarily on a separate church-state issue—contained a provision transferring the reapportionment function from the legislature to a bipartisan commission (Chapter XIII). One of the plans before the Pennsylvania constitutional convention which convened in December 1967, submitted by an Americans for Democratic Action chapter, proposed as a backstop for legislative failure a kind of bipartisan commission—the two legislative leaders of each party plus the governor.[37]

Of special interest is the reapportionment provision in the Maryland draft constitution, to be submitted to popular referendum in May 1968.[38] It extends to a one and one-half party state the bipartisan commission idea in a form purer than Missouri's pseudo-bipartisan commission (Chapter XIII). A preparatory committee for the Maryland convention had placed near-plenary reapportionment power in the governor. The convention, however, adopted a plan for a nine-man bipartisan commission, none of whom may be holders of elective office, selected as follows: the four legislative leaders (majority and minority in each house) each appoint two, the governor appoints one. The commission is to initiate reapportionment by preparing a plan, and the legislature then has an opportunity to substitute a plan of its own. If the legislature does not do so, or cannot override a governor's veto, the commission plan goes into effect. Thus a governor who prefers the bipartisan plan, and has more than two-fifths support in the legislature (three-fifths being necessary to override a veto), could preserve the work of the commission.

In states which like Maryland are one and one-half party states, it may not be possible to get agreement to give the weaker party half of the partisan seats on a bipartisan commission. An alternative for such states

37. While this book was in press the convention proposed a bipartisan commission, with a tie breaker picked by the partisans or selected by the supreme court.

As an aftermath of the Iowa Supreme Court's invalidation of multimember districts (*Kruidenier v. McCulloch*, discussed in Chapter XVIII), the legislature set up a temporary bipartisan subdistricting commission, the state chairman of each political party appointing five. It successfully subdistricted, in most instances on the basis of local party agreements, and also used a computer to suggest alternative arrangements. Iowa Legislature Subdistricting Commission "Report to Legislature," May 1, 1967.

38. Text and supporting comments are given in Committee Memorandum No. LB 2. Cf., *Report of the Constitutional Convention Commission* 128 (1967).

would be to create a modified bipartisan commission constructed perhaps as follows: three members appointed by the majority party in the legislature (party controlling lower house in event of a split); two members appointed by the minority party in the legislature; two persons appointed by the highest state court; two persons appointed by the governor from nominees submitted by the state committees of each party. No matter which party controlled the governorship, a commission so constructed could neither thwart the reasonable demands of a majority party, nor run roughshod over the minority party.

New Jersey's first use of her new system did reveal one defect which should be considered by those states which may adapt it to their own use. Bipartisanship failed at the last minute because of the way the New Jersey Supreme Court handled complainants who requested changes in the plan reported by the bipartisan commission. Although certain senate districts were inside the 15 percent outer "negotiation" boundary which had been deemed satisfactory in California, the New Jersey Supreme Court, nevertheless, on purely mathematical grounds ordered some major realignments of politically sensitive counties to achieve a "better" mathematical result. The court admitted that it was operating in the dark, and there was no evidence on whether or not the requested change was also in the direction of feathering complainants' political nests. Evidence of this sort would, of course, come before the bipartisan commission and may be taken account of in its deliberations; it is not and cannot be well carried forward to the court.

Therefore, to prevent bipartisan understandings worked out by careful commission deliberation from being upset by casual and uninformed judicial action, the New Jersey-type commission system should be amended to modify but not eliminate the judicial role. If the mathematics of the plan submitted by the commission fall within a reasonable outer boundary, the plan should be adopted unless challengers can show invidious *political* effect. In other words, challengers should not be allowed to perpetuate an unintellectual battle over population percentage points under a census which in many instances will already be inaccurate by more than the percentage points in dispute. This proposed rule is essentially the same rule which the United States Supreme Court has worked out to handle challenges to multimember districts.[39]

Bipartisan methods commend themselves for two further reasons beyond the simple desire to have an assured method to accomplish reapportionment. One concerns the integrity of the judicial process and popular faith in it. Use of formal bipartisan methods rather than direct reliance

39. See the multimember district cases for Georgia and Hawaii, Fortson v. Dorsey, 379 U.S. 433 (1965) and Burns v. Richardson, 384 U.S. 73 (1966).

on the courts would avert the speculations and rumors concerning political affiliations and interests of the judges which were an important part of the historical record in this period in such states as Michigan and Illinois. The other concerns gerrymandering. As discussed more fully in Chapter XVIII, judicial review of gerrymandering charges regarding any plan which on its face is mathematically "equal" is so difficult as to be nearly impossible in the ordinary instance. Bipartisanship built into the reapportionment process at the outset can be an important guarantee of fairness in the end result and can obviate the need for an after the fact and often bootless judicial review of "unfair" features of a concededly numerically equal plan.

In short, reapportionment must be approached as an *institutional* problem of government, not as a narrow quest for a private voter right of equality defined solely in mathematical terms. As an institutional problem, we have just begun to experiment with devices for nonlegislative apportionment. As the experimentation proceeds, at least one eye should always be kept on the possibilities for building bipartisanship into whatever device seems most suited to a given state, whether it be pre-trial process, ad hoc judicial commissions or masters, formal commissions appointed from party nominees, ex officio commissions, or other combinations.

XV

The "Dirksen Amendment" Campaign–I

Humpty Dumpty sat on a wall,
Humpty Dumpty had a great fall.
All the king's horses, and all the king's men,
Couldn't put Humpty Dumpty together again.

(To be read mellifluously)

Judicial rulings compelling drastic political changes can be expected to induce sharp political reactions, and the Supreme Court's *Reapportionment Decisions* of June 15, 1964, nullifying both houses of most state legislatures in the nation, were no exception. Extremist positions tended to dominate much of the discussion of the constitutional crisis in legislative reapportionment, beginning with *Baker* v. *Carr*. Extremism reached its highest point in congressional agitation for and against some tampering with the judicially announced rule of "one man-one vote." Some damned the Supreme Court as an unconscionable usurper in the field of politics. Others welcomed the new rulings as a sort of political "Lydia Pinkham," which must be preserved at all costs as a sovereign specific for the many ills of the body politic.

By mid-August 1964 the House Judiciary Committee under Chairman Emanuel Celler had held eight days of hearings on a package of more than 130 bills introduced by 99 members, but did not report out a bill.[1] At this point, Congressman William M. Tuck of Virginia bypassed the Celler committee. With the aid of the Rules Committee headed by his fellow Virginian Howard W. Smith, he brought to the House floor a bill to strip the federal courts of all power over state legislative apportionment. After amendment to extend its prohibition to pending cases, the bill was passed on August 19 by a vote of 218 to 175.[2]

1. Strangely, this interesting series of hearings containing much interesting comment on congressional power over federal court jurisdiction was never published.
2. H.R. 11625, 88th Cong., 2d Sess. (1964), renumbered 11926 as modified and passed by the House of Representatives, 110 *Cong. Rec.* 19580–19667 (daily ed. Aug. 19, 1964).

Meanwhile, on the Senate side, a measure introduced by Minority Leader Everett M. Dirksen of Illinois as a rider to the Foreign Aid bill had been undergoing revision in consultation with Majority Leader Mike Mansfield of Montana, Deputy Attorney General Nicholas deB. Katzenbach, and Solicitor General Archibald Cox. As initially proposed on August 3, the rider was an attempt to impose on the courts a temporary moratorium on further apportionment litigation. The revised version created a presumption in favor of some delay, but left the courts free to proceed if they felt the public interest required it.[3] The margin by which the Tuck bill passed the House was thought by many observers to be designed to place the modified Dirksen-Mansfield "breathing spell" measure in the position of being an acceptable compromise.

Lost in the shuffle, as the weeks went by, was a proposed constitutional amendment by Congressman William M. McCulloch which had attracted major attenton in early July. If initiated by a two-thirds vote in both houses of Congress and ratified by the legislatures of three-fourths of the states, it would have permitted a state to apportion one house of its legislature on factors other than population, *provided* such deviation in one house from the Supreme Court's equal population district rule was approved by the people in a popular referendum.[4]

Two enduring issues concerning basic lines of power in the American political system derive from these hectic events in Congress in the first four months after *Reynolds* v. *Sims* and merit separate discussion. The first is the extent of congressional power to modify judicial policy in areas of constitutional law by modifying the jurisdiction of the federal courts. A subsidiary aspect of this issue is the question of the lesser power to impose a temporary moratorium on further litigation in such a field as apportionment, as initially attempted by Senator Dirksen and Majority Leader Mansfield. The second issue, perhaps more difficult conceptually, is the question of the power of Congress, or of a federal constitutional convention (should one be called), to draft an amendment to the Constitution to modify the Supreme Court's rule of equal population districts for both houses of state legislatures. A subsidiary aspect of this issue is whether it is possible in a field such as this to draft a limited amendment, one which would do no more than restore part of the status quo ante and not set in motion a new chain of uncertainties and unsettling developments. In short, whether or not there be a plenary *power* to draft and ratify an amendment in the "one man-one vote" field, would it be *practicable* to attempt to do so?

3. 110 *Cong. Rec.* 17138 (daily ed. Aug. 3, 1964), 110 *Cong. Rec.* 18567–68 (daily ed. Aug. 12, 1964).
4. H. R. J. Res. 1055, 88th Cong., 2d Sess. (1964).

A. Congressional Power Over Federal Court Jurisdiction

One of the shimmering realities of the American system of separation of powers, known to all students of elementary courses in civics is that the independence of federal judges is a prime guarantor of a rule of law rather than a rule of contemporary passion. The independence, bolstered by life tenure, is deemed to be a necessary bulwark of the American system of judicial review. There is much truth in this analysis. Empirically it is supported by the simple fact that short-run support for the federal judiciary and the Supreme Court tends to shift back and forth in unsettling fashion between the "Conservative" and "Liberal" camps, depending on which one's interests are being fostered or repressed by the current line of Court decisions.

Because of this widespread recognition of the Court's moderating role, attempts to tamper with the federal judicial system through use of congressional or executive power invoke instinctive reactions of shock and disbelief. Even so popular a President as Franklin D. Roosevelt learned this to his surprise in 1937 in the ill-fated Court-packing controversy. Too few persons realize, however, that the Constitution itself, after specifying the Supreme Court's appellate jurisdiction in Article III, adds the qualifying phrase "with such Exceptions, and under such Regulations as the Congress shall make." Further, although the Constitution defines national judicial power in terms of the categories of "cases" and "controversies" encompassed, the parceling out of this jurisdiction to "such inferior Courts as the Congress may from time to time ordain and establish," is left to congressional discretion.

It was on these foundations that the congressional proposals to modify or postpone federal court reapportionment jurisdiction in the summer of 1964 were founded. In other words, in lieu of attempting to put new language into the Constitution by the amending process in order to allow some consideration of nonpopulation factors in apportionment, the easier and more direct route seemed to be simply to enact a statute ousting federal courts from jurisdiction over reapportionment, or at least postponing it. To achieve this end the Congress would have had to do three things: (1) exclude from the original jurisdiction of the lower federal courts power to entertain apportionment cases in the first instance; (2) prevent the Supreme Court from hearing reapportionment cases in the first instance as part of that Court's original jurisdiction; (3) prevent the Supreme Court from exercising appellate jurisdiction over reapportionment cases in state courts. Although the matter is not free from doubt, an analysis of these three possible routes of congressional action suggests that at least under precedents so far developed Congress has substantial power in regard to the first and third categories. Here as in so many areas of "ultimate confrontation" in the separation of powers area, control over the outcome may rest more on the current balance of power and popular feeling than on clear constitutional command.

1. CONGRESS AND LOWER FEDERAL COURT JURISDICTION

Three fairly recent clusters of cases are relevant to the question of congressional power over lower federal court jurisdiction, and particularly the power to strip lower federal courts of jurisdiction over a constitutional issue such as apportionment. Two of the case clusters support a theory of plenary power in Congress; one does not.

The pro-congressional power cases are those dealing with the Norris-La Guardia Act and with the World War II Price Control Act. The former Act severely limited federal court jurisdiction to grant injunctions in labor disputes, but was upheld in a Supreme Court opinion in which Justice Owen J. Roberts said: "There can be no question of power of Congress thus to define and limit the jurisdiction of the inferior courts of the United States." [5] The Price Control Act set up a special Emergency Court of Appeals to handle claims of invalidity of the price regulations, and barred the regular district courts from considering such questions. In sustaining this limitation of federal district court jurisdiction, Chief Justice Harlan Fiske Stone for the Court said: "Article III left Congress free to establish inferior federal courts or not as it thought appropriate. It could have declined to create any such courts, leaving suitors to the remedies afforded by state courts, with such appellate review by this Court as Congress might prescribe." [6]

The third cluster of cases dealt with the Portal-to-Portal Act of 1947, passed after Supreme Court interpretation of federal wage and hour laws as including underground travel in mines had resulted in a flood of suits for back pay. In the Act, Congress rejected the Supreme Court interpretation, thus seeking to make the claims groundless, and also barred such back pay suits from all federal and state courts. Litigants then claimed that the Act, in its retroactive operation, deprived them of property without due process of law, in violation of the Fifth Amendment. If Congress does have plenary power wholly or partially to close the doors of federal

5. Lauf v. E. G. Shinner & Co., 303 U.S. 323, 330 (1938).
6. Lockerty v. Phillips, 319 U.S. 182 (1943).

courts, the short answer to all these suits would have been to dismiss them for want of jurisdiction without reaching the due process issue. Professor Henry M. Hart and Herbert Wechsler [7] found, however, that the federal courts of appeal and most district courts treated the due process question as open to decision despite the separate provision in the Act withdrawing federal court jurisdiction, and then went on to reject the due process claim on the merits. Judge Harrie Brigham Chase for the Second Circuit Court of Appeals put the matter this way:

> We think, however, that the exercise by Congress of its control over jurisdiction is subject to compliance with at least the requirements of the Fifth Amendment. That is to say, while Congress has the undoubted power to give, withhold, and restrict the jurisdiction of the courts other than the Supreme Court, it must not so exercise that power as to deprive any person of life, liberty, or property without due process of law or to take private property without just compensation.[8]

The question before the Celler committee in 1964 was whether these precedents permitted a restricted congressional power to bar federal district courts from hearing complaints that certain state legislative apportionment systems violate plaintiffs' rights under the equal protection of the laws clause of the Fourteenth Amendment. Under the broad language in the opinions upholding the Norris-La Guardia Act and the Price Control Act one would anticipate no lack of congressional power. The counterargument would be that neither of these acts were designed to bar plaintiffs totally from raising important constitutional claims. When violation of constitutional rights was alleged under the Portal-to-Portal Act the courts hesitated to rest their decisions solely on the ground of congressional withdrawal of jurisdiction. It would seem then that courts have not yet given a definitive answer to the question concerning the extent to which Congress can close the doors of the inferior federal courts to *any* kind of claim, including allegations of a violation of a personal constitutional right to liberty, equality, or property.

2. CONGRESS AND SUPREME COURT ORIGINAL JURISDICTION

In contrast to the substantial arguments which can be made in favor of a broad congressional power over lower federal court jurisdiction, there seems to be no way of justifying a restrictive statute over the Supreme Court's original jurisdiction. The Constitution clearly specifies two head-

7. Henry M. Hart and Herbert Wechsler, *The Federal Courts and the Federal System* (Brooklyn: The Foundation Press, 1953).
8. Battaglia v. General Motors Corp., 169 F.2d 254, 257 (2d Cir. 1948).

ings of original jurisdiction for the Supreme Court. There are no qualifying phrases or authorization to Congress to make an exception.

Lack of congressional power by statute to limit the Court's original jurisdiction would be immaterial, however, if the original jurisdiction clause itself were construed not to cover a suit to enjoin a *state official* from holding an election under an allegedly unconstitutional state apportionment statute. Not every suit which in some way *affects* a state is deemed, in the constitutional sense, to be a suit to which a "state" is a "party," as that term is used in Article III or in the analogous clause in the Eleventh Amendment which prevents federal courts from entertaining certain suits "against" a "state."

The important question is to ascertain what the Supreme Court original jurisdiction clause means when it speaks of cases "in which a State shall be a Party." The answer can be found by making two lines of analysis: first, by analyzing the original jurisdiction clause in the context of the entire Article III of which it is an interrelated part; second, by analyzing the meaning of the analogous "suit against a state" clause in the Eleventh Amendment. The first line of analysis yields the conclusion that the Supreme Court's original jurisdiction did not extend generally to *any* suit involving a state, but only to the limited categories specifically mentioned earlier in Article III. None of these categories have any bearing on apportionment litigation. They are: controversies between two or more states, controversies between a state and citizens of another state, and controversies between a state or citizens on the one hand and foreign citizens or their subjects on the other hand.

The second line of analysis, under the analogous language in the Eleventh Amendment, immediately encounters the doctrine of *Ex Parte Young*.[9] Under the *Young* doctrine suits in federal courts against various state officials to curb their allegedly illegal conduct have usually been allowed, despite the Eleventh Amendment's prohibition on suits against a state. The theory is that if the official's action is unlawful under the federal Constitution then it is not "state action" for the purpose of the Eleventh Amendment, and the suit to restrain the threatened unconstitutional action is not a suit "against the state." It is simply a suit to hold the official within the proper bounds of his power.

Without pursuing these two lines of analysis further, the short of the matter can be said to be this. The original jurisdiction of the Supreme Court does not extend to reapportionment cases for three reasons. First, if viewed as suits against a state by the state's own citizens, they would be barred by the Eleventh Amendment, as broadly construed by the Supreme Court. Second, if not viewed as being a suit against a "state" within the meaning of the Eleventh Amendment, then the suits, by analogy,

9. 209 U.S. 123 (1908).

should not be viewed as suits involving a "state" as a "party" within the meaning of those terms as used in the Supreme Court's original jurisdiction clause in Article III, Section 2, Paragraph 2. Third, wholly apart from the Eleventh Amendment, both the text and the interpretations of Article III indicate that the original jurisdiction of the United States extends only to a limited category of suits in which a state is a party, and could not be stretched to cover a state legislative apportionment suit brought by the state's own citizens. This third reason should remain as an effective barrier to such suits, even if the barrier posed by the doctrine of state immunity from suit by its own citizens—which rests on judicial interpretation and not on the express language of the Eleventh Amendment or of Article III—be repealed by judicial re-interpretation.

3. CONGRESS AND SUPREME COURT APPELLATE JURISDICTION

Many persons view with horror any congressional tampering with the Supreme Court. In legal circles the view has been fairly widely held, however, that the express grant of power to Congress in Article III to regulate and to make "exceptions" to the appellate jurisdiction of the Supreme Court, coupled with the famous *Ex Parte McCardle* [10] case shortly after the Civil War, does give to Congress a plenary power over the Court's appellate jurisdiction. In *McCardle*, the Supreme Court for the third time [11] avoided the issue of the constitutionality of Reconstruction legislation by acquiescing in a habeas corpus repeal statute that had the effect of withdrawing from the Court jurisdiction over a case already argued and awaiting final decision. *McCardle* could be viewed as a war-related political question case, although, to be sure, the opinion of Chief Justice Salmon P. Chase does not read that way.

The assumption that under the *McCardle* precedent Congress has a broad power in this area is evidenced by conflicting proposals a few years ago to amend the Constitution to *deprive* Congress of its authority to make exceptions to the appellate jurisdiction of the Supreme Court,[12] and proposals to *exercise* the power by making specific exceptions as in the current reapportionment controversy.[13] Several writers, however, have

10. 74 U.S. (7 Wall.) 506 (1868).
11. Two earlier unsuccessful attempts were Georgia v. Stanton, 73 U.S. (6 Wall.) 50 (1867) and Mississippi v. Johnson, 71 U.S. (4 Wall.) 475 (1867).
12. See, e.g., Justice Owen J. Roberts, "Now is the Time: Fortifying the Supreme Court's Independence," 35 A.B.A.J. 1 (1944). A constitutional amendment was proposed by Senator John M. Butler with the support of several bar associations and passed the Senate but was tabled in the House of Representatives. S. J. Res. 44, 83rd Cong., 1st Sess. (1953); see 79 A.B.A. Rep. 242 (1954).
13. Senator William E. Jenner attracted much attention a few years ago with his proposal to eliminate Supreme Court appellate jurisdiction in several categories of cases, including state subversive activities legislation and state bar admissions, S. 2646, 85th Cong., 2d Sess. (1958). See also Charles Warren, "Legislative and Judicial

expressed considerable doubt concerning the breadth and current applicability of the *McCardle* precedent. As Justice Roberts once observed concerning the *McCardle* case, it was done for "political reasons and in a political exigency to meet a supposed emergency." [14] Others have implied that if the *McCardle* case cannot be treated as an exceptional political question case it is simply wrong. The thought is that the "exceptions" clause only gives Congress some power of tidying up and easing the Supreme Court's burden on inconsequential matters; the clause does not give Congress power to upset the separation of powers system by impeding or blocking the Court's central power of constitutional adjudication.

In view of the special setting of the *McCardle* case and the fact that its short opinion discusses none of the larger issues, it seems reasonable to suggest that the Supreme Court has not definitively resolved the apparent conflict between the "exceptions" clause of Article III and the spirit of the rest of the Article as developed in our tradition of judicial review. The most recent Supreme Court reference to the matter suggests as much. In *Glidden Co.* v. *Zdanok*, there is a dictum in the opinion of the Court written by Justice John Marshall Harlan that seemingly accepts the *McCardle* precedent.[15] To this, Justice William O. Douglas, in dissent, reacted by saying: "There is a serious question whether the *McCardle* case would command a majority view today." [16] Justice Harlan himself went on to note that, despite the *McCardle* precedent, the Court refused to apply a withdrawal of jurisdiction statute "to a case in which the claimant had already been adjudged entitled to recover by the Court of Claims, calling it an unconstitutional attempt to invade the judicial province by prescribing a rule of decision in a pending case." [17] He cited an old Reconstruction period case, *United States* v. *Klein*.[18]

4. THE WISDOM OF CONGRESSIONAL ACTION BY STATUTE AGAINST COURT DECISIONS

Precedents thus far developed regarding congressional power to withdraw or postpone federal court jurisdiction in such constitutional law areas as state legislative apportionment leave the matter in a rather unsatisfactory state. When one shifts, however, from consideration of congressional

Attacks on the Supreme Court of the United States—A History of the Twenty-Fifth Section of the Judiciary Act," 27 *Am. L. Rev.* 1, 161 (1913), and Charles Warren, *The Supreme Court in United States History*, 2 vols. (rev. ed; Boston: Little, Brown, 1935).
14. Roberts, *supra* note 12, at 3.
15. 370 U.S. 530, 567 (1962).
16. *Id.* at 605, n. 11.
17. *Id.* at 568.
18. 80 U.S. (13 Wall.) 128 (1872).

power to consideration of the *wisdom* of congressional action of this sort, doubts may disappear. For Congress by statute to tamper with federal court jurisdiction over federal constitutional issues would mean a shift from a system of separation of powers to a system of parliamentary supremacy. Such a step is not to be taken lightly no matter how extreme the provocation or how ill-considered a given court decision may be thought to be—whether the matter be reapportionment, Bible-reading in public schools, or criminal procedure. Ad hoc redefinition of judicial jurisdiction impelled by the passions of the moment could turn the unique American institution of judicial review into a political football. By this same token, even though President Franklin D. Roosevelt's Court-packing bill probably was technically legal and constitutional, he was a dubious friend of American democracy to submit it. The authorized and orderly process for modifying a particular judicial interpretation of the Constitution is to change the text of the Constitution itself by amendment.

Of course, as a *New York Times* editorial writer phrased it in the summer of 1964, "timetables for change fixed by Federal judges in many states are so immediate" [19] as to raise a prospect of political eggs being scrambled which never could be unscrambled. For this reason, even those members of Congress preferring the route of constitutional amendment felt that some temporary "holding action" was needed in order not to make a constitutional amendment a bootless act. This was the thought behind the Dirksen-Mansfield moratorium plan to which even the Department of Justice gave temporary blessing. It is difficult, if not impossible, however, to distinguish the basis for congressional power to order for a specified time period a court moratorium on further apportionment litigation, from the basis for congressional power completely to withdraw court jurisdiction in apportionment matters. If Congress by statute had power to withdraw jurisdiction from lower federal courts and the Supreme Court, then a temporary statutory moratorium on *exercise* of the jurisdiction would of course be a lesser included power. But if the power to withdraw jurisdiction is doubtful, then a qualified moratorium would not seem to stand on any stronger legal footing.

In a situation of this sort consideration could be given to memorializing the Court to use the doctrine of judicial abstention in order to obtain a grace period for consideration of a constitutional amendment. After all, in

19. *New York Times*, Aug. 6, 1964, p. 28, col. 2. The sentence from which the quoted words are taken was deleted from the editorial in some editions of the *Times* that day. It reads in full as follows: "The difficulty is that the timetables for change fixed by Federal judges in many states are so immediate that it may be hard to persuade hostile Congressmen they have any choice except to act with indecent speed before adjournment."

an area which is much simpler conceptually, i.e., desegregation of public education, the Supreme Court itself after deciding the merits in 1954 scheduled a special hearing on remedies, and delayed for a year the entry of a final order which, when entered, was phrased in terms of "all deliberate speed" rather than immediate compliance.[20] But for Congress to attempt to direct the course of judicial action simply by passing a statute would be a very grave step.

5. THE "SENSE OF CONGRESS" RESOLUTION OF 1964

As events unfolded in the summer of 1964 as an immediate reaction to the Supreme Court's June decision in *Reynolds* v. *Sims* and its companion "one man-one vote" cases, attention centered primarily on two measures. One was a bill introduced by Congressman Tuck and immediately dubbed by some the "court ripper" bill designed to strip the federal courts of all jurisdiction in state legislative apportionment litigation.[21] The other was the milder Dirksen-Mansfield moratorium proposal. As already noted, some supporting precedents could be found for the *constitutionality* of the Tuck bill. But even if it was not clearly unconstitutional by existing precedents, it did appear to those who did have some reservations concerning the breadth of the new "one man-one vote" rule, to be at least "anti-constitutional" in the fundamental sense of running counter to the general spirit of the American constitutional system. It would have cut the heart out of the federal courts' central and vital power of constitutional adjudication. The measure generated a storm of protest outside of Congress, if not inside Congress.

The moratorium proposal was quite a different matter. As revised in conferences with Deputy Attorney General Katzenbach and Solicitor General Cox and co-sponsored by Majority Leader Senator Mansfield, the Dirksen-Mansfield "rider" or amendment to the Foreign Aid Bill was quasi-advisory and in the nature of a "stay." [22] Upon application of any interested party, courts were to grant a stay, "in the absence of highly unusual circumstances." The stay would have permitted use until January 1, 1966, of unmodified apportionment provisions. It further would have allowed a legislature in regular session or the people, by the process of state constitutional amendment, a reasonable opportunity to reapportion after a state's apportionment provisions had been declared unconstitutional. The revised "rider" also endorsed in principle federal court action

20. Brown v. Board of Education, 349 U.S. 294 (1955).
21. 110 *Cong. Rec.* 17138 (daily ed. Aug. 3, 1964) (introduced); 110 *Cong. Rec.* 17482 (daily ed. Aug. 5, 1964) (reported by Judiciary Committee).
22. 110 *Cong. Rec.* 18567–68 (daily ed. Aug. 12, 1964); and see *New York Times*, Aug. 13, 1964, p. 19, cols. 1–2.

on state legislative apportionment. It authorized federal district courts to apportion a state if the state failed to reapportion during the period of the stay.

If one can rise above the emotionalism the controversy aroused, and eschew oversimplified appeals in terms of rural sinners and urban saints in favor of a concern for fair representation, the revised Dirksen-Mansfield proposal may be seen to have presented a special case. The separation of powers objection might still be asserted. But Justice Department officials were persuaded, apparently, that the revised language could rest on congressional power under Section 5 of the Fourteenth Amendment, which authorized legislation implementing the substantive provisions of Section 1 [23]—a power particularly relevant when massive restructuring of government is at issue rather than mere vindication of a simple, personal civil right. On policy grounds, it could have been argued that the Dirksen-Mansfield "rider" would have done no more than urge courts to grant at least a short period for the conceptually difficult area of legislative apportionment, i.e., a grace period comparable to the longer one already voluntarily granted by the courts in the area of desegregation of public schools.

But, also on policy grounds, the Dirksen-Mansfield "rider" was too broad. It would have blocked *all* federal court apportionment action during the period of the stay, not merely action designed to put at least one house of a state legislature on a straight population basis. As such, it was not coterminous with the main line of discussion of the *Reapportionment Decisions*, or with the proposed McCulloch constitutional amendment, which sought to except only one house from the strict equal population district rule. The true issue was not one of restoring Old Sarum-type rotten boroughs. Rather, the issue was whether the complementary goals of majority rule and fair representation of parties and groups can be attained adequately by using a bicameral formula that considers only bare numbers.

In public discussion and in discussions inside Congress itself, the Tuck "court ripper" bill and the Dirksen-Mansfield temporary moratorium bill were not sharply differentiated. Indeed, the emotional reaction engendered by the extremism of the Tuck bill tended to spread without diminution to the moratorium proposal.

True, Walter Lippmann in his several columns on the matter always kept the two proposals separate, and in measured tones in a column labelled "The Dirksen Breather" he approved the moratorium idea:

> The real issue, as I see it, is whether reapportionment of the State legislatures, which is necessary but also a far-reaching change of habit

23. *New York Times*, Aug. 16, 1964, § E, p. 3, col. 7.

and custom, should be propelled by something more than the Federal courts alone,—whether, that is to say, this great change in the political balance of power should have also the approval of Congress and be subjected to the test of a Constitutional Amendment. Taking this to be the purpose of the Dirksen proposal, it seems to me sound and in the end desirable.[24]

More typical and somewhat harsh was a featured special column in the *Washington Post* by Dean Eugene Y. Rostow and Professor Thomas I. Emerson of the Yale Law School under the title "An Old Tool of Tyrants: Method of Congress in Attacking Reapportionment Seen as Blow at the Constitution Itself." Repeatedly linking the two measures as the "Dirksen-Tuck proposals" the authors called them "wrong in principle, wrong as constitutional law and wrong as a procedure for considering changes in constitutional law." After asserting that "nothing will be done by the courts now that cannot be undone later by constitutional amendment," they cast the issue in stark terms:

> Ultimately, then, the issue raised by the congressional fight over reapportionment is whether the institution of judicial review is to be cast aside. There may be some who would welcome that eventuality, but we are confident that that view is shared by only a small sect.[25]

With much justification Senator Dirksen, who was the primary proponent of the moratorium idea, could have said that with friends like Congressman Tuck he did not need enemies in this area. Although the Tuck bill was approved in the House in August 1964, in a vote which was a mixture of earnestness and of tactical planning to open the way for a less stringent compromise measure, the vote backfired. The denouement of the Dirksen-Mansfield "rider" debate was passage by the Senate in a colorful session on September 24, 1964, of a weakened "sense of Congress" version introduced by Majority Leader Mansfield alone.[26] This measure then died when the House failed to take further action before adjournment.

One may speculate what might have resulted had the House, on the eve of the Democratic National Convention in August, passed the Dirksen-Mansfield compromise measure rather than the Tuck bill. Had this been done, the Congress might have come back from the Democratic National Convention with its business so arranged as to make almost certain the enactment of the Dirksen-Mansfield compromise. By September 1 the Congress might have been able to move on to the more

24. *Washington Post*, Aug. 18, 1964, p. 11, cols. 1–3.
25. *Washington Post*, Aug. 30, 1964, p. E1, cols. 1–8, p. E3, cols. 1–5.
26. 110 *Cong. Rec.* 22051 (daily ed. Sept. 24, 1964).

important corollary matter of the content of a possible constitutional amendment. Instead, the drastic Tuck bill produced an angry reaction, the Convention recess gave opponents time to marshal their forces, the Dirksen-Mansfield measure suffered a fatal loss of momentum, and the door was opened to a successful filibuster by Senate liberals led by the other Senator from Illinois, Paul Douglas.[27]

Out of this welter of activity, however, a "sense of Congress" for some delay was clearly expressed by both houses. Its effect, or lack of effect, on the courts was signalled by the federal district court's action in the Virginia case in ordering reapportionment by December 15, 1964, and cutting in half the terms of certain senators,[28] and by Chief Justice Warren's denial of a stay.[29]

B. The Constitutional Amendment Campaign

Although the Tuck withdrawal-of-jurisdiction bill and the Dirksen-Mansfield moratorium proposal failed in 1964, not to be renewed, the move continued for a constitutional amendment to permit continuation of a modified "federal plan" in those states desiring it. To those not attuned to the real power centers in Washington, and to the problems of state ratification, the drive seemed to gain increasing momentum in 1965. But the fun, really, if not the fight, had gone out of it. Although the measure had a reasonable prospect for achieving two-thirds support in the Senate, it was hopelessly blocked in the lower house by a combination of two forces. One was the opposition of Congressman Emanuel Celler, Chairman of the House Judiciary Committee, who had even refused to allow the extensive House Reapportionment Hearings of 1964 to be published. The other was the sharply enhanced liberal Democratic control caused by the 1964 election and the influx of a number of new Democratic faces, appropriately labeled the "Goldwater freshmen."

27. The highlights with interesting quotations from both sides of the aisle are captured in a column by Dan Cordtz in the *Wall Street Journal*, Sept. 25, 1964, p. 16, col. 4. One of the filibuster leaders, using the language of consensus rather than majoritarianism, summed up the matter as follows: "What it all proves, I think, is that unless the country feels very strongly in favor of a certain piece of legislation, it can be beaten —and that's as it should be." Said Senator Dirksen: "You need a highly emotional issue, like civil rights, or a bill with lots of appeal (Comsat) to get cloture. Otherwise, any determined group can make a filibuster work. It's as simple as that."

And so, ironically, an opponent of unqualified "one man-one vote" was beaten by the minority tactic of the filibuster.

28. Mann v. Davis, 238 F. Supp. 458 (E.D. Va. 1964).

29. *New York Times*, Oct. 29, 1964, p. 1, col. 5.

In addition, the proposed amendment had an ever-dwindling chance of ratification in the state legislatures because there were "Goldwater freshmen" there too, in addition to the changes judicially forced. Indeed, it had no chance at all unless sent to ratifying conventions rather than to the state legislatures, which were being rapidly remade by lower court action. It would have taken a negative vote in one house of only thirteen of the state legislatures to defeat the measure. In popular referenda, however, the federal plan idea has consistently had strong popular support. Oddly enough, none of the principal amendment drafts provided for ratification by the more popular process of conventions rather than the more indirect process of state legislative action.

The campaign reached its peak in August 1965 when the Senate fell only seven votes short of the necessary two-thirds for initiation of the constitutional amendment. Despite a similar defeat in 1966, the proponents persisted in 1967 with a new approach seeking to have two-thirds of the states, as provided in the amending clause of the Constitution, petition Congress to call a constitutional convention on reapportionment. It became increasingly doubtful, however, that an amendment, even if initiated, and ratified, would have a major impact. Judicial refinements of the "one man-one vote" principle in regard to gerrymandering, multi-member district systems, and devices to achieve equitable minority representation emerged as more enduring issues potentially affecting all states in each successive reapportionment. Nevertheless, this persistent reapportionment amendment campaign did raise a number of interesting issues, throwing light on both the immutability of judicial review and the viability of the amending clause in the Constitution.

1. THE PRELUDE

As early as December 1962, the 16th Biennial General Assembly of the States held by the Council of State Governments proposed a series of three "states rights" amendments, one being on reapportionment. In their combined effect they were deemed to be so extreme that all three were disapproved by the American Bar Association's House of Delegates at its annual meeting in the summer of 1963. The proposed reapportionment amendment, approved 26 to 10 with ten states abstaining, would have reversed *Baker* v. *Carr*. It specified that no part of the federal Constitution applied to legislative apportionment and deprived federal courts of jurisdiction over state legislative apportionment. A second proposed amendment, approved 37 to 4 with four states abstaining, would have authorized bypassing Congress in the constitutional amendment procedure. It provided that any proposal supported by two-thirds of the state legislatures should be submitted for ratification (by the usual process of state legislative action or special convention action in three-fourths of the states) without a congressional two-thirds vote. A third proposal, which squeaked through 21 to 20 with five states abstaining, would have authorized a special Court of the Union. Its members were to be the 50 chief justices of the state supreme courts, and it would review United States Supreme Court decisions on matters "reserved to the states or to the people" by the Constitution.[30]

It was not until the Supreme Court nullified the little "federal plan" for the states in its equal population ruling of June 1964 that serious consideration was given to a constitutional amendment. Even then the central purpose of the amendment campaign of Senators Dirksen (at least in his later 1965 drafts), Jacob K. Javits of New York, Frank Church of Idaho, and Congressman William M. McCulloch remained clouded for the country as a whole, and perhaps remains clouded to the present day. The halo effect of the General Assembly of the States proposals of 1962, of the court moratorium proposal of 1964, and the Congressman Tuck "court ripper" bill of 1964, had poisoned the well. It is doubtful if one voter in ten in 1965 and 1966 conceived of the campaign, in its better moments, as a "federal plan" campaign—and a federal plan subject to recurring popular referenda at that—rather than a campaign to completely eradicate "one man-one vote," as almost universally and persistently reported in the press.

The American Bar Association, which had condemned all three of the "states rights" amendments proposed by the General Assembly of the States in 1962, was authorized by its House of Delegates to support the idea of a modified federal plan amendment at the Senate Reapportionment Hearings in the spring of 1965.[31] The state senate of "federal plan" California, as noted in Chapter XIV, was busily engaged in this same period in sending emissaries to other state capitols to whip up enthusiasm for memorializing Congress on the federal plan idea.

2.   REAPPORTIONMENT AMENDMENT—QUEST FOR A MIDDLE POSITION

Extremism had not been exhausted in the 1964 battle over Congressman Tuck's court jurisdiction bill or the Dirksen-Mansfield moratorium pro-

30. See articles by Frank E. Shanahan, Jr., "Proposed Constitutional Amendments: They Will Strengthen Federal-State Relations," and by Charles L. Black, Jr., "Proposed Constitutional Amendments: They Would Return Us to Confederacy," 49 A.B.A.J. 631, 637 (1963). The first article contains the texts of the proposals. See also Fred P. Graham, "The Role of the States in Proposing Constitutional Amendments," 49 A.B.A.J. 1175 (1963); Charles L. Black, Jr., "The Proposed Amendment of Article V: A Threatened Disaster," 72 Yale L. J. 957 (1963); William F. Swindler, "The Current Challenge to Federalism: The Confederating Proposals," 52 Geo. L. J. 1 (1963).
31. Hearings Before the Subcommittee on Constitutional Amendments of the Senate Committee on the Judiciary, 89th Cong., 1st Sess. 357 (1965).

posal. A desire still continued in some quarters in 1965 simply to slap the Supreme Court. On the other hand, the tendency to portray all proposals for modification of the Supreme Court's rulings in blackest terms as an indistinguishable mass continued. This was Armageddon and democracy itself was at stake. Even a foreign observer used to the hyperbole of American politics might have wondered a bit at the spectacle of "senior federal plan" Senators being unable to muster even a syllable of support for a "junior federal plan" for the states.

Something like an intelligible middle position began to emerge, however, as the Senate Subcommittee on Constitutional Amendments proceeded to hold hearings on a series of proposed reapportionment constitutional amendments early in the 1965 session.[32] Exemplifying this approach were two proposals, one by Senator Javits of New York and the other by Senator Church of Idaho.

The key to the Javits-Church approach was to permit one house of a bicameral state legislature to be on a mixed representation basis, rather than on numbers alone, *provided* the plan is approved decennially by statewide popular referenda.[33] In succeeding drafts the better known proposal of Senator Dirksen incorporated these features also.

A *Washington Post* editorial discussed this approach approvingly as follows:

> Such a carefully limited plan would not amount to going back to the "rotten-borough system" which Douglas so vigorously deplored. Rather, it would merely allow the states some of the discretion that they have always exercised in shaping their own governments.[34]

Viewed philosophically, this limited amendment proposal itself had some features of a "one man-one vote" or "direct democracy" approach.

32. *Id.*, generally. The testimony of 74 witnesses and the numerous statements submitted comprise more than 1000 pages.
33. S.J. Res. 44, 89th Cong., 1st Sess., introduced Feb. 8, 1965, by Senator Javits. It reads in pertinent part as follows: "Nothing in this Constitution shall prohibit the people of a State from apportioning the membership of one house of a bicameral legislature upon the basis of factors other than population, from giving reasonable weight to factors other than population in apportioning the membership of a unicameral legislature, or from providing for any such apportionment following each enumeration provided for in article 1, section 2 of this Constitution if such apportionment or provision is submitted to a vote of the people through a statewide referendum held in accordance with law and with the provisions of this Constitution, and such apportionment or provision is approved by a majority of those voting on that issue."
S.J. Res. 38, 89th Cong., 1st Sess., introduced Feb. 2, 1965, by Senator Church. It reads in pertinent part as follows: "Any State having a legislature composed of more than one house may depart from the principle of equal representation in one house by adopting another reasonable system of representation with the approval of a majority of the electorate, provided review be permitted periodically."
34. *Washington Post*, March 8, 1965, p. A 14, col. 2.

Arguably, it was in accord with the underlying thrust of *Baker* v. *Carr* itself, if the thrust of that decision be taken as a step to "returning politics to the people." Such a basic purpose of returning politics to the people and breaking up frozen apportionment systems, which seems central to *Baker* v. *Carr* and to most subsequent reapportionment litigation, has roots in the liberal Populist movement for governmental reform in the Midwestern and Western states several decades ago, and also in the Progressive movement, with which the name of La Follette is so prominently associated. Progressivism was based in part on an awareness that governmental forms and institutions are intrinsically imperfect; that electoral district systems can be rigged to produce political inequity with or without an "equal population" rule; that internal legislative maneuvering can defeat or thwart dominant popular feeling; that minority factions often can gain exaggerated strength by holding a balance of power in key election districts and in the internal operation of the legislature, and so forth. The works of Hofstadter [35] and Ranney and Kendall [36] list these elements and many more. Out of the Progressive movement came devices for "direct democracy," in contrast to the customary indirect democracy of representative legislatures based on apportionment systems and district elections. The devices for direct democracy included the initiative, the referendum, the recall, the direct primary. Except for the direct primary these devices were not intended to displace entirely the traditional form of representative democracy, but to serve as a "gun behind the door."

There are pros and cons on "direct democracy" devices, and like all governmental institutions they are themselves imperfect. However, a study several years ago indicated that disasters predicted by opponents of direct democracy have not occurred.[37] To be sure, in the area of civil rights there are critical special problems. Interesting conceptual problems of majority rule (as expressed through a statewide "one man-one vote" referendum) and of minority rights surround the famous California Proposition 14 case, denying to the people the power to *repeal* by constitutional amendment process an *anti*discrimination law regarding housing.[38] But use of popular referenda is especially relevant where the issue is not simply a personal civil right, but is a question of whether a given apportionment system produces a *representative* expression of the popular will on

35. Richard E. Hofstadter, *The Age of Reform* (New York: Knopf, 1955).
36. Austin Ranney and Willmoore Kendall, *Democracy and the American Party System* (New York: Harcourt Brace, 1956).
37. Joseph La Palombara and Charles B. Hogan, "Direct Legislation: An Appraisal and Suggestion," 45 *Am. Pol. Sci. Rev.* 400 (1951).
38. Mulkey v. Reitman, 387 U.S. 369 (1967). The court's theory, in part, was that instead of being a straight statutory repealer, Proposition 14 prevented re-enactment of an antidiscrimination law except by the process of further constitutional amendment.

public policy issues in such fashion as to approximate a *direct* expression of popular will. In apportionment, this is the issue.

All was not sweetness and light, however, as proposal followed proposal. The idea of limiting court jurisdiction in reapportionment matters, even though such action would open the way for re-creation of frozen rotten boroughs as sitting legislatures failed to respond to future population change, was abandoned only under pressure. The first sentence of Senator Dirksen's initial draft seemed to point in this direction.[39] Equally unappealing from the standpoint of a premise of "returning politics to the people" were draft amendments which would give a state carte blanche to put one house of the legislature on a mixed representation basis, by a one-time referendum vote, and then keep it that way until a majority of sitting legislators could be motivated to make a further change. Without provision for decennial popular review, the way would have been opened for a fresh political freeze. The slogan "SOS"—newly translated as "Save Our Seats"—probably would carry the day.

Absence of provisions for such decennial popular review was a serious deficiency in the initial Dirksen draft, in the 1965 American Bar Association reapportionment resolution,[40] and in one of the resolutions introduced by Senator Church.[41]

39. S.J. Res. 2, 89th Cong., 1st Sess., introduced Jan. 6, 1965, by Senator Dirksen for himself and thirty-seven other Senators. It reads in pertinent part as follows: "The right and power to determine the composition of the legislature of a State and the apportionment of the membership thereof shall remain in the people of that State. Nothing in this Constitution shall prohibit the people from apportioning one house of a bicameral legislature upon the basis of factors other than population, or from giving reasonable weight to factors other than population in apportioning a unicameral legislature, if, in either case, such apportionment has been submitted to a vote of the people in accordance with law and with the provisions of this Constitution and has been approved by a majority of those voting on that issue."
40. The American Bar Association resolution, approved by the House of Delegates at its annual mid-winter meeting, Feb. 8, 1965, reads in pertinent part as follows: "Now, therefore, *be it resolved*, that the American Bar Association approves and endorses an amendment to the Constitution of the United States to the effect that one house of a bicameral state legislature may be apportioned in part by reference to geography, county and city lines, economic conditions, history, and other factors in addition to population, provided that such a plan of apportionment is approved by a majority of voters of the State, and . . . ."
41. S.J. Res. 37, 89th Cong., 1st Sess., introduced Feb. 2, 1965, by Senator Church and following the text of a General Assembly of the States (Council of State Governments) proposal of December 1964. It reads in pertinent part as follows: "Section 1. Nothing in this Constitution shall prohibit any State which has a bicameral legislature from apportioning the numbers (sic) of one house of such legislature on factors other than population: Provided, That the plan of such apportionment shall have been submitted to and approved by a vote of the electorate of that State.

"Section 2. Nothing in this Constitution shall restrict or limit a State in its determination of how membership of governing bodies of its subordinate units shall be apportioned."

In addition to the growing awareness of the need to build into a reapportionment amendment a provision for decennial popular review of any modified federal plan, there was also increasing pressure to build some standards into the federal amendment itself so that a state could make only "reasonable" deviations in one house from an equal population district principle. There was a strong feeling in some quarters against giving a state full discretion to return one house to a system of full county equality even if such a plan were approved periodically by statewide popular referenda.

In short, it was not overly difficult, as the *Washington Post* had noted editorially, to state the case for a limited reapportionment amendment keyed to the popular referendum idea and aimed essentially at reversing the Colorado apportionment case while leaving the other five basic Supreme Court decisions untouched. The Colorado case, as noted in Chapters X and XI, was itself a "majorities in conflict" case and the Court's decision never has received an adequate rationalization. The Supreme Court's decision outlawing Colorado's modified federal plan, even though it had been approved by a two-to-one margin in a statewide "one man-one vote" election, is tenable only if the whole reapportionment struggle be reduced to the simple principle of an individual "civil right" to vote. By thus reducing it one also eliminates the representation issues, which cannot be totally ignored without making a mockery of the apportionment process.

All this underlay the drafting and redrafting of proposed reapportionment amendments in the spring of 1965 for presentation to Senator Birch Bayh's Subcommittee on Constitutional Amendments. The hearings themselves were handled with scrupulous fairness by Senator Bayh, and in the late spring he tried to take the lead in devising a compromise amendment, but the effort failed.[42] As draft followed draft, it became apparent that it was easier by far to express a philosophic opposition to the Colorado decision than to draft an amendment which would do no more than touch that one decision.

42. In a speech in Fort Wayne, Indiana, on May 18, 1965 (Office Release), Senator Bayh proposed four "safeguards" which became the basis for an aborted attempt to produce a new draft amendment. They were: (1) Compliance with the Supreme Court's requirement for equal population districts as a precondition for authority to apportion one house on a basis other than population; (2) A requirement that legislatures desiring to apportion one house on a basis other than population submit a specific apportionment plan for the people to approve or reject; (3) Mandatory return to the equal population principle unless periodically—say, every 10 years—the people approve a legislative plan for apportioning one house on some other basis; (4) Approved apportionment plans should be subject to judicial review to prevent violation of other constitutional guarantees.

3. DEBATES AND DEFEATS: 1965–1966

The 1965 Reapportionment Amendment Hearings before Senator Bayh's Senate Subcommittee on Constitutional Amendments culminated in a Senate vote on August 4, 1965. The tally was 57 to 39 in favor of Senator Dirksen's draft amendment, thus falling seven votes short of the necessary two-thirds of the Senators present and voting required for initiation of a constitutional amendment.[43] The measure had been gotten to the floor by an unusual route. Senator Bayh's Subcommittee had reported S.J. Res. 2, as amended, to the full Senate Judiciary Committee. It discussed the measure on July 14 and 29, 1965, but took no action. Senator Dirksen on July 22, 1965, then offered S.J. Res. 2 as an amendment in the nature of a substitute for a pending measure, S.J. Res. 66, designating August 31–September 6, 1965, as "National American Legion Baseball Week." [44] Requiring only a majority vote, the substitute was agreed to, and the Dirksen amendment was before the Senate. This legislative tactic was not unique, although the press twitted the Senate majority for using it. The Twenty-Fourth Amendment (abolition of poll tax) had gotten to the floor in this manner as a substitute for the joint resolution establishing a national monument in memory of Alexander Hamilton; and the Civil Rights Bill of 1960 had been tacked onto a bill for relief of the Stella Reorganized Schools in Missouri.

With the exception of Senator Javits's draft, the Dirksen draft was the only one of the measures considered by the Subcommittee to be brought to the floor. The Dirksen measure, which had undergone some modification since introduced in January 1965, read as follows at the time of the Senate debate (the minor changes made after the debate and before the vote, on motion of Senator Hruska, being shown in brackets):

> SECTION 1. The people of a State may apportion one house of a bicameral legislature using population, geography, or ["or" changed to "and"] political subdivisions as factors, giving each factor such weight as they deem appropriate, or giving similar ["similar" changed to "reasonable"] weight to the same factors in apportioning a unicameral legislature, if in either case such plan of apportionment has been submitted to a vote of the people in accordance with law and with the provisions of this Constitution and has been approved by a majority of those voting on that issue. When the first ["the first" changed to "a"] plan of apportionment [phrase "based on factors of

43. 111 Cong. Rec. 18660 (daily ed. Aug. 4, 1965).
44. 111 Cong. Rec. 17189–91 (daily ed. July 22, 1965). See also S. Rep. No. 191, 90th Cong., 1st Sess. 3–4 (1967).

population, geography, and political subdivisions" inserted] is submitted to a vote of the people under this section there shall also be submitted, at the same election, an alternative plan of apportionment based upon substantial equality of population.

SEC. 2. Any plan of apportionment which has been approved under this article shall be resubmitted to a vote of the people, or, another plan may be submitted under the provisions of section 1, at the November general election held two years following each year in which there is commenced any enumeration provided for in section 2 of article I, and upon approval by a majority of those voting thereon, such plan of apportionment shall continue in effect until changed in accordance with law and with the provisions of this Constitution.[45]

Senator Javits's draft came before the Senate as a proposed amendment in the nature of a substitute for the Dirksen draft, but was rejected by a vote of 85 to 12.[46] It too had been modified since first introduced in February 1965, and read as follows at the time of the Senate debate and vote:

SECTION 1. The people of a State may apportion one house of a bicameral legislature, or a unicameral legislature, using geography or political subdivisions as well as population as factors, if such plan of apportionment bears a reasonable relationship to the needs of the State, is consistent with the provisions of this Constitution except for the provisions of this article, and has been submitted to a vote of the people in a statewide referendum held in accordance with law and with the provisions of this Constitution and has been approved by a majority of those voting on that issue. When a plan of apportionment is submitted to a vote of the people under this article there shall also be submitted, at the same election, an alternative plan of apportionment based upon substantial equality of population.

SEC. 2. Any plan of apportionment which has been approved under this article shall be resubmitted to a vote of the people in a statewide referendum, or, another plan may be submitted under the provisions of section 1, at the November general election held two years following each year in which there is commenced any enumeration provided for in section 2 of article I, and upon approval by a majority of those voting thereon, such plan of apportionment shall continue in effect until changed in accordance with law and with the provisions of this Constitution.[47]

There were several differences between the Javits and the Dirksen drafts. Senator Javits said that under his formula population was to be the

45. S.J. Res. 66, 89th Cong., 1st Sess. (1965), as amended to substitute the Dirksen amendment (S.J. Res. 2, as amended) for its original terms.
46. 111 Cong. Rec. 18330 (daily ed. Aug. 2, 1965); 111 Cong. Rec. 18608–9 (daily ed. Aug. 4, 1965).
47. Amendment to amended S.J. Res. 66, 89th Cong., 1st Sess. (1965) (introduced by Senator Javits).

base for apportioning the second house as well as the first house, but could be mixed with geographic or political subdivision considerations. Court review was expressly preserved, he said, on the question of "reasonableness," i.e., whether the mixed standard bore a reasonable relationship to the needs of the state. His substitute averted any possibility of discrimination on grounds of race by making clear that only the Court's interpretation of the Fourteenth Amendment in regard to reapportionment was being modified and that no other provision of the Constitution was being altered. The substitute also provided that each mixed representation plan submitted to popular referendum must be accompanied by a strict equal population plan, thus giving the voters a choice, whereas the Dirksen proposal so required only on the initial submission of a mixed representation plan.[48]

a. *Opposing Camps*

However, neither the discussion in the Senate from July 20 to August 4, nor the "D-Day" debate on August 4 with Senator Dirksen of Illinois marshaling the proponents and Senator Douglas of Illinois marshaling the opponents, focused on these differences or on details of draftsmanship. At the outset the breadth of the Dirksen amendment was characterized in overdrawn terms by Senator Douglas, who asserted that its objective was "to reverse the decision of the Supreme Court in the Alabama case." [49] With this beginning, neither in the press nor on the floor was the issue portrayed as an attempt really to leave five of the "big six" reapportionment decisions of 1964 untouched, including the Alabama case, *Reynolds* v. *Sims*, and to reverse only the Colorado case, *Lucas* v. *Colorado General Assembly*. The purport of the amendment language was to give the voters in a state via the popular referendum route an option to deviate from the strict population equality in one house if desired.[50]

The Dirksen forces were not always adroit in portraying the asserted narrow character of the Dirksen amendment or correcting the historical record. Their tactics were characterized by a Chaplinesque stumblebum quality which failed to appeal to those not already possessed of reservations about the self-sufficiency of the "one man-one vote" slogan. They were long on earnestness, short on ingenuity in draftsmanship, and totally incapable of creating a counter-slogan which, by giving pause, might have brought more persons into an effective dialogue on the real difficulties of

48. 111 *Cong. Rec.* 18330 (daily ed. Aug. 2, 1965); 111 *Cong. Rec.* 18595–98, 18600–601 (daily ed. Aug. 4, 1965).

49. 111 *Cong. Rec.* 17189 (daily ed. July 22, 1965). See also similar statement of Senator Daniel K. Inouye of Hawaii, 111 *Cong. Rec.* 18164–67 (daily ed. Aug. 29, 1965).

50. See detailed discussion of *Reynolds* and *Lucas* in Chapter XI *supra*.

creating effective representation systems. Senator Dirksen was the main actor on the proponents' side, with Senator Roman L. Hruska of Nebraska as a major lieutenant. He had an easy majority, but he needed a two-thirds vote for proposal of an amendment.

In various ways the proponents kept saying that the "whole burden" of their argument was to go "back to the people." [51] But they were handicapped by the very recent memory of real malapportionment abuses in a majority of the states and by some continued deficiencies in their revised draft in addition to its differences from the Javits draft. For example, Senator Tydings had very appropriately proposed that in keeping with a theme of popular control a reapportionment amendment should provide for ratification by state ratifying conventions rather than by state legislatures, but his proposal was defeated in the Judiciary Committee.[52]

The opposition to the amendment idea was led by Senator Paul Douglas with strong support from Senator William Proxmire of Wisconsin and Senator Joseph D. Tydings of Maryland. If the posture of proponents was Chaplinesque, the posture of the opponents had an extravagant quality. Wrapping themselves in the flag, they offered "one man-one vote," defined as close equal population districts, as an ultimate civil right not susceptible of modification. Two constantly recurring themes were the integrity of judicial review and return to original virtue. They repeated the canard that all states between 1790 and 1890 were "equal population" states at the time of admission and that the original constitutions of 36 of the 50 states were on this basis for both houses.[53]

The fact that at least one house would remain on a pure population basis was met by suggesting that a possible veto power in the one house which was not placed on a strict equal population district principle would be almost as bad as population malapportionment of both houses. More difficult to handle was the fact that even if the Dirksen amendment were ratified, no change in the one man-one vote rule would occur without periodic popular referenda in the state which wished to adopt a mixed representation system. The rebuttal took the form essentially of expressing distrust of popular referenda, Senator Douglas stating: "Referendums have become, in this day of modern communications and propaganda techniques, the tools of special interests rather than acceptable vehicles for the expression of an informed popular will." A more basic objection noted was that except in those states such as Colorado and California, which have the popular initiative, a proposal to place one house of the

---

51. 111 *Cong. Rec.* 18635 (daily ed. Aug. 4, 1965).
52. 111 *Cong. Rec.* 18238 (daily ed. July 30, 1965).
53. 111 *Cong. Rec.* 17396–97 (daily ed. July 23, 1965). But for a different tabulation see Chapter IV *supra*, Chart 3.

legislature on a mixed representation basis could emanate only in the existing legislature, which itself might not yet have been reconstructed on an equal population district basis.

Another tactic was to concede that some flexibility was desirable and to assert, by selective quotation of dicta, that the Supreme Court's 1964 *Reapportionment Decisions* really allowed much flexibility. This argument, of course, now sounds rather hollow in the light of the mathematical stringency insisted upon in later, clarifying court decisions in 1966-1967, as noted in Chapter XVII.

An additional tactic of the opponents, given voice by Senator Robert F. Kennedy of New York and others, was to attempt to saddle the Dirksen amendment with all of the problems emanating from Southern repression of the Negro vote. The serious problems of Negro nonregistration which have been the target of several civil rights acts, including the Voting Rights Act of 1965, are essentially separable, however, from representation forms in the context of a reapportionment amendment. As noted in Chapter XVIII, racial gerrymandering and Southern dilution of Negro representation by use of large multimember districts is part of the apparent Southern desire, as Senator Kennedy phrased it, "to keep the Negro a political cripple indefinitely." [54] The problem is real, but has no unique relation to the Dirksen amendment because the tactics mentioned may coexist as easily with "one man-one vote" districts as with disproportional districts.

b. The "Lonely Middle"

The principal exception to the tendency to cast the "D-Day" debate in sterile terms of total support or total opposition to the Dirksen amendment was the band of twelve who supported the proposal which Senator Javits submitted as a substitute for the Dirksen amendment and which was rejected 85 to 12. In precise terms the exception would be confined really to the six members who distinguished between the two amendments by supporting the Javits draft but opposing the Dirksen draft. They were Senators Clinton P. Anderson of New Mexico, Ross Bass of Tennessee, Bayh of Indiana, Javits of New York, Thomas J. McIntyre of New Hampshire, and Edmund S. Muskie of Maine. Had this group also supported the Dirksen amendment, the required two-thirds majority of those present and voting still would not have been achieved; the final Dirksen vote would then have been 63 to 33, still one vote short.

Of course, the bona fides of any vote cast for a measure which is known to be foredoomed to defeat is subject to question; and it is true that Senator Bayh, and perhaps Senator Muskie, for example, were in the position

54. 111 *Cong. Rec.* 18616 (daily ed. Aug. 4, 1965).

of being rather liberal Senators from rather conservative constituencies. Regarding Senator Bayh, a "courtesy vote" factor may have been present. The Javits draft did not meet Senator Bayh's condition of requiring "prior compliance," but Senator Javits had supported Senator Bayh's opposition in the Subcommittee to the Dirksen draft. Taken at face value, however, some of the remarks of this group were of special interest, particularly those of Bayh himself.

Senator Bayh clearly asserted his preference for a middle position rather than an either/or position on the question of a reapportionment amendment and referred to his own aborted plan to submit a draft. Its two main features, he indicated, would have been expressly to authorize discretion in state legislatures to make some deviations in the face of such situations as Colorado's distant western slope, but to require as a precondition of any easing up on the equal population district principle an initial compliance with it for both houses. Practically, of course, his second requirement makes an odd if not illogical bedfellow with his first requirement. His purpose may have been to ensure that an unreconstructed legislature would not control the content of the mixed reapportionment plan submitted to popular referendum. But such a purpose, it seems, could have been handled more expeditiously by authorizing a popular initiative or convention process as alternatives for legislative action in proposing the apportionment plan. "I still wish that we could provide for some leeway," he said, but "the deck is stacked against those of us who wish to have safeguards and yet also some leeway." [55] In this quote is succinctly summarized the whole story of the reapportionment amendment movement from 1964 to 1966.

In sum, if Senator Bayh of Indiana was young Hamlet, seeking some way of accommodating the abstract judicial premise of equal voter rights and the democratic premise of popular control of constitutional change, Senator Douglas of Illinois was the old liberal lion fighting yet another battle—to be his last—for ultimate virtue. Senator Tydings played the role of the lion's cub, gaining recognition on broader plains than his native Maryland. Such politically moderate supporters of the amendment idea as Senator Hugh Scott of Pennsylvania and Senator Javits of New York were in a delicate position. They were somewhat muted by the nature of their constituencies, especially in the light of the mischaracterization of the amendment's terms as resurrecting the malapportionments of the past and disrupting the progress being made in Negro voting. (And yet the Dirksen amendment was supported by Senators Frank J. Lausche of Ohio, Leverett Saltonstall of Massachusetts, Thomas H. Kuchel and George Murphy of California, Dirksen of Illinois and Scott himself on

55. Id. at 18605.

the final vote.) Senator Dirksen, successful architect of many coalitions but now faced with a two-thirds requirement, had at last encountered an uncoalescable issue, even though he started with at least majority support assured.

The intellectual community remained disaffected, and perhaps this was the crucial factor. Having seen old and seemingly impregnable malapportionments toppled, it was not yet overly concerned with the niceties of effective representation and the thought that the pendulum might swing too far in the opposite direction. And it realized that many supporters of the amendment idea were motivated as much by self-interest linked to the past as by a desire to achieve a more perfect system.

c. Revision and Defeat, 1966

Although the August 4 vote on the reapportionment amendment looked to some like a near miss—only one vote short if the Dirksen and Javits strength could have been pooled in a common, acceptable draft—the matter was effectively dead. If the proponents in a year of effort in two congressional sessions were unable to characterize the issue as something less than an attack on a supposed American birthright, and to find adequate language to stake out a middle-ground position, it was unlikely that a few more months of effort would make a difference.

An anticlimax was played out, however. On August 11, 1965, a week after "D-Day," Senator Dirksen introduced a revised draft which was to become the basis for further negotiations with Senator Javits and a second defeat on the Senate floor in April 1966. The revised draft, S.J. 103, provided for ratification only by legislatures at least one house of which was in compliance with the equal population principle, and sought to capture and magnify the nonarithmetic aspects of Chief Justice Warren's opinion in Reynolds v. Sims. It spoke of a purpose of "effective representation," [56] and referred to "geography and political subdivisions" [57] as legitimate considerations along with population as the representation basis for one house. Under its terms a proposal for a mixed representation formula for one house could be submitted to a statewide popular referendum only by a legislature at least one house of which was in compliance with the equal population principle (same requirement as for initial ratification of the amendment itself). Further, each such proposal would have to be accompanied by an alternative equal population plan in order to give the people a choice. The full text read as follows:

56. See Reynolds v. Sims, 377 U.S. 533, 565 (1964) where Chief Justice Warren refers to "fair and effective representation for all citizens" as the "aim" and also speaks of "full and effective participation."
57. Id. at 578, 580 where "political subdivision" representation is suggested as a basis for justifying "some deviations" from strict population equality.

SECTION 1. The legislature of each State shall be apportioned by the people of that State at each general election for Representatives to the Congress held next following the year in which there is commenced each enumeration provided for in section 2 of article I. In the case of a bicameral legislature, the members of one house shall be apportioned among the people on the basis of their numbers and the members of the other house may be apportioned among the people on the basis of population, geography, and political subdivisions in order to insure effective representation in the State's legislature of the various groups and interests making up the electorate. In the case of a unicameral legislature, the house may be apportioned among the people on the basis of substantial equality of population with such weight given to geography and political subdivisions as will insure effective representation in the State's legislature of the various groups and interests making up the electorate.

SEC. 2. A plan of apportionment shall become effective only after it has been submitted to a vote of the people of the State and approved by a majority of those voting on that issue at a statewide election held in accordance with law and the provisions of this Constitution. If submitted by a bicameral legislature the plan of apportionment shall have been approved prior to such election by both houses, one of which shall be apportioned on the basis of substantial equality of population; if otherwise submitted it shall have been found by the courts prior to such election to be consistent with the provisions of this Constitution, including this article. In addition to any other plans of apportionment which may be submitted at such election, there shall be submitted to a vote of the people an alternative plan of apportionment based solely on substantial equality of population. The plan of apportionment approved by a majority of those voting on that issue shall be promptly placed in effect.[58]

Negotiations with the Javits camp failed, however, and no new hearings were held. Some thought was given to convening a conference of legal and political scholars to make a fresh start on the broader dimensions of modern representation theory and devise appropriate language for the "safeguarded flexibility" which Senator Bayh had called for in the Senate debate in 1965. Because of problems of time, money, and interest nothing came of the idea.

Ratification Only by Properly Apportioned Legislatures. In order to avert the suggestion that a reapportionment amendment itself might be declared unconstitutional if ratified by state legislatures some houses of which were not yet in full compliance with the new equal population rule, the Dirksen amendment was modified without opposition on motion of Senator Frank Church of Idaho to provide that it could be ratified only

58. S.J. Res. 103, 89th Cong., 1st Sess. (1965).

by states which had placed both houses on this basis.[59] As a condition of ratification, the Dirksen draft had required prior compliance in at least one house, but not in both houses. Actually, the near-universal modifications of legislatures which had occurred by this time made the point rather academic.

Senator Bayh, however, still held out for the broader rule that whether or not a state was in prior compliance and thus eligible to *ratify* the amendment, it would have to be in prior compliance before it could *utilize* the provisions of the Amendment. In the floor discussion he again reiterated his concern for "one man-one vote" extremism and said: "If we could have incorporated the one word 'reasonable' and required prior compliance, I would have been willing to support those who believe the Supreme Court interpretation has gone too far." [60]

One might wonder, however, whether a requirement of prior compliance in both houses would make much sense *if* the process of initial ratification were by state ratifying conventions (which Senator Dirksen had rejected), and *if each* submission to popular referendum of the question of adopting or retaining a mixed representation system in one house were accompanied by an alternative equal population plan. If there also were provision for submission of a population equality plan by the popular initiative process rather than by the sitting legislature, a rule of prior compliance in both houses would seem to require a useless act.

"Popular Will" v. *"Moral Law."* After several days of desultory discussion the Senate voted 55 to 38 in favor of the Dirksen amendment, thus again falling seven votes short of the required two-thirds majority of those present and voting. The discussion by the opposing forces led by Senators Dirksen and Douglas assisted by Senators Proxmire and Tydings, produced few new ideas.[61] The primary effort of the Dirksen forces was to

59. 112 *Cong. Rec.* 7997, 8002 (daily ed. April 19, 1966). The amendment was offered at least partly in response to a recently published article which had suggested that malapportioned legislatures were incompetent to ratify a federal reapportionment amendment. Peter H. Wolf, "An Apportionment Amendment: Can It Be Legally Ratified?" 52 *A.B.A.J* 326 (1966).

60. 112 *Cong. Rec.* 8180 (daily ed. April 20, 1966).

61. An interesting side feature, however, was the attempt by Senators Douglas, Proxmire, and Tydings to have Senator Dirksen disclose the financial backers of his Committee for Government of the People (successor to the National Commission on Constitutional Government) which was formed in January 1966 to stir up popular and state legislative support for a reapportionment amendment. It conducted an extensive campaign of mailings and press releases under the guidance of the California-based public relations firm of Whitaker and Baxter. An interesting account of the Committee's operation by Robert Sherrill, published in the St. Petersburg *Times*, was inserted in the *Congressional Record* by Senator Douglas. The article included the comment that "the pressures advocated by W&B are proper enough: letters to the editor, letters to congressmen and State legislators, work through local organizations." Nevertheless, the opposing Senators on several occasions wondered whether the group was

twit the opposition for marching under the banner of "one man-one vote" but being afraid of statewide popular referenda on the issue of representation forms.[62] Another noted that the amendment would do no more than permit the people "if they so wish, to again take account of the multitude of diverse factors which require consideration in any adequate system of representation." [63] In one of the more sophisticated statements which accords well with the actual post-reapportionment experience in many states,[64] Senator Thruston B. Morton of Kentucky cautioned against viewing the "one man-one vote" principle as a nostrum, a sacred cure-all for the problems of state governments. He said:

> Redistricting all houses of all legislatures in all States will not change many facts.
> Redistricting will not keep pollution from entering a river upstream and defiling the waters of that river as it flows downstream. It will not prevent legislators from facing conflict of interests in the votes they cast. It will not magically open new and painless sources of revenue so desperately needed by the States. It will not fill in the chuckholes in State roads, it will not educate children, it will not pay teachers more, it will not even bring the conference football championship to the State university. Neither, I might add, will adoption of the pending joint resolution solve these problems.
> So let us get away from the world of imagery and wishful thinking and factless persuasion and talk a little sense. No one wants to abandon majority rule in favor of minority rule. This joint resolution certainly would not do that—no matter what anybody may try to tell us.[65]

To the proponents Senator Douglas had a ringing response, convincing to his followers and perhaps to the country at large, but which proceeded from a premise wholly antithetical to the premise of the Dirksen supporters. The reapportionment amendment supporters proceeded from the premise, not always succinctly portrayed, that the issue was not simply the right to vote but the creation of effective representation forms in regard to which there were reasonable alternatives. The premise of Senator Douglas and his followers was that equal population districts, or perhaps elections at-large, were the only representation forms which were "moral"

in compliance with the lobbying laws, but Senator Dirksen dismissed the request as a "red herring." 112 Cong. Rec. 7938–39, 7988 (daily ed. April 19, 1966).

62. 112 Cong. Rec. 8166 (daily ed. April 20, 1966) (remarks of Senator Len B. Jordan of Idaho).

63. 112 Cong. Rec. 7966 (daily ed. April 19, 1966) (remarks of Senator James B. Pearson of Kansas).

64. See Chapter XX, and Bill Kovach, "Some Lessons of Reapportionment," 37 The Reporter 26 (Sept. 21, 1967).

65. 112 Cong. Rec. 7990 (daily ed. April 19, 1967).

or "ethical," let alone merely "reasonable" or "constitutional." In short, a rule of equal population districts was viewed as being just as much an inviolable *personal* right as such specific guarantees in the Bill of Rights as freedom of speech or right of jury trial or prohibition of cruel or unusual punishment. Referring to the equal population rule, Senator Douglas said:

> I maintain that this is a natural right, an ethical right—yes, using the term in its proper way, a God-given right, that people should be equal in the sight of God and equal in the sight of law—that no majority should take away from an individual.[66]

Thus cast, in absolute, even spiritual, terms not only was there no basis for compromise but the opposing sides were not even agreed on the nature of the issue and thus were "talking past one another" as one Senator said.[67] Indeed, the full thrust of the Douglas peroration was to deny that guarantees like freedom of speech and equal protection, though put into the Constitution by the amending process, could ever be amended out of the Constitution. Senator Douglas had virtually said as much before Senator Bayhs' subcommittee earlier. Under persistent questioning by Senator Hruska, in which Bayh joined to some extent, Douglas had refused to agree with the proposition that the First Amendment is itself amendable. He had said, "Let me say, I would oppose this being done. Secondly, I don't think it could be done, because this principle underlies the Constitution of the United States." [68]

The Douglas characterization of the reapportionment issue obviously gave no basis for viewing the United States Senate itself as even a tolerable institution, however firmly founded historically. And, consequently, Senator Douglas did go on in the Senate debate to refer to the rule of state equality as "wrong morally," to speak of the big states as being "chained in this body," and to bemoan the fact that exemption of Senate representation from coverage of Article V prevented utilizing the amending process to reconstitute the Senate and bring it into accord with "moral law." [69]

The Dirksen amendment was voted down a second time—and this was

66. *Id.* at 8003.
67. *Id.* at 7994 (remarks of Senator Pearson).
68. *Hearings Before the Subcommittee on Constitutional Amendments of the Committee on the Judiciary of the United States Senate,* 89th Cong., 1st Sess. 53 (March 4, 1965).
69. 112 *Cong. Rec.* 8005 (daily ed. April 19, 1966). Quaere, however, whether Article V's prohibition of changing a state's equal representation in the Senate without its consent would bar an amendment transferring all important Senate powers to the House, leaving the states with equal voice in a "senatorial" advisory body analogous to the English House of Lords or the upper house of the West German government.

really the third round, if the defeat of the moratorium measure in 1964 be taken as the kickoff of the struggle. But Senator Dirksen's closing peroration, adapted from General Douglas A. MacArthur, that "old soldiers never die; they just fade away," presaged continuation of the struggle in the altered form of a drive for a constitutional convention.

XVI

The "Dirksen Amendment" Campaign–II

"Some men look at constitutions with sanctimonious reverence
and deem them like the ark of the covenant, too sacred to be
touched. . . . Each generation . . . has a right to choose for itself the form of government it believes the most promotive of its
own happiness. . . . A solemn opportunity of doing this every
19 or 20 years should be provided by the constitution. . . ."

Thomas Jefferson

"I maintain that this [equal population districts for both houses
of state legislatures] is a natural right, an ethical right—yes, using
the term in its proper way, a God-given right. . . ."
"In my opinion, and that of other observers, there is little real
expectation that the Congress will call a convention even if two-
thirds of the State legislatures pass the applications. It cannot, I
believe, be forced to do so."

Senator Paul Douglas

C. In Retrospect: To What Extent Is the Constitution Amendable?

1. IMPOSSIBILITY OF DRAFTING A SIMPLE
APPORTIONMENT AMENDMENT

On two occasions in recent history, one being the *Reapportionment Decisions* and the other being the *School Prayer Decisions* in 1962 and 1963,[1]
rulings of the Supreme Court have evoked not only strong feeling but a
drive to amend the Constitution to undo the decision. On reapportionment, congressional failure led to a drive for a constitutional convention.
Laying aside the *wisdom* of trying to reverse the decisions, it has proved
in each instance far easier to criticize the Court's decisions than to draft a
satisfactory "repealing" amendment. The real lesson therefore of the ill-

1. Engel v. Vitale, 370 U.S. 421 (1962); School Dist. v. Schempp, Murray v. Curlett,
374 U.S. 203 (1963).

fated reapportionment amendment campaign, and the campaign against the prayer decisions which centered on the Becker amendment, may be this: It is simple to make a major constitutional modificaton by judicial decision. It is devilishly difficult thereafter to draft a constitutional amendment which will only undo the one unpopular decision and not affect anything else or create new problems. To those favoring judicial restraint in the Holmes-Frankfurter tradition this fact provided one of their stronger arguments for a judicial policy of treading softly in new thickets.

In regard to the proposed prayer amendments, one problem was that if the amendment used the phrase "nonsectarian" a round of fresh uncertainty in school boards and courts would follow; and if the amendment itself tried to define nonsectarian the prospects for agreement were dim.[2] The principal draft of Congressman Frank J. Becker did not raise this problem but did create at least one major uncertainty in authorizing school prayers on a "voluntary basis."[3] The language also applied to any "institution, or place." What is "voluntary" when attendance is compulsory as in public schools, penal institutions, and military service? The difficulties with the various reapportionment amendment drafts (Ch. XV) were perhaps more serious.

Constitutional amendments, with a few exceptions, are noted for their brevity if not their clarity. And lack of clarity, of course, is less consequential when only in futuro effect is intended. Examples of the latter include the vague but pregnant due process and equal protection of the laws concepts of the Fourteenth Amendment. These really do little more than authorize a large on-going creative natural law process of law "finding." But consider the following examples of problems which arise in trying to devise a text for an amendment which would do no more than modify the Colorado case, *Lucas* v. *Colorado General Assembly*,[4] and leave the other 1964 *Reapportionment Decisions* untouched.

First, should there be express provision for judicial review, or no provision, thus relying on the general tradition of judicial review as expanded or contracted by changing judicial concepts of activism and restraint? The opening sentence of the initial Dirksen draft of S.J. Res. 2, until deleted in Subcommittee, seemed to point in the opposite direction of actually impeding judicial review. If review is specified, might this not deprive the

2. See colloquy between Congressman Byron G. Rogers and Professor Paul A. Freund in *Hearings on School Prayers Before the Committee on the Judiciary of the House of Representatives*, 88th Cong., 1st Sess. 1657 (1963).
3. See H. R. J. Res. 693, 88th Cong., 1st Sess. (1963), commonly referred to as the "Becker amendment," Section 1 of which was as follows: "Nothing in this Constitution shall be deemed to prohibit the offering, reading from, or listening to prayers or biblical scriptures, if participation therein is on a voluntary basis, in any governmental or public school, institution, or place."
4. 377 U.S. 713 (1964).

Court of its traditional capacity to control its work, and to avoid untimely handling of awkward questions, by manipulating such flexible concepts as "standing to sue" and "justiciability"? Granted that in *Baker* v. *Carr* the Court limited the political question doctrine in regard to legislative re-apportionment, should not the extent of the limitation be for the Court itself to decide? The political question doctrine is one of the few instruments of self-defense the Court possesses.

Second, should the amendment seek to regulate the manner in which the people of a state give their assent to placing one legislative house on a basis other than strict equal population districts? Specifically, should the people simply vote on the general idea of having a federal plan or a modified federal plan, with details left to the legislature or a state constitutional convention, or should the people vote on a specific plan? If the latter, should there be provision for a choice among plans, or for successive presentation of different plans?

Third, should there be provision for further popular review in each state of the federal plan idea regardless of the outcome of the initial vote? Specifically, should there be provision for a decennial referendum in each state on the question of adopting a federal plan or continuing a federal plan already in existence? In this event the question would recur of whether the voters should have a choice among competing plans or be allowed simply to cast a yes-no vote on one measure.

In lieu of detailed specification of the number and character of referenda required to adopt and continue a federal plan, would it be preferable and simpler to create as part of the federal amendment a popular initiative process for each state for this topic? Under existing state law only a minority of states authorize the initiative process.

Fourth, to what extent should the federal amendment seek to define the number and character of nonpopulation factors which could be incorporated in a modified federal plan or mixed apportionment formula? Some of the Dirksen and Javits drafts spoke simply of "reasonable weight to factors other than population." [5] The American Bar Association proposal spoke of apportionment "in part by reference to geography, county and city lines, economic conditions, history, and other factors." [6] Apart from the difficulty of getting agreement on a list of limiting standards, the incorporation of such provisions in an amendment raises several policy questions. Would the list impede the process of tailoring an apportionment system to the needs of a particular state? Would the list impede the normal process of judicial review which otherwise could be relied upon to

5. S.J. Res. 2 (Dirksen), S.J. Res 44 (Javits), 89th Cong., 1st Sess. (1965).
6. See full text in chapter XV, note 40.

negate either specifically impermissible standards such as race or generally unreasonable standards?

Fifth, as a corollary to the question of attempting to channel the number and character of "other factors" which could be considered for the nonpopulation house of the legislature, should the amendment seek to limit in mathematical terms the extent of permissible deviation from an equal population district premise? Taking this route might ease the "standards" problem by obviating the need for any specification of the kinds of nonpopulation factors which could be utilized. Although a rule of reason could and should be judically maintained, there would be more room for traditional and realistic political negotiation and no need to prove that each district line was "rational" in the sense of being a logically consistent derivation from a specified list of factors. An amendment capturing this thought might read somewhat as follows:

> Nothing in this Constitution or judicial interpretations thereof shall limit the right and power of the people of a state, expressed through statewide referendum, to apportion one house of the state legislature by population and the second house by a mixture of population and nonpopulation considerations provided the resultant deviations from mean population in the districts for the second house not exceed an average deviation of ____ percent and a maximum deviation of ____ percent, and provided further . . . [decennial review, etc.].

Such a text would do several things. First, in keeping with the suggested direct democracy approach, it provides that ratification shall be by state ratifying conventions, not state legislatures. Second, the text authorizes, but does not require, implementing federal legislation to provide a reapportionment petition procedure for those states, unlike Colorado, which lack the initiative procedure. Third, no deviation from the existing rule of equal population districts for both houses of a bicameral legislature could occur except in regard to one house, and this deviation is subject to initial popular approval and an opportunity for regular popular review thereafter.

Fourth, the clause concerning average and maximum percentage deviation would place some outer boundaries on the amount of deviation in the second house from a straight population principle without attempting the impossible task of defining a finite list of permissible nonpopulation factors. The *average* deviation concept is a more meaningful mathematical measure of "malapportionment," although it is usually ignored in favor of focusing on the extremes. Such a draft has some virtues of simplicity and flexibility but some persons justifiably may doubt the advisability of inserting a specific mathematical figure in the federal Constitution.

Should the permitted mathematical variation in the second house be only slightly in excess of the 15 percent maximum deviation figure commonly mentioned under the *Reynolds* doctrine, or should it be permitted to range up to a 100 or 200 percent deviation? Also, if the federal plan or modified federal plan amendment were to be limited by a guideline expressed in mathematical terms, would not the *average* deviation concept be more appropriate than a maximum deviation concept?

This list of the kinds of problems which arise in attempting to devise a text for a narrow reapportionment amendment is not exhaustive. It does serve to document the proposition that even with more congressional support than the amendment proponents were able to muster, the task of devising a satisfactory text would not have been easy. Incorporating very many of the suggestions listed above could have produced not a constitutional amendment but an election code.

2. COULD UNREAPPORTIONED LEGISLATURES RATIFY A REAPPORTIONMENT AMENDMENT?

No constitutional amendment has ever been declared unconstitutional, although for a time the Supreme Court seemed to treat the matter as being subject to judicial review.[7] A repudiation of the idea that constitutional amendments are themselves subject to judicial review can be found in the last Supreme Court treatment of the amending power in *Coleman v. Miller*,[8] which involved the initiated but unratified Child Labor Amendment. Only eight justices sat for this case. The Court ruled that both the issue of undue time lapse since congressional initiation, and the power of the Kansas legislature to give approval after having initially rejected the amendment were "political questions" for Congress, not the Court, to decide. (On a further issue of the power of the lieutenant governor to break a tie in the Kansas senate, the Court was evenly divided and made no ruling.) A solid block of four justices, including Justices Black and Douglas, went further, stating their view in strong terms that the amending process was " 'political' in its entirety, from submission until an amendment becomes part of the Constitution, and is not subject to judicial guidance, control or interference at any point." [9]

If the Supreme Court should ignore the quoted *Coleman* dictum, and be willing to review a reapportionment amendment, would the fact of ratification by some "malapportioned" state legislatures be deemed such a

7. See e.g., National Prohibition Cases, 253 U.S. 350 (1920); Leser v. Garnett, 258 U.S. 130 (1922); Dillon v. Gloss, 256 U.S. 368 (1921); Hawke v. Smith, 253 U.S. 221 (1920); United States v. Sprague, 282 U.S. 716 (1931).
8. 307 U.S. 433 (1939).
9. *Id.* at 456.

"bootstrap" operation as to jeopardize the amendment's constitutionality? The essence of the argument would be that the amendment was a minority imposition on the American people. At least two preliminary counter-arguments could be made: first, the amendment would be proposed only if supported by a two-thirds vote in both houses of Congress; second, even after ratification a reapportionment amendment of the Javits or Dirksen type would contemplate deviation from the Supreme Court's equal population district standard only if the deviation be approved by a statewide popular referendum.

a. *Powers of Malapportioned Legislatures*

The starting premise is that a "malapportioned" legislature is competent to discharge its customary tasks as the legislative organ of the state including, as the Supreme Court indicated in the Maryland case,[10] enactment of reapportionment measures. Indeed, this proposition follows inexorably from the proposition frequently announced both before and after the 1964 *Reapportionment Decisions* that reapportionment is a legislative function and that the problem is to galvanize the legislature to act. Obviously there is no need for a legislature to exercise this function—and reapportion decennially—*unless* the passage of time has eroded this pre-existing apportionment and made the current legislature a "malapportioned" legislature. Accordingly, following the Supreme Court's lead, virtually every court which has dealt with reapportionment has accorded primacy to legislative action. Typically, reapportionment has been handled by statute, legislatures exercising a generic power, or a remedial power sanctioned by federal equity, to replace nullified parts of a state constitution's apportionment formula with a new plan. The courts take over only when the malapportioned legislature fails to act in appropriate fashion on reapportionment.[11]

A special question may arise, however, concerning the power of a malapportioned legislature to *initiate* a *state* constitutional change on apportionment—or, by analogy, to *ratify* a proposed *federal* amendment on apportionment, which is the present question. In regard to the former

10. 377 U.S. 656, 675–76 (1964).
Some courts have invoked an "avoidance of chaos and confusion rule" as a way of protecting acts of malapportioned legislatures from attack by criminals seeking to invalidate the law they violated, e.g., State v. Bomar, 381 S.W. 2d 297 (Tenn. 1964); Dawson v. Bomar, 322 F.2d 445 (6th Cir. 1963), cert. den. 376 U.S. 933 (1964). This is a variation of the familiar "de facto officer" rule which supports the validity of acts of an unqualified or "improper" officer if he is exercising the powers of a proper, i.e., de jure, office. See Kidd v. McCanless, 200 Tenn. 273, 292 S.W. 2d 40 (1956). The "de facto officer" doctrine must be stretched to cover the malapportionment situation because under malapportionment there is no de jure office.
11. See Appendix A and individual state comments.

question, the general tendency in the post-*Reynolds* era was to make no distinction between the power of a malapportioned legislature to reapportion itself by statute, or by instituting a state constitutional convention. Malapportioned legislatures have instituted constitutional conventions either to sanction a plan already put in force by the malapportioned legislature, as in Connecticut, or to make a fresh start, as in New Jersey, Hawaii, and Maryland. In a preliminary phase of Tennessee reapportionment a challenge to a legislative call of a constitutional convention was dismissed on the ground that even though the convention, like the legislature, would be malapportioned, it only would have power to propose and not to take final action.[12]

The more precise analogy in state precedents, however, to the undecided question of power of a malapportioned state legislature to ratify a federal amendment, is the question of the power of a malapportioned legislature itself to propose a state constitutional amendment on apportionment. A federal district court in Nebraska refused either to enjoin submission of a constitutional amendment proposed by the malapportioned legislature, or to rule on the amendment's validity prior to expression of popular feeling.[13] By contrast a Georgia federal district court ruled that a malapportioned legislature was incompetent to submit a state constitutional reapportionment amendment.[14] The ruling was effectively mooted by an intervening election before appeal to the United States Supreme Court was effected. Subsequently the Supreme Court partially vacated the ruling and remanded the matter in a short per curiam opinion which seemingly had the effect of placing the matter in limbo and robbing the lower court order of any precedential effect. Justice Arthur M. Goldberg found the Court's remand order "mystifying" and wanted to make it crystal clear that the Court was wiping the slate clean and leaving open the question of the powers of a malapportioned legislature to initiate constitutional change.[15]

If a malapportioned legislature is incompetent to initiate a constitutional amendment, as the Georgia federal district court ruled, then what

---

12. West v. Carr, 212 Tenn. 367, 370 S.W.2d 469 (1963).

13. League of Nebraska Municipalities v. Marsh, 209 F. Supp. 189, 194–95 (D. Neb. 1962). One legislature was told that prior to its own reapportionment it should take no action on any "federal plan" national amendment. Petuskey v. Rampton, 243 F. Supp. 365 (D. Utah 1965).

14. Toombs v. Fortson, unreported order of June 30, 1964. The order was entered despite the innocuous nature of the proposed new constitutional clause on reapportionment. It did no more than fix the size of the two houses, repeal all other provisions, and empower the legislature to reapportion as it wished—under the over-all restraint, of course, of the federal equal population principle.

15. Fortson v. Toombs, 379 U.S. 621, 636. Justice Harlan in a separate opinion could find "nothing . . . in the Constitution, or in any decision of this Court which requires a state to *initiate* complete or partial constitutional change only by some method in which every voice in the voting population is given an opportunity to express itself."

of provisions in some state where 8 percent of the people may initiate constitutional change by petition? Does equal opportunity to utilize the petition process make the difference?

In a complicated series of events in Hawaii concerning a reapportionment plan passed by the legislature, a federal district court disallowed both interim use of the plan and its contemplated submission to the voters as a constitutional amendment.[16] But the ruling was based on alleged federal constitutional defects in the plan, i.e., denial of equality of voter representation by using multimember districts to create "monoliths," [17] rather than an intrinsic lack of power in a malapportioned legislature to propose constitutional amendments. The district court's ruling concerning multimember districts was reversed by the Supreme Court for lack of appropriate proof of invidious effect, but the machinery for a constitutional convention set in motion by the legislature under district court pressure was allowed to stand.[18] Thus the question of power of a malapportioned legislature to submit a reapportionment plan directly to the people again was mooted.

Of special significance may be the more recent ruling of the Supreme Court in the famous disputed Georgia governorship election, *Fortson* v. *Morris*.[19] There the Court upheld, 5-4, the power of the malapportioned Georgia legislature (partially reapportioned but under court mandate to reach full compliance) to elect the governor of Georgia in 1966 when no candidate received the necessary majority of the popular vote.

b. *Legislatures and Federal Amendments*

Looking to the future, the precise issue of power of a malapportioned state legislature to ratify a reapportionment amendment to the *federal* Constitution would never be aired if a majority of the Court adhered to the view of four justices in the *Coleman* v. *Miller* case in 1939 that constitutional amendment disputes are "political" questions not judicially reviewable. The easing of the political question disability in *Baker*, however, might presage a willingness to review the merits of the question. If so, the larger question would be the power of a "malapportioned" legislature to ratify *any* constitutional amendment. A recent essay seeking to maintain the thesis that a malapportioned legislature could not ratify a reapportionment amendment conceded that the argument was equally applicable to ratification of *any* amendment.[20] The central premise given for the argu-

16. Holt v. Richardson, 238 F. Supp. 468, 240 F. Supp. 724 (D. Hawaii 1965).
17. 240 F. Supp. at 730.
18. *Ibid.*
19. 385 U.S. 231 (1966); and see above pp. 136–37, 221 n. 59.
20. Peter H. Wolf, "An Apportionment Amendment: Can It Be Legally Ratified?" 52 A.B.A.J. 326 (1966).

424   DEMOCRATIC REPRESENTATION

ment was that the Constitution, including judicial construction, is higher law and invalidates governmental actions inconsistent with its announced commands and prescriptions.

In realistic terms, therefore, the question would be whether a legislature reconstructed after the 1964 *Reapportionment Decisions* could ratify *any* constitutional amendment in the 1970s before reapportioning itself again under the 1970 census.[21] A rule that such a legislature could *not* ratify *any* amendment would come close to being a reductio ad absurdum-type of rule. Since many legislatures would be regularly affected, the rule would force periodic suspension of Article V in regard to legislative ratification and force use of the alternative route of state ratifying conventions, which itself might be suspect if the same districts were used. Consistency of principle under such a Caesar's wife rule would seem to require also the nullification of all bills enacted by lame-duck legislatures, even if properly apportioned. Further, there would be little basis for distinguishing, and continuing to observe, the rule that a malapportioned legislature could pass general legislation and even elect a governor, as in Georgia.

Attempts have been made to make the argument more plausible by suggesting two limitations.[22] One limitation is that there would be no standing for citizen challenge of a malapportioned legislature's ratification of most amendments, other than a reapportionment amendment, because of lack of the required degree of personal interest. (The argument assumes of course that conceded voter standing for direct attack on state legislature apportionment could be extended to cover the somewhat different question of the ratification process for a federal reapportionment amendment.) However, prior to the *Coleman* v. *Miller* four-justice dictum against any further judicial review whatsoever of constitutional amendment questions, the Court in a series of suits had litigated a number of questions concerning the validity of the prohibition amendments (Eighteenth and Twenty-first) and woman suffrage amendment (Nineteenth) without being troubled by standing or justiciability considerations.[23] And some recent cases suggest a trend to ease requirements of standing so that citizens may more easily litigate public law issues, e.g., church-state cases [24] and reapportionment cases themselves.

The second limitation is to confine the asserted disability to those legislatures judicially declared malapportioned. Absent such a ruling an unre-

---

21. It seems unlikely, though not impossible, that the Fourteenth Amendment will be construed to require reapportionment more often than the regular decennial census—or five year census, if that becomes the regular practice at the Census Bureau.

22. Wolf, *supra* note 20, at 331.

23. See note 7, *supra*.

24. E.g., Engel v. Vitale, 370 U.S. 421 (1962); School Dist. v. Schempp, 374 U.S. 203 (1963). But cf. Flast v. Gardner, 271 F. Supp. 1 (S.D.N.Y. 1967).

constructed or malapportioned legislature could still validly ratify a federal reapportionment amendment. This limitation is based on the sound principle that otherwise amendments would have no finality; they would be subject to retroactive invalidation, causing uncertainty and confusion. However, this limitation brings with it new problems of arbitrariness. It introduces the chance factor of differential plaintiff and judicial vigor in different states in timing and pressing reapportionment suits. And the limitation also would operate differently in different states because of divergencies among the judges on what constitutes "malapportionment," a 10 or 15 percent deviation (and much more in the "first round" cases after *Reynolds* v. *Sims*) being acceptable in some states but not in others. Not to put too fine a point on it, the argument against ratification by malapportioned legislatures has an instinctive appeal but it concededly sweeps in too much if not limited; and the limitation process involves logical inconsistencies.

However, to avoid all doubts, it can be expected that any future reapportionment amendment, like the Dirksen "last try" in 1966, would contain a provision for ratification by ratifying conventions rather than state legislatures. Here too, however, a further reductio ad absurdum-type objection is possible. Ratifying conventions, after all, are not the same thing as a statewide, "one man-one vote" popular referendum. Delegates may be elected in the same districts as legislators.[25] The state convention then would be in outward form a carbon copy of the state legislature. Because its members are delegates rather than legislators, and would be chosen only on the basis of their commitment to vote yes or no on the amendment in question, the factor of distortion of popular will caused by unequal size districts would be diluted, but not totally eliminated. And not eliminated at all would be the vice common to all district systems, and often productive of distortions greater than those caused by surplus pluralities ("wasted votes"). The statewide popular majority actually may lose in a district system if its strength is heavily concentrated in a minority of districts.

In short, under the bonds of Article V we are chained to hard choices, and it may not be satisfactory to use "reductio ad absurdum" as an all-encompassing exoneration for the ills of our present practice.

c. *Should We Amend Article V?*

Perhaps it is time to take a fresh look at Article V itself. Some of the problems of the issues raised above would be mooted by terminating en-

25. Everett S. Brown, *Ratification of the Twenty-First Amendment to the Constitution of the United States: State Convention Records and Laws* 515–19 (Ann Arbor: University of Michigan Press, 1938).

tirely the practice of state legislative ratification and using only state ratifying conventions. Additional problems would end if the entire ratification section of Article V were rewritten to authorize statewide popular
referenda as the sole method for ratification of federal amendments. All
problems would vanish and "one man-one vote" theory would be fully
honored by going further and authorizing *nationwide* popular referenda as
the sole ratification device for federal constitutional amendments. Thus
only can we avoid the distorting feature of surplus pluralities stemming
from the state-unit factor which would still be present in the half-way
house device of intrastate referenda. In ratification of federal amendments by state legislatures (or by state ratifying conventions if similarly constructed), there are as many districts—and consequent distortions—as there are state legislative districts, approximately 6000. In
ratification by statewide popular referenda there are still, in effect, fifty
districts—the states themselves. Only in ratification by nation-wide popular referenda is there a single undistorted *national*-constituency response
to the national issue of changing the only Constitution common to us
all.

Such a shift, of course, may be too great a change for a "federal" or
"states rights" heritage to accept all at once. But if "one man-one vote"
be taken seriously, the choice should be between such a truly national ratification process and use of statewide referenda. In the former the "federal" interest would be preserved by the role of the United States Senate
in the initiation process; in the latter the "federal" principle would be
preserved because the states would still be acting as equal state units in
the ratification process. Neither ratification form now utilized under Article V—by state legislatures or by state conventions commonly elected
from the very same districts—is conceptually consistent with the "one
man-one vote" revolution.

D. The Attempted "Call" of a Constitutional Convention

One of the best-known "dead letter" clauses in the federal Constitution is
that part of Article V which authorizes constitutional amendment by the
process of a constitutional convention. A convention "shall" be called by
Congress on "application" of two-thirds of the states, with subsequent ratification accomplished by the usual alternatives of approval by three-
fourths of the states acting either through legislative action or state ratifying conventions. It is understandable that the Founding Fathers, sitting
in a Constitutional Convention, should have wished to authorize further

constitutional conventions as an alternative for constitutional change by congressional initiation. It is also understandable that the convention device has never been used; piecemeal constitutional revision, which is all the people have ever desired, is more expeditiously handled by congressional initiation. The convention clause of Article V has become, therefore, only a "protest clause"—a device for popular protest against congressional refusal to initiate a given amendment. It is available to any who muster enough strength to convince both houses of one or more state legislatures to petition Congress to call a convention. The "application" or petition usually specifies the one amendment desired. A well-known but unsuccessful drive a few years ago, for example, sought a convention for the purpose of imposing a 25 percent ceiling on income taxation.[26]

Failure of the Dirksen forces in 1965 and 1966 to muster a two-thirds Senate vote for initiation of a reapportionment amendment led to renewed vigor on the part of those who contemporaneously were seeking to open up the convention route for a reapportionment amendment, and perhaps a prayer amendment too. By early 1967 thirty-two states had petitioned in one form or another for a constitutional convention to modify the requirement that both legislative houses be based on equal population districts.[27] However, the nearer the count got to the necessary figure of two-thirds (34 state petitions), the more voices were heard in Congress and elsewhere questioning the "validity" of the petitions, the duty of Congress to act even if petitions were received from 34 or more states, and the availability of any court remedy to force Congress to act if it were disinclined to call a convention.

Some of the problems with the convention clause,[28] which have been discussed in introductory political science classes as a parlor game for years, include the following: (1) What is the permissible time lapse between the first petition and the 34th petition, i.e., how far back can we go in making the "two-thirds" count? In the case of the drive for a reappor-

26. Staff of House Committee on the Judiciary, *Problems Relating to State Applications for a Convention to Propose Constitutional Limitations on Federal Tax Rates*, 82nd Cong., 2d Sess. 5 (Comm. Print 1952).

27. American Enterprise Institute, Special Analysis Series No. 5, *A Convention to Amend the Convention?* 11–16 Washington, D.C., June 16, 1967.

As of September 1967 the following 32 states had petitioned for a convention: Alabama, Arizona, Arkansas, Colorado, Florida, Georgia, Idaho, Illinois, Indiana, Kansas, Kentucky, Louisiana, Maryland, Minnesota, Mississippi, Missouri, Montana, Nebraska, Nevada, New Hampshire, New Mexico, North Carolina, North Dakota, Oklahoma, South Carolina, South Dakota, Tennessee, Texas, Utah, Virginia, Washington, Wyoming.

28. Cyril F. Brickfield, *Problems Relating to a Federal Constitutional Convention* in House Committee on the Judiciary, 85th Cong., 1st Sess. (Comm. Print 1957); Arthur E. Bonfield, "Proposing Constitutional Amendments by Convention: Some Problems," 39 *Notre Dame Lawyer* 659 (1964).

tionment convention, some petitions dated back to 1963 and were a response to the 16th Biennial General Assembly of the States' resolutions in December 1962, calling for three so-called "states rights" amendments, one of which suggested removal of state reapportionment jurisdiction from the federal courts.[29]

(2) How similar must the wording or substantive content of the state petitions be in order to constitute a single movement and be counted together in satisfying the two-thirds requirement? In the case of the drive for the reapportionment convention some early petitions followed the 1962 General Assembly of the States in opposing court jurisdiction. Others, like the final Dirksen draft, only sought an optional departure from the Colorado case, i.e., one house could be placed on a mixed representation basis by popular referendum process. (The 17th Biennial General Assembly of the States in December 1964 recommended this approach and dropped opposition to court jurisdiction.)

(3) Associated with the second question is the broader question of whether Article V contemplates state specification of the very amendment desired, or only designation of the amendment topic. At the practical level, of course, no one goes to the great exertion of having states petition Congress for a constitutional convention unless he at least has a particular topic in mind, and he usually wishes to specify how it should be handled.[30] In fact, state petitions have been rather specific in their wording.

It has been argued, however, that specification of the text of the amendment desired prevents the petition from being a valid "application" to Congress under Article V. The ground asserted is that Article V should contemplate an open convention and free deliberation.[31] But the text of Article V simply refers to congressional initiation or state petition-convention initiation, as alternative and equally available modes for proposing "amendments" to the Constitution. And the origin of Article V more rebuts than supports the asserted restrictive interpretation. The state

29. *Hearings Before the Subcommittee on Constitutional Amendments of the Senate Committee on the Judiciary*, 89th Cong., 1st Sess. 357 (1965); Council of State Governments, "Amending the Constitution to Strengthen the States in the Federal System," 36 *State Government* 10 (1963).
30. Brickfield, *supra* note 28, at 7–8, 75; Fred P. Graham, "The Role of the States in Proposing Constitutional Amendments," 49 A.B.A.J. 1175 (1963).
31. Charles L. Black, "The Proposed Amendment of Article V: A Threatened Disaster," 72 *Yale L. J.* 957 (1963); Bonfield, *supra* note 28, at 677–78. See also Arthur John Keeffe, "Article V Revisited," 53 A.B.A.J. 674 (1967).
  Professors Black and Bonfield are so anxious to unhorse the idea of a reapportionment convention that they virtually unhorse the state petition process itself. Further, there may be a certain *chutzpah* quality in the argument of some supporters of the narrow view: the state applications cannot be counted as a single application to achieve two-thirds unless they express a common interest and do so within a fairly concentrated time period; but if too specific they are per se invalid!

petition clause of Article V was not an historical accident, but was added in response to criticism after the Committee on Style and Revision had reported a draft confining initiation of amendments to Congress. George Mason feared that under this draft "no amendments of the proper kind would ever be obtained by the people, if the government should become oppressive," [32] which he deemed likely. James Madison and Alexander Hamilton in *The Federalist* noted that Article V as modified to include the state petition process "equally enables the general and the state governments to originate the amendment of errors, as they may be pointed out by the experience on one side or on the other," and that nothing in this regard is left to the "discretion" of Congress.[33]

(4) Associated with the third question is the specific question whether a convention would be limited to the topic or topics mentioned in the petitions. Would it be the intent of Article V to hold a convention for the sole purpose of voting yes or no on Senator Dirksen's final reapportionment amendment draft, or on any other draft? On the other hand, if a federal reapportionment convention had general authority, might it not confound all 34 of the state petitioners who brought it into being by proposing a rule even more stringent than the judicial interpretation of "one man-one vote?"

Perhaps the reasonable path would be to separate the question of specificity in the state petitions from the question of limiting the powers of the delegates in convention assembled. In all candor, the former is unavoidable. Indeed, specificity in state petitions may be helpful in pinpointing the area for discussion and illustrating the ease or difficulty of capturing the desired change in constitutional language. The latter question of convention powers is much more difficult, and involves the corollary question of congressional powers.

(5) What is the congressional role in the "call" of a constitutional convention? Here there are a number of subsidiary questions. Is Congress the exclusive judge of the validity and sufficiency of the petitions, or could the matter be litigated? Can Congress give guidance to the convention in the form of limiting the range of topics or even limiting the range of choices to be considered regarding a given topic? Undoubtedly Congress has some role to play in passing the necessary enabling act, but the question of subject matter controls would depend on unpredictable variables of popular feeling and of judicial willingness to get deeply involved in the amending process.

32. Max Farrand, editor, *The Records of the Federal Convention* I: 202–3 (New Haven: Yale University Press, 1911).
33. James Madison, *The Federalist* No. 43: 294, 302; Alexander Hamilton, *The Federalist* No. 85: 164, 168–69 (New York: Tudor Publishing Co., 1947).

(6) Would congressional refusal to call a convention be a "political question" beyond the reach of judicial power, or could Congress by court order be forced to act? In 1965 at an early stage in the reapportionment amendment struggle, Senator Douglas predicted that Congress would not—and implied that he would not—honor a "call" for convention "even if two-thirds of the State legislatures pass the applications." He doubted that Congress could "be forced to do so." [34]

It is true that despite both *Baker* v. *Carr* on state legislative reapportionment and *Wesberry* v. *Sanders* on congressional redistricting, there is no precedent for orders by a federal court directed to the President or Congress. Both *Baker* and *Wesberry* could be enforced by *federal* court orders against *state* legislatures. Considerations both of power to enforce the order, and of separation of powers at the national level of government, might induce a court to avoid a clash with Congress on the call of a constitutional convention. Such considerations led the Supreme Court in the past to refuse to enjoin President Andrew Johnson from enforcing Reconstruction legislation.[35] To be sure, in 1952 the Court did invalidate President Harry S. Truman's seizure of steel mills during a strike, but the injunction was directed to the Secretary of Commerce and in any event was a negative order rather than a command to act.[36]

(7) How is the convention to be composed? Article V seems to vest plenary power in Congress in providing for the size, composition, and manner of election of the convention. By analogy to a common practice in setting up state constitutional conventions, Congress might simply provide for election of a convention in the same manner and in the same districts as Congress itself is elected. However, this would mean that the portion of the national convention corresponding to the Senate would be grossly malapportioned. And though Article V may expressly authorize Senate malapportionment by exempting it from constitutional amendment, it does not authorize convention malapportionment. It would be an anomaly, particularly in the reapportionment field, to set up a national convention to deal with state legislative apportionment which was itself malapportioned. The problem would be minimized by modeling a national convention on the House of Representatives and basing it solely on congressional districts, but this would still overrepresent the smallest states. In a properly apportioned national convention—following the emerging rule of thumb of some courts that any district deviation of more than 10 percent (or even less) is suspect—some smaller states could have

34. Statement of Senator Paul Douglas before the Subcommittee on Constitutional Amendments of the Senate Judiciary Committee, 89th Cong., 1st Sess. (mimeo March 4, 1965).
35. Mississippi v. Johnson, 71 U.S. (4 Wall.) 475 (1866).
36. Youngstown Sheet & Tube Co. v. Sawyer, 343 U.S. 579 (1952).

no delegates of their own unless the convention were made quite large.

For example, if Alaska were to be given one vote in a national convention and if all other states were to be given voting strength in direct proportion to that of Alaska's (dividing each state's 1960 population by that of Alaska—226,167), there would be 804.7 votes cast at the convention. New York's present congressional delegation is 41. At the convention New York would cast 74.2 votes. Other states now having only one representative in the House are Delaware, Nevada, Vermont, and Wyoming. They would cast 2.0, 1.3, 1.7, and 1.5 votes, respectively. Only Alaska's vote would remain unchanged. Alternatively, if the size of the convention were to be limited to 435 and no state were to be guaranteed at least one vote, and if votes were apportioned according to a strict system of ratios, Alaska, Nevada, and Vermont would be the only states not having a whole vote of their own. Vermont might have a full vote, however, if a 10 percent deviation were deemed permissible, because its population is within 10 percent of the ratio. (The ratio is determined by dividing 435 into the 1960 population of the United States. The resulting ratio is 412,237.)

(8) A special question, not highlighted until the current reapportionment controversy, is whether a malapportioned legislature is competent to *petition* for a convention to consider limiting the new "one man-one vote" rule. Of the 32 states making application by early 1967, 26 were under a court order to reapportion at the time the petition was approved.[37] This question is analogous to the question of whether a malapportioned legislature would be competent to *ratify* a federal reapportionment amendment. The retroactivity problem may be less serious at the proposal stage than at the ratification stage. But there remains the problem of arbitrariness and disuniformity stemming from differential lower court rulings on what constitutes a properly apportioned legislature, and also the logical necessity of applying such a rule of disability to all petitions for a constitutional convention, regardless of subject matter.

Even without exhausting all of the possible complexities, the state petition and federal convention route to constitutional amendment emerges as a veritable "can of worms," and seems unlikely to be used successfully. For this reason many find it difficult to take seriously this portion of Article V, despite the clear intent of the Founding Fathers to keep open an amendment route not subject to congressional control. Although few persons now may share the sense of nation-state tensions which gave rise to the addition of the state petition clause to Article V, situations can be

37. Johnny H. Killian, *Memorials to Congress on Constitutional Convention*, Library of Congress Legislative Reference Service (March 21, 1967).

imagined where the disposition of congressional forces, including a Senate filibuster, could block initiation of an amendment which, if submitted, would receive adequate support for ratification.

Perhaps by analogy to the practice in some states we should explore the advisability of proposing federal amendments by some process of popular initiative, or by proposal in two successive Congresses by an absolute majority (or even simple majority), in lieu of the present requirement of a two-thirds vote.

Near the end of 1967 the drive for a national convention for reapportionment seemed destined to fail because at the peak of interest even the most generous count fell two states short of the required 34. The broad questions listed surrounding the convention process, and the more detailed questions which could be derived from them, may be destined to remain unanswered—as they have through more than 175 years of American constitutional history.

E. Reprise: The Relevance of Article V

The drive to have Congress initiate a reapportionment amendment and the ensuing drive to accomplish the same goal by constitutional convention seems to have failed. In retrospect the proposals seemed destined to failure from the outset. Some of the particular proposals had little merit; others, centering on limited modification of the "one man-one vote" principle and on recurring popular referenda, were more appealing in principle but difficult to incorporate in appropriate constitutional text. But, apart from the particular merits of alternative draft amendments to give new direction to our representation theory and practice, the most striking thought that emerges from this controversy is the extreme disfavor, amounting almost to derision, with which the amendment proposals were met.

As the reapportionment amendment controversy fades, it leaves us with these far broader issues: Is the amendment article (Article V) irrelevant to the larger public law controversies of our day? Is it totally irrelevant where modification of a Supreme Court decision is involved? With regard to the latter issue, it is certainly too late in the day to pretend that courts do not dramatically and effectively change the Constitution. Indeed, it has been common lore in introductory American Government classes for decades that vigorous use of the unique American system of judicial review explains the infrequency of formal amendment—or the petty character of most additions except for the Bill of Rights and the Civil War Amendments. Supreme Court justices on occasion admit to "amending" the Constitution, or at least accuse their brethren of it, which amounts to the same thing.[38]

The dimensions of the issue can best be delineated by a series of rhetorical questions: Why are proposals to "amend" the Constitution to modify a particular "Supreme Court amendment" to, or expansion of, the Constitution deemed dishonorable or a "retribution," [39] or a "casting aside" of judicial review? [40] How do Article V and judicial review compare in *democratic* theory? Is judicial review incompatible with Article V, or vice versa? Does the possibility of a "bad" constitutional amendment make the process of constitutional amendment impure? What of a "bad" exercise of judicial review? Is the Court to be deemed infallible, correctible only by itself?

Is Article V suited only to tinkering with the grosser mechanical details of our system, e.g., no presidential third term, presidential disability and succession, District of Columbia voting for President and Congress, the poll tax, and the like? Are weighty public policy matters, such as theories and problems of representation beyond the reach of Article V? If some issues are effectively beyond the reach of Article V, are they beyond the reach of the people?

At the very least, is there cause for concern when a proposal for a constitutional amendment leads more to a national diatribe than to a national dialogue? The present-day champions of the Court, and viewers-with-alarm of the amending process are classifiable as political "liberals." But liberals have not always been on the side of the Court, nor have "conservatives" always opposed it. Indeed, the Court was frequently so pro-property from the Civil War to the New Deal that attacking the Court, in the name of democracy, was a standard liberal pastime. Hence, the present degree of anti-Article V feeling, in the cause of keeping Court decisions inviolate, is historically anomalous. Court decisions have changed, yes. But has democratic theory regarding "ultimate control" changed that much? Control made too "ultimate" is not "control" at all. Jefferson, for example, thought the Constitution should be revised every twenty years [41]—and he did not have in mind using the process of *Marbury* v. *Madison*.

In these contexts the reapportionment amendment campaign in Con-

38. See, e.g., Justice Black in Bell v. Maryland, 378 U.S. 226, 248 (1964) and Justice Harlan in Reynolds v. Sims, 377 U.S. 533, 591 (1964).
39. *New York Times*, June 29, 1964, p. 1, cols. 2–3, p. 20, col. 1.
40. *Washington Post*, Aug. 30, 1964, p. E 1, cols. 1–8, p. E 3, cols. 1–5.
41. Saul K. Padover, editor, *Thomas Jefferson on Democracy* 67 (New York: New American Library of World Literature, 1953).

gress and the subsequent constitutional convention campaign, though the former at least was always a lost cause, leave disturbing implications for the future. The implications arise neither from the intrinsic rightness or wrongness of the amendment proposals, nor from the arguments with which they were met on policy grounds. They arise from the size of the chorus who were more inclined to jeer than to argue, and who seemed to feel that any constitutional amendment proposal is positively unclean when modification of a particular Court decision is at issue. For example, even after the constitutional convention idea had been discussed frequently in Congress and elsewhere, an article nevertheless appeared bearing the sinister title: "The Quiet Campaign." [42] But what is more quiet than judicial review, and indeed, more narrowly channeled by limitations on standing to be heard? In short, the defeat of the reapportionment amendment idea tends to confirm the impracticality of efforts to modify by constitutional amendments any major Court decision, no matter how sharp may be the Court's break with prior constitutional understanding.

So, though we start with the question of a reapportionment amendment we end with a much larger question: Is Article V of the Constitution irrelevant to the grander issues of constitutional form and policy which we call constitutional law? Is a Supreme Court vote (5-4, 6-3) always sufficient, no matter how ill-founded in history, text, or general expectation the newly announced principle may be? As noted in Chapters VIII and XI neither the congressional district opinions nor the reapportionment opinions have foundation in the text of the Constitution when put in the context of the times in which the texts were drafted, as conceded by scholars on both sides of the reapportionment issue.[43]

However, the same can be said about a great many of the formative decisions of the Court, e.g., the remaking of the interstate commerce clause into a clause authorizing substantial national regulation of *intra*state activity,[44] the remaking of the First Amendment with the aid of the Fourteenth Amendment's "incorporation doctrine" into a ban against state as well as congressional interference with freedoms of expression,[45] the transformation of the Fourteenth Amendment's ban against state discrimination into a ban also against private discrimination,[46] the transforma-

42. Theodore Sorenson and Paul Simon, "The Quiet Campaign," *Saturday Review* 17, 20 (July 15, 1967).

43. Alfred H. Kelley, "Clio and the Court: An Illicit Love Affair," in 1965 *Supreme Court Review* 119; William W. Van Alstyne, "The Fourteenth Amendment, the 'Right' to Vote, and the Understanding of the Thirty-Ninth Congresses," *id.* 33 (Philip B. Kurland, editor, Chicago: University of Chicago Press, 1965).

44. Wickard v. Filburn, 317 U.S. 111 (1942); Katzenbach v. McClung, 379 U.S. 294 (1964); Heart of Atlanta Motel v. United States, 379 U.S. 241 (1964).

45. Gitlow v. New York, 268 U.S. 652 (1925).

46. Evans v. Newton, 382 U.S. 296 (1966). See also note 38 *supra*.

tion of the prohibition against compulsory self-incrimination into a virtual prohibition against voluntary disclosure while in police custody [47] and others. Although views differ concerning the propriety of some of these decisions, the confession decisions being especially controversial, they are as a group vigorous, well-expressed, Constitution-flexing decisions which have done much to keep the Constitution in step with changing times and changing values.

The unique American process of judicial review, so foreign to our English or continental forebears, is for us a traditional and valued process. Few now fail to perceive and admit that it is a major form of American policy-making. But is it not a condition of the exercise of such great power that it be deemed to be *honorably* subject to the process of constitutional amendment? Need a constitutional amendment proposal to modify in some respect a given Court decision be deemed a "retribution" or even a "correction"? Would it not be enough to view Article V (particularly where ratification is by the popular process of ratifying conventions) as an alternative and legitimate avenue for policy-making? Or is the question, thus posed, simply quaint? [48]

47. Massiah v. United States, 377 U.S. 201 (1964); Escobedo v. Illinois, 378 U.S. 478 (1964); Miranda v. Arizona, 384 U.S. 436 (1966).
48. A condition, of course, of viewing our Constitution as formally amendable as well as judicially construable is that the amending clause itself is deemed subject to inquiry and possible change.

XVII

Remaining Thorns in the Political Thicket–I

"Every plan has a political effect, even one drawn by a seventh grade civics class whose parents are all nonpartisans and who have only the United States census data to work with. Even though they drew such a plan with the most equal population in districts, following the maximum number of political subdivision boundaries and with the most regular shapes, it could very well result in a landslide election for a given political party."

> A. Robert Kleiner, Democratic Member
> Michigan Bipartisan Apportionment Commission
> (National Municipal League Speech), 1966

"We are doubtful, however, that the deviations evident here ['from 14.84% over-represented to 11.64% under-represented'] are the kind of 'minor' variations which *Reynolds* v. *Sims* indicated might be justified by local policies counseling the maintenance of established political subdivisions in apportionment plans."

> Supreme Court per curiam opinion, *Kilgarlin* v. *Hill*
> (Texas Legislative Apportionment Case), 1967

Conceptual confusion concerning both ends and means, which has plagued reapportionment practice and litigation since *Baker* v. *Carr*, emerges ever more sharply in the "second round" of reapportionment activity inspired by the "one man-one vote" principle of *Reynolds* v. *Sims*. And the conceptual confusion is unlikely to be settled before the "third round" of reapportionment after the 1970 census.

By comparison to the pre-*Baker* period, all recent reapportionments are "equal," but some are much more "equal" than others. Some have been accepted without much fuss, some have been challenged; *and* many of the challenges do not turn solely, or at all, on the degree of arithmetic equality in district population. Why? The answer, like the answer to most difficult constitutional questions, may be found by reverting to the goals and purposes of reapportionment itself. As stressed in Chapter II, and to an extent in succeeding chapters, apportionment and districting are the key components of our chosen type of *political representation system*. Some other types might be equally "democratic." Examples range from a mass meeting system of decision-making to use of a pure proportional representation system; but considerations of practicality obviate use of the former and the latter is thought to have special problems of its own.

A. Perspective

The goal of all types of political representation systems is to provide both responsiveness to popular feeling and a power to govern, the latter consideration dictating operation by majority rule rather than by an endless quest for a total consensus. But though majorities are to rule, minorities are to be heard and are to participate in the legislative deliberation process by which the ever-changing majorities on specific measures ebb and flow. Speaking of political minorities, Morris L. Ernst has referred to "that tender and essential feeling of having a spokesman of their choosing in the halls of the mighty." [1] Without getting into refined, interesting questions of the extent to which reality approaches this oversimplified model of political representation and governance, it seems clear that our democratic faith assumes at least a rough approximation of the model.

Hence, though we have tended to talk primarily of district elections and majority rule, our central concern is *proportionality in political representation*. Groups, and coalitions of groups, including the majority coalition itself, are to be heard in rough *proportion* to their popular strength in the deliberative-governance process. Of course, a district system tends to "pay off" only to large groups. Only a large group has much prospect of obtaining a plurality and winning a seat, thus making political parties the dominant groups. To an important degree, however, subgroups such as ethnic minorities, occupational classifications, and economic class categories tend to identify more with one party than another. They thus receive their political representation, at least in a rough way, through one political party or the other; the concern for "proportionality" continues. A set of legislative districts—whether or not "equal" in population—in which a political party consistently polls close to 40 percent of the vote but seldom musters more than 20 percent of the seats, denies effective political representation in terms of legislative bargaining power to the

1. Morris L. Ernst, Letter to Editor on "The Right to Be Heard vs. The Right to Vote," 51 A.B.A.J. 508 (1965).

minority (or to the set of minorities which make up the party). Equally important, by denying to the minority even its proper minority share of positions of influence, it impedes the minority's quest for majority status and may turn a nominal two-party system into an actual one-party system.

In the post-*Reynolds* era the issues that are emerging most sharply are ones concerning effectiveness of political representation and the bases for a "fair shake" in political party competition. None of the issues are readily resolvable in terms of the "equal population" side of the "one man-one vote" principle. They do take on added force under the "full participation" side of that same principle. Indeed, "one man-one vote" is both a mighty axe against the malapportionment of numbers of our past, and a source of sharply heightened expectations concerning political equity in the future. Herein, perhaps, lies the true reapportionment revolution.

Enduring issues include (1) the definition of the apportionment base itself, i.e., gross population or something less; (2) the choice to be made among alternative types of districting, i.e., single-member, multimember, floterial, or mixed; (3) avoidance of conscious or accidental racial gerrymandering; (4) avoidance of conscious or accidental political gerrymandering; (5) justiciability of districting and gerrymandering issues, i.e., whether the Fourteenth Amendment is satisfied when bare numbers are made "equal," without judicial inquiry into equality of voter influence on legislative outcomes; (6) the relevance of such special devices to achieve more proportionate representation of all groups as cumulative voting, limited voting, the "place" system within multimember districts; (7) the role of computers; (8) various lesser issues such as timing and frequency of apportionment, judicial deadlines and sanctions, scope of parties entitled to be heard, and the like.

Continued Primacy of Arithmetic. The necessary starting point for a discussion of reapportionment issues is still the equal population concept. The degree of arithmetic equality required in district populations conditions the entire reapportionment process. It provides a foundation for the exercise of discretion in drawing district lines, and for avoiding or achieving a gerrymander. There is a paradox here, however, which gives discussions of districting problems a "double-think" quality. A tight arithmetic equality standard may *restrict* experimentation with special devices for minority representation, such as cumulative voting, limited voting, and weighted voting, and at the same time, it may *ease* the path to a gerrymander by giving reapportioners *carte blanche* to ignore all traditional district lines and communities of interest in carving out new enclaves of "equal population."

The burden of proof also has shifted in regard to alleged misuse of legislative discretion in apportionment and districting. Before 1964 the chal-

lengers to then-existing apportionments had only to show population disparity among the districts; the state then had the burden of showing that
all population disproportionalities were the product of a rational formula
consistently applied. Since 1964 the persons alleging misuse of legislative
discretion in apportionment find that the discretion is protected by a
strong presumption of constitutionality so long as the one factor of population proportionaility—i.e., "substantial equality"—is present. It is up to
the challengers to amass hard-to-come-by proof either of evil legislative intent or of minority repression in the actual operation of the challenged
plan.

B. When Is Equality "Substantial"?

Although a "rule of reason" is the glory of the common law in many
areas, it is not a rule which makes a congenial bedfellow with an equality
concept. If "equal" is not truly equal, it is not equal. An undefined something else becomes the standard. The key Supreme Court term, "substantial equality," is therefore a contradiction in terms, except in the area of
racial desegregation. There it may be taken to connote gradualism over a
time period in achieving an agreed goal of full equality of status and opportunity. But in adopting "substantial equality" as the implementing
measure of a constitutional "one man-one vote" principle, the Supreme
Court was not connoting gradualism, but attempting to put its finger on
the essence of the right. In thus adopting as the basic standard something
less than rigidly equal lumps of population, while at the same time seemingly eschewing the political realities of effective representation, the Supreme Court was assigning legislatures and lower courts a challenging but
also an intellectually frustrating task.

1. SUPREME COURT'S INITIAL GUIDELINES

As discussed in some detail in Chapter XI, the Supreme Court was far
from clear in the 1964 *Reapportionment Decisions* concerning the precise
content of the "one man-one vote" principle. In the leading state legislative reapportionment case the Court, speaking through Chief Justice
Warren, said:

. . . we mean that the Equal Protection Clause requires that a State make an honest and good faith effort to construct districts, in both houses of its legislature, *as nearly of equal population as is practicable*.[2]

This statement was qualified not only by its own undefined concept of "practicability," but by several caveats sprinkled through the opinion. Arithmetic exactness is not required, political subdivisions as representation units received favorable mention, some deviations might be permissible under a rational state policy, and effective representation was a basic aim. Perhaps the strongest statement was Chief Justice Warren's warning that a freewheeling revision of districts, not following any traditional or natural boundaries, would be "an open invitation to partisan gerrymandering."[3]

All of this was not so much a constitutional formula as a conundrum. Logically, a near-exact population equality in districting *is* possible if that is the only goal sought. But reapportioners were to be allowed to consider the other elements listed, provided "population is [not] submerged as the controlling consideration."[4]

In one of the "big six" cases of 1964, the Colorado case, the Court seemed to come close to accepting a population variance ratio of 1.73 to 1 and a maximum deviation from average district of 30 percent, when coupled with a minimum electoral percentage of 45.1. In this case the Court invalidated a state senate in which the population variance ratio was 3.67 to 1 and in which the most deviant district was 166 percent larger than the ideal or average district. The lower house also became unconstitutional because of the Court's theory of nonseverability; but the Court suggested that standing by itself the lower house was "at least arguably apportioned substantially on a population basis."[5]

a. *"Equality" in Cases Appealed to the Court on Other Grounds*

Nor did the Court clarify the "equality" idea in the first series of cases to come to it after 1964, raising such districting issues as multimember districting or racial gerrymandering. Admittedly, the population equality issue was not raised in these cases and could not have been reached under conventional rules of review even had the Court wished. Nevertheless, it was natural that population deviations accepted by lower courts and not deemed worthy of inclusion in an appeal should not pass unnoticed. In a series of per curiam rulings in the 1965 Term, the Supreme Court sum-

2. Reynolds v. Sims, 377 U.S. 533, 577 (1964).
3. *Id.* at 579.
4. *Id.* at 581.
5. Lucas v. Colorado General Assembly, 377 U.S. 713, 730 (1964).

marily approved or refused to review lower court disposition of nonpopulation issues in a number of states where the deviations from arithmetic equality exceeded 20 percent.[6] In the Maryland case, the state Court of Appeals in 1966 had discussed the apportionment plan's maximum deviation figure of 36 percent as follows:

> According to the decisions, 36% is, of course, high. However, as we stated above, the Supreme Court has recognized that some divergences from population-based representation are permissible, so long as they are the result of legitimate considerations incident to the effectuation of a rational state policy, based principally upon population. . . . The parties to this appeal and the counsel who represent them have, for the main part, been vitally interested for the last several years, in matters pertaining to apportionment, and have made careful studies of the decisions and writings thereon. They all agree that Bill 5 is constitutionally permissible. In light of the above and our own careful consideration of the matter, we are unwilling to strike down the Bill for the comparatively few "suspect" variances, which, in our view, clearly result from an earnest effort to accomplish a reasonable statewide apportionment, and, at the same time, accord some slight independent representation to individual, existing political subdivisions.[7]

Attempted Supreme Court review on the ground that even this plan was tighter than constitutionally required, was denied.

The only two cases in which apportionment plans went to oral argument in the Supreme Court in the first two years after *Reynolds* v. *Sims* were the Georgia and Hawaii multimember districting cases.[8] In the former case, *Fortson* v. *Dorsey*,[9] the attack on use of a mixed single-member and multimember district system for the Georgia senate did not include an attack on arithmetic equality grounds even though the population variance ratio was 1.8 to 1 and 6 of 54 senatorial districts deviated

6. Burnette v. Davis, 382 U.S. 42 (1965), *affirming*, 245 F. Supp. 241 (E.D. Va. 1965); Nolan v. Rhodes, 383 U.S. 104 (1966), *affirming*, 251 F. Supp. 584 (S.D. Ohio 1965); Harrison v. Schaefer, 383 U.S. 269 (1966), *affirming*, 251 F. Supp. 450 (D. Wyo. 1965); Hughes v. Maryland Committee for Fair Representation, 384 U.S. 950 (1966), *denying petition for certiorari*, 217 A. 2d 273 (1966). See also Crawford County Bar Association v. Faubus, 383 U.S. 271 (1966), *affirming*, 251 F. Supp. 998 (E.D. Ark. 1965), wherein the maximum deviation was 13.9 percent.
7. Hughes v. Maryland Committee for Fair Representation, 241 Md. 471, 217 A. 2d 273, 281 (1966).
8. In a third case in which the Supreme Court heard oral argument in the immediate post-*Reynolds* period, Toombs v. Fortson from Georgia, the issue was not an attack on an apportionment plan as such, but only the question of whether a malapportioned legislature could submit a constitutional amendment on apportionment. Hence, the case could contribute nothing to speculation concerning the Court's concept of the arithmetic equality standard.
9. 379 U.S. 433 (1965).

from the population of the ideal or average size district by more than 15 percent. The Court refused to disturb the plan. Similarly, in *Burns* v. *Richardson*,[10] the revised Hawaii senate with a mixture of single-member and multimember districts was not attacked on arithmetic equality grounds even though a 28 percent deviation could be shown. Nor was the unrevised lower house under attack even though it had a maximum population deviation of 49 percent.[11]

2. INITIAL LOWER COURT IMPLEMENTATION

Absent an authoritative statement from the United States Supreme Court, lower courts moved in various directions in the period between 1964 and 1966. A truly surprising range of mathematical variation developed in judicially ordered or judicially approved plans—many of which are destined to remain in force until after the 1970 census. In some states a theory of compensating inequalities in the apportionment for two houses was used as a basis for rationalizing some district inequalities, as in Vermont.[12] In Utah, however, the federal district court upheld an apportionment which lacked the feature of compensating inequality, the same county being the most underrepresented in the apportionment plans for both houses.[13]

By the end of 1966, at least 25 states had plans judicially approved for permanent or temporary use (often with no assurance of further revision prior to the 1970 census) in which the districts in at least one house exceeded a 15 percent variation from average size districts. The states included Alabama, Alaska, Arizona, Colorado, Connecticut, Florida, Georgia, Hawaii, Idaho, Maine, Maryland, Montana, Nevada, New Mexico, Ohio, Oklahoma, Pennsylvania, South Carolina, Tennessee, Utah, Vermont, Virginia, Washington, Wisconsin, Wyoming. Apportionment plans in some additional states fell in this category without judicial ruling, e.g., New Hampshire and West Virginia. Maximum deviation percentages included the following: Colorado, 30 percent; Hawaii (49 percent if lower

10. 384 U.S. 73 (1966).
11. The Hawaii house had not been changed since it was originally apportioned on the basis of 1958 registered voters. On the 1958 base its deviation figures would be: population variance ratio, 2.09 to 1; maximum district deviation from average, 36 percent. However, because there should be a common apportionment base for each house of the legislature at any given time, the Hawaiian lower house in the context of the *Burns* case should be measured by the 1964 registered voter base which underlay the challenged new senate apportionment, thus yielding the following deviation figures for the house: population variance ratio, 2.8 to 1; maximum district deviation from average, 49 percent.
12. Buckley v. Hoff, 243 F. Supp. 873 (D. Vt. 1965).
13. Petuskey v. Rampton, 243 F. Supp. 365 (D. Utah 1965).

house be measured by 1964 registered voters which was the base used for the senate revision); Idaho, 32 percent; Maryland, 36 percent; New Mexico, 29 percent; Washington, 20 percent; Wisconsin, 32.5 percent (as judicially revised on eve of *Reynolds,* no further action taken).

a. *Severability*

With such uncertainty concerning the central question, "how equal is equal?" it is not surprising that plans in some states were approved on solely arithmetic bases deemed invalid in other states. More critically, the variant arithmetic rules of thumb concerning equality were the key also to the much-discussed "severability" issue, i.e., how much of a state's preceding apportionment standards and customs could co-exist with "one man-one vote." Federal overriding of state constitutional apportionment practices is directly proportional to the degree of rigidity in the federal population equality standard. This factor, as discussed in Chapter XII, was a key element in the Michigan reapportionment case that bounced back and forth several times between a bipartisan commission and the federal and state courts between 1964 and 1966.

b. *Tendency Toward Rigidity*

There was, however, a gradually emerging tendency, likewise exemplified in Michigan and in some congressional districting suits which raised analogous issues,[14] for the courts to move toward an increasingly rigid mathematical equality standard. This tendency flowed naturally from the Supreme Court's disinclination in *Reynolds* v. *Sims* to treat the reapportionment issue as involving problems of fair representation of groups, beyond the creation of equal-size piles of faceless census statistics. Under the narrow characterization of the reapportionment issue in *Reynolds,* lower courts *logically* have little choice but to stick fairly close to population equality.

Raw population equality is the *one* apparently certain standard which, if met, will yield an apportionment plan or order virtually irreversible on appeal. As courts perceived this, their tendency was to move in the direction of a nonintellectual, almost nit-picking, stress on equal population percentage points. This was so even at the cost of countenancing some overt or covert gerrymandering, continuance of some antiminority multimember districting practices, and casual disregard of political subdivision lines and the communities of social and political interest they often contained. Paradoxically, a tight mathematical equality rule which provides an excuse for disregarding prior district lines and natural boundaries,

14. Drum v. Seawell, 250 F. Supp. 922 (M.D. N.C. 1966); Preisler v. Secretary of State, 257 F. Supp. 953 (W.D. Mo. 1966).

coupled with the very real difficulties of mounting a successful attack on gerrymandering, may enhance rather than minimize opportunities for unfair districting practices.

3. SUPREME COURT'S REVISED GUIDELINES: 1967

In a series of state legislative and congressional districting decisions early in 1967, the Supreme Court was confronted with the tension between the *logical necessity* to be rigid on the equality standard, which derived from obscurity in *Reynolds v. Sims* concerning elements of fair representation other than raw district population, and the *actual implementation* of the "one man-one vote" principle which had yielded the disuniformity noted above.

a. Swann v. Adams

The leading case was *Swann v. Adams* from Florida, argued in December 1966 and decided in January 1967. However, neither the parties' briefs nor oral argument, nor the Court's own sources of information on the reapportionment realities of the preceding two years, were commensurate with the dimensions of the issue. The apportionment plan which Florida had adopted with much travail, and which the federal district court had accepted as a substitute for earlier disapproved plans, was *on arithmetic grounds* one of the tighter approved plans in the nation. And, arithmetic equality was the only issue in the case under *Reynolds* "substantial equality" guideline despite the fact that from a representation standpoint interesting questions could have been raised concerning districting details and concerning the gross winner-take-all effect of giving Miami (Dade County) 22 lower house members elected at-large.[15]

Under Florida's proposed apportionment the maximum district deviations for the senate and house respectively were 15.09 percent and 18.3 percent, yielding population variance ratios of 1.3 to 1 and 1.4 to 1. In the course of the oral argument, it was apparent from the questioning of counsel by Supreme Court Justice Byron R. White, who subsequently wrote the opinion for the Court, that Justice White was under the im-

15. Brief for Amici Curiae, Swann v. Adams, 385 U.S. 440 (1967), No. 136, at 5–12.
The petitioners claimed: (1) that giving Dade County 22 representatives without subdistricting would dilute the votes of residents of single representative counties such as Monroe. Thus, a resident of Dade County would have 22 times as much voting power because he would be represented that many times; (2) that if subdistricted, the voices of racial and political minorities would be represented. In an at-large election the heavy Democratic white majority would submerge the pockets of Republican and Negro strength within the major urban counties. Two of the amici—one Republican and one Democrat—were from Monroe, a single representative county. One, a Republican, was from Dade County.

pression that Florida's figures were exceptionally deviant in comparison to the post-*Reynolds* reapportionment in most other states. Attorney General Earl Faircloth, arguing the case for Florida, neither in his brief nor in his oral presentation, possessed the full range of information to set the record straight. And there is not the slightest indication in the Supreme Court's subsequent opinion that the Court realized that invalidation of Florida's plan also would imply invalidation of post-*Reynolds* judicially approved plans in nearly half the states. (As listed above, 25 state plans at this time exceeded a 15 percent deviation and a majority of them also exceeded Florida's 18 percent deviation.)

The Supreme Court did invalidate Florida's apportionment and for the first time since the 1964 *Reapportionment Decisions* attempted to rephrase the arithmetic equality standard. The change from the *Reynolds* formulation was dramatic. In place of the "substantial equality" formulation and the number of uncertain caveats with which Chief Justice Warren had sprinkled his *Reynolds* opinion, the new formulation seemed to be: no deviations other than de minimis deviations are permissible unless special justification be shown. The Court did not define the percentage point at which a deviation ceases to be de minimis and requires special justification, nor did it indicate what justification, if any, would support mathematical deviations exceeding a "de minimis" level.

Justice White also showed a tendency to focus on a comparison of the two most extreme districts, rather than on the more conventional measure of the percentage by which districts deviate from the average or ideal. In statistical terms there is an important distinction between a percentage figure denoting variation from the norm, and one that expresses the "range" between the largest and the smallest districts. The latter will always be a higher percentage figure than the former. Using the "range" concept rather than the maximum deviation concept, Justice White formulated the Court's apparent guideline as follows:

> . . . De minimis deviations are unavoidable, but variations of 30% among senate and 40% among house districts can hardly be deemed de minimis and none of our cases suggests that differences of this magnitude will be approved without a satisfactory explanation grounded on acceptable state policy. . . .[16]

Justices John Marshall Harlan and Potter Stewart dissented sharply on the burden of proof-presumption of unconstitutionality issue:

> This holding seems to me to stand on its head the usual rule governing this Court's approach to the validity of legislative enactments, state as well as federal, which is of course that they come to us with a

16. Swann v. Adams, 385 U.S. 440, 444 (1967).

strong presumption of regularity and constitutionality. . . . Accordingly, I do not believe the burden is on the State to justify every aspect of a complex plan completely restructuring its legislature, on pain of its being declared constitutionally invalid by the judiciary.[17]

In practice the Court's new formulation of the federal apportionment standard in *Swann* may outlaw all deviations exceeding 5 percent (which of course becomes 10 percent when a "range" concept is used) so long as vigorous plaintiffs are available to show that a revision of one or two lines will make the deviations more nearly "de minimis." For that matter, if special "justification" cannot be shown there is no reason in terms of districting mechanics for permitting maximum deviations of one percent (or "ranges" of two percent). Michigan, using single-member districts and cutting county lines where necessary, has demonstrated that a state senate can be constructed in which the maximum district deviation is 0.58 percent.

De minimis deviations in district population equality always can be brought to near-zero simply by ignoring traditional political subdivision lines and using census tracts as the sole building blocks for legislative districts. Further, it is difficult to articulate community of interest factors with any precision as possible justifications for particular deviations, even if such factors are included within the Court's undefined "acceptable state policy" phrase. For example, can preservation of a county line at a cost of making the maximum deviation 3 percent higher (e.g., 13 percent rather than 10 percent) be justified by showing that by being kept intact the county "balances" another county with a different political party persuasion and different economic interest? That the *Swann* formulation may presage such an absolute equality standard for construction of legislative districts is buttressed by two congressional district per curiam rulings made the same day, and by the Supreme Court's reversal a month later of a federal district court's approval of a Texas reapportionment plan.

b. *The* Swann *Fallout*

Congressional Districts. On the same day as the *Swann* decision, the Supreme Court nullified an Indiana congressional districting plan even though the maximum deviation from the average district was only 12.8 percent,[18] and sustained a Missouri federal district court which had nulli-

17. *Id.* at 447–48 (Harlan, J., dissenting).
18. Duddleston v. Grills, 385 U.S. 455 (1967).
    Perhaps the earliest example of a "tight equality" approach in judicially devised congressional districting was the 1.45 percent maximum deviation plan ordered for Maryland by a three-judge federal district court in May 1966. Maryland Citizens Committee for Fair Representation v. Tawes, 253 F. Supp. 731 (D. Md. 1966). How-

fied a Missouri congressional district plan in which the maximum deviation was only 9.9 percent.[19] By simply citing the *Swann* ruling as authority the Supreme Court showed its tendency to use the same population equality yardstick for both state legislative apportionment and congressional districting. (Arguably, a tighter equality requirement might be supportable for congressional districts to counterbalance the area-based United States Senate.) In each of these cases the complaining parties either had themselves suggested, or could point to, an alternative plan not adopted by the legislature under which deviations would have been less. In neither case, as in *Swann*, was any consideration given to representation factors other than the gross population of the districts at issue.

The opinion of the Missouri federal district court, reaching the conclusion which the Supreme Court affirmed, may be especially instructive. In responding to the contention that the population discrepancies did not exceed 9.9 percent, District Judge John W. Oliver refused " ' to be drawn into a sterile controversy over averages and percentages,' " since the words "as nearly as practicable" were not to be used as " 'an escape hatch for the reluctant.' " He concluded by refusing to hold that "the constitutional right of equal representation may be but slightly, and therefore permissibly, abridged on the theory that percentage figures and ratio numbers make unexplained and substantial [9.9 percent] population deviations and variances look smaller." [20] The rule emerges that if a population deviation, regardless of size, can reasonably be reduced, it is unconstitutional. Thus a new maxim of "constitutional equity" is born: That which may be made more equal is not equal!

The Texas Legislature. The Supreme Court's invalidation of the Texas reapportionment, without oral argument, rested on a more complicated record but is equally instructive. The Court did not reach certain issues concerning floterial districting, and allegations of racial and political gerrymandering. Rather, it overruled the district court because some districts deviated from the average population by minus 14.84 percent and plus

---

ever, this order was flawed by the fact that the real issue was Baltimore City's retention of three Congressmen, even though its population entitlement was less. Unlike the legislature's 14.9 percent maximum deviation plan which the court rejected, the court's plan in effect retained three Congressmen for Baltimore City at the cost of cutting up surrounding suburban counties.

19. Kirkpatrick v. Preisler, 385 U.S. 450 (1967).

20. Preisler v. Secretary of State of Missouri, 257 F. Supp. 953, 974 (W.D. Mo. 1966).

This approach was continued in the invalidation of yet another legislatively devised congressional district plan which had a maximum deviation from average of only 3.13 percent. Preisler v. Secretary of State of Missouri, Civ. No. 1064 (W.D. Mo. December 29, 1967). Circuit Judge M. C. Matthes, dissenting, said these deviations were "truly of a 'de minimis' nature."

11.64 percent.[21] The Court also noted that 55 of the total of 116 representatives would be elected from eight multimember districts in which the population per representative varies from the ideal by more than 5 percent. In addition, 12 of the 52 single-member districts deviated by more than 10 percent from the average size district.

In sustaining the plan the lower court had placed on the plaintiffs the burden not only of demonstrating the amount of population deviation but also of "negat[ing] the existence of any state of facts which would sustain the constitutionality of the legislation." [22] The Supreme Court said that under the authority of the *Swann* decision the approach should be just the reverse: "unless satisfactorily justified by the court or by the evidence of record, population variances of the size and significance evident here are sufficient to invalidate an apportionment plan." [23]

Apart from placing on the challengers the burden of showing why population deviations ranging from plus 11 percent to minus 14 percent were inequitable, the district court had a second major theme. It further justified the state plan as the product of "a bona fide attempt to conform to the state policy requiring legislative apportionment plans to respect county boundaries whenever possible." [24]

Without ruling whether in some circumstances such a state policy could justify a 14.84 percent deviation, the Supreme Court on several grounds rejected the district court's reasoning here too. First, since state policy concededly permitted cutting of some county lines to avoid "undue" population deviations, it was incumbent on the state to show why a few more should not be cut to reduce the 11 and 14 percent deviations—but the Court gave no indication where this process should stop. Second, since state policy permitted formation of multimember and floterial districts, it also was incumbent on the state to show why further use of this device could not reduce deviations while at the same time preserving county lines. Third, the Court said, the state and district court had failed to particularize the "county lines" justification sufficiently, i.e., to relate it to "specific inequalities among the districts" and especially to the "particular deviations" at issue. Lastly, the district court had not given "satisfactory grounds" for rejecting two other plans in the record which "respected county lines but which produced substantially smaller deviations from the principle of *Reynolds* v. *Sims*." [25]

21. Kilgarlin v. Hill, 386 U.S. 120, 121–22 (1967). For further mathematical details see the district court opinion, Kilgarlin v. Matrin, 252 F. Supp. 404, 454–55 (S.D. Tex. 1966).
22. *Id.* at 414.
23. Kilgarlin v. Hill, 386 U.S. 120, 122 (1967).
24. *Id.* at 122–23.
25. *Id.* at 122.

An Emerging Rule of Near-Absolute Equality? By relying on a presumption of invalidity, unrebutted by special justification, the Supreme Court in the Texas case, as in the Florida case, avoided a specific ruling that deviations approaching 15 percent are per se unconstitutional. But the true message here seems to be that the arithmetic equality principle is tightening, that special justifications will be rigorously reviewed, and that the special justifications themselves must not produce more than a "minor" variation (the *Swann* "de minimis" phrase was not repeated in *Kilgarlin*). It was therefore, more an exercise of personal hope than appreciation of implications for Circuit Judge Leonard P. Moore in a later New York case to insist in the face of these decisions that the Supreme Court has not yet made "absolute mathematical equality" the rule, for that would be an "abject judicial surrender of jurisdiction to the mindless computer." [26]

In short, *Swann* and *Kilgarlin,* and the accompanying rulings in the Missouri and Indiana congressional district cases seem to signal a rather rigid development [27] of the so-called "one man-one vote" principle of the 1964 *Reapportionment Decisions.* Such a development follows logically from the Court's starting premise. The Court has characterized the reapportionment issue as being a matter only of equalizing gross population clusters, rather than as being one of achieving fair and effective political representation.

Nevertheless, it would have been a distinct surprise even for the victorious plaintiffs' counsel in 1964—who were attacking legislatures where the population variance ratios for at least one house commonly exceeded

26. Wells v. Rockefeller, 273 F. Supp. 984, 989 (S.D. N.Y. 1967).
27. Further evidence of such a trend can be seen in some subsequent lower court rulings under the apparent influence of the *Swann* opinion. That the "special justification" language in *Swann* may be just shadowboxing is suggested by the action of a Massachusetts federal district court, a month after *Swann,* in voiding a congressional district plan with maximum deviations of plus 11.7 percent and minus 12.4 percent instead of re-opening to give the state an opportunity to try to "justify." Dinis v. Volpe, 264 F. Supp. 425 (D. Mass. 1967), aff'd 88 S. Ct. 697 (1968).
A maximum deviation of more than 10 percent in Mississippi's new state legislative districts was held per se unconstitutional unless specially justified. Connor v. Johnson, 265 F. Supp. 492 (S.D. Miss. 1967). Federal district courts themselves revised Tennessee's and Florida's congressional districts within maximum percentage deviations of 2.17 percent and 1.20 percent respectively. Baker v. Ellington, 273 F. Supp. 174 (M.D. Tenn. 1967); Gong v. Kirk, Civ. No. 64–143 (S.D. Fla. August 2, 1967), aff'd, 88 S. Ct. 695 (1968). However, the maximum deviation from average under the Florida plan actually may not be 1.20 percent but 8.78 percent under a corrected computation brought to the Supreme Court's attention on appeal.
See also Drum v. Seawell, 250 F. Supp. 922 (M.D. N.C. 1967), where federal district court action by nullifying the legislature's 8.9 percent maximum deviation plan succeeded in evoking from the legislature a 2.3 percent maximum deviation plan for congressional districts. Gerrymandering allegations concerning the latter plan were summarily rejected.

20 to 1—to have been told that the new rule prevented following county boundaries whenever the resulting deviations approached 10 to 15 percent. And it might have produced shock to be told that a 10 to 15 percent "county boundary" plan would be unconstitutional solely because a differently arranged "county boundary" plan would hold deviations under 10 percent. Suppose, for example, that counties A and B are grouped and C and D are grouped; the resulting maximum deviation is 15 percent; and each of the closely balanced political parties thereby receives one seat. If it could be shown that grouping counties A with D and B with C would reduce the deviation to 10 percent, must the change be made—even if the political representation result would be to give one party two seats and the other none? Would the latter result be all right if it were the result of a computer-prepared population equality plan, but not all right if it were the product of a partisan apportionment done by the majority party in the legislature? From the standpoint of an ultimate concern for representative government, should not the latter result be suspect no matter what apportionment method is used?

Nor does it ease the apparent new rule of rigidity appreciably to suggest that in *Swann* and *Kilgarlin* the Court was just reaching for a requirement that the legislature "show the background of its work a little bit." Realistically, *is* a political negotiation process inside some limit such as 10 or 15 percent reducible to "rational" justification? The answer must be no, if rational is defined as "logically consistent derivation from precise principles articulated in advance."

Thus is raised again the crucial distinction in constitutional process and judicial review between "reasonableness of result" and "rationality of design" as discussed in Chapters VI, VII, and XI. Few pieces of legislation —indeed, little that government does—is "rational" in the above sense. Many of the results nevertheless represent "reasonable" accommodations of conflicting and even irreconcilable principles, e.g., "make all district populations equal," but "don't submerge a minority in a district controlled by its opponents, or let one political party take all the marbles."

As an aftermath of Chief Judge William J. Campbell's bipartisan pretrial in Illinois (Chapter XII), or the New York and New Jersey bipartisan commission operations (Chapter XIII), could a "rational" justification have been given for each deviation? There were trade-offs, adjustments, and balancing, with each party watching but not controlling the other. Far from being things to be viewed with distaste, these features are the prime virtues of a bipartisan process. In the eyes of most local observers, the resulting plans were equal, representational, politically fair, and conducive to producing a base for a two-party rather than a one-party system.

Perhaps at this point we come back again to the overriding importance of *reapportionment method*. Under the *Swann* and *Kilgarlin* revisions of the equal population principle, should not the use of a bipartisan commission, rather than use of partisan methods, itself be a self-sufficient justification for deviations which though still "minor" exceed "de minimis"? Should not there be a conscious policy of actually limiting judicial review of a bipartisan commission plan if it is within or close to a 15 percent maximum deviation, such as the 1967 New Jersey plan (discussed in Chapter XIII)? Instead the New Jersey Supreme Court spoke disparagingly of "so-called community interests, partisan history, and residence of incumbents" and said it had "no doubt that the last mentioned considerations are wholly irrelevant to the subject." [28] To the contrary, what else is worth talking about once mathematical deviations are so miniscule as to disappear even for the nearsighted? By making an unexplained minor tinker of some lines to get a bit better arithmetic equality the New Jersey court invited suspicion as to the real reasons for its own action.

The Instability of an "Equal as Possible" Standard. A prime goal of litigation over constitutional claims as well as private claims is that finality be achieved as speedily as possible. And in general government matters, apart from litigation, there is much truth in the familiar observation that it is sometimes as important to have a decision as to have the ideally just decision.

From this perspective a very real hazard of an "equal as possible" constitutional standard for apportionment is that plaintiff attack is made too easy on mere showing that a more "equal" plan is possible. Further, under the "standing" rules of *Baker* v. *Carr* any dissatisfied voter can be a plaintiff and thus prevent finality in apportionment, even though the two major parties and all significant groups are satisfied with a particular plan having 5, 10, or 13 percent maximum deviation. In both *Swann* and *Kilgarlin*, and in the concurrent Indiana and Missouri congressional districting cases, the plaintiffs succeeded by making a simple arithmetic proof, without having to relate it to any demonstrable representation purpose.

Absent a need to show representation purpose or actual discrimination, there is no logical reason why diligent plaintiffs could not mount a plausible attack on any plan with more than a one percent deviation, and do so every five years if the five-year census becomes common. Under a "substantial equality" principle such instability need not occur—particularly if the burden of proof be allocated to the plaintiff to show actual discrimination in plans where the maximum deviation is no more than 10 to 15 percent. But in *Swann* and the associated cases early in 1967 the Supreme Court may already have passed this possible stopping point.

28. Jackman v. Bodine, 49 N.J. 406, 231 A. 2d 193, 200 (1967).

4. NOTE ON MATHEMATICAL MEASURES OF EQUALITY COMMONLY
USED IN STATE LEGISLATIVE APPORTIONMENT AND
CONGRESSIONAL DISTRICTING

Thus far in this work the courts' commonly used mathematical measures
of apportionment-districting equality—and the figures for particular plans
—have been noted frequently, but the measures themselves have not been
subjected to critical analysis. While reserving a full-dress critique to the
statistician, some anomalies and insufficiences in "judicial arithmetic" may
be noted here, both as a footnote to the emerging rule of mathematical
rigidity, and as a prelude to a more sophisticated approach toward specific
districting and representation issues.

The simplest measure is the *population variance ratio* (PVR). Because
it only compares the population of two districts, the largest and the
smallest, it can be computed even if full population details of a plan are
not available. It is descriptively incomplete in comparing only extremes; it
also may be misleading if used in isolation. A more descriptive measure is
to compute for each district the percentage deviation from average
("ideal") district population. Then the plus and minus *maximum percentage deviations* can be reported, and also the *average percentage deviation* can be computed.

A simple hypothetical case can illustrate the unreliability of the population variance ratio test in comparison to percentage deviations test in sig-
nifying voter overrepresentation or underrepresentation. Let us assume
that in two legislative bodies of 100 districts each, the first has 50 districts
of 120,000 and 50 districts of 80,000, and that the second has 90 districts
of 100,000 but five of 65,000 and five of 135,000. The population variance
ratio in the latter instance is more than 2 to 1, yet 90 of the 100 districts
are perfect. The ratio figure for the former is only 1.5 to 1, yet all of the
districts have a 20 percent deviation.

Another common measure is the minimum population potentially represented by a bare majority of a legislative house, also called the (fictional) *electoral percentage*. It ignores voting realities and is computed by
cumulating the total population represented by the half of the legislature
(plus one district) which comes from the smaller districts. A "perfect
score" is presumably near 50 percent. A detailed critique of this measure
is given in the "Numbers Game" subsection of Chapter VII. There we
showed that a 10 percent maximum deviation rule could produce an electoral percentage of 46.1 if each district deviated by 10 percent, half above
and half below the norm. And yet the Supreme Court of Maine, more in-

tent on honor-roll arithmetic than on representation realities, said in 1966 that "at least 50%" was the basic principle.[29]

The population variance ratio itself can be expressed as a percentage, rather than a ratio, to give the spread—as a percentage—between largest and smallest district. For example, in the above illustration with districts varying from 80,000 to 120,000 and the ideal being 100,000, the maximum deviation from average is 20 percent but the top to bottom "range" (or "variation," to use Justice White's term in *Swann v. Adams*) is 50 percent of the lower limit. Failure to separate these measures causes confusion in determining whether or not a given percentage is a "minor" departure from "equality."

An amusing example of a confusion of this sort occurred in congressional deliberations in 1967 on H.R. 2508, a bill introduced by Congressman Emanuel Celler to fix mathematical and other standards to guide state legislatures in congressional districting. The key provision was that the "district with the largest population . . . shall not exceed by more than 30 per centum the district with the smallest population." (After the 1970 census the figure was to become "10 per centum.") Draftsmen had intended by this language to express the common rule of thumb of a permissible 15 percent maximum deviation, either way, from average population, and discussion proceeded along these lines.

Actually, the language used is in one sense *tighter*, and in one sense *looser*, than a conventional 15 percent maximum deviation standard. For example, with 100,000 as the norm, a 15 percent deviation will permit districts ranging from 85,000 to 115,000. But if there be an 85,000 district, a rule that the largest shall not exceed the smallest by more than 30 percent imposes a ceiling of 110,500, rather than 115,000. (The reason is that 30 percent of 85,000 is 25,500, not 30,000.) On the other hand, the bill's formula would permit a maximum deviation approaching 30 percent on one side of the norm if the most deviant district on the other side deviated by only 3 or 4 percent.

Chairman Celler of the House Judiciary Committee who had introduced the bill was belatedly surprised to discover that the "30 per centum" figure in the measure would not validate the congressional districts in his own state. Even though the New York districts were reasonably within a 15 percent deviation limit (ranging from plus 15.1 to minus 14.4, the spread or *sum* of these deviations being 29.5 percent), they would have been invalid under the bill because the largest district (471,001) was 34.5 percent in excess of the smallest district (350,186). In other words, using the *smallest* district's population as the base, and adding 30 percent, would yield a maximum upper limit of 455,242, which

29. Opinion of the Justices, 216 A. 2d 651 (Me. 1966).

would have been only 11.2 percent above the ideal district size of 409,324. As a result the measure was altered but never was enacted because after many fruitless sessions the House and Senate conferees deadlocked.[30]

a. *Distinction Between State Legislative Apportionment and Congressional Districting*

Lastly, mention should be made of several mathematical formulae which are always mentioned in connection with apportionment of congressional seats to the states, and are frequently mentioned in regard to apportionment and districting of state legislative seats. These formulae, or "methods," are ways of handling the problem of fractional remainders in the congressional apportionment process and include the following: major fractions; equal proportions; harmonic mean; smallest divisors; and greatest divisors.[31]

Although the statement may come as a surprise to some people, it can be said that *all of these mathematical formulae are now irrelevant to apportionment and districting of state legislative seats.* The reason is that these formulae cannot be used unless there are *agreed fixed districts* at the outset *among which a finite* number of seats are to be "apportioned" on as equal a basis as possible—without cutting up a district or a legislator. There are three steps in setting up congressional seats, and such formulae as "equal proportions" can play a role only in the second step: (1) create the representative areas (districts), each of which has at least one representative (the Constitution makes each state such a fixed "district"); (2) allocate the fixed number of remaining representatives among the districts by some formula such as "equal proportions"; (3) within each district (state) create subdistricts of equal population for each representative allocated to the primary district (state).

These three steps have no analogue, at least since 1964, in the process of setting up state legislative seats because the crucial first step—agreed fixed districts—is missing. Counties and cities, or even fixed groupings of such units, can no longer be used as fixed districts. To satisfy the tight equality requirements of *Reynolds* v. *Sims* and *Swann* v. *Adams* most states will have to cut and recut at least some political subdivision lines, or group and later regroup city and county units. In other words, the "one man-one vote" requirement for state legislatures is a statewide *every-seat-equal* requirement, and all district lines are fluid.

For congressional seats, by contrast, the requirement is only an *intrastate* (really intra-"district") *equality*, rather than a nationwide every-seat-

30. *New York Times*, Oct. 16, 1967, p. 1, col. 5. See also H.R. Rep. No. 435, 90th Cong., 1st Sess., 1, 2, 5 (1967); S. Rep. No. 291, 90th Cong., 1st Sess. (1967).
31. Laurence F. Schmeckebier, *Congressional Apportionment* 12 (Washington: Brookings Institution, 1941). The author also mentions ten "discarded methods." *Id.* at 73.

equal requirement. Accepted without question are all of the inequalities caused under step one by gross differences in state populations, and caused under step two by arbitrary mathematical allocation of fractional remainders.[32]

Hence, the whole process of setting up state legislative seats is exactly like the third step listed above in the process of setting up congressional seats. Steps one and two of the congressional seat process now have no counterparts in the state legislative seat process. Thus the effect of *Reynolds* and *Swann* is to destroy any basis for using the term "apportionment" to describe the process of setting up legislative seats of equal population! There is now simply a kaleidoscoped process of using the current population and the current number of legislative seats as the basis for creating a current, but temporary, set of equal population districts. Some of the lines may coincide with some pre-existing city or county boundaries; but such result is fortuitous, and *not* the result of "apportioning" seats to those units as such.

With no enduring districts analogous to the "state districts" in congressional apportionment-districting, with rapidly shifting population, with frequent revision of districts, the whole process of setting up and revising state legislative seats is generically *redistricting*, not reapportionment. With few really meaningful or enforceable ground rules, with a welter of important but conflicting interests, and with the *Swann-Kilgarlin* tightening of the arithmetic equality requirement, the process unavoidably comes to resemble a "floating crap game," as one experienced "reapportioner" privately remarked. And the stakes are public office, for one partisan or another, depending on which set of "equal" lines is drawn.

32. The congressional apportionment formula under Article I, Section 2 of the Constitution automatically produces major inequalities among congressional districts, *viewed nationally*, by guaranteeing one seat to each state regardless of population and allocating a fixed number of remaining seats without cutting state lines or using floterial districts. These inequalities far exceed a rule of thumb of 10 or 15 percent, and are not confined to the single-Congressman states. Of course, in the populous states with many Congressmen the inequalities tend to average out and become minimal.

For example, on the basis of the 1960 census the nationwide ideal population for a congressional seat is 412,234 (national population divided by 435 seats). The ideal populations for New York and California congressional seats (state population divided by seats assigned to it) are 409,326 and 413,611, respectively, which vary only by —0.7 and +0.3 percent from the national ideal. Other states vary markedly. Some at the low population end are the following: Alaska, 226,167; Nevada, 285,278; New Hampshire, 303,460; Hawaii, 316,386; North Dakota, 316,223; Idaho, 333,595. All of these except the first two are two-Congressman states. Some at the high population end are the following: Maine, 484,633; Nebraska, 470,443; New Mexico, 475,511; Arkansas, 446,568; Delaware, 446,292. Of these, only Delaware is a one-Congressman state. Expressed in percentage terms the state deviations from a nationwide "one man-one vote" norm, even using the state's ideal district size, range for the first group from 19.1 (Idaho) to 44.9 (Alaska); and for the latter group from 8.5 (Delaware) to 17.6 (Maine).

XVIII

Remaining Thorns in the Political Thicket–II

"It might well be that, designedly or otherwise, a multi-member constituency apportionment scheme, under the circumstances of a particular case, would operate to minimize or cancel out the voting strength of racial or political elements of the voting population."

Justice William J. Brennan, Jr., *Fortson v. Dorsey*, 1965

"*Fortson* and *Burns* both involved multi-member constituency apportionments, whereas the Delaware apportionment calls for single member districts . . . . Perhaps partisan gerrymandering may be more discernible in one instance than the other . . . . Nevertheless, to allow a legislature to deprive any group of fair representation in any manner would be to condone invidious discrimination . . ."

District Judge Caleb M. Wright (concurring in part, dissenting in part), Delaware Reapportionment Case, 1967

Frequently in the course of constitutional development one problem is solved or at least ameliorated only at the cost of creating or worsening another problem. Both reapportionment cases and racial equality cases illustrate the point. For example, in the crucial struggle for Negro equality and effective integration into the mainstream of American life, the aim for almost a century was to achieve a "color-blind Constitution" and racially neutral governmental policies. This standard was achieved in the 1954 *School Desegregation Decisions* and later cases. But it was then perceived that unless affirmative policies of intermixture based on racial identity were devised, the ultimate goal of effective integration would remain only a shimmering ideal.

The label for the new racial problem is "de facto segregation." It emanates from segregated housing patterns based on "informal" forces rather than legal command, from differing levels of educational opportunity and training, from continuance of private prejudice or at least private inertia in devising new avenues for effective integration, and of course from differing levels of economic security. This last factor conditions all freedom of movement, all access to skills training, and all social opportunity as well. De facto segregation is correctable—within the short time span dictated by the pressure of rising expectations—only through racially based programs under a "color-conscious Constitution." We have seen therefore a sudden scramble to restore racial designation in record-keeping so that desegregation progress may be measured. There is a new ambivalence among persons realistically concerned with civil rights concerning the propriety of "benevolent" racial quotas, which has caused *The Reporter* to remark editorially, "How confused all the old and new pieties have become." [1]

Similarly, in reapportionment, which like the racial problem raises issues which go to the foundation of our concepts concerning a democratic society, there is a new post-*Reynolds* tension between faith in the equality of numbers and awkward realities of districting arrangements. The most striking aspect of the malapportionments of the past was the simple fact of failure to reapportion. Legislative inaction in the face of major population growth and shift created a mixture of "rotten boroughs" and districts with inflated population. To be sure, the particular arrangement of district lines themselves did operate in some instances to favor some interests and repress others. Malrepresentation stemming from the makeup of district lines did not, however, become of central importance in most states. Lines themselves were seldom changed, and the inequities thus caused were overshadowed by gross malapportionment of the total population.

Just as a "color-blind Constitution" seemed to be the solution to problems of racial discrimination and segregation, so a mandate to the legislature to reapportion regularly seemed to be the solution to the malapportionment problem. This much was accomplished by the 1964 *Reapportionment Decisions*. However, it may now be perceived that a mandate to reapportion, coupled with a rule of tight arithmetic equality for all districts, creates new opportunities for unfairness in representation (gerrymandering). First, the reapportionment process and revision of districts will recur much more often than in the past. Second, the mandate of tight arithmetic equality, by requiring abandonment of many district lines based on traditional political subdivision boundaries, enhances opportunity for gerrymandering. Third, the exigencies of frequent redistricting under a tight arithmetic equality standard may be eased by resorting to various combinations of multimember districting—a choice which may be influenced by the reapportioners' appreciation of the partisan advantages which may flow from the winner-take-all characteristic of multimember districts.

1. *The Reporter*, Oct. 19, 1967, pp. 10–12.

C. Districting Choices, Gerrymandering Possibilities, Judicial Roles

As an unavoidable corollary of judicial entry into the political thicket to force frequent redistricting under an ever-tightening arithmetic equality rule, there arises the issue of the extent to which courts should police *partisan execution* of the *judicial command* to redistrict, or should promote apportionment processes that minimize the need for it, such as use of bipartisan commissions or bipartisan pre-trial (Illinois example). At this point we are brought back to *Baker* v. *Carr* and its central issue of "justiciability." It is obvious that the central goal of the *Baker* plaintiffs, and plaintiffs in reapportionment cases generally, is a *political representation* goal. The aim is to force change in apportionment and districting practices so that the political influence of the challengers may be reflected in the state legislature. To be frank, this means a plaintiff goal of electing partisan legislators in closer proportion to plaintiffs' strength than is afforded by the challenged districting system. Such a goal is perfectly legitimate; indeed, it is the essence of a democratic election system.

The new question therefore is: Can courts, by labeling such claims non-justiciable, view their Fourteenth Amendment mission to be discharged by forcing arithmetic equalization of districts, while leaving all issues of actual districting practices and gerrymandering to resolution by political action? Logically as well as politically the answer is no. Political relief from a legislature in which a majority of the incumbents are ensconced in safe, equal, but politically unfair districts may be as bootless a quest in the 1970s as was the pre-*Baker* quest, through political action, to break the rural stranglehold on state legislatures. For courts to limit their concern to bare population equality would be to build a reapportionment edifice of judicial bricks without straw.

The Supreme Court has not yet precisely faced and resolved this issue in any case in which there was full briefing and oral argument. There are conflicting intimations in the post-*Reynolds* Supreme Court and lower court rulings on how to handle this "new frontier of justiciability" issue. Before reviewing and assessing these conflicting intimations a definition of the scope of the issue is in order.

1. WHAT IS GERRYMANDERING?

Whenever "gerrymandering" is mentioned heads nod sagely for the conversation is then on familiar ground. Perhaps few persons recall the story of how an ancient Massachusetts "salamander" district was dubbed a "gerrymander" because of Governor Elbridge Gerry's hand in it, albeit a reluctant one.[2] But all are familiar with the practice of devising odd-shaped districts for political advantage—which is the historically derived and common popular usage of the term gerrymandering. Cartoonists, especially, have a field day in making "snakes," "turkey foots," "frying pans," and the like, emerge from sets of revised districts. "Checker-board square" is the assumed ideal. Any significant deviations from such symmetry are deemed unclean and unjustifiable.

It may come as a surprise, therefore, to be told that this common understanding is highly unfortunate. It is unfortunate because it tends to preclude intelligent discussion of unfair partisan practices and results, in districting. It immediately casts attention in the wrong direction—toward superficialities of shape and size, rather than toward the political realities of district composition. These realities, as Robert Luce has so aptly observed, turn on the "accident of sleeping place."[3] It is the particular nature of this "accident of sleeping place" for a party's supporters which determines whether a set of symmetrical districts is fair, or is a clean-sweep gerrymander for that party. Not to perceive this is to confuse form with function, and even to prevent the asymmetrical designs dictated by considerations of political balance and minority representation, and dictated as well by normal preferences for giving some recognition to natural boundaries and political subdivisions.

Clearly misleading and wrong, therefore, are such definitions of gerry-

---

2. Although the particulars of the story vary, the term "gerrymander" probably arose from the following sequence of events: following a redistricting of Essex County, Massachusetts, Governor Elbridge Gerry signed the districting bill into law even though he was opposed to the soon-to-be-attacked provisions of the bill. A dialogue then occurred between portraitist Gilbert Stuart and another party, the identity of whom seems to be in conflict. Looking at a map of the redistricting printed in the *Boston Weekly Messenger* of March 6, 1812, Stuart noticed one fairly compact district encircled by another of distorted outline. He then sketched in a head, wings and claws and noted the likeness to a dragon. The other party considered it more like a salamander whereupon Stuart is alleged to have said, "Better call it a 'Gerrymander.'" It is ironic that a term bearing his name became such an epithet of opprobrium, since Gerry signed the bill only because he doubted the propriety of a governor's assertion of his veto power over a matter of such character. See Robert Luce, *Legislative Principles* 397–98 (Boston: Houghton, Mifflin, 1930).
3. *Id.* at 393.

mandering as the following: (1) "the creation of legislative districts of grotesque form to produce a maximum number of districts with majorities for the party in charge of districting"; (2) "the application of contorted physical shapes for an intended partisan gain." [4] Little better is the following: "districting by political faith or race, not geography." [5] This last smacks of the "three monkeys" principle that gross results are acceptable if innocently caused.

More to the point are definitions of gerrymandering which speak of the "art of political cartography." [6] In simplest language, gerrymandering should be taken to encompass *all* apportionment and districting arrangements which transmute one party's actual voter strength into the maximum of legislative seats and transmute the other party's actual voter strength into the minimum of legislative seats. *Gerrymandering is discriminatory districting. It equally covers squiggles, multimember districting, or simple nonaction, when the result is racial or political malrepresentation.*

a. Myth of Compactness

A rule of compactness and contiguity, if used merely to force an explanation for odd-shaped districts, can have much merit.[7] Erected as a firm enforceable requirement, however, a rigid compactness-contiguity rule shifts attention from the realities of party voting to mere physical geography. Indeed, it would undercut the spirit of Chief Justice Earl Warren's oft-quoted statement about "people, not trees or acres," being the representational concern, if "people" denotes politically alert citizens.

For example, a recent article by a geographer sets forth a device for measuring gross perimeter of districts, and a geometric index of compactness.[8] These, combined with a 15 percent maximum deviation rule, are applied to create a set of suggested districts. The inference is that gerrymandering is thereby avoided and that fair districting is achieved, but there is not one line about the *political* effect of the proposed districts.

4. V. O. Key, *American State Politics: An Introduction* 64–65 (New York: Knopf, 1956); Charles P. Edwards, "Theoretical and Comparative Aspects of Reapportionment and Redistricting: With Reference to Baker v. Carr," 15 *Vand. L. Rev.* 1265, 1278 (1962).
5. Robert C. Brooks, *Political Parties and Electoral Problems* 437 (New York: Harper Brothers, 1923).
6. Andrew Hacker, *Congressional Districting* 54 (Washington: Brookings Institution, 1964).
7. In this spirit the Rhode Island Supreme Court has referred to constitutional requirement of "compactness" as being "peripheral in its thrust," forbidding a "complete departure" but leaving to legislative determination the degree of compactness which is "possible" in the total representation picture. Opinion to the Governor, 221 A.2d 799 (R.I. 1966).
8. Joseph E. Schwartzberg, "Reapportionment, Gerrymanders, and the Notion of 'Compactness,'" 50 *Minn. L. Rev.* 443 (1966).

Thus the crucial question about districting and gerrymandering—the impact on parties, policies, and programs, and on effective political competition—is not even considered.

The reality is that odd-shaped districts sometimes *may* facilitate unfair advantage of one party over another. The reality also is that odd-shaped districts *may be* one way, short of some proportional representation device, of avoiding "wasted votes," i.e., of ensuring some minority representation by recognizing a few relatively safe enclaves for the weaker party. In the latter instance questions of representation theory can be raised as to whether it is preferable for a minority to have its own voice in the legislature, or to be voiceless except through the dominant party. But in any event a rigid compactness rule will not provide satisfactory answers.

b. *Inseparability of Gerrymandering by Discriminatory Multimember or Single-Member Districting*

In a phrase, gerrymandering is *discriminatory districting*. For those states accustomed to using single-member districts for both houses of the legislature no further amplification is necessary. But what of those states which use some multimember districts, or that special variety of multimember districting known as floterial districts?

A "floterial district" has been defined as a "legislative district which includes within its boundaries several separate districts or political subdivisions which independently would not be entitled to additional representation but whose conglommerate population entitled the entire area to another seat in the particular legislative body being apportioned." [9] Although forbidden in Illinois in 1848 and Iowa in 1857, floterial districts have been common in the South. [10] In theory, they are a way of achieving greater arithmetic equality in situations where there are political subdivisions of varying sizes whose populations do not neatly accord with the representation ratio, while at the same time preserving the integrity of the boundaries of traditional political subdivisions.

The Supreme Court in *Reynolds* v. *Sims* suggested that use of floterial as well as multimember districts might be permissible to achieve some flexibility. However, Justice Douglas in his concurring opinion in *Kilgarlin*, the 1967 Texas reapportionment case, warned that multimember districting "allows the majority to defeat the minority on all fronts." [11]

Conceding that "all districting is gerrymandering," in the special sense to be noted below, there is still a major difference between the mild ma-

9. Davis v. Mann, 377 U.S. 678, 686 n.2 (1964).
10. Luce, *supra* note 2, at 377; A. Z. Reed, "The Territorial Basis of Government Under the State Constitutions," 40 *Columbia University Studies*, 553 (New York: Columbia University Press, 1911).
11. 386 U.S. 120, 126 (1967).

jority party biases which may unavoidably accompany use of single or multimember districting systems, and exaggerated biases. There is moral concern and there may well be constitutional concern when a majority can "defeat the minority on all fronts." It should be immaterial whether the defeat is accomplished by gross multimember districting which Justice Douglas had in mind (Texas districts ranged from single-member up to 14-member) or by partisan creation of single-member districts. Functionally, there is no distinction. From the standpoint of minority representation (racial, political, or other) or party competition, the two forms of discrimination are simply alternative sides of a double-edged sword wielded by the controlling group. It follows then that there can be no logical distinction between these two forms of voter discrimination in regard to justiciability. If one is justiciable, so is the other.

c. All Districting Is "Gerrymandering"

To be brutally frank, whether or not there is a gerrymander in *design*, there normally will be some gerrymander in *result* as a concomitant of all district systems of legislative election. (A precondition of gerrymandering is use of a district system for election of legislators, or, of course, use of a winner-take-all at-large system. It cannot occur in a pure proportional representation system.) Marked disparities between a party's actual voting strength and its proportion of seats gained may be noted even under relatively equalized districts. For example, in 1966 in California a minority of the statewide congressional vote produced Democratic majorities in both houses of the reapportioned legislature, and a 21 to 17 edge in the unrevised congressional districts. By contrast, a Republican plurality of only 41,000 in a statewide total of nearly 900,000 produced a five to two Republican edge in congressional seats in Iowa. In New Jersey's revised congressional districts Democrats gained a nine to six edge in 1966 despite a Republican plurality in the popular vote.[12]

In a functional sense it may thus be said that *districting is gerrymandering*. The generalization applies both to single-member districting and to multimember districting. The former has been observed for years to create at least a mild bias in favor of the dominant party because it tends to win a higher percentage of districts than its statewide popular vote percentage. The latter creates a similar bias because of the winner-take-all feature. The normal majority party bias in single-member districts can be exaggerated by conscious partisan line skewing. This same bias in multimember districts can be exaggerated by increasing the number of legis-

12. See generally, Republican National Committee, *The 1966 Elections* (Washington, D.C., 1967).

lators elected in each district, e.g., use of six-member districts, or higher, rather than two-member districts.

Perceiving these generic elements of districting makes the problem of achieving a just representation system no easier, but does permit the right questions to be asked. First, what range of "gerrymander in result" is tolerable? Some play in the joints of the political system is accepted. But hardly acceptable under democratic theory, or constitutional theory, are repeated inversions of popular minorities into governmental majorities, or distortions of two to one or greater in the ratio of votes cast to seats gained. Second, what kinds of reapportionment method will minimize *both* gerrymandering by design and in result? This question was explored in Chapters XII to XIV, and the discussion culminated with a plea for consideration of bipartisan methods in apportionment-districting.

Third, failing use of bipartisan methods, and there often will be failure as states persist in using traditional partisan methods of districting, the next focus of inquiry emerges: Will courts curb gerrymandering excesses in the process of policing the equal population mandate for construction of American legislatures? In short, we are now brought back to *Baker* v. *Carr*. Rephrased, the key question is whether the old "political question" doctrine still lives to protect gerrymandering from judicial review, or whether gerrymandering, like unequal district population, poses a justiciable issue.

2. JUDICIAL RESTRAINT ON RACIAL GERRYMANDERING BY DISCRIMINATORY DISTRICTING

Without conceding that "racial" gerrymandering and "political" gerrymandering can be distinguished in principle in terms of justiciability, substantive violation of the Fourteenth Amendment, or adverse impact on legislative representation, the discussion will proceed first to explore judicial handling of racial gerrymandering, to be followed by an analysis of political gerrymandering. This approach is dictated by the cases; some courts seem to be much more unconcerned in the presence of partisan gerrymandering than of racial gerrymandering. Accustomed to dealing with racial matters in general, courts are now inclined to pursue race questions into the new area of the "political thicket." But being unaccustomed to dealing with the claims of nonethnic partisan minorities, courts try to ignore the fact that having entered the thicket they cannot depoliticize the effects of judicial apportionment orders merely by closing judicial eyes and ears.

(As an aside it should be stressed that here we are discussing alleged racial gerrymandering of legislative districts. Totally irrelevant are cases which loosely speak of "gerrymandering" of school districts to defeat racial integration. There we deal simply with one species of direct infringement of a conceded constitutional "racial" right, because the effect is the same as if the state set up racially segregated schools.[13] By contrast, in allegations of racially gerrymandered legislative districts the problem is to define the content of the constitutional right itself.)

"Racial" gerrymandering of legislative districts, properly viewed, is a type of "political" gerrymandering because the *political* effect on the minority group is the central concern. Therefore, rules on the burden of proving discrimination and on the needed depth of proof, suggested in the racial gerrymandering cases, provide patterns likewise for judicial handling of political gerrymandering cases.

The justiciability of racial *gerrymandering* claims is founded on the broader principle that racially discriminatory governmental action *in general* gives rise to claims that courts will hear. Regarding the merits of the claims, a proven classification on racial grounds is virtually a per se violation of equal protection, despite some recent weakening of the "colorblind Constitution" concept.

It follows that use of multimember districts, or careful drawing of single-member districts to weaken the *political* influence of Negro voters is an abuse of the equality spirit of the "one man-one vote" doctrine. No court seems to dispute this principle, although actual invalidations have been few.

a. Wright v. Rockefeller

In its first encounter with an alleged racial gerrymander of a legislative district, the Supreme Court in *Wright* v. *Rockefeller* [14] in 1964, found no difficulty in treating the issue as justiciable. It then left untouched the challenged Manhattan Island congressional districts for lack of adequate proof of racial motive or effect. The justiciability conclusion may have been eased by the Court's pre-*Baker* ruling in *Gomillion* v. *Lightfoot*,[15]

13. See Northcross v. Board of Educ. City of Memphis, 302 F.2d 818, 823 (6th Cir. 1962), *cert. denied*, 372 U.S. 944 (1962); *id.*, 333 F.2d 661, 664 (6th Cir. 1964); Monroe v. Board of Comm'rs of City of Jackson, Tennessee, 380 F.2d 955 (6th Cir. 1967).
14. 376 U.S. 52 (1964).
15. 364 U.S. 339 (1960). Cases often cast longer shadows forward than is apparent when measured only by their facts. For example, after the lower court decision in *Gomillion*, the present writer on September 29, 1959, penned the following retrospectively clairvoyant note to the officials of the American Municipal Association (now National League of Cities) for whom he had consulted: ". . . if the Supreme Court takes the case it would be a fairly safe bet that several of the justices would somehow get around the 'political question' precedents . . . . If a majority of the Court should

the "Tuskegee racial gerrymander case." Actually, as discussed in Chapter V, *Gomillion* was not a legislative district gerrymander at all. It involved, rather, a detachment of Negro territory from the city of Tuskegee (the reverse of the common practice of annexation) an act not illegal per se but illegal in this instance because impermissibly grounded on race.

Wright v. *Rockefeller* did involve a true legislative gerrymander allegation. Plaintiffs argued that the four congressional districts on Manhattan Island had been devised by the legislature with racial composition in mind, to the detriment of Negro and Puerto Rican representation. Although the attack seemingly was centered on the Harlem district, all four must be considered together, and were so considered in plaintiffs' proof, because of their unavoidable interconnection as created and as prospectively subject to change. Of the four districts, three had a predominantly white population and white Congressmen. They ranged from 94.9 percent white (i.e., non-Negro and non-Puerto Rican) in the case of then-Congressman John V. Lindsay's "silk stocking" 17th district, down to 72.5 and 71.5 percent white in the other two districts. The fourth district was then-Congressman Adam Clayton Powell's 18th district (Harlem) which was 86.3 percent Negro-Puerto Rican.

There was no challenge to the arithmetic disparity in the population of the four districts. The range from 382,320 to 445,175 was within the state's policy of a 15 percent maximum deviation from state average. Rather, stress was placed on uneven configuration of district lines and on racial composition.

Politically the districts were also split three to one, Congressman Lindsay being the only Republican. Phrased another way, two minority interests, not one, were involved: the Negro interest in one of the three Democratic districts, and the Republican interest in one of the three white districts. Further, because important Negro leaders, including Adam Clayton Powell himself, intervened as defendants to support the constitutionality of the plan, it is not wholly unlikely that at least some backers of the suit were as much interested in destroying the safe Republican "communal constitutency" as in breaking up the safe Negro "communal constituency." It may be suggested that had the Negro and Republican minority communal interest been centered in one district rather than split, plaintiffs' case in *Wright* would have been conceptually easier, however unlikely such a possibility might be from the standpoint of political realities.

vote to hold the statute unconstitutional it could be a very important case from the municipal-urban viewpoint. . . . From the standpoint of present-day construction of the Fourteenth Amendment it would be difficult to distinguish between 'unconstitutional' disenfranchisement of Negroes and 'constitutional' disenfranchisement of the urban voter in regard to legislative districts generally."

The fatal gaps in plaintiffs' proof were twofold. First, a likely explanation for the composition of the districts was that the Republican-controlled legislature devised the districts more along partisan political lines, to avoid a Democratic clean sweep of the four Manhattan districts, than along racial lines. Second, and more important, the interest in effective Negro representation itself was much clouded by the fact that Negro parties and intervenors were on both sides of the case. They were divided by the issue of which was preferable from the standpoint of Negro representation, a safe Negro district whereby the Negro one-fourth or one-third of Manhattan Island elects its own spokesman; or four racially mixed districts not subject to Negro voter control, but in which Negroes may achieve a balance of power influence over all four Congressmen?

Out of this mélange, and with Congressman Powell's status in mind, the district court said it found plaintiffs' theories of unconstitutionality "difficult to pin down." It warned that a court should ever be watchful lest it be made "the pawn of warring political factions." [16]

b. *Race and "Equal Representation"*

Although it was overshadowed in the 1963 Term of the Supreme Court by *Wesberry* and *Reynolds*, which announced the equal population district standard for congressional districts and state legislative districts, in retrospect, *Wright* v. *Rockefeller* emerges as the key case in our present "second round" of apportionment litigation.[17] A strong presumption for substantial population equality in districting, which is the essence of *Wesberry* and *Reynolds*, can be supported either by a simple civil rights theory of equal voter "value," or a more sophisticated theory of actual malrepresentation of interests presumptively flowing from gross population imbalance. Once over the hurdle of population equality the "representation" aspect of "equal representation" immediately requires special attention lest a gerrymandered "equality" make a mockery of "one man-one vote." Failure to deal with problems of gerrymandering i.e., discriminatory equal

16. 211 F. Supp. 460, 464–65 (S.D. N.Y. 1962).
17. On authority of *Wright* v. *Rockefeller*, the Supreme Court sustained a federal district court dismissal of another early racial gerrymandering attack on New York congressional districts, *Honeywood* v. *Rockefeller*, 214 F. Supp. 897 (E.D. N.Y. 1963). The federal district court had again placed a heavy burden of proof on the Negro plaintiffs to show not only the racial effect of the districting but also to rebut the possibility of nonracial explanations. The record in *Honeywood*, however, was weaker than the record in *Wright* because the primary basis suggested to support the charge that the legislature was motivated by racial considerations was that a congressional district line change had moved a few hundred Negroes from a district which was 6 percent Negro to one which was 23 percent Negro. Although not mentioned by the court, one might suggest that the change could be viewed as a benefit by enhancing the possibility that Negro interest would have significant influence in at least one district.

population districting, will give the *Reapportionment Decisions* the thrust of "one-half a pair of pliers." [18]

Wright identifies, although it does little to illuminate, such current issues as the following: (1) *standing* to assert a claim based on "malrepresentation of interests" as distinguished from "malapportionment of people"; (2) relevant categories of *proof* of malrepresentation apart from numbers inequality; (3) use of *presumptions* to allocate and shift the crucial burden of proof on legislative motive and on the operative effect of a particular set of districts. From *Wright* comes this overriding question— made sharper by the racial context but not confined to *racial* political interests: To what extent is it constitutionally permissible, proper, or perhaps necessary in representation theory, to create homogeneous "communal constitutencies"?

Muddled Race Precedents. Despite the long line of racial discrimination cases beginning with the white jury cases in 1880 and coming down through the recent cases concerning desegregation of schools and public facilities generally, the precise nature of a plaintiff's "standing to sue" and the precise nature of the basis for invalidating statutes based on or significantly recognizing race is surprisingly murky. Hence the character of the relevant proof is also unclear. In *Strauder* v. *West Virginia*,[19] the Supreme Court invalidated the conviction of a Negro defendant on a mere showing that the conviction was by a mandatory all-white jury. Clearly the general interest of Negroes in equal opportunity to serve on juries was not the essence of the defendant's claim. If the decision rests on a sub silentio assumption of prejudice is not the danger of prejudice equally present in a fairly drawn all-white jury that tries a Negro defendant? And yet the Court has disclaimed any governmental duty to include Negroes on a Negro defendant's jury. In *Brown* v. *Board of Education* the Court seemed impressed by the simple fact of segregation; it is doubtful that proof of instructional superiority in the Negro schools would have averted a declaration of unconstitutionality.

Thus racial classifications (and by extension any identifiable nonracial classifications) in legislative districting may be viewed alternatively as (1) impermissible when *intentionally* arranged by the legislature; (2) impermissible where a racial effect (special benefit or harm) can be shown; (3) impermissible because harm is presumed by operation of law simply as a result of a racial classification, e.g., statutes separating a minority group could be said to testify to its inferiority; (4) impermissible as a constitu-

18. Phil C. Neal, "Baker v. Carr: Politics in Search of Law," in 1962 *Supreme Court Review* 252, 278 (Philip B. Kurland, editor, Chicago: University of Chicago Press, 1962).
19. 100 U.S. 303 (1880).

tional absolute regardless of intent or effects, which is perhaps simply a shortened statement of the third point. To say that harm flowing from racial classification is presumed by operation of law, rather than to say that such classification is bad regardless of demonstrable present injury, enables us to give at least lip service to conventional requirements about "standing to sue." No one may claim protection of the Constitution unless someone has been hurt, and normally the plaintiff must show personal harm.[20]

The Nub of Wright. Dissenting District Judge Thomas F. Murphy was impressed with plaintiffs' demonstration of the racial composition of the districts, and the way in which line changes would alter the racial composition. Despite a "total absence of direct proof," he felt that this demonstration made out a prima facie case of racial intent entitling plaintiffs to victory unless the state could show that the particular racial composition was the accidental product of lines drawn more from political or other considerations than from racial considerations. Thus, he would place on the state the difficult burden of proving a negative. He did hint, however, that the state might win by proving "that the lines were drawn as part of a political compromise between the major parties to insulate certain sections for 'traditional purposes.'"[21] The district court majority and Justice Hugo L. Black, speaking for the Supreme Court majority, were unwilling to aid the plaintiffs with a "prima facie" rule and found that the plaintiffs had failed to prove that "the New York Legislature was either motivated by racial considerations or in fact drew the districts on racial lines."[22]

Because *Wright* was a *legislative representation* case rather than an all-white jury case or a segregated public facility case, the question naturally arises whether plaintiffs would or should have won their case even if they could have proven racial motivation, or "racial lines" in fact. Justice Black noted the problems caused by the simple fact of Negro and Puerto Rican residence concentrations. And he seemed to leave open the question of constitutionality of a conscious policy of evenly dividing minority groups among districts, which might be the only way to avoid the Negro "communal constituency" which plaintiffs were challenging in this case. He also noted the split on representation values among the Negro parties themselves, which clouded the constitutional issue of discrimination. He said:

20. For a detailed discussion of the justiciability, standing, and burdens of proof problems raised by *Wright*, see Note, "Wright v. Rockefeller and Legislative Gerrymanders: The Desegregation Problems Plus A Problem of Proof," 72 *Yale L.J.* 1041 (1963).
21. 211 F. Supp. at 472–73.
22. 376 U.S. at 56.

As the majority below pointed out, the concentration of colored and Puerto Rican voters in one area in the county made it difficult, *even assuming it to be permissible,* to fix districts so as to have anything like an equal division of these voters among the districts. Undoubtedly some of these voters, as shown by this lawsuit, would prefer a more even distribution of minority groups among the four congressional districts, but others, like the intervenors in this case, would argue strenuously that the kind of districts for which appellants contended would be undesirable and, because based on race or place of origin, themselves be unconstitutional.[23]

The nub of the problem in *Wright* may be this: in terms of results, spreading Negroes or other minorities may help them *educationally,* but may hurt them *politically* in terms of safe seats. Racial desegregation cases therefore may yield unappealing precedents for racial gerrymandering cases. And there is a further insistent factor, which the law of representation cannot ignore. Getting "one of their own" into high political office has long been viewed as the final token of full integration of ethnic minorities into American society.[24]

Douglas and the Real Issues. Justice William O. Douglas's opinion cryptically posed some of the *real* questions about racial gerrymandering and, to an extent, political gerrymandering. He would move from nullification of "rotten boroughs" to nullification of "racial boroughs," for each is "at war with democratic standards." He would not want to copy the experience of India, Cyprus, and Lebanon. Devising constituencies in recognition of the social fragmentation of a country, he indicated, imposes the danger of fragmented government.[25] And yet too rigid a policy of discouraging ethnic representation may express itself as Hitler's submergence of all interests in the central "Volk myth" or Stalin's "Russification" of various subnationalities in the Soviet Union.

It is all very well for Douglas to say that "racial electoral registers, like religious ones, have no place in a society which honors the Lincoln tradition." [26] But this is not the issue. Without endorsing all the aims of Black Power—which was not even on the horizon when Douglas wrote—a recognition or at least a tolerance of the interaction of residence and race, residence and religion, residence and economic views, is *also* a function of

23. *Id.* at 57–58 (emphasis added).
24. Samuel Lubell, *The Nature of American Politics* (New York: Harper, 1952).
25. See W. J. M. MacKenzie, *Free Elections* 34–35, 94–95 (Oxford: Clarendon Press, 1958) who warns against the danger of communal elections based on European and African experience because excessive communalism may defeat nationalism and jeopardize self-government.
26. 376 U.S. at 66.

a democratic *political* representation system. "Political" interests never exist in isolation as pristine entities divorced from sex, race, economic class, vocation, and so forth.

In short, Douglas does help by directing attention away from bare population equality, [27] and by noting the tension between ethnic-interest group realities and community unity. Before he finishes he traps himself in two ways. He rejects the need to prove racial motive in legislative districting and says that "racial segregation that is state-sponsored should be nullified *whatever may have been intended.*" [28] (This thought may be similar to several recent civil rights opinions suggesting that whatever the state *permits* the state *endorses.*[29]) He also adds the caveat that an election district consisting of a racial bloc may be all right if it is an "actual neighborhood." [30]

Where then does Justice Douglas leave us? Ethnic representation is to be vigorously discouraged. Districts that produce ethnic representation are bad even without racial motive. Yet, "actual neighborhoods" (and why would not Harlem fit this category?) even if ethnic, are permissible election districts! Traversing the political thicket obviously is not a task for the thin-skinned.

c. *Racial Questions in* Reynolds-*Inspired Reapportionments*

The handful of racial gerrymandering cases since *Wright* v. *Rockefeller* confirms the *justiciability* of pleas of racial discrimination in legislative districting, and the great difficulty of defining what constitutes racial discrimination. In none of the cases has there been any significant discussion of opposing theories of effective Negro representation, i.e., communal constituencies versus mixed constituencies, nor any explicit consideration of the extent to which one or the other theory should be embodied into constitutional law in the context of a particular case.

Defeat in Virginia. The farthest departure from the communal ethnic constituency idea occurs in multimember districting, but to date no alleged Negro gerrymander has been invalidated on that ground. One

27. *Id.* at 59 n.1 where Justice Douglas said: "Nor does the Constitution require a scheme for exact equality in districting, let alone a 'mathematically-based procedure for districting which produces contiguous districts nearly equal in population.' See Weaver and Hess, A Procedure for Nonpartisan Districting: Development of Computer Techniques, 73 *Yale L.J.* 288, 307 (1963)."

28. *Id.* at 61 (emphasis added).

29. Evans v. Newton, 382 U.S. 296 (1966); Bell v. Maryland, 378 U.S. 226, 286 (1964) (Goldberg, J., concurring). See also Pennsylvania v. Brown, 270 F. Supp. (E.D. Pa. 1967), the famous Girard College case in which a federal district court in July 1967 voided the trust limitation to white male orphans as impermissible "state action," even though an earlier court had substituted private trustees for the public trustee (City of Philadelphia) selected by Mr. Girard.

30. 376 U.S. at 67.

major attempt concerned the alleged Virginia racial gerrymander which the Supreme Court refused to review in 1965.[31] Richmond Negro citizens challenged that portion of an "equal population" apportionment statute which combined the City of Richmond (219,958) and Henrico County (117,339) into one multimember district to elect eight lower house members at-large. They also challenged the refusal to district Richmond itself into single-member districts. Their "proof" of racial discrimination consisted essentially of indicating (a) that Negroes constituted 42 percent of Richmond's population but only 29 percent of the enlarged district population; (b) that such a combination of political subdivisions was unprecedented where each was large enough to qualify for separate representation; (c) that use of single-member districts inside Richmond would ensure election of a Negro as one of the five delegates, and perhaps as one of the two senators.

Regarding their claim that Richmond and Henrico County were improperly joined, the Negro plaintiffs said, citing *Gomillion* v. *Lightfoot*,[32] that attempts to nullify Negroes' political effectiveness are invalid, whether by "zoning them *out* of the city of Tuskegee" or "zoning them *into* a large district in which their number will be overwhelmed."[33] But on this branch of the case their cause was hurt, probably, by a concurrent attack on the same Richmond-Henrico multimember plan by white Henrico plaintiffs who claimed that one reason for the enlarged district was to submerge the growing Republican vote in Henrico County.[34] As the Negro plaintiffs tried to point out, it could be said that this feature made the Richmond-Henrico district doubly bad, as a repression of both Negro and Republican groups in favor of white Democratic dominance.[35] But it blunted the claim of racial gerrymander by suggesting a nonracial, partisan explanation for the creation of the enlarged multimember district.

Regarding the intra-Richmond single-member district claim, the federal district court got around any inference of adverse racial intent by pointing out that multimember districts were traditional in Virginia for cities and counties entitled to more than one legislator. Also, the Richmond city council was elected at-large "without question by either race."

Tradition, therefore, blunted the inference of racial *intent*. And the court ignored the question of racial *effect* because any corrective measures

31. Burnette v. Davis, 382 U.S. 42 (1965).
32. 364 U.S. 339 (1960).
33. Jurisdictional Statement (Negro Appellants) Thornton v. Davis, United States Supreme Court, October Term, 1965, No. 241, p. 22.
34. Jurisdictional Statement (White Appellants) Burnette v. Davis, United States Supreme Court, October Term, 1965, No. 241, pp. 7, 12.
35. Brief, Mann v. Davis, United States District Court for the Eastern District of Virginia, Civil Action No. 2604, 1965, p. 10; Jurisdictional Statement, *supra* note 33, at 11, 13.

would have to be founded implicitly, if not explicitly, on grounds of race. "No line may be drawn to prefer by race or color," said Circuit Judge Albert V. Bryan for the court.

Thus, the dilemma of the Harlem cases, *Wright* v. *Rockefeller*, continues. Negro plaintiffs fall between two stools. They cannot win on a racial intent theory because of difficulty of proof and existence of alternative nonracial explanations for the lines drawn. They cannot win on a racial effect theory, because even if adverse racial effect is obvious, a corrective redistricting would require conscious consideration of racial identity—a practice impermissible under the traditional color-blind Constitution concept.

Victory in the Deep South. By contrast, allegations of anti-Negro gerrymandering of legislative districts occasionally have been upheld without need for elaborate proof or extended comment, by federal district courts in the Deep South, sitting in areas more known for Negro voter repression than New York or even Virginia. In Alabama in 1965 a federal district court, intimately aware of the local scene, voided some new multicounty, multimember districts for the state legislature on the ground that the combinations were not needed for population equalization and could be explained only as racial gerrymandering.

Operating more on judicial notice than on proof of record the court said:

> The House plan adopted by the all-white Alabama Legislature was not conceived in a vacuum. If this court ignores the long history of racial discrimination in Alabama, it will prove that justice is both blind and deaf.
> The conclusion is inescapable that Elmore, Tallapoosa and Macon [the last including the City of Tuskegee of *Gomillion* fame—Ed.] were combined needlessly into a single House district for the sole purpose of preventing the election of a Negro house member.[36]

Each could have been a separate single-member district county, yielding some Negro representation, but were grouped into one three-county, three-man district. The court noted other similar instances.

But what of *Wright* v. *Rockefeller* and the Virginia case where Negro plaintiffs with similar complaints had lost? In *Wright* both the lower court and the Supreme Court had seemed to agree that racial intent would be bad, but had refused to infer racial intent from proof of obvious racial effect because alternative explanations for the lines existed. The

36. Sims v. Baggett, 247 F. Supp. 96, 109 (M.D. Ala. 1965).

court in Alabama likewise found obvious racial effect, and went on to "find" racial intent. But it really seemed to infer the latter from the former, with the aid of judicial notice of the state's anti-Negro customs which helped to make implausible any nonracial explanation. The district court in the same case turned aside "strong inferences" that the other house, the Alabama senate, had been racially gerrymandered too. The court's explanation, both frank and quaint, was that an earlier senate plan "carefully formulated" by the court itself as a sort of dry-run "produced results from which it would have been possible to infer a motive of racial discrimination, which we knew did not exist." [37]

A second Alabama case a year later sustained a racial gerrymander charge against a Democratic party county executive committee's resolution which switched the method of elected committeemen from a district system to an at-large system.[38] Under the old system 16 of the committeemen were elected from single-member districts and five at-large; as revised the 16 districts continued only as residence units and all 21 committeemen were elected at-large. The defense, presented it would seem as an afterthought, was that the change was to comply with the "one man-one vote" population equality requirement. However, the federal district court found racial motive and effect because: (1) there was no suit forcing modification of the prior system; (2) the more natural change would have been to retain the 30 year-old district (beat) system and equalize the district; (3) no action had been taken until the registration efforts under the Voting Rights Act of 1965 had produced Negro majorities in four of the 16 districts.

Despite the fact that the court's ruling on the Alabama senate gave Negro plaintiffs only a partial victory on their racial gerrymandering charge in the state legislature case, it is hard to down the feeling that the real distinction between the two Alabama cases and *Wright v. Rockefeller* is geographical. In regard to racial discrimination in education we have tended to devise two Fourteenth Amendments, a mild one for the North, a strict one for the South; racial legislative district allegations may fit this same pattern. The North-South difference turns on the past legalized mistreatment of the Negro in the South, which as a consequence now requires affirmative pro-Negro state measures to eradicate the ongoing effect of state-caused "Jim Crow" inequalities. Such precedents as this Alabama case may mean, therefore, little more for Northern Negro-impacted legislative districts than the Southern education cases mean regarding Northern Negro-impacted school zones. In the South, as an aftermath of slavery

37. *Id.* at 107 n.17.
38. Smith v. Paris, 257 F. Supp. 901 (M.D. Ala. 1966).

and "Jim Crow" laws there must be affirmative corrective measures. In the North, where de facto school segregation is the product of "voluntary," i.e., not legally coerced residence patterns, court orders have tended to be much less stringent.[39]

Recurrent, Unproven Racial Gerrymandering Allegations. The comment just made concerning the apparent greater disposition on the part of courts to agree with plaintiffs' racial allegations in the South than in the North should not of course be taken to mean that Southern Negro plaintiffs will always win in their challenges to alleged racial gerrymandering. In the Texas state legislative apportionment case in 1966, charges of racial gerrymandering were turned aside by the federal district court as unproven. The Negro racial gerrymandering allegation was really a variant of a primary attack on use of multimember districts which were alleged to have both invidious racial and political effects. Although the multimember districts were used primarily in urban areas where Negroes were a significant portion of the population, the court felt that the districts themselves provided an inadequate basis for concluding that invidious racial gerrymandering had occurred. The court did not discount the possibility, however, that such proof could be made by showing Negro vote repression in elections actually held under these districts. In short, racial intent had not been shown and until an election was held possible invidious racial effect could not be measured.[40]

The need to carefully support a racial gerrymandering allegation even in such a Deep South state as Mississippi is evidenced by the Supreme Court's refusal in 1967 to review a federal district court's dismissal of a challenge to Mississippi's congressional districts.[41] The suit was brought with Northern support by the Mississippi Freedom Democratic Party and the Lawyer's Constitutional Defense Committee, and supported by data on the racial composition of revised congressional districts which indicated that the districts would produce an all-white Mississippi congressional delegation. Under the 1960 census, Mississippi was 42 percent Negro. As of the date of this suit, 64 percent of potential white voters were registered and 32 percent of potential Negro voters. Plaintiffs in their brief had asserted that to be representative of racial composition of the state, a Mississippi congressional delegation of five members should include two

39. Compare Deal v. Cincinnati Bd. of Educ., 369 F. 2d 55 (6th Cir. 1966); Tometz v. Waukeegan Bd. of Educ., Illinois Supreme Court (1967), with United States v. Jefferson City Bd. of Educ., 372 F. 2d 836 (5th Cir. 1966); Hobson v. Hansen, 269 F. Supp. 401 (1967).
40. Kilgarlin v. Martin, 252 F. Supp, 404, 437–40 (S.D. Tex. 1966). See also Hainsworth v. Martin, 386 S.W. 2d 202 (Tex. 1965), *vacated and remanded*, 382 U.S. 109 (1965).
41. Connor v. Johnson, 386 U.S. 483 (1967).

Negroes. The district court ruled, however, that plaintiffs had "wholly failed" [42] their burden of proof. The only evidence of legislative intent was a sheaf of newspaper reports on what a few legislators had thought or said. The actual Negro-white composition of the districts was the product, the court said, of necessary redistribution of population to achieve equal population districts.

In a companion federal district court challenge to Mississippi's revised state legislative districts, racial questions were not reached. The districts, one of which deviated by as much as 32.55 percent from average district size, were invalidated under the tightened arithmetic equality rule of *Swann* v. *Adams*, the federal district court interpreting *Swann* as making suspect all deviations from average district size in excess of 10 percent.[43]

3. JUDICIAL RESTRAINT ON POLITICAL GERRYMANDERING BY DISCRIMINATORY DISTRICTING

Gerrymandering by race or by partisan or political interest affiliation each has the purpose of unfairly distorting political representation in legislative assemblies. The two are not logically separable, therefore, in terms of a judicial disposition to review the matter (justiciability) or in terms of problems of proof and of defining the substantive standard of unconstitutionality. In practice, however, the two lines of cases concerning racial and political gerrymandering have diverged sharply. Some courts have taken the position that political gerrymandering allegations are not even justiciable, while others—sometimes the same court—have kept alive the idea that discriminatory use of multimember districts (a special gerrymandering form) may be both justiciable and unconstitutional.

Two lines of political gerrymandering cases result. One consists of allegations of discriminatory multimember districting; here courts, including the United States Supreme Court, have tended not to foreclose justiciability (the *Fortson* line). The second concerns single-member districting challenges; here several courts, arguably including the Supreme Court, have ruled against justiciability (the *Lomenzo* line). But some judges have argued for justiciability of single-member district challenges on the ground that the generic unfairness issue is the same as in calculated use of multimember districting, and on the ground that the United States Su-

42. Connor v. Johnson, Civil Action No. 3830 unreported decision of the United States District Court for the Southern District of Mississippi, September 1966, set forth in full at Jurisdictional Statement, Connor v. Johnson, United States Supreme Court, October Term, 1966, No. 999, pp. 27, 37.
43. Connor v. Johnson, 265 F. Supp. 492 (S.D. Miss. 1967).

preme Court has not yet allowed the issue to be fully briefed and argued.[44]

a. *Supreme Court Rulings on Political Gerrymandering in the Context of Multimember Districting*

Use of multimember and floterial districts was not at issue in the 1964 *Reapportionment Decisions*. However, in dicta in several of the opinions the Court indicated that use of floterial and multimember districts might be permissible even when the latter introduced a major "at-large election" factor.[45]

Fortson v. Dorsey. The Supreme Court's first encounter with the issue occurred in 1965 when the state of Georgia in *Forston v. Dorsey* [46] appealed a lower court ruling invalidating mixed use of multimember and single-member districts in Georgia's senate reapportionment plan. The districts were not challenged as being inadequately proportionalized under the *Reynolds* equal population mandate. Nor was it argued that minorities were submerged in the large multimember districts. Rather the plaintiffs pointed to inequities in representation between single-member districts and multimember districts. They stressed the Fulton County (Atlanta) district in which seven senators were elected at-large, but resided in and represented seven "subdistricts" within the county. The district court found invidious discrimination because the residents of a single-senator county could elect and control their senator, whereas the voters in one of Fulton County's nominal subdistricts, by virtue of the at-large voting system, could have foisted on them as "their senator" a man who had lost in his subdistrict but had prevailed in the countywide vote.[47] The Supreme Court reversed the district court, finding "highly hypothetical" the asserted discrimination and pointing out that despite the district residence feature, a senator whose "tenure depends upon the county-wide elec-

44. Prior to *Baker v. Carr* there was very little solid case law either on the justiciability of gerrymandering by discriminatory drawing of district lines, or on gerrymandering by discriminatory use of multimember districts to submerge minorities. As indicated in Chapter V, in the pre-*Baker* era when all challenges to legislative apportionment were deemed nonjusticiable by most courts, whether involving overt discriminatory districting or simple nonaction, there were always a few exceptions to the rule of nonjusticiability. Most of the seeming exceptions, however, involved attempted enforcement of quite precise state constitutional standards on reapportionment without reaching the question of political fairness.
45. See e.g., Reynolds v. Sims, 377 U.S. 533, 579 (1964); Davis v. Mann, 377 U.S. 678, 686 (1964); Lucas v. Colorado General Assembly, 377 U.S. 713, 731 n.21 (1964).
46. 379 U.S. 433 (1965).
47. Subsequently, and before *Fortson* was reversed in the Supreme Court, the same federal district court which had decided *Fortson* rejected an argument that a multi-member district is intrinsically bad because of its *internal* winner-take-all effect. Reed v. Mann, 237 F. Supp. 22 (N.D. Ga. 1964).

torate . . . must be vigilant to serve the interests of all the people in the county," thus making him the "county's and not merely the district's senator." [48]

Fortson at first blush seemed to be a vehicle for clarifying important districting issues left open by the 1964 *Reapportionment Decisions*, but the handling and outcome of the case were a marked disappointment. It was not widely realized that plaintiffs' contentions were very narrow and did not reach the crucial issue of unfair impact on political representation needs in the multimember counties, flowing from the winner-take-all aspect of the at-large election system. There were two minorities in Fulton County who were adversely affected by the seven-senator at-large system: Negro voters and the growing Republican party. Complaining parties were primarily Fulton County Republicans—in the context of the times, Goldwater Republicans, and therefore not in good posture to present the Negro anti-gerrymandering interest. They also did not present their own political interest, feeling perhaps that too overt a discussion of the political realities of "one man-one vote" might offend the Court. In consequence, the case went to the United States Supreme Court with a mere ten-page plaintiffs' brief and six-page motion to affirm.

Oral argument was also a debacle. One of the first questions asked by Justice Arthur M. Goldberg of Edwin F. Hunt, counsel for the victorious plaintiffs in the district court, was whether the suit involved questions of invidious repression of voting interests on racial or political party grounds. The Bench leaned forward and awaited eagerly the response, as did the courtroom spectators, because this seemed to be getting down to the nub of "one man-one vote" as a political representation concept. Mr. Hunt's response, however, was that he did "not want the Court yet to say" that the interest of minorities in effective representation "is a constitutionally protected right." The Bench visibly relaxed, and indeed seemed to lose interest. Sensing victory, counsel for the state, Assistant Attorney General Paul Rodgers, did not utilize all of his allotted time—the first such instance in the reapportionment cases.

However, in the opinion written by Justice William J. Brennan, Jr., reversing the district court, the Supreme Court itself sought to salvage something of the plaintiffs' potential case. The Court emphasized that on this record it could not hold the statute unconstitutional on its face. It then added the following tantalizing invitation for further litigation on more complete records of the question of representational fairness:

> We treat the question as presented in that context, and our opinion is not to be understood to say that in all instances or under all cir-

cumstances such a system as Georgia has will comport with the dictates of the Equal Protection Clause. It might well be that, *designedly or otherwise,* a multi-member constituency apportionment scheme, under the circumstances of a particular case, would operate to *minimize or cancel out the voting strength of racial or political elements of the voting population.* When this is demonstrated it will be time enough to consider whether the system still passes constitutional muster.[49]

This comment occurred in a multimember districting context, and therefore referred to multimember districting. But at the core of it seems to be a concern that *any* districting system, regardless of intent, *not operate to underrepresent* either racial or nonracial political interests. The comment seems to rest on the existence of a constitutional right of fair group representation in single or multimember districts, i.e., a political equity interest as a corollary of "one man-one vote."

Burns v. Richardson. A year later in the Hawaiian reapportionment appeal, *Burns v. Richardson,*[50] another challenge to a mixed multimember and single-member districting system failed for lack of adequate proof of invidious discrimination. But Justice Brennan, writing again for the Court, revived and amplified his *Fortson* dictum, stressing at several points in the opinion the interim and qualified nature of the Supreme Court's reversal of another federal district court which had found fault with multimember districting.[51]

In *Burns,* a vigorous federal district court, in an effort to compel prompt reapportionment of the Hawaiian senate, had not only held Hawaiian legislators' toes to the fire in the spring of 1965, but had also kept in close touch with legislative deliberations while issuing a series of guiding orders on substantive districting questions. The district court nullified the legislature's end product, because the senate multimember districts did not "complement the makeup of the house, to provide the vital equality of voter representation," but rather constituted "monolithic political units of representation." [52] "Such artificially concentrated political power," the

49. *Id.* at 439 (emphasis added).
50. 384 U.S. 73 (1966).
51. A third federal district ruling against multimember districting in the early post-*Reynolds* period—concerning Pennsylvania's reapportionment—was vacated by the United States Supreme Court after the state supreme court had entered the field. Drew v. Scranton, 229 F. Supp. 310 (M.D. Pa. 1964), *vacated and remanded,* 379 U.S. 40 (1964). The district court had ruled that "one man-one vote" means that each voter must vote for the same number of legislators. Otherwise some voters would have only one legislator looking out for their interests; others would have two, three, or four. It also expressed concern, as did the Pennsylvania Supreme Court, regarding submergence of minority groups in large multimember districts. Butcher v. Bloom, 203 A.2d 556 (Pa. 1964).
52. Holt v. Richardson, 240 F. Supp. 724, 729, 730 (D. Ha. 1965).

court said, "negates any notion of equality of representation for the minorities entrapped therein, as well as for all other electors of the state. . . . " [53]

Because of the manner in which the case had been handled in the district court, the state's appeal came up to the Supreme Court with a record inadequate to demonstrate the precise way in which particular multimember districts adversely affected political parties and ethnic, economic, or other interests. This kind of case calls for new kinds of data: detailed profiles of the challenged districts in terms of interest group and political party alignments, especially the latter; relevant past election results; reasonably objective predictions concerning the future political performance of the new districts in the light of all available data; and, ideally, a detailed profile of the "representation performance" of the new districts in an actual election. Thus, the supporters of the federal district court's ruling were forced into a rather theoretical argument almost bordering on the proposition that multimember districts are per se bad.

In the Supreme Court oral argument the Bench indicated that whatever its interest might be in representation realism, and in pursuing questions of discriminatory single-member and multimember districting beyond the easy test of arithmetic equality, it desired hard evidence. It was not inclined to erect presumptions of unconstitutionality based on logical speculations concerning minority submergence in large multimember districts, or the possibly exaggerated legislative influence of those majorities in a position to control a large multimember district. Chief Justice Warren, for example, asked "What groups are prejudiced by multimember districts," and "whether there was evidence of gerrymandering of any district lines." In response there was much plausible reasoning and reliance as in the briefs on "practical political realism" [54] but little hard proof.

Arguing in behalf of the governor and against multimember districts, Washington attorney Dennis G. Lyons pointed out that "voting" and "representation" are different concepts, and that the latter involves considerations of "aggregate human need." This thought would support use of single-member districts in order to produce a broad spectrum legislature rather than a monolith controlled by the majorities who controlled a few key multimember districts. However, as opposing counsel R. G. Dodge arguing for the lieutenant governor and the senate said, the Supreme Court has not yet squarely held that there is "a federal right to be represented."

Reacting to this line of argument, Justice Brennan for the Court said: "There may . . . be merit in the argument that by encouraging bloc voting multi-member districts diminish the opportunity of a minority

53. *Id.* at 730.
54. Brief for John A. Burns, Governor of the State of Hawaii, p. 77.

party to win seats. But such effects must be demonstrated by evidence." [55] Thus again, for lack of proof, the Court turned aside an allegation that mixed use of multimember and single-member districts amounted to a gerrymander producing unfair political representation results. But after re-iterating the above-quoted *Fortson* v. *Dorsey* dictum, Justice Brennan added the following additional warnings concerning the possible unconstitutionality of multimember districting in particular circumstances:

> It may be that this invidious effect can more easily be shown if, in contrast to the facts in *Fortson*, districts are large in relation to the total number of legislators, if districts are not appropriately subdistricted to assure distribution of legislators that are resident over the entire district, or if such districts characterize both houses of a bicameral legislature rather than one. But the demonstration that a particular multi-member scheme effects an invidious result must appear from evidence in the record.[56]

Another Anti-Multimember District Dictum. Not since *Burns* in 1966 has the Supreme Court addressed itself, after full briefing and oral argument, to the question of alleged political gerrymandering by use of multimember districts. In the 1967 Texas legislative apportionment case (Chapter XVII), handled per curiam and without oral argument, the Supreme Court reversed, solely on arithmetic equality grounds, the district court's acceptance of the plan despite challenges to its multimember districting features. Although the Supreme Court did not have to reach the multimember districting issues, it did take pains to say: "Our cases do not foreclose attempts to show that in the particular circumstances of a given case multi-member districts are invidiously discriminatory." In a concurring opinion Justice Douglas more explicitly added this warning:

> . . . I reserve decision on one aspect of the problem concerning multi-member districts.
>
> Under the present regime each voter in the district has one vote for each office to be filled. This allows the majority to defeat the minority on all fronts. . . .
>
> I am not sure in my own mind how this problem should be resolved.[57]

The challengers had failed to convince the district court that the multimember districts had effected both a political and racial gerrymander.[58]

55. 384 U.S. at 88 n.14.
56. *Id.* at 88.
57. Kilgarlin v. Hill, 386 U.S. 120, 122 (1967).
58. Kilgarlin v. Martin, 252 F. Supp. 404 (S.D. Tex. 1966). The district court doubted the justiciability of a "political" gerrymander, and felt that a racial gerrymander had not been intended and could not be proven to be a necessary result of the multimem-

Multimember Districts Ruled Unconstitutional in Iowa. In one instance where a lower court had invalidated a multimember districting scheme the United States Supreme Court did not grant review and reverse, in contrast to its action in *Fortson* and *Burns*. The case was *Kruidenier* v. *McCulloch* [59] from Iowa in which a several hundred page record was compiled in the spirit of the *Fortson* v. *Dorsey* warnings that a cancelling out of "the voting strength of racial or political elements" must be "demonstrated" and not merely asserted. Plaintiffs, two Republicans and two Democrats, objected to the mixed use of single and multimember districts in Iowa's hastily enacted 1964 temporary reapportionment plan (re-enacted in 1965 without significant change on this point), particularly the provision for the election of eleven representatives at-large in Polk County (Des Moines).

Construing *Fortson's* "political elements" term broadly, plaintiffs sought to adduce proof of submergence in Polk County of three minorities: the "rural minority"; the suburban "communities of interest" (using Democratic suburban leaders as witnesses); and the Republican minority (using as witness a defeated Republican candidate who had "won" in her residence area but lost in the county at large). The Democratic party clean sweep of Polk's (and other) multimember seats in 1964 made the Republican minority claim especially pressing. Reliance on it alone seemed inadvisable, however, because the Polk eleven at-large plan was created by the 1964 Republican legislature and was merely continued by the 1965 "Goldwaterized" Democratic legislature. Plaintiffs sought to support these claims with political profile data based on 1964 party registrations and voting behavior, and with testimony comparing single-member districts and large multimember districts in such matters as constituent-legislator relationships, campaign problems, the role of campaign funds and the length of the ballot.

In a confusing mixture of opinions a 5 - 4 state supreme court majority, without relying on the record compiled by the plaintiff, held void in principle the *mixed use* of single and multimember districts for any legislative house unless specially justified. The majority placed its ruling both under the state constitution and the Fourteenth Amendment of the federal Constitution. Regarding the state constitution, the majority felt that multimember districts offended the old, "uniform operation" [60] of laws clause, which they seemingly reconstructed now in the light of the new

ber districts until an election had been held under the challenged plan. (The district court did object to some floterial districts because the component parts did not have their proportionate share of a seat; it ordered modification for the future or conversion to plain multimember districts.)

59. 385 U.S. 851 (1966).

60. Kruidenier v. McCulloch, 258 Iowa 1121, 142 N.W. 2d 355 (1966).

federal "one man-one vote" theory. The thought was that the resident of a multimember district has greater "voting power" than a single-member district resident both in regard to legislators and in regard to the legislature's committee system. "He has a much greater opportunity to find legislators to espouse his cause and a much greater chance that one or more of his representatives will be on the committee to which his legislation is assigned." [61]

The court's reasons for invalidity under the Fourteenth Amendment's equal protection clause were essentially the same and were presented much more elaborately. Noting that in *Fortson* v. *Dorsey* and *Lucas* v. *Colorado General Assembly* the United States Supreme Court had indicated that a mixed single-member and multimember districting system was not per se unconstitutional, the Iowa majority said:

> [The United States Supreme Court has] not considered the problem
> from the standpoint of the resident of a single-member district. . . .
> In view of the deep concern the Supreme Court has repeatedly shown
> for the rights of the individual and for ultimate fairness, we believe it
> will hold such scheme violates the Equal Protection Clause when the
> argument here advanced is presented. Consistent application of the
> principles announced in Reynolds v. Sims seems to compel that re-
> sult.[62]

Significantly, the Iowa court would place the burden of proof on the proponent of a mixed single-member and multimember district system in regard to both state and federal constitutional claims.

Four justices dissented from this per se invalidation of *mixed* use of single-member and multimember districts, but joined the majority on the invalidation of the eleven-member Polk County district on the basis of some of the plaintiffs' special proofs. They were impressed with (a) voter difficulty in making an intelligent choice in the face of the long and cumbersome ballot; (b) lack of identifiable constituencies within the county; (c) the fact that multimember district residents have no "personal" representative. But they specifically rejected plaintiffs' proofs on submergence of large Republican and rural minorities in the Polk County eleven-man district.

Thus, in *Kruidenier* both wings of the state supreme court avoided the real issue of political discrimination. But for different reasons both wings agreed on invalidation of the eleven-man Polk County district. Five justices focused on comparative voting power—including influence in the legislature—of residents of different-size constituencies, and voided all districting systems which permit voters to be represented by differing

61. *Id.* at 364.
62. *Id.* at 363.

numbers of legislators. Four justices thought they were taking a narrower position by focusing on the differing degree of intimacy in constituent-legislator relationships between large and small constituencies. Actually, their "lack of identifiable constituencies" argument is as applicable to a two-man district as to an eleven-man district. Thus the logic of the minority's position took them beyond the majority to a flat requirement of single-member districting.

From the standpoint of representation theory in regard to minorities, and the proper content of constitutional rules concerning representation, the Iowa case perhaps was more interesting, and certainly had a more complete and provocative factual record, than *Fortson* or *Burns*. But Supreme Court review was not forthcoming. The state court majority seemingly had rested its opinion both on the "uniform operation" clause of the Iowa constitution and the "equal protection" clause of the federal Constitution. Hence the United States Supreme Court could and did invoke the customary rule of nonreview where a state court decision can be said to rest on an "adequate state ground" without relation to federal law.[63] It did this even though it was obvious that the state clause took on all its meaning, as the Iowa court itself said, from new federally inspired viewpoints on "one man-one vote," and even though the state court's opinion was devoted mainly to the Fourteenth Amendment.

Another interesting but little noticed case on the "frontier of equal protection" was the Supreme Court's affirmance of a federal district court's refusal to hear a challenge to a South Carolina anti-"bullet voting" provision.[64] South Carolina and a few other states have had a requirement

63. In those fields where broad constitutional principles find their home in equivalent clauses in the federal Constitution and state constitutions, the "adequate state ground" rule can be a slippery way of avoiding clarification of the federal law and of finalizing state rulings. Tactically, in the "equal protection" area regarding apportionment, and perhaps also in the church-state separation area, a court which is not contravening any established federal policy may immunize from federal review a decision striking out on a new path, by invoking the state constitution as an "adequate state ground."

64. Boineau v. Thornton, 235 F. Supp. 175 (E.D.S.C. 1964) (complaint dismissed), *aff'd per curiam* 379 U.S. 15 (1964). An unsuccessful petition for rehearing stressed the anomaly of the Court's action in affirming this South Carolina case without oral argument at a time when oral argument had been scheduled in the Georgia multi-member district case (*Fortson v. Dorsey*), and a request for review was pending in a Pennsylvania multimember district case (*Drew v. Scranton*, subsequently vacated to permit the state courts to act). Commenting on these cases in 1964, the present writer made the following remark, which in its main thrust is still appropriate in 1967: "All three of these cases raise interrelated aspects of one central problem, *i.e.*, the relation of the new 'one man-one vote' philosophy to multi-member district systems, to the subleties of gerrymandering which may be associated with such systems, and to voting arrangements within multi-member districts. . . . If well handled, full dress oral argument in *Dorsey, Drew*, and *Boineau*, could [have illuminated] for the first time, the political realities and deeper philosophical issues of representation that have been ignored so far in most reapportionment litigation." See my Reapportionment Sym-

that, in at-large voting in multimember districts, each voter in order to
have his votes counted must vote for *all* offices even though his own party
has nominated only one or two men. In Richland County, which was to
elect ten state legislators, the Democrats nominated a full slate, but the
Republicans nominated only two. The gist of the complaint was that this
system could be mathematically shown to endanger and possibly frustrate
equal vote weighting and majority rule. For example, let us assume, as in
South Carolina, that with ten men to be elected at-large in a county to a
given class of office such as state legislator, party A puts up only two men
and party B puts up a full slate of ten. If the percentage of total voters
who favor party A's two men are a majority and if they cast their "other"
votes for the same B party men, then this group of voters will elect *all* its
choices (2A, 8B). However, if this same majority of total voters who favor
party A's two men should happen to spread their "other" votes evenly
over the full ten-man slate of party B, then the men nominated by party
A will lose unless they have the support of more than 72 percent of the
total number of voters. Between these two mathematical extremes lie the
actual voting patterns. But the crucial point is that even with support of
a majority of the voters, party A's two men may lose if their supporters
spread their remaining votes at random over the party B slate. To this
extent, provisions like this South Carolina statute leave majority rule to
chance.

The Supreme Court is in no hurry, obviously, to consider detailed questions of "one man-one vote" in the context of districting practices and
representation results. At the same time, the Court has taken great pains
to leave open opportunity for attacks on multimember districting.

b. *Supreme Court Rulings on Political Gerrymandering in the
Context of Single-Member Districting*

In marked contrast to its several dicta concerning possible unconstitutionality of politically discriminatory multimember districting, the Supreme Court has either created or allowed to develop the surprising doctrine that challenges to allegedly politically discriminatory single-member
districting are not even justiciable, unless the factor of race is also present.
If this doctrine does exist—and so far there are only two cryptic Supreme
Court per curiam rulings to support it—it has no intellectual appeal. At
least one federal district court judge has forthrightly said as much in a
1967 Delaware case [65] which had perhaps the most carefully developed
"gerrymandering record" of any post-*Reynolds* case.

posium article "Reapportionment in the Supreme Court and Congress: Constitutional
Struggle for Fair Representation," 1963 *Mich. L. Rev.* 209, 221 n.35 (1964).
65. Sincock v. Gately, 262 F. Supp. 739, 855 (D. Del. 1967) (Caleb M. Wright, J.,
dissenting).

To distinguish between discrimination by multimember districting and discrimination by single-member districting, to judicially police the former but not the latter, would be analogous to repressing burglary and being unconcerned about robbery.

Lomenzo and Political Gerrymandering Allegations in New York. The view that political discrimination by single-member districting is nonjusticiable derives from the involved sequence of state legislative apportionment litigation in New York after a Republican lame-duck legislature produced four plans in December 1964 (Chapter XIII). Plan A, the plan eventually put in force by the federal district court as a temporary plan, was attacked, as were the other plans, on political gerrymandering and other grounds. But at the outset of the hearing the court announced that political gerrymanders "do not raise questions under the Federal Constitution"; [66] hence the parties were asked not to waste time on this point.

In further amplification of this thought Circuit Judge Sterry R. Waterman asserted in the court's subsequent February 1965 opinion that *Reynolds* v. *Sims* concerned only "arithmetic," and that political gerrymandering claims are not within the purview of *Reynolds* unless "unequal populations" among districts can also be shown.[67] He then turned to the just-decided Supreme Court case of *Fortson* v. *Dorsey* and its dictum regarding possible unconstitutionality of schemes that minimize "voting strength of racial or political elements." He baldly asserted that that case "makes it clear that the Supreme Court has refrained from condemning partisan gerrymandering as unconsitutuional." [68]

To the contrary, nothing is less clear. The one thing clear about *Fortson*, as indicated earlier in this chapter, is that plaintiffs did not raise the issue of partisan gerrymandering, and that the Supreme Court in a dictum went out of its way to drag it in to preserve it for the future when adequate proof might be shown.[69]

Multiple appeals were taken to the Supreme Court from this New York ruling and the further litigation it inspired. One state appeal was from that part of the district court's action which had voided Plans B, C, and D because of their fractional voting features and their impermissible apportionment base (actual voters in a given election). In response, one of the Democratic plaintiffs took a protective cross-appeal on Plan A—to be in a

66. WMCA v. Lomenzo, 238 F. Supp. 916, 925 (S.D. N.Y. 1965).
67. *Id.* at 926.
68. *Ibid.*
69. In subsequent proceedings in the state courts, Plan A was nullified as a permanent plan on the narrow ground that the lower house under this plan was larger than permitted by the state constitution, and that this size limitation had survived the 1964 *Reapportionment Decisions.* The lower state court indicated that political gerrymandering allegations could present a justiciable *state law* issue, but made no final ruling on the charges.

position to discuss it further if the Supreme Court reopened—but did not press the political gerrymandering issue. Actually, the political gerrymandering issue had quickly become academic for the plaintiffs. The federal district court had nullified Plans B, C, D on non-gerrymandering grounds, the state courts had nullified Plan A for violating the state constitution's size limitation on the assembly, and the federal court had then restricted Plan A's operation to one year only. The election for the special one-year terms was less than a month away when the Supreme Court in October 1965 acted on some of the appeals (but not those just mentioned) and summarily approved without opinion this interim arrangement.

Justice John Marshall Harlan, however, filed a cryptic concurring opinion in WMCA v. Lomenzo in which he said this action by the Court regarding Plan A "necessarily affirms" also the district court's rejection of the contention that "partisan 'gerrymandering' may be subject to federal constitutional attack under the Fourteenth Amendment"—a principle which he found to be "eminently correct." [70] Some months later in June 1966 (New York meanwhile having been reapportioned by Judicial Commission) the Court disposed of the still-pending state appeal on old Plans B, C, D, and plaintiff's protective cross-appeal on Plan A, by "vacating as moot" the federal district court's February 1965 ruling insofar as it concerned these remaining issues.[71]

Is it proper to draw out of this involuted sequence of events, which confused the litigants as well as the public, a Supreme Court ruling against Fourteenth Amendment policing of political gerrymandering? Apparently the district court's negative ruling on justiciability cannot be said to have been erased when the Supreme Court in June 1966 disposed of remaining appeals by vacating portions of the judgment, because no party was pressing the gerrymandering issue at that time. It certainly can be said that the district court's nonjusticiability ruling concerning gerrymandering never was reviewed on the merits after briefing and oral argument. Perhaps it never was reviewed on the merits at all in view of the unique circumstances of the Supreme Court's so-called "affirmances" of the district court in the appeals disposed of on the eve of the 1965 special election. The parties were not even given the opportunity to argue the point at the district court level! Despite Justice Harlan's solo opinion in Lomenzo, the Court's October 1965 action would seem more properly to be viewed merely as putting the Supreme Court's blessing on a temporary accommodation worked out by the federal district court to keep New York's government functioning.

70. WMCA v. Lomenzo, 382 U.S. 4, 5–6 (1965).
71. Lomenzo v. WMCA, 384 U.S. 887 (1966).

Michigan Gerrymandering Appeal; No "Substantial Federal Question." In *Badgley* v. *Hare* [72] the Supreme Court again without hearing argument refused to review allegations of political gerrymandering by careful drawing of single-member district lines. This argument arose out of the tense post-*Reynolds* reapportionment struggle in Michigan. As detailed in Chapter XII, within hours after the 1964 *Reapportionment Decisions* Michigan's so-called Bipartisan Commission and court process produced a Democratic reapportionment plan—more by default of the Republican commissioners, who had not anticipated the rigor of *Reynolds*, than by design. It was, and may still be, the tightest population equality plan in the nation for a state legislature. After the plan had—with the aid of the Goldwater presidential candidacy—produced Democratic majorities in both houses of the legislature in 1964, the matter was reopened. But an impasse in the Bipartisan Commission and the Michigan Supreme Court left in effect the Democratic plan, commonly called the Austin-Kleiner plan.

In the Michigan Supreme Court Republicans had been denied discovery process, whereby they had hoped to document gerrymandering intent by ascertaining the process by which the plan had been created. Nor had they received a conventional trial on the issues they sought to take to the United States Supreme Court, because of the confusing interaction of the Commission and the state supreme court, and the limited reapportionment jurisdiction of the latter under the state constitution. These issues were: allegations of political gerrymandering; allegations of undue breaking up of communities of interest and cutting of political subdivision lines; the claim that an overly tight equality standard had been used as justification for districting freedom; the claim that they had received no adequate hearing on these matters in the state court.

As presented to the United States Supreme Court, therefore, there was an inadequate record, and the parties disagreed even on the simple matter of whether there had been a deadlock in the Michigan Supreme Court, or a majority disposition. The 132 pages of state supreme court opinions presented as an appendix to the plaintiffs' submission were a formless mass.

Plaintiffs necessarily were reduced to arguing that certain results of the plan evidenced a gerrymander. They showed, for example, a four-district area where by odd shapes, and splitting counties to join Democratic cities the Austin-Kleiner plan produced two Democratic senators and two Republican senators. And they showed that a more symmetrical and compact arrangement, cutting one less county and being even a bit tighter regarding population equality, would produce four Republican senators.[73] How-

72. 385 U.S. 114 (1966).
73. Jurisdictional Statement, Badgley v. Hare, *ibid.*, pp. 22–25.

ever, the suggested alternative arrangement, instead of clinching plaintiffs' case, invites further inquiry whether a four-senator Republican sweep in this area would be any less discriminatory than a "gerrymandered" two-two split. Such an inquiry can be answered adequately only by relating political details of the area in question to party posture in the state as a whole. On the latter question, the Austin-Kleiner plan in 1964 had enabled the Democratic party to capture 65 percent of the house with 58 percent of the vote. But the plaintiffs' case in the Supreme Court in November 1966 probably was not helped—assuming judges read the newspapers—by the fact that two weeks before the Court disposed of the case, the political parties had gained legislative seats in close proportion to their popular strength in the second Michigan legislative election under the Austin-Kleiner plan.

The case came to the United States Supreme Court for mandatory review under the process known as "appeal" in the technical sense, rather than for discretionary review under the process known as petition for certiorari.[74] The appeal was "dismissed for want of a substantial federal question," without citing any authority or attaching any explanation. Does this disposition mean that a majority of the Supreme Court, following the lead of Justice Harlan in his *Lomenzo* comment and despite the Court's strong language in *Fortson, Burns,* and *Kilgarlin,* has conclusively decided to treat discriminatory *single-member* districting as presenting no justiciable Fourteenth Amendment issue? Authorities can be cited on each side of this question.

Significantly, the "orthodox view" expressed by some treatise writers that such a dismissal is a ruling on the merits (unlike the "neutral" effect of a denial of certiorari) has never been expressly stated or explained by a majority of the Supreme Court itself.[75] If full review of a supposedly mandatory "appeal" from a state court is not granted by votes of four or

74. An "appeal" will lie to the Supreme Court in two instances: (1) where a federal statute or treaty has been challenged and found unconstitutional; (2) where a state statute has been challenged but upheld as not repugnant to the federal Constitution, laws, or treaties.

"Appeal" has its roots in the old "writ of error" process for review. Being a supposedly mandatory review, the idea may naturally arise that the Supreme Court's disposition of the case, no matter in what form, should be a ruling on the merits. Cohens v. Virginia, 19 U.S. (6 Wall.) 264, 408–12 (1821).

A denial of a petition for writ of certiorari has universally been held not to be an adjudication of the merits. See, e.g., Justice Frankfurter in Maryland v. Baltimore Radio Show, 338 U.S. 912 (1950).

75. For the orthodox view see Charles Alan Wright, *Federal Courts* 431 (St. Paul, Minnesota: West, 1963), who cites Robert L. Stern and Eugene Gressman, *Supreme Court Practice* 164 (Washington: Bureau of National Affairs, 1962), who cite only Barton v. Senter, 353 U.S. 963 (1957). The case hardly supports the orthodox view because it was an unexplained summary affirmance of a lower court, not a dismissal. See also Note, "The Insubstantial Federal Question," 62 *Harv. L. Rev.* 488 (1949).

more justices, the only other alternatives the Court now allows itself are to summarily affirm the lower court judgment, or to summarily dismiss for want of a substantial federal question. To be sure, Justice Brennan speaking for himself has said the votes by which the Court in conference chooses between these two options are "on the merits." Seizing on this statement, one district court judge in a case not dealing with reapportionment has said that an insubstantial federal question dismissal "amounts to an affirmance of the case on the merits." [76]

But how can this be? If a "dismissal" is an "affirmance" the Court may as well abolish the "insubstantial federal question" category and dispose of "appeals" in only two ways: full review, or summary affirmance of the lower court judgment.[77] Practically, however, the Court needs more than such an either-or approach in disposing of the mounting volume of "appeals," for the sake of docket control if nothing else. The Court may have doubts concerning justiciability, the adequacy of record compiled below, or the clarity of the lower court rulings. In developmental constitutional law areas, it may not feel the time is ripe for embracing the doctrine advanced by the appellant.

The Michigan reapportionment case seems to be an especially inappropriate vehicle for concluding that an "insubstantial federal question" dismissal is an endorsement of Justice Harlan's view in *Lomenzo* on nonjusticiability of political gerrymandering. For one thing, there was no clear counterpart in the confusing opinions of the Michigan Supreme Court to the specific ruling of the federal district court in *Lomenzo* that political gerrymandering was nonjusticiable.[78] In view of the paucity of the record, and the illogic under *Baker* v. *Carr* and *Fortson* v. *Dorsey* of limiting justiciability, the United States Supreme Court could have been saying merely that plaintiffs had not proved a Fourteenth Amendment violation.[79] Further, the cryptic dismissal of the Michigan case is hardly an

76. Port Authority Bondholders Protective Committee v. Port of New York Authority, 270 F. Supp. 947, 950–51 (S.D. N.Y. 1967) citing Eaton v. Price, 360 U.S. 246, 247 (1958) (separate memorandum of Justice Brennan).
77. Dismissal may properly occur, of course, where the technicalities of the "appeal" statute are not satisfied. But it has long been obvious that "insubstantial federal question" dismissals cover a far broader range than that. See Reynolds Robertson and Francis R. Kirkham, *Jurisdiction of the Supreme Court of the United States* 101 et seq. (Richard F. Wolson and Philip B. Kurland, editors, New York: Mathew Bender & Co., 1951); Stern and Gressman, *supra* note 75, at 90 et seq.
78. Indeed, in one of the few specific comments on the question in the series of Michigan opinions, Michigan Supreme Court Justice Paul L. Adams, in an opinion endorsed by Justice Eugene F. Black, expressed doubts that Justice Harlan's *Lomenzo* comment was a "definitive statement" of the position of the United States Supreme Court on "gerrymandering," especially in view of the later *Fortson* dictum. *In re* Apportionment of the Michigan Legislature, 137 N.W. 2d 495, 512–14 (1965).
79. Such an approach may be consistent, oddly enough, with the statement of Justice Harlan, joined by Justice Stewart, calling for dismissal of a racial gerrymandering case

appropriate vehicle for signaling a conclusive Supreme Court judgment on a novel but crucial issue of constitutional law.

In any event, of course, because the "stare decisis" doctrine of standing by past decisions is not so much an iron maiden as a flexible guideline, it would take only a different vote at a future time to reverse an anti-justiciability precedent supposedly derived from the "insubstantial federal question" dismissal of the Michigan political gerrymandering claim. Even Supreme Court judgments reached after full briefing and oral argument and supported by careful opinions may have short life. After dodging as an "insubstantial federal question" (two "appeals" being dismissed on this ground) the constitutionality of the compulsory flag salute for public school children, the Supreme Court declared it constitutional in 1940, and then reversed itself in 1943 and declared it unconstitutional.[80]

c. *Political Gerrymandering Muddle in the Lower Courts*

Although the Supreme Court has yet to explain its position on the justiciability of political gerrymandering, several lower courts have held political gerrymandering allegations to be nonjusticiable. Several of these rulings occurred even before the Supreme Court arguably reinforced Justice Harlan's *Lomenzo* comment by dismissing the Michigan political gerrymander appeal (*Badgley*) for want of a "substantial federal question." And the viewpoint has persisted even though the *Fortson* dictum was further amplified and supported in 1966 in the Hawaiian reapportionment case, *Burns* v. *Richardson*, and in 1967 in the Texas legislative reapportionment case, *Kilgarlin* v. *Hill*.

In few of these cases, which concerned both state legislative apportionments and congressional districting, was the matter of justiciability subjected to extensive discussion. And in several instances the courts buttressed their ruling of nonjusticiability (based on Justice Harlan's *Lomenzo* statement) with the statement that partisan gerrymandering had not been convincingly proven anyway. Examples include the congressional districting rulings in Kansas and Texas, and the Texas state legislative ap-

on "insubstantial federal question" grounds. They could not have been saying that racial gerrymandering is nonjusticiable, because neither demurred from the Court's review of the racial gerrymandering charges in *Wright* v. *Rockefeller*. They could have been saying that the Negroes had not proved their case. See Hainsworth v. Martin, 386 S.W. 2d 202 (1964) where the majority, in light of intervening circumstances, vacated a lower court judgment which also had denied the Negro claims.

80. Minersville School District v. Gobitis, 310 U.S. 586 (1940); West Virginia State Bd. of Educ. v. Barnette, 319 U.S. 624 (1943). See also the pre-*Gobitis* dismissals for want of a substantial federal question: Leoles v. Landers, 302 U.S. 656 (1937); Herring v. State Bd. of Educ., 303 U.S. 624 (1938). See Paul A. Freund, *On Understanding the Supreme Court* 9 et seq. (Boston: Little, Brown, 1951).

portionment ruling.[81] Other negative rulings on the justiciability of political gerrymandering occurred in an Alabama state legislative apportionment case,[82] a Pennsylvania local apportionment case where the court's negative statement seems broad enough to cover all types of districting,[83] and a New Jersey congressional districting case. In the New Jersey case, however, the state supreme court did wonder whether "too much has been read into" the *Lomenzo* statement of Harlan, in the light of the subsequent *Fortson* and *Burns* precedents, and indicated that exceptions to the rule of nonjusticiability "may well appear with experience." [84]

These negative rulings on justiciability perhaps are a product of a natural desire not to grasp the sharpest nettles in the political thicket. But if allowed to stand in the forthcoming round of state reapportionment and congressional redistricting after the 1970 census, then the 1964 "one man-one vote" rulings may be a hollow victory for those groups—racial, partisan, or "political" in the broad sense of the term—who are in the minority under an existing apportionment system. Pre-*Baker* legislatures would not apportion *at all* without judicial pressure; post-*Reynolds* legislatures may not, and in some instances seemingly have not, reapportioned *fairly* without judicial pressure.

A concern for fairness in "equalized" reapportionments can be seen in the critical comments on the Harlan *Lomenzo* statement and the *Badgley* dismissal made by all judges of a three-judge federal district court in a massively prepared political gerrymandering case in Delaware. Unfortunately, this case was not appealed to the Supreme Court, because after an extensive discussion of gerrymandering, and explicit findings that some anti-Republican gerrymandering had occurred, the court gave the plaintiffs

81. Meeks v. Avery, 251 F. Supp. 245 (D. Kan. 1966); Bush v. Martin, 251 F. Supp. 484 (S.D. Tex. 1966).
    An anti-Republican gerrymander in the Dallas area seems to have been fairly well documented with reliable "voting histories" data in the Texas congressional districting case, but the federal district court in the companion Texas state legislative apportionment case took a dim view of such data on the ground that voting behavior may shift frequently and unpredictably.
82. Sims v. Baggett, 247 F. Supp. 96, 104 (M.D. Ala. 1965). The political gerrymandering claim here was really only a weak corollary of an attack based mainly on racial gerrymandering grounds.
83. Newbald v. Osser, 425 Pa. 478, 230 A.2d 54 (1967). Butcher v. Bloom, 420 Pa. 305, 216 A.2d 457 (1966). The Pennsylvania Supreme Court majority apportionment of the state when the legislature failed to act was criticized by dissenting Justice Michael Musmanno as a political gerrymander. He did not consider the issue of justiciability of gerrymandering either under the federal or state constitutions. However, where the court itself reapportions as in *Bloom*, it should avoid gerrymandering, whether or not it would review a gerrymandering charge against a legislatively devised reapportionment.
84. Jones v. Falcey, 48 N.J. 25, 222 A.2d 101, 105–6 (1966).

a victory on the alternative ground that certain minor deviations from arithmetic equality were unconstitutional.[85]

On the facts Circuit Judge John Biggs, Jr.'s massive 112-page opinion for the court denied some claims of an anti-Republican gerrymander by the Democratic legislature but supported several claims on the basis of proof primarily in the form of detailed party election performance data. In regard to "rural New Castle County" (that part not covered by the city of Wilmington), he found one gerrymandered district but denied the charge as to the area as a whole despite the fact that of 15 contested seats the Democrats captured two-thirds with less than 50 percent of the popular vote.[86] In the city of Wilmington he found non-compactness and an anti-Republican gerrymander in regard to a "galloping horse" district. He denied a charge of political gerrymandering in regard to a "lop-eared rabbit" district in Kent County, although it was shown that Republicans in 1962 with 48.1 percent of the vote captured one of the three senatorial seats and in 1964 with 42.1 percent of the vote captured no seats. As between the city of Wilmington and the remainder of New Castle County he found a gerrymander in awarding a fractional house seat and a fractional senate seat (New Castle having the major fraction in each instance by the court's population estimates) to heavily Democratic Wilmington rather than to closely balanced New Castle.

On the "law" of gerrymandering, Judge Biggs with apparent reluctance, concluded that Justice Harlan's *Lomenzo* comment, augmented by the Court's dismissal of *Badgley*, "seems" to indicate that "political gerrymandering" is "not cognizable under the Fourteenth Amendment." However, being "not certain of the correctness" of this conclusion, the district court had made gerrymandering findings, he said, so that its "mistake, if it be such, can be corrected on appeal." [87] And yet, in giving the plaintiffs a victory on an alternative (and arguably specious) tight arithmetic ground, the court seemingly made appeal by plaintiffs impossible; and no appeal was taken by the state from the court's unequal population ruling.

85. Sincock v. Gately, 262 F. Supp. 739 (D.Del. 1967).
    Following extensive findings of fact, the court invalidated the apportionment plan on population grounds both as to the allocation of seats to the major political subdivisions within the state, but also as to the subdistricting within those major subdivisions. Statistical tables are at 757–86 *et seq.* Before subdistricting, the maximum deviations for the apportionment plan were: +6.69, −11.74 for the senate; +7.36, −4.3 for the house. Given the subdistricting, however, maximum deviations were as high as +12 percent and −16 percent. At 821–28 the court considered the discrepancies and required invalidation of the apportionment plan because of population inequality.
86. *Id.* at 812, 814. When the additional (uncontested) seat is included the totals become Democrats, 52,269 votes, 11 seats; Republicans, 51,931 votes, 5 seats. *Id.* at 815.
87. *Id.* at 833.

Separate views on the justiciability of political gerrymandering were filed by the two other judges. District Judge Caleb R. Layton III felt that despite *Lomenzo* and *Badgley* the Supreme Court "has not spoken on the question of gerrymandering." [88] He moved from this to the odd conclusion that despite *Baker v. Carr* the matter should be presumed to be "a political, not a constitutional issue" until the Supreme Court expressly authorized adjudication.

This was too much for District Judge Caleb M. Wright. Agreeing that the Supreme Court has not "spoken" on this "significant problem", and putting more weight on the Court's explicit dicta in the *Fortson* and *Burns* cases than on its "summary treatment" of the matter in *Lomenzo* and *Badgley*, he would proceed to adjudicate partisan gerrymandering questions.[89] He continued:

> Concededly, gerrymandering is fairly deep in the "political thicket." Nevertheless, to allow a legislature to deprive any group of fair representation in any manner would be to condone invidious discrimination. . . . Since the discrimination worked by partisan gerrymandering is as sinister as that worked by malapportionment—both operate to nullify the voting power of certain elements of the citizenry—it would seem that the rationale of Baker v. Carr requires that those whose votes are debased by partisan gerrymandering be afforded the protection of the Fourteenth Amendment.[90]

Thus is posed one of the major reapportionment issues for the 'seventies. It is unlikely that the issue of justiciability of political gerrymandering will be laid to rest until the Supreme Court speaks specifically to the point. In the light of past reversals of Court position, it also is unlikely that seriously aggrieved parties with a provable case will cease suing even if the Court's first explicit response is to leave political gerrymandering by single-member districting within the "political thicket." Indeed, how can parties so aggrieved rest, so long as both multimember district gerrymandering and racial gerrymandering remain justiciable?

"Backdoor" Invalidations of Political Gerrymandering. The unsatisfactory character under "one man-one vote" theory of a rule that political gerrymandering is nonjusticiable is evidenced by the fact that some of the courts taking this position under the authority of Justice Harlan's

88. *Id.* at 855.
89. *Id.* at 855–56.
90. *Id.* at 857. The Rhode Island Supreme Court also has noted the apparent conflict between Justice Harlan's *Lomenzo* statement and Justice Brennan's *Fortson* dictum. Finding no facts of gerrymandering anyway, the court did not resolve the conflict. Opinion to the Governor, 221 A. 2d 799 (R.I. 1966). The "backdoor" invalidations of gerrymandering, noted in the next section, do reflect the spirit of Judge Wright's remarks, and seem to be a covert dissent from *Lomenzo* and *Badgley*.

Lomenzo statement have nevertheless found ways to invalidate some plans where the primary issue was political gerrymandering. The capacity of judges to develop legal fictions to get around adverse precedents is an important creative aspect of any legal system, and may rebut the ethical view that "honesty is the best policy." The legal fiction developed to handle "nonjusticiable" political gerrymandering claims is, however, rather narrow. The idea of backdoor invalidation of gerrymandering has at least two facets.

One facet, as illustrated in rulings by New Jersey's Supreme Court and a Kansas federal district court, is ingenious—perhaps even ingenuous. In essence it is that a plan which cuts local subdivision lines, and is alleged to have thereby created a political gerrymander, is presumptively unconstitutional *if* it can be shown that the same degree of population equality could have been achieved by an alternative plan cutting fewer local political subdivision lines. For example, in nullifying on pseudo-arithmetic grounds a congressional districting plan which was challenged as being an anti-Republican gerrymander, the New Jersey Supreme Court said:

> . . . [A] limited deviation may be acceptable if it is needed to stay with [sic] the lines of existing political subdivisions and thus to avoid the spectre of partisan gerrymandering. . . . But . . . if equality would be more nearly achieved by shifting whole municipalities to a contiguous district, the draftsman has not achieved equality "as nearly as practicable," unless some other constitutionally tenable reason (if there is any) can be shown to justify the disparity.[91]

The court did allow one-time use of the plan in 1966, and it did produce a Democratic 9 - 6 sweep of the congressional seats even though the statewide Republican popular vote exceeded the Democratic vote, 1,045,641, to 1,020,779.

The thought expressed in the quoted statement of the New Jersey Supreme Court was derived from an earlier sequence of Kansas litigation where an anti-Democratic gerrymander by the Republican legislature was one of the charges. The Kansas federal district court did invalidate the state legislative apportionment, but not the congressional districting, on pseudo-arithmetic grounds. It noted that if political subdivisions are ignored, very close population equality is possible and said: "[W]here a state legislature undertakes a plan of reapportionment which ignores political subdivision lines, it is not permissible . . . to deviate from the equal population principle. . . . "[92] In the congressional districting case,

---

91. Jones v. Falcey, 48 N.J. 25, 222 A.2d 101, 107–8 (1966).
92. Long v. Avery, 251 F. Supp. 541, 553 (D. Kan. 1966).

where the anti-Democratic gerrymandering charge was more strongly pressed, the court repeated this statement but found no violation.[93]

A variant of the "backdoor" approach to invalidation of gerrymandering occurred in a North Carolina congressional districting case, where a conceded policy of protecting incumbents, rather than a conventional interparty gerrymander, invoked the court's displeasure.[94] A redistricting commission, operating under this policy reported a plan with a 6.15 percent maximum deviation. The legislature accepted it in substance but tinkered two districts, thus raising the population disparity to 8.91 percent. A federal district court voided the legislature's plan (though permitting its use in 1966) nominally because the commission had shown that a more equal plan was possible, and that the legislature's changes were not rationally related to any proper purpose. But the court seemingly was motivated as well by its dislike of the "tortuous lines" which an "overemphasis" on protecting incumbents had produced.

The difficulty with these rulings—especially the one made by the New Jersey Supreme Court where gerrymandering clearly seems to have been the real motivation for the decision—is that they amount to judicial shadowboxing with an important constitutional issue. The real elements of the gerrymandering claim are concealed, rather than analyzed and made the ground for a reasoned decision responsive to both representation theory and the constitutional mandate of voter equality.

A somewhat different facet of this "backdoor" approach is exemplified by the federal district court's handling of the challenged legislative reapportionment in Delaware in 1967, discussed in the preceding section. There, gerrymandering charges were analyzed at length, some gerrymandering was found as a matter of fact, but invalidation was placed on arithmetic equality grounds. The population deviations were relatively minor, and took on real meaning only by being placed in gerrymandering context in the court's long and careful opinion. It is difficult to avoid the conclusion that gerrymandering was the real decisional basis, even though disavowed by the court in the Delaware case under authority of the Supreme Court's supposed nonjusticiability rulings in *Lomenzo* and *Badgley*.

In short, for some lower courts political gerrymandering does not seem to be a completely "nonjudicial" issue, even though for the moment it may be technically "nonjusticiable" under a broad interpretation of *Lomenzo* and *Badgley*. Unfortunately, it is also true that if the reapportioners in a case like Delaware's had been a bit tighter arithmetically, and sacrificed only one or two more seats to the opposition party, they would

93. Meeks v. Avery, 251 F. Supp. 245, 251 (D. Kan. 1966).
94. Drum v. Seawell, 250 F. Supp. 922 (M.D. N.C. 1966).

have deprived the court of the opportunity to make a "backdoor" anti-gerrymandering ruling on pseudo-arithmetic equality grounds.

d. *Reapportionment, Gerrymandering, and the Crucial Burden of Proof Problem*

The *Fortson* and *Burns* cases, taken together, are quite instructive on two related questions which affect challenges to discriminatory *multimember* districting, and which will affect future challenges to discriminatory *single-member* districting. Such challenges can be expected to continue despite the apparent nonjusticiability rule derived from *Lomenzo* and *Badgley*. These questions are: (a) whether the essence of unconstitutional districting is bad legislative intent or bad operating result; and (b) how to allocate the burden of proof when districting is challenged on non-arithmetic grounds. There is much talk of bad legislative *intent* being the touchstone of unconstitutionality in the racial gerrymandering cases. But *Fortson* and *Burns* seem to make bad *effect* the touchstone of potential unconstitutional discriminatory districting.

The concern for *intent,* which seems to be confined to racial gerrymandering cases, may have a special explanation. It overlaps with the idea that racial classifications are per se bad regardless of effect. Intent seems to be demonstrated by the mere fact that the legislature has created a racial classification, i.e., has operated in a situation (as argued by plaintiffs in *Wright* v. *Rockefeller*) where racial data are so clear the legislature should have realized that it was creating a racial classification. (Of course as already noted in discussing *Wright,* a focus on intent apart from a showing of injury poses a problem of rationalizing a plaintiff's personal "standing to sue"—a problem generic to race cases generally.)

The *Fortson-Burns* focus on *effects,* suggesting that apportionment schemes that minimize racial or political voting strength either "designedly or otherwise" may be unconstitutional is more in accord with the corollary legal principle of confining "standing to sue" to persons who can show actual harm. It also avoids the danger that a primary focus on intent would prevent successful challenge to districting discrimination. A tight arithmetic equality rule itself requires and justifies drastic change in prior districts. If those who district in discriminatory fashion "cover their tracks" by having an anonymous staff attend to political details, evidence of intent may be unavailable, and gerrymandering would be immune to effective judicial review.

Up to and including the 1964 *Reapportionment Decisions* courts handled the burden of proof problem so that once plaintiffs had made the easy showing, on the basis of census figures, of significant disparities in district population, the burden of proof shifted to defenders of the legislatively chosen apportionment system. They had to show that all disparities were not only reasonable but also explicable as the logical result of a consistently followed and identifiable set of apportionment factors—the "rational plan" idea. The results of the cases suggest that this burden of proof was unbearable.

Now, however, the roles are reversed. In the post-*Reynolds* period a legislatively chosen apportionment plan which on its face is "equal" is itself entitled to a presumption of constitutionality. The burden is on the challenger not only to suggest but to *prove* that the system "was designed to or would operate to minimize or cancel out the voting strength of racial or political elements of the voting population." [95] In the Hawaiian reapportionment case Justice Brennan said that the lower court was wrong in insisting "that the legislature 'justify' its proposal," [96] and went on to say that the legislature's discretion on apportionment policy is subject to constitutional challenge only when the challengers can show that the apportionment plan is defective in the respects just indicated.

By analogy, all *proponents* of legislative discretion to utilize winner-take-all districting (i.e., multimember or floterial districts), or allegedly discriminatory single-member districting, or weighted or fractional voting systems, or special residence requirements under an at-large voting system, are now in the fortunate position of the Hawaiian legislature—assuming of course that the population distribution in the particular plan adheres to the principle of proportionate equality. Also by analogy, the *challengers* of such special districting or voting arrangements would be in the position of the Hawaiian challengers. They would have the burden of showing either evil intent or minority repression in actual operation of the special districting or voting arrangements. Insofar as such a burden of proof may not be easily borne, a fair amount of maneuver and perhaps some very clever gerrymandering may be "constitutional" in practice if not principle—whether done by multimember or single-member districting.

In short, our burden of proof rules may in effect be redefining our substantive concept of "equal representation," which has been the watchword of the reapportionment revolution. In those post-*Reynolds* cases where "equality" is the focus and a plan is attacked on the ground that a further tinker will reduce the population percentage deviation a bit the Supreme Court is disposed to presume the worst and force a change as in

95. Burns v. Richardson, 384 U.S. 73, 88 (1966), paraphrasing Fortson v. Dorsey, 379 U.S. 433 (1965).
    On proof problems and the role of presumptions in constitutional litigation see Kenneth L. Karst, "Legislative Facts in Constitutional Litigation," 1960 *Supreme Court Review* 75; Dean Alfange, Jr., "The Relevance of Legislative Facts in Constitutional Law," 114 *U. Pa. L. Rev.* 637 (1966).
96. 384 U.S. at 89.

Swann v. *Adams*. But where "representation" is the focus and the plan is attacked on the ground that a political gerrymander has resulted, the Supreme Court is disposed to presume the best and impose a stringent burden of proof (as in *Fortson, Burns, Kilgarlin*), or deny justiciability altogether (as may have happened in *Lomenzo* and *Badgley*).

e. Proposal: All Gerrymandering is Justiciable, Subject to a Reasonable Burden of Proof

The foregoing discussion deals with the heart of the reapportionment revolution so far as the judiciary is concerned; and the courts of course have been the impelling forces in the revolution. If "one man-one vote" is also to mean "one vote-one *value*," then courts cannot be unconcerned with the manner of exercise of the districting *duty* which their orders impel and the districting *discretion* which tight arithmetic equality requirements create. It is simply untrue that once equal population districts are achieved, fair representation problems vanish or become de minimis.[97] For we have seen statewide popular minorities become legislative majorities in such states as New Jersey and California, and narrow popular majorities become gross legislative majorities in such states as Iowa.[98] And at the city council level in almost all large cities a near clean-sweep result for the dominant party has become almost proverbial, whether the council is elected under an at-large system, a single-member district system, or a mixed single and multimember district system.

Responding to this challenge, the Supreme Court and lower courts have conceded the justiciability under federal law of claims of gerrymandering by discriminatory racial or multimember districting, although there have been few actual invalidations because of the stringent burden of proof. There is no sound reason—grounded on principles of representation or on a practical desire not to overburden courts with difficult cases—not to extend federal justiciability to discriminatory single-member districting also. If fears that courts would have to "wallow" in the political thicket underlay the apparent nonjusticiability rulings in *Lomenzo* and *Badgley*, the self-sufficient rebuttal is that a stringent burden of proof will avert the danger.

With *Baker* v. *Carr* courts "lost their innocence" in regard to legislative

97. This has been borne out by post-*Reynolds* experience, notwithstanding early predictions that gerrymandering problems would evaporate or become inconsequential with "one man-one vote." Carl A. Auerbach, "The Reapportionment Cases: One Person, One Vote—One Vote, One Value," 1964 *Supreme Court Review* 1, 65 (Philip B. Kurland, editor, Chicago: University of Chicago Press, 1964); Andrew Hacker, *Congressional Districting* 133 (Washington: Brookings Institution, 1964).

98. See earlier discussion in this chapter and in Chapter XIII regarding 1966 election results in these states. Michigan, despite gerrymandering claims, is an interesting exception.

apportionment. They now cannot logically review questions of bare arithmetic population equality and ignore discriminatory districting. It is one thing to stand aloof and leave the political thicket to politicians. A policy of nonreview in the pre-*Baker* era left the courts neutral. It is quite another thing to pursue vigorously a policy of forcing reapportionment and redistricting, and then to refuse to examine the resulting handiwork. A bare "body count" judicial review is not enough in reapportionment; for that can amount to a combination of complicity in malrepresentation and refusal to share responsibility.

We also can see a paradoxical "role reversal" among some Supreme Court justices in the reapportionment field. From the arithmetic equality approach of the 1964 cases, made ever tighter by the recent 1967 ruling, reapportioners get a mandate to act and a very broad districting discretion. But from Justice Harlan, dissenter in both *Baker* and *Reynolds*, but author of the *Lomenzo* nonjusticiability statement, reapportioners get protection against having their acts scrutinized. The occasional indications of concern about multimember district gerrymandering come not from Justice Harlan but from Justices Brennan and Douglas. It would seem, therefore, that Justice Harlan's dissents in *Baker* and *Reynolds*, unlike Justice Frankfurter's *Baker* opinion, were informed more by a sense of history than by a sense of representation theory and practice. It seems plausible to say that today Justice Felix Frankfurter would be among those calling for some policing of districting discretion.

Finally, apportionment and districting arrangements have a more than casual impact on effective competition in the marketplace of political ideas. For without a fair opportunity to elect representatives, freedom of political association yields no policy fruits. Thus, First Amendment freedom of speech and of association as well as Fourteenth Amendment interests may be thwarted by discriminatory districting systems.[99]

---

99. Policies of nonjusticiability, as has recently been observed in a general essay on judicial roles, may "exclude those most in need of access from the opportunity to have grievances heard." Victor G. Rosenblum, "Justiciability and Justice: Elements of Restraint and Indifference," 15 *Cath. U. L. Rev.* 141 (1966).

XIX

Remaining Thorns in the Political Thicket—III

"A . . . danger in the use of [a single] hypothesis lies in the temptation toward oversimplification. . . . causation is never single, always plural."

Allan Nevins
The Gateway to History

A detailed discussion of reapportionment issues for the 1970s could go on almost endlessly, because in politics as in sex the marvel of each age is the vigor and ingenuity with which men apply themselves to create fresh approaches to old themes. Of overweening importance may be some matters already covered, such as the problem of defining and achieving the special kind of "equality" which is called for in this field (Chapter XVII), and the problem of gerrymandering in the broadest sense of the term (Chapter XVIII). Also, reapportionment methods, and particularly the importance of bipartisanship (Chapter XIV), may have greater impact on reapportionment than objectively stated standards.

There are, however, a number of other issues which in particular situations may have a drastic effect on the method and quality of reapportionment, and on effective representation. All of them are relevant to the policy choices which reapportioners must make, whether or not the resulting choice is subject to the judicial review tenets discussed in the two preceding chapters. Using only gross categories, and ignoring continuing procedural details,[1] additional major issues include the following: (1) the ap-

1. Procedural issues include: (1) court change in the size of the legislature; (2) extension of time for a valid apportionment plan; (3) severability and continued validity of some parts of state constitutional apportionment clauses, particularly provisions designed to retard gerrymandering freedom; (4) such details as provision for holdover legislators, shortening terms, staggering terms in new plans; (5) powers of malapportioned legislatures; (6) special procedural issues such as intervenor policy, evidentiary rules, use of pre-trial conferences, etc.

In general, size may be changed and has been except where prohibited by a state constitutional provision. Butcher v. Bloom, 420 Pa. 305, 216 A.2d 457 (1966); *In re* Orans, 15 N.Y. 2d 339, 206 N.E. 2d 854 (1965). Courts have often made reasonable

portionment base; (2) districting choices (floterial, single, or multimember districts) and devices for minority representation; (3) the role of computers; (4) emerging "higher mathematical" measures of representation which question the legitimacy of all mixed districting systems.

The holding of constitutional conventions in many states, inspired by the need to revise the reapportionment article of the state constitution, is a noteworthy post-*Reynolds* development. However, it will not be specially treated here because much of the data is not yet available and because the substantive problems of reapportionment standards remain much the same whether the reapportioning instrument be a court, a state legislature, a convention, or a constitutional amendment directly proposed and ratified without convention process. Of course, state constitutional change is needed in many states to institute regularized post-*Reynolds* apportionment procedures, and to authorize future use of special bipartisan or "nonpartisan" reapportionment commissions. These latter alternatives were major features of the recent constitutional convention deliberations in such states as New Jersey, New York, Maryland, and Pennsylvania, as noted in Chapters XIII and XIV.

D. Apportionment Base

In *Reynolds* v. *Sims* and its companion cases the question of the appropriate apportionment base was not at issue. The discursive opinions in these cases seem to leave open a variety of alternatives—total population, citizen population, qualified voters, or registered voters. All of these bases have been used and approved since *Reynolds*. The Supreme Court has accepted New York's use of citizen population [2] and expressly approved Hawaii's use of registered voters,[3] at least on an interim basis and in absence of proof of discriminatory effect. Use of registered voters as the apportionment base has been approved also in Vermont,[4] and use of qualified voters (population over 21) has been approved in Tennessee.[5]

time extensions, in some instances as late as 1968. Harris v. Anderson, 194 Kan. 302, 400 P.2d 25 (1965); Toombs v. Fortson, 241 F. Supp. 65 (N.D. Ga. 1965). Terms have been shortened, but some courts have been sympathetic to the holdover situation and have allowed flexibility. Butcher v. Bloom, *supra*; Stout v. Bottorff, 246 F. Supp. 825 (S.D. Ind. 1965). Malapportioned legislatures have generally been deemed to have full power to act—including reapportionment measures and the election of the Georgia governor when the 1966 election produced no popular majority (See pp. 423, 136.)

2. WMCA v. Lomenzo, 387 U.S. 4 (1965).
3. Burns v. Richardson, 384 U.S. 73 (1966).
4. Buckley v. Hoff, 243 F. Supp. 873 (1965).
5. Baker v. Carr, 247 F. Supp. 629 (N.D. Tenn. 1965).

From the standpoint of representation theory one can marshall some interesting arguments pro and con on the issue of using some apportionment base narrower than total population. If legislators are viewed as lobbyists for governmental service for their areas, then total population may be the appropriate apportionment base. At the same time, because the Bureau of the Census counts people where it finds them, use of total population may produce a serious distorting effect because of such factors as military population, state institution population, college student population, tourists, and so forth. The distortions may be avoided by use of a narrower apportionment base such as qualified voters or registered voters, and this narrower base may better reflect the concept of a legislator as the representative of the conscious political viewpoints of his constituency. If a legislator is a delegate—and if he is not, why then do we worry about apportionment?—is he the delegate of the majority who voted for him, or of all those who took part in the election, or of all those who were entitled to take part in the election, or of all those entitled to participate in the election, including their dependents? Or should he be viewed as the delegate of the total population in his district, including that of the state prison, the state mental hospital, the federal military installation, and the colleges?

An exception to lower court and Supreme Court permissiveness in regard to the apportionment base is the ruling in New York invalidating an apportionment based on votes cast in the previous gubernatorial election.[6] A similar negative view was taken in Arizona regarding a state constitutional provision authorizing extra representation on the basis of ballots cast in the gubernatorial election.[7] In the New York case the federal district court remarked on the novelty of using actual election votes as an apportionment base, and noted that New York City would receive approximately two percent less representation under this base than under a total population base. Perhaps the most serious objection to using actual votes in a given election as an apportionment base is that voter turnout is subject to regional vagaries such as weather, local organization, and local contests. On the other hand, an incentive for voter turnout in some areas would be a healthy thing. Machine politics is sometimes made easier by low and controlled voter turnout.

Use of a later census than the 1960 census would seem to be unobjectionable provided it is used uniformly, and a court in Kansas has so held.[8] More questionable is a partial deviation from the 1960 census base to justify an ad hoc situation. In creating multimember districts in Harris County, Texas, the legislature allocated seven members to the twenty-

6. WMCA v. Lomenzo, 238 F. Supp. 916, 924 (1965).
7. Klahr v. Goddard, 250 F. Supp. 537, 547 (D. Ariz. 1966).
8. Harris v. Shanahan, 192 Kan. 629, 390 P.2d 772 (1964).

second district even though its 1960 population was slightly less (417,238) than that of the twenty-fourth district (417,396), which was given six members. The court cited testimony indicating that the legislature had adequate reason to believe that the former district had grown faster since 1960 and had greater growth potential.[9]

In Tennessee, the county delegations who subdistricted counties used two different bases—straight population or estimated qualified voters. Turning aside a plaintiff argument that a two-base system was per se unconstitutional, the federal district court said that proof of actual discrimination or of particular inequities was needed.[10] In the Delaware reapportionment case (Chapter XVIII), technically decided on arithmetic equality grounds, the federal district court did support its assertions that a political gerrymander had occurred by considering post-1960 population data. The court said that where a difference of a few hundred people will determine whether one area or another gets a disputed seat, the population growth in the two areas since the last census—if known—should be considered.[11] Approaches such as these may be relevant in special situations where award of a seat to one or another part of a state is the sole issue; but unless carefully handled, such approaches raise a problem of possible intrastate inequity by use of a dual standard.

E. Districting Choices and Minority Representation

Instinct tells us that all multimember district systems run the risk of providing the dominant party or faction with an opportunity to make a clean sweep of all seats. And yet, conversion to a single-member district system may not wholly avert this danger. It takes but slight reflection to realize that if the dominant party's supporters are spread relatively evenly, that party can win each district under a single-member district system too. Choice between these two is further complicated by empirically unverified lists of pros and cons concerning the representation effectiveness of single-member versus multimember districts in the literature on parties and elections.

Nor does a selection between these two exhaust the range of districting

9. Kilgarlin v. Martin, 252 F. Supp. 404, 430–31 (S.D. Tex. 1966). See also Sincock v. Gately, 262 F. Supp. 739 (D.Del. 1967).
10. Baker v. Carr, 247 F. Supp. 629, 639 (M.D. Tenn. 1965).
11. Sincock v. Gately, 262 F. Supp. 739, 799, 814 (D. Del. 1967). See Wells v. Rockefeller, 273 F. Supp. 984, 991–2 (S.D. N.Y. 1967): "Let them use *any* available population figures they can muster" (emphasis added).

choices. Floterial (overlapping) districts have been used for years in a few states. Multimember districts themselves may be modified by addition of local residence requirements or by a requirement that each candidate run for a "place," rather than against all other candidates. If proportionate representation of minority groups, in order to enhance their influence on legislative outcomes, is deemed to be of prime importance, less common variants such as limited voting, cumulative voting, or pure proportional representation, command attention.

1. SINGLE-MEMBER VERSUS MULTIMEMBER DISTRICTS

There has been a strong trend toward adoption of single-member districts, but multimember districts also have been used since colonial times and are still common. A survey several years before *Baker v. Carr* indicated that in the then 48 states, 88 percent of state senators and 55 percent of lower house members were elected in single-member districts.[12] On the eve of *Baker v. Carr* another survey indicated a three to one preference (3179 to 927) for single-member districts over multimember districts for lower houses in 49 states (excluding Nebraska). But in terms of legislators there was a close division (3179 from single-member districts and 2704 from multimember districts), because each multimember district elected on the average nearly three legislators. For the state senates (including unicameral Nebraska) there was a marked preference for single-member districts: only 127 were multimember, electing 305 legislators; 1589 were single-member.[13] Accurate post-*Reynolds* counts are not yet possible, but the reapportionment revolution seems to have enhanced the pressure for single-member districts, especially within state metropolitan areas, e.g., Maryland, Michigan, Ohio, Oklahoma, Pennsylvania, Tennessee.

Speculative evaluations of single-member districts, only occasionally supported by detailed empirical inquiry, have produced at least nine supposed effects of single-member districts, and inferentially nine opposite effects of multimember districts.[14] Five of the supposed effects of single-member districts may be said under critical analysis to relate more to the factor of

12. Maurice Klain, "A New Look at the Constituencies," 49 *Am. Pol. Sci. Rev.* 1105, 1113–16 (1955).
13. Paul T. David and Ralph Eisenberg, *State Legislative Redistricting: Major Issues in the Wake of Judicial Decision* 20 (Chicago: Public Administration Service, 1962).
14. See Ruth C. Silva, "Compared Values of the Single- and the Multi-Member Legislative District," 17 *Western Pol. Quart.* 504, 506–9 (1964), and authorities cited, on whom I have relied heavily at this point. See especially James D. Barnett, "Unitary-Multiple Election Districts," 39 *Am. Pol. Sci. Rev.* 65–67 (1945); Duncan Black, "The Theory of Elections in Single-Member Constituencies," 15 *Canadian J. Econ. & Pol. Sci.* 158–75 (1949); Maurice Duverger, *Political Parties* 44–45, 59–60 (New York: Wiley, 1954).

small *size* of the district than to the fact that only one legislator is elected. Hence these factors are correctable, to the extent that they do exist, simply by having smaller legislatures and larger districts, while at the same time retaining the single-member tradition. These five supposed effects are: (1) localism; (2) less able candidates; (3) weak and decentralized parties; (4) emphasis on candidates rather than parties or issues; (5) a particular kind of legislative responsibility to the electorate, which may give the legislator some independence from his own party (a factor obviously overlapping with the two preceding points).

A sixth supposed effect of single-member districts—shorter legislative tenure—is rebutted by some empirical studies.[15] A seventh—more gerrymandering opportunity—is not shown in practice to have any more relation to single-member than to multimember districts. A large multimember district, by eliminating line-drawing within the area covered by the district, eliminates that kind of gerrymandering associated with line-drawing. But as pointed out by several writers, and documented by studies of several states, large multimember districts may facilitate gerrymandering within the state as a whole if a winner-take-all voting system is employed within each district.[16] An eighth and ninth supposed effect of single-member districts—a less representative legislature, and maintenance of a two-party rather than a multiparty system—relate (like the foregoing gerrymandering claim) as much to the kind of *electoral system* employed as the number of legislators in a district.

The almost universal American electoral system, used in both single and multimember districts, is *single-ballot-plurality voting*. (The alternative of using some form of proportionate electoral system to improve representativeness can be used, of course, only in multimember districts or with at-large voting.) In other words, under the simple plurality system, each voter casts the same number of votes as there are offices to be filled, and the candidates with the highest numbers of votes win. If there are numerous candidacies and no provision for a run-off election, the resulting split in the popular vote, even in a single-member district, may elect candidates whose winning pluralities are less than a majority of the total number of votes cast for a given office. In either a single-member or multimember system, a simple plurality rule may enable the dominant party to capture seats in excess of its popular voting strength.

Mis-representativeness, i.e., undue repression of the weaker party, seems

15. Charles S. Hyneman, "Tenure and Turnover of the Indiana General Assembly I & II," 32 *Am. Pol. Sci. Rev.* 51, 54, 311, 312–13 (1938); and his "Tenure and Turnover of Legislative Personnel," 195 *Annals* 21 (1938).
16. Silva, *supra* note 14, at 513; Howard D. Hamilton, "Legislative Constituencies: Single-Member Districts, Multi-Member Districts, and Floterial Districts," 20 *Western Political Quarterly* 321, 325–28 (1967).

to be greater in multimember than in single-member districts according to several studies, thus bearing out the logical expectation, although at least one recent study finds important local exceptions to this generalization. In states with a fairly strong tradition of a two-party government, the dominant party's weakest nominee in a multimember district may prevail over the minority party's strongest nominee. In the 1962 legislative elections in Pennsylvania, for example, only two of the state's 41 multimember districts split their representation between the two parties; 39 districts were one-party monopolies. Evidence of this clean-sweep tendency in multimember districts has been found in Colorado, Ohio, Michigan, and two-party parts of Texas.[17] "In general," Professor Ruth C. Silva has stated, "the more members per district, the greater the disproportion between each party's share of the statewide vote and its share of seats in the chamber." [18]

Professor Howard D. Hamilton has also found that a party sweep is the "usual occurrence" in multimember districts.[19] However, his survey of election results in Indiana, Michigan, and Ohio suggests that the corollary is not necessarily true, i.e., that a conversion to single-member districts would always yield party seats, in the legislature as a whole, in closer proportion to party statewide vote. In pre-reapportionment Ohio, for example, Democratic sweep of multimember districts partly offset Republican dominance in single-member districts.

The Hamilton survey also indicated that apart from the impact on statewide party totals flowing from use of multimember districts, a use of single-member districts—or a series of small multimember districts—will provide greater minority party representation inside metropolitan areas than use of large multimember districts. For example, in Multnomah County, Oregon, a division into five small multimember districts in 1955 resulted in election of seven Republicans and nine Democrats to the Oregon lower house. This provided some minority party representation within the county, which as one large multimember district would normally have had an all-Democratic delegation. Within each of the five small multimember districts, however, there was a strong tendency for one party to take all of the seats.

The results of additional studies of districting in four metropolitan areas—Atlanta, New Orleans, Miami (Dade County) and Oklahoma

17. See William P. Irvin, "Colorado: A Matter of Balance"; H. Dicken Cherry, "Texas: Factions in a One-Party Setting"; Herbert Waltzer, "Apportionment and Districting in Ohio: Components of Deadlock"; Karl A. Lamb, "Michigan Legislative Apportionment," in Malcolm E. Jewell, editor, *The Politics of Reapportionment* 64, 120, 173, 267 (New York: Atherton, 1962). See also Jewell, "Minority Representation: A Political or Judicial Question," 53 *Ky. L. J.* 267 (1965).
18. Silva, *infra* note 60, at 767.
19. Hamilton, *supra* note 16, at 325; see also Hamilton, "Some Observations in Ohio: Single-Member Districts, Multi-Member Districts and the Floating Fraction," *Reapportioning Legislatures* 73 (Columbus, Ohio: Charles E. Merrill, 1966).

City—in the main are in accord with the foregoing generalizations and qualifications.[20] For the Miami, Florida, metropolitan area, which became a 22-man multimember district under reapportionment, Professor Manning J. Dauer has recommended adoption of the Multnomah County, Oregon, system of using several small multimember districts to provide better representation within the metropolitan area.[21]

The decision to subdistrict large metropolitan areas, or to leave them as multimember at-large monoliths, may crucially affect representativeness, and hence governmental tone, of states where one huge metropolitan area has almost half of the state's population. California House Speaker Jesse M. Unruh, although himself from southern California, favored subdistricting, including subdistricting of Los Angeles County which went from one to 15 senators (one shared with Orange County) under reapportionment. He said:

> It may have been the intention of the Supreme Court to end the domination of state legislatures by small, rural counties, but, surely, it could not have been intended that prevailing partisan political sentiment in one county should dominate the entire state.[22]

Although the foregoing studies, as well as the logic of the matter, indicate that multimember districts do tend to operate as political monoliths, their effect on statewide party totals will be affected by such variables as party member residence distribution in a given state and the manner of construction of the multimember districts themselves. The Oregon experience does seem to bear out this hypothesis: the larger the district, the greater the distortion. So far as constitutionality is concerned, the Supreme Court precedents discussed in Chapter XVIII in cases from Georgia, Hawaii, and Texas [23] indicate that all forms of multimember districting are still permissible. They are subject to judicial challenge, however, if a plaintiff can demonstrate serious racial or political mis-representativeness in the operation of the districting system.

20. Morris W. H. Collins, Jr., Manning J. Dauer, Paul T. David, Alex B. Lacy, Jr., George J. Mauer, *Evolving Issues and Patterns of State Legislative Redistricting in Large Metropolitan Areas* (Oklahoma City: Oklahoma City University Institute of Metropolitan Studies, 1966).
21. Manning J. Dauer, *Multi-Member Districts in Dade County: Study of a Problem and a Delegation* (Tallahassee: Florida State University Institute of Governmental Research, 1965).
   Compare similar comments with respect to local government in George E. Berkley, "Flaws in At-Large Voting," 55 *Nat. Civ. Rev.* 370 (1966).
22. Speech on "1965 Legislative Session" before Greater Los Angeles Press Club, April 15, 1965, p. 4.
23. Fortson v. Dorsey, 379 U.S. 433 (1965); Burns v. Richardson, 384 U.S. 73 (1966); Kilgarlin v. Hill, 387 U.S. 120 (1967).

2. FLOTERIAL DISTRICTS

A variant of the multimember district option is use of a floterial district. As noted in Chapter XVIII, floterial districts, like multimember districts, have been questioned because of their gerrymandering possibilities, but to date have not been found per se invalid by the United States Supreme Court. In the lower courts there has been a varied reaction to floterial districts when challenged under the newer equal population and fair representation concepts flowing from the ambiguous "one man-one vote" idea. Although definitions vary, a floterial district in essence is not merely a multi-unit district, but an overlapping district; i.e., one or more units within a multi-unit floterial district have independent representation, in addition to their share of the floterial seat(s) assigned to the area as a whole. For example, unit A may have one seat, unit B may have no seat of its own, but A and B combined may share another seat.

Floterial districts were part of the 1965 Virginia reapportionment plan. A federal district court, although it approved the plan in general, was troubled by the manner of electing two delegates in a four-unit area, consisting of three counties and one separated city (under Virginia's unusual city-county separation system).[24] One delegate was elected from Rockingham County and the City of Harrisonburg, with a combined population of 53,363 (ideal single seat quota being 39,669). Shenandoah and Page counties with a combined population of 37,397 were given no separate representation. However, all four units were combined, for a second seat, into a floterial district of 90,760. The court, on purely arithmetic grounds, felt that although the overpopulated Rockingham-Harrisonburg area was compensated through its share of the floterial seat, "Shenandoah with Page suffers from a clear under-representation."[25] The court's solution was to convert the single-member district and the floterial district into one multi-member district, encompassing the four units and electing both delegates at large.

Thus on arithmetic grounds the revised district's 90,760 population was less than 15 percent in excess of an "ideal" two-seat quota of 79,368. However, in *political* terms, not considered by the court, the question is whether the court's solution would correct what it termed "clear under-representation" of Shenandoah-Page. Rockingham-Harrisonburg, if united in interest, could outvote Shenandoah-Page and still take both seats.

It was just this consideration, apparently, which led a federal district court in Tennessee to question seven floterial districts, even though not

24. Mann v. Davis, 245 F. Supp. 241 (E.D. Va. 1965).
25. *Id.* at 246.

challenged by the parties; it did not, however, convert them into multi-member districts. (The court termed them direct-floterial districts, i.e., districts which elect a floterial representative even though one or more counties within the district also elect a separate representative of their own.) The court said:

> . . . Although there is possible discrimination against counties, there is no discrimination between districts, and it is with the districts that we are primarily concerned. Although this discrimination could be eliminated through the use of at-large elections, still, in a practical sense, the same counties which control the election of the direct and floterial representatives under the present Act would still control the election of the increased number of floterial representatives in at-large elections.[26]

A federal district court in Indiana invalidated a floterial district system on the ground that it impaired and diluted the weight of votes of those voters residing in the smaller counties in multicounty floterial districts.[27] The court's decision was placed on arithmetic grounds only, although one commentator has said the "floterials facilitated gerrymandering" by the Democratic-controlled Indiana legislature, while preserving a facade of "strict equality-of-representation ratios." Speaking of the now-invalidated plan he said:

> Each of the eight most populous counties is an MMD [multi-member district] and is joined to one or more adjacent counties to form a floterial district. . . . Some districts combine Republican-inclined rural or suburban counties with a strongly Republican urban county to form a graveyard. Others add rural or suburban Republican counties to an urban Democratic stronghold to submerge rural and suburban Republicans.[28]

The court paid special attention to one three-county floterial district—Marion, 424,090; Hendricks, 19,116; and Morgan, 23,304. Marion was entitled to, and received, seven senators of its own under a 1965 reapportionment act. It shared an eighth senator with little Morgan and Hendricks. The court found an undue impairment of the worth of a vote in the two smaller counties, stating that in the Marion County seven-senator district there was one senator for every 60,584 voters, while in the three-county one-senator floterial district there was one senator for every 466,510 voters.

The court refused to compute "equality," as the legislature had done, by

26. Baker v. Carr, 247 F. Supp. 629, 640 (M.D. Tenn. 1965).
27. Stout v. Bottorff, 246 F. Supp. 825 (S.D. Ind. 1965).
28. Hamilton, *supra* note 16, at 335.

dividing the total population of the three counties by the area total of eight senators. This approach yields a supposed population-per-seat figure of 96,542, which is only a three percent deviation from the statewide mean. The court said such an approach "avoids reality," [29] because the voters in Hendricks and Morgan have no share in the seven senators assigned to Marion. Hence, on "true" arithmetic grounds the Hendricks-Morgan voters had less than one-ninth of the weight of Marion voters.[30]

This Indiana floterial may also be an instance where arithmetic alone comes close to proving adverse political effect. The residents of the two smaller counties, insofar as their views differed from the views in the larger county, would be as powerless as the tail on a dog to control the political movement of the whole.

In the important *Kilgarlin* v. *Hill* case concerning the 1965 Texas reapportionment (already considered arithmetically in Chapter XVII and regarding alleged gerrymandering aspects in Chapter XVIII), the multiple challenges included an attack on floterial districting. The federal district court followed the lead of Virginia and ordered a conversion of the floterial districts into multimember districts, without considering the point noted by the court in Tennessee that the smaller counties may be just as disadvantaged in a large multimember district as in a large floterial district.[31] The Texas court said the sub-units within the floterial districts did not have their proportionate share of a seat.

An interesting aspect of the Texas case is that the court did not declare floterial districting under all circumstances to be per se unconstitutional under *Reynolds* v. *Sims*, as urged by the plaintiffs—which, of course, would have put the federal district courts in Texas and Tennessee in conflict on this point. Under conventional analysis, any use of floterial districts produces wildly disproportionate population variance ratios [4.63 to 1 in the Texas plan under attack]. The essence of the idea is to combine into one district some sub-units, at least one of which already has sufficient population for at least one seat in its own right. Hence there is automatic unconstitutionality *if* the arithmetic analysis seemingly called for by *Reynolds* v. *Sims* is confined to comparing the grossly inflated population of a floterial district with the population of the smallest district.

The thought of the federal district court in Texas is well illustrated by its

29. 246 F. Supp. at 830.
30. The problem of arithmetically measuring representativeness in floterial districts has also troubled others. Professors Schubert and Press's wholly mathematical analysis of relative malapportionment among the states initially ranked Indiana in fiftieth position. When they recomputed, adjusting for the overlapping feature, Indiana ranked tenth. Glendon Schubert and Charles Press, "Measuring Malapportionment," 58 *Am. Pol. Sci. Rev.* 302 and 966 (1964).
31. Kilgarlin v. Martin, 252 F. Supp. 404 (S.D. Tex. 1966).

objection to a floterial district consisting of Nueces County (221,573) and Kleberg County (30,052). The former ("dominant") county had three seats of its own; the latter ("appurtenant") county had representation only through the floterial seat it shared with the dominant county. Because the state quota for a single seat was 63,864, Kleberg's population entitled it to approximately one-half control of one seat. However, as combined with Nueces in a floterial district with a population of 251,625, Kleberg's residents had only one-eighth control of one seat.

But though nullifying this district, the court took pains to point out that in some combinations, with proportionate control allocated to each sub-unit, a floterial district could be constitutional. For example, Kleberg could be combined with another county (or counties) whose population, plus that of Kleberg, would only total one seat ratio, thus preserving Kleberg's "right" to a half-interest in a seat. Alternatively, Kleberg might be combined twice: firstly as part of a multimember district where its population would give it one-fourth control over one seat; secondly as part of a floterial district where its population would give it a one-quarter share of the floterial seat. In this double combination Kleberg's right to a half-interest in a legislator (because its population is half of a full seat quota) would still be preserved. Kleberg would have a total influence of one-half of a "representative," expressed through two one-fourth shares in two representatives, in two different districts!

The Texas court, though noting the wild population variance ratios which floterial districts necessarily produce (if the floterial district, without adjustment, be treated as the state's largest district), apparently thought that this factor need not be controlling. It stressed instead "equality" *inside* the floterial district, which could be provided by giving each sub-unit its appropriate fractional share of a fictional representative, as outlined above. The Texas federal district court did not consider the additional question—noted by the Indiana federal district court in its invalidation of floterials in that state—of relative equality of citizens who are represented only through the floterial district, and those who have this representation plus one or more representatives of their own.

In summary, despite the Supreme Court's permissive but not carefully considered statements in the dicta in the 1964 *Reapportionment Decisions*,[32] floterial districts pose even more serious "equality" problems—both arithmetically and politically—than do multimember districts. Regarding the latter, the Supreme Court in such cases as *Fortson* v. *Dorsey* and *Burns* v. *Richardson* [33] has imposed on the challengers a burden of

32. Reynolds v. Sims, 377 U.S. 533, 579 (1964); Davis v. Mann, 377 U.S. 678, 686–87 & n.2 (1964).
33. 379 U.S. 433 (1965); 384 U.S. 73 (1966).

demonstrating actual submergence of minorities. However, in the floterial district situation, arithmetic analysis alone may point to actual political discrimination. Residents in the smaller sub-units of a floterial district have only a minuscule effect on the one representative assigned to a huge floterial district, when compared to voters in smaller districts elsewhere in the state. Inside their floterial district they must combat the political force of the larger units already well-organized for the purpose of electing the separate representatives assigned to these larger units. In short, the "representation" half of "equal representation" is especially troublesome in floterial district situations.

3. RESIDENTIAL SUBDISTRICTS, ROTATION, AND "PLACE" REQUIREMENTS

a. *Candidate Residence Requirements in Multimember Districts*

The "monolith" character of large multimember districts can be partially moderated by retaining the at-large voting feature but requiring candidates to reside in residential subdistricts. Such devices have had special appeal in the South. A Georgia system in which the nominal residence areas inside a seven-senator district were assumed to be reasonably equal in population, was left undisturbed by the Supreme Court in *Fortson v. Dorsey*. As noted in Chapter XVIII, the challenge was on a narrow intercounty equity ground, intra-multimember district problems being ignored. If it matters where within a large legislative district a given legislator lives—and this is the *raison d'être* for a residence requirement—a single-member district situation is being approximated; the equal representation spirit of *Reynolds v. Sims* should apply and require equal population in the residence subdistricts.

Even if the residence subdistrict populations are equal, it might be argued that the "representation" facet of "equal representation" was still being offended. The voters of the multimember district, although voting as a unit for their representatives in the final election, are not able to choose the ideal candidates at the nomination stage. In other words, the requirement that each nominee must come from a personal residence subdistrict materially restricts political freedom of the multimember district voters as a whole at the crucial nomination stage. This narrowing of the range of possible nominees would be considerably aggravated, of course, if the residence subdistricts were grossly unequal in population.

Despite the anomaly under *Reynolds v. Sims*—and its developed equal population rigidity described in Chapter XVII—of allowing unequal size candidate districts inside multimember districts, the United States Supreme Court did just that in a series of local government apportionment cases in May 1967. The Court refused to say that the Fourteenth Amendment's "one man-one vote" doctrine applies with equal force to local legislative bodies. It did say that even if the Amendment applied, it would not nullify a consolidated city-county council, four of whose members were elected at-large without residence requirement, and seven of whom were elected at-large from residence units (former boroughs of the county) in which population varied from 733 to 29,048.[34] It is doubtful that this judicial permissiveness extends to unequal residence districts for state legislatures. As discussed in more detail in Chapter XX this unusual local government decision—insofar as it is capable of being rationalized at all—may rest on a Court desire to allow much experimentation with representation forms at the local level in order to foster such "good government" goals as city-county consolidation and other "metro" developments.

"*Negative Residence*" *Provisions.* Another variant of juggling residence requirements is the so-called "negative residence" clause found in an occasional state legislative apportionment statute. Such clauses require that in a multimember, multicounty district, one or more of the representatives must reside in the smaller counties.

A South Carolina provision of this sort, modified by a fractional population ratio feature, was permitted on an interim basis only, but the case did not reach the Supreme Court.[35] A negative residence provision in Maryland's reapportionment statute was nullified by the state's highest court on the ground that the voters in the two-county, two-senator district at issue "are confined in their choice by the county residences of the candidates, even though the counties have manifestly unequal populations, instead of having the right to choose between candidates from substantially equal subdistricts." [36] The court found internal inequity among voters in the two-county district and also noted that the result was that some votes would be

34. Dusch v. Davis, 387 U.S. 112 (1967). See also Board of Supervisors of Suffolk County v. Bianchi, 387 U.S. 97 (1967); Moody v. Flowers, 387 U.S. 97 (1967); Sailors v. Board of Education of the County of Kent, 387 U.S. 105 (1967). See p. 581 below.

35. O'Shields v. McNair, 254 F. Supp. 708 (D. S.C. 1966). The provision was that in all multimember, multicounty districts, no one county could have more than one senator residing within the county unless it had 175 percent or more of the population base per senator. Litigation against the negative residence provision continued in 1967. A similar feature in an intermediate Florida plan passed by the special sessions of the Florida legislature in March 1966 was allowed to stand without discussion. Swann v. Adams, No. 186-62-M Civil-DD (S.D. Fla. March 18, 1966).

36. Sec. of State v. Bryson, 224 Md. 418, 429, 224 A.2d 277, 282 (D. Md. 1966), invalidating the following provisions: "In any Senatorial District comprising more than one county and having two senators, not more than one resident of any one county may be nominated by one political party at the primary election, unless the population of that one county exceeds the population of all the remaining counties in the district in the aggregate."

magnified, others diluted, by reason of the disparities in population between counties in those multicounty districts subjected to the negative residence provision.

The motivation for negative residence provisions is to ensure some voice in the legislature for the smaller counties in a multicounty district. However, the device is just as questionable under "one man-one vote" principles as use of candidate residence subdistricts of unequal population. A small portion of the population is being preferred over a larger portion.

b. *Rotation Provisions*

Another device—equally questionable on constitutional grounds—for ensuring some small-county voice in multicounty districts is to provide that one or more of the seats rotate among the counties, regardless of their relative population size. Rotation was practised in North Carolina for decades under a statute authorizing party committees in multicounty senatorial districts to make rotation agreements. Approximately a half-dozen such agreements continued after the 1966 reapportionment of the North Carolina senate. However, the constitutionality of the device seemed so doubtful under *Reynolds* v. *Sims* that no serious consideration was given to authorizing lower house seat rotation when multicounty house districts were created for the first time in 1966.[37]

Although the Supreme Court has not ruled on rotation, a federal district court held a Georgia senate seat rotation statute unconstitutional under the Fourteenth Amendment in 1962.[38] Even if a particular rotation plan did operate to average out representation in proportion to population over the cycle of rotation, it would still seem to be subject to constitutional attack. A voter's constitutional right under present apportionment standards is a continuous right not an occasional right.

c. *"Place" Voting in Multimember Districts*

The "place" system is a seemingly constitutional method for avoiding some of the disadvantages of multimember districting, such as the winner-take-all tendency, while still retaining the basic form of multimember districts. Under the system, all candidates in a multimember district designate the "place" (or post, or position) for which they are running. Each seat is a "place," normally designated by number. A candidate runs only against the others who have designated the same place; all voters in the county may vote for each place.

37. John L. Sanders, "Structuring Representation in Legislatures—Unique Devices," a speech given at the annual meeting of the National Municipal League, Boston, November 14, 1966.
38. Cullen B. Gosnell, "Small Counties Rule," 47 *Nat. Mun. Rev.* 332–34 (1958); Toombs v. Fortson, 205 F. Supp. 248, 257 (N.D. Ga. 1962).

Unlike the restricted residence system, and rotation system, the place system is not subject to invalidation on simple unequal-population grounds, because all voters stand in the same relation to all "places." There are no residence subdistrict features, or rotation among counties.

Although its origins are obscure, the place system has been particularly common in the South because of the Southern tradition of frequent use of multimember districts, and has been continued apparently without judicial restraint in some reapportionment plans enacted since the 1964 *Reapportionment Decisions.*[39]

There are several obvious general effects of the place system. In presenting the voter with a series of grouped candidacies, rather than one long list, it may allow more deliberate voting, although it does channel the range of permissible choices. It has several advantages from the standpoint of candidates. Through jockeying, and refiling if permitted, a candidate may have some choice in selection of opponents, and of course the "personal" although not the geographic range of the campaign is reduced by having fewer opponents. Incumbent legislators can separate themselves in different "places." This may lead to harmony among incumbents, and some immunization from opposition because challengers will tend to compete for other places. Formation of legislative slates may be facilitated.

Racial implications of place systems are more complicated. Insofar as construction and election of balanced slates is facilitated, minority interests may receive conscious and benevolent consideration if that be the desire of the party slate builders. But the place system may harm Negro candidacies by spotlighting the place for which Negro candidates have filed.

More significantly, the adoption of a place system stops the "bullet voting" ("single shot" voting) practice which Negro and other minorities may use to advantage in multimember district voting without a place system. By bullet voting we mean the minority group practice in multimember districts of voting for fewer than the total number of offices to be filled. The practice may enable election of a candidate favored by a minority, if the votes of the majority are scattered over many candidates. This possible outcome of bullet voting apparently led to the adoption of the place system in 1960 in Shelby County, Tennessee, as a device to stop Negro bullet voting. But a proposal to adopt the place system in North Carolina's 1966 reapportionment act failed, in part because of opposition of Negro leaders.

39. Roy E. Young, *The Place System in Texas Elections* (Austin: University of Texas, 1965). The system has also had extensive use in Alabama, Arkansas, Florida, Mississippi, and occasionally elsewhere. See also the following papers presented at the annual meeting of the National Municipal League, Boston, November 14, 1966, which have been helpful in the preparation of this section: Malcolm E. Jewell, "The Place Method in State Legislative Elections"; John L. Sanders, "Structuring Representation in Legislatures—Unique Devices."

4. WEIGHTED AND FRACTIONAL VOTING

Weighted voting and fractional voting plans retain some unequal population districts for the primary purpose of ensuring a voice in the legislature for the smaller political entities. Thus, they are similar in purpose to special candidate-residency subdistricts and rotation in multimember districts, as discussed above. In weighted and fractional voting, equalization still rules, so the proponents claim. Equalization takes the form of allocating to each legislator a number of *votes* proportional to the unequal population of the represented district, rather than of equalizing district population (as in single-member districting) or of assigning additional legislators to unequally populous districts (as in multimember districting). In pure weighted voting each district has a single legislator to cast the "weighted votes." If a district's bloc of weighted votes is divided among two or more legislators, the form may be referred to as modified weighted voting; it provides additional "voices" as well as "votes" for the populous districts.

Arithmetically, fractional voting is based on the same principle as weighted voting, but is significantly different in one respect. In a fractional voting system, no legislator has more than one vote; thus a major district realignment occurs just as in single-member districting. However, underpopulated political subdivisions are preserved as representation units by assigning a legislator to them and giving him a fractional vote, e.g., if the unit's population is half of the state quota for a full seat, the legislator receives a half-vote.

Although the general American custom has been to elect legislators only from single or multimember districts, the device known as "weighted voting" was discussed seriously as long ago as the 1840s in the legislature of Kentucky. In Kentucky's constitutional convention at this time the following virtues were suggested for weighted voting, although the plan was not adopted: (1) it would preserve separate and independent representation for each unit; (2) it would minimize gerrymandering; (3) it would prevent creation of communities of disinterest which occurs when sections of different sentiment are placed together solely for mathematical quota purposes; (4) it would give every citizen a better voice in the councils of state; (5) by preserving separate representation for each county, jealousy and ill-will between counties would be minimized.[40] Weighted voting, which is based squarely on an arithmetic principle of equal voter right, is not to be confused with the plural voting system used in England until 1948,

40. See Francis N. Thorpe, A *Constitutional History of the American People*, 1776–1880 II: 107–9 (Washington, D.C.: U.S. Government Printing Office, 1898).

whereby "second votes" were awarded on the basis of business, residence, or presentation of a university degree.[41]

Since the Supreme Court's decision in *Baker* v. *Carr*, weighted or fractional voting devices have been considered for the state legislative apportionment in several states, but for a variety of reasons never implemented.[42] A federal district court in Washington entered an order for weighted voting (later rescinded) unless there was timely reapportionment by a special session. Although reserving judgment on the political wisdom of the plan, the court said that weighted voting "ultimately satisfies the constitutional test of 'one person-one vote' as enunciated by the Supreme Court." [43] A state court in New Mexico, although finding no problem under the federal Constitution, nullified a weighted voting plan because it was thought to be inconsistent with state constitutional clauses providing that for various purposes various percentages of "members" shall cast votes.[44] A subsequent attempt to amend the state constitution to permit weighted voting failed in 1965.

a. *New York's Fractional Plan*

In New York, a fractional voting provision for the lower house was included in two of three plans nullified by a federal district court.[45] Under the plan most preferred, all districts being single-member, 127 assemblymen would cast full votes, 47 would cast fractional votes ranging from three-fourths to one-sixth. In nullifying fractional voting the court expressly reserved judgment on its possible use for local government reappor-

41. W. J. M. Mackenzie, *Free Elections* 31 (London: George Allen & Unwin, 1958).
42. At an early stage of the Alabama reapportionment litigation in 1962, a memorandum on weighted voting as a possible judicial remedy for malapportionment was submitted by Professor C. Dallas Sands at the request of Judge Richard T. Rives. (See Memorandum Brief filed in Sims v. Frink, Civ. No. 1744-N, July 5, 1962). The matter was never pursued in Alabama but Professor Sands's memorandum concluded with this comment on the possible representation virtues and mechanics of weighted voting:
"The practice of allowing thinly populated areas to have delegates who could act as their spokesmen in order to assure that their interest be not overlooked can be defended without sacrifice of democratic principle if the weight of a delegate's vote in legislative decision making is not out of proportion to the population of the area he represents. The technique for reform that has been suggested here would make it possible to give all regions a voice in debate without sacrificing equal rights of citizens to participate in the power of decision. This technique could not have been employed in earlier times because of the sheer burden of the arithmetical work that it would then have entailed. This is no longer a problem, however, with modern tabulating machines and computing equipment."
43. Thigpen v. Meyers, 231 F. Supp. 938, 941 (W.D Wash. 1964).
44. Cargo v. Campbell, Santa Fe County District Court, Civ. No. 33272 (January 8, 1964).
45. WMCA v. Lomenzo, 238 F. Supp. 916 (1965).

tionment. One member of the three-judge federal panel subsequently indicated a preference for weighted voting as an interim measure, but it was neither enacted nor ordered.[46]

The fractional voting suggested for New York was the creation of Governor Nelson A. Rockefeller's Citizens' Committee on Reapportionment, which was the source of the four reapportionment plans enacted by the December 1964 lame duck New York legislature (Chapter XIII). Although recommending fractional voting as a feasible stop-gap measure, the Citizens' Committee did not recommend weighted voting because of problems it saw in the operational aspects of the plan inside a legislature, i.e., concern about committee chairmanships, committee voting, and the adequacy with which a multi-vote legislator could represent his constituents. Though possessed of many votes, an assemblyman would have only one voice.[47]

The Citizens' Committee's thoughts about the possible operational problems of weighted voting were echoed by the federal district court in its negative ruling on the constitutionality of the fractional voting device, but the court refused to follow the Committee in distinguishing between the two. Rather, the court in WMCA v. Lomenzo [48] felt the smaller districts with a fractional vote but a full voice would be overrepresented. The state's appeal from this aspect of the federal district court's ruling was never resolved by the United States Supreme Court on the merits, because in June 1966 (after permanent reapportionment had been achieved by judicial commission action) the Supreme Court, on agreement of all the parties, "vacated as moot" the judgment of the district court in this regard.[49]

b. *Evaluation*

Weighted voting and fractional voting may be evaluated from two standpoints: the degree to which they achieve the arithmetic equality called for by *Reynolds* v. *Sims*, and their adequacy as representation devices in terms of the realities of legislative operation.

Arithmetically viewed, weighted and fractional voting are in line with the Supreme Court's announced goal of "substantial equality of population"; moreover, they achieve this while maintaining concern for the Court's corollary interest in "integrity of various political subdivisions." Both allow use of fixed units that may help to minimize the gerrymandering evils of "indiscriminate districting" in pursuit of population equality.

46. WMCA v. Lomenzo, 246 F. Supp. 935, 956 (1965).
47. *Report of the Citizens' Committee on Reapportionment to Governor Nelson A. Rockefeller* 36–40 (1964). The chairman was William Hughes Mulligan, Dean of Fordham University Law School.
48. WMCA v. Lomenzo, 238 F. Supp. 916, 923 (S.D. N.Y. 1965).
49. Lomenzo v. WMCA, 384 U.S. 887 (1966).

Viewed in operational terms, however, weighted and fractional voting may be subject to some reservations. Under weighted voting, one legislator possessed of many votes may wholly dominate a committee; and he would be an especially potent force in the compromise and adjustment process in the legislature as a whole. The latter effect, of course, is also possible under a multimember district system if the members from one district act in unison, but the former is not. Weighted voting may thus have even greater "monolith" tendencies than those which induced a federal district court to object to Hawaii's multimember district system.

None of the operational problems associated with weighted voting flow from fractional voting, except to a de minimis degree. Major reapportionment still occurs, and each populous area receives its full quota of legislators, most legislators have a full vote and also a full voice for all legislative purposes, i.e., committee operation, general negotiation, "lobbying" for constituents, and the like.

One aspect of weighted and fractional voting merits special stress. If attack on them extends beyond arithmetic proportionality, which is the primary test of *Reynolds* v. *Sims,* to political realities—impact on candidates and campaigns, and on effective citizen representation inside the legislature—then the same rules of judicial review should apply as those now used for review of multimember districting. As noted in Chapters XVII and XVIII, a recent line of leading cases concerning multimember districting (*Fortson* v. *Dorsey, Burns* v. *Richardson, Kilgarlin* v. *Hill*) indicates that if arithmetic equality of voter weight can be shown to be achieved by a given districting system, the crucial burden of proof then passes to the challenger to prove actual adverse effect on the "voting strength of racial or political elements of the voting population." [50]

Fractional voting is on a somewhat special footing, and was not at all carefully considered in the one negative federal district court ruling, *WMCA* v. *Lomenzo.* The court noted the possible awkwardness of adopting the plan to committee operations, and stressed the apparent overrepresentation of the fractional vote district. Paradoxically, the overrepresentation argument may be reversed to suggest that small district residents are underrepresented in a fractional vote system because the only legislator to whom they may personally appeal has such slight influence. The underrepresentation argument requires analysis of what other alternatives are open to the residents of a small underpopulated district. There are different views on what is considered preferable from the standpoint of representation interests: retaining identity and having a fractional vote but a full voice; or losing local identity by making each resident an equal voting member of a larger district, where he may be a powerless appendage or

50. Burns v. Richardson, 384 U.S. 73, 88 (1966).

where he may occasionally have real influence if election contests are close.

Without attempting to list all possible arguments on the merits and demerits of weighted and fractional voting, a few large considerations may be noted. The overrepresentation-underrepresentation argument could be a serious one. But it also might fall within the "de minimis" inequity category suggested by Justice Byron R. White in *Swann* v. *Adams* [51] if in a particular plan the fractional vote districts were few and the fractions did not range below one-half or one-third. Of course, with any fraction, a fractional vote legislator normally could break a tie. And in single and multi-member district systems, particular districts may have only fractional influence, even though our "whole-number syndrome" retards analysis of this sort. As one state court judge observed in turning aside a challenge to a local government weighted voting system:

> All legislators cannot serve on all committees and the work of some will involve more important matters than the work of others. No matter what the plan of legislative apportionment may be, no citizen can be assured that his representative will serve on one committee or another, or as a particular matter that his voting power in committee will be proportionate to his voting power in the legislative body as a whole.[52]

As was observed in the discussion of floterial districting, the representation realities which tended to be glossed over in the Supreme Court's stress in *Reynolds* on "equal population districts" come to the fore in persistent fashion when alternatives to single-member districting—which has its own insufficiencies as well as benefits—are considered. Because of these uncertainties, and the uncertainties which the Court has itself created regarding multimember districting, the "real" rationale of *Reynolds* v. *Sims* perhaps has not yet emerged.

5. SPECIAL MINORITY REPRESENTATION DEVICES

"Nothing is more certain," wrote John Stuart Mill, "than that virtual blocking out of the minority is no necessary consequence of freedom, but instead is diametrically opposed to the first principle of democracy: representation in proportion to numbers." He continued: "A majority of the electors should always have a majority of the representatives; but a minority of the electors should always have a minority of the representatives." [53]

51. 385 U.S. 440 (1967).
52. Town of Greenburgh v. Board of Supervisors of Westchester County, 53 Misc. 2d 88, 277 N.Y. 2d 885, 893 (Sup. Ct. 1967).
53. John Stuart Mill, *Considerations on Representative Government* 151, 146 (New York: Holt, 1874).

Often demanded but achieved only erratically, minority representation claims doubtless will continue to be pressed under reapportionment as under malapportionment. All of us are minorities at one time or another. And the desire for equal (in this context, proportionate) treatment is as deep as the instinct which impels parents of more than one child to give identical gifts as a condition of family harmony. Minority representation interests encompass both ethnic minorities and party minorities. Ethnic minorities are more easily identified, but both minority groups have identical goals: more effective political representation.

Minority representation interests flow through all of the discussion of apportionment and districting. Provision of a "voice" for geographic subunits which have minority representation interests underlie such special devices as candidate subdistrict residence requirements, rotation provisions (but not in the "place" system), and weighted and fractional voting. Three special devices designed expressly to foster minority representation are limited voting, cumulative voting, and proportional representation. Because they are so closely interrelated in concept, they will be discussed together, even though only one—cumulative voting—has been used at the state legislature level.

a. *Limited Voting*

Limited voting, a device which has had some use at the local level in this country, restricts either the number of nominees of a political party or the votes of a citizen to fewer than the number of offices to be filled, thus guaranteeing a seat to the largest minority in the constituency.[54] The so-called "minority representation laws" of Pennsylvania in regard to county boards, and of Connecticut in regard to local units generally, are essentially limited voting laws. For Pennsylvania's three-man county commissions, each voter has only two votes, each party thus normally nominates only two persons, and the boards almost universally consist of two members of the majority party and one member from the minority party.[55]

In Connecticut, in a plan currently undergoing court attack on one man-one vote grounds, the minority is guaranteed a fixed number of positions, e.g., with a nine-man town council the minority party receives three seats, whether it polls as little as one percent or as much as 49 percent of the total vote.[56] Arguably, Connecticut's fixed ratio system achieves some mi-

---

54. See generally, Enid Lakeman and James D. Lambert, *Voting in Democracies* (London: Faber and Faber, 1955); W. J. M. MacKenzie, *Free Elections* (London: George Allen & Unwin, 1958).
55. Pa. Stat. Ann. Title 16, 501 (St. Paul: West Publishing Co., 1956).
56. Conn. Gen. Stat. Ann., Title 9, 167(a) (St. Paul: West Publishing Co., 1967). See discussion in Lester B. Snyder and Richard N. Pearson, "Effect of Malapportionment Cases on Political Subdivisions of the State," 39 *Conn. B. J.* 1, 26 (1965).

nority representation at too high a cost. It may not adequately relate proportional party vote to the ratio allocation of seats, but then neither does a single or multimember district system, although we have become accustomed to the disproportional results of these more common systems.

Since 1961, the New York City Council has been operating under a revised representation system using limited voting for one portion of the council. By a vote of 689,405 to 283,982 in 1961, New York City voters created ten new city council seats in addition to the 27 population-based seats. Two each were allocated to the city's five boroughs (counties), to be elected at-large in each borough, under a limitation that each party could nominate only one candidate in each borough and that each voter could vote for only one in each borough. Thus the system guarantees one seat in each borough to the minority party. The provision survived attack on constitutional grounds in the New York courts in 1963, and the United States Supreme Court dismissed the appeal without comment [57] prior to the 1964 *Reapportionment Decisions*. A parallel attack in federal district court also failed [58] subsequent to the 1964 decisions.

Because the new councilmen are allocated two to each borough, rather than on a population basis, an apparent conflict is created between the goal of minority representation and the goal of "equal voter weight," if the latter is approached solely in terms of equal population districts. The 1960 populations of the four largest boroughs ranged from 2,627,313 in Brooklyn to 1,424,551 in the Bronx; the fifth borough, Staten Island, is only 221,991.

The votes of Staten Island in the 37-man City Council (Staten Island also has one district councilman on a population basis in addition to its two at-large seats) do not materially threaten to take control away from the dominant mass of New York City population. But it is obvious that the system is questionable if the only appropriate constitutional principle is one requiring every district to approximate the average size district within a narrow range. The price of nullifying the limited voting system on this ground would be denial of the slight degree of minority representation which the limited voting provision does provide.

However, the trial judge in the initial state court litigation focused on a different aspect. Limited voting, he said, "strikes at the very heart of our democratic process." What he meant by "democratic process" is not well articulated. If the term is taken to mean a consideration of the many elements that enter into the creation and operation of a fair and effective sys-

57. Blaikie v. Power, 243 N.Y.S. 2d 185, 193 N.E.2d 55 (1963). The appeal was dismissed "for want of a substantial federal question." 375 U.S. 439 (1964). Was this dismissal a ruling on the merits, hence "validating" limited voting? See discussion, Chapter XVIII, *circa* footnotes 74–80.
58. Blaikie v. Wagner, Costello v. Rockefeller, 258 F. Supp. 364 (S.D. N.Y. 1965).

tem of democratic representation, then the judge has an oversimplified view of democracy. Use of a system whereby a Republican minority in New York City normally numbering about 35 percent (which even elected a mayor in 1965) is given approximately 14 percent of the council seats rather than none is not obviously undemocratic. Rather, limited voting in the New York City Council context poses a question of competing "democratic" values.

b. Cumulative Voting

All discussions of special minority representation devices for American state legislatures tend to focus on the cumulative voting system which Illinois has employed since 1872 for the lower house of its state legislature. The device continues under the reapportionment of 1965 (Chapter XII).

Under the Illinois system lower house members are elected from three-member districts and each voter may vote for three candidates; if he prefers he may "cumulate" his three votes on one candidate or divide them between two candidates. Members of a minority party in a given district will tend to cast all three of their votes for one minority party candidate; majority party members will tend to cast one and one-half votes for each of two dominant party nominees. (A party seldom nominates more than one or two candidates.) Experience indicates that by this process a minority party which has 25 percent support or higher in a district can normally elect one of the three district legislators.[59]

In the Illinois practice, party leaders frequently agree in advance on the number of nominees so that often there are only three—two for the dominant party, one for the minority party. It has been charged that through interparty collusion the third legislator (minority party man) in a district may be a "kept" man, e.g., the West Side bloc of Republicans in Chicago often vote with Democrats on key issues. Professor Silva's tabulation for the five campaigns between 1954 and 1962 showed that the voters of one or both parties had no real choice in the process of choosing a representative in more than one-third of the districts.[60] Because this practice—which

59. See George S. Blair, *Cumulative Voting: An Effective Electoral Device in Illinois Politics* (Urbana: University of Illinois Press, 1960); "The Case for Cumulative Voting in Illinois," 47 *Northwestern L. Rev.* 344 (1952); "Cumulative Voting: Patterns of Party Allegiance and Rational Choice in Illinois Legislative Contests," 52 *Am. Pol. Sci. Rev.* 123 (1958); Charles S. Hyneman and Julian D. Morgan, "Cumulative Voting in Illinois," 32 *Ill. L. Rev.* 12 (1937); See also Lakeman and Lambert, *supra* note 54, at 79–82; MacKenzie, *supra* note 54, at 57–59.
60. Ruth C. Silva, "Relation of Representation and the Party System to the Number of Seats Apportioned to a Legislative District," 17 *Western Pol. Quart.* 742, 753–55 (1964).
In 1966, when Democrats put up two candidates in every district except one, the result in a few instances was to shift a minority Democratic seat from an old liner to a new and frequently younger man. Letter to author from Professor Samuel K. Gove,

is not a generic feature of cumulative voting—makes the primary the real election and also places paramount control in the party leaders, cumulative voting has been criticized for allowing too little voter freedom. However, the system has had the beneficent effect of preventing gross over-representation or underrepresentation of the Republican and Democratic parties in the state legislature. The division of party seats in the legislature has closely reflected the popular vote division. The system tends to make each party a statewide party, carrying the Democratic party into Republican hardcore areas downstate and carrying the Republican party into hardcore Democratic areas in Chicago.

Because some of the alleged defects of the cumulative voting system as operated in Illinois are not intrinsic and could be moderated by statutory revision of the primary and general election process, it is surprising that the Illinois system has not been copied, even on an experimental basis, in other states. Professors Sawyer and MacRae have made this comment:

> . . . some "good government" groups . . . proposed that parties be required to run full slates. This would, of course, negate the basic purpose of this scheme of minority representation. In addition, several writers have implied that a non-contested election represented collusion, but this is not necessarily so. Such a case may indeed be the best strategy for each party, and may represent the *only* way in which nearly proportional representation can be assured.[61]

They suggest a modification whereby party voters would determine the rank of party candidates on a party list, and the party's total vote in the general election (without regard to candidates) would determine how many from the party list were elected.

Cumulative voting is readily adaptable to any state which now elects one house in three-man multimember districts. Indeed, the same districts could be used for election of the state senate, making them single-member districts for this purpose, which was the former practice in Illinois. Without going all the way to pure proportional representation, cumulative voting may be a way of achieving a goal of fair and effective representation along with a "one man-one vote" equalization process. It is in a sense an American two-party version of PR. Also, because cumulative voting gives each

Director of the University of Illinois Institute of Government and Public Affairs, January 17, 1967. Although cumulative voting has strong support in Illinois, Professor Gove is critical: "It is divisive in the party, tending to create intra-party conflict. It also leads to inter-party collusion . . . ." Alternatively, Clyde Flynn, staff assistant to Senator Everett M. Dirksen of Illinois, has suggested that some of the better representatives were those from the minority party in a district, because the safety of the seat attracted good men.
61. Jack Sawyer and Duncan MacRae, Jr., "Game Theory and Cumulative Voting in Illinois: 1902–1954," 56 *Am. Pol. Sci. Rev.* 936, 946 (1962).

voter as many votes as there are offices to be filled, and gives him full freedom to cast these votes as he wishes among available candidates, this device would seem to be immune to many of the challenges against limited voting. A possible question would be the power of party committees to fix the number of nominees, if that aspect of the system continued. However, if such a challenge were accepted, consistency would require the Supreme Court likewise to nullify all restricted residence provisions for candidates in multimember districts.

In accord with the purposes sought by cumulative voting and analogous minority representation devices, Morris L. Ernst has made this comment:

> I wonder if the Bar has been sufficiently inventive to design a course of conduct somewhere in between the workable but undemocratic provision in the Federal Constitution [federal plan] and the mathematical absolutism of one man, one vote. I have suggested to newly formed nations a formula that minority parties might get *in toto* one-third of the votes, a figure insufficient to express power but sufficient to give people that tender and essential feeling of having a spokesman of their choosing in the halls of the mighty.[62]

c. *Proportional Representation (Pure)*

Pure proportional representation cannot be ignored in a discussion of minority representation devices, even though it is unlikely to be adopted for an American state legislature—or to be used more widely for local legislatures. As discussed in Chapter III, a pure proportional representation system is in accord with basic tenets of representation theory. Indeed, it may be the only way of making good on "one man-one vote" if that is interpreted: "one man, one vote, each vote to be as *effective* a vote as possible." However, because proportional representation, in European experience, sometimes fails to create governing majorities and effective leadership, and transforms a two-party system into a multiparty system, PR seldom has found favor in this country. Limited voting and cumulative voting, by contrast, do not impede effective leadership or weaken the two-party system.

Pure proportional representation maximizes the number of votes that "count" and minimizes the number of votes that are "lost." It does this in the well-known Hare system, by using a single transferable vote (the voter indicating his preferences among candidates by marking in rank order) under the following formula:

$$\frac{\text{Votes Cast}}{N+1} + 1 = \text{Single Seat Quota.}$$

62. Morris L. Ernst, 51 A.B.A.J. 508 (1965).

"N" signifies the number of seats to be filled. In the counting process, surplus ballots (above the quota) of winning candidates and ballots of bottom candidates are redistributed by second, third, fourth choices, and so forth. Thus, if 100,000 votes are cast to elect 9 legislators, only 9991 votes would be "lost," in contrast to a possible "loss" of more than 49,000 votes in a single-member district plurality system. In other words, at the end of the counting process, with 100,000 votes cast, there would be nine piles of 10,001 votes for the winning candidates and one pile of "lost" votes.

Several other forms of proportional representation,[63] including the "list" system, have been used in Europe in preference to the Hare system. In the list system voters cast their ballots for party slates rather than for individual candidates, and a party elects a proportion of its slate equivalent to its proportion of the total vote cast. The list system gives the voter less freedom of choice, strengthens party organization, but does not solve the problem of avoiding a proliferation of parties and of creating effective governing majorities.

Although never used for a state legislature in this country, a proportional representation system has been used in more than twenty cities from coast to coast.[64] Perhaps best known is the use of PR in five New York City elections between 1937 and 1945.[65] In addition to the two major parties, four minor parties received representation: American Labor, City Fusion, Communist, and Liberal. The election of some Communists may have been a major reason for abandoning proportional representation, by popular referendum, and returning to a district system.[66]

In a provocative but little noticed article a few years ago, Professor Charles V. Laughlin proposed a system designed to "have all the fairness of proportional representation and yet retain the advantages of separate districts." [67] His proposal combines districts and the list system. Candidates would be nominated and voted on by districts, each voter in the state having one vote. There would be no requirement that a candidate reside in his district, and a candidate could be nominated in more than one district, but party leaders would decide the total number to nominate in a given

63. See Silva, *supra* note 60, at 757–66 and sources cited therein for a succinct discussion.
64. *Id.* at 759 and n. 54. See also Clarence G. Hoag and George H. Hallett, Jr., *Proportional Representation—The Key to Democracy* 105–57 (New York: National Municipal League, second edition, 1940).
65. Belle Zeller and Hugh A. Bone, "The Repeal of P.R. in New York City—Ten Years in Retrospect," 42 *Am. Pol. Sci. Rev.* 1127 (1948).
66. Although PR was criticized journalistically for fanning racial feeling, more sober studies indicate that PR "neither lessened nor intensified minority group tensions." Silva, *supra* note 60, at 762. Compare Warren Moscow, *Politics in the Empire State* (New York: Knopf, 1948).
67. Charles V. Laughlin, "Proportional Representation: It Can Cure Our Apportionment Ills," 49 *A. B. A. J.* 1065 (1963).

district. The district votes would not "elect," but would determine the position of a candidate on his party's statewide list, i.e., each candidate would be ranked according to the total number of votes received in all the districts in which he was nominated. The final lists determining "election" would be limited to the two parties receiving the largest statewide vote, thus avoiding party proliferation. A party would "elect" from the top of the list a percentage of candidates corresponding to its percentage of the statewide popular vote. The proposal also contains a provision for election of independent or minor party candidates on an intradistrict basis, if they receive sufficient votes, the seats thus filled being deducted from the number apportioned between the two major parties.

Although assertedly capable of being superimposed on any existing districting plan, the proposed system has certain problems. If some multimember, and hence more populous districts continued, candidates running in those constituencies with larger vote pools would seem to have a better chance of appearing high on the eventual state party list. A popular candidate who gathers more votes than he needs thereby weakens the prospect that other candidates in the multimember district will even "make the list."

A simpler and perhaps more reliable way of combining the fairness of PR with the advantages of separate districts is the mixed district and list system in use in West Germany since World War II (described in detail in Chapter IV).[68] Part of the legislature is elected from single-member districts, and part by PR from party lists. A party's district victories are deducted from its list entitlement. Thus, the list aspect keeps the major parties in proper balance, and also offers some prospect for election of minor party candidates.

Although conversion of entire state legislatures to a proportional representation system either of the Hare-type or the list-type is highly unlikely, some form of PR perhaps should receive consideration as a device for larger multimember districts. PR used in large multimember districts would avoid the winner-take-all tendency, while at the same time preserving whatever districting flexibilities may be associated with use of multimember districts.

F. Role of Computers

The panacea of the 'sixties is the computer. We hear of its being used in surprisingly varied situations, from controlling variables in master plan

68. See James K. Pollock, "A Sensible Approach," 54 *Nat. Civ. Rev.* 357 (1965).

preparation to preparation of soap opera scripts (the latter probably being far simpler). We are apt to forget the message in IBM's New York World's Fair exhibit that "people are everything; the computer is only a tool." In legislative redistricting a computer, following only a population equalization principle of "one man-one vote," could run a legislative district line right across Central Park in midtown Manhattan (and in one trial run did so). Such excrescences may be avoided by more careful programming. But it is a hard-core fact that every line drawn on a map, whether blindly or designedly, has partisan implications different from any other kind of line that could be drawn. The point takes on added meaning in light of the additional fact that many alternative sets of equally "equal" districts are possible.

It follows that an awareness of the complexity of the political process, of theories and problems of effective representation, of group dynamics and the like, is the paramount factor in intelligent reapportionment-redistricting; knowledge of computers is secondary. Indeed, without an awareness of the complexity of the political process, computers will not be fed a sufficiently broad range of information to produce meaningful print-outs and raise the level of discussion about the nature of proposed, alternative sets of districts. If we are to consider only bare numbers of people, a computer is not needed; a calculating machine would suffice, although it would lack, of course, the "magic" of the "computer" label.

a. Computer Utilities

The proper approach must be to appreciate the computer for what it is. A computer is essentially a rapid computation device, which makes arithmetic computations accurately, rapidly, and with incredible volume. If properly programmed, it may be helpful in revealing or disproving possible correlations in those instances where values can be expressed numerically. It is also limited, as is a subjective essay, by the level of imagination, knowledge, and biases of the system designer or programmer. Reapportionment and redistricting involve representation, and as stated repeatedly in this book, representation is the political heart of any democratic system of government. Before we can make practical and effective use of computers, we need more basic theoretical work and many more empirical studies on the nature and function of political representation in a mass democracy that combines socially stratified residence with a highly mobile population.

In short, representation theory, and a sophisticated understanding of actual practices of political representation both in the election process and in the legislature, must lead and dominate the use of computer technology. There may well be significant "feedbacks" in the sense that preparation of computer programs, and running of trial programs, will be an aid to precision in identification of data and clarification of concepts. But despite the aura that surrounds the magic word "computer," there should not be an equal partnership between reapportioners and computer technicians, any more than the partnership between entrepreneur and accountant is an equal partnership. As articulated by one student of the law-science "interface":

> [M]en of law and men of politics must keep firmly in mind that in the legal-political arena, the scientist enjoys no special position of eminence. His views are worthy of belief only to the extent that he is knowledgeable on the particular legal or political issue at hand.[69]

Computers, for example, may play an important role in testing (and perhaps suggesting) alternative reapportionment plans, *provided* the data (including political data) are sufficiently detailed and the programming and parameters sufficiently flexible. There should be data, and appropriate machine instructions, so that the following factors could be incorporated in the print-out concerning alternative plans: use of existing districts as a starting point for alteration (i.e., the factor of incumbency and existing political relationships); prospective political party results, based on projecting past voting behavior patterns into the new sets of alternative districts; political equity factors (also called the proportional representation factor), by which I mean the relationship between the percentage of seats captured by a party and its percentage of the statewide legislative vote; maximum preservation of existing county, city, and perhaps even township boundaries. The last may not be possible under the tighter arithmetic equality concepts announced in 1967 by the Supreme Court (Chapter XVII), and in some instances may not be desirable, but the possibilities should be known. In addition, there should be print-outs on the homogeneity-heterogeneity of district population in terms of age, education, income, occupation, race and other ethnic classifications, religious affiliation, etc., if known. In short, the print-out should cover all of the political terrain, because *each* of the factors influences elections—and we are constructing, after all, election districts *in a system where no lines are neutral.*

As Professor Stuart S. Nagel has observed, it is "almost an abuse of a computer not to take advantage of its great versatility." [70] In the post-

---

69. Leo A. Huard, "Law and Science: Marriage, Divorce or Meretricious Relationship?" 5 *Santa Clara L. Rev.* 1, 17 (1964). See also Ralph E. Lapp, *The New Priesthood: The Scientific Elite and the Uses of Power* (New York: Harper & Row, 1967).
70. Stuart S. Nagel, "Simplified Bipartisan Computer Redistricting," 17 *Stan. L. Rev.* 863 (1965). The availability of politically meaningful social science data with which to "stuff" computers has improved markedly in recent years. See, e.g., *Social Science Data Archives* (New York: Council of Social Science Data Archives, 1967); Karl A.

Reynolds era in cases on multimember districting, gerrymandering, and minority representation, concern for "representation performance" is superseding the initial primary stress of *Reynolds* v. *Sims* on simple population equality in districting. Whether or not made justiciable and subjected to detailed court review, these claims (concerns) are ones to which the political process should at least be sensitive. The political sophistication which a goal of fair and effective representation requires—whether or not there be an enforceable constitutional right to an effective vote—can be aided greatly by computer technology. The use may be partisan or bipartisan, preferably the latter.

In California, for example, Democrats made an impressive start in the use of computers in the spring of 1965 to construct and test various plans for apportionment and districting, particularly for the districting of the Los Angeles region.[71] Masses of data on past voting patterns in various elections, and voter profiles in terms of residence, sex, race, party affiliation, and economic status were fed into computers so that quick answers could be given to such questions as these: We need 500 more for District X; where can we find 500 with four-to-one split in our favor, at least half of whom must be Negro and with an even sexual mix? Or, what will suggested District Y do for us in a legislative election, or presidential election, or in a gubernatorial election; and what ethnic range of candidates could we successfully run? The Republicans were trying to do the same; however, their desire at one point to borrow Democratic cards suggests they were a little behind in organization, if not in money; and they did not control the key legislative committees where the work was centered.

This kind of informed planning and negotiation in the reapportionment-

Fox, "The Functional Economic Area," paper delivered at Regional Science Association meeting, Ann Arbor, November 13–16, 1964.

Especially provocative is a technique combining a television screen and a computer. Accordingly, plans may be displayed and can be modified according to suggestions made by on-the-scene participants, and prospective political performance of the districts can be shown if adequate data are in the computer. See paper presented by Chandler Harrison Steven, "On the Screen; Man-Machine Interaction," National Municipal League annual meeting, Milwaukee, November 13, 1967.

71. Comments in this paragraph summarize the author's observations in California in 1965. For an interesting commentary from the majority (Democratic) side, see the paper entitled "The Computer as an Aid to Legislative Reapportionment" by William Below, consultant to 1965 California Assembly Committee of Elections and Reapportionment, delivered at Computers in Redistricting Conference (American Law Institute and American Bar Association), Washington, D.C., October 22–23, 1965. For a report from the minority (Republican) side, see Stephen D. Slingsby, "The Gerrymander," Ph.D. dissertation, Graduate School for Claremont Colleges, 1966.

Another example of proper and helpful use of computers to backstop political decision-makers occurred in Iowa in 1967 where the University of Iowa's Computer Center implemented guidelines given by a bipartisan commission and prepared optional plans. See also comments on computer use in Connecticut and Minnesota in Chapter XIII.

redistricting process is research, it is political realism. This is a vital aspect of representation analysis. As stated before in this work, every line drawn on a map, even by a blindfolded, neutral draftsman (and only a blind-folded draftsman can be neutral) inevitably makes one or more policy choices by favoring one interest against another. Persons and parties should and do care how their interests are affected by line-drawing. Computerology of the sort described above is really only a process for *more exact* and more prompt description of district composition.

The political and social profile information which a data-full and well-programmed computer can provide should be made generally available so that the public may be informed, and may have some chance of making rational judgments. If used in this way to yield *detailed political and social profiles of existing and proposed election districts* computers can serve to elevate the level of discussion by reapportionment negotiators and the general public. An even better use of such detailed computer print-outs would be in the context of bipartisan methods of reapportionment, as discussed in Chapters XII through XIV. Although computers proved unhelpful in the bipartisan pre-trial process of Illinois reapportionment worked out by Chief Judge William J. Campbell, the problem seems to have been one of time and programming, rather than any generic incapacity of computers as an information source for apportionment and redistricting.

A number of computer programs in relation to redistricting now exist.[72] Only one, that of Professor Stuart S. Nagel, makes a conscious attempt to include as one of the parameters in the program a direction for the computer to produce districts which, on the basis of political profile data also placed in the computer, will produce districts likely to preserve an existing party balance in the legislature, or to produce some other party balance deemed reasonable by the programmers in the light of over-all partisan trends in the state.[73] Although never used for an actual state reapportionment, computer input, parameters, and programming of this type should be the focus for experimentation in the 'seventies. Only this kind of sophistication would make computer districting programs responsive to the range of issues and districting options dictated by representation theory, and by the perceived needs of the parties and the public generally, including political and ethnic minorities.

72. Nagel, *supra* note 70; James B. Weaver and Sidney W. Hess, "A Procedure for Nonpartisan Districting: Development of Computer Techniques," 73 *Yale L. J.* 288 (1963); Henry F. Kaiser, "An Objective Method for Establishing Legislative Districts," 10 *Midwest J. Pol. Sci.* 200 (1966); Edward Forrest, "Apportionment by Computer," 7 *Am. Behavioral Scientist* 23 (1963).

See also *Course of Study on Computers in Redistricting* (mimeo) prepared for Computers in Redistricting Conference, American Law Institute—American Bar Association, Washington, D.C., October 22–23, 1965.

73. Nagel, *supra* note 70.

b. The "Nonpartisan" Myth

Quite different from this recommended approach is the program of James B. Weaver and Sidney W. Hess, which has received extensive financial support from the National Municipal League for implementation and refinement. As described in a 1963 article and apparently little modified since, the program seems to be an adaptation of a pre-existing "canned program" for optimum location of regional warehouses to minimize freight costs on nationwide orders—an example of the kind of dominance of man by machine which it will be the initial task of the last third of the twentieth century to avoid. The program centers on population equality and a special "compactness" measure, the latter being the most interesting element of the program. Rejecting geographical concepts of compactness, the authors attempt to program the computer so that it will produce districts (actually alternative sets of districts) of "maximum compactness around centers of population," [74] i.e., districts in which the median distance of citizens from their residence to the district's population center is as small as possible. It is this aspect of the program, a sort of "center of population gravity" idea, which enabled Weaver and Hess to adapt the warehouse heuristic to political districting:

> The chosen measure of compactness makes it possible to take advantage of certain mathematical similarities between the redistricting problem and a problem already programmed on computers—that of assigning customer orders to specific warehouse locations so as to minimize freight costs. This program, supplemented for this specific use by various additional steps and subcalculations, assigns EDs (customers) to LD centers (warehouses) in a manner minimizing moment of inertia (freight cost).[75]

This technique has many problems. One is the special measure of compactness used. Even in mathematical terms, this "center of population gravity" approach is only one of several available compactness formulae. Another compactness formula, for example, would be to devise districts with the least perimeter possible.[76] Any mathematical approach to compactness is of interest only in regard to its political significance as applied to reapportionment problems. The "center of population gravity" approach places particular emphasis on distance each voter resides from the

74. Weaver and Hess, *supra* note 72, at 292.
75. *Id.* at 301–2.
76. See e.g., Joseph E. Schwartzberg, "Reapportionment, Gerrymanders, and the Notion of 'Compactness,' " 50 *Minn. L. Rev.* 443 (1966). Professor Henry F. Kaiser, at the ALI-ABA Computer Conference, *supra* note 72, described a multiplicity of possible mathematical measures of compactness.

district's population center, and makes lines of communication from the "town hall" as short as possible. It may be questioned whether in an age of electronic communication, home distribution of newspapers, and decrease in town meeting-style government this factor is as important in the design of representation systems as it is in the design of warehouse systems (where costs rise directly as distance from the warehouse increases). Paradoxically, if the computer starts with a district several times longer than it is wide, and curved or quarter-moon shaped, this program may produce a district in which the voters are closely arranged about a center of population which actually lies in a rival district!

A second recurrent problem is the multiplicity of possible "acceptable" districts which a simple computer program could produce. Using various maximum population deviations up to 5 percent as the index, and building on census tracts or census enumeration districts, the program could produce hundreds or thousands of combinations of possible "equal" sub-districts for a large area. Even with the Weaver-Hess compactness index there still could be possibly a hundred or more combinations.[77]

Of course, if the Supreme Court's concept of "substantial equality" were flexible enough to permit the computer to avoid cutting lines of pre-existing political subdivisions, computer programming would produce a far smaller number of possibly acceptable sets of alternatives. However, as the Supreme Court's constitutional standard in *Swann* v. *Adams* and other 1967 cases has been redefined in the direction of absolute population equality with de minimis deviations, such parameters become unfeasible. Paradoxically, the tighter the population equality standard, the more difficult it is to devise computer programs to "take over" the function of re-apportionment and produce only a small number of "equal districts" for a state or a sub-area of a state (unless the computer be rigged in unconscionable fashion). Alternative sets of "equal" districts will be devised in too great profusion to be helpful, unless a great many controls—including political controls—be fed into the computer.

A third problem with the Weaver-Hess program is its billing as "A Procedure for Nonpartisan Districting." [78] The authors do recognize that: "Districts can be absolutely equal in population and still be gerryman-

---

77. As an aftermath of the federal district court's invalidation of Delaware's reapportionment in 1967 (*Sincock* v. *Gately*, Chapter XVIII), the Weaver-Hess organization was asked to propose possible new districting arrangements through use of their computer program. The problem immediately arose as to what additional factors might be included to reduce the multiplicity of possibly acceptable "equality" plans to a manageable number.

78. See the article describing the program, *supra* note 72. The organization formed to promote the program, with the aid of Ford Foundation money channeled through the National Municipal League, is labeled CROND, meaning Computer Research on Nonpartisan Districting.

dered . . . Nor will a gerrymandered district always be identifiable by its shape, in spite of the usual connotation of the term." [79] But the authors seem not to recognize that (a) generically no district lines are neutral, i.e., devoid of partisan implications favoring one group more than would an alternative and equally constitutional line; (b) closing one's eyes to political realities of population composition in devising a computer program may make the program innocently partisan, but never nonpartisan; (c) under their own precept quoted above, an "equal" set of districts modified only by their special compactness concept may "still be gerrymandered." Indeed, their own program will produce not one set of districts but several, each with different political implication—and who is to choose? In this connection the following comment on the Weaver-Hess program was made by Professor Stuart S. Nagel, author of a proposed more sophisticated "bipartisan computer" program:

> . . . their program as of April, 1965 does not consider equality and compactness simultaneously, it does not guarantee contiguity, and it has no political features. The Weaver-Hess program is thus nonpartisan only in the sense that it is unpredictable as to which party it will favor.[80]

Professor Henry F. Kaiser, whose presentation was one of the highlights of the ALI-ABA conference,[81] provided another needed eye-opener for those who view mathematicians-statisticians as "objective." He pointed out that although any given mathematical formula is itself objective in its execution of a given task, the crucial process of selecting mathematical starting points is highly judgmental and subjective. Different starting points may yield different results, e.g., whether to stress moment of inertia, sum of squares, product of squares, coefficient of variation, and many others, singly or in combination. He subjected to detailed criticism the Weaver-Hess program, seeing a built-in rural bias in the moment of inertia formula for compactness. And he criticized the Schubert-Press attempted mathematical measure of malapportionment [82] as being based on a faulty perception of the mathematical properties of a coefficient of variation, and as using outmoded skewness-kurtosis concepts. Who is "right" mathematically? Clearly, before we entrust very much to mathematical formulae and computing machines, there is need for a Supreme Court of Mathematics —as great a need as for a Supreme Court of Law.

Although Weaver and Hess do realize the political limitations of their program (unlike many politically naive computer experts) the title of

79. Id. at 296 n.31.
80. Nagel, supra note 70, at 874 n.12.
81. Conference, supra note 72.
82. Schubert and Press, supra note 30.

their article conveys the opposite impression. So great is public confusion about computers, and so great is public respect for anything presented in seemingly complicated and refined mathematical formulae, that billing any computer program as "nonpartisan" poses a real danger. In the 'sixties, or in the apportionments of the 'seventies, wide segments of the public may be "sold" and may accept a reapportionment plan as wonderful, and also fair and "nonpartisan," just because a computer program was used in its preparation. It is seriously misleading to state or imply that computerized districts are nonpartisan. As Professor Myron Q. Hale has aptly phrased it: "Each of the 'scientific methods,' etc., has an explicit or implicit political value 'built in.' "[83]

Let us therefore use computers in the reapportionment-redistricting field. If we feed them ten times or one hundred times more data and more varied instructions they can become vital tools for detailed, accurate *description* of the varied elements that make up political representation. But let us stop talking about nonpartisanship, and thus avoid making the three monkeys the symbol of twentieth-century computer redistricting technology.

G. The Unsettling "Higher Math" of "One Man-One Vote"

1. FRUITLESS REFINEMENTS OF POPULATION EQUALITY MEASURES

In the early phases of the reapportionment revolution, attention focused on the simple fact of major population disparities among legislative districts, i.e., disparities between a district's share of the total population of the state and its share of the legislative seats. The measures most frequently referred to by the courts—population variance ratio, maximum deviation from average district, and fictional electoral percentage [84]—appear frequently in this work and have been subjected to a brief critique at the end of Chapter XVII. In addition, several writers have suggested various more refined methods of working with bare population data in order to improve intrastate descriptions of malapportionment and interstate com-

83. Letter to author from Professor Myron Q. Hale, Ohio State University Department of Political Science, July 10, 1967, who has done extensive work and computer experimentation in Ohio reapportionment. See also Hale's "Computer Methods of Districting," in Howard D. Hamilton, ed., *Reapportioning Legislatures* (Columbus, Ohio: Charles E. Merrill, 1966); and Hale, ed., "Representation and Reapportionment," *Political Studies*, No. 2, Ohio State University Department of Political Science, March 1965.

84. Manning J. Dauer and Robert G. Kelsay, "Unrepresentative States," 44 National Municipal Review 571 (1955).

parisons. One study lays special stress on the rural-urban conflict from 1910–1960 and is historically helpful in identifying counties substantially malapportioned with respect to their state legislatures.[85] Another study seeks a single malapportionment index for each county, relating the county's percentage of seats in both houses to the county's percentage of the state's population. Thus, as of 1962, Wayne County, Michigan (Detroit) had 34.082 percent of the state's population, and 34.542 and 20.580 percent respectively of the house and senate seats, yielding an average in both houses of 27.561 percent. Subtracting Wayne's two-house power percentage from its population percentage shows a "power deficit" of 6.521 percent.[86]

Justices Tom C. Clark and John Marshall Harlan in their *Baker* v. *Carr* [87] dissent sought a "total representation" measure for each county in both houses, by expressing the county's "representation" in terms of the total number of seats (or parts of seats) it controlled. Justice Clark handled the problem of multicounty districts simply by pro-rating district seats among the number of counties in the district without regard to disparities in county populations. Justice Harlan found this technique faulty, and would pro-rate multicounty seats in proportion to the population size of the member counties.

Yet another computation, still focusing only on raw population data, but using multiple formulae (mean, standard deviation, inverse coefficient of variation, skewness, kurtosis) sought measures both of intrastate malapportionment and of comparative interstate malapportionment. However, as noted earlier in this chapter, the tricky problem of handling multicounty, multimember, and floterial districts caused difficulty in computing the "apportionment ideal" for each state; after initial publication in June 1964 a corrective tabulation was published in December 1964. In that revision Tennessee of *Baker* v. *Carr* fame moved from forty-fourth place to eighth place and Indiana moved from fiftieth to tenth place.[88]

All of the foregoing attempted measures of malapportionment rest on a simple "population equality" premise. Insofar as "representation" enters in, it does so only on the hypothesis that there is a direct and significant

85. Paul T. David and Ralph Eisenberg, "*Devaluation of the Urban and Suburban Vote: A Statistical Investigation of Long-Term Trends in State Legislative Representation*" (Charlottesville, Virginia: University of Virginia Bureau of Public Administration, 1961).
86. Alan L. Clem, "Measuring Legislative Malapportionment: In Search of a Better Yardstick," 7 *Midwest J. Pol. Sci.* 125, 141 (1963); also see his: "Problems of Measuring and Achieving Equality of Representation in State Legislatures," 42 *Neb. L. Rev.* 622 (1963).
87. 369 U.S. 186, 262, 340 (1962).
88. Schubert and Press, *supra* note 30.

correlation between effective citizen representation in the legislature and population equality in the apportionment and districting process. A correlation of sorts undoubtedly exists, but it is only a part of the problem of ascertaining and obtaining fair and effective representation *in the sense of equal opportunity to influence legislative outcomes*. It is just such a quest for more sophisticated representation indices that motivates plaintiffs in the "second round" reapportionment cases to challenge districting options, gerrymandering, winner-take-all problems, and the like. Further, the increasing rigidity in the equal population principle, exemplified in *Swann v. Adams* and other 1967 Supreme Court cases, undercuts the old formulae in another way. A focus on county units becomes inappropriate if conventional subdivisions must be ignored and district lines become fluid in pursuit of a moving target of rigid decennial population "equality." In short, if strict population equality is the only concern, some of the early apportionment formulae are not needed. Alternatively, if effective representation in the legislature is the primary concern, apportionment measures based solely on raw population are quite incomplete, if not irrelevant.

2. THE NEW MATHEMATICS OF EFFECTIVE REPRESENTATION

Quite different and extremely provocative are some newer measures of apportionment and *representation*. These measures question the validity of all apportionments in which districts of varying population are "equalized" in relation to the legislature by adding extra seats to the more populous units, i.e., by making them multimember districts or (for some New York county boards) weighted voting districts. The United States Supreme Court recognized the new formulae without comment in a footnote to the 1967 challenge to Texas single-member and multimember districts of varying sizes.[89]

This new approach has its roots in recent analyses of effective power relationships, using techniques akin to those of game theory. It has only belatedly been applied in any meaningful way to reapportionment matters, because many practitioners of such theories have ignored political representation theory. The pioneers tended to be mathematicians or apolitical social scientists; some political scientists among them, enamored with game theory approach as with a new toy, were almost pridefully scornful of the "traditional" theory content of their own profession.

The game theory approach, in turn an adaptation of probability theory,

89. Kilgarlin v. Hill, 386 U.S. 120, 125 n.3 (1967), citing John F. Banzhaf III, "Multimember Electoral Districts—Do They Violate the 'One Man, One Vote' Principle," 75 *Yale L.J.* 1309 (1966).

can be used to analyze various possible voting combinations of legislators, or blocs of legislators.[90] "Voting power" can be expressed as the frequency with which a given legislator or bloc of legislators can cast a deciding vote, i.e., be in a position to "pivot" or be an essential member of a minimal winning coalition. This kind of analysis can be applied to measure power in any situation where a one-to-one relationship does not exist, because "players" possess unequal numbers of votes. For example, the electoral college can be treated as a "legislature" in which the players have weighted votes ranging from 3 (the smallest states) up to 43 (New York in 1960).[91]

None of this has direct relation to representation. The focus is on the power of the players (legislators), rather than on the individual citizen on whom our "one man-one vote" interest centers, both in representation theory and in the *Reapportionment Decisions*. John F. Banzhaf III, however, has taken the additional step of devising mathematical measures of *citizen* influence in multimember district systems where differing sizes of constituencies are awarded varying numbers of representatives.[92] The focus now is on measures of *citizen influence to effect legislative outcomes*. The findings are startling, showing that a citizen in a four- or five-man multimember district (e.g., Hawaii and Wyoming senates) has more effective representation than citizens in the single-member districts in the ratio of 2 to 1 and 2.24 to 1 respectively. And for 13- and 14-man multimember districts (Arkansas and Texas lower houses) the ratios become 3.61 to 1 and 3.74 to 1 (See Chart No. 10).

These *influence* ratios are shockingly higher than the *population* variance ratios which in conventional gross population arithmetic of apportionment were thought to be permissible. A 15 percent maximum population deviation in single-member districts, even if each district deviates by that much, yields only a 1.35 to 1 ratio. If a 5 percent maximum deviation rule emerges for single-member districts under the Supreme Court's 1967 tightening trend, the population variance ratio falls to 1.10 to 1.

Although technical, the formulae adapted by Mr. Banzhaf, and his find-

90. See L. S. Shapley and Martin Shubik, "A Method for Evaluating the Distribution of Power in a Committee System," 48 *Am. Pol. Sci. Rev.* 787 (1954); William H. Riker, "Some Ambiguities in the Notion of Power," 58 *Am. Pol. Sci. Rev.* 341 (1964).
91. Irwin Mann and L. S. Shapley, "Values of Large Games, v.1: Evaluating the Electoral College Exactly," Rand Corporation memorandum, RM–3158 P R (1962). See also William H. Riker and Lloyd S. Shapley, "Weighted Voting: A Mathematical Analysis for Instrumental Judgments," paper presented at 1965 annual meeting of American Society for Political and Legal Philosophy; Samuel Krislov, "The Power Index, Reapportionment and the Principle of One Man, One Vote," 1965 *M.U.L.L.* 37; William H. Riker, "Bargaining in a Three-Person Game," 61 *Am. Pol. Sci. Rev.* 642 (1967).
92. Banzhaf, *supra* note 89.

CHART 10

UNEQUAL VOTER INFLUENCE UNDER MULTIMEMBER DISTRICTING

	Number of Legislators per District	Number of Districts in State	Percentage Effective Representation Compared with Single-Member District	Percent Deviation in Effective Representation with Respect to Average *
Arkansas House 1	1	17	100	−30
	2	15	141	− 1
	3	6	173	+22
	4	3	200	+41
	5	2	224	+58
	13	1	361	+154
Georgia Senate 2	1	23	100	−14
	2	4	141	+22
	3	2	173	+49
	7	1	263	+128
Hawaii Senate 3	1	1	100	−48
	2	1	141	−18
	3	2	173	0
	4	4	200	+16
Texas House 4	1	52	100	−22
	2	9	141	+ 9
	3	4	173	+34
	4	3	200	+55
	5	1	224	+74
	6	2	245	+90
	7	1	264	+105
	8	1	283	+119
	10	1	316	+145
	14	1	374	+190
Wyoming Senate 5	1	10	100	−21
	2	4	141	+11
	3	1	173	+36
	4	1	200	+57
	5	1	224	+76

* Minus sign (−) indicates underrepresentation, lack of sign indicates overrepresentation.
1. Yancey v. Faubus, 251 F. Supp. 998 (D.Ark. 1965), affd. 383 U.S. 271 (1966).
2. Dorsey v. Fortson, 228 F. Supp. 259 (N.D.Ga. 1964), reversed [thus restoring legislature's plan] 379 U.S. 433 (1965).
3. Holt v. Richardson, 240 F. Supp. 724 (D.Hawaii, 1965), vacated and remanded [thus restoring legislature's plan] 384 U.S. 73 (1966).
4. Kilgarlin v. Martin, 252 F. Supp. 404 (S.D. Tex. 1966), reversed 386 U.S. 120 (1967), but number of members in each multimember district was not at issue.
5. Schaefer v. Thomson, 251 F. Supp. 450 (D.Wyo. 1965).

ings, can be summarized somewhat succinctly. They may be the "new math" approach to quantifying "effective representation" in the 'seventies, and helpfully augment, if not replace, the equal population syndrome of the essential first phase of the reapportionment revolution. The Banzhaf approach can most easily be appreciated by first considering the mathematics of weighted voting, and then multimember districting.[93] In both instances voters are in districts of unequal size; in each instance there is a corrective, taking the form of increasing either the number of legislators or legislative votes (or a third possibility is modified weighted voting, which adds some legislators and some votes). The important question is this: Is citizen influence on legislative outcomes really equalized, where district populations are unequal, by these devices?

Assuming an apportionment quota of 1000, if we give ten "seats" or "votes" to a 10,000 population district we have achieved a linear proportionality. It is another question whether "effective citizen influence" likewise progresses in linear fashion so that the over-all legislative influence of a citizen of the 10,000 population district is equal to the influence of a citizen in the 1000-man district. Only if this is so do we avoid "one man-one vote" problems. In fact, as tested by mathematics responsive to the issue of *effective citizen influence on legislative outcomes*, the answer is a resounding "no."

Assuming the route of straight weighted voting, the analysis takes the form of ascertaining the frequency with which each legislator may cast a deciding vote (i.e., be a necessary member of a minimal winning coalition). The most heavily weighted legislators (from the more populous districts) always have more influence. In some instances the lightly weighted legislators—and the district citizens they represent—will have no influence.

An example would be a pre-reapportionment 5-district legislature, each legislator possessing one vote, but with one district having 50,000 population and the remaining four having 10,000 each. Applying weighted voting as a corrective still yields a 5-district, 5-man legislature; but one man now has five votes, the remaining four each have one vote. The five-vote man now has all the voting power and the other four have none. By contrast, if five seats are allocated to the largest district, whether on a subdistricted basis or at-large, the prospect of disagreement within the delegation may preserve the possibility that legislators from the smaller districts may on

93. Part of the summary which follows is adapted from the author's chapter on "Representation Values and Reapportionment Practice: The Eschatology of 'One Man-One Vote,'" in *Representation* (NOMOS XI) (J. Roland Pennock, editor, New York: Atherton Press, 1968), and his 1966 consulting memoranda on reapportionment for New York State Office for Local Government.

occasion have some effective voting power—even though their power still may not be properly proportionalized.[94]

The effect just described applies only to *legislator* voting power in weighted voting systems. There is a second effect, concerning *citizen* influence on legislative outcomes, which applies both to weighted voting and multimember district systems. Under both systems it can be demonstrated that there is an exaggeration of the effective citizen influence in favor of the citizens in the larger districts.

In this instance the mathematics involves a square root analysis. A citizen who resides in the single-member district can vote for one legislator only. The citizen in the larger multimember district is a "smaller frog in a bigger puddle" but he has influence regarding several legislators. If each legislator tried to follow his constituents' wishes he, figuratively, would poll his constituency on each issue. (Unless this "delegate model" is followed, there is little reason to worry about the mathematics of district population regarding representation; and the re-election factor, of course, does lend a delegate characteristic to most legislators.) The *measure* of effective citizen influence is the frequency with which the citizen can be a member of a minimal constituency majority determining the action of one, or more, legislators—or blocs of weighted votes.

Thus analyzed, it can be shown that citizens in larger multimember districts have more influence on legislative outcomes than do citizens in either smaller multimember districts or single-member districts, *even though* the district populations are proportionately equal. The larger the multimember district, i.e., the more legislators it elects, the greater the individual citizen's influence on legislative outcomes. The total or over-all influence on legislative outcomes of the voter in a multimember district (or his "effective representation") can be shown to be *proportional to the square root of the population of the district*, and thus varies with district size.[95] (Actual computation can be simplified by using the square root of the number of legislators assigned rather than using the actual populations of the multimember districts since the difference will be minimal.)

A further comment may help to clarify the concepts involved. Laying aside for the moment the number of legislators allocated to a district, it is true that voter influence has an inverse relationship to district population, i.e., voter influence goes down as district population goes up. *But* voter influence does not go down (i.e., vary inversely) in exact *linear proportion* to

94. John F. Banzhaf III, "Weighted Voting Doesn't Work: A Mathematical Analysis," 19 *Rutgers L. Rev.* 317, 338–40 (1965), suggesting that in New York's Nassau County under weighted voting three of the six legislative districts were without effective influence for many years.
95. To better visualize this consult the detailed tabulations and examples in Banzhaf, *supra* note 89, at 1320–23.

district population shift. Rather it goes down more slowly and decreases inversely to the *square root* of the district population. For example, if district population goes from 50,000 to 100,000, voter influence superficially would seem to be half, but this is not so because the square root of 50,000 is more than half of the square root of 100,000. Therefore, to preserve parity with the voters in the 50,000 district, the voters in the 100,000 district do not need to have twice the number of legislators of the 50,000 district. Under current apportionment practice, they do receive a doubled quota of legislators and are thus overcompensated, and their citizens acquire exaggerated influence on legislative outcomes.

The deviations in effective citizen influence on legislative outcomes under this analysis are significant, and are affected minimally by actual district population deviations of 15 percent or even higher. Indeed, this kind of analysis suggests that a conventional arithmetic equality battle over population deviation percentage points of 10–15 or even 15–20 percent is bootless *if* multimember districts of varying sizes, or a mixture of single-member and multimember districts, are used. Such multimember districting itself magnifies "citizen influence" disparities way beyond the disparities produced by moderate deviations from population equality.

A glance at Chart No. 10 (third column) on multimember districts in five states shows that citizens in the 13-man district have more than three-and-a-half times more effective representation in the Arkansas lower house than citizens in the single-member districts. The overrepresentation ratios in regard to effective citizen representation in favor of the citizen of the largest multimember district in the other legislative houses shown in the chart are as follows: Georgia, 7-man district, 2.64 to 1; Hawaii, 4-man district, 2 to 1; Texas, 14-man district, 3.74 to 1; Wyoming, 5-man district, 2.24 to 1. And the ratio is more than 4.51 to 1 in Florida's 22-man at-large district for Dade County (Miami), which continued in the plan accepted by the lower court after the Supreme Court decision in *Swann* v. *Adams*, although, to be sure, the point now being discussed was not at issue.

The degree of misrepresentation can also be expressed in terms of the percentage of the population of the entire state which resides in the under-represented districts. Assuming a proportional allocation of population under the *Reynolds* doctrine, the figures would be as follows: Arkansas, 65 percent of the population underrepresented; Georgia, 70 percent; Hawaii, 36 percent; Texas, 55 percent; Wyoming, 60 percent.

To this line of analysis the objection might be raised that political factors, including political party operation, affect the abstract model in real life. The complete answer, however, is that *if* political factors are to be considered here, they likewise must be considered in relation to the actual operation of equal population districts under the simple arithmetic approach which has dominated reapportionment litigation to date.[96] The point should be made also that voting as a bloc by all members of a given multimember district legislative delegation is *not* an essential assumption in the analysis made by Mr. Banzhaf. With unanimity the effect is the same as with weighted voting. Without it, the disparity in effective influence between citizens in single-member districts and citizens in multimember districts is only slightly reduced.

The essence of the matter is that in mathematical analysis made at the level of the Supreme Court's "sixth grade arithmetic" of 1964, on which the reapportionment revolution was based, multimember systems with varying sizes of districts (or weighted voting) may satisfy the simple "one man-one vote" proportionality principle. If analyzed at a more sophisticated mathematical level, unexpected (disproportional) variants appear in abstract measures of *citizen power to influence legislative results*. Further, if we focus on equality (i.e., proportionality) of power to influence *actual* legislative results—which some have argued is the root issue, rather than the single question of equality of district populations—a further anomaly appears. We are then seeking a goal which, on mathematical grounds, cannot be achieved under any mixed districting system (i.e., where voters elect different numbers of legislators). And on political grounds also the goal is unlikely to be achieved unless district lines and district populations be carefully analyzed and adjusted with political composition and "political equity" in mind. Despite the apparent contrary assumption of *Reynolds v. Sims*, full citizen equality in affecting legislative *outcomes* is not a natural corollary of simple proportionalization of district population.

96. The well-known tendency of district systems to overrepresent the dominant party can also be expressed in a mathematical formula. If all of the districts are single-member, if at least 90 percent of the popular vote is distributed among no more than two parties, and if the popular strength of the two parties is equally distributed throughout the state, it can be shown that the ratio of the seats won by the parties is approximately equal to the ratio of the cubes of the statewide popular vote each receives. M. G. Kendall and A. Stuart, "The Law of Cubic Proportion in Election Results," 1 *Brit. J. Soc.* 163 (1950).

XX

The Outreach and Impact of "One Man-One Vote"

"The conception of political equality from the Declaration of Independence, to Lincoln's Gettysburg Address, to the Fifteenth, Seventeenth, and Nineteenth Amendments can mean only one thing—one person, one vote."

> Justice William O. Douglas, *Gray v. Sanders* (1963)

"The science of government is the most abstruse of all sciences.
. . . It is the science of experiment. . . .

"The fact that each of the seven councilmen must be a resident of the [grossly unequal] borough from which he is elected, is not fatal. . . .

". . . the history . . . of the area and population . . . demonstrates the compelling need, at least during an appreciable transition period, for knowledge of rural problems in handling the affairs of one of the largest area-wide cities in the United States."

> Justice Douglas, *Local Apportionment Cases* (1967)

A. Local Government Apportionment

Not until the spring of 1967 did local government apportionment receive full consideration in the United States Supreme Court. Even then the initial series of four cases did not result in a definitive statement on the applicability of the "one man-one vote" concept to local government.* However, inspired by *Baker* v. *Carr* [1] and *Reynolds* v. *Sims*,[2] lower courts in Maryland, Michigan, Wisconsin, New York, Virginia, and elsewhere held that the Fourteenth Amendment's "one man-one vote" principle was applicable to all local bodies possessed of legislative power,[3] and also to bodies

* Applicability was confirmed by a decision while this book was in press. See Note, p. 581.
1. 369 U.S. 186 (1962).
2. 377 U.S. 533 (1964).
3. Ellis v. Mayor and City Council of Baltimore, 352 F.2d 123 (4th Cir. 1965); Brouwer v. Bronkema, 377 Mich. 616, 141 N.W.2d 98 (1966); State *ex rel.* Sonneborn v. Sylvester, 26 Wis. 2d 43, 132 N.W.2d 249 (1965); Seaman v. Fedourich, 262

544

with mixed legislative-executive power such as the New York City Board of Estimate.[4] School boards were also covered within the "one man-one vote" principle in several decisions.[5] A series of cases in California in 1963–1965 nominally were placed on state law grounds,[6] although the influence of the new federal approach toward the Fourteenth Amendment was obvious. There were some deviant voices,[7] but in national perspective they were in a minority.

The logic of those lower courts holding that the equal population principle applies with equal force to local legislative districts as for state legislative apportionment was simple. It rested on what seemed to be the initial constitutional premise of both *Baker* and *Reynolds* (see Chapter VI and XI), that a reapportionment case is generically a voting case, resting on the interests of individual citizens in having their votes counted and weighted equally. As Chief Justice Earl Warren said, "people, not land or trees or pastures, vote."[8] If "one man-one vote" cases are civil rights cases and nothing more, then state and local legislative apportionment cannot be separated because the Fourteenth Amendment applies equally to state and local activity. Under a single federal constitutional clause a citizen cannot logically have two dimensions of voting rights, any more than he can have two dimensions of free speech rights.

One of the better early opinions was that of Judge Fred N. Searl in a Michigan county board case,[9] in the course of which he also exploded the defense theory that the Supreme Court's old decision in a 1907 city consolidation case, *Hunter v. Pittsburgh,* precluded the application of "one man-one vote" to local government. In that case the Court upheld a consolida-

N.Y.S.2d 244, 16 N.Y. 2d 94 (1965); Dusch v. Davis, 361 F.2d 465 (4th Cir. 1966). See tabulation in Clifford I. Dobler and Herbert S. Duncombe, "The Apportionment of County Governing Bodies," in *County Handbook-1967* (Washington, D.C.: National Association of Counties, 1968). And see Josephine Y. King, "The Reynolds Standard and Local Reapportionment," 15 *Buffalo L. Rev.* 120 (1965); Jack B. Weinstein, "The Effect of the Federal Reapportionment Decisions on Counties and Other Forms of Municipal Government," 65 *Columbia L. Rev.* 21 (1965).
4. McMillan v. Wagner, 239 F. Supp. 32 (S.D.N.Y. 1964), not, however a final decision.
5. See, e.g., Delozier v. Tyrone Area School Board, 247 F. Supp. 30 (W.D.Pa. 1965); Strickland v. Burns, 256 F. Supp. 824 (M.D.Tenn. 1966).
6. Griffin v. Board of Supervisors, 388 P.2d 888, 384 P.2d 421 (Calif.); Miller v. Board of Supervisors, 405 P.2d 857 (1965). See John F. Gallagher, "Apportionment in California Counties," *California Government Series No. 6* (Davis, Calif.: University of California (Davis) Institute of Governmental Affairs, 1964).
7. See, e.g., Knudson v. Kelvering, 377 Mich. 666, 141 N.W.2d 120 (1966); Avery v. Midland County, Texas, 406 S.W.2d 442 (1966); Moody v. Flowers, 256 F. Supp. 195 (M.D.Ala. 1966).
8. Reynolds v. Sims, 377 U.S. 533, 580 (1964).
9. Brouwer v. Bronkema (Kent Co., Mich. Cir. Ct., Sept. 11, 1964) 13 National Municipal League, Court Decisions on Legislative Apportionment 81. This apparently was the first local apportionment case decided after *Reynolds.*

tion even though a majority of the voters in the smaller city opposed it and said: "[T]he State is supreme, and its legislative body, conforming its action to the state constitution, may do as it will, unrestrained by any provision of the Constitution of the United States . . . ." [10] But as Justice Felix Frankfurter wrote in the Tuskegee gerrymander case in which the Court voided the detachment of Negro territory from the City of Tuskegee: "When a state exercises powers wholly within the domain of state interests, it is insulated from Federal judicial review. But such insulation is not carried over when state power is used as an instrument for circumventing a Federal political right." [11]

Under the impetus of this view, Wisconsin county boards were thoroughly revamped in 1965 under a statute passed in response to a state supreme court ruling. The court invalidated Wisconsin's traditional system of giving townships and city wards equality on county boards regardless of their widely differing population.[12] New York's similar system of equal ward and town (township) representation on county boards was invalidated by both state and federal courts; [13] and city council districts in New York also were subjected to the equal population rule.[14] The result was extensive local experimentation with new representation forms, making New York local government a sort of redistricting laboratory for the nation. Forms used have included single-member districts, multimember districts, combinations of these two systems, combinations including floterial districts, pure weighted voting, modified weighted voting.[15]

1. THE CRYPTIC CASES OF MAY 1967

When the Supreme Court in four cases in May 1967 refused to meet the issue squarely, it surprised close observers of the local districting scene, especially in view of the Court's tendency to tighten the "one man-one vote" concept for congressional districting and state legislative apportionment. Two of the four cases—*Moody* v. *Flowers* concerning the Houston County (Alabama) Board and *Board of Supervisors* v. *Bianchi* concerning the Suffolk County (New York) Board—were dismissed on a technical point.[16] They were said to involve only "local" law rather than law of

10. 207 U.S. 161, 179 (1907).
11. Gomillion v. Lightfoot, 364 U.S. 339, 347 (1960).
12. State ex rel. Sonneborn v. Sylvester, *supra* note 3.
13. Augostini v. Lasky, 262 N.Y.S. 2d 594, 46 Misc.2d 1058 (1965); Bianchi v. Griffing, 238 F. Supp. 997 (E.D.N.Y. 1965).
14. Seaman v. Fedourich, *supra* note 3.
15. See "Information Bulletins on Reapportionment of Local Government Legislative Bodies" issued periodically since 1966 by New York State Office for Local Government, Albany, N.Y.
16. 387 U.S. 97 (1967).

statewide application and hence should not have been heard by a three-judge federal district court with direct review by the Supreme Court; the proper path was trial before a single federal district judge, review by an intermediate federal Court of Appeals, and then a review petition to the Supreme Court.[17] In the other two cases—*Sailors* v. *Kent Board of Education*[18] from Kent County, Michigan, and *Dusch* v. *Davis*[19] concerning the consolidated City of Virginia Beach—the Supreme Court "reserved the question whether the apportionment of municipal or county legislative agencies is governed by *Reynolds* v. *Sims.*"[20] But even "assum[ing] *arguendo*" that it does apply, said Justice William O. Douglas for the Court, the systems challenged in these two cases were not shown to be unconstitutional.

a. *The Michigan School Board Case*

The *Sailors* case concerned an unusual pyramidal system of selecting the five members of the county board of education. Local district school boards inside the county—themselves elected at-large—each sent one delegate to a biennial meeting, regardless of the size of the local district. In Kent County the largest unit to send a delegate was the City of Grand Rapids (201,777); the four smallest local school districts to send delegates had populations ranging from 99 to 145. Delegates to this biennial meeting "elected" the five-man county board. Plaintiffs attacked this system of selection of the county board on the ground that it was similar in effect to Georgia's unequal county-unit system of electing statewide officers which the Supreme Court had invalidated in 1963 in *Gray* v. *Sanders*[21] (Chapter VIII).

In the Supreme Court the plaintiffs' case against the Kent Board of Education collapsed on two grounds. First, although the record was not as clear as one might wish, it indicated that all important powers were exercised by the intracounty local boards which were elected at-large. The county board, on which the attack centered, apparently had a power (sub-

17. For Suffolk County at least this was a close ruling. And even though the Solicitor General himself raised the jurisdictional point in his amicus brief, in a later case he referred to the Court's ruling as a "narrow reading" of the three-judge jurisdictional rule. In the Suffolk case the challenged rule of town equality on the county board was not merely a local charter policy; the charter conformed with general state policy, and if invalidated, a "back-up" provision in general state law would have preserved the rule of town equality. Brief for the United States as Amicus Curiae, pp. 118–30, Sailors v. Board of Education of the County of Kent, 387 U.S. 105 (1967). Brief for the United States as Amicus Curiae, Avery v. Midland County, Texas, United States Supreme Court, October Term, 1967, No. 39, p. 71.
18. 387 U.S. 105 (1967).
19. 387 U.S. 112 (1967).
20. *Id.* at 114.
21. 372 U.S. 368 (1963).

ject to review) of changing local school district lines; but it was active mainly in providing special education services, e.g., remedial programs for retarded and delinquent children. It was not, therefore, a body possessing conventional "legislative" powers. Second, the Supreme Court viewed the pyramidal system of selecting the Kent County Board as an *appointive* rather than an elective system. Hence, it was wholly beyond the reach of the "one man-one vote" concept.

On its special facts the decision in the *Sailors* case may be plausible, but the reasons advanced for rejecting the challenge have uncertain predictive value for the future. To call a "pyramidal" system of election an "appointive" system is an odd use of the word "appointive." Under our electoral college system, the President technically may be "appointed" rather than elected, but this is a special instance grounded in the compromises at the constitutional convention. The key factor in the *Sailors* case may have been the Court's feeling that the county board performed "essentially administrative functions"; though important, they were not "legislative in the classical sense." [22] As Justice Douglas, who wrote the Court's opinion, summarized:

> At least as respects non-legislative officers, a State can appoint local officials or elect them or combine the elective and appointive system as was done here. If we assume *arguendo* that where a State provides for an election of a local official or agency—whether administrative, legislative, or judicial—the requirements of *Gray* v. *Sanders* and *Reynolds* v. *Sims* must be met, no question of that character is presented.[23]

Justice Douglas seems to be saying two things: a state may "appoint" nonlegislative officers to avoid "one man-one vote"; but if there is an election, "one man-one vote" applies regardless of the character of the duties of the elective officials. The latter thought is easily accepted, and in *Gray* and *Reynolds* we have precedents for application of the "one man-one vote" concept to both elected executive and elected legislative officials. The former thought is more questionable since it is hard to believe that the Court was saying that a state legislature could shift local officials en masse from an elective to an "appointive" basis to avoid the rigors of "one man-one vote." Such a conversion would seriously endanger prospects for minority representation, either ethnic or political.

b. *The Consolidated City of Virginia Beach Case*

Far more important than the *Sailors* case as an indication of Supreme Court posture on local government "one man-one vote" problems is the

22. 387 U.S. at 110.
23. *Id.* at 111.

Dusch v. *Davis* case. As a result of the consolidation of the City of Virginia Beach (in Virginia) and adjoining Princess Anne County, an eleven-man council was created. At the time of the case the council consisted of four members nominated and elected wholly at-large, and seven members elected at-large but required to be residents of districts whose populations varied from 733 to 29,048. A lower federal court invalidated the plan.[24]

In vigorous defense of this plan, Harry Frazier III entertained the Supreme Court by stressing the town's unique aspects, geographic, ecological, and political. Prior to consolidation the City of Virginia Beach was a small resort town. Princess Anne was a large county, with some population spill-over from the City of Norfolk in one corner; but it consisted mainly of a large undeveloped wildlife area, and some agricultural areas. It included a part of famous Dismal Swamp which is on the Eastern Flyway for migratory birds. Another section, Pungo, reportedly has exceptionally fine bear hunting. At least in part the consolidation was motivated by a desire to prevent Norfolk from annexing adjacent populous areas of the county.

Although these features made the oral argument an hilarious affair, they seemed to have played no part in the Court's decision. After all, many states have unusual underpopulated geographic areas, with poor communications, but such factors have been given no weight in the Supreme Court's state legislative apportionment decisions. And Justice William J. Brennan, Jr., intimated during oral argument that he was unimpressed with Mr. Frazier's "uniqueness" argument because such a test would require "long trials for 20,000 or more local units."

Rather, in saying that even if the Fourteenth Amendment rule announced in *Reynolds* v. *Sims* applied to local government it would not nullify the candidate local residence provision in the Virginia Beach plan, the Court seems to have had something else in mind. Its theme seems to have been the desirability of leaving open broad areas for experimentation in representation forms at the local level. In short, instead of focusing on the question of bear hunting in little Pungo, the Court seems to have placed the Virginia Beach consolidation case in the context of the urban-metropolitan governmental muddle.

The unresponsiveness of present local government forms to urban-suburban social and political problems, and the need for creativity in devising better arrangements, is one of the themes of our times. In the course of oral argument, for example, Justice Byron R. White asked Mr. Frazier whether a "one man-one vote" equalization principle—thus barring an ar-

24. 361 F.2d 495, 497 (4th Cir. 1966), the court saying that under the 7–4 plan "the imbalance in representation in the council is obvious." Similarly in Maryland the unconstitutionality of restricting county board candidates to unequal residence districts was thought to be so clear that the point was conceded. Montgomery County Council v. Garrott, 222 A.2d 164 (Md. 1966).

rangement like the 7-4 plan—would have led to defeat of the consolidation proposal in the popular referendum. Mr. Frazier answered yes. This point is perhaps the key to the *Dusch* case. It is reflected in Justice Douglas's closing lines in his opinion for the Court. The restrictive candidate residence provision, he said, "seems to reflect a detente between urban and rural communities that may be important in resolving the complex problems of the modern megalopolis in relation to the city, the suburbia, and the rural countryside." [25] Even more explicitly in *Sailors* he wrote for the Court as follows:

> Viable local governments may need many innovations, numerous combinations of old and new devices, great flexibility in municipal arrangements to meet changing urban conditions. We see nothing in the Constitution to prevent experimentation.[26]

In announcing this policy position, the Court ignored rather than distinguished the rigid, arithmetic equality approach of the state legislative apportionment and congressional districting cases. True, as Justice Douglas mentioned in *Dusch*, on the record before it in *Fortson* v. *Dorsey* the Court had sustained Georgia's candidate residence requirement in its system of at-large election of seven senators in Fulton County (Atlanta). However, Justice Douglas passed over the vital fact that the seven candidate residence districts were assumed to be reasonably equal (Chapters XVII and XVIII).

Further, if the decision in *Dusch* evinces a Court disposition to go beyond equal population arithmetic and consider results, what of the "gerrymandering" possibilities which are implicit in Virginia Beach's 7-4 plan? As Chief Justice Warren had asked in oral argument, might it not "get out of hand?" What is to prevent a dominant group in the two largest subdistricts (called "boroughs" in this plan), whose populations respectively were 29,048 and 23,731, from placing and electing a "patsy candidate" in the remaining much smaller subdistricts, thus sweeping all council seats? The populations of the remaining five districts were: 13,900, 8091, 7211, 2504, 733. Justice Douglas seems to have been sensitive to this possibility, but dismissed it in a footnote with the observation that the same result could occur even if the districts were abolished. The two largest subdistricts, he said, "if united in their efforts, could elect all 11 councilmen, even though the election were at large." [27] Yet only three months earlier in his separate opinion in the Texas state legislative apportionment case, Justice Douglas had expressed concern about at-large elections in multi-

25. 387 U.S. at 117.
26. 387 U.S. at 110–11.
27. 387 U.S. at 117 n.5.

member districts, because this "allows the majority to defeat the minority on all fronts."[28]

From the standpoint of effective representation, the central problem in both state and local districting stems from the Court's premise, expressed in *Fortson* v. *Dorsey*, that at-large elections are per se constitutional unless the challengers can show "invidious discrimination." Thus, the constitutional rule of *Dusch* may be: apparent discrimination stemming from use of such special districting features as candidate residence districts of unequal population is not unconstitutional if the same apparent discrimination would accompany a pure at-large system—*unless* there is *particularized* proof of cancelling out "the voting strength of racial or political elements."[29] But this possible rule is subject to the *caveat* noted above that the Court may be treating local government as a "special case," and would not permit equivalent flexibility in constructing unequal candidate residence districts for state legislatures.

2. ORAL ARGUMENT—JUDICIAL UNEASE IN THE LOCAL POLITICAL THICKET

In many respects the more than five hours of oral argument in the Supreme Court in these four local apportionment cases in the spring of 1967 were more interesting and enlightening than the brief, cryptic opinions subsequently written for the Court by Justice Douglas. (The New York and Alabama county board cases, *Bianchi* and *Moody*, received full treatment in argument even though subsequently dismissed on a technical jurisdiction point as noted above.) This may be one of those frontier areas of the law where one can sense the Court's difficulty better from Bench-counsel repartee in the courtroom than from the formal record and decisions. The Bench in general discussed the issues as though they *were* agreed on the proposition that "one man-one vote" applied to local government, but were troubled by the great variety of local government situations and by questions of where and how far to apply the principle.

a. Concern for Minority Representation

Francis X. Beytagh, assistant to the United States Solicitor General who presented the government's amicus curiae views, began with the proposition that the "one man-one vote" principle applies locally to "all elective bodies set up by law." Justice Potter Stewart immediately intervened, continuing the role he assumed early in reapportionment litigation of acting as spokesman for the minority representation side of the majority rule coin.

28. Kilgarlin v. Hill, 386 U.S. 120, 126 (1967).
29. Fortson v. Dorsey, 379 U.S. 433, 439 (1965).

He remonstrated at what he felt was the excessively majoritarian thrust of the government's amicus brief. He suggested that the government was pushing so hard to bring local government within a rigid equal population principle as to make "enlightened and progressive experimentation impossible," e.g., devices to achieve a "proportional representation" result so that the local legislature would mirror the full range of citizen opinion. He suggested that in the field of representation the constitutional requirement of equal protection must be responsive to "an infinite variety" of local circumstances. In this opening repartee with Mr. Beytagh, Justice Stewart thus hinted at important aspects of the opinions subsequently written for the Court by Justice Douglas.

Anomalously, there is one representation form potentially responsive to the twofold interest of preserving a distinctive voice for small component parts of a county (or of a limited function special purpose district), while at the same time vindicating the "one man-one vote" principle arithmetically. That form is pure or modified weighted voting (Chapter XVIII). It was briefed and was present in one of the cases—*Suffolk County* (New York) v. *Bianchi*—but never was reached in oral argument. The weighted voting argument was scheduled for presentation by Richard C. Cahn, who was supporting both the applicability of "one man-one vote" to local government and the permissibility of Suffolk County's plan of modified weighted voting. However, he argued late in the five-and-a-half-hour sequence and by that time it appeared that the Court might be inclined to dismiss all except the Virginia Beach case on the ground that none of the challenged boards possessed meaningful power. A series of questions from the Bench had elicited so little indication that the Houston County (Alabama) Board possessed meaningful governmental power that at intermission one of the audience filing out was heard to say: "Those old boys on that Board of Revenue down there just don't know how low-down, no-account they are!" Hence, Mr. Cahn exhausted his time in an effort to show that at least New York county boards were significant legislative bodies—an effort made bootless by the Court's dismissal of this case and the Houston County case on jurisdictional grounds.

b. *The Problem of "General" and "Special" Local Bodies, and Functional Classification*

Justices Abe Fortas and Potter Stewart wondered if petty special function bodies like conservation districts should be included. This led Mr. Beytagh to suggest a modified rule to the effect that there should be a rebuttable presumption in favor of applying "one man-one vote" to all local elective bodies; and he conceded that it might be a "rational" exception to have one member elected from each section of a conservation district, regardless of population. Justice Tom C. Clark then wondered about tax equalization boards, which are normally appointive but which have far more important policy impact than some petty elective boards. On the question of administrative-legislative distinctions, Justice White brought out the fact that the Fourteenth Amendment's "one man-one vote" principle was not limited to "legislative functions" but also applied to executive officials, as indicated by the 1963 case, Gray v. Sanders, concerning Georgia's county-unit system of electing the governor and some other statewide offices.

What then about state judges elected from unequal population districts, Justice Brennan asked. Judges would not be covered, Mr. Beytagh replied, reverting to the twofold test of "one man-one vote" applicability hypothesized in the Solicitor General's brief. Under this test the equal population principle would apply to those elective bodies which were "representative" in nature.[30] The word "elective" seemed clear, but Justice Brennan wondered what the term "representative office" meant in this context. Without attempting a full definition, Mr. Beytagh replied that judges would not be included because they "don't speak for the public."

Justice Brennan pursued this problem of functional classification in the argument concerning the Houston County Board, asking Charles S. Rhyne, counsel for the plaintiffs, whether "representative" means "more than simply elected by the people." Mr. Rhyne responded that the "one man-one vote" principle should apply to all elective officials—including judges and tax equalization boards—because "all governmental powers are important." Justice Stewart seemed to feel that this response was rather broad and he asked Mr. Rhyne whether public utilities, with extensive governmental powers, including the power of condemnation, should be included. And he asked the crucial question whether an unrestricted application of the "one man-one vote" principle would logically limit the people's discretion to make some governmental policy-making bodies appointive rather than elective. This produced a peroration from counsel about the value of "one man-one vote" in a democratic society, but no enlightenment on the "outreach" problems obviously troubling the Bench.

Paul O. Strawhecker, defending the Michigan system of electing the Kent Board of Education, was asked essentially the same question by Justice Douglas, who wondered if a state could "substantially abolish elections" by setting up a "system of pyramiding up to the top from one local election." Mr. Strawhecker gave the proper response, although the point was not pursued, i.e., that this idea would raise not so much a question of equal protection under the Fourteenth Amendment as a question of the proper form of state government under the guarantee of a "republican

30. Brief for the United States as Amicus Curiae, Sailors v. Board of Education of the County of Kent, 387 U.S. 105 (1967).

form of government" in Article IV of the federal Constitution. For Justice Felix Frankfurter, of course, this is the clause most relevant to all representation-apportionment questions (Chapter V); and the issues in the disputed Georgia governorship election in 1966, when the legislature selected the governor, also may be said to lend themselves better to treatment under this clause than under the equal protection clause (Chapter VI, pp. 136–37, n.43).

In his rebuttal Mr. Rhyne sought to articulate one all-embracing principle in response to the probing questions from the Bench. He reverted to the concept of no taxation without representation and pointed out that the populous City of Dothan inside Houston County pays 69 percent of the county's tax bill even though it has only one seat on the board. This only invited a further barrage. Justice White pointed out that since the tax system was fixed by the state legislature, even a reapportioned county board could not change it. Justice Fortas, looking beyond the case at hand, asked how the question of who pays taxes is relevant in determining the outreach of "one man-one vote." There is, of course, no constitutional principle of no taxation without representation, else there could be no separate District of Columbia. More seriously, if a principle of this sort were to be derived from the Fourteenth Amendment as a deduction from "one man-one vote," it logically would require election of boards of assessment and boards of tax equalization, as well as election of the body which actually fixes the tax rate.

This extended sequence of oral argument was more fascinating in many ways than any of the reapportionment arguments since *Baker* v. *Carr*. The Bench, the Solicitor General, and at least some of the counsel, were ready now to grapple with philosophic issues of representation and responsive governmental structure going beyond the "equal population" simplicity of the earlier "one man-one vote" principle. If "one man-one vote" was to apply locally, what bodies would it reach—and how stringently and for what purposes? As Justice Fortas so aptly phrased it: "The real question is: what is local government?"

3. THE TEXAS COUNTY BOARD CASE

Yet another local government "one man-one vote" case received full review in the United States Supreme Court in November 1967—*Avery* v. *Midland County, Texas*.[31] The county board (locally called a "commissioners' court" but referred to here as a board) consisted of the county judge elected at-large who was ex officio presiding officer in addition to his other duties, and four commissioners. The latter were elected in districts of such

31. Decided against the county while this book was in press. See Note, p. 581.

unequal size that three of the four were chosen by a mere 2.6 percent of the qualified voters. The distribution of the county population among the four districts was as follows: first district (the City of Midland), 97.01 percent; second, 1.22 percent; third, 0.59 percent; fourth, 1.18 percent. Although some of the functions of the board apparently were oriented more to the rural portions of Midland County than to the City of Midland, the total range of power was extensive, including authority regarding a county hospital, regional public housing authorities, and tax equalization (there being no state equalization agency).

This districting arrangement went through an interesting sequence of litigation in the state courts.[32] The trial court held the plan unconstitutional and ordered creation of an equal population plan. An intermediate appellate court reversed on the ground that the "one man-one vote" doctrine had not yet been authoritatively applied to local government by the United States Supreme Court. The Texas Supreme Court rejected this viewpoint and held the existing unequal districts unconstitutional. But unlike the trial court, the state supreme court did not require creation of a strict equal population plan. It said that recent developments had narrowed the county board's major functions to the non-urban areas of the county, and suggested that in reconstituting the board a number of factors in addition to population could be considered: (1) qualified voters; (2) land areas; (3) geography; (4) miles of county road; (5) taxable values. Most of these factors, except for the first, would be impermissible, obviously, in regard to state legislative reapportionment or congressional districting (Chapters VIII and XI).

In oral argument in the Supreme Court, the supporters of the original grossly unequal district plan in Midland County were subjected to a withering crossfire. The facts were more stark than in any of the local government cases argued in May 1967. Chief Justice Warren questioned: "Don't you have the situation where one of your million acre ranches controls the entire county?" Arguing on behalf of the county, W. B. Browder, Jr., had to say, "To some extent, yes." [33]

Unlike two of the May 1967 cases—Suffolk County and Houston County—there was no three-judge federal court jurisdiction problem because *Midland* came up from a state court system. The only "jurisdictional" doubt (really a "finality" question) was whether Midland County might reapportion itself satisfactorily under the state court order, making further litigation unnecessary. The Solicitor General's position was that the

---

32. The unreported trial court opinion is set forth at page 130 of the Record certified to the United States Supreme Court. For the intermediate appellate court and state supreme court opinions see 397 S.W.2d 919 and 406 S.W.2d 422 (1967).
33. *Washington Post* (AP), November 15, 1967, p. 3, cols. 6–7.

case was ripe for review, because under the Texas Supreme Court's reapportionment order a pure population reapportionment was not required. However, the Solictor General's position seemed to beg the question, for *if* the "one man-one vote" principle does *not* require as close equality at the local level as at the state level, then a mixed districting formula, including some nonpopulation factors, could settle the matter in "satisfactory" fashion.

The *Midland* case also was unlike the Kent County (Michigan) school board case because concededly the Texas board was elected and not appointed. It was unlike the Virginia Beach case because there was no at-large election feature. To reassure Justice Stewart, the Solicitor General in his amicus brief in the *Midland* case said that neither the propriety of "proportional representation schemes" nor "weighted voting" was involved in the Texas case. Adopting the government's position in *Midland* would not preclude the Court, he said, from considering such questions in appropriate situations, citing the Court's earlier dismissal of the appeal in the New York City Council limited voting case.[34]

Continuing one of the themes of oral argument in the spring, 1967, cases, Chief Justice Warren asked a series of questions concerning the powers of the Midland County board. The board did seem to have significant policy-making powers, even though by custom the board did not exercise much power within the City of Midland. Justice Fortas's prime focus was on the question of whether strict equal population districting, in view of the City of Midland's population dominance, would result in "inability of the county to get roads and other improvements." In other words, was the Texas system a "conscious policy" of wealth equalization through malapportionment—just as New York State, as he noted, in effect subsidizes less developed states? How much "rational variance" from population equality do such subsidy considerations permit, if any?

Arguing for a strict population apportionment, the Solicitor General alluded to the other side of the coin, i.e., the effect of malapportionment on limiting and stunting urban growth. The point was not pursued, but it does raise a significant policy question. Suppose, for example, that there was a significant suburban fringe in the county, outside the boundaries of the City of Midland. Under malapportionment, with a minority of the county's total population controlling the board, a countywide viewpoint could not be brought to bear upon city-fringe disputes. On the other hand, on the unusual facts of *Midland*, if the board were reapportioned under a

34. Brief for the United States as Amicus Curiae, Avery v. Midland County, Texas, United States Supreme Court, 1967 Term, No. 39, p. 72 n.87, citing in turn Blaikie v. Power, 13 N.Y.2d 134, 193 N.E.2d 55 (1963), *appeal dismissed*, 375 U.S. 439 (1964).

strict population equality plan it could become a City of Midland monolith, with the city controlling all or most of the seats.

4. THE POSSIBLE CREATIVE ROLE OF A LOCAL GOVERNMENT "ONE MAN-ONE VOTE" PRINCIPLE

Both the May 1967 local government cases in the Supreme Court and the later *Avery* v. *Midland County* case, because of their special facts and manner of handling by the Court, leave many questions unanswered concerning the eventual reach of the "one man-one vote" principle in regard to local government agencies and officials. First, although the *Dusch* case concerning the consolidated City of Virginia Beach indicates that at-large elections and even grossly unequal candidate residence districts are available as valid reapportionment patterns, at least prima facie, the possibility of overturning such systems by detailed proof of invidious discrimination continues. And it may be easier to marshal such proof at the local level than at the state level. With a smaller area to look at, and total control of the unicameral local legislature at stake, the focus is sharper than in regard to state legislatures. In short, Justice Brennan's *Fortson* v. *Dorsey* dictum about fair and effective representation of "racial or political elements" may bear fruit at the local level. There is something rather stark about a 55 to 60 percent majority regularly sweeping to a 10 to 0 majority on a county board or city council.

Second, although weighted voting and fractional voting seem to be dead at the state legislative level, these devices still are receiving much attention at the local level in New York State. Third, because local legislative bodies are unicameral, it could be argued that courts should adhere to a tighter standard of population equality than in regard to state legislatures. The argument could be supported by pointing to the fact that local government district lines are rather arbitrary anyway, in contrast to the interest in preserving some local political subdivisions and communities of interest in constructing state legislative seats. However, the stress in *Dusch* v. *Davis* and in *Sailors* v. *Kent Board of Education* on preserving much room for local experimentation severely undercuts this thought.[35]

Because local legislative bodies are unicameral, there may be and proba-

---

35. In his opinion in *Reynolds* in 1964, Chief Justice Earl Warren intimated that congressional districts (though only one-half of the Congress is on a population principle) might be subjected to a tighter arithmetic standard than state legislative districts (377 U.S. 533, 578), but the Court's handling of cases in these fields in 1967 did not continue this thought. Indeed, the Court's opinion in *Swann* v. *Adams* which permitted only de minimis deviations from arithmetic equality for state legislatures was cited as authority for summary disposition of two congressional districting cases (Chapter XVII).

bly should be an enhanced concern for creation of mixed electorates. For example, the Twenty-ninth American Assembly in 1966 made this recommendation:

> As the principle of "one man, one vote" is applied, innovations in districting policies to improve patterns of representation are desirable. Districting problems vary greatly from state to state and from area to area within states. Creative use of single-member districts and multi-member districts, alone or in combination, may help solve problems of fair representation, especially in urban areas.[36]

As a step beyond this suggestion for mixed districting to create mixed electorates, it may be more feasible at the local level than at the state level to achieve a broad spectrum legislature by use of specific devices which guarantee some minority representation. After all, an attempt to achieve this goal merely by mixed districting—electing some legislators from small districts and others from large districts—could be subject to "higher math" attack (Chapter XIX). Effective citizen influence on legislative outcomes is unequal whenever election districts of differing size are used for a single legislative house. Minority representation devices which could be considered include the following: cumulative voting; alternative forms of limited voting already in use for the New York City Council and for some local governments in Connecticut and Pennsylvania; and pure proportional representation, despite the common American dislike of this form.

Raising our sights somewhat, application of "one man-one vote" concepts to local government in some states may greatly invigorate local political systems by making them more competitive. It may also yield new structural forms for more effective local government integration.[37] Reformation of those county boards which traditionally have been elected from malapportioned local districts (townships or "towns" in some states), and reformation of at-large boards by creating equal subdistricts,[38] may produce a ready-made instrument for metropolitan regional government. A county board on which all sections of the county—city, suburbs, rural areas—are equally represented in proportion to their population would have a high claim to receive those powers needed for effective metropolitan government. Most "metro" suggestions have in the past been distasteful to local

36. "State Legislatures in American Politics" 6, Report of the Twenty-ninth American Assembly, April 28–May 1, 1966 (Harriman, New York: Arden House, 1966).
37. See my article, "New Constitutional Forms for Metropolis: Reapportioned County Boards; Local Councils of Governments," 30 *Law and Contemporary Problems* 57 (1965).
38. United States Bureau of the Census, *Governing Boards of County Governments: 1965* (Washington, D.C.: U.S. Government Printing Office, 1965).

politicians, and except in Tennessee,[39] few metro proposals have fared well. The county, as a traditional unit, may be more acceptable. To be sure, a single county is not coterminous with the full reach of the metropolitan area in some places. However, as a starting point, the county is at least broader in concept than the city. And with reformed and reinvigorated county boards, the path to intercounty functional co-ordination should be eased.

Such a development focusing on the county also may offer the only hope for bringing together into one electorate the central city Negro ghetto and the white suburban ring. It may offer the only real basis for approaching problems on a reasoned local-regional basis, rather than on a crash basis between city machine and White House. A primary result of local "one man-one vote" reformation may be, therefore, to refurbish the county as a key building block for effective urban and regional government.

B. "Malapportioned" Judicial Election Districts

Should the "one man-one vote" principle, in addition to covering legislative and executive elections, be extended to require equalizing the population of districts from which some state judges are elected? Justice Brennan wondered about this in repartee with counsel during oral argument in the local government apportionment cases in the spring of 1967; and it was not an idle question. There have been a few suits, although the Supreme Court has not yet been asked to review the matter.

First, where the judges of a court serving an entire state (or a designated part thereof) are separately elected from subdistricts in the area served by the court, it may be argued that "one man-one vote" requires that each of these election districts be substantially equal in population. In short, the bench is analogized to a legislature elected from districts. Second, where a number of courts of equivalent jurisdiction serve several parts of the state, it may be argued that a right of equal service on the part of the citizens requires that the number of judges for each of the courts be proportional to the size of the population served. This kind of "equal protection" argument goes beyond voting situations; it would apply equally to a system in which judges were appointed.

39. See U.S. Advisory Commission on Intergovernmental Relations, *Alternative Approaches to Governmental Reorganization in Metropolitan Areas* (1962); U.S. Advisory Commission on Intergovernmental Relations, *Performance of Urban Functions: Local and Areawide* (1963).

The first of these two questions was raised in a suit in Illinois. Prior to a 1962 amendment to the state constitution's judicial article, the Illinois Supreme Court was even more malapportioned than the legislature. Cook County (Chicago) shared one justice with four other counties, although this group had 59.7 percent of the state's population. The remaining six were spread downstate, giving the bench a Republican cast. Under the amendment, Cook County received three justices and four others were spread downstate, but implementation was to be gradual as incumbents retired. Even as revised there still was a population variance ratio between Cook County and the smallest judicial district of 1.53 to 1; but this feature was not challenged even though ratios that large are now frowned on for legislative districts (Chapter XVII).

In an attempt to expedite Cook County's acquisition of three state supreme court justices, a suit was filed against the state Electoral Board invoking the new *Reynolds* v. *Sims* doctrine of equal population for election districts. The necessary first step in this case, *Romiti* v. *Kerner*,[40] was to articulate a federal right to equal population in judicial election districts. Plaintiffs relied here, as in legislative apportionment, on the Supreme Court's dominant tendency to characterize apportionment questions as involving essentially questions of personal voting rights. From this premise they derived an across-the-board principle that all citizens must stand in the same relation to all elective governmental bodies, *regardless* of the kind of *function* performed by the body. The equal population principle had been applied to "legislative bodies" in apportionment cases, and to "executive" officials in Georgia's county-unit case. Indeed, this Georgia system of nonpopulation vote weighting also had been used for statewide judicial officers, although this point had not been singled out for attention in *Gray* v. *Sanders*[41] (Chapter VIII).

Thus, plaintiffs asked, why not now announce a general application of the "one man-one vote" principle to the judiciary? The rule urged was that if an election is authorized for any governmental body, the Fourteenth Amendment's equal protection clause requires population equalization and equal voter status. To be sure, some judges are appointive rather than elective, but so are some executive officials. In those states with appointive judiciaries the "one man-one vote" principle still is vindicated through citizen control of the officials who in turn appoint the judges—an example of "representative government." In states with elective judges there is "direct pure democracy,"[42] provided the districts are equal or elections are at-

40. 256 F. Supp. 35 (N.D. Ill. 1966).
41. 372 U.S. 368 (1963).
42. Brief of Defendant, Paul Powell, p. 42, *Romiti* v. *Kerner*, *supra* note 40. Secretary of State Powell, one of several state officials on the Electoral Board, had himself realigned as a party plaintiff.

large. In point of fact, among thirty-two states which elect judges for their high courts, there are twenty-four at-large systems, four district systems like Illinois, three at-large systems qualified by restricted candidate residence provisions, and one hybrid system of three from districts and two at-large. Among eighteen states using an appointive system, the governor appoints in thirteen states (qualified by legislative approval in six) and the legislature, or part thereof, appoints in five states.[43]

The defendants, including the Illinois State Bar and Chicago Bar Associations as amici curiae, sidestepped *Gray v. Sanders* on which plaintiffs placed heavy reliance. Defendants centered on the proposition that the essence of the reapportionment cases was to develop a "one man-one vote" principle in the context of "representative" bodies, thus functionally excluding the judiciary. As phrased in one brief:

> [S]ince the judiciary is in no sense a representative organ of our government, it is abundantly clear, we submit, that popular equality is of little moment in the process of judicial selection. Instead, the nature of the judicial process is such that the prime concern is to ensure that only competent lawyers will be chosen who will impartially and ably decide cases and dispense justice, and be encouraged to remain on the bench.[44]

And they pointed out that a rule of population equalization of districts every ten years or more frequently would undermine principles of long judicial tenure and professionalization.

None of these interesting questions was resolved in the *Romiti* suit. Prior to the federal district court's decision, the death of one downstate judge and resignation of another (the latter occurring after oral argument) freed two seats for transfer to Cook County in the 1966 elections. Because Cook was to be entitled to three resident supreme court judges when the 1962 judicial article amendment was fully implemented, this left in issue only the seat of Justice Walter V. Schaefer. He had been elected in 1961 in the old supreme court district which Cook County, with 85 percent of the population, shared with four smaller counties, including Lake County. Under the incumbent-protection provisions of the 1962 amendment, Justice Schaefer, a resident of Lake County, would not stand for re-election until 1970, would stand unopposed, and still would not have to be a resident of Cook County.

Under the changed circumstances the court felt that only one central issue remained—the residence of Justice Schaefer. There being no proof of injury or discrimination, the court could find no violation of the federal

43. See detailed appendix in Brief of Defendant William J. Scott (State Treasurer), *Romiti v. Kerner, supra* note 40.
44. *Id.* at 9.

equal protection clause in allowing a judge to stand for election in a district in which he was not a resident. The court noted too, that the dominant bloc of votes in Justice Schaefer's election in 1961 had come from Cook County. Even granting the principle of *Lucas* v. *Colorado General Assembly* (Chapter XI) that a popular referendum provides no shield for legislative malapportionment, the Illinois judicial district plan ratified in 1962 was a step correcting much malapportionment, and it did not indefinitely postpone "full equality of voting rights for voters" [45] in the new Cook County district.

Thus the federal district court was able to dismiss the complaint in *Romiti* on narrow grounds, without reaching the broad constitutional questions raised by the plaintiffs. The judges did add the comment that they had "little doubt that, in a proper case, there is a valid distinction between applying the 'one man, one vote' rule in a legislative reapportionment case" and applying it "to the election of a state supreme court judiciary." [46] Significantly, the court did not simply dismiss the case under a broad rule that judicial election districts are wholly immune from "one man-one vote" attack. It examined the facts and found no meaningful inequity, in a manner similar to the United States Supreme Court's handling of the local apportionment issue in the Virginia Beach case, *Dusch* v. *Davis*.[47]

Under authority of the *Romiti* decision, and for lack of proof of special discrimination, the same court dismissed a companion suit filed by Negro entertainer Dick Gregory and Sherman H. Skolnick.[48] These plaintiffs had alleged debasement of the votes of Cook County Negroes and Jews on the ground that 83 percent and 95 percent respectively of the members of these two groups in Illinois were concentrated in underrepresented Cook County. Hence their complaint seemed oriented specially toward Justice Brennan's dictum in *Fortson* v. *Dorsey* warning against submergence of the voting strength of minorities in a districting system.

There have been only a handful of suits in other states attempting to invoke the "one man-one vote" doctrine in the judicial field. Of special significance is a 1964 Georgia suit, *Stokes* v. *Fortson*,[49] brought by some voters and the Republican nominee for solicitor general (prosecutor) in one of Georgia's several judicial circuits. Each circuit contains a superior court with a resident judge and solicitor who are nominated in the circuit, but elected at-large in the state. The case thus raised the question of potential repression of Negro and Republican judicial candidates for lower

45. Romiti v. Kerner, *supra* note 40, at 45.
46. *Id.* at 46.
47. 387 U.S. 112 (1967), discussed above.
48. Skolnick v. Kerner, 260 F. Supp. 316 (N.D. Ill. 1966).
49. 234 F. Supp. 575 (N.D. Ga. 1964).

court posts in the South by this device of statewide election rather than election confined to the area of the court's jurisdiction. Although the federal district court turned aside the challenge, it did admit that "the statewide electorate may override the choice of the circuit." [50]

Indeed, it was this possibility, by analogy, which had led this very same three-judge court a few months earlier to invalidate Fulton County's system of electing seven senators at-large in the county but from restricted residence districts (Chapter XVIII).[51] Without even mentioning the Fulton County senators case, the district court sustained Georgia's judicial election system on the ground that the "one man-one vote" doctrine for legislative and executive officials does not extend to the judiciary. It said:

> Manifestly, judges and prosecutors are not representatives in the same sense as are legislators or the executive. Their function is to administer the law, not to espouse the cause of a particular constituency.[52]

Subsequently this federal district court's decision in the Fulton County senators case was reversed by the United States Supreme Court, *Fortson* v. *Dorsey*,[53] on the ground that the senators really served the whole county, and no repression of particular groups had been shown (Chapter XVIII). The judicial election decision was not reviewed by the Supreme Court. Had it been reviewed the Court would have been faced squarely with the question of applicability of the "one man-one vote" doctrine to judicial elections. It could not have approved the at-large system on the same theory it applied to the Fulton County senators case because the judges— unlike the senators—were elected not to serve the entire at-large electorate, but only to serve in the area in which they resided and were nominated.[54]

Quite different from these judicial election cases are two cases concerned not so much with equal voter control of judges as with allocation of judicial manpower among populous and less populous districts. In *Romiti* plaintiffs wanted their proportionate share of influence, measured by the population of their district, in the selection of the bench of the highest state court. In *Stokes* plaintiffs wanted to have the local judge elected locally, rather than by the entire state electorate in which local voters might be an insignificant part. But in Ohio and New York cases, federal district courts were asked to rule that the equal protection clause of the Fourteenth Amendment requires distribution of judges on a per-capita basis. It so happened that the judges in each instance were elective, but citizen *service* by the judiciary rather than citizen *control* of the judiciary was at issue. Plain-

50. *Id.* at 577.
51. Dorsey v. Fortson, 228 F. Supp. 259 (N.D. Ga. 1964).
52. Stokes v. Fortson, *supra* note 49, at 577.
53. 379 U.S. 433 (1965).
54. Occasional special assignment elsewhere was permissible, however. *Id.* at 578.

tiffs in Ohio were not voters but litigants who alleged delay in hearing their personal injury suits; and New York plaintiffs were a mixture of lawyers and litigants.

In dismissing the Ohio suit as posing a political and not justiciable question the court said:

> Judges do not represent people, they serve people. They must, therefore, be conveniently located to those people whom they serve. Location then, is one of many significant factors which the legislature may properly consider when carrying out its constitutional mandate to create an effective judicial system.[55]

Similarly in dismissing the New York suit the court said:

> In contrast to legislative reapportionment, population is not necessarily the sole, or even the most relevant, criterion for determining the distribution of state judges. The volume and nature of litigation arising in various areas of the state bears no direct relationship to the population of those areas.[56]

Obviously such suits do not raise "one man-one vote" issues, however interesting they may be as suggesting an eventual outreach of equal protection to create a *constitutional* right of equal governmental service—a doctrine that would have interesting implications in the social welfare field and in poverty areas. (See Chapter VII for discussion of various facets of equal protection.)

Romiti and *Stokes*, perhaps, do raise some "one man-one vote" issues. The Georgia decision is especially unsatisfactory because it potentially denies to local voters control over their elective local circuit judge. And the dismissal of the *Romiti* case would hardly have been intellectually satisfying if the result had been to leave six-sevenths of the Illinois Supreme Court under the control of downstate voters numbering less than half of the population. The important focus for determining the outreach of the "one man-one vote" doctrine is not policy-making, because all officials— including judges obviously—share in policy-making. Rather, at some point we get down to appearances and a concept of per se invalidity. If *any set* of offices, including judicial offices, is made elective, thus creating expectations of direct citizen control over the officers, how can it be just to give some voters more influence than others by the device of malapportionment?

---

55. Buchanan v. Rhodes, 249 F. Supp. 860, 865 (N.D. Ohio 1966).
56. New York State Association of Trial Lawyers v. Rockefeller, 267 F. Supp. 148, 153–54 (S.D. N.Y. 1967).

C. "One Man-One Vote" and the Electoral College System of Presidential Elections

The single-constituency election is the original home and perhaps the one true home of "one man-one vote"—the Supreme Court having first announced this principle in *Gray* v. *Sanders*,[57] which freed the Georgia governorship and other statewide offices from the county-unit system of vote weighting. With a single constituency and one office to be filled, any system of vote weighting by unit vote or electoral vote device raises the possibility of denying the prize of office to the person most preferred on a simple head-count plurality basis. It was natural, therefore, for an attempt to be made to litigate under "one man-one vote" precepts the constitutionality of the electoral college system of electing our President and Vice President.

The presidential election is a single-constituency election; and the states with their allocated electoral vote are a direct analogue to the Georgia counties with their allocated unit vote. In each instance (prior to the invalidation of Georgia's county-unit system) the election of President or governor would be determined not by the over-all popular plurality, but by a majority of the electoral or unit vote. Also, under each plan the electoral or unit vote is not allocated to the states or counties strictly in accord with their relative population (Chapter VIII). In the electoral college system of indirect election of the President, each state has as many electoral votes as it has seats in both houses of Congress. Thus Alaska (226,167 population) with one Representative and two Senators has three electoral votes, while New York (16,782,304 population) with 41 Representatives and two Senators has 43 electoral votes—thus yielding a disparity in voter weight between these two states of 5 to 1. Disparities in voter weight are less under the electoral college system than under the invalidated Georgia county-unit system (99 to 1 in the latter). Nevertheless the constitutional requirement of allocating two Senators and at least one Representative to each state (and hence three electoral votes) regardless of population, does give exaggerated influence to voters in smaller states under the conventional arithmetic equality measures of *Reynolds* v. *Sims*. Because nonpopulation allocation of electoral votes to states is fixed in the Constitution itself, radical change can be accomplished only by constitutional amendment.

There is, however, a second crucial distorting feature of our present elec-
57. 372 U.S. 368 (1963).

toral college system which is not fixed in the Constitution, namely the state-controlled practice of using a "general ticket system" for determining allocation of the electoral vote inside each state.[58] Under this system which states have used almost universally since the early part of the last century,[59] a presidential candidate who wins a plurality of the popular vote captures the entire electoral vote of that state.

It is primarily this intrastate winner-take-all system which regularly causes great disparities between a presidential candidate's percentage of the nationwide popular vote and his percentage of the total electoral college vote. It also raises the spectre of electing a minority President, and actually did have this result in 1888 when Benjamin Harrison's 48 percent of the popular vote yielded 58 percent of the electoral vote against his opponent, Grover Cleveland.[60] Even when a minority presidency is avoided, the non-population allocation of the electoral vote, as greatly exaggerated by the "general ticket" or winner-take-all system, causes a great disparity between a candidate's percentage of the nationwide popular vote and his percentage of the electoral college vote. In 1960 Kennedy, with 49.71 percent of the popular vote to Nixon's 49.55 percent, captured 303 electoral votes to Nixon's 219 (Senator Harry F. Byrd captured 15).[61] Other recent examples of popular vote and electoral vote disparity are: Johnson, 1964, 61 percent of the popular vote, 90 percent of the electoral vote; Eisenhower, 1956, 57.4 percent of the popular vote, 86 percent of the electoral vote;

58. See Neal R. Peirce, *The People's President: The Electoral College in American History and the Direct Vote Alternative* (New York: Simon & Schuster, 1968).
See also, Robert L. Tienken, "Proposals to Reform Our Electoral System" (Library of Congress Legislative Reference Service, American Law Division, 1966); "The Electoral College: Operation and Effect of Proposed Amendments to the Constitution of the United States" (Memorandum prepared by the staff of the Subcommittee on Constitutional Amendments of the Committee on the Judiciary of the United States Senate, 87th Congress, 1st Sess., 1961).
59. See my "Electoral College Procedure," 3 *Western Pol. Sci. Quart.* 214 (1950).
60. Brief of Petitioner, p. 26, Delaware v. New York, *petition denied*, 385 U.S. 895 (1966). The elections of 1824 and 1876 are not certain examples of electing minority Presidents. In the former, there was no effective two-party system; in the latter there was evidence of voting fraud on both sides.
61. Brief of Petitioner, *supra* note 60, at 23. The eleven-man Democratic elector slate of Alabama consisted of six unpledged electors who finally voted for Senator Harry F. Byrd (D. Va.) and five loyalist electors for Kennedy. Since the votes cannot be separated in counting, the highest popular vote for an unpledged elector would be placed under the "Byrd" column and the highest vote for a pledged elector would be placed under the "Kennedy" column. Under this method of counting, however, votes for the Democratic elector slate are actually counted twice with resultant inflation of both the Kennedy and unpledged popular vote totals. An alternative is to divide the highest Democratic elector vote, 5/11 to Kennedy and 6/11 unpledged. If that is done, Kennedy's Alabama total drops to 147,295 and he trails Nixon in the national popular count.

Eisenhower, 1952, 55.1 percent of the popular vote, 83 percent of the electoral vote.

Views do vary on what persons or groups are helped or hurt by the electoral college system. Arithmetically, the system obviously favors the smaller states.[62] Practically, however, the system often has been said to favor the larger states, and more specifically the balance of power minorities within the larger states whose vote may determine the allocation of the entire electoral vote of the state. This large-state bias also has been said to extend to candidate selection and campaign emphasis.[63]

In 1966 a suit was filed directly in the Supreme Court, *Delaware v. New York et al.,*[64] asking that the "one man-one vote" principle be extended to presidential elections. Twelve other states joined Delaware as plaintiffs after the suit was filed—Arkansas, Florida, Iowa, Kansas, Kentucky, Oklahoma, North Dakota, Pennsylvania, South Dakota, Utah, West Virginia, and Wyoming—thus making it a suit by 13 states against 37 states (plus the District of Columbia, which received electoral votes in 1961 under the Twenty-third Amendment). The suit of course could not reach the constitutionally fixed nonpopulation allocation of the electoral vote. The attack centered rather on the state-controlled "general ticket system" of allocating the total electoral vote of a state to the candidate with a mere plurality in the popular vote.

Such a suit would have been unthinkable a few years ago. But the disposition of the Court to enter the "political thicket" of legislative apportionment in *Baker v. Carr* and its concern for equal voter weight in invalidating the Georgia county-unit system in 1963, seemed to make plausible a suit against the "general ticket" aspect of the electoral college.[65] The redress contemplated by Delaware took three forms. As an interim measure the Court might require a division of the electoral vote inside each state in proportion to the popular vote of each state. Second, the Court could re-

62. For more sophisticated mathematical analyses see Irwin Mann and L. S. Shapley, "Values of Large Games, v. 1: Evaluating the Electoral College Exactly," Rand Corporation memorandum, RM–3158 P R (1962); for an alternative treatment, see John F. Banzhaf, "One Man, 3.312 Votes: A Mathematical Analysis of the Electoral College," *Villanova L. Rev.* (Spring, 1968).

63. From 1868 to 1964, 29 states had neither a presidential nor a vice presidential candidate, whereas New York had 24, Indiana 12, and Illinois and Ohio 10 each. Brief, *supra* note 59, at 33–36.

64. 385 U.S. 895 (1966). The present writer was one of the draftsmen of the 97-page Complaint and Brief as Special Counsel to Attorney General David P. Buckson of Delaware, along with James C. Kirby, Jr., Professor of Law at Northwestern University Law School, and the Washington, D.C., law firm of Gosnell, Durkin & McGrath.

65. See Neal R. Peirce, "The Electoral College Goes to Court," 35 *The Reporter* 34 (1966).

quire election of presidential electors in districts, e.g., congressional districts, as a way of preventing an automatic winner-take-all result in each state. Neither of these remedies would have touched the nonpopulation allocation of the electoral vote. But each could have moderated the gross disparities in national popular vote and electoral vote totals, because of the well-known tendency of any district system to exaggerate the influence of the dominant party. As a third remedy the Court could have invalidated the general ticket system and then, as in state legislative apportionment cases, deferred any final decree in order to give Congress time to consider an appropriate change by constitutional amendment.

Although plaintiffs' theory of standing and justiciability required careful articulation,[66] the more serious problem was to identify a substantive federal constitutional right which was being violated by state use of the general ticket system. Two theories of federal substantive right were articulated. One was directed to the general ticket system's distorted intrastate allocation of the electoral vote, i.e., the winner-take-all feature. This feature discriminates against minority voters (those casting votes for the losing candidate) by treating their votes as though they have been cast for the winning candidate. In other words, allocating all of a state's electoral votes to the candidate receiving a bare 51 percent of the popular vote achieves the same result in national electoral vote totals as though the candidate had captured 100 percent of the popular vote of that state. Hence, in the several states dominated by one political party, minority party voters' activity at the polls is at best a moral protest, rather than a meaningful discharge of a constitutional privilege equally held and equally exercised by all democratic citizens.

The second theory, which really amounted to putting the first theory in national perspective, was that the general ticket system arbitrarily makes state lines Chinese walls, to the detriment of some partisans but not others. By conventional equal protection clause precepts, it is argued, state use of the general ticket system discriminates between *two classes* within the jurisdiction of the state: voters for the presidential candidate who musters a *plurality* in the state, and voters for the *losing* candidate or candidates. Votes of the latter group are prevented totally from having any national impact, i.e., from being joined at least indirectly with votes of fellow partisans in other states (which would be the case under either a proportional system or a subdistrict system). Votes of the former group by contrast are magnified in national impact by the state unit vote or "manufactured unanimity" rule. They also are effectively joined with votes of fellow partisans

66. The theory of standing was that Delaware as parens patriae was serving as a collective spokesman for aggrieved voters in Delaware, as well as for its own interest, although the latter was somewhat tenuous.

in other states where the party has managed to muster a plurality, no matter how narrow. Yet this diametrically opposite treatment of votes of "plurality" candidate voters in a state, and votes of "losing candidate" voters in that state, occurs in a situation where *all* are voting with reference to the *single national purpose of filling one office.*

In terms of constitutional foundation, these arguments were based not only on the restraints imposed on states by the Fourteenth Amendment but also on general equity principles which the Court may use in an original jurisdiction suit between states, and on the Fifth Amendment. The latter nominally only applies to the federal government, but it was asserted that states are acting quasi-federally in regard to the electoral college, just as they are under the federal constitutional amendment process.[67] However, because the Supreme Court's original jurisdiction, contrary to popular impression, is wholly discretionary, the Court in a brief order without reasons or citation of precedents, refused to entertain the suit.[68]

Despite the Court's refusal to hear the suit, our present system of electing a President and Vice President is completely insupportable under current "one man-one vote" theory. Distortions caused by nonpopulation allocation of electoral votes, and especially by the winner-take-all effect of the general ticket system inside each state, are serious. Indeed, they are more egregious than the distortions in many of our now-invalidated legislative malapportionments. Likewise, a district system of electing presidential electors would be insupportable under "one man-one vote" theory. Under our present system there are 51 state units intermediate between voter and final count, thus distorting the effect of his vote. Under the district system, if each presidential elector were assigned to a district, there would be 538 intermediate units causing distortion.

The proportional system under which the electoral vote in each state would be divided among the presidential candidates in proportion to their percentage of the popular vote in that state would come closest to minimizing distortion, while retaining the basic state unit allocation of the electoral vote. However, such a proportional system would tend to help the Democratic party and hurt the Republican party, according to a study

67. Hawke v. Smith, 253 U.S. 221 (1920); National Prohibition Cases, 253 U.S. 250, 386 (1920).
68. Of thirteen original jurisdiction suits disposed of by the Court from 1960 to October 1966, eight were disposed of in the following manner: "Motion for leave to file bill of complaint denied."
That part of the argument in the brief directed to the general ticket system's repression of "minority voters" inside a state perhaps could have been aired in a lower court suit inside a given state, thus easing problems of standing and justiciability. However, effective relief would need to be national and uniform in order to put all voters on an equal plane vis-à-vis the presidency. See also Penton v. Humphrey, 264 F. Supp. 250 (S.D. Miss. 1967).

made a few years ago.[69] The reason is to be found in the long shadow still cast by the Civil War, which as a matter of political pathology has produced for the Democratic party the so-called "Solid South." Assuming a fairly competitive party system outside the South, but continued Democratic party dominance in the South, a proportional system of intrastate division of the electoral vote could mean that the non-Southern electoral vote would be divided fairly evenly between the two national parties, allowing Democratic electoral votes in the South to determine the outcome of the presidential election.

An even more undemocratic feature of the electoral college system is the provision that in the event no candidate receives a majority of electoral votes the power of selecting the President passes to the House of Representatives, with each state delegation casting a single vote. Thus, because Alaskan voters and New York voters each control only one vote for President at this stage, the former would exert 74.2 times the voting power of the latter (ratio of the two states' census population). The House has not exercised this function since 1800. But third party presidential candidacies, such as that of former Alabama Governor George C. Wallace in 1968, always raise this prospect.

Why, however, should we retain any aspect of our electoral college system of electing our President and Vice President? Constitutions are not immutable, and we have seen in the last half-dozen years a virtual revolution in the composition of districts both for state legislatures and the House of Representatives. In keeping with the new "one man-one vote" spirit, why should we not amend our Constitution and convert to a system of direct popular election for the presidency? A major overhaul probably would occur promptly—and probably in the direction of a direct popular vote system—*if* the system again should operate to elect a minority President. Further, the likelihood of another minority President may not be remote, even without third-party challengers. In the past we have had a two-party system, but in effect, many one-party states. Insofar as there now is a trend toward two-party operation in some previous one-party states, elections can be expected to be closer than in the past with a corresponding greater danger that the electoral college will "elect" a minority President even in a two-candidate election.

Two major problems stand in the way of easy conversion to a direct national election system for the presidency. One is the problem of uniformity

69. Ruth C. Silva, "The Lodge-Gossett Resolution: A Critical Analysis," 44 *Am. Pol. Sci. Rev.* 86, 92 (1950); and see her statement in *Hearings on Nomination and Election of President and Vice President,* 334–39, Senate Judiciary Subcommittee, 84th Cong., 1st Sess. (1955).

of voting qualifications among the states; the second is the problem of local corruption in vote counting.[70] If we adopted direct popular voting and continued to allow the states to fix voting qualifications and to conduct elections, the chance factor of differing voter qualifications and dishonest vote counting could determine the outcome of a close presidential contest. Differing qualifications and local corruption can have some impact now, state by state. But under direct popular voting the impact would be immediate, direct, and national. Could we expect the people to remain unconcerned if a bloc of 16-21-year-old voters in one or two states provided the winning margin for the presidency; or if the winning margin were provided by a bloc of 100,000 votes in one or two large boss-run cities?

The essence of the direct popular vote idea for the presidency is that we are dealing with a *national* election for a single *national* office. Each voter has a right to expect that he will stand in the exact same relation to this national office as any other voter. Such an equal and fair voter status can be achieved only if there are uniform standards of voter qualification, uniformly administered, and a nationally safeguarded ballot with a nationally safeguarded fair count. In short, a natural next step in our developing "one man-one vote" theory would be a constitutional amendment setting up a uniform and nationally policed system for presidential elections.

D. "One Man-One Vote" in Frontierland and Shadowland

Beyond these areas of local government, judicial election districts, and the presidency, there is a further range of problems which have begun to receive attention but have not received authoritative treatment in the Supreme Court.

Party Committees. Courts have been loath to extend the "one man-one vote" doctrine to the election of a county or state political party committee and chairman. In the typical situation committeemen are elected in districts of unequal population, and the committeemen in turn elect the chairman. Plaintiffs have failed to get a court order requiring election of

---

70. Failure to require such uniform qualifications is the primary defect in the otherwise commendable "direct popular vote" proposal of the American Bar Association, *Electing the President: A Report of the Commission on Electoral College Reform* (1967), endorsed by the House of Delegates at the mid-winter meeting, February 1967.

the county chairman by popular vote of all registered party voters;[71] and they have failed in an attack on election of the state chairman by state committeemen apportioned on a county equality basis.[72] Even if there were to be a "party committee reapportionment," should the apportionment base be registered party membership, as was apparently contemplated in attempted suits in New York[73] and New Jersey,[74] or total population as in Rhode Island's system[75] of keying state party committee membership to the population-based state legislative districts?

In denying relief courts have been only mildly troubled by the fact that malapportioned party organizations frequently have power to select party nominees for public office in event of death or withdrawal of the candidates nominated in "one man-one vote" primaries. In New Jersey the state party chairmen have power also to appoint half of the bipartisan reapportionment commission, a tie breaker being judicially appointed (Chapter XIII). In contrast to this general hands-off attitude regarding party chairmen and committees—which one court buttressed by reference to the Supreme Court's hesitancy in applying "one man-one vote" to local government[76] —an Alabama federal district court has scrutinized racial discrimination in party committee structure.[77]

State Constitutional Conventions. Because state constitutional conventions only propose texts for ratification and do not decide policy issues, a court in Tennessee shortly after *Baker* v. *Carr* refused to bar a constitutional convention even though it would be malapportioned, like the legislature.[78] The ruling was in keeping with the tendency in the period immediately following the reapportionment rulings, to accord power to malapportioned bodies to legislate in all fields, including reapportionment, and even to propose constitutional amendments (see extensive discussion in Chapter XVI). Necessity may have dictated leniency in the interim period of adjusting to "one man-one vote," but its continuance is highly questionable. Because voters only can ratify or defeat constitutional change in the form proposed by state conventions or legislatures, the "proposers" rather

71. Lynch v. Torquato, 228 F. Supp. 268 (W.D. Pa. 1964), *affirmed,* 343 F. 2d 370 (3d Cir. 1965).
72. Rogers v. State Committee of the Republican Party, 96 N.J. Super. 265 (Superior Court N.J. 1967).
73. Davis v. Sullivan, 261 N.Y.S.2d 697, 47 Misc.2d 60 (1965).
74. Rogers, *supra* note 72.
75. Gallant v. LaFrance, 222 A.2d 567 (1966).
76. Rogers, *supra* note 72, at 855–56.
77. Smith v. Paris, 257 F. Supp. 901 (M.D. Ala. 1966), discussed in Chapter XVIII.
 Do party "loyalty oaths" extracted as a condition of allowing a candidate to run under a party label raise any "one man-one vote" questions? Indeed, do loyalty oaths support the "representation" facet of the "one man-one vote" concept? See Canton v. Todman, 367 F.2d 1005 (3d Cir. 1966).
78. West v. Carr, 212 Tenn. 367, 370 S.W.2d 469 (6th Cir. 1963).

than the "ratifiers" possess significant—perhaps dominant—powers to shape constitutional revision.[79]

"One Man-One Vote" Miscellany. Penumbral areas where plaintiffs may attempt to support their public policy goals by appeal to "one man-one vote" precepts extend potentially to all systems of direct or indirect election, to quasi-governmental bodies where a "representation" function is present, and even to areas where "services" arguably should be proportioned to population in the areas served. A plea of a constitutional right to equal—i.e., population-apportioned—services of an elective judiciary has made little headway in suits in Ohio and New York, as already noted.[80]

Closer to the line and somewhat analogous to the party committee cases is a New Jersey decision concerning a system of equal unit representation rather than population representation of district boards of education in a state federation of education set up by statute.[81] A primary function of the federation was lobbying in the legislature for education interests, and it was empowered to defray costs by levying assessments on the district boards. Although a trade union suit was dismissed for lack of standing—the union being upset concerning certain lobbying positions of the federation—the "representation" function being performed and the direct relation to the public decision-making process do seem to raise interests closely allied to the "one man-one vote" concept.

Of more general interest is a New York decision upholding the fairly common policy of using a more restricted electorate for school district elections than for general elections. To vote a person had to show: (a) parenthood (or guardianship) of a child in a public school; or (b) ownership or lease of real property (or status as a spouse of such a person—a mere lodger or boarder being excluded). The unsuccessful plaintiff was an unmarried adult residing with his rent-paying parents. Characterizing the suit as "frivolous" the court said the plaintiff could not complain of taxation without representation because he owned no property in the district; nor could he complain regarding educational policy because he had no children.[82] But is interest in the educational policy of a community confined to parents? And is not local education supported in part by grants from general state funds to which all contribute through some species of taxation?

---

79. See 68 W. Va. L. Rev. 314 (1966). See also Blount v. Board of Supervisors of Elections, 247 Md. 342, 230 A.2d 639 (1967).

80. See notes 55–56 *supra.* A Maine court has ordered that jury panels not only be apportioned among various towns on a population basis, but represent a cross-section of occupational and other groupings. Such a policy, however, rests on jury system policies, not voting system policies.

81. New Jersey State AFL-CIO v. State Federation of District Boards of Education, 93 N.J.Super. 31, 224 A.2d 519 (Superior Court, 1966).

82. Kramer v. Union Free School District, 259 F. Supp. 164 (E.D. N.Y. 1966).

E. Policy Impact of Malapportionment and Reapportionment

1. PUBLIC POLICY AND MALAPPORTIONMENT: ORTHODOX VIEW AND CAVEATS

Seeing in *Baker* v. *Carr* the "death knell of minority state government," [83] many commentators predicted that reapportionment would lead to a great resurgence of state government, a heightened concern for urban problems at state capitals, and less need for direct federal-local relations to solve urban problems. These thoughts have been common in social science and popular literature for decades, and were highlighted in the 1955 report of the Kestnbaum Commission on intergovernmental relations.[84] They are repeated in a report on apportionment issued by the United States Advisory Commission on Intergovernmental Relations.[85]

This conventional wisdom about malapportionment may be especially pertinent regarding the South. In 1948 the typical Southern legislature was described as "chiefly a body of Democratic, small-town or rural white men, a majority of whom represent a minority of the white population of the state." [86] Indeed, the South may be the true home of pre-*Baker* v. *Carr* malapportionment, several observers seeing an apparent correlation between district population disparities and government unresponsive to current needs.[87] A belated development of the middle class, and delayed industrialism and urbanism may have been contributing factors.

Outside the South, however, the popular impression about the effects of malapportionment encounters difficulties. New York and California have

83. Address by Charles S. Rhyne, past president of the American Bar Association, general counsel of the National Institute of Municipal Law Officers, and one of the counsel in *Baker* v. *Carr*, delivered before the New York University Alumni Association a few months after *Baker*.
84. Commission on Intergovernmental Relations (Kestnbaum Commission), *Report to the President* (1955). See also Gordon E. Baker, *Rural Versus Urban Political Power* (New York: Random House, 1955).
85. U.S. Advisory Commission on Intergovernmental Relations, *Apportionment of State Legislatures* (1962).
86. H. C. Nixon, "The Southern Legislature and Legislation" 10 *J. of Pol.* 410, 412 (1948).
87. William C. Havard and Loren P. Beth, *The Politics of Mis-Representation* (Baton Rouge: Louisiana State University Press, 1962). See also Malcolm E. Jewell, *Legislative Representation in the Contemporary South* (Durham: Duke University Press, 1967); Allen P. Sindler, ed., *Change in the Contemporary South* (Durham: Duke University Press, 1963).

been widely honored for keeping government current with developing needs, with economic growth, and with technological change. Yet both were malapportioned prior to the 1964 *Reapportionment Decisions*. Indeed, with the exception of Connecticut and Vermont, the California senate was the single most malapportioned body in the nation. By contrast, perennially well-apportioned Massachusetts frequently has been portrayed in recent times as one of the most corrupt states in the nation.[88]

Few empirical studies existed prior to the *Reapportionment Decisions*, but there were a handful of reports which seemed to question the popular idea that state deficiencies regarding social legislation and urban problems were caused primarily, or even significantly, by the single factor of malapportionment. Separate studies of urban-rural conflict in the Illinois and Missouri legislatures conducted by Professors George D. Young and David R. Derge indicated that "the city's bitterest opponents in the legislature are political enemies from within its own walls, and those camped in the adjoining suburban areas." The research supported these findings: [89]

1. Nonmetropolitan legislators seldom vote together with high cohesion against metropolitan legislators.
2. Metropolitan legislators usually do not vote together with high cohesion.
3. Metropolitan legislators are usually on the prevailing side when they do vote together with high cohesion.

Tangentially relevant also are some reports of the United States Advisory Commission on Intergovernmental Relations. These reports suggest that voter apathy and tax fears have been primary causes of unprogressive government. Even under reapportionment, continued reliance upon federal programs and funds may seem to be the path of political wisdom for state and local politicians; indeed, reports on state and local government finances reveal an increasingly heavy reliance on federal funds.[90] One study, for example, surveys the relatively dismal record of attempts in the period 1950–1961 to achieve city-county consolidation or other major governmental integration in eighteen metropolitan areas. Ten of the eighteen plans failed to pass the popular referendum hurdle, even though the vote was

88. Edward R. F. Sheehan, "Brooke of Massachusetts," 228 *Harper's* 41 (June 1964).
89. David R. Derge, "Metropolitan and Outstate Alignments in Illinois and Missouri Legislative Delegations," 52 *Am. Pol. Sci. Rev.* 1065 (1958), incorporating findings of George D. Young, "The 1958 Special Session of the Missouri General Assembly," Missouri Political Science Association Newsletter, No. 3 (1958).
90. State and local government funds received from the federal government increased from slightly under $1 billion in 1942 to $7 billion in 1960, and jumped to $13 billion in 1966. Bureau of the Census, *Statistical Abstract of the United States* 423 (1967).

not statewide but was confined to the metropolitan area.[91] Another common idea seriously questioned by the Advisory Commission study of "metro plan" defeats is that reorganization plans carry in urban areas but fail to get a concurrent majority—where that is also required—in the outer reaches of the proposed new district.[92]

Population-Weighted Recomputation of Legislative Votes. A handful of legislative roll call vote studies also suggests the need for caution in attributing all sins of past unprogressive government to malapportionment and maldistricting, and in expecting major change in this regard under reapportionment. On the eve of *Wesberry v. Sanders* [93] which applied the "one man-one vote" principle to the lower house of Congress, one study weighted Congressmen's votes on four issues by the population of their districts, and recomputed the results. Recomputation rather surprisingly suggested that the "liberals" benefited from the then-existing congressional maldistricting.[94] A more detailed study weighted, by district population, 267 roll call votes in the 87th and 88th Congresses (1961–1965) on which Presidents Kennedy and Johnson took a position. Under the weighting scheme Administration support declined in 196 instances, increased in 71 instances. In nine instances weighting would have changed the outcome—once in favor of the Administration's position and eight times against it.[95] A study of twenty-two roll call votes in two sessions of the unreapportioned Texas legislature, using this same technique of recomputing legislators' votes according to the population of their districts, indicates that the outcome would have differed on only one measure.[96] Studies of this sort necessarily ignore the differences in nominations, campaigns, and elections that might have resulted from reapportionment or redistricting, but are one clue to the relation between apportionment and political behavior. Unfortunately, similar studies do not exist for all states, so that hypotheses concerning re-

91. U.S. Advisory Commission on Intergovernmental Relations, *Factors Affecting Voter Reactions to Governmental Reorganization in Metro-Areas* 21 (1962); see especially comments on St. Louis.
92. *Id.* at 27.
93. 376 U.S. 1 (1964).
94. Andrew Hacker, *Congressional Districting* 97 (Washington: Brookings Institution, 1963). Hacker analyzes four roll call votes of the 87th Congress, each proposal having vigorous Administration support. The Administration lost three of the four. After weighting the votes, it still would have lost the three but by greater margins, and would also have lost the fourth (the successful Administration attempt to expand the membership of the powerful House Rules Committee).
95. Letter to author from Professor Joel Margolis, University of Wisconsin, May 6, 1967. Unlike Hacker, Margolis included in his tallies only the votes on Congressmen who actually voted "yea" or "nay" on a given piece of legislation.
96. Clarice J. McDonald, "Legislative Malapportionment and Roll Call Voting in Texas: 1960–1963," M.A. Thesis, University of Texas, 1964.

gional variations in the impact of malapportionment cannot be empirically verified.

2. THE NEW EMPIRICISM: WHAT CONNECTION BETWEEN APPORTIONMENT AND PUBLIC POLICY?

A very recent series of political science findings—most published since the 1964 *Reapportionment Decisions*—has now virtually exploded our conventional notions about malapportionment and bad government. Several researchers set out to ascertain, on a careful statistical basis, the answer to a question Duane Lockard asked in 1963: "Do states with fair apportionment respond to urban appeals more readily?" [97]

All used similar techniques of selecting an interstate measure of malapportionment and of then making correlations for each state on a number of variables associated with legislative output, with environment, and with structural features such as party competitiveness and divided party control between governors and legislatures. Legislative output variables of course cover the full range of legislative activity, but the principal ones selected related to levels of spending for welfare and education, to taxation, to state aid for cities, and to highway policy. Environmental variables considered included urbanization, industrialization, income, educational level of citizenry. Malapportionment indices used varied, but all related exclusively to raw district population data. They are the Schubert-Press scale (which however does arbitrarily weigh the state senate at 1.5), the David-Eisenberg vote value of urban counties, the electoral percentage (Chapter XIX, Sec. G).

The recurring theme in the findings was that state differences in wealth and urbanization and their associated factors, rather than malapportionment, were statistically associated with state policy differences. Thomas R. Dye's summary of his more than 90 measures of policy in the fields of education, welfare, highways, taxation, and regulation of public morality is typical:

> On the whole, the policy choices of malapportioned legislatures are not noticeably different from the policy choices of well apportioned legislatures. Most of the policy differences which do occur turn out to be a product of socio-economic differences among the states rather than

97. Duane Lockard, *The Politics of State and Local Government* 319 (New York: Macmillan, 1963). Similarly in 1963 I pointed out that the growing empirical research was still too much concerned with "the more gross and easily identified aspects of political behavior" and unfortunately cast little light on apportionment questions. See my "Apportionment Standards and Judicial Power," 38 *Notre Dame L.* 367, 388 (1963).

a direct product of apportionment practices. Relationships which do appear between malapportionment and public policy are so slight that reapportionment is not likely to bring about any significant policy changes.[98]

Similarly Richard I. Hofferbert found "no significant relationship between apportionment and public policy." Examining some additional structural variables, he also found no significant relationship between "apportionment and divided control, divided control and public policy, or between the party in power and public policy." [99] A report by David Brady and Douglas Edmonds likewise conformed with Dye's statement and also produced an unexpected finding about interparty competition in malapportioned states: "Democrats controlled more state legislatures and generally held more seats in malapportioned states." [100] Even excluding the South in the period studied, 1957–1961, Republicans did better in well-apportioned states and progressively poorer in the medium to poorly apportioned states.

Problems of research design in this area are major, including not only the danger of oversimplification in loose use of ecological correlations, but also the need to bring many more institutional arrangements—e.g., districting, coattail effects of gubernatorial and presidential candidates—within the range of study. The survey research technique of depth interviewing, despite its expense, may help to penetrate the secrecy of the ballot and of legislators' motives; it is a needed next step in research into the realities of representation.

The question of party competition merits special attention. Despite the lack of significant correlations between past malapportionment and policy,

98. Thomas R. Dye, Politics, Economics, and the Public: Policy Outcomes in the American States 280 (Chicago: Rand McNally & Company, 1966). See also Herbert Jacob, "The Consequences of Malapportionment: A Note of Caution," 43 Social Forces 261 (1964); John P. White and Norman E. Thomas, "Urban and Rural Representation, 17 W. Pol. Quart. 724 (1964); Alvin D. Sokolow, "After Reapportionment: Numbers or Policies?" delivered at annual meeting, Western Political Science Association, March 24–26, 1966; John G. Grumm, "Structure and Policy in the Legislature," paper delivered at Southwestern Political Science Association annual meeting, Dallas, March 26, 1967.
99. Richard I. Hofferbert, "The Relation Between Public Policy and Some Structural and Environmental Variables in the American States," 60 Am. Pol. Sci. Rev. 73, 81 (1966).
A related area of research concerns the kinds of issues which produce partisan divisions in state legislatures. Professor Hugh L. LeBlanc reports that money and labor bills produce sharper partisan divisions than business regulation or health and welfare issues. Paper on "Voting in State Senates: Party and Constituency Factors," delivered at Southwestern Political Science Association annual meeting, Dallas, March 24, 1967.
100. David Brady and Douglas Edmonds, "The Effects of Malapportionment on Policy Output in the American States," 17, 10-A (mimeo), University of Iowa Laboratory for Political Research, 1966.

it would seem that one result of reapportionment should be to invigorate party competition—both intraparty and interparty— which should in turn have a policy effect and perhaps an over-all invigorating effect on state government. Regarding interparty competition, this hypothesis is not precluded by the Brady-Edmonds study, which simply identified party status in legislatures at three different periods under varying degrees of malapportionment among the states. Hofferbert does make the statement that he found no significant relationship between "apportionment and partisan competition," [101] but it turns out that he did not even look at legislatures. He devised a measure of interparty competitiveness for each state by utilizing contests for President, governor, and United States Senator. However interesting this measure may be as a comparative index of party competitiveness among the states, it tells nothing of the party makeup or personality makeup either of malapportioned or reapportioned legislatures. The hypothesis may still be supportable therefore that we should pay special attention to interparty competition under reapportionment, *and* to districting choices which may maximize prospects for party competition.

This *inter*party competition hypothesis does conflict with the finding of Dye in the 1954–1964 period. He includes this factor as well as the level of voter participation and malapportionment in the list of variables with which no significant policy correlation can be demonstrated. Also, Dye, unlike Hofferbert, does incorporate party legislative control in his index of interparty competition. He does not, however, attempt to isolate the additional variable of the choice between single-member and multimember districting, nor consider the possible major impact of reapportionment on *intra*party competition, access to office, and political style. Also, Dye did find that an increase in party competition results in an increase in voter turnout even when socioeconomic factors are controlled; and that urban underrepresentation is significantly related to party competition, voter participation, and partisanship.[102] Further, regarding the apparent lack of correlation of party competition with policy, Dye does introduce the caveat that quantification necessitates a simplification of complex processes subtly affecting a state's political system.

Even more supportable is the hypothesis that *intra*party competition will be enhanced by reapportionment and will have an invigorating effect. *Intra*party competition for the increased number of seats, particularly in the suburbs which lack a party boss tradition, could be especially important as a source of new blood, and this already has occurred in some states. Professors Steiner and Gove did find that one effect of the 1955 reapportionment of the Illinois legislature was to increase competition in the Republican

101. Hofferbert, *supra* note 99.
102. Dye, *supra* note 98, at 55, 71, 73, 259.

party in suburban Cook County.[103] None of the new empirical studies have dealt meaningfully with intraparty competition and reapportionment.

Under both the interparty and intraparty competition hypotheses, districting choices become crucial, particularly the basic choice between single and multimember districts, and also the role of such modified proportional devices as cumulative voting (Chapter XIX). Particularly to be feared may be multimember district monoliths in the large metropolitan areas which are the prime beneficiaries of reapportionment. On the basis of interviews in six states in the spring of 1967—Ohio, Tennessee, Colorado, Texas, Indiana, Kentucky—Professor Jewell[104] concluded that in addition to "broader representation of partisan and racial interests" single-member districting "enhances the prospects that metropolitan legislative delegations will be more heterogeneous in socioeconomic" terms as well.[105] There was some indication of greater candidate independence from party organizations and other endorsing groups, and closer ties to his constituency. Because questions of who will receive and who will pay will continue to agitate and divide metropolitan communities, single-member districting has an important representation function to perform, for as Jewell concluded, "districting increases the likelihood that these conflicts and differences will be fully represented in the legislative delegations."

Journalistic accounts of reapportionment impact vary, but some journalists have tended simply to transfer the "single cause" fallacy from malapportionment to reapportionment. A good example is a *Time* 1967 story which featured Maryland but neglected to mention that along with reapportionment Maryland unexpectedly had acquired a suburban, hard-hitting Republican governor as replacement for the last "old-South" governor from the state's Eastern Shore.[106] By contrast, Governor George Romney in Michigan, with the tightest reapportionment in the nation, nevertheless has had great difficulty with needed tax programs.[107]

An interpretive story in *The Reporter*, however, good enough for the anthologies, looked at Tennessee five years after *Baker* v. *Carr* and found a

103. Gilbert Y. Steiner and Samuel K. Gove, *Legislative Politics in Illinois* (Urbana: University of Illinois Press, 1960).
104. Malcolm E. Jewell, "The Effects of Legislative Districting in Metropolitan Counties," paper delivered at annual meeting of National Municipal League, Milwaukee, November 13, 1967.
105. Views differ on whether election of some Negro legislators under subdistricting adequately counterbalances the Negroes' loss of the claim on all urban legislators which they had under former at-large systems. But it seems that whites are doing the wondering, and Negroes prefer districting. See Bill Kovach, "Some Lessons of Reapportionment," *The Reporter*, September 21, 1967, p. 32.
106. *Time*, May 19, 1967, p. 25.
107. *New York Times*, April 2, 1967, p. 64, col. 1.

decidedly mixed bag. Tennessee lost its forty-two-year-old "monkey law" which prohibited teaching evolution, and it acquired daylight saving and a beginning on control of strip mining and air pollution. But a long list of central city measures failed, and a city spokesman declared: "With reapportionment . . . the new balance of power may rest with the present suburban area . . . leaving the core city politically impotent once again." [108]

At best reapportionment may create an "atmosphere for action," [109] but the product may not be predictable, a thought tentatively confirmed by preliminary reports from the National Municipal League's five year study of state legislatures and reapportionment.[110] In the South, where the research is considerably simpler than in the North, Republican gains and the stirrings of a two-party system are especially noteworthy. Suburban gains are obvious North and South but the effect is not uniform. In California the senate's "club ethic" survived a dramatic shift of seats to the Los Angeles area and had a distinct moderating effect on policy changes in the 1967 session—testifying to the strength of internal legislative cultures and their capacity to mould the new recruit. In Ohio there were signs of emergence of a new coalition: suburban-rural vs. the central city. But in New York, suburban gains did seem to provide the narrow edge for Democratic party control of one house, a new air in both parties, and some increase in state aid. Within a few years this new research may yield the kind of detailed knowledge of our representation system that was needed a decade ago on the eve of the reapportionment revolution.

108. Kovach, *supra* note 103, at 32, quoting Herbert J. Bingham, Executive Secretary, Tennessee Municipal League.

109. Allen Dines (Democratic Speaker of the House, Colorado), "A Reapportioned State," 55 *Nat. Civ. Rev.* 70, 74 (1966).

110. The comments that follow are derived from the following preliminary reports made by professors at the annual meeting of the National Municipal League, Milwaukee, November 14, 1967: Florida, Manning J. Dauer; California, Alvin D. Sokolow; Ohio, Myron Q. Hale; New York, Richard Lehne.

Note: While this book was in press the Supreme Court on April 1, 1968, decided *Avery v. Midland County, Texas* (pp. 554–57 above), specifically holding that the Fourteenth Amendment's "one man-one vote" principle applies to local government. Oral argument evidence of judicial unease in the local thicket (p. 551 above), was reflected in the Court's 5-3 vote, and in Justice Fortas's sharp dissent. He referred to "one man-one vote" as a "shibboleth" and a "hatchet," and showed great concern for the "representation" side of "equal representation" at the local level. But he did not suggest that what he called the "simplistic" aspects of the doctrine be modified for congressional or state legislative districts.

Justice White for the majority followed those lower courts which had already decided that the new Fourteenth Amendment principle necessarily applies locally too. He added two qualifications. One was that a "special purpose unit" could be exempted. The other was a reaffirmation of the Court's decision in *Dusch v. Davis* (p. 548 above), a decision which seems to rest on far looser arithmetic equality concepts than are being enforced against state legislatures. Pending further elaboration this rule emerges: "one man-one vote" applies locally too—more or less.

XXI

Conclusion

"In a really equal democracy, every . . . section would be represented, not disproportionately, but proportionately. A majority of the electors would always have a majority of the representatives, but a minority of the electors would always have a minority of the representatives. Man for man, they would always be as fully represented as the majority."
John Stuart Mill, *Considerations on Representative Government*

"The dictatorship of the majority . . . [is a] . . . bugaboo which haunts the books of political theorists but has never been found in the flesh in modern history."
Sydney Hook, *The Parodoxes of Freedom*

"We now propose the following rule: the process of governmental policy-making will be so constructed that every group of 'significant' size will have an opportunity to veto threatened deprivations of its freedom. . . .
"Thus the making of governmental decisions is not a majestic march of great majorities united upon certain matters of basic policy. It is the steady appeasement of relatively small groups."
Robert A. Dahl, *A Preface to Democratic Theory*

THE MATRIX OF THEORY

The ten themes delineated in Chapter I of this work, re-read in the light of all that has been portrayed, serve also to introduce the conclusion. We start with democratic theory and it points to the inevitability of "one man-one vote," or something signified by that slogan. The most appealing facet of the term is the right to vote, as a common right of citizenship, and courts and theorists are on most solid ground and most self-assured when dealing with it. To this is related the much more subtle concept of fair and effective representation.

Dominant in Chief Justice Earl Warren's opinions in the 1964 *Reapportionment Decisions* is the ideal that as nearly as possible all men should count as one politically, however different their other circumstances. Such an idea has been one of the vital components of American political development. The broadening of the franchise is one basic level in an egalitarian political ideal. A second level concerns voting rules regarding the filling of elective office once the breadth of the franchise has been settled. Practically, if not logically, the ideal becomes associated here with a simple plurality principle inside a given constituency, because of the impossibility of getting unanimity and the likelihood that control of the many by the few could result from more complicated choice systems. This is all that was involved in the 1963 Georgia county-unit case, *Gray* v. *Sanders.*

The third level of attempted application of egalitarianism to political institutions is the difficult one, i.e., its application to the election of a bicameral (or unicameral) representative assembly. Here a simple principle of egalitarianism becomes rather uninformative; it fuses, or should fuse, with corollary questions regarding the nature and problems of representative government. There is an inner tension—indeed, inconsistency—in the oft-mentioned "equal representation" phrase. An equal *basis* for representation, itself not an easy concept, is not the same thing as equal *representation.* Egalitarianism in this area denotes an approach to the quantum of an *individual act,* such as voting. Representation, i.e., effective political representation, denotes an *end result* in a system where not all can be winners but all want to be heard proportionately. Were it not for our inheritance of the district system for creating legislative assemblies, and some important corollary values associated with it, "one man-one vote" applied to representative government would seem to point to some form of proportional representation.

To put the matter another way, the basic premise of political equality, when applied to representative assemblies, must include a concept of political equity at the operative level of allocation of legislative seats as well as the more obvious concept of equal population. Neither at-large voting with its winner-take-all tendency nor single-member districting with its tendency to over-reward the dominant party automatically yields political equity. Numerically equal districts (or proportional in the case of multimember districts) do cure malapportionment of people; they may leave untouched, or affect in odd ways, the corollary problem of malrepresentation of parties and interests. "Black Power" demands for proportional legislative power now highlight the issue in some areas, but the problem is as old as apportionment.

The history of America, far more than the history of any Communist nation, has been to a surprising extent a long romance with an egalitarian ideal. Egalitarianism was bolstered considerably by the exigencies of frontier life. It is nourished also by our still-developing national moral sense and the exigencies of twentieth-century mass democracy.

REPRESENTATION REALITIES

We start then with theory, specifically with comfortable theories of political equality and consensual government. And, responsively, the first round of the reapportionment revolution proceeded on a population-equalization basis with little else considered (Chapters VIII-XIV, generally). With this beginning we are soon plunged into an expanding series of disputes bringing us ever nearer to the realities of representation and its effect on public policy (Chapters XVII-XX, generally).

First, there is the definition of the population equality standard itself. Once a 15 percent maximum deviation from average district seemed sufficiently stringent; the standard is now moving below 10 percent—but why not one percent, or less? Second, the tighter the arithmetic equality standard the greater the amount of redistricting which is required. Because this is really *constituency creation*, two lines of discretion emerge: structural options, such as the single-member—multimember dispute; ecological options, such as the homogeneity-heterogeneity dispute in district composition. Third, because no district lines are politically neutral, the inevitable policy choices raise issues of racial and political gerrymandering. Fourth, these issues in turn raise questions of the capacity or willingness of courts to illuminate and adjudicate the more refined representation issues once egregious population malapportionment has disappeared.

Fifth, an interesting "higher math" approach is emerging which suggests that all systems of mixed districting for one legislative house create disproportional citizen influence on actual legislative outcomes. Of equal interest is the return to first principles which this approach induces. If proportional citizen influence on possible legislative outcomes is the true "one man-one vote" goal—a concept of equalizing political opportunity—then what of such limiting devices as seniority rule and extraordinary majority requirements inside legislatures? What, indeed, of a logical "one man-one vote" outreach to all elective "policy" positions including not only local government boards but judges? Sixth, expanded political science empiricism now reports studies which find the link between particular apportionment systems and policy decisions rather tenuous. But these studies do open the way to a better understanding of the components of political party competition, and the possibility of enhancing both interparty and intraparty competition and vigor through districting devices.

Seventh, and especially important, a series of factors have combined to focus attention on *apportionment method*, e.g., a growing awareness of: the difficulty of articulating precise apportionment standards in advance, the unlikelihood of detailed court review of gerrymandering charges, and the grossly political character of every districting decision. Specifically, there has been renewed attention to the technique of a bipartisan commission as a safeguard against conscious or innocent gerrymandering, with tie breaker added to ensure accomplishment of the mission (summarized at end of Chapter XIV). This approach frankly recognizes apportionment-districting to be an institutional problem of government, and politically volatile, which should neither be left to partisan disposition by the sitting legislature and governor, nor farmed out to a supposedly neutral body of platonic "guardians."

Last, there is the diversion of the reapportionment amendment campaign to allow one state house, with popular approval, to depart somewhat from the strict equal population rule (Chapters XV, XVI). For all the hyperbole and extravagant showmanship on both sides of the issue, the campaign does pose meaningful issues both of representation theory and of constitutional revision: for example, can a continued federal plan for Congress be juxtaposed with a straight equal population rule for the states? Can the distinction rest forever on an accident of history, or is "one man-one vote" something less than a universal moral-political principle? In terms of constitutional change, the campaign tells much about our deep acceptance of far-reaching judicial articulation of basic norms, and our deep suspicion of formal textual change.

THE CHANGING POLITICAL MAP

Part of the shape of things to come is obvious, much is not. Some preliminary observations worth reassessing after the 1970 census may be the following. In the South the sharp increase in urban-suburban seats has brought a better-educated, more vigorous breed of politicians onto the scene, and in some states has planted the seeds of a two-party system. In the North sharp Republican losses in rural areas have been at least partially compensated by gains in the suburbs. The reapportionment upheaval, by throwing many incumbents together in revised districts has allowed both parties in some states to clean out some deadwood. In most populous states the primary beneficiaries of reapportionment, in terms of seats gained, have been suburbs not central cities. In many states reapportionment opens the way for a new brand of coalition politics among three groups, no one of which can dominate the legislature—central city, suburbs, rural-small town.

Because central cities tend to be Democratic strongholds, while rural-small town areas tend to retain a Republican allegiance, the effect of reapportionment in many states outside the South has been to shift the battle for state political control to the suburbs, where both major parties have a mixed record of successes and failures. Most significantly, such a shift reunites the traditional multiple components of ruling power—wealth, economic leadership, class position, education, professions, middle class. But problems of the core city—increasingly ghettoized—continue to grow. For these problems the reapportionment revolution provides no answers, although it does change the rules of the game of coalition politics which cities always have had to play.

IMPLICATIONS FOR A FEDERAL "COMMUNITY"

A much larger question, and one on which there is often more hopeful piety than wisdom, is the relation of reapportionment to state response to modern governmental needs, and to state roles in the modern American federal system. It may be that "there are not now large numbers of people who have their heart set on serving in the legislature." [1] And decades of greater federal vigor and resources have created in some a conditioned reflex like that of Mayor Charles P. Taft of Cincinnati who said: "I would rather do business with Washington." [2] But it also may be that we have not been clear enough in our thinking concerning state roles that are viable and ones that are not in modern federalism. The phrase "last chance for the states" [3] invites this question: What chance was there in the first place in the light of congressional commerce, revenue, and war powers, and inherent state jurisdictional limitations? Until some realistic appraisal is made of those state roles which may be both legitimate and viable in the latter part of the twentieth century, the states will be in a "can't win" position. They will either attempt too much and fail, or do a little, perhaps reasonably well, and still be criticized for not matching Washington.

Statehood and state legislatures, malapportioned or well apportioned, are grounded in American federalism. Both the meaning and implications of that hoary tradition, and the need to update it along with other parts of our oft-called "living Constitution" are seldom explored. However, the size, complexity, and diversity of the country still seems to support a fundamental American commitment to a rough regionalism. The desire for sub-units of authority and creativity in large heterogeneous countries seems to transcend political systems and is present to a surprising extent even in Russia and Communist China.

States still have vital roles in the provision of a meaningful framework for cross-county and interstate metropolitan matters. Federal aid to states

1. Samuel K. Gove, "Reapportionment and Illinois Public Policy," 23 Ill. Bus. Rev. 6, 7 (1966).
2. Roscoe C. Martin, The Cities and the Federal System, 167 (New York: Atherton Press, 1965).
3. Joseph D. Tydings, "The Last Chance for the States," Harper's 71 (March 1966).

and localities is an area of vast complexity where state enabling legislation is frequently necessary. Although a statewide perspective on use of federal funds has not always been forthcoming, such perspective and harmonization can come only from state legislatures or agencies under its direction. Politically, the regenerative force of the state as an independent proving ground for national office has always been a vital aspect of American federalism.

All of this is intimately related to the reapportionment revolution. Reapportionment *plus* creative districting arrangements going beyond a narrow focus on population equality alone offers an opportunity to bring within the state legislature—*and* local governing bodies and congressional delegations too—the full range of interests and spokesmen in all fields of modern government: service, regulation, metropolitan structure. And reapportionment touches in a vital way the structure of our mixed nation-state political party system by creating, under optimal districting arrangements, the basis for vigorous and effective interparty and intraparty competition. Reapportionment can be an integrative and invigorating force both within and between governmental levels. It may not be the answer to all of our governmental needs and frustrations because, as recent empirical research demonstrates, the forces that shape policy are complex and not uniquely related to governmental form. But it has never been tried. If we cannot manage all this through more effective institutions of representation we very likely cannot manage it, honorably, at all.

The many-faceted reapportionment revolution is thus an auspicious stage in an ongoing process of perfecting representative democracy. It has opened the way for an overdue modification of some questionable features of our political system and for a recrystallization on a sounder basis of values and institutions—if we move with care and maintain a focus on the intricacies of representation and effective party competition. There are no simple formulae for making power just and politics clean; or for assuring both majority rule and equitable minority representation. "One man-one vote" is the symbol really of an aspiration for fairness, for avoidance of complexity, for intelligibility in our representational process in a mass democracy—indeed, for a sense of meaningful membership in the *polis*. These are legitimate aspirations. The task of honoring them has only begun. The problem, and the challenge, before us is that of building a political system which so mixes unity and diversity, majoritarianism and consensus, interest representation and safeguards against balance of power tactics, as to yield a stable, fair, dynamic power to govern.

Appendix A

State Legislative Apportionments: 1962–67

EXPLANATORY NOTE:

The following appendix shows the apportionment position of the states as of January 1962 on the eve of *Baker* v. *Carr,* and at successive periods until a "final" reapportionment was achieved. Action through mid-summer 1967 is incorporated. In most instances the last figures shown indicate the apportionments the state will have until the 1970 census requires further revision. The accompanying text for each state capsules briefly the some-times intricate series of events on the path to at least partial compliance with the "one man-one vote" principle. The arithmetic measures used are those commonly stressed by the courts (see Ch. XVII).

In the right hand column the use of a 15 percent deviation figure as a basis for analysis and comparison is not meant to imply that all districts inside a 15 percent deviation are constitutional. This figure has been a common "guide" for some commentators and lower court judges but as noted in Chapter XVII a tighter population equality concept may be emerging.

Because there is no complete and authoritative reporting source on legislative apportionment there are occasional gaps in the data for some states and there may be errors or discrepancies in some figures reported. Needed computations have been performed primarily by my research assistant, Gordon W. Hatheway, Jr.

SOURCES:

The arithmetic data and accompanying comments are based on the author's files; Robert L. Tienkin, "Apportionment of State Legislatures" (Legislative Reference Service of Library of Congress, mimeo, January 10, 1965), successive revisions by Johnny H. Killian to April 4, 1966, and Killian files to mid-summer 1967; National Municipal League, "Compendium on Legislative Apportionment" (mimeo, January 1962 and special tabulations of October 15, 1963, and April 15, 1964); Chart as of January 1, 1965, with

589

session changes through August 12, 1965, prepared by Legislative Reference Service of Library of Congress and published in 111 *Cong. Rec.* 27195 (daily ed., October 22, 1965); National Municipal League, "Apportionment in the Nineteen Sixties" (mimeo 1967).

ALABAMA

Date		Population Variance Ratio	Electoral Percentage	Maximum Percent Deviation From Average		Districts (and/or Legislators) With More Than 15 Percent Deviation From Average (Where Data Available)	
						Districts	Legislators
1/62	(S)	41.2	25.1	+582	−83.4		
	(H)	15.6	25.7	+239	−78.7		
11/62	(S)	20.0	27.6	n.c.	−65.5		
	(H)	4.7	37.9	+164	−65.8		
11/65	(S)	1.46	47.8	28.7	−13.9	3 of 26	3 of 35 sen.
	(H)	1.63	47.7	+22.7	25.0	11 of 43	16 of 106 rep.

COMMENT: In June 1964 in the leading case of Reynolds v. Sims, 377 U.S. 533 (1964), the United States Supreme Court affirmed the federal district court's interim reapportionment plan which had been taken from parts of two plans proposed by the legislature in 1962. Sims v. Frink, 208 F. Supp. 431 (M.D. Ala. 1962). A November 1965 apportionment took effect with 1966 elections. For the senate the court approved a legislative plan. For the lower house the court made modifications. Sims v. Baggett, 247 F. Supp. 96 (M.D. Ala. 1965). Paid, nonvoting "legislative agents" were provided for counties without a resident legislator. The court and court-approved plans were to be in effect for the 1966 elections, and until the 1970 census if not overruled. (For further discussion, see Ch. IX.)

ALASKA

Date		Population Variance Ratio	Electoral Percentage	Maximum Percent Deviation From Average		Districts (and/or Legislators) With More Than 15 Percent Deviation From Average (Where Data Available)	
						Districts	Legislators
1/62	(S)	19.1	35.0	+408	−59.3		
	(H)	2.2	47.7	+36.4	−39.6		
9/65	(S)	1.56	50.9	+28.7	−12.6	3 of 11	3 of 20 sen.
	(H)	n.c.	n.c.	n.c.	n.c.	10 of 19	11 of 40 rep.

COMMENT: Following the *Reynolds* decision in the United States Supreme Court, the governor convened a gubernatorial advisory board and reapportioned the senate on September 3, 1965. (The house had been reapportioned by the governor in 1961 according to state constitutional provision.) The senate reapportionment was challenged on the ground that the state constitution only authorized the governor to reapportion the house. The senate apportionment in the constitution was area-based, permanent, and could be changed only by constitutional amendment. The state supreme court ruled that the governor had implicit authority to reapportion the senate. It reasoned that the state constitutional convention would have given the governor the power (as it had for the house) had it been able to foresee the decisions of the Supreme Court in *Baker* and *Reynolds*. Wade v. Nolan, 414 P. 2d 689 (1966). (For further discussion, see Ch. XIV.)

ARIZONA

Date		Population Variance Ratio	Electoral Percentage	Maximum Percent Deviation From Average		Districts (and/or Legislators) With More Than 15 Percent Deviation From Average (Where Data Available)	
						Districts	Legislators
1/62	(S)	85.8	12.8	+613	−91.7		
	(H)	5.3	46.0*	+87	−64.4		
1965	(S)	7.1	40.0	+31.0	−17.7		28 of 31 sen.
Spec.	(H)	n.c.	n.c.	n.c.	n.c.		
Session							
2/66	(S)	1.27	52.3	+6.5	−15.6	1 of 30	1 of 30 sen.
	(H)	1.27	50.6	+6.5	−15.6	1 of 30	2 of 60 rep.

* Estimated, because district boundaries drawn locally.

COMMENT: Court issued own plan for both houses after a 1965 special session had reapportioned senate but not house. Klahr v. Goddard, 250 F. Supp. 537 (D. Arizona 1966). Court also required the parties to submit subdistricting plans for two large multimember counties, Maricopa and Pima (Tucson and Phoenix), in senate and house. The court adopted the parties' agreed plan for Maricopa but when the parties disagreed on Pima the court adopted the attorney general's plan. 254 F. Supp. 997 (D.Ariz. 1966). District lines are drawn so that senate and house districts coincide, there being two representatives for each senator within a district, most senatorial districts being single-member, with a few multimember.

ARKANSAS

Date	Population Variance Ratio		Electoral Percentage	Maximum Percent Deviation From Average		Districts (and/or Legislators) With More Than 15 Percent Deviation From Average (Where Data Available)	
						Districts	Legislators
1/62	(S)	2.3	43.8	+59	−29.4		
	(H)	6.4	33.3	+78	−72.9		
7/65	(S)	1.26	49.2	+13.7	−9.5		0
	(H)	1.34	48.2	+13.9	−14.8		0

COMMENT: Federal district court held apportionment in both houses unconstitutional in Yancey v. Faubus, 238 F. Supp. 290 (D.C.E.D. Arkansas 1965). An apportionment board consisting of the governor, the secretary of state and the attorney general reapportioned the legislature. The court upheld this plan despite complaints about use of multimember districts. Yancey v. Faubus, 251 F. Supp. 998 (D.C.E.D. Arkansas 1965), aff'd. Crawford County Bar Association v. Faubus, Alexander v. Faubus, 383 U.S. 271 (1966). (For further discussion, see Ch. XIV.)

CALIFORNIA

Date	Population Variance Ratio		Electoral Percentage	Maximum Percent Deviation From Average		Districts (and/or Legislators) With More Than 15 Percent Deviation From Average (Where Data Available)	
						Districts	Legislators
1/62	(S)	422.5	10.7	+1432	−96.4		
	(H)	4.2	44.7	+55	−63.9		
10/65	(S)	1.33	48.9	+13.1	−14.9		0
	(H)	1.32	48.6	+13.5	−14.3		0

COMMENT: Federal district court held senate apportionment invalid. Silver v. Jordan, 241 F. Supp. 576 (D.C.S.D. California 1964), aff'd. 381 U.S. 415 (1965). State supreme court declared house apportionment invalid. Silver v. Brown, 46 Cal. Rptr. 308, 405 P. 2d 132 (1965). Standards set: no district to deviate by more than 15 percent from average; minimum electoral percentage to be at least 48 percent. Court approved legislative reapportionment of October 1965 after modifying some districts to correct "technical errors." Silver v. Brown, 48 Cal. Rptr. 609, 409 P. 2d 689 (1966). (For further discussion, see Ch. XIV.)

COLORADO

Date		Population Variance Ratio	Electoral Percentage	Maximum Percent Deviation From Average		Districts (and/or Legislators) With More Than 15 Percent Deviation From Average (Where Data Available)	
						Districts	Legislators
1/62	(S)	7.3	29.8	+51	−66.6		
	(H)	8.1	32.1	+37	−70.6		
1963	(S)	3.67	33.0	+66	−54.9		
Session	(H)	1.73	45.1	+30	−24.4		
7/64	(S)	1.4	46.9	+21.1	−16.9	6 of 35	
	(H)	1.7	45.3	+30.2	−24.8	17 of 65	
2/67	(S)	1.15	50.1	+7.5	−6.2	0	
	(H)	1.28	53.8	+13.4	−11.7	0	

COMMENT: After the state supreme court refused to take affirmative action, Stein v. General Assembly, 150 Colo. 380, 374 P. 2d 66 (1962), suit was instituted in federal court challenging the apportionment of the legislature. Lisco v. McNichols, 208 F. Supp. 471 (D. Colo. 1962). The court decided it had jurisdiction but deferred action because of lack of evidence concerning alternative plans, proximity of elections, and the presence of reapportionment initiative measures on the November ballot. On November 6, 1962, the voters approved one of two amendments to the constitution regarding reapportionment. The 1963 legislature implemented the amendment by statute. The federal district court then upheld the constitutionality of the amendment and statute. Lisco v. Love, 219 F. Supp. 922 (D. Colo. 1963). In one of the 1964 *Reapportionment Decisions*, the United States Supreme Court reversed, Lucas v. General Assembly of Colorado, 377 U.S. 713 (1964).

On remand, the federal district court ruled that the new amendment was not severable and therefore the whole apportionment must fail, that multi-member counties could be subdistricted, and that there was sufficient time for the legislature to reapportion. Lucas v. General Assembly of Colorado, Civil Action No. 7501 (D. Colo. June 26, 1964). The special session of the legislature convened on July 1, 1964, and the reapportionment for both houses enacted by it was approved by the federal district court on July 13, 1964. 232 F. Supp. 797 (1964). However, the court refused to enjoin proceedings in the state courts contesting the subdistricting features of the plan. The state supreme court determined that since the ratified amendment to the state constitution had been declared unconstitutional, the pre-existing provision of the state constitution forbidding subdistricting was controlling. In view of the pending 1964 elections the order was stayed until the convening of the 1965 legislature. White v. Anderson, 155 Colo. 291, 394 P. 2d 333 (1964); MacDonald v. Love, 155 Colo. 344, 394 P. 2d 345 (1964). The court subsequently reaffirmed its ruling, *In re* House of Representatives, 157 Colo. 76, 400 P. 2d 931 (1965). In an effort to save the subdistricting provisions of the ratified constitutional amendment, the federal court's ruling was appealed to the United States Supreme Court. The Supreme Court affirmed the lower court's findings as to the constitutionality of the new apportionment on federal grounds, but remanded the subdistricting issue for determination under the state court ruling. General Assembly of Colorado v. Lucas, 379 U.S. 693 (1965). The 1965 legislature enacted a new apportionment which consisted of the 1964 enactment without the subdistricting provision. Multimember districts would hold at-large elections. In November 1966 a constitutional amendment to authorize subdistricting was approved. In February 1967 the legislature reapportioned both houses, each district being single-member. (For further details see Ch. X.)

CONNECTICUT

Date		Population Variance Ratio	Electoral Percentage	Maximum Percent Deviation From Average		Districts (and/or Legislators) With More Than 15 Percent Deviation From Average (Where Data Available)	
						Districts	Legislators
1/62	(S)	6.7	33.4	+138	−62.6		
	(H)	424.2	12.0	+840	−97.8		
1/65	(S)	1.52	47.9	+23.0	−19.2	7 of 36	7 of 36 sen.
	(H)	2.1	43.8	+38.4	−34.5	67 of 177	67 of 177 rep.

COMMENT: Federal district court invalidated apportionments of both houses. Butterworth v. Dempsey, 229 F. Supp. 754 (D.C.D. Connecticut 1964), *aff'd.,* Pinney v. Butterworth, 378 U.S. 564 (1964). Court ordered special legislative session which was held from August 3 to September 10, 1964, but enacted nothing. On September 24, the court cancelled the November 3 elections and on October 29 ordered another special session to propose a valid apportionment plan and to call a constitutional convention by January 30, 1965. The 1962 legislature was held over until the special 1965 elections. The court also appointed special master to apportion if legislature was unable or unwilling to do so. On January 5, 1965, legislature authorized a constitutional convention. On January 22, the legislature enacted a bipartisan special apportionment. The court approved the new plan, lifted the 1965 election order and held the legislature over until the 1966 elections. Butterworth v. Dempsey, 237 F. Supp. 302 (D.C.D. Connecticut 1965). A new constitutional provision was approved by the people and proclaimed by the governor on December 14, 1965. The provision did little more than confirm the bipartisan agreement on reapportionment. (For further discussion, see Ch. XIII.)

DELAWARE

Date	Population Variance Ratio	Electoral Percentage	Maximum Percent Deviation From Average		Districts (and/or Legislators) With More Than 15 Percent Deviation From Average (Where Data Available)	
					Districts	Legislators
1/62	(S)	16.8	22.0	+167	−84	
	(H)	35.4	18.5	+357	−87.3	
6/63	(S)	15.5	29.9	+305	−80.9	
	(H)	12.2	27.6	+203	−83.4	
7/64*	(S)	1.34	52.6	+11.8	−16.3	2 of 18	2 of 18 sen.
	(H)	1.26	49.0	+9.2	−13.6	0

* Invalidated; may be replaced in 1968.

COMMENT: In 1962, a federal district court intimated that both houses were unconstitutionally apportioned but withheld decision until August 7, 1962, to give the legislature a chance to act. The court indicated that it would prefer a constitutional amendment rather than a legislative reapportionment enactment. Sincock v. Terry, 207 F. Supp. 205 (D. Del. 1962). A special session of the legislature approved a constitutional amendment on July 30, 1962. It would be effective if approved by the ensuing legislature. The 1963 legislature approved the constitutional amendment. In the interim, the court refused either to dismiss the pending action or grant affirmative relief. 210 F. Supp. 395 (D. Del. 1962); 210 F. Supp. 396 (D. Del. 1962). Upon ratification by the 1963 legislature, the suit was reopened and the court found both the old and new constitutional provisions unconstitutional. Sincock v. Duffy, 215 F. Supp. 169 (D. Del. 1963). The plan was found defective on population grounds, a "federal analogy" argument being rejected. An October 1, 1963, deadline was set for a new reapportionment. The United States Supreme Court affirmed, Roman v. Sincock, 377 U.S. 695 (1964). On July 6 and 8, 1964, the legislature enacted new apportionments for the house and senate, respectively. The new statutes were challenged on political gerrymandering and population inequality grounds but the court withheld judgment until after the 1964 elections. Sincock v. Roman, 233 F. Supp. 615 (D. Del. 1964). The apportionment subsequently was invalidated on population grounds only, although the federal district court made extensive findings of fact and law as to the political gerrymandering charges. The court declined to rule that gerrymandering was a justiciable issue, but made the findings should the Supreme Court care to pass on the issue. Sincock v. Gately, 262 F. Supp. 739 (D. Del. 1967). A further reapportionment is anticipated in 1968. (For further discussion, see Chs. IX and XVIII.)

FLORIDA

Date		Population Variance Ratio	Electoral Percentage	Maximum Percent Deviation From Average		Districts (and/or Legislators) With More Than 15 Percent Deviation From Average (Where Data Available)	
						Districts	Legislators
1/62	(S)	98.0	12.3	+618	−92.7	36 of 38	36 of 38 sen.
	(H)	108.7	14.7	+498	−94.5	66 of 67	92 of 95 rep.
1/63	(S)	38.1	14.1	+407	−89.2		
	(H)	23.3	22.9	+151	−93.8		
7/65	(S)	1.53	46.4				23 of 58 sen.
	(H)	4.04	41.6				42 of 109 rep.
3/66	(S)	1.3	48.4	+10.6	−15.1	1 of 37	1 of 48 sen.
	(H)	1.4	50.4	+15.3	−18.3	3 of 117	7 of 117 rep.
2/67	(S)	1.1	50.9	+5.0	−5.1	0 of 17	0 of 48 sen.
	(H)	1.1	49.6	+4.6	−5.6	0 of 24	0 of 119 rep.

COMMENT: On July 23, 1962, a federal district court held the apportionment of both houses unconstitutional and indicated that a pending amendment to the state constitution was similarly invalid. Sobel v. Adams, 208 F. Supp. 316 (S.D. Fla. 1962). The legislature met in special session and withdrew from voter consideration the amendment tentatively invalidated by the federal court. In its place a new constitutional amendment was proposed which would be submitted to the electorate at the 1962 general elections. Two statutes were enacted which would provide for implementation of the amendment if approved by the voters. These plans were accepted by the federal district court. Id. at 319 (supplemental order of September 5, 1962). The amendment was defeated by the voters in the 1962 general election. Another special session was summoned but deadlocked and adjourned after twenty days.

In an advisory opinion sought by the governor, the state supreme court ruled that the legislature could reapportion by statute notwithstanding the limitations of the state constitution. Opinion of the Justices, 150 S. 2d 721 (Fla. 1963). Another special session was then summoned, and it enacted a reapportionment for both houses. On February 7, 1963, the plan was approved by the federal court. Sobel v. Adams, 214 F. Supp. 811 (S.D. Fla. 1963). The act also was attacked unsuccessfully by certain Negro voters seeking subdistricting of all multimember districts. Lucas v. Adams (M.D. Fla. 1963), 13 National Municipal League, Court Decisions on Legislative Apportionment 14, affirmed per curiam, 378 U.S. 555 (1964).

On November 6, 1964, the voters rejected the proposed constitutional amendment which would have validated the 1963 act. After a federal court set a July 1, 1965, deadline for a valid plan, a special session of the legislature passed a reapportionment which became law without the governor's signature on July 7.

On December 23, 1965, a federal district court invalidated the plan on population grounds but allowed the 1966 elections to be held under it. Swann v. Adams, 258 F. Supp. 819 (1965). A carry-over provision respecting the seats of certain senate incumbents was invalidated while a residency clause was upheld in the same opinion.

On February 25, 1966, the United States Supreme Court reversed that part of the district court's order which would have allowed the 1966 elections to be conducted under the invalidated plan. 383 U.S. 210 (1966). The legislature then met in special session and passed another reapportionment for both houses on March 9. The plan was upheld by the federal district court. Swann v. Adams, 258 F. Supp. 819, 826 (S.D. Fla. 1966) (supplemental order). On January 9, 1967, the Supreme Court reversed on grounds that population deviations had not been sufficiently justified. Swann v. Adams, 385 U.S. 440 (1967).

On remand a special session of the legislature made further proposals, including a weighted voting plan. In an order of February 14, 1967, the federal district court rejected the state's proposal and adopted a court plan devised by a political science professor. Swann v. Adams, 263 F. Supp. 225 (S.D. Fla. 1967).

GEORGIA

Date		Population Variance Ratio	Electoral Percentage	Maximum Percent Deviation From Average		Districts (and/or Legislators) With More Than 15 Percent Deviation From Average (Where Data Available)	
						Districts	Legislators
1/62	(S)	42.6	22.6	+664	−82.1		
	(H)	98.8	22.2	+864	−90.9		
11/62	(S)	1.8	48.2	+30.1	−28.0	6 of 54	6 of 54 sen.
	(H)	n.c.	n.c.	n.c.	n.c.		
2/65	(S)	n.c.	n.c.	n.c.	n.c.	n.c.	n.c.
	(H)	2.0	42.7	+24.0	−36.9	68 of 141	120 of 205 rep.
7/67	(S)	Unavailable					
	(H)	"					

COMMENT: Following the Supreme Court's decision in *Baker*, suit was instituted in federal court challenging the apportionments of both houses. The court found the apportionment of both to be invidiously discriminatory, yet hesitated to declare that both must be apportioned on population grounds without other judicial guidance. Toombs v. Fortson, 205 F. Supp. 248 (N.D. Ga. 1962). Subsequently the court required that one house be apportioned on a population basis and suggested that a special session of the legislature be convened or else the court would have to judicially reapportion. Toombs v. Fortson, Civil Action No. 7883 (N.D. Ga. 1962). The legislature met in special session and enacted a reapportionment for the senate while leaving the house unchanged. In addition, a constitutional amendment was proposed validating the legislative action which was submitted to the electorate and approved on November 6, 1962. The aspect of the new senate apportionment providing for some single-member counties but for countywide voting in multimember counties was challenged successfully in a federal district court. Dorsey v. Fortson, 228 F. Supp. 259 (N.D. Ga. 1964). The Supreme Court reversed, holding that combining single-member districts and multimember districts in one plan did not by itself show vote dilution, and that in the absence of proof of population inequality the challenge must be dismissed. Fortson v. Dorsey, 379 U.S. 621 (1965).

After *Reynolds*, the 1962 suit was reopened challenging the constitutionality of the house apportionment. The apportionment was held invalid and elections were enjoined under the existing apportionment. In addition, the legislature was required to reapportion the house during the 1965 session. Toombs v. Fortson, Civil Action No. 7883 (N.D. Ga. June 30, 1964). The portion of the order prohibiting legislative consideration of a constitutional amendment on reapportionment was appealed to the Supreme Court where it was vacated, for reasons not made clear in the several opinions of the justices. In any event, the election at which a possible constitutional amendment could have been ratified had already been held. Fortson v. Toombs, 379 U.S. 621 (1965).

The legislature reapportioned the house in 1965. Plaintiffs then challenged the house apportionment in federal court, and the court requested that apportionments of both houses be considered on a theory of interrelationship. On April 1, 1965, the federal district court invalidated the apportionments of both houses but allowed their use on an interim basis for the 1966 elections. (It was the legislature elected under these "invalidated apportionments" that was held by the United States Supreme Court to have the power to choose Lester G. Maddox as governor of Georgia after neither Mr. Maddox nor front-runner Howard H. "Bo" Calloway had received a popular vote majority in the November 1966 election.) Fortson v. Morris, 385 U.S. 231 (1966). In addition, the federal district court required that new apportionments be enacted by the end of the 1968 legislative session or May 1, 1968, whichever occurred first. Toombs v. Fortson, 241 F. Supp. 65 (1965). The deadline was then reset by the federal court for July 1, 1967. The first election under a new and "permanent" plan will be November 1968.

HAWAII

Date		Population Variance Ratio	Electoral Per- centage	Maximum Percent Deviation From Average		Districts (and/or Legislators) With More Than 15 Percent Deviation From Average (Where Data Available)	
						Districts	Legislators
1/62	(S)*	7.47	21.0	+151.4	—66.3	6 of 6	25 of 25 sen.
	(H)*	4.53	38.5	+91.7	—59.5	15 of 18	42 of 51 rep.
4/65	(S)**	1.37	49.7	+28.1	—6.6	1 of 8	1 of 25 sen.
	(H)**	2.81	43.0	+44.2	—48.7	9 of 18	21 of 51 rep.

* These figures are based on 1960, *total population*. The following figures derive from the Hawaiian *registered voters* base (1960):

Population Variance Ratio (S) 10.88 (H) 2.07
Electoral Percentage (S) 27.9 *** (H) 46.5
Maximum Deviation (S) +83.1 —83.2 (H) +18.1 —43.3

** Temporary senate plan, and original house plan, current registered voter basis.
*** Because of multimember districts, this is theoretical percentage necessary to elect 60 percent of senate.

COMMENT: At statehood in 1959 the Hawaiian legislature was reapportioned. Following the decision by the Supreme Court in *Reynolds*, the state attorney general determined that the apportionment of both houses was unconstitutional. Haw. Att. Gen. Ops. 64-33–64-37 (July 6, 1964). The state supreme court then held the senate apportionment invalid, declined to rule on the house, allowed the 1964 elections to be conducted under the old apportionment, and indicated its preference for a constitutional amendment rather than a legislative reapportionment enactment. Guntert v. Richardson, 47 Haw. 662, 394 P. 2d 444 (1964). A special session of the legislature was convened on July 23, 1964, but was unable to reapportion.

Suit was then filed in the federal district court. The court denied a motion for preliminary injunction to stay the holding of the 1964 elections and deferred trial until January 11, 1965, unreported (D. Hawaii 1964). On February 17, the federal court invalidated the constitutional provision concerning apportionment of the senate and also the provision concerning the manner in which the senate apportionment could be changed. The house apportionment was upheld. Holt v. Richardson, 238 F. Supp. 468 (D. Hawaii 1965). On April 14, the legislature sent to the court a plan for provisional reapportionment of the senate, to be embodied in a constitutional amendment to be submitted to the electorate. The plan was rejected. 240 F. Supp. 724 (D. Hawaii 1965). The court then banned any legislative business other than reapportionment until a valid plan was enacted, and reasserted its preference for a constitutional amendment. The former portion of the court's order was stayed by Justice William O. Douglas on May 21, 1965. On appeal to the Supreme Court, the federal court's invalidation of the senate plan was reversed. Burns v. Richardson, 384 U.S. 73

(1966). (For discussion of *Burns* see Chs. XVII and XVIII.) In November 1966 the voters approved the call of a constitutional convention for 1968 which is expected to include apportionment on its agenda.

IDAHO

Date		Population Variance Ratio	Electoral Percentage	Maximum Percent Deviation From Average		Districts (and/or Legislators) With More Than 15 Percent Deviation From Average (Where Data Available)	
						Districts	Legislators
1/62	(S)	102.1	16.6	+517	−94.0		
	(H)	17.0	32.7	+48	−91.2		
1/63	(S)	n.c.	n.c.	n.c.	n.c.		
	(H)	11.3	44.2				
1965 Spec. Session	(S)	n.c.	n.c.	n.c.	n.c.		
	(H)	1.47	47.9				
3/66	(S)	1.41	46.9	+19.0	−15.4	4 of 35	4 of 35 sen.
	(H)	1.56	46.7	+32.0	−15.4	7 of 42	10 of 70 rep.

COMMENT: In a post-*Baker* suit the Idaho Supreme Court upheld the apportionment of both houses. Caesar v. Williams, 84 Idaho 254, 371 P. 2d 241 (1962). A 1963 reapportionment of the house decreased materially the population variance ratio and electoral percentage. An unsuccessful suit challenging this apportionment was brought in federal court. Hearne v. Smylie, 225 F. Supp. 645 (D. Idaho 1964). The United States Supreme Court reversed in a per curiam opinion on June 22, 1964, one week after the major *Reapportionment Decisions* in *Reynolds* and its companion cases. 378 U.S. 563 (1964).

On remand plaintiffs sought the convening of a special session of the legislature which would be ordered to reapportion before the 1964 elections, or an order that the elections be held at-large. On June 23, 1964, the federal district court ruled that proceedings would be stayed until thirty days following the end of the 1965 legislative session. The United States Supreme Court dismissed an appeal from the stay, the legislature having reapportioned in the interim. Hearne v. Smylie, 381 U. S. 420 (1965). A federal district court held a 1965 legislative reapportionment to be unconstitutional for the senate and tentatively acceptable regarding the house. Hearne v. Smylie (D. Idaho 1965), 22 National Municipal League, Court Decisions on Legislative Apportionment 128. On March 12, 1966, the legislature created a new apportionment for the senate and two plans for the house, the first of which was preferred. Although the state constitution prohibits division of any county in forming legislative districts, a number of the districts were made up by division of counties. On April 1, the federal district court accepted this plan. (D. Idaho 1966), 25 National Municipal League, Court Decisions on Legislative Apportionment 76.

ILLINOIS

Date		Population Variance Ratio	Electoral Per- centage	Maximum Percent Deviation From Average		Districts (and/or Legislators) With More Than 15 Percent Deviation From Average (Where Data Available)	
						Districts	Legislators
1/62	(S)	10.6	28.7	+226	−69.2		
	(H)	4.7	39.9	+181	−39.7		
9/65	(S)	1.14	50.4	+6.7	−7.0	0	0
	(H)	1.19	49.1	+8.6	−8.3	0	0

COMMENT: United States Supreme Court, citing *Reynolds*, reversed lower court approval of modified federal plan and remanded. Germano v. Kerner, 378 U.S. 560 (1964). Lower court took no action until after 1964 elections. Then federal court voided the area-based senate apportionment plan. Germano v. Kerner, 241 F. Supp. 717 (Jan. 22, 1965). (D.C.N.D. Ill.) Next month state supreme court also voided senate composition. People *ex rel.* Engle v. Kerner, 32 Ill. 2d 212, 205 N.E.2d 33 (1965). Court warned that it would apportion if the legislature did not. Principal parties unsuccessfully petitioned federal court, asking it to defer to state court. Germano v. Kerner, 241 F. Supp. 715 (D.C.N.D. Ill. 1965). United States Supreme Court reversed, directing federal court to retain jurisdiction but stay its hand pending action by state court or legislature. Scott v. Germano, 381 U.S. 405 (1965). Legislature deadlocked. State and federal judges on August 25, 1965, approved an apportionment plan drawn up in a federal pre-trial conference supervised by District Chief Judge Campbell. On September 9, 1965, the state supreme court ordered it into effect. People *ex rel.* Engle v. Kerner, 33 Ill. 2d 11, 210 N.E. 2d 165 (1965), appeal dismissed, 384 U.S. 981 (1966), and Germano v. Kerner, 247 F. Supp. 141 (D.C.N.D. Ill. 1965). This action helped pave the way for ending the deadlock also on lower house reapportionment. By similar joint action of the two courts the deadlock was also broken on congressional districts. People *ex rel.* Scott v. Kerner, 211 N.E. 2d 736 (1965) and Kirby v. Illinois State Electoral Board, 251 F. Supp. 908 (D.C.N.D. Ill. 1965).

Pre-*Reynolds* house note: The 1963 legislature and the governor deadlocked on bills apportioning the lower house. The result was an at-large election, under the state constitution, for all 177 members after the commission too failed to agree. The legislature enacted measures to provide for the election and the courts refused to intervene. People *ex rel.* Spence v. Carpentier, 30 Ill. 2d 43, 195 N.E. 2d 690 (1964); Daniels v. Carpentier, 30 Ill. 2d 590, 198 N.E. 2d 514 (1964); Swanson v. Illinois, 226 F. Supp. 699 (D.C.N.D. Ill. 1964). Each party nominating convention selected 118 candidates instead of 177 and cumulative voting was not used. (For further discussion, see Ch. XII.)

INDIANA

Date	Population Variance Ratio	Electoral Per-centage	Maximum Percent Deviation From Average		Districts (and/or Legislators) With More Than 15 Percent Deviation From Average (Where Data Available)	
					Districts	Legislators
1/62	(S)	4.4	40.4	+76	−54.9*	
	(H)	5.4	34.8	+96.2	−66.2*	
2/64	(S)	4.38	38.5	+80	n.c.*	
	(H)	9.85	36.5	+212	n.c.*	
2/65	(S)	1.38	49.4			
	(H)	1.41	48.1			
11/65	(S)**	1.27	49.5	+12.8	−11.2	o	o
	(H)**	1.26	48.7	+13.5	−10.0	o	o

* Based on figures given in Stout v. Hendricks, 228 F. Supp. 568, 580–83 (S.D. Ind. 1964). The National Municipal League, "Compendium on Legislative Apportionment" (New York, 1962) lists the following figures for this date: for the senate, +84, −58.2; for the house, +70, −68.6. The National Municipal League, in a supplement published April 15, 1964, lists the same "minus" maximum deviation for April 1964 as for January 1962.

** Over-21 population basis. On a total population basis the figures would be: (S) 1.33, 49.1 percent, +14.5 −15.0 percent, o; (H) 1.27, 48.9 percent, +10.3 −11.1 percent, o.

COMMENT: The 1921 apportionment plan was invalidated in 1963. Stout v. Hendricks, 228 F. Supp. 568 (S.D. Ind. 1964). A new plan had been enacted by the legislature and became law when the gubernatorial veto was held to be defective. State ex rel. Bogard v. Hendricks (Superior Court of Marion County, No. S63-7713, February 11, 1964) (unreported). That plan went into effect for the 1964 elections. The 1963 plan was held unconstitutional in 1965 by a federal district court. Stout v. Bottorf, unreported (S.D. Ind. February 26, 1965). A subsequent legislative reapportionment was invalidated by the same court. Stout v. Bottorf, 246 F. Supp. 825 (S.D. Ind. 1965). The plan failed because of a floterial district provision.

The legislature then enacted four plans for each house and a federal district court in Stout v. Bottorf, 249 F. Supp. 488 (S.D. Ind. 1965), ordered two into effect. The court's determination was based in large part on how many districts in the plan under consideration varied by more than 10 percent from the ideal district population. All plans were based on an "over-21" population basis.

IOWA

Date	Population Variance Ratio	Electoral Per-centage	Maximum Percent Deviation From Average		Districts (and/or Legislators) With More Than 15 Percent Deviation From Average (Where Data Available)	
					Districts	Legislators
1/62	(S) 9.0	35.2	+373	−46.2		
	(H) 16.8	26.9	+421	−69.7		
3/64*	(S) 3.2	38.9				
	(H) 2.2	44.8				
6/65**	(S) 1.71	45.2	+31.7	−23.0		21 of 61 sen.
	(H) 2.23	44.8	+39.8	−36.5		39 of 124 rep.
5/67	(S) 1.72	40.1	+32.6	−23.3	21 of 61	21 of 61 sen.
	(H) 2.24	48.5	+39.7	−37.4	37 of 124	37 of 124 rep.

* First temporary plan of March 1964 declared unconstitutional on February 11, 1965.
** Second temporary plan, 1965 session, voided because of multimember districting provision.

COMMENT: After delaying its final order until a proposed constitutional amendment had been rejected, a federal district court invalidated both houses on January 14, 1964, and the United States Supreme Court affirmed as part of the *Reapportionment Decisions* of June 1964. Davis v. Synhorst, 225 F. Supp. 689 (S.D. Iowa 1964), *aff'd. sub nom.* Hill v. Davis, 378 U.S. 565 (1964). In the interim between January and June the legislature had enacted a new plan which the federal district court had approved as a temporary plan. Davis v. Synhorst, 231 F. Supp. 540 (S.D. Iowa 1964). After the new federal standards became known in June 1964 the federal district court declared the plan unconstitutional. Davis v. Cameron, 238 F. Supp. 462 (S.D. Iowa 1965).

The legislature initiated a proposed constitutional amendment which needed to be approved by the next legislature before being submitted to the voters, and also enacted a new temporary apportionment. The state supreme court voided the mixed use in this plan of multimember and single-member districts in the same house, and the United States Supreme Court denied review. Kruidenier v. McCulloch, 142 N.W. 2d 355 (1966), *cert. den.*, 385 U.S. 851 (1966). (See Ch. XVIII for further discussion.) Subdistricting of multimember districts was accomplished in May 1967 by use of an ad hoc bipartisan commission.

KANSAS

Date		Population Variance Ratio	Electoral Per- centage	Maximum Percent Deviation From Average		Districts (and/or Legislators) With More Than 15 Percent Deviation From Average (Where Data Available)	
						Districts	Legislators
1/62	(S)	21.3	26.8	+529	−70.5		
	(H)	33.2	18.5	+293	−88.8		
2/64	(S)	1.2	50.1	+14	−15	0	0
	(H)	28.7	19.4				
3/66	(S)*	n.c.	n.c.	n.c.	n.c.	n.c.	n.c.
	(H)**	1.25	48.8	+11.0	−11.2	0	0

* If tested by 1965 state census the figures became: 1.5, 48.6 percent, +24.6 −17.2. New senate apportionment anticipated in 1968.
** Based on 1965 state census.

COMMENT: Following partial reapportionment of the senate in 1959 and the house in 1961, suit was brought to declare the apportionments invalid. A state trial court held the senate and part of the house apportionment plans unconstitutional and asked for at-large elections for the twenty house seats declared unconstitutional on July 26, 1962. The order was stayed so that the 1963 legislature could act. On appeal the state supreme court deferred decision pending legislative action. Harris v. Shanahan, 191 Kan. 1, 378 P. 2d 157 (1963). The 1963 legislature reapportioned the senate but a bill reapportioning the house failed in the senate. Subsequently the state supreme court held the apportionment of both houses unconstitutional. Harris v. Shanahan, 192 Kan. 183, 387 P. 2d 771 (1963). The senate apportionment failed only because the city of Leawood inadvertently had been omitted in the bill signed by the governor. The court thought the senate apportionment otherwise "commendable." Id. at 791. A special session of the legislature reapportioned both houses in February 1964. The apportionment of both houses was then approved on March 30, by the state supreme court. Harris v. Shanahan, 194 Kan. 629, 390 P. 2d 772 (1964).

However, following Reynolds, suit was instituted to have the previously approved legislative reapportionment declared unconstitutional. Finding the task of implementing Reynolds "distasteful," the state supreme court nevertheless bowed to superior authority. It declared the apportionment of the house unconstitutional and ordered that a valid plan be created in time for the 1966 elections. Harris v. Anderson, 194 Kan. 302, 400, 400 P. 2d 25 (1965), 382 U.S. 894 (1965). In the interim, suit had been instituted in a federal district court after Reynolds, challenging the apportionment of both houses.

On December 28, 1965, the federal court deferred to the state courts the issue of the apportionment of the house, but held the apportionment of the senate unconstitutional. Long v. Avery, 251 F. Supp. 541 (D. Kan. 1965) (reported in 1966). The court ordered a valid apportionment for the senate in time for the 1966 elections, but on February 10, 1966, it moved the deadline to April 1, 1968, so that incumbent senators could serve out their four-year terms. In an opinion issued February 24, 1966, the court noted that if senators were unable to serve this would cause disruption of some state agencies whose membership was composed of senators. (D. Kan. 1966), 25 National Municipal League, Court Decisions on Legislative Apportionment 117. On March 2, 1966, the legislature completed a reapportionment for the house. The population statistics used for this house apportionment were based on the 1965 state census.

KENTUCKY

Date		Population Variance Ratio	Electoral Per-centage	Maximum Percent Deviation From Average		Districts (and/or Legislators) With More Than 15 Percent Deviation From Average (Where Data Available)	
						Districts	Legislators
1/62	(S)	2.9	42.0	+165	−43.6	19 of 38	19 of 38 sen.
	(H)	6.0	34.1	+123	−62.9	69 of 100	69 of 100 rep.
4/64	(S)	1.9	46.6	+51	−22.4	11 of 38	11 of 38 sen.
	(H)	2.0	44.8	+33.2	−33.6	34 of 100	34 of 100 rep.

COMMENT: No action instituted since Reynolds, as of mid-1967.

LOUISIANA

Date		Population Variance Ratio	Electoral Per-centage	Maximum Percent Deviation From Average		Districts (and/or Legislators) With More Than 15 Percent Deviation From Average (Where Data Available)	
						Districts	Legislators
1/62	(S)	8.0	33.0	+197	−62.6		32 of 39 sen.
	(H)	17.4	34.1	+287	−77.2		
6/63	(S)	n.c.	n.c.	n.c.	n.c.		n.c.
	(H)	8.34	33.1	+80.4	−78.4	61 of 80	82 of 105 rep.
1966	(S)	1.46	48.3	+16.5	−20.4	3 of 27	4 of 39 sen.
	(H)	1.46	46.7	+21.2	−17.3	5 of 49	7 of 105 rep.

COMMENT: A 1963 reapportionment of the house was upheld by the state supreme court. LeDoux v. Parish Democratic Executive Committee, 244 La. 981, 156 S. 2d 48 (1963). Previously a federal district court, on June 28, 1963, had upheld a partial challenge to the same house reapportionment. Daniel v. Davis, 220 F. Supp. 601 (E.D. La. 1963). On February 8, 1966, a federal district court stayed a challenge to the apportionments of both houses, but ordered a valid reapportionment for both in time for the November 1966 elections. The court would order at-large elections or would judicially reapportion if the valid reapportionments were not forthcoming. Bannister v. Davis, No. 2818, Civil Action; Spencer v. McKeithan, No. 3316, Civil Action (E.D. La. 1966). The legislature reapportioned both houses late in 1966.

MAINE

Date		Population Variance Ratio	Electoral Per- centage	Maximum Percent Deviation From Average		Districts (and/or Legislators) With More Than 15 Percent Deviation From Average (Where Data Available)	
						Districts	Legislators
1/62	(S)	2.83	46.9	+60	−54.0		23 of 34 sen.
	(H)	5.5	39.7	+105	−62.8		
1964	(S)	n.c.	n.c.	n.c.	n.c.		n.c.
	(H)	3.43	42.9	+105.6	−40.0	45 of 114	56 of 151 rep.
8/67	(S)	1.21	51.0	+8.7	−10.4		0
	(H)	n.c.	n.c.	n.c.	n.c.	n.c.	n.c.

COMMENT: The house was reapportioned by the legislature in 1964 under a constitutional revision ratified in 1963. The 1961 apportionment of the senate was not changed at this time although the constitutional commission had recommended changes.

A constitutional amendment for senate reapportionment was proposed by the legislature in January 1966 after being approved in an advisory opinion by the state supreme court. Opinion of the Justices, 216 A. 2d 651 (1966). It specified the following guidelines: one senator per 30,000 population, maximum deviation of 10 percent, county lines to be followed as much as possible. The proposal was ratified in November 1966. The legislature created an advisory nine-man Senatorial Apportionment Commission consisting of the leaders of each party in each house, four professors, and the dean of the University of Maine Law School. When the Democratic governor and the Republican legislature deadlocked, the state supreme judicial court reapportioned the senate on August 1, 1967, closely following a plan proposed by the Commission. In re Apportionment of Senate, 233 A. 2d 137 (1967).

MARYLAND

Date		Population Variance Ratio	Electoral Percentage	Maximum Percent Deviation From Average		Districts (and/or Legislators) With More Than 15 Percent Deviation From Average (Where Data Available)	
						Districts	Legislators
1/62	(S)	31.8	14.2	+360	−83.5		
	(H)	12.5	25.3	+181	−77.0		
10/65	(S)	1.40	47.4	+18.2*	−15.8*	4 of 16*	8 of 43 sen.*
	(H)	1.89	48.0	+35.9*	−29.1*	7 of 29*	10 of 142 rep.*

* Subsequently there was some subdistricting of the senate and house multimember districts, thus changing both the number of districts and the population. Exact figures are not available.

COMMENT: In 1962 the Maryland Court of Appeals upheld a lower state court determination regarding the validity of the senate apportionment (federal plan theory) and the validity of a house reapportionment. Maryland Committee for Fair Representation v. Tawes, 229 Md. 406, 184 A. 2d 715 (1962). In one of the landmark decisions of 1964 the Supreme Court reversed and held invalid both legislative houses. 377 U.S. 656 (1964). A valid reapportionment was ordered for the 1966 elections. After the regular session of the 1965 legislature adjourned sine die, a special session was called and passed a reapportionment signed into law October 27, 1965. Two plans were passed for the senate, the first being preferred by the legislature. One plan was passed for the house. On December 29, 1965, the Circuit Court of Anne Arundel County voided the first senate plan on population grounds and accepted the second senate plan and the house plan. Maryland Committee for Fair Representation v. Tawes, No. 13, 920 Equity (Cir. Ct., Anne Arundel County). The Maryland Court of Appeals and the Supreme Court affirmed. 217 A. 2d 273 (1966), 384 U.S. 950 (1966). (For further discussion, see Ch. IX.)

MASSACHUSETTS

Date		Population Variance Ratio	Electoral Percentage	Maximum Percent Deviation From Average		Districts (and/or Legislators) With More Than 15 Percent Deviation From Average (Where Data Available)	
						Districts	Legislators
1/62*	(S)	2.3	44.6	+55	−33.6		
	(H)	13.9	45.3	+130	−83.9		
1963**	(S)	n.c.	n.c.	n.c.	n.c.		
	(H)	7.2	45.9	+43.4	−80.0	28 of 170	38 of 240 rep.

* Under a legal-voter population base, the January 1962 figures are as follows: (S) 1.3, 50.5, +8.4, −14.0; (H) 7.7, 46.1, deviations undetermined.
** Legal voter base.

COMMENT: Disregarding the two island counties which have always had one representative each, the PVR for the house is 1.09 to 1. However, there are PVR's of up to 1.9 to 1 within subdistricts of counties. Reapportionment was under way in mid-1967, the state supreme court withholding action to give the legislature an opportunity to reapportion under the 1965 state census.

MICHIGAN

Date		Population Variance Ratio	Electoral Percentage	Maximum Percent Deviation From Average		Districts (and/or Legislators) With More Than 15 Percent Deviation From Average (Where Data Available)	
						Districts	Legislators
1/62	(S)	12.4	29.0	+234	−72.1		
	(H)	4.0	44.0	+90	−52.4		
6/64	(S)	1.01	52.5	+0.58	−0.40	0	0
	(H)	1.17	50.6	+1.46	−2.82	0	0

COMMENT: A state supreme court dismissal of a suit to require reapportionment of the senate, Scholle v. Hare, 360 Mich. 1, 104 N.W. 2d 63 (1960), was vacated and remanded to the state court by the United States Supreme Court for reconsideration in the light of Baker. 369 U.S. 429 (1962). On remand, the Michigan Supreme Court declared the senate reapportionment unconstitutional on population grounds, declared no legislation to exist under which state senators could be elected in 1962, enjoined the August 1962 primaries, and declared that unless a valid apportionment were enacted, the 1962 elections would be at-large. Scholle v. Hare, 367 Mich. 176, 116 N.W. 2d 350 (1962). Justice Potter Stewart stayed the order pending appeal on July 31, 1962, and the elections took place under the old system. A state constitutional revision provided a new apportionment system in 1963. Among the provisions was a requirement that the senate apportionment be based 80 percent on population and 20 percent on area and that reapportionment be handled by bipartisan commission. A federal district court upheld the provisions of the 1963 amendment on March 16, 1964. Marshall v. Hare, 227 F. Supp. 989 (E.D. Mich. 1964). After the bipartisan commission deadlocked the state supreme court adopted one of the individual commissioner plans suggested to it as complying most closely with the state constitution, but withheld judgment on federal constitutional issues. In re Apportionment of the Michigan State Legislature, 372 Mich. 480, 128 N.W. 2d 350 (1964).

On June 17, 1964, two days after Reynolds, the state supreme court withdrew its approval of the plan and directed the commission to prepare a plan based on population, within two days. 373 Mich. 250, 128 N.W. 2d 722 (1964). On June 22, 1964, the United States Supreme Court denied certiorari in the case dating back to 1960 in which the state supreme court had held the 1952 apportionment invalid, Beadle v. Scholle, 377 U.S. 990 (1964), and also reversed the federal district court's holding in favor of the validity of the 1963 constitutional amendments. Marshall v. Hare, 378 U.S. 561 (1964). On the same day, the bipartisan commission again being deadlocked, the state supreme court chose a different individual commissioner plan and ordered it into effect. In re Apportionment of the Michigan State Legislature, 373 Mich. 250, 128 N.W. 2d 722 (1964). The 1964 elections were conducted under this plan. A suit challenging the plan on partisan gerrymandering grounds, inter alia, was brought after the 1964 elections and the state supreme court ordered the commission to draw a reapportionment comporting with both state and federal constitutional provisions. 376 Mich. 410, 137 N.W. 2d 495, 376 Mich. 483, 138 N.W. 2d 16 (1965). On December 31, 1965, the commission reported it was deadlocked and the state supreme court assumed jurisdiction. On March 8, 1966, after a confused series of opinions, the Michigan Supreme Court in effect indicated that it too was deadlocked. The 1966 elections were conducted under the 1964 plan and that plan will probably remain in effect until after the 1970 census. (For further discussion, see Ch. XII.)

MINNESOTA

Date	Population Variance Ratio		Electoral Per- centage	Maximum Percent Deviation From Average		Districts (and/or Legislators) With More Than 15 Percent Deviation From Average (Where Data Available)	
						Districts	Legislators
1/62	(S)	3.8	40.1	+95	−48.0		38 of 67 sen.
	(H)	11.9	34.5	+281	−67.6		87 of 135 rep.
6/66	(S)	1.44	+48.1	+25.3	−12.9	1 of 67	1 of 67 sen.
	(H)	1.52	−47.2	+12.7	−25.6	4 of 135	4 of 135 rep.

COMMENT: On December 5, 1964, a federal district court invalidated the apportionment of both houses. Honsey v. Donovan, 236 F. Supp. 8 (D. Minn. 1964). The 1965 legislature passed a reapportionment for both houses in its closing days which was vetoed by the governor on May 24, 1965. Suit was instituted in state court attacking the validity of the gubernatorial veto on the ground that the bill did not need gubernatorial approval because the legislature was acting in response to a federal court order. The state supreme court reversed a trial court determination in favor of the contention, leaving the veto in force. Duxbury v. Donovan, 272 Minn. 424, 138 N.W. 2d 692 (1965). The original plaintiffs then asked the federal court to reapportion the state. The court refused, deferring to the expertise of the legislature and the governor. Honsey v. Donovan, 249 F. Supp. 987 (D. Minn. 1966). On May 21, 1965, the governor signed a legislative reapportionment into law after having exercised his veto a second time on May 4. The new enactment made certain modifications in district lines demanded by the governor. (For further discussion, see Ch. XIII.)

MISSISSIPPI

Date		Population Variance Ratio	Electoral Per- centage	Maximum Percent Deviation From Average		Districts (and/or Legislators) With More Than 15 Percent Deviation From Average (Where Data Available)	
						Districts	Legislators
1/62	(S)	8.8	34.6	+184	−67.9		
	(H)	16.7	29.1	+282	−77.8		
12/66	(S)	1.67	48.5	+32.6	−20.7	12 of 41	16 of 52 sen.
	(H)	1.89	45.4	+41.6	−25.4	22 of 72	24 of 122 rep.
3/67	(S)	1.26	48.5	+12.5	−10.7	0 of 36	0 of 52 sen.
	(H)	1.24	48.5	+9.7	−11.1	0 of 52	0 of 122 rep.

COMMENT: The 1962 reapportionment was declared unconstitutional in Connor v. Johnson, 256 F. Supp. 962 (S.D. Miss. 1966). The governor called the legislature into special session and a new reapportionment was passed and approved by the governor on December 1, 1966. The apportionment was challenged and voided in Connor v. Johnson, 265 F. Supp. 492 (S.D. Miss. 1967). The court then ordered its own apportionment into effect but stated that the legislature was free to reapportion at any time, providing constitutional standards were met.

MISSOURI

Date		Population Variance Ratio	Electoral Per-centage	Maximum Percent Deviation From Average		Districts (and/or Legislators) With More Than 15 Percent Deviation From Average (Where Data Available)	
						Districts	Legislators
1/62	(S)	1.6	47.7	+22	—24.1	12 of 34	12 of 34 sen.
	(H)	13.4	20.3	+99	—85.8	143 of 163	143 of 163 rep.
9/65	(S)	1.09	52.1	+4.6	—3.8		0
	(H)	n.c.	n.c.	n.c.	n.c.		n.c.
3/66	(S)	n.c.	n.c.	n.c.	n.c.		n.c.
	(H)	1.21	48.6	+8.6	—10		0

COMMENT: Apportionments of both houses were held unconstitutional in December 1964 in Jonas v. Hearnes, 236 F. Supp. 699 (D.C.W.D. Mo. 1964). On September 11, 1965, a special senate apportionment commission, as authorized in the constitution, consisting of gubernatorial bipartisan appointees, reapportioned the senate. On July 15, 1965, the legislature reapportioned the house and proposed an amendment validating the apportionment act which was rejected by the voters on August 17, 1965. A special session proposed an amendment creating a special house apportionment commission, also consisting of gubernatorial bipartisan appointees, which was approved by the voters on January 14, 1966. The new commission apportioned the house on March 23, 1966. (For further discussion, see Ch. XIII.)

MONTANA

Date		Population Variance Ratio	Electoral Per-centage	Maximum Percent Deviation From Average		Districts (and/or Legislators) With More Than 15 Percent Deviation From Average (Where Data Available)	
						Districts	Legislators
1/62	(S)	88.4	16.1	+556	—92.6		47 of 56 sen.
	(H)	14.0	36.6	+74	—87.6		63 of 94 rep.
8/65	(S)	1.47	46.8	+16.8	—20.8	5 of 31	6 of 55 sen.
	(H)	1.67	47.9	+24.7	—25.1	8 of 38	13 of 104 rep.

COMMENT: A federal district court took judicial notice of apportionment discrimination, but deferred to the legislature. Herweg v. 39th Legislative Assembly (D.C.D. Mont. Jan. 13, 1965), 27 National Municipal League, Court Decisions on Legislative Apportionment 2. The legislature was unable to reapportion. The court after pre-trial hearings on suggested plans then ordered its own plan into effect. Id., 246 F. Supp. 454 (D.C.D. Mont. 1965). A constitutional amendment was ratified in 1966 specifying population-based apportionment in each house following each census but subject to any amendment to the federal Constitution. It also authorized subdividing counties, thus enabling creation of single-member districts.

NEBRASKA
(Unicameral)

Date	Population Variance Ratio	Electoral Percentage	Maximum Percent Deviation From Average		Districts (and/or Legislators) With More Than 15 Percent Deviation From Average (Where Data Available)	
					Districts	Legislators
1/62	2.7	36.6	+57	−42.5		
1963	1.7	43.9				
3/65	1.57	47.9			11 of 50	11 of 50 sen.
2/66	1.20	49.3	+12.7	−6.5		0

COMMENT: On July 17, 1964, a federal district court invalidated a mixed 80 percent population–20 percent area apportionment amendment and the 1963 act based on it. League of Nebraska Municipalities v. Marsh, 232 F. Supp. 411 (D.C.D. Neb. 1964). The legislature reapportioned in March 1965 but that plan also was voided. Id., 242 F. Supp. 357 (D.C.D. Neb. 1965). A revised plan enacted by the legislature early in 1966 was upheld by both state and federal courts. Carpenter v. State, 179 Neb. 628, 139 N.W. 2d 541 (1966); League of Nebraska Municipalities v. Marsh, 253 F. Supp. 27 (D.C.D. Neb. April 12, 1966).

NEVADA

Date	Population Variance Ratio	Electoral Percentage	Maximum Percent Deviation From Average		Districts (and/or Legislators) With More Than 15 Percent Deviation From Average (Where Data Available)	
					Districts	Legislators
1/62	(S) 223.6	8.0	+658	−96.6		
	(H) 22.1	35.0	+63	−91.9		
11/65	(S) 1.47	50.4	+11.3	−21.2	5 of 13	5 of 20 sen.
	(H) 1.53	47.5	+18.5	−22.4	9 of 16	20 of 40 rep.

COMMENT: Federal court invalidated apportionment of both houses and ordered a special legislative session. Dungan v. Sawyer, 250 F. Supp. 480 (D.C.D. Nev. 1965). In November 1965 the legislature apportioned both houses. Federal court, despite reservations, approved the plan. 253 F. Supp. 352 (D.C.D. Nev. 1966).

NEW HAMPSHIRE

Date		Population Variance Ratio	Electoral Per- centage	Maximum Percent Deviation From Average		Districts (and/or Legislators) With More Than 15 Percent Deviation From Average (Where Data Available)	
						Districts	Legislators
1/62	(S)	2.6	45.3	+64	−37.3		
	(H)	222.4	43.9	+284	−99.7		
1965	(S)	1.20	51.7	+11.2	−13.2		0
Session	(H)	2.20	45.8	+63.0	−30.6	52 of 100	80 of 400 rep.

COMMENT: Pre-*Reynolds* challenge to the 1961 apportionment was dismissed in 1962, the state supreme court upholding both the use of tax payment as the basis for senate apportionment and the system of part-time representation for the house. Levitt v. Maynard, 104 N.H. 244, 182 A. 2d 897 (1962); Levitt v. Att. Gen., 104 N.H. 100, 179 A. 2d 286 (1962). The population of the smallest district that has a representative is 8 (sic), which is the basis for the 1962 population variance ratio calculation above. However, towns with a population of less than 822 are not represented every year but are entitled to one two-year term every ten years.

A constitutional convention meeting before and after *Reynolds* proposed reapportionment amendments which were ratified in November 1964. The system of part-time representation was abolished. The legislature reapportioned under the amendments in 1965.

NEW JERSEY

Date		Population Variance Ratio	Electoral Per- centage	Maximum Percent Deviation From Average		Districts (and/or Legislators) With More Than 15 Percent Deviation From Average (Where Data Available)	
						Districts	Legislators
1/62	(S)	19.0	19.0	+222	−83.2	5 of 14	8 of 29 sen.
	(H)	3.0	46.5	+42	−51.2	9 of 21	11 of 60 assem.
4/65	(S)	1.61	47.0	*	*	5 of 14	8 of 29 sen.
	(H)	n.c.	n.c.	n.c.	n.c.	n.c.	n.c.
7/67	(S)	1.29	50.2	+10.8	−13.8		0
	(H)	1.37	47.3	+13.6	−17.2	3 of 80	3 of 80 assem.

* The *average* disparity under this plan was 9.4 percent.

COMMENT: The assembly was reapportioned in 1961 following a state supreme court decision which warned that failure to reapportion would give rise to a cause of action under the state constitution and the Fourteenth Amendment of the federal Constitution. Asbury Park Press v. Wooley, 33 N.J. 1, 161 A. 2d 705 (1960). After *Baker* v. *Carr* a lower court turned aside a challenge to the apportionment of both houses. Jackman v. Bodine, 78 N.J. Super. 414, 188 A. 2d 642 (1963). Following the subsequent decision of the United States Supreme Court in *Reynolds* v. *Sims*, the state supreme court unanimously reversed the lower court as to the senate and noted that it was not yet time to pass on the apportionment of the assembly. 43 N.J. 453, 205 A. 2d 713 (1964). In denying a motion for extension of time for enacting a new apportionment, the state supreme court indicated that the assembly plan was valid as a temporary measure. 44 N.J. 312, 208 A. 2d 648 (1965).

The senate first attempted a solution by adapting its rules to provide for weighted voting for its present members. The state supreme court invalidated this measure, holding that the apportionment could not be changed by changing the senate rules. 43 N.J. 491, 205 A. 2d 735 (1964). On April 12, 1965, the legislature enacted a temporary plan for the senate which was upheld as an interim measure only. 44 N.J. 414, 209 A. 2d 825 (1965).

An apportionment plan was adopted by a constitutional convention and ratified in November 1966. Provision was made for a bipartisan reapportionment commission to make future reapportionments. The commission consists of ten members with the chief justice of the New Jersey Supreme Court appointing an eleventh member to act as a tie breaker if necessary. The commission deadlocked in the spring of 1967 and an eleventh member was appointed. A compromise plan was adopted by the full commission, 8-3. The apportionment was challenged by dissenting members of the commission and by the attorney for the original plaintiffs. After ordering several minor adjustments, the state supreme court approved the plans for temporary use. Jackman v. Bodine, 231 A. 2d 193 (1967). (For detailed discussion, see Ch. XIII.)

NEW MEXICO

Date		Population Variance Ratio	Electoral Percentage	Maximum Percent Deviation From Average		Districts (and/or Legislators) With More Than 15 Percent Deviation From Average (Where Data Available)	
						Districts	Legislators
1/62	(S)	139.9	14.0	+783	−93.7		
	(H)	15.5	27.0	+103	−86.7		
12/63	(S)	n.c.	n.c.	n.c.	n.c.		
	(H)	8.6	42.0				
6/65	(S)	3.08	19.9				
	(H)	1.74	46.3	+36.2	−38.2	9 of 70	9 of 70 rep.
2/66	(S)	2.37	42.2	+44.4	−39.0	28 of 42	28 of 42 sen.
	(H)	n.c.	n.c.	n.c.	n.c.	n.c.	n.c.
3/66	(S)	1.79	45.8	+29.1	−27.6	18 of 42	18 of 42 sen.
	(H)	n.c.	n.c.	n.c.	n.c.	n.c.	n.c.

COMMENT: A state court in 1963 held unconstitutional New Mexico's existing apportionment and fixed a Nov. 1, 1963, deadline for reapportionment by the legislature, subsequently extended to Dec. 13, 1963. Cargo v. Campbell (Santa

Fe County District Court, September 1963), 6 National Municipal League, Court Decisions on Legislative Apportionment 79. The legislature reapportioned, but incorporated a weighted voting plan, weighting each legislator's vote by the actual population of his district. The plan was nullified by the state court because it was thought to be inconsistent with a state constitutional clause providing that for various purposes various percentages of "members" shall cast votes. Cargo v. Campbell (Santa Fe County District Court, January 8, 1964), 10 National Municipal League, Court Decisions on Apportionment 179.

On August 27, 1964, a suit was filed in federal district court challenging the constitutionality of the existing senate apportionment but the court deferred action to give the 1965 legislature an opportunity to reapportion under the new Supreme Court standards announced in *Reynolds* v. *Sims*. Lindsay v. Campbell, unreported (D. N.Mex. 1964). The 1965 legislature reapportioned and retained a weighted voting provision, subject to a state constitutional amendment to authorize weighted voting. The proposed amendment, and hence the reapportionment, was rejected in a September 28, 1965, referendum. On October 11, the federal district court fixed a deadline of March 1966 for senate reapportionment. The legislature's February 1966 reapportionment of the senate was voided by the federal district court on March 17, 1966. The court imposed its own plan, to remain in effect until after the 1970 census unless changed by further, valid, state action. Beauchamp v. Campbell (D. N.Mex. 1966), 23 National Municipal League, Court Decisions on Apportionment 90.

NEW YORK

Date		Population Variance Ratio	Electoral Percentage	Maximum Percent Deviation From Average		Districts (and/or Legislators) With More Than 15 Percent Deviation From Average (Where Data Available)	
						Districts	Legislators
1/62	(S)	2.2	36.9 *	+48	−33.6		
	(H)	21.0	38.2 *	+34	−86.6		
12/64	(S)	1.15	49.4	+7.2			
	(H)	1.21	49.3	+10.8			
3/66	(S)	1.16	49.1	+9.4	−6.2	o	o
	(H)	1.21	49.2	+8.8	−10.3	o	o

* If computed by citizen population, which is New York's apportionment base, the figures become: senate, 41.4; assembly, 33.4.

COMMENT: Apportionments of both houses were attacked as violative of the federal Constitution in 1962. The suit was dismissed before *Baker* v. *Carr* as presenting a nonjusticiable question. WMCA v. Simon, 202 F. Supp. 741 (S.D. N.Y. 1962). On authority of its intervening decision in *Baker*, the Supreme Court reversed and remanded. 370 U.S. 190 (1962). On remand, the federal district court sustained the rationality of the apportionments challenged. 208 F. Supp. 368 (S.D. N.Y. 1962). The Supreme Court reversed in one of the *Reapportionment Decisions* of June 1964. WMCA v. Lomenzo, 377 U.S. 633 (1964). On July 27, 1964, on remand, the federal district court set an April 1, 1965, deadline for a valid reapportionment, allowed the 1964 election to be conducted under the invalidated plan but limited the legislators elected to one-year terms, and directed new elections in November 1965 under a new and valid reapportionment. The reduction of terms provision was appealed and affirmed. 246 F. Supp. 953 (S.D. N.Y. 1964), *affirmed sub nom.*, Hughes v. WMCA, 379 U.S. 694 (1965).

Governor Nelson Rockefeller meanwhile had appointed a Citizens' Committee on Reapportionment to recommend apportionment plans. A lame-duck session of the legislature, in December 1964 enacted four plans in order of preference. In February the federal district court voided Plans C and D because of fractional voting provisions for the assembly. Plan B was invalidated because it used the 1962 gubernatorial vote as the apportionment base rather than total population. Plan A, the plan least preferred by the legislature, was accepted. WMCA v. Lomenzo, 238 F. Supp. 916 (S.D. N.Y. 1965). The November 1965 elections were therefore ordered to be conducted under Plan A. However, on April 14, 1965, the New York State Court of Appeals affirmed a lower court decision holding Plan A to be in violation of the state constitution because the legislature had changed the size of the lower house. The constitution set a 150-member ceiling on assembly membership; Plan A provided for a 165-member assembly. *In re* Orans, 15 N.Y. 2d 339, 258 N.Y.S. 2d 825, 206 N.E. 2d 854 (1965), *affirming* 257 N.Y.S. 2d 839 (Sup. Ct. 1965). On May 10 and May 24, the federal district court reaffirmed its order regarding the November 1965 elections, despite the state court rulings. Legislative leaders sought a stay of the district court order which was denied. Travia v. Lomenzo, 381 U.S. 431 (1965). Contending that "no final and binding" federal order requiring an election had been issued, the New York Court of Appeals on July 9, 1965, enjoined the holding of November elections. Glinski v. Lomenzo, 16 N.Y. 2d 27, 209 N.E. 2d 277 (1965).

On July 13 the federal district court reaffirmed its previous order and enjoined all persons from interfering with the holding of the November elections. WMCA v. Lomenzo, 246 F. Supp. 953 (S.D. N.Y. 1965). A petition for a stay was denied by Justice John Marshall Harlan on July 16 because of the earlier June 1 denial of stay by the Supreme Court. Travia v. Lomenzo, 381 U.S. 431 (1965). Appeals were taken from all orders, state and federal. The affirmance in WMCA v. Lomenzo, 382 U.S. 4 (1965) indicated an affirmance of the finding of constitutionality with respect to Plan A. The dismissal of Rockefeller v. Orans, 382 U.S. 10 (1965), indicated that Plan A was temporary because of the state court holding of invalidity and that any final plan must comport with applicable and valid state constitutional standards. The affirmances in Travia v. Lomenzo, 382 U.S. 9 (1965) and Screvane v. Lomenzo, 382 U.S. 11 (1965) indicated that the federal court could validly implement its orders respecting the holding of November elections by injunction, even against the state's highest court. The appeal left pending, Lomenzo v. WMCA, was the challenge to the invalidation of Plans B, C, and D, which eventually was vacated as moot on June 20, 1966, 384 U.S. 887. On December 13, the district court's order of July 13 enjoining interference with the November elections was affirmed. Travia v. Lomenzo, 382 U.S. 4 (1965).

On November 2, 1965, a one-year legislature was elected under Plan A. A new apportionment had been ordered by the trial division of the state supreme court on August 24, 1965. A deadline of February 1, 1966, was set, and subsequently extended to February 15 by the Court of Appeals. *In re* Orans, 47 Misc. 493, 262 N.Y.S. 2d 893, *affirmed*, 24 A.D. 2d 265 N.Y.S. 2d 49 (1965). After the legislature deadlocked, the Court of Appeals appointed an ad hoc reapportionment commission which submitted a plan on March 13, 1966. On March 21, the Court of Appeals held the plan valid over all objections. *In re* Orans, 17 N.Y. 2d 721, 269 N.Y.S. 2d 971, 216 N.E. 2d 834 (1966).

On November 2, 1965, the voters decided in favor of calling a constitutional convention to meet in 1967 and, among other things, devise a new apportionment formula. The 1966 elections were held under the commission apportionment plan. The 1967 convention delegates were similarly selected. A convention proposal to transfer apportionment power from the legislature to a bipartisan commission failed when voters in November 1967 rejected the entire proposed new constitution, primarily because of a church-state issue. (For further details see Chs. IX and XIII.)

NORTH CAROLINA

Date	Population Variance Ratio		Electoral Per- centage	Maximum Percent Deviation From Average		Districts (and/or Legislators) With More Than 15 Percent Deviation From Average (Where Data Available)	
						Districts	Legislators
1/62	(S)	6.0	36.9	+199	−50.6		
	(H)	18.2	27.1	+116	−88.7	88 of 100	105 of 120 rep.
1/63	(S)	2.3	47.6				
	(H)	n.c.	n.c.	n.c.	n.c.	n.c.	n.c.
1/66	(S)	1.32	48.8	+12.7	−14.8 *	0	
	(H)	1.33	47.5	+14.4	−14.0 *	0	

* The *average* district population disparity for the senate was 6.49; for the house, 6.73.

COMMENT: On November 30, 1965, the federal court invalidated legislature's apportionment and ordered new plans by January 31, 1966. Drum v. Seawell, 249 F. Supp. 877 (M.D.N.C. February 18, 1966). *Id.*, 250 F. Supp. 922 (M.D.N.C. 1966).

NORTH DAKOTA

Date		Population Variance Ratio	Electoral Per- centage	Maximum Percent Deviation From Average		Districts (and/or Legislators) With More Than 15 Percent Deviation From Average (Where Data Available)	
						Districts	Legislators
1/62	(S)	8.9	31.9	+225	−63.6		
	(H)	3.2	40.2	+52	−51.7		
1965	(S)	1.39	47.1	+19.4	−14		5 of 53 sen.
Reg.	(H)	1.39	47.1	+19.4	−14		10 of 106 rep.
Sess.							
8/65	(S)	1.24	46.8	+10.1	−12.1	0	
	(H)	1.24	46.8	+10.1	−12.1	0	

COMMENT: Federal court invalidated apportionment in both houses. Paulsen v. Meier, 232 F. Supp. 183 (D.N.D. 1964). In 1965 the legislature reapportioned but this was voided and the court substituted its own plan. 246 F. Supp. 36 (D.N.D. 1965).

OHIO

Date		Population Variance Ratio	Electoral Per- centage	Maximum Percent Deviation From Average		Districts (and/or Legislators) With More Than 15 Percent Deviation From Average (Where Data Available)	
						Districts	Legislators
1/62	(S)	1.9	41.0	+52	−20.8		
	(H)	9.4	30.3	+37	−85.6		
10/65	(S)	1.21	49.6	+8.8	−9.9	0	0
	(H)	1.33	47.3	+13.5	−13.5	0	0

COMMENT: In 1963 a federal district court had approved Ohio's apportionment on a federal plan theory but the United States Supreme Court reversed as part of the package of 1964 Reapportionment Decisions. Nolan v. Rhodes, 218 F. Supp. 953 (S.D. Ohio 1963), rev'd. per curiam, 378 U.S. 556 (1964).

The court on October 15, 1964, then invalidated the apportionment of both houses but allowed them to remain in effect for the 1964 elections in order to give the 1965 legislature a chance to act. Nolan v. Rhodes, unreported (S.D. Ohio 1964). A special session of the legislature proposed an amendment on December 10, 1964, but it was rejected by the people on May 4, 1965. The 1965 legislature was unable to agree on further action. On September 16, 1965, the federal court asked the parties for plans by October 15. An Apportionment Board composed of the governor, the auditor, and the secretary of state submitted a plan which was accepted as a temporary plan on October 27, 1965. Blosser v. Rhodes, 251 F. Supp. 584 (S.D. Ohio 1965), *aff'd.*, 383 U.S. 104 (1965). (For further discussion, see Ch. XIV.)

A constitutional amendment to provide a firmer basis in state constitutional law for this 1965 plan, and to enlarge the Apportionment Board, was defeated in May 1967, perhaps because an unpopular bond issue also was on the ballot. In June the Ohio Supreme Court upheld the power of the Apportionment Board to adopt the 1965 plan even though other parts of the Ohio apportionment formula had been invalidated in the 1964 *Reapportionment Decisions.* State *ex rel.* King v. Rhodes, 11 Ohio St. 2d 95, 228 N.E. 2d 653 (1967). In November 1967 the people ratified a constitutional amendment which had passed in the legislature with some bipartisan support, and which was substantially similar to the amendment defeated in May 1967. It specifies single member districts and a 5 percent maximum deviation, with deviations up to 10 percent permitted where necessary to avoid cutting county lines.

OKLAHOMA

Date		Population Variance Ratio	Electoral Per- centage	Maximum Percent Deviation From Average		Districts (and/or Legislators) With More Than 15 Percent Deviation From Average (Where Data Available)	
						Districts	Legislators
1/62	(S)	26.4	24.5	+554	−75.2		
	(H)	14.0	29.5	+216	−77.9		
6/64	(S)	1.51	49.4	+27.5	−15.4	3 of 48	
	(H)	1.26	48.6	+12.6	−10.5	0	

COMMENT: The United States Supreme Court affirmed lower court decision invalidating the apportionment in both houses. Moss v. Burkhart, 220 F. Supp. 149 (W.D. Okla. 1963), *aff'd.*, Williams v. Burkhart, 378 U.S. 558 (1964). The district court on remand in the summer of 1964 accepted only that part of a proposed state amendment pertaining to the size of the senate and declared the rest invalid. Under court direction and without legislative action both an apportionment and subdistricting plan were devised. The attorney general and a court aide played major roles. Reynolds v. State Election Board, 233 F. Supp. 323 (W.D. Okla. 1964). Attempts to appeal were fruitless, and the new plan was used in the November 1964 election. The 1965 legislature made minor modifications in some districts, subdistricting some holdover multimember districts, and incorporated the court's plan in a single statute. (For further discussion, see Ch. XII.)

OREGON

Date		Population Variance Ratio	Electoral Per-centage	Maximum Percent Deviation From Average		Districts (and/or Legislators) With More Than 15 Percent Deviation From Average (Where Data Available)	
						Districts	Legislators
1/62	(S)	2.5	47.3	+25.4	−49.3	10 of 19	10 of 30 sen.
	(H)	2.1	48.0	+34.5	−35.7	8 of 28	12 of 60 rep.

COMMENT: No court action since *Reynolds* affecting the whole state. On January 26, 1966, the state supreme court ruled that the subdistricting of Multnomah County was unconstitutional. Cook v. McCall, 242 Ore. 480, 410 P. 2d 505 (1966). The court ordered next legislature to redraw districts on a more equal basis, and to eliminate at-large representation.

PENNSYLVANIA

Date		Population Variance Ratio	Electoral Per-centage	Maximum Percent Deviation From Average		Districts (and/or Legislators) With More Than 15 Percent Deviation From Average (Where Data Available)	
						Districts	Legislators
1/62	(S)	10.7	33.1	+145	−77.1		
	(H)	31.1	37.7	+158	−91.8		
11/63	(S)	2.7	43.4				
	(H)	18.0	42.7				
2/66	(S)	1.21	50.1	+9.9	−9.3	0	
	(H)	1.35	47.0	+16.0	−14.1	1 of 203	

COMMENT: Federal district court held unconstitutional new pre-*Reynolds* apportionment acts, objecting to mixed use of multimember and single-member districts and to population provisions. Drew v. Scranton, 229 F. Supp. 310 (M.D. Pa. 1964). On September 29, 1964, the state supreme court invalidated apportionment of both houses. Butcher v. Bloom, 415 Pa. 438, 203 A. 2d 556 (1964). The federal court was ordered to defer to the state court. Scranton v. Drew, 379 U.S. 40 (1964). Legislature was unable or unwilling to apportion. On February 4, 1966, the state supreme court issued its own plan for the 1966 elections, to remain in force until replaced. Butcher v. Bloom, 420 Pa. 305, 216 A. 2d 457 (1966).

RHODE ISLAND

Date		Population Variance Ratio	Electoral Percentage	Maximum Percent Deviation From Average		Districts (and/or Legislators) With More Than 15 Percent Deviation From Average (Where Data Available)	
						Districts	Legislators
1/62	(S)	96.9	18.1	+151	−97.9		
	(H)	39.0	46.5	+121	−94.4		
7/67	(S)	1.22	50.3	+18.6	−12.2	2 of 50	2 of 50 sen.
	(H)	1.31	49.4	+18.6	−9.7	6 of 100	6 of 100 rep.

COMMENT: Following *Baker* the state supreme court held the apportionment unconstitutional but noted its inability to reapportion. It warned that if the legislature did not reapportion, a federal court might. Sweeney v. Notte, 95 R.I. 68, 183 A. 2d 296 (1962). After *Reynolds* the legislature, with the aid of a study commission, reapportioned in 1966 and re-enacted the measure over the governor's veto. Responding to a request from the governor for an advisory opinion, the state supreme court said it did not have adequate facts to rule on political gerrymandering charge, referred to a presumption of constitutionality, and upheld the act. Opinion to the Governor, 221 A. 2d 799 (1966).

SOUTH CAROLINA

Date		Population Variance Ratio	Electoral Percentage	Maximum Percent Deviation From Average		Districts (and/or Legislators) With More Than 15 Percent Deviation From Average (Where Data Available)	
						Districts	Legislators
1/62	(S)	25.1	23.3	+317	−83.6		
	(H)	3.4	46.0	+53.5	−55.1		
2/66	(S)	1.42	47.6	+13.5	−19.8	4 of 27	5 of 50 sen.
	(H)	n.c.	n.c.	n.c.	n.c.	20 of 46	26 of 100 rep.

COMMENT: A federal district court invalidated the senate apportionment and set April 1, 1966, as the deadline for approval of a valid plan (December 3, 1965). O'Shields v. McNair, 254 F. Supp. 708 (W.D. S.C. 1966). The court on February 28, 1966, accepted one of three plans submitted by a regular session of the legislature, but ordered a new apportionment within two years. The court reduced the terms of those elected in 1966 from four to two years and questioned a "residency" clause. The apportionment of the house was sustained at the same time. O'Shields v. McNair, 254 F. Supp. 708 (W.D. S.C. 1966).

SOUTH DAKOTA

Date		Population Variance Ratio	Electoral Percentage	Maximum Percent Deviation From Average		Districts (and/or Legislators) With More Than 15 Percent Deviation From Average (Where Data Available)	
						Districts	Legislators
1/62	(S)	4.3	38.3	+122	−48.9		
	(H)	4.7	38.5	+84	−61.2		
1965	(S)	1.39	47.1	+16.1	−16.7	2 of 29	2 of 35 sen.
Session	(H)	1.40	46.7	+19.5	−14.1	3 of 39	4 of 70 rep.

COMMENT: State legislature reapportioned in 1965. No court action. Attempt to petition the plan to a referendum failed.

TENNESSEE

Date		Population Variance Ratio	Electoral Percentage	Maximum Percent Deviation From Average		Districts (and/or Legislators) With More Than 15 Percent Deviation From Average (Where Data Available)	
						Districts	Legislators
1/62	(S)	6.0	26.9	+120	−63.2		
	(H)	23.0	28.7	+121	−90.8		
9/63	(S)	1.33	48.4 *				
	(H)	1.45	46.0 *				
5/65	(S) **	1.34	48.9	+15.9	−13.9	1 of 33	1 of 33 sen.
	(H) **	1.53	47.0	+27.9	−16.4	6 of 93	5 of 99 rep.

* The 1963 apportionment is based on over-21 population. On a total population basis the electoral percentages for the senate and house, respectively, would be 49.1 and 48.5 percent.
** Calculated with floterial districts.

COMMENT: A federal district court suit challenging apportionments of both houses was dismissed for lack of jurisdiction and failure to state a justiciable question. Baker v. Carr, 179 F. Supp. 824 (M.D. Tenn. 1959). In its first landmark reapportionment decision, the United States Supreme Court reversed, holding that reapportionment suits present justiciable federal questions. 369 U.S. 186 (1962). The legislature was called into special session on May 29, 1962, and enacted new apportionments for both houses on June 7. These plans were invalidated by the federal district court on June 22, but were allowed as interim plans pending a new apportionment, the deadline for which was set for June 3, 1963. 206 F. Supp. 341 (M.D. Tenn. 1962). The same special session provided for the calling of a state constitutional convention to be held in 1965 if the electorate approved. In the November 1962 elections the proposal was approved. The delegates were to be chosen on the basis of the 1961 apportionment. This method of choosing delegates was attacked on the ground that the 1961 apportionment had already been held unconstitutional. The state supreme court dismissed the challenge, holding it to be premature because the convention would have power only to propose and not to decide. West v. Carr, 212 Tenn. 367, 370 S.W. 2d 469 (1963), *appeal dismissed*, 378 U.S. 557 (1964).

The 1963 legislature again reapportioned both houses. The federal district court on October 10, 1963, approved the house plan and invalidated the senate plan because it ignored fractional remainders. 222 F. Supp. 684 (M.D. Tenn. 1963). The court then tentatively adopted the plaintiffs' plan for the senate, after deleting a provision for a floterial district, but allowed time for submission of alternative plans. Further plans were submitted, but the court then stayed all proceedings pending the decision of cases before the Supreme Court. On June 27, 1964, following *Reynolds*, the court rejected the alternative senate plans, accepted the plaintiffs' senate plan, declared the house apportionment invalid, and tentatively accepted the plaintiffs' house plan. On August 28, 1964, the court gave its final approval to the plaintiffs' house plan. It noted that the 1965 legislature was not prohibited from enacting a valid reapportionment if it wished to avoid the court's plan.

The special session of the 1965 legislature reapportioned both houses. On November 15, 1965, the federal district court approved the apportionment of both houses after attacks on degree of population equality, apportionment base, subdistricting, and floterial districts were dismissed. 247 F. Supp. 629 (1965). Certain proposed amendments to the state constitution were adopted by the electorate in the November 1966 general elections. Several changes were made including the following: subdistricting of multimember districts was required, legislators are required to live in the district they represent rather than in the county where their district is located; if the Supreme Court ever decides to allow representation on bases other than population, provision is made for use of geographic and other nonpopulation elements.

TEXAS

Date		Population Variance Ratio	Electoral Per- centage	Maximum Percent Deviation From Average		Districts (and/or Legislators) With More Than 15 Percent Deviation From Average (Where Data Available)	
						Districts	Legislators
1/62	(S)	8.4	30.3	+303	−52.8		
	(H)	3.1	38.6	+65	−46.9		
6/65	(S)	1.23	49.4	+10.7	−10.1	0	
	(H)	1.31	47.4	+11.6	−14.8	0	

COMMENT: The legislature reapportioned both houses in 1961. After the Supreme Court's *Reynolds* decision a federal district court on December 16, 1964, found provisions of the apportionments of each house unconstitutional and fixed a deadline of August 2, 1965, for a valid reapportionment. Kilgarlin v. Martin (S.D. Texas 1964), 15 National Municipal League, Court Decisions on Legislative Apportionment 121. Concurrently, a state court dismissed a suit to require subdistricting of all multimember districts. Plaintiffs alleged that the "place system" in these multimember districts tended to discriminate against racial minorities. Hainsworth v. Martin, 386 S.W. 2d 202 (Tex. Civ. App. 1965). The United States Supreme Court subsequently vacated the lower court order and remanded the case because the legislature had reapportioned in the interim in response to the federal court order. Hainsworth v. Martin, 382 U.S. 109 (1965).

The legislative reapportionment of both houses was accomplished on June 9, 1965, and the senate plan went unchallenged. The federal district court also upheld the reapportionment of the house except for the floterial district system. Kilgarlin v. Martin, 252 F. Supp. 403 (S.D. Tex. 1966). The 1966 elections were permitted under the partially invalidated house plan, but the court stated that if the plan went uncorrected until August 1, 1967, the court would require that the counties in the floterial districts be reconstituted into multimember districts with election of all representatives from those counties to be held at-large. Allegations of racial and political gerrymandering were held not proved. The Supreme Court affirmed all holdings of the lower court except its validation of population deviations (in the districts other than the floterial districts) of +14.84 percent and −11.64 percent. The state was held not to have carried its burden of proof to justify anything more than "minor" population deviations as required by Reynolds. Kilgarlin v. Hill, 386 U.S. 120 (1967). Justice William O. Douglas in a concurring opinion expressed concern about the fairness of multimember districts, but reserved the question.

UTAH

Date	Population Variance Ratio		Electoral Per- centage	Maximum Percent Deviation From Average		Districts (and/or Legislators) With More Than 15 Percent Deviation From Average (Where Data Available)	
						Districts	Legislators
1/62	(S)	6.9	21.3	+81	−73.9		
	(H)	27.8	33.3	+133	−91.4		
5/65	(S)	1.75	48.1	+16.1	−33.5	9 of 13	11 of 28 sen.
	(H)	1.55	47.6	+7.2	−30.8	6 of 19	8 of 69 rep.

COMMENT: A federal district court invalidated the apportionment of both houses but allowed the November 1964 election to be held under the old plan to give the 1965 legislature an opportunity to reapportion. Petuskey v. Clyde, 234 F. Supp. 960 (D.C.D. Utah 1964). The 1965 legislature's reapportionment was sustained except for a holdover provision affecting 11 senators which was invalidated. The court ordered that all senators be elected in 1966. Petuskey v. Rampton, 243 F. Supp. 365 (D.C.D. Utah 1965).

VERMONT

Date	Population Variance Ratio		Electoral Per-centage	Maximum Percent Deviation From Average		Districts (and/or Legislators) With More Than 15 Percent Deviation From Average (Where Data Available)	
						Districts	Legislators
1/62	(S)	6.4	47.0	+43	−77.3		
	(H)	827.5	11.9	+1991	−97.4		
6/65 *	(S)	1.60	49.0	+23.2	−22.8	3 of 12	4 of 30 sen.
	(H)	1.30	48.7	+11.5	−14.3	0	

* The November 1965 apportionment for the house was based on registered voters.

COMMENT: A federal district court invalidated apportionments of both houses but allowed 1964 elections under old plan. Buckley v. Hoff, 234 F. Supp. 191 (D.C.D. Vt. 1964). It limited the 1965 legislature strictly to apportionment and required a valid plan by March 31, 1965. While an appeal was pending in the Supreme Court the order was changed to allow all forms of legislation between January 1 and July 1, 1965, and to extend terms to July 1, 1965. As thus modified the order was affirmed. Parsons v. Buckley, 379 U.S. 359 (1965). The legislature's action adopting an apportionment plan was approved on June 24, 1965, thus ending almost two centuries of town representation. Buckley v. Hoff, 243 F. Supp. 873 (D.C.D. Vt. 1965).

VIRGINIA

Date	Population Variance Ratio		Electoral Per-centage	Maximum Percent Deviation From Average		Districts (and/or Legislators) With More Than 15 Percent Deviation From Average (Where Data Available)	
						Districts	Legislators
1/62	(S)	5.5	37.7	+188	−47.9		
	(H)	7.1	36.8	+259	−49.8		
1962	(S)	2.6	41.1	+165	−37.7		
Session	(H)	4.4	40.5	+240	−44.8		
12/64	(S)	1.37	48.2	+18.3	−13.5	1 of 31	1 of 40 sen.
	(H)	1.53	47.0	+20.0	−21.8	10 of 55	10 of 100 del.

COMMENT: Following the Supreme Court's decision in *Baker*, suit was instituted in federal court challenging the apportionments of both houses. The court nullified the apportionments and enjoined further elections under the existing apportionments. Mann v. Davis, 213 F. Supp. 577 (E.D. Va. 1962). This order was stayed, first by the district court and then by Chief Justice Earl Warren sitting as Circuit Justice, pending review by the United States Supreme Court.

The Supreme Court affirmed in one of the 1964 *Reapportionment Decisions*, 377 U.S. 678. On remand the federal district court ordered a special session convened to create a valid plan by January 1966. In addition, the terms of incumbent senators were reduced from four years to two. 238 F. Supp. 458 (E.D. Va. 1964), order on mandate, 238 F. Supp. 459; stay denied without opinion, Davis v. Mann, 379 U.S. 694 (1964). A special session was convened on November 30, 1964, and a new apportionment was enacted two days later. A challenge to the 1964 apportionment was brought on racial gerrymandering and multimember districting grounds. The gerrymandering challenge was dismissed as not proved. The challenge to the multimember districts was dismissed, the court finding justification for the scheme solely on equal population grounds. Mann v. Davis, 245 F. Supp. 241 (E.D. Va. 1965), *affirmed sub nom.*, Burnette v. Davis, 382 U.S. 42 (1965). (For further discussion, see Chs. IX and XVIII.)

WASHINGTON

Date	Population Variance Ratio		Electoral Per-centage	Maximum Percent Deviation From Average		Districts (and/or Legislators) With More Than 15 Percent Deviation From Average (Where Data Available)	
						Districts	Legislators
1/62	(S)	7.3	33.9	+152	−65.5		
	(H)	4.6	35.3	+102	−56.4		
2/65	(S)	1.45	47.6	+22.0	−16.1	4 of 49	4 of 49 sen.
	(H)	1.61	46.7	+18.2	−26.9	7 of 56	12 of 99 rep.

COMMENT: A federal district court voided the apportionment of both houses on September 13, 1962. Thigpen v. Meyers, 211 F. Supp. 826 (W.D. Wash. 1962), *aff'd*. 378 U.S. 544 (1964). After *Reynolds*, the federal district court enjoined holding of further elections and instituted a temporary weighted voting plan on July 23, 1964. 231 F. Supp. 938 (W.D. Wash. 1964). Both orders were rescinded in October to give the incoming January 1965 legislature an opportunity to reapportion, and transaction of all other non-essential legislative business was prohibited until the reapportionment plan was enacted. Thigpen v. Meyers (W.D. Wash. 1964), 12 National Municipal League, Court Decisions on Legislative Apportionment 170, 173. The legislature adopted a bipartisan apportionment plan worked out between the parties on February 26, 1965, and the district court approved the plan on March 9, 1965. Thigpen v. Kramer (W.D. Wash. 1965), 17 National Municipal League, Court Decisions on Legislative Apportionment 136. There was no appeal. (For further discussion, see Ch. XIII.)

WEST VIRGINIA

Date		Population Variance Ratio	Electoral Percentage	Maximum Percent Deviation From Average		Districts (and/or Legislators) With More Than 15 Percent Deviation From Average (Where Data Available)	
						Districts	Legislators
1/62	(S)	3.4	46.7	+336	−36.4		
	(H)	9.0	40.0	+112	−76.9		
1964	(S)	2.0	46.7	+34.5	−31.0	6 of 17	12 of 34 sen.
Session	(H)	2.4	46.0	+46.4	−37.7	18 of 47	21 of 100 rep.

COMMENT: On February 7, 1964, the state supreme court invalidated apportionment of both houses. Robertson v. Hatcher, 135 S.E. 2d 675 (1964). The legislature reapportioned in 1964.

WISCONSIN

Date		Population Variance Ratio	Electoral Percentage	Maximum Percent Deviation From Average		Districts (and/or Legislators) With More Than 15 Percent Deviation From Average (Where Data Available)	
						Districts	Legislators
1/62	(S)	2.8	45.0	+73	−37.7	16 of 33	16 of 33 sen.
	(H)	4.5	40.0	+121	−50.7	54 of 100	54 of 100 assem.
5/64	(S)	1.4	48.4	+14.5	−16.0*	1 of 33	1 of 33 sen.
	(H)	2.4	45.4	+32.5	−43.7*	27 of 100	27 of 100 assem.

* The *average* percentage deviation became for the senate 6.6 percent and for the assembly 11.3 percent.

COMMENT: The state supreme court held apportionment of both houses invalid and also invalidated an apportionment act on February 28, 1964. State *ex rel.* Reynolds v. Zimmerman, 22 Wis. 2d 544, 126 N.W. 2d 551 (1964). The legislature passed a new act and the governor vetoed it. On May 14, 1964, the state supreme court issued its own plan on the eve of *Reynolds* v. *Sims. Id.*, 23 Wis. 2d 606, 128 N.W. 2d 16 (1964). It allowed six days for filing of objections or requested changes. The parties filed no objections or motions but four requests for changes were filed by others, e.g., criticism of splitting the City of Glendale in the Milwaukee suburbs among three senatorial districts and three assembly districts. Without a hearing the court rejected all comments because all suggested changes would have increased population disparities. The court then ordered its plan into effect for the 1964 elections. *Id.*, 23 Wis. 2d 606, 128 N.W. 2d 349 (1964). There has been no action since *Reynolds* as of mid-1967.

WYOMING

Date	Population Variance Ratio		Electoral Per- centage	Maximum Percent Deviation From Average		Districts (and/or Legislators) With More Than 15 Percent Deviation From Average (Where Data Available)	
						Districts	Legislators
1/62	(S)	9.8	26.9	+147	−74.4		
	(H)	3.4	35.8	+70	−50.6		
1963	(S)	9.8	24.1				
Session	(H)	2.6	46.4	+46.7	−43.3	10 of 23	12 of 61 rep.
7/65	(S)	2.08	47.4	+35.9	−34.5	5 of 17	7 of 30 sen.
	(H)	n.c.	n.c.	n.c.	n.c.	n.c.	n.c.

COMMENT: A federal district court invalidated the senate apportionment and upheld the house apportionment. Schaefer v. Thomson, 240 F. Supp. 247 (D. Wyo. 1964). The 1965 legislature was unable to reapportion. On October 8, 1965, the court reapportioned the senate. Id., 251 F. Supp. 450 (D. Wyo. 1965). Intervenors appealed and sought subdistricting of multimember counties. The United States Supreme Court affirmed the district court's order without opinion on February 28, 1966. Harrison v. Schaefer, 383 U.S. 269 (1966).

Appendix B

Congressional Districting as of *Baker* v. *Carr*, 1962

EXPLANATORY NOTE FOR APPENDIX B AND APPENDIX C:

Appendix B, below, seeks to tabulate the "arithmetic" of congressional districts uninfluenced by the *Baker* v. *Carr* decision of March 1962. Although confined to state legislative apportionment, the decision did influence some legislatures in the direction of greater equalization of congressional districts even before the Supreme Court ruled on congressional districts in 1964 in *Wesberry* v. *Sanders*. Therefore some late 1962 redistricting figures are not included in the "1962" tabulation.

The tabulation of congressional district figures for the 1968 election has some gaps because full data for some states were unavailable, and because recently invalidated plans of some states must be replaced in time for the November 1968 election.

The right-hand column in Appendix B is based on the 15 percent "rule-of-thumb" figure which until recently has been mentioned in court opinions and comments as a tolerable outer boundary for population deviations. The right-hand column in Appendix C, however, is based on the 5 percent figure which Congress considered but did not enact in its deliberations on a new congressional districting bill in 1967. Also it may be noted that the Supreme Court in 1967 invalidated an 11 percent Indiana plan and sustained a lower court invalidation of a 9 percent Missouri plan. (See Ch. XVII.)

SOURCES:

The arithmetic data are based on the author's files; 25 *Cong. Quart.* 2580 (Dec. 15, 1967); 24 *Cong. Quart.* (Special Report, Sept. 16, 1966); incidental CQ Weekly Reports, 1962–67; National Municipal League, "Apportionment in the Nineteen Sixties" (mimeo 1967).

Congressional Districting as of *Baker* v. *Carr*, 1962

State	Population Variance Ratio	Maximum Percent Deviation From Average		Districts With More Than 15 Percent Deviation From Average
Alabama	1.5	+21.4	−17.2	2 of 8
Alaska	At-Large			
Arizona	3.3	+52.9	−54.3	2 of 3
Arkansas	1.7	+28.8	−25.4	4 of 4
California	2.0	+424.4	−27.0	9 of 38
Colorado	3.2	+49.1	−55.4	2 of 4
Connecticut	2.2	+63.2	−24.5	5 of 6
Delaware	At-Large			
Florida	2.8	+60.3	−42.5	5 of 12
Georgia	3.0	+108.9	−31.0	6 of 10
Hawaii	At-Large			
Idaho	1.6	+22.9	−22.9	2 of 2
Illinois	1.6	+31.6	−33.6	9 of 24
Indiana	2.4	+64.6	−31.4	6 of 11
Iowa	1.3	+12.3	−10.4	0 of 7
Kansas	1.4	+23.9	−14.3	1 of 5
Kentucky	1.7	+40.8	−19.2	4 of 7
Louisiana	2.0	+31.6	−35.2	4 of 8
Maine	1.1	+4.3	−4.3	0 of 2
Maryland	3.2	+86.3	−37.3	7 of 8
Massachusetts	1.3	+11.6	−12.3	0 of 12
Michigan	6.9	+85.3	−71.4	14 of 19
Minnesota	1.3	+13.2	−12.0	0 of 8
Mississippi	2.1	+39.9	−32.3	3 of 5
Missouri	1.3	+17.3	−12.4	1 of 10
Montana	1.5	+18.7	−18.7	2 of 2
Nebraska	1.3	+12.8	−14.0	0 of 3
Nevada	At-Large			
New Hampshire	1.2	+9.3	−9.3	0 of 2
New Jersey	2.3	+44.8	−36.9	9 of 15
New Mexico	At-Large			
New York	1.3	+15.1	−14.4	1 of 41
North Carolina	1.8	+18.7	−36.9	4 of 11
North Dakota	1.1	+5.4	−5.4	0 of 2
Ohio	2.6	+79.5	−41.6	14 of 24
Oklahoma	2.4	+42.5	−41.3	4 of 6

Oregon	2.0	+18.2	—40.0	3 of 4
Pennsylvania	1.8	+31.9	—27.7	9 of 27
Rhode Island	1.2	+7.0	—7.0	0 of 2
South Carolina	1.8	+33.9	—31.4	3 of 6
South Dakota	2.7	+46.3	—46.3	2 of 2
Tennessee	2.8	+58.2	—43.6	6 of 9
Texas	4.4	+118.5	—48.5	20 of 23
Utah	1.8	+28.6	—28.6	2 of 2
Vermont	At-Large			
Virginia	1.7	+36.0	—21.1	4 of 10
Washington	1.5	+25.2	—16.0	2 of 7
West Virginia	1.4	+13.4	—18.6	1 of 5
Wisconsin	2.2	+40.1	—34.2	Not Available
Wyoming	At-Large			

Appendix C

Congressional Districting Effective for 1968 Elections

EXPLANATARY NOTE AND SOURCE NOTE:

See explanatory note and sources for Appendix B.

State	Population Variance Ratio	Maximum Percent Deviation From Average		District With More Than 5 Percent Deviation From Average
Alabama	1.15	+8.4	−6.1	5 of 8
Alaska	At-Large			
Arizona	1.13	+5.2	−6.6	2 of 3
Arkansas	1.02	+1.6	−0.6	0 of 4
California	Not Available			Not Available
Colorado	1.22	+12.6	−7.4	2 of 4
Connecticut	1.19	+14.1	−4.3	1 of 6
Delaware	At-Large			
Florida	1.12	N.A.	N.A.	N.A.
Georgia	1.38	+15.5	−16.4	8 of 10
Hawaii	At-Large			
Idaho	1.21	+9.4	−9.4	2 of 2
Illinois	1.14	+7.5	−6.1	6 of 24
Indiana	1.23	+7.2	−12.8	4 of 11
Iowa	1.25	+12.3	−10.4	2 of 7
Kansas	1.15	+4.2	−9.6	1 of 5
Kentucky	1.10	+5.5	−3.8	1 of 7
Louisiana	1.25	+13.7	−9.1	N.A.
Maine	1.09	+4.3	−4.3	0 of 2
Maryland	1.03	+1.5	−1.1	0 of 8
Massachusetts	1.02	N.A.	N.A.	0 of 12
Michigan	1.03	+1.3	−2.1	0 of 19
Minnesota	1.29	+13.2	−12.0	5 of 8
Mississippi	1.06	+3.2	−2.8	0 of 5
Missouri	1.04	N.A.	N.A.	0 of 10
Montana	1.06	+3.1	−3.1	0 of 2
Nebraska	1.31	+12.8	−14.0	2 of 3
Nevada	At-Large			
New Hampshire	1.21	+9.3	−9.3	2 of 2

New Jersey	N.A.	N.A.	N.A.	N.A.
New Mexico	At-Large			
New York	Invalidated. The following new plan is being appealed:			
	1.14	+6.5	—6.6	10 of 41
North Carolina	1.04	N.A.	N.A.	0 of 11
North Dakota	1.11	+5.4	—5.4	2 of 2
Ohio	Invalidated. Appeal not expected on this new plan:			
	1.02	+1.4	—1.1	0 of 24
Oklahoma	1.04	N.A.	N.A.	0 of 6
Oregon	1.16	+6.0	—8.6	2 of 4
Pennsylvania	1.35	+15.0	—14.9	16 of 27
Rhode Island	1.22	+7.0	—7.0	2 of 2
South Carolina	1.12	+6.1	—5.4	4 of 6
South Dakota	1.07	+3.4	—3.4	0 of 2
Tennessee	1.04	N.A.	N.A.	0 of 9
Texas	1.16	N.A.	N.A.	N.A.
Utah	1.03	+1.5	—1.5	0 of 2
Vermont	At-Large			
Virginia	1.11	+5.8	—3.8	2 of 10
Washington	1.26	N.A.	N.A.	N.A.
West Virginia	1.39	+13.4	—18.5	N.A.
Wisconsin	1.07	+3.4	—3.4	0 of 10
Wyoming	At-Large			

Table of Cases

Subject Index

For cases, *see* Table of Cases.

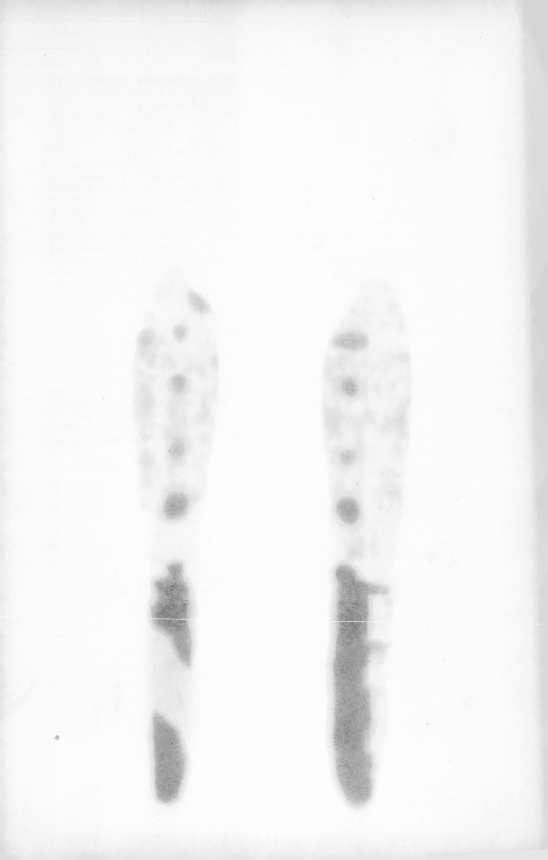